Home Cookin'

The Lions Clubs Cookbook
Volume 3

Another special collection of favorite recipes
from Lions Clubs members
from across the nation.

Compiled by
Cookbooks Unlimited
Loveland, Colorado

Published and Printed By
Cookbook Publishers, Inc.
P.O. Box 15920
Lenexa, Kansas 66285-5920

ISBN Number: 0-9638796-5-0

First Printing   October 1999   10,000 books

> *A recipe that is not shared with others,*
> *will soon be forgotten,*
> *but when it is shared*
> *it will be enjoyed by future generations.*

Dedication

We dedicate this book to all Lions Clubs members...a very special group of people who are committed to building a brighter future for their community and their fellow man.

Our very sincere thanks go to all those Lions members who so generously contributed their favorite recipes for this outstanding cookbook. Without their efforts, this book would not have been possible.

Thank you also, to all those persons who purchase one of these cookbooks. It is your support of the Lions Club organization that makes their efforts so successful.

We hope you enjoy the many outstanding and delicious recipes that so many people from so many different parts of the country have chosen to share with you in this fabulous book.

Our sincere thanks,

Francis & Linda Sedlacek
Cookbooks Unlimited

WHO IS A LION?

He has achieved success who has lived well, laughed often and loved much; who has gained the respect of intelligent men and the love of little children; who has filled his niche and accomplished his task; who has left the world better than he found it, whether by an improved poppy, a perfect poem or a rescued soul; who has never lacked appreciation of earth's beauty or failed to express it; who has always looked for the best in others and given the best he has; whose life was an inspiration, whose memory a benediction. He Is A Lion!

> *Lions Motto:*
>
> # WE SERVE

Lions are more than 1.4 million strong...men and women...young and old. You will find them in 185 countries from the hinterlands of Australia and Brazil to thriving urban centers like New York City and Milan. They speak dozens of languages and differ in nature and customs.

But Lions share a common spirit...and, since 1917, have been united for a single cause; helping those less fortunate.

Today Lions are tackling the tough problems facing our world...problems like blindness and drug abuse, lack of training for the disabled and underprivileged, and elder care.

And Lions are succeeding because they have embraced all those committed to building a brighter future for the world and for themselves. With a new generation of enlightened members, Lions are working smarter, faster and with more direction and commitment than ever before.

We are the Lions.

We Serve.

...that's why WE SERVE!

We Serve
www.lionsclubs.org

A Concern for the World's Youth

For young people whose circumstances don't offer opportunity or direction, Lions youth programs offer more than fond memories — they offer inspiration for the future.

Every summer, thousands of disadvantaged and disabled youths, for whom summer camp would otherwise be just a dream, attend Lions-sponsored camps. Here they learn that people do care; that the future does hold possibilities; and that they can make their own opportunities.

The Lions-Quest "Skills for Growing" program for elementary school students and the "Skills for Adolescence" curriculum for middle school students have helped millions of young people around the world acquire the skills of self-esteem they need to live productive, happy, drug-free lives.

Through the Lions International Youth Exchange program, more than 5,000 youngsters travel yearly to a foreign country to live with a host family. There they learn to appreciate and understand cultures different from their own...and find the inspiration to help build a world that includes tolerance, compassion and sensitivity for all those who are different than themselves.

Lions Clubs in 185 countries sponsor more than 4,500 Leo clubs worldwide. The more than 113,000 members, ages 12 to 28, perform various community service activities and support a special worldwide Literacy and Culture Project.

GENERATION OF HELP

Our youth programs ensure a bright future!

We Serve

www.lionsclubs.org

2075-99

Campaign "SightFirst"

Worldwide, Lion Clubs are recognized for their service to the blind and visually impaired. This service began through a challenge issued by Helen Keller to become "knights of the blind in the crusade against darkness" during the Lions 1925 International Convention.

Established in 1990, SightFirst works to prevent and reverse blindness worldwide by closing the gap between existing health care services and those that remain desperately needed.

Today, more than 40 million people in the world are blind. Remarkably, 80 percent of these cases could have been prevented or are curable with proper treatment. The problem, however, is that the vast majority of people who are blind live in developing countries that lack the basic resources—clean water, sanitary living conditions, medical facilities—to fend off preventable diseases that cause blindness.

Working in cooperation with dedicated eye care professionals and eye health experts, governments and other concerned organizations, Lions have mobilized communities in every corner of the world to help fill the gap between all that is being done and all that needs to be done to overcome the tragedy of blindness wherever it strikes.

Financial support for SightFirst projects is provided by Campaign SightFirst, which depends on the fundraising activities of local clubs, donations by individual Lions, and the contributions of governments, foundations, and corporations.

Other Sight-Related Activities

In addition to the SightFirst program, Lions Clubs continue to support other sight-related activities:

- In the U.S., Canada, and United Kingdom, Lions co-sponsor with 460 LensCrafters stores the *Give the Gift of Sight,* a special used eyeglass collection and recycling program.

- Lions provide 600,000 free professional glaucoma screenings and make 25,000 corneal transplants possible each year.

- Lions establish and support a majority of the world's eye banks, hundreds of clinics, hospitals, and eye research centers worldwide.

- Lions provide thousands each year with free quality eye care, eyeglasses, Braille-writers, large print texts, white canes, and guide dogs.

- Lions operate the vast majority of eye banks throughout the world and have donated hundreds of millions of dollars toward research, training, and rehabilitation for people who are blind.

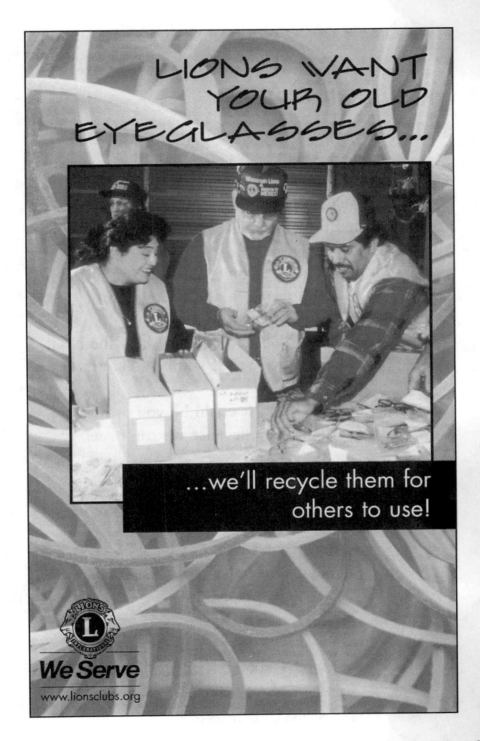

Be A Lion

Can you imagine how it would be,
If it was dark and you couldn't see?

It would be hard to read or write,
Yet, some take for granted their gift of sight.

I'm not one of these people, I assure you of this,
My eyesight, to me, I surely would miss.

I joined the Lions Club because they help the blind.
You can join too, would you be so kind?

One of these days, it could be you or me,
needing some help because we can't see.

Call a member and make a start.
Say you'll be happy to do your part.

Be a Lion...Join today...
And help someone else along the way.

by
Doris (Criket) Kimbrell
Iron City Lions Club
Iron City, Tennessee

Join a Lions Club and make a difference in your life and the lives of countless others.

By participating in a local Lions club, you can help meet pressing needs in your own community and have a meaningful impact on the health and well-being of people around the world.

For more information about joining a Lions Club, contact your local Lions Club (look for an address or phone number in the back of this cookbook)

or contact

Lions Clubs International
300 - 22nd Street
Oak Brook, IL 60523-8842
Phone (708) 571-5466

Lions Make A Difference

TABLE OF CONTENTS

FAVORITE RECIPES
FROM MY COOKBOOK

Recipe Name	Page Number

FOOD QUANTITIES FOR 25, 50, AND 100 SERVINGS

FOOD	25 SERVINGS	50 SERVINGS	100 SERVINGS
Rolls	4 doz.	8 doz.	16 doz.
Bread	50 slices or 3 1-lb. loaves	100 slices or 6 1-lb. loaves	200 slices or 12 1-lb. loaves
Butter	½ lb.	¾ to 1 lb.	1½ lb.
Mayonnaise	1 c.	2 to 3 c.	4 to 6 c.
Mixed filling for sandwiches (meat, eggs, fish)	1½ qt.	2½ to 3 qt.	5 to 6 qt.
Mixed filling (sweet-fruit)	1 qt.	1¾ to 2 qt.	2½ to 4 qt.
Jams & preserves	1½ lb.	3 lb.	6 lb.
Crackers	1½ lb.	3 lb.	6 lb.
Cheese (2 oz. per serving)	3 lb.	6 lb.	12 lb.
Soup	1½ gal.	3 gal.	6 gal.
Salad dressings	1 pt.	2½ pt.	½ gal.
Meat, Poultry, or Fish:			
Wieners (beef)	6½ lb.	13 lb.	25 lb.
Hamburger	9 lb.	18 lb.	35 lb.
Turkey or chicken	13 lb.	25 to 35 lb.	50 to 75 lb.
Fish, large whole (round)	13 lb.	25 lb.	50 lb.
Fish, fillets or steaks	7½ lb.	15 lb.	30 lb.
Salads, Casseroles, Vegetables:			
Potato salad	4¼ qt.	2¼ gal.	4½ gal.
Scalloped potatoes	4½ qt. or 1 12x20" pan	8½ qt.	17 qt.
Mashed potatoes	9 lb.	18-20 lb.	25-35 lb.
Spaghetti	1¼ gal.	2½ gal.	5 gal.
Baked beans	¾ gal.	1¼ gal.	2½ gal.
Jello salad	¾ gal.	1¼ gal.	2½ gal.
Canned vegetables	1 #10 can	2½ #10 cans	4 #10 cans
Fresh Vegetables:			
Lettuce (for salads)	4 heads	8 heads	15 heads
Carrots (3 oz. or ½ c.)	6¼ lb.	12½ lb.	25 lb.
Tomatoes	3-5 lb.	7-10 lb.	14-20 lb.
Desserts:			
Watermelon	37½ lb.	75 lb.	150 lb.
Fruit cup (½ c. per serving)	3 qt.	6 qt.	12 qt.
Cake	1 10x12" sheet cake 1½ 10" layer cakes	1 12x20" sheet cake 3 10" layer cakes	2 12x20" sheet cakes 6 10" layer cakes
Whipping cream	¾ pt.	1½ to 2 pt.	3 pt.
Ice Cream:			
Brick	3¼ qt.	6½ qt.	12½ qt.
Bulk	2¼ qt.	4½ qt. or 1¼ gal.	9 qt. or 2½ gal.
Beverages:			
Coffee	½ lb. and 1½ gal. water	1 lb. and 3 gal. water	2 lb. and 6 gal. water
Tea	¹⁄₁₂ lb. and 1½ gal. water	⅙ lb. and 3 gal. water	⅓ lb. and 6 gal. water
Lemonade	10 to 15 lemons, 1½ gal. water	20 to 30 lemons, 3 gal. water	40 to 60 lemons, 6 gal. water

SNACKS, APPETIZERS, BEVERAGES
SNACKS

CHEESE BISCUITS (WAFERS)

½ lb. sharp Cheddar cheese, grated
2 sticks margarine, softened

2 c. plain flour
2 c. Rice Krispies
Dash of cayenne pepper

Preheat oven to 350°. Blend cheese and margarine. Slowly add flour to mixture. Add pepper and Rice Krispies and mix with hands into a ball. Will be firm.

Drop by teaspoon onto cookie sheet and mash flat with a fork or hand. Needs to be very thin to be crispy. Bake from 10 to 12 minutes (depending on oven) until edges are golden brown and until firm to touch. When cool, place in airtight container. Makes 6 to 7 dozen biscuits.

A family holiday favorite. They disappear *very* quickly!

Lion Sylvia James, Foley Lions Club
Foley, AL, USA

CHEESE STRAWS

2 (8 oz.) Cracker Barrel extra sharp cheese
2 sticks margarine
3 c. plain flour

Dash of salt
Dash of red pepper
Dash of paprika

Mix well until very firm. Place in cookie pastry press with choice of attachment. Press out strings to desired lengths on baking sheet. Bake in 350° oven on top rack for 15 minutes.

Nancy White, North Tazewell Lions Club
North Tazewell, VA

CHEESE STRAWS BY JOHN

1 lb. sharp Cheddar cheese, grated
3 sticks butter, softened
3 c. flour

¼ tsp. cayenne pepper
1 tsp. salt

Combine all and mix well. Preheat oven to 275°. Bake one pan at a time for 30 to 35 minutes. Remove to a bowl lined with paper towels.

John Hamner, Bellville Lions Club
Bellville, GA, USA

CHEESE CRISPS

1 c. butter
2 c. all-purpose flour
½ tsp. salt
¼ tsp. cayenne pepper

2 c. (8 oz.) shredded sharp
   Cheddar cheese
3 c. rice crisp cereal

In a mixing bowl, cream the butter until fluffy. Slowly mix in flour, salt, and cayenne pepper. Stir in cheese and cereal. Shape into 1½ inch balls and place on ungreased baking sheet. Bake at 350° for 15 to 17 minutes or until slightly browned. Serve warm or cold. Yields 3 dozen.

Mrs. Charlotte M. Garner, Pascagoula Evening Lions Club
Pascagoula, MS

PITA CRISPS

⅓ c. oil
1 tsp. ground cumin
¼ tsp. cayenne pepper

Salt
4 pita breads

Heat the oven to 400°. Combine the oil, cumin, cayenne pepper, and ¼ teaspoon salt. Split the pitas in halves. Brush the cut side of each half with the flavored oil. Stack the pitas and cut them into quarters. Spread them on a baking sheet in a single layer and bake until golden brown, about 10 minutes. Transfer to a rack to cool.

Per pita crisp: 41 calories, 1 g protein, 2 g fat, 57 mg sodium, 4 g carbohydrate, 0 mg cholesterol.

Lion John J. Hess, Clarence Lions Club
Clarence Center, NY, USA

TRASH (DO DADS)

1 box Wheat, Rice, and Corn
   Chex
1 box cheese crackers (Cheez-its)
1 pkg. pretzels
2 (12 oz.) cans mixed nuts
A few pecan halves (or broken)
1 c. bacon drippings

1 stick margarine
2 Tbsp. garlic salt
1½ Tbsp. Accent
1 Tbsp. Tabasco sauce
3 Tbsp. Worcestershire sauce

Heat bacon drippings and margarine till warm. Add garlic salt, Accent, Tabasco, and Worcestershire. Stir well. In a very large pan, combine other ingredients. Pour liquid ingredients gradually over ingredients, stirring gently with wooden spoon. Cook at 250° for 1 hour. Turn or stir gently; cook for 1½ more hours. After cooling, put in Ziploc bags or any airtight container.

This is good to share with friends at Christmas (or any other time). Everyone enjoys it. It will keep for 2 to 3 weeks or longer if tightly sealed.

Emily Groover, Bellville Lions Club
Bellville, GA, USA

2

CRISPIX MIX

1 lb. butter
2 c. brown sugar
1 c. Karo syrup (white)
2 tsp. vanilla

2 boxes Crispix cereal
2 (12 oz.) cans mixed nuts
2 c. pecans
2 c. raisins

Boil butter, sugar, and syrup for 5 minutes. Add vanilla. Put cereal, nuts, and raisins in 2 jelly roll pans. Pour syrupy mixture over top and stir well. Bake in oven 1 hour at 200°. Stir every 15 minutes.

Something different and delicious.

Mrs. Jan Callaghan, Elburn Lions Club
Elburn, IL, USA

SNACK MIX

6 c. Crispix cereal
1 (10 oz.) can mixed nuts
1 (10 oz.) pkg. mini-pretzels

¾ c. butter or margarine
¾ c. packed brown sugar

Combine dry ingredients. In a saucepan, melt butter over low heat. Add brown sugar; cook and stir until dissolved. Pour over cereal; stir to coat. Place one-third on a greased baking sheet (15x10 inches). Bake at 325° for eight minutes. Stir and bake for 6 more minutes. Spread on waxed paper to cool. Repeat with mixture.

Can be done on two large baking sheets or three smaller ones.

This is good to make at holiday time.

Leola C. Jurrens, Downtown Bartlesville Lions Club
Bartlesville, OK, USA

OYSTER CRACKER SNACKS

2 (12 oz.) bags oyster crackers
1 pkg. Hidden Valley Ranch
   dressing

2 tsp. dill wed
1 tsp. garlic powder
¾ c. oil

Mix together Hidden Valley Ranch dressing, dill weed, garlic powder, and oil. Spread crackers on cookie sheet. Pour ingredients mixture over crackers. Toss. Let stand for about 2 hours, stirring occasionally.

James Cunningham, Graysville-Proctor Lions Club
Glen Easton, WV, USA

What would you change if this day were your last?

SNACK CRACKERS

½ tsp. garlic powder
1 tsp. dill weed
1 pkg. Hidden Valley Original mix

¾ c. salad oil
2 pkg. oyster crackers

Mix first 4 ingredients together. Add crackers. Put in metal or glass bowl (not plastic). Let stand for 2 hours, stirring every 15 minutes.

Betty Rutledge, Bryan Lioness Club
Bryan, OH

PRETZELS, HOT BUTTERED

1½ c. flour
¼ tsp. salt
½ tsp. sugar

1⅛ tsp. dry yeast
½ c. warm water

Topping:

¼ c. warm water
1 Tbsp. baking soda
1½ Tbsp. unsalted butter, melted

Coarse salt
Savory topping

Place dry ingredients in mixer bowl; mix well to blend. Add water and mix until dough becomes a ball, cleaning sides. Transfer to a lightly greased covered bowl. Allow to rest for 30 minutes at room temperature.

Preheat oven to 500°. Prepare a lightly greased baking sheet. Transfer dough to a lightly greased work surface. Divide into 4 parts. Let set for 5 minutes. Roll each piece into 30 inch rope and form into pretzel shape. Place on baking sheet and allow to rest for 10 minutes.

Prepare wash by dissolving soda in warm water. Invert pretzels, dip in wash, and place back on baking sheet, washed side up. Sprinkle lightly with coarse salt, covering thoroughly. Bake 8 or 9 minutes, turning pan once. Remove from oven and brush liberally with melted butter; dust with savory topping. Onion, garlic, or tomato toppings can be used.

John Hamner, Bellville Lions Club
Bellville, GA, USA

A little example can have a big influence.

CHEESY SOFT PRETZELS

1½ c. all-purpose flour
½ c. shredded Cheddar cheese
2 tsp. baking powder
1 tsp. sugar
¾ tsp. salt

2 Tbsp. cold butter or margarine
⅔ c. milk
1 egg, beaten
Coarse salt

In a bowl, combine flour, cheese, baking powder, sugar, and salt. Cut in butter until crumbly. Stir in milk just until moistened. Knead on a floured surface for 1 minute; divide in half. Roll each portion into a 12x8 inch rectangle; cut each into 8 inch long strips. Fold strips in half, pinching the edges, and twist into pretzel shapes. Place on greased baking sheets. Brush with egg and sprinkle with coarse salt. Bake at 400° for 12 to 15 minutes or until golden brown. Serve immediately. Yield: 1½ dozen.

CHOCOLATE PRETZEL RINGS

48 to 50 pretzel rings
1 (8 oz.) pkg. chocolate kisses

¼ c. M&M's

Place the pretzels on greased baking sheets; place a chocolate kiss in the center of each ring. Bake at 275° for 2 to 3 minutes or until chocolate is softened. Remove from the oven. Place an M&M on each, pressing down slightly so chocolate fills the ring. Refrigerate for 5 to 10 minutes or until chocolate is firm. Store at room temperature. Yield: About 4 dozen.

"If you like chocolate-covered pretzels, you'll love these simple snacks. They're fun to make anytime of year because you can color coordinate the M& M's to each holiday."

Maria Gaso, Bentleyville Lioness Club
Bentleyville, PA, USA

LETTER PRETZELS

1 pkg. dry yeast
½ c. warm water
1 tsp. sugar
½ tsp. salt

1⅓ c. flour
1 beaten egg
Coarse salt for top

Dissolve yeast in water with sugar. Stir in flour and salt. Knead and divide into 12 pieces. Roll to 18 inch rope and shape into your favorite letters. Place on greased baking sheet and brush with beaten egg; sprinkle with coarse salt. Bake for 13 minutes at 425°.

This is special for children.

Pat Worden, South Jefferson Lions Club
Adams, NY

CARAMEL CRACKERS

2 (9 oz.) boxes Ritz Bits
½ c. butter or margarine
½ c. light corn syrup
1 tsp. baking soda

1 c. dry-roasted peanuts
1 c. granulated sugar
1 tsp. vanilla

Preheat oven to 250°. Combine crackers and nuts in a greased, large, shallow baking pan. In a saucepan, bring butter, sugar, and corn syrup to a boil and cook for 5 minutes. Remove from heat; add vanilla and soda. Pour caramel mixture over crackers and nuts; stir well. Bake 1 hour, stirring every 15 minutes. Pour onto waxed paper and break apart; allow to cool. Store in airtight container. Makes approximately 9 cups of snack mix.

Mary L. Coon, Hutchinson Breakfast Lions Club
Hutchinson, KS, USA

BROWN SUGAR CRACKERS

Melt ¾ cup butter.

Add:

1 c. brown sugar
¼ c. honey

⅛ c. water

Bring above to a boil. Simmer on low for 5 minutes.

Add to following and stir well:

1 tsp. vanilla

½ to ¾ c. chopped nuts

Line cookie tray with foil. Spray foil with cooking spray. Place ½ box Club crackers close together on foil. Drizzle mixture on crackers. Bake at 350° for 10 minutes.

Lion Sandy Clever, East Prospect Lions Club
East Prospect, PA, USA

POPCORN CAKE

½ c. butter
1 (16 oz.) bag marshmallows
¼ c. peanut butter
4 qt. popped popcorn

1 c. dry roasted peanuts
1 (10 oz.) pkg. chocolate candy
coated peanuts

Melt butter, marshmallows, and peanut butter in large pan until completely melted. Cook one more minute. Pour over popped corn and peanuts; mix in the chocolate candy. Pour into a buttered angel food cake pan to shape and turn out on foil covered cardboard cake plate when set. Do not bake. Decorate with candy canes at Christmas, small flags at 4th of July, etc.

PDG Bud Myers, Guiding Lion, Sunrise Lions Club
(chartered June, 1999)
Mexico, MO

CARAMEL CORN

1 c. butter or oleo
2 c. brown sugar (not packed)
½ c. dark corn syrup

1 tsp. salt
6 qt. popcorn

Bring to a boil (stirring constantly); boil 5 minutes (not stirring). Remove from heat. Stir in 1 teaspoon vanilla and ½ teaspoon baking soda. Mix together and pour over popcorn. Pour in shallow pan. Bake in oven at 250° for 1 hour. Stir every 15 minutes. Let cool and break apart on a newspaper. Store in a tight container.

Anne Johnson, Sunrise Lions Club
Mexico, MO

HAM CRESCENT SNACKS

1 can refrigerator crescent rolls
4 thin slices ham

4 tsp. prepared mustard
1 c. shredded Swiss cheese

Unroll dough into 4 long rectangles. Press perforations to seal. Place ham slices on rectangles. Spread ham with mustard and sprinkle with cheese. Starting at longest side, roll up jelly roll fashion. Cut into ½ inch slices. Place, cut side down, on ungreased cookie sheet. Bake for 15 to 20 minutes or until lightly browned at 375°.

This is an easy, delicious appetizer.

Mrs. Duane (Pam) Bennett, Mad River Lions Club
Riverside, OH, USA

PECAN LOG

1 box vanilla wafers
1 c. condensed milk

½ c. pecans

Crumble wafers. Add condensed milk and chopped fine pecans. Make a long roll. Refrigerate about 3 hours; cut in pieces.

Melba Johnson, Brookhaven Alpha Lions Club
Brookhaven, MS

People with a disability have a unique ability to teach us how to live.

CARAMELIZED APPLE SLICES

Simple, elegant, and versatile, too. Enjoy these tart sweet apples warm with a dollop of whipped cream, over ice cream or on a generous slice of gingerbread.

2 cooking apples (such as Granny
   Smith)
4 Tbsp. butter

¼ c. brown sugar
1 tsp. vanilla extract

Peel the apples and cut into thick slices. In a frying pan, melt the butter over low heat. Stir in the brown sugar and vanilla and cook until sugar dissolves, about 3 minutes. Add the apples and toss gently to coat. Cover and cook until the apples are tender, about 10 minutes. Makes 4 servings.

Per serving: 194 calories, 0 g protein, 12 g fat, 7 mg sodium, 23 g carbohydrate, 31 mg cholesterol.

Mrs. Mike Nowicki, Clarence Lions Club
Clarence Center, NY, USA

GLAZED FRUIT

1 lb. mixed fresh fruit with stems
   (such as grapes, kumquats,
   and strawberries)

⅛ tsp. cream of tartar
2 c. sugar

Oil a large baking sheet very lightly. Wash fruit and dry completely. Leave stems intact. Dissolve cream of tartar in 1 cup water in a deep saucepan. Add sugar and bring to a boil over high heat. Boil until syrup reaches hard-crack stage (300°). Dip base of pan in cold water to stop cooking. As soon as syrup stops bubbling, begin dipping fruit. Hold each piece by the stem and quickly dip into the syrup. Let excess drip back into pan and then put on baking sheet. Leave until set. Serve after dinner with espresso or coffee. Makes about 50 pieces.

Per piece: 19 calories, 0 g protein, 0 g fat, 0 mg sodium, 5 g carbohydrate, 0 mg cholesterol.

Work time: 30 minutes. Total time: 30 minutes.

The holidays are the perfect time for glazed fruit. The coating, which softens quickly in humid weather, stays crisp in winter's dry air. The glaze will last 2 to 4 hours, so you can dip the fruit before your guests arrive and serve the candylike treats after dinner.

A few words of caution: Sugar reaches high temperatures. Be extra careful when dipping fruit and never leave hot syrup in the reach of children.

Joanne M. Wetzler, Clarence Lions Club
Clarence Center, NY, USA

PINEAPPLE TARTS

1 beaten egg
½ c. milk
¼ c. pineapple juice

1 heaping tsp. baking powder
3 heaping Tbsp. sugar
¼ tsp. salt

Mix enough flour to make a batter just thick enough to stick to the sliced pineapples. Fry in skillet with Crisco.

Lion Ida Rohrer, Moundbuilders Lions Club
Newark, OH, USA

Be as gracious in receiving as you are in giving.

❧ ❧ ❧

What you will be tomorrow depends on the choices you make today.

❧ ❧ ❧

The bonds of matrimony aren't worth much unless the interest is kept up.

APPETIZERS

HOT PEPPERED SHRIMP

2 sticks margarine
1 small can black pepper

Enough medium shrimp to cover
bottom of casserole

Place margarine in large, shallow casserole dish and microwave until melted. Place 1 layer unpeeled shrimp in the melted margarine. Cover shrimp with 1 small can of black pepper.

Cover and microwave until shrimp meat pulls away from the shell just along the back ridge. If shrimp is held up to the light, you will be able to clearly see the separation from the shell. Be very careful not to overcook shrimp. Be prepared by having on hand very cold iced tubs of cold beverages.

Do not allow children or sissy adults to eat this dish as it is very hot!

Vivian Houser, Foley Lions Club
Foley, AL

SHRIMP AND RED PEPPER APPETIZER ALA CHARLOTTE

1 clove fresh garlic, minced
1 lb. medium size shrimp
1 jar red roasted peppers, cut
    into long strips
1 c. black olives, sliced

2 Tbsp. fresh parsley, chopped
½ c. olive oil
2 tsp. red wine vinegar
½ lb. Feta cheese, crumbled

Saute shrimp and garlic with oil; discard oil after cooking. Put in bowl with remaining ingredients (except cheese). Chill for at least 4 hours. After chilling, add Feta cheese to top of bowl.

Can be used as appetizer, on a relish tray, or as a side dish - delicious!! Good with warm French bread.

Jeri Maynard, Hudson Nottingham West
Hudson, NH, USA

Prejudice distorts what it sees, deceives when it talks,
and destroys when it acts.

EASY APPETIZER

2 pkg. crescent rolls
2 (8 oz.) pkg. cream cheese
½ c. plain yogurt

½ pkg. Ranch dressing
½ c. mayonnaise

Toppings (your choice):

Shredded cheese
Raw veggies
Chopped tomato

Shrimp
Chopped egg
Chopped olives

Spread unrolled crescent rolls in a 12x18 inch tray or flat pan. Bake at 350° for 8 to 10 minutes. Let cool.

Mix cream cheese, mayonnaise, yogurt, and dry Ranch dressing. Spread over baked dough. Sprinkle with your choice of toppings: Cheese, veggies, shrimp, crumbled hard-boiled eggs, olives, etc.

A very easy appetizer. Just use your imagination to create your choice of toppings.

Nancy Poole, Bend Lions Club
Bend, OR

STUFFED MUSHROOMS

Black pepper to taste
⅛ tsp. thyme
¼ tsp. garlic salt
Chopped green onions

Chopped crabmeat
Fresh mushrooms
½ tsp. melted butter
Mozzarella cheese, finely chopped

Wash mushrooms and remove stems. Combine ingredients, chop, and stuff into mushrooms. Sprinkle cheese on top and bake at 425° for 15 to 20 minutes. Remove from oven and serve immediately.

Dianne Gibson, Mayfield Lions Club
Mayfield, KY, USA

To avoid the mistakes of youth, draw from the wisdom of age.

Winners never quit and quitters never win.

WALNUT STUFFED MUSHROOMS

16 to 24 medium sized
   mushrooms
2 Tbsp. butter or margarine
Garlic salt
1 Tbsp. finely minced fresh onion
2 tsp. Worcestershire sauce

1 Tbsp. mayonnaise
3 Tbsp. Parmesan cheese
3 Tbsp. finely chopped walnuts
Fresh parsley for garnish

Clean mushrooms. Remove stems and set aside. Brush mushroom caps with part of butter and lightly sprinkle them with garlic salt. Chop stems and saute with onion in remaining butter. Add other ingredients and fill caps with this mixture.

Place in ovenproof dish and bake at 400°F. for 10 minutes or until mushrooms are tender and tops are browned. Garnish with a sprinkle of fresh chopped parsley or a parsley sprig and serve.

PDG James R. Schiebel, Hilton Lions Club
Hilton, NY, USA

SAUSAGE-BACON ROLL-UPS

1 large loaf white bread
1 lb. mild or hot sausage
1 (8 oz.) pkg. cream cheese

1 to 2 lb. bacon, slices cut in
   halves
1 small onion, chopped

Trim crust off bread and cut slices in halves. Brown sausage with onion and drain well. Mix cream cheese with sausage while still warm. Spread mixture on bread slices and roll-up. (May be frozen at this point.) Wrap with bacon and secure with toothpick. Bake at 400° until brown and crispy.

Katherine Rawls, Brookhaven Alpha Lions Club
Bogue Chitto, MS, USA

QUICK PIZZA TRIANGLES

1 (15 oz.) pkg. refrigerated pie
   crusts

Filling:

4 oz. (1 c.) Mozzarella cheese
¾ c. sliced pepperoni, chopped

¾ c. pizza sauce
1 tsp. dried Italian seasoning

Heat oven to 450°F. Place pie crusts on cutting board. Cut each crust into quarters, making 8 wedges.

In medium bowl, combine all filling ingredients; mix well. Place 1 heaping tablespoon filling on half of each crust wedge. Fold unfilled sides of wedges over filling. With fork, press edges to seal. Place on ungreased cookie sheet. Bake at 450°F. for 12 to 14 minutes or until crust is golden brown. Makes 8 pizza pockets.

Lion Kathy Dobson, Mount Airy Foothills Lions Club
Mount Airy, NC, USA

ALMOND HAM ROLL-UPS

1 (8 oz.) pkg. cream cheese
2 Tbsp. mayonnaise or salad
   dressing
1 tsp. instant minced onion
1 tsp. Worcestershire sauce
¼ tsp. dry mustard
¼ tsp. paprika

½ tsp. pepper
½ tsp. hot sauce
1 Tbsp. finely chopped almonds,
   toasted
1 (12 oz.) pkg. thinly sliced boiled
   ham

Combine all ingredients except ham, stirring until blended; spread 1 tablespoon mixture on each ham slice. Roll up jelly roll fashion, starting at short end. Wrap in plastic wrap and freeze. It can be frozen as long as a month ahead.

Thaw at room temperature 1 hour before serving. Cut each roll into ¼ inch slices. Yield: 5 dozen.

JoAnn Jones, Mathews Lions Club
North, VA

SWEET BOLOGNA APPETIZER

1 lb. sliced bologna
1 Tbsp. mayonnaise
2 (8 oz.) pkg. Philadelphia cream
   cheese

4 to 5 Tbsp. horseradish

Mix mayonnaise, cream cheese, and horseradish. Spread between 3 to 4 slices of bologna, stacked. Refrigerate. When cool, cut each stack into 8 pie shaped pieces. Garnish with parsley. *Enjoy.*

The Prayer of a Bachelor

Oh Lord: I pray to thee, please send a wife.
I've had enough of the single life.
No more, oh Lord, will I stingy be
If only you'll send a good cook to me.

Lois Leber, East Prospect Lions Club
East Prospect, PA, USA

HOT AND SPICY FLANNIGANS

1 lb. ground beef
1 lb. hot sausage
1 can Campbell's nacho soup

1 can Campbell's cheese soup
1 pkg. pepperoni
Cocktail rye bread

Brown beef and sausage together. Drain. Add both cheese soups. Spread on cocktail bread and put pepperoni on top. Place on cookies sheet. Bake in oven at 350° for 15 minutes or until heated through. Also can microwave.

FETA FRITTATA

A practical dish if ever there was one, a frittata can be served hot, warm, or room temperature and is good for breakfast, lunch, or supper. Cut in thin wedges, it also makes a fine hors d'oeuvre.

1 onion
1 green pepper
8 eggs
Salt and pepper

2 Tbsp. oil
3 oz. Feta cheese (about ½ c.), crumbled

Slice onion. Cut green pepper into strips. Beat eggs with 1 tablespoon water, ¾ teaspoon salt, and ½ teaspoon pepper. In an ovenproof frying pan, heat oil over medium heat. Add onion, green pepper, and ½ teaspoon salt; cover and cook until tender, about 10 minutes. Reduce heat to low. Pour in egg mixture and crumble Feta cheese on top. Cook until sides and bottom of frittata are set, but top is still runny, about 10 minutes.

Meanwhile, heat broiler. Broil frittata until top is golden and puffed, about 2 minutes. Makes 4 servings.

Per serving: 185 calories, 11 g protein, 14 g fat, 670 mg sodium, 3 g carbohydrate, 296 mg cholesterol.

Barbara Joy Hess, Clarence Lions Club
Clarence Center, NY, USA

WON TON

1 pkg. won ton skins
1 lb. ground beef
½ c. water chestnuts, diced
¼ c. green onions, chopped
Sealer (1 Tbsp. cornstarch and ¼ c. water)

2 Tbsp. soy sauce
1 tsp. sesame oil
1 Tbsp. dry sherry
1 egg, beaten

Sweet and Sour Sauce:

1 (8 oz.) can crushed pineapple
½ green pepper, diced
3 Tbsp. sugar

3 Tbsp. vinegar
1 Tbsp. cornstarch

Chop and mix water chestnuts and onions. Mix with beef in a bowl. Add soy sauce, sesame oil, dry sherry, and egg. Mix well. Place filling in won ton skin and fold, envelope style. Deep-fry to a light brown color. Add Sweet and Sour Sauce ingredients and thicken with cornstarch.

Won tons may be made ahead and frozen. Thaw and serve warm or cold. Sauce may also be warm or cold.

Sarah Wehling, Bothell Lions Club
Bothell, WA, USA

PICKLED ONIONS

1 lb. small white boiling onions
1½ c. water
1½ c. vinegar (white)
¼ tsp. salt

Pinch of red pepper (optional)
½ Tbsp. pickling spice (add more
   if desired)

Peel onions and cut X on top of each. Pack in jar with tight lid. Mix all other ingredients and pour over onions. Store in cool dark place at least one week.

Lion Ernie Freitas, Rio Rico Santa Cruz Valley Lions Club
Rio Rico, AZ, USA

HOLIDAY APPETIZER PIE

8 oz. pkg. cream cheese
2 Tbsp. milk
½ c. sour cream
2½ oz. jar dried beef, finely
   chopped

2 Tbsp. green pepper, finely
   chopped
2 Tbsp. minced onion
½ tsp. pepper

Soften cream cheese. Mix all ingredients together. Spoon into 8 inch pie plate. Bake at 350° for 15 minutes. May top with chopped nuts if desired.

Kim Lindsey, Mayfield Lions Club
Mayfield, KY, USA

GROUND BEEF SNACK QUICHES

¼ lb. ground beef
⅛ to ¼ tsp. garlic powder
⅛ tsp. pepper
1 c. biscuit/baking mix
¼ c. cornmeal
¼ c. cold butter or margarine
2 to 3 Tbsp. boiling water
1 egg

½ c. half & half cream
1 Tbsp. chopped green onion
1 Tbsp. chopped sweet red
   pepper
⅛ to ¼ tsp. salt
⅛ to ¼ tsp. cayenne pepper
½ c. finely shredded Cheddar
   cheese

In a saucepan over medium heat, cook beef, garlic powder, and pepper until meat is no longer pink; drain and set aside. In a bowl, combine the biscuit mix and cornmeal; cut in butter. Add enough water to form a soft dough. Press onto the bottom and up the sides of greased miniature muffin cups. Place teaspoonfuls of beef mixture into each shell. In a bowl, combine the egg, cream, onion, red pepper, salt, and cayenne; pour over beef mixture. Sprinkle with cheese. Bake at 375° for 20 minutes or until a knife inserted near the center comes out clean. Yield: 1½ dozen.

The only things we really lose are those things we try to keep.

CRAB PUFFS

Boil together:

½ c. water   ½ tsp. salt
½ c. butter

Add ½ cup flour all at once. Stir until smooth. Remove from heat. Add 2 eggs, one at a time, beating after each. Add the following optional seasonings - parsley, Worcestershire sauce, chopped onion, mustard, and celery. Stir in gently 1½ cups crabmeat. Drop by teaspoon into hot fat (375°) and cook until lightly browned. Drain on paper.

Freeze individually on a cookie sheet until frozen, then transfer to a Ziploc freezer bag. To reheat, place in oven at 325° for 8 minutes.

This is a recipe that's great to do ahead of time. Always a hit when served.

JoAnn Jones, Mathews Lions Club
North, VA

ZUCCHINI OMELET APPETIZER

2 zucchini, sliced   ¼ tsp. salt
Flour for dredging   Pepper
4 to 6 eggs, slightly beaten   ⅛ tsp. thyme (ground)
1 Tbsp. Parmesan cheese

Dredge zucchini lightly in flour. Heat olive oil in skillet and cook zucchini in it until crisp. Combine eggs, Parmesan, salt, pepper, and thyme. Pour over zucchini. Cook until well set on both sides. Turn over once.

Sarah Wehling, Bothell Lions Club
Bothell, WA, USA

TENDER CHICKEN NUGGETS

"These tender chunks of chicken with a tasty corn flake crumb coating are fun to make - and eat."

1 c. crushed corn flakes   ¼ c. prepared Ranch salad
½ c. grated Parmesan cheese   dressing
½ tsp. salt   1 lb. boneless, skinless chicken
¼ tsp. pepper   breasts, cut into 1 inch cubes
⅛ tsp. garlic powder   Additional Ranch dressing

In a shallow bowl, combine the first five ingredients. Place dressing in another bowl. Toss chicken cubes in dressing, then roll in corn flake mixture. Place in a greased 11x7x2 inch baking pan. Bake, uncovered, at 400° for 12 to 15 minutes or until juices run clear. Serve with additional dressing for dipping. Yield: 4 servings.

Barbara K. Hugus, West Milford Lions Club
West Milford, WV, USA

COCKTAIL MEATBALLS

1 lb. ground beef
1/3 c. minced onion
1 egg
1 tsp. salt
1/2 tsp. Worcestershire sauce
1 (12 oz.) bottle chili sauce

1/2 c. dry bread crumbs
1/4 c. milk
1 Tbsp. snipped parsley
1/8 tsp. pepper
1/4 c. shortening
1 (10 oz.) jar grape jelly

Mix ground beef, bread crumbs, onion, milk, egg, and next 4 ingredients; gently shape into 1 inch balls.

Melt shortening in large skillet; brown meatballs. Remove meatballs from skillet; pour off fat. Heat chili sauce and jelly in skillet, stirring constantly, until jelly is melted. Add meatballs and stir until thoroughly coated. Simmer, uncovered, 30 minutes. Makes 5 dozen appetizers.

The secret's in the sauce.
Mrs. Jim (Judie) Thryselius, Elburn Lions Club
Elburn, IL, USA

PARTY MEATBALLS

Meatballs:

5 lb. bag Italian meatballs (1.2 oz size)

Sauce:

2 bottles chili sauce
2 Tbsp. A.1. Steak Sauce
1/2 c. vinegar (white or apple cider)
1 c. brown sugar
1 large can tomato sauce

1 large can chunk pineapple with juice
1 small jar sweet gherkin pickles with juice

Mix all ingredients together. Pour over meatballs. Bake 1 to 1 1/2 hours at 350°.

Lioness Marie C. Beatty, East Anne Arundel Lioness Club, 22A
Pasadena, MD, USA

People that care are people who share.

COCKTAIL MEATBALLS

1 lb. ground beef
½ c. dry bread crumbs
⅓ c. minced onions
¼ c. milk
1 egg
1 Tbsp. snipped parsley

1 tsp. salt
⅛ tsp. pepper
½ tsp. Worcestershire sauce
¼ c. shortening
1 (12 oz.) bottle chili sauce
1 (10 oz.) jar grape jelly

Mix ground beef, bread crumbs, onion, milk, egg, and next 4 ingredients; gently shape in 1 inch balls. Melt shortening in large skillet; brown meatballs. Remove meatballs from skillet; pour off fat. Heat chili sauce and jelly in skillet, stirring constantly, until jelly is melted. Add meatballs and stir until thoroughly coated. Simmer, uncovered, for 30 minutes. Makes 5 dozen appetizers.

Elizabeth Maddock, Canaan Northwest Lions Club
Canaan, CT, USA

MEATBALLS AS APPETIZERS

½ lb. ground beef
1 small onion, minced
Dash of garlic salt
½ tsp. salt

Dash of pepper
1 tsp. Worcestershire sauce
1 tsp. soy sauce

Yield: 3 dozen.

Sarah Wehling, Bothell Lions Club
Bothell, WA, USA

NOEL NIBBLERS

1 lb. ground beef
¼ c. finely chopped onion
½ tsp. salt
1 lb. frankfurters, cut into 1 inch
    pieces

1 (10 oz.) jar apricot or peach
    preserves
1 c. barbecue sauce
1 (20 oz.) can pineapple chunks,
    drained

Combine meat, onion, and salt; mix lightly. Shape into 1 inch meatballs. Brown in large skillet. Add frankfurters. Combine preserves and barbecue sauce. Simmer for 20 minutes, stirring occasionally. Add pineapple and heat thoroughly. Makes approximately 10 dozen appetizers.

Donna King, York Springs Lions Club
York Springs, PA

Don't just spend time with your children. "Invest it."

PORK SCRAP (SPREAD)

2 lb. ground pork
3 onions, chopped
1 clove garlic
¼ tsp. nutmeg

¼ tsp. cinnamon
¼ tsp. cayenne
½ tsp. ground cloves
Salt and pepper

Mash pork with masher down into water about ¼ inch over meat. Add spices. Bring to a boil, then simmer 2 hours. Keep adding water, as needed, to ¼ inch over meat. Spoon off excess grease, then stir well. Let set. Store in containers in refrigerator or freezer.

Great with saltines or on bread with pickled cucumbers/onions.
Lion Ernie Freitas, Rio Rico Santa Cruz Valley Lions Club
Rio Rico, AZ, USA

MOCK CHOPPED LIVER

3 medium onions
¼ c. oil
2 c. cooked green beans, drained
  (fresh or frozen)

4 hard-boiled eggs
10 walnuts, chopped
1 tsp. salt
¼ tsp. pepper

Dice and saute onions in oil until light gold in color. Mix with green beans, eggs, and nuts and chop until of a fine consistency or grind in meat grinder. Add salt and pepper and chill. Serve on lettuce leaf or mold to serve with crackers or party rye. Yield: 6 servings.
Joan Katz, Stafford-Missouri City Lions Club
Stafford, TX, USA

LIVER PATE

1 lb. chicken livers
¼ medium onion
¼ tsp. salt

1 (8 oz.) pkg. cream cheese
Garlic salt (to taste)

Cook 1 pound chicken livers, onion, and salt until livers are soft enough to mash. Mash while still warm. Add cream cheese and garlic salt and mix well. Keep refrigerated. Serve with crackers.
Audrey Leisgang, Ashwaubenon Lioness Club
Green Bay, WI, USA

A child may not inherit his parent's talent but he will absorb their values.

PICANTE PIMENTO CHEESE SPREAD

1½ lb. sharp Cheddar cheese, shredded
3 oz. American cheese, grated
1 Tbsp. onion, finely chopped
1 (4 oz.) jar chopped pimentos (undrained)

½ c. mayonnaise
Black pepper (to taste)
1 (8 oz.) jar hot picante sauce

Stir all ingredients together thoroughly and chill.

Good served with corn chips or as a sandwich spread.

Doris (Cricket) Kimbrell, Iron City Lions Club
Iron City, TN, USA

CHILI CHEESE LOG

3 c. grated Cheddar cheese
4 oz. cream cheese, softened
¾ tsp. Worcestershire sauce

¼ tsp. pepper
Lots of chili powder

Put Cheddar cheese, cream cheese, Worcestershire sauce, and pepper into mixing bowl. Beat until soft and smooth. Roll into two rolls. Make diameter a bit smaller than a round cracker so slices will fit on top. Sprinkle waxed paper liberally with chili powder. Roll to coat each log well. Wrap in wax paper. Chill in refrigerator for three or four days to blend. Put slices on round crackers or serve with a cheese knife and assorted crackers. Freezes well.

Lion Micheal and Ruth (Sauskojus) Bartolf, Oxbow and District Lions Club
Oxbow, Saskatchewan, Canada

CHEESE BALL

2 (8 oz.) pkg. softened cream cheese
3 tsp. mayo
3 tsp. dry onion soup mix

½ lb. shredded sharp cheese
1 c. crushed nuts (walnuts or pecans)

Mix together with hands and form into a ball. Roll and coat with nuts.

Lion Nelson Bonager, East Prospect Lions Club
East Prospect, PA, USA

REUBEN CHEESE DIP

1 (8 oz.) can sauerkraut, drained
2 bags corned beef, cut up
½ c. Miracle Whip or mayo

2 c. shredded Swiss cheese
2 c. shredded Cheddar cheese

Mix together and spread in a 9x9 inch pan sprayed with Pam. Bake at 350° for 25 minutes. Serve on rye or cocktail bread or crackers.

Janet Paule, Bryan Lioness Club
Bryan, OH

GJETOST FONDUE

3 c. shredded Gjetost cheese
3 Tbsp. flour
1½ c. dry white wine
1 (8 oz.) can crushed pineapple

French bread cubes
Wedges of apples, peaches, pears, mandarin orange sections

Stir together cheese and flour in a medium mixing bowl. Set aside. In a 3 quart saucepan, heat wine till just boiling. Reduce heat to medium. Add the cheese and flour mixture, ½ cup at a time, stirring after each addition till the cheese is melted. Stir in undrained crushed pineapple. Makes 3 cups.

Sarah Wehling, Bothell Lions Club
Bothell, WA, USA

CHEESE FONDUE

¼ c. butter
2 c. milk
1 lb. American cheese, cubed
1 (2 oz.) jar pimentos

¼ c. flour
½ pkg. dry onion soup mix (mix with ¼ c. water for 5 minutes)

Heat butter and milk together in a saucepan. Put all other ingredients in the blender and add hot milk and butter. Blend until smooth. Pour into fondue pot. Serve with French or Italian bread, cubed.

You may fry bread cubes in butter and sprinkle with garlic salt.

Linda Fox, Saginaw Lions Club
Saginaw, TX

BRAUNSCHWEIGER DIP

1 lb. or less Braunschweiger
1 large pkg. sour cream

1 pkg. Lipton onion mix

Mix all the ingredients together with mixer. *Great on crackers!*

BRAUNSCHWEIGER BALL

½ lb. Braunschweiger
2 tsp. minced onion
1 Tbsp. horseradish

¾ c. fine dry bread crumbs (optional)
8 oz. pkg. softened cream cheese

Mix all ingredients together and form into a ball. May be rolled in chopped nuts or decorated with whole nuts. Refrigerate several hours or overnight. Serve with crackers.

Liz Birchen, O'Fallon Lions Club
O'Fallon, MO, USA

2075-99

HOT JEZEBEL

10 to 12 oz. pineapple preserves
10 to 12 oz. apricot preserves
5 oz. prepared horseradish (not creamed)

1 tsp. dry mustard
8 oz. brick cream cheese

Mix first 4 ingredients and pour over 8 ounce brick cream cheese on plate surrounded by crackers.

Mixture is really enough for 2 bricks of cream cheese.

A Lion Banner Night favorite appetizer.

Judy Hoffman, Southport Lions Club
Indianapolis, IN

MEXICAN CAVIAR

2 (4½ oz.) cans chopped ripe olives, drained
2 (4 oz.) cans chopped green chilies, drained
2 ripe tomatoes, peeled and chopped
1 small sweet onion, finely chopped

1 tsp. garlic salt
3 tsp. olive oil
3 Tbsp. red wine vinegar
1 tsp. pepper
1 or 2 tsp. sugar
Dash of seasoning salt

Combine all ingredients and refrigerate in tightly covered container overnight. Serve with Scoops corn chips.

Nettie Favara, Greenwood Lions Club
Greenwood, MS, USA

CHILI DIP

½ lb. Velveeta cheese (mild Mexican flavor)

1 can chili (without beans)
1 can hot tamales

Melt cheese in small crock pot in microwave. Unwrap tamales and mash. Add tamales and chili to cheese. Mix well and return to microwave. Heat for about 3 minutes on HIGH. Return to heating element of crock pot and serve hot with corn chips or tortilla chips.

Nettie Favara, Greenwood Lions Club
Greenwood, MS, USA

All of creation bears God's autograph.

HUMMUS - GARBANZO DIP AND SPREAD

Time: 15 minutes.

2 c. cooked garbanzo beans
¼ c. cooking liquid
¼ c. tahini
2 Tbsp. olive oil

2 Tbsp. lemon juice
1 tsp. minced garlic
½ tsp. sea salt

Combine in food processor or blender cooked garbanzo beans, 2 table-spoons reserved cooking liquid, lemon juice, and olive oil. Blend until well mashed, adding more cooking liquid if needed.

Blend in the tahini, garlic, and seasonings. Do not overblend. The texture should be creamy and rough at the same time. If using a blender, it may be necessary to process in several smaller batches. Cover and refrigerate until ready to serve. Serves 6.

Serve with raw vegetable dippers or as a spread for pita bread. Will keep several days refrigerated. Freezes very well.

Comments: Beans must be cooked ahead.

PDG Jim Schiebel, Hilton Lions Club
Hilton, NY, USA

SPINACH DIP

4 oz. cream cheese, softened
1 c. mayonnaise
1 c. shredded Parmesan cheese

1 box frozen chopped spinach,
thawed and squeezed
1 small onion, chopped

Mix together. Bake at 350° for 20 minutes.

Lion Paul and Vale Welsh, East Prospect Lions Club
East Prospect, PA, USA

SOUTHERN SALSA DIP

1 (250 g) pkg. Philadelphia
cream cheese, softened
2 Tbsp. real mayonnaise
1 (120 ml) can diced green chilies
1 c. chopped, seeded tomato

¼ c. finely chopped onion
1 clove garlic, crushed
1 tsp. chili powder
¼ tsp. salt
Freshly ground pepper to taste

Blend cream cheese and mayonnaise. Stir in remaining ingredients. Cover and chill several hours to blend flavours. Serve with crisp vegetables and nachos. Makes 2 cups.

Micheal and Ruth Bartolf, Oxbow and District Lions Club
Oxbow, Saskatchewan, Canada

DIP FOR CHIPS

½ c. cottage cheese
1 c. sour cream
1 hard cooked egg, chopped
1 Tbsp. catsup
1½ tsp. horseradish

1 tsp. Worcestershire sauce
½ small clove garlic
½ tsp. dry mustard
½ tsp. salt

Mix and chill.

Sarah Wehling, Bothell Lions Club
Bothell, WA, USA

B L T DIP

1 lb. bacon, fried crisp and
crumbled

1 large tomato, diced
1 c. mayonnaise

Mix all together.

Tastes like a BLT sandwich without lettuce. Fritos Scoopers make a great dipper for this simple dip.

Mrs. Jan Callaghan, Elburn Lions Club
Elburn, IL, USA

DILLY DIP

1 c. sour cream
1 c. mayonnaise
1 tsp. Beau Monde seasoning

1 Tbsp. dill weed
1 Tbsp. chopped parsley
1 Tbsp. chopped onion

Mix all together and put in refrigerator overnight.

Great with snack crackers or potato chips.

Lion Amy L. Kastle, Kirwin Lions Club
Kirwin, KS, USA

YUMMIE CHIP DIP

1 lb. dairy cheese (extra sharp)
4 hard-boiled eggs
1 small jar pimentos

1 small onion
½ c. butter, melted
½ c. Miracle Whip salad dressing

Put cheese, eggs, pimentos, and onion through a food processor or grinder. Stir in butter and Miracle Whip.

Also makes a great cracker spread.

Veronica Nye, Scio Lions Club
Scio, NY, USA

SHRIMP DIP

1 can tomato soup
1 (8 oz.) cream cheese
½ pkg. unflavored gelatine
¼ c. water (dissolve gelatine in water)

½ c. onions, chopped fine
½ c. celery, chopped fine
½ c. green peppers, chopped fine
2 lb. shrimp, chopped
1 c. mayonnaise

Heat soup and dissolve cream cheese in it until it melts, then mix all together.

Lion Jane McCune, Huffman Lions Club
Huffman, TX

SHRIMP DIP

1 (8 oz.) pkg. Philadelphia cream cheese
1 (8 oz.) ctn. sour cream
1 can (small) shrimp, drained, or
1 c. finely chopped shrimp

½ small onion, chopped fine
2 Tbsp. mayonnaise

Use a fork to mash the cream cheese. Add sour cream, onions, and mayonnaise. Blend in shrimp and marinate for a few hours before serving.

Lion June Taylor, Foley Lions Club
Foley, AL, USA

DIANE'S CRABMEAT DIP

2 (8 oz.) pkg. cream cheese, softened
2 cans flaked crabmeat
1 tsp. minced onion

2 Tbsp. "Outerbridges" sherry pepper sauce
Shredded Mozzarella cheese

Mix first four ingredients well. Place in shallow casserole dish or pie plate. Cover with shredded cheese. Bake in 350° oven approximately 15 to 20 minutes until heated through and cheese is melted and bubbly - do not brown. Serve with assorted crackers, Melba toast, etc.

If unable to find Outerbridges sherry pepper sauce, substitute with 1½ tablespoons cooking sherry and ½ tablespoon hot sauce of your choice (Tabasco, Louisiana hot sauce, etc.).

Easy, easy, easy - always gets rave reviews at parties; can be made ahead up to cooking point and frozen until needed.

Diane Pettit, East Haddam Community Lions Club
East Haddam, CT, USA

Correction may mold us, but encouragement will motivate us.

EASY HOT CRAB DIP

1 can cream of mushroom soup
½ block Velveeta cheese (mild
   Mexican - more if desired)

1 lb. fresh crab (claw works well)
Old Bay seafood seasoning
Toast cups

Melt cheese and soup over low heat (burns easily). Pick crab for shells. Add to cheese mixture. Add seasoning to taste. Serve in chafing dish. Heat and top with cheese.

To make toast cups: Roll bread with rolling pin; cut into 4 squares or 4 rounds. Doesn't matter if some crust is on. Dip in melted margarine and scrape excess on side of pot. Mold in small muffin tins. Bake until brown around edges at 325° for 12 to 13 minutes. Spoon crab mixture into toast cups.

I serve this at parties. It is always a hit.

Martha C. Daniel, Bellville Lions Club
Bellville, GA, Evans County, USA

CLAM CASINO DIP

1 lb. bacon
1 stack Ritz crackers, crushed
2 chopped green pepper
2 chopped onions

2 stalks chopped celery
3 cans minced clams
¼ lb. butter or margarine
3 stacks Ritz crackers

Fry 1 pound bacon. When crisp, remove bacon from pan and cool on paper towel. Add ¼ pound butter to bacon drippings and melt butter. Add green peppers, onions, and celery and saute until tender. Add the stack of Ritz crackers after they are crushed. Add 1 drained can of clams and 2 cans with juice. Add crisp bacon. Mix all ingredients. Pour into greased 1½ quart pan. Bake at 350°F. for 30 minutes. Serve with extra Ritz crackers for dipping.

PDG James R. Schiebel, Hilton Lions Club
Hilton, NY, USA

ANCHOVY DIP

1½ c. mayonnaise
½ c. sour cream
10 anchovy fillets, finely chopped
3 Tbsp. chopped parsley

2 Tbsp. lemon juice
1 large clove garlic, minced
4 whole scallions, finely chopped

In medium bowl, mix all ingredients until well-blended. Refrigerate at least 1 hour (or overnight). Serve with chips and raw vegetables, such as celery and carrot sticks, cherry tomatoes, broccoli and cauliflower florets, and zucchini. Makes 2 cups.

Work time: 15 minutes. Total time: 15 minutes.

Per 1 ounce serving: 171 calories, 1 g protein, 18 g fat, 214 mg sodium, 1 g carbohydrate, 18 mg cholesterol.

Lion John J. Hess, Clarence Lions Club
Clarence Center, NY, USA

MEXICAN FRITOS DIP

1 lb. ground round
1 pkg. taco seasoning mix
1 can refried beans
1 c. sour cream
½ medium size bottle mild taco sauce
1 c. sharp Cheddar cheese, grated

Brown meat. Drain. Mix in the taco seasoning mix and can of refried beans with meat. Put mixture in a shallow baking dish. Mix sour cream and taco sauce and pour over the meat mixture. Sprinkle cheese on top and bake at 350° for 20 minutes. Best when served warm. Serve with dip size Fritos.

This disappears quickly at parties.

Janet Brown, Covington Lions Club
Covington, GA, USA

MEXICAN DIP

1 lb. ground beef
½ lb. Mexican Velveeta, cubed
⅔ c. Miracle Whip
¼ c. onion, chopped

Season to taste and brown meat; drain. Add remaining ingredients and mix well. Spoon mixture on 9 inch pie plate. Bake 10 minutes at 350°. Stir and continue to bake 5 minutes longer. Serve with corn chips.

Mrs. Duane (Pam) Bennett, Mad River Lions Club
Riverside, OH, USA

KZ'S PIZZA PAN TACO DIP

8 oz. cream cheese
8 oz. cottage cheese
1 pkg. taco seasoning
Tomatoes, sliced black olives, and green onions
12 oz. shredded cheese

Mix cream cheese and cottage cheese. Spread over 2 (14 inch) pizza pans (aluminum throw aways). Sprinkle 1 package taco seasoning over cheese mixture. Cover with a mixture of diced tomatoes, sliced black olives, and diced green onions. Spread shredded cheese over all. Serve with chips, Fritos, and crackers for dippers. *Summer party favorite.*

Judy Hoffman, Southport Lions Club
Indianapolis, IN

When you think you've arrived, you still have a long way to go.

2075-99

7-LAYER TACO DIP

1 pkg. tortilla chips
1 lb. hamburg
1 pkg. taco seasoning mix
1 can refried beans
1 (16 oz.) container sour cream

2 large tomatoes
1 bunch scallions
1 small can sliced black olives
1 large (8 oz.) pkg. fancy blend
   cheeses

Cook hamburg. Drain. Put back in frypan. Add water and taco seasoning according to package directions. Simmer till liquid is gone. On a cookie sheet, spread refried beans with a rubber spatula. Next layer: Hamburg (use hands to make sure it is crumbled), sour cream (spread with rubber spatula), cheese (sprinkle liberally), tomatoes (cut in small pieces), scallions (sliced thin - just the greens), and black olive slices (drained). Use tortilla chips and dip into mixture.

Every party or family gathering I am asked to make this. Funny thing is, I don't eat it as I don't like tomatoes or onions.

Linda E. Bernier, Nottingham West Lions Club
Hudson, NH, Hillsboro County

TACO DIP

16 oz. sour cream
1 pkg. Taco Bell seasoning
Chopped tomatoes

Shredded sharp Cheddar cheese
Green onion tops
Corn chips

Mix and spread on plate. Top with remaining ingredients. Serve with corn chips.

Lion Gloria Bonager, East Prospect Lions Club
East Prospect, PA, USA

TACO DELIGHT

8 oz. cream cheese

8 oz. sour cream

Mix them together and lay mixture on bottom of glass dish. Spread taco sauce on top of mixture. Cook 1 pound hamburg. Spread over taco sauce. Spread lettuce, cheese, and tomatoes on top of hamburg. Eat with nachos.

Debra James, Beckmantown Lions Club
West Chazy, NY

The best way to stay on your feet is to get down on your knees.

TACO DIP

1 (8 oz.) pkg. cream cheese
2 Tbsp. sour cream
2 c. chopped lettuce
1 chopped tomato
Green pepper and/or onions
    (optional)

1 jar taco sauce
Shredded cheese
Taco chips

Soften cream cheese with sour cream. Spread in a deep dish pie plate. Layer chopped lettuce over, then chopped tomato and green pepper and/or onions. Pour taco sauce over it and cover with shredded cheese. Serve with taco chips or potato chips or crackers. *Simple and good.*

Mollie Bangs, South Jefferson Lions Club
Adams, NY

TACO DIP

3 medium avocados
3 Tbsp. lemon juice
Picante sauce
8 oz. pkg. sour cream
¼ c. mayonnaise
Salt/pepper
Pinto beans (fresh cooked are
    best, approx. 4 c.)*

3 medium tomatoes, chopped
Chopped black olives
Shredded Longhorn cheese
Garlic powder
Finely chopped onion

Make guacamole with avocado, lemon juice, and picante sauce and season with garlic powder and salt. Mix mayonnaise with beans; season with picante sauce, garlic powder, and onions. Spread on platter (½ inch thick). Spread guacamole on top of beans; spread sour cream next. Top with tomatoes and olives and cover with cheese. Serve with nacho chips.

Great recipe for parties for all ages.

* Note: One large can refried beans can be used in place of fresh cooked beans.

Shirleen Willis, Stafford-Missouri City Lions Club
Stafford, TX, USA

Worry is the interest you pay on borrowed trouble.

Never let a bleak past cloud a bright future.

MEXICAN PIE

1 large can refried beans or 2
  small (15 or 16 oz.) cans
1 (4 oz.) can chopped green
  chilies (undrained)
1 ctn. guacamole
1 (16 oz.) sour cream
1 env. taco seasoning mix
Grated cheese
Diced tomatoes
Sliced green onions (some green,
  2 bunches)
1 small can black olives

In bowl, combine beans and chilies; spread on large serving plate. Layer guacamole over beans. Mix sour cream and taco seasoning. Layer over guacamole. Sprinkle with cheese. Put tomatoes over this. Sprinkle onion over this. Sprinkle olives over this. Refrigerate until served. Serve with tortilla chips. Delicious.

Martha C. Daniel, Bellville Lions Club
Bellville, GA, Evans County, USA

TACO OLE BY LAWRY'S SALT

1 lb. ground beef, browned and
  drained
1 pkg. taco mix by Lawry's

Add to meat, then follow package instructions for cooking. Add 1½ cups sour cream and reheat. Serve over corn chips. Top with grated cheese, torn lettuce, chopped tomatoes, and any other topping you like on tacos.

Other ideas: Chopped ripe olives, salsa, chilies, or onions.

Sarah Wehling, Bothell Lions Club
Bothell, WA, USA

NEW MEXICAN-STYLE NACHOS GRANDE

½ lb. chorizo sausage, crumbled
2 Tbsp. minced onion
1 c. prepared refried beans
½ lb. tortilla chips
¼ lb. Monterey Jack cheese
¼ lb. Cheddar cheese
3 jalapeno peppers, sliced
1 c. guacamole
½ c. sour cream
¼ c. sliced black olives

In a large frying pan over medium heat, cook the chorizo sausage until brown, about 10 minutes. Drain on paper towels. Set aside. Pour off all but ½ tablespoon fat. Add the onion and cook 2 minutes. Stir in the refried beans and heat through, about 5 minutes. Heat the broiler. Spread chips on a baking sheet. Grate the cheeses (you should have 1 cup of each) and sprinkle over chips, then top with peppers. Broil until cheese melts, 2 to 3 minutes. Put bowls of guacamole, beans, chorizo, and sour cream in center of a large platter and arrange nachos around them. Scatter olives over nachos. Makes about 40 nachos.

Work time: 50 minutes. Total time: 50 minutes.

Per nacho: 92 calories, 3 g protein, 7 g fat, 210 mg sodium, 5 g carbohydrate, 10 mg cholesterol.

Mrs. Lucy Aiken, Clarence Lions Club
Clarence Center, NY, USA

MEDITERRANEAN NACHOS

3 pita breads (each about 6
   inches in diameter)
1 large clove garlic
¾ lb. tomatoes, seeded and diced
   (about 1¾ c.)
6 oz. Mozzarella cheese, shredded
   (about 1½ c.)

2 Tbsp. chopped fresh parsley
1 Tbsp. balsamic vinegar
1½ tsp. chopped fresh basil (or
   ½ tsp. dried basil, crumbled)
¼ tsp. salt
Pinch of crushed red-pepper
   flakes

Heat oven to 400°. Cut each pita horizontally in half. Cut each half into quarters. Arrange pieces, cut-side up, on a cookie sheet. Bake until golden brown, 5 to 6 minutes. Remove, but keep oven on. Gently rub tops of pita quarters with garlic clove, taking care not to break pitas. Arrange them on an ovenproof plate.

In a medium bowl, combine tomatoes, Mozzarella, parsley, vinegar, basil, salt, and red-pepper flakes. Spoon mixture onto pita pieces. Bake until cheese melts, about 5 minutes. Makes 6 servings.

Per serving: 175 calories, 9 g protein, 6 g fat, 370 mg sodium, 20 g carbohydrate, 22 mg cholesterol.

Lion John J. Hess, Clarence Lions Club
Clarence Center, NY, USA

SALSA AND CHIPS

Salsa:

1 large can tomatoes, diced
1 small can diced green chilis
1 jalapeno pepper, diced
1 bunch green onions, chopped

½ tsp. garlic
2 Tbsp. cilantro
Dash of cayenne pepper
Salt to taste

Mix all ingredients in large bowl; let stand for one hour before serving. Very good as topping for tacos, omelettes, and can be used in con queso. Add more jalapeno pepper and cayenne to make *hot*.

Chips:

1 bag corn or flour tortillas
Seasoned salt

Oil

Heat oil. Cut tortillas into wedges. Fry individually, turning till lightly browned on both sides. Salt chips lightly. Use above salsa as dip.

It's not how long you live, but how you live.

TACO FOLDOVERS

1 (15 oz.) refrigerated pie crusts

Filling:

¼ c. mayonnaise
¼ c. thick and chunky salsa
1 c. cubed, cooked chicken
1 c. chopped tomato

¼ c. sliced green onions
4 oz. (1 c.) shredded Cheddar
  cheese

Heat oven to 450°F. Place pie crusts on ungreased cookie sheet; remove plastic sheets.

In small bowl, combine mayonnaise and salsa; mix well. Spread mayonnaise mixture evenly over each pie crust. Sprinkle half of each crust with remaining ingredients. Fold untopped half of each crust over filling; do not seal. Bake at 450°F. for 14 to 18 minutes or until golden brown. If desired, top with shredded lettuce, sliced ripe olives, sour cream, and additional salsa. Makes 6 foldovers.

Lion Denalee Baylor, Mount Airy Foothills Lions Club
Mount Airy, NC, USA

SALSA ROLL-UP HORS D'OEUVRES

1 pkg. (10) large burrito shells
1 pt. sour cream
1 c. shredded Cheddar cheese

1 c. Old El Paso mild salsa
1 pkg. dry Ranch salad mix

Combine all ingredients. Spread thin layer on each burrito. Roll burrito tightly. Place in glass dish with waxed paper between layers. Cover and refrigerate 24 hours. Remove from refrigerator and slice into 1 inch pieces. Place on serving tray.

Lioness Carolyn Kellner, East Anne Arundel Lioness Club
Glen Burnie, MD, USA

PARTY PINWHEELS

2 (8 oz.) pkg. cream cheese,
  softened
1 pkg. Hidden Valley Original
  Ranch dressing mix

3 green onions, minced
5 or 6 flour tortillas
½ c. red pepper, diced
1 can sliced black olives, drained

Mix first 3 ingredients. Spread on tortillas. Sprinkle on remaining ingredients. Roll and wrap tightly. Chill 2 hours, covered. Cut off roll ends. Cut rolls into ½ to 1 inch slices.

Lion Ronald Robinson, Graysville-Proctor Lions Club
Proctor, WV, USA

SPINACH TORTILLA ROLLS

1 c. sour cream
1 (8 oz.) pkg. cream cheese, softened
3 green onions, chopped
2 (10 oz.) pkg. frozen chopped spinach, thawed and squeezed dry

1 small buttermilk Ranch dressing mix
¼ or ½ c. *real bacon bits*
Salt, seasoned to taste
Dill, seasoned to taste
Garlic powder seasoned to taste
1 (10 oz. medium) pkg. tortillas

Sauce:

Picante salsa
Sour cream

Green onion

Combine ingredients. Spread ¼ inch (or "so") thick on tortillas. Roll tightly. Wrap in plastic wrap. Refrigerate for at least 4 hours or longer. Slice diagonally on platter with sauce.

Sauce: Mix together.

Makes a lot! Big hit with everyone.

Deborah Kromish, Community Lions Club
East Haddam, CT

TORTILLA APPETIZERS

8 oz. sour cream
8 oz. cream cheese, softened
4 oz. can El Paso green chillies, drained
4 oz. can chopped black olives, drained

1 c. mild Cheddar cheese
½ c. green onion, chopped
¼ tsp. garlic and season salt
1 pkg. flour tortillas

Mix all ingredients and spread on tortilla. Roll up like cinnamon rolls. Put in plastic wrap. Refrigerate for 2 hours. Slice ¼ to ½ inch thick with electric knife. Serve and enjoy.

This recipe is great for picnics or get-togethers.

Maria Gaso, Bentleyville Lioness Club
Bentleyville, PA, USA

TORTILLA ROLL-UPS

2 pkg. soft large flour tortillas
2 pkg. (8 oz.) cream cheese
1 pkg. salami (chip beef or whatever kind of meat)

1 c. green pepper
1 c. green onion
¼ c. black olives

Soften the cream cheese. Mince up salami, green pepper, and black olives and add to cream cheese. Mix well. Spread spoonful on each flour tortilla to cover it. Roll up each individual tortilla. Refrigerate overnight. Cut up each roll into bite-size pieces and serve as appetizer.

VEGETABLE DIP

1½ c. cottage cheese (12 oz. size)
1 Tbsp. onion flakes
1 Tbsp. parsley flakes
1 tsp. seasoned salt
½ c. mayonnaise
1 tsp. dill weed
1 tsp. garlic salt

Put in blender and mix well. Use on veggies!

This is yummy on fresh veggies!!

Lion Edie Aas, Jasper-Quarry Lions Club
Jasper, MN, USA

GARLIC VEGETABLE DIP

½ c. sugar
2 tsp. garlic powder
2 tsp. salad oil
4 tsp. Dijon mustard
1 c. Miracle Whip

Mix first four ingredients well until sugar is dissolved. Add Miracle Whip and mix well. Keeps 2 to 3 weeks in refrigerator. Serve with raw vegetables.

Mrs. Tim (Linda) Lyons, Elburn Lions Club
Batavia, IL, USA

ANN'S DIP

1 tsp. parsley
½ tsp. dill weed
1 tsp. chopped green onions
 (chives)
1 c. mayonnaise
½ tsp. garlic
2 drops of Tabasco
1 tsp. Beau Monde seasoning
1 c. sour cream

Blend all ingredients together and refrigerate for at least two hours. Garnish with parsley and chives. Recipe is easily doubled.

Serve with vegetables, chips, or use as a salad dressing. Will keep up to a month in refrigerator.

Lion Ann Frechette, Lake of the Woods Lions Club
Kenora, Ontario, Canada

HERB DIP WITH VEGETABLES

1 c. mayonnaise
¼ c. snipped parsley
¼ c. snipped chives
1 Tbsp. tarragon vinegar or white
 wine vinegar
1 tsp. anchovy paste or mashed,
 drained anchovy fillets
1 clove garlic, quartered
⅛ tsp. ground pepper
½ c. sour cream

Place ½ of the mayonnaise and remaining ingredients, except sour cream, in a food processor and process. Stir in sour cream and remaining mayonnaise.

Sarah Wehling, Bothell Lions Club
Bothell, WA, USA

34

APPLE DIP

1 pkg. Skors
½ c. brown sugar (light)
½ c. granulated sugar

¼ c. sour cream
8 oz. cream cheese

Combine all ingredients. May serve at once or let stand for 1 to 2 hours. Skors will be softer if set longer. This may be used for other fruits.

Emily Groover, Bellville Lions Club
Bellville, GA, USA

CARAMEL DIP FOR FRESH FRUIT

1 (8 oz.) pkg. cream cheese
¾ c. brown sugar

¼ c. white sugar
2 tsp. vanilla

Mix together with electric mixer till smooth.

Good with any kind of fresh fruit and easy.

Mrs. Jan Callaghan, Elburn Lions Club
Elburn, IL, USA

CARAMEL DIP

1 (8 oz.) cream cheese
¾ c. brown sugar
¼ c. sugar

1 tsp. vanilla
Chopped nuts (optional)
Apple slices

Soften cream cheese. Combine all ingredients. Mix well. Serve with apples and other fruits.

CHILI-CHEESE DIP

2 (8 oz.) pkg. cream cheese
2 cans chili with beans
Sliced jalapenas (as desired)

8 oz. shredded Monterey Jack
    cheese

Spread cream cheese in a 9x13 inch pan. Layer chili on top of cream cheese. Layer peppers on top of chili. Cover with shredded cheese. Bake at 350° for about 15 minutes until cheese is melted. Serve with tortilla chips.

Dianne Englert, Jefferson City Capital Lions Club
Jefferson City, MO, USA

CHEESE BALL

2 (8 oz.) pkg. cream cheese
1 c. grated Cheddar cheese
1 pkg. onion soup mix

4 Tbsp. sweet pickle relish
1 pkg. sour cream mix (I use 4
    Tbsp. sour cream)

Mix together. Shape and coat with chopped nuts or parsley.

Pam Caldwell, Mexico Sunrise Lions Club
Mexico, MO

MEX-TEX DIP

3 medium size ripe avocados
2 Tbsp. lemon juice
½ tsp. salt
¼ tsp. pepper
1 c. sour cream
½ c. mayo
1 pkg. taco seasoning mix
2 cans bean dip (plain or
    jalapeno)

4 large tomatoes, chopped
1 large bunch green onions,
    chopped
1 can black olives, chopped
1 pkg. sharp Cheddar cheese,
    grated to make 2 c.
Large tortilla chips

Peel, pit, and mash avocados with lemon juice, salt, and pepper. Combine sour cream, mayo, and taco seasoning mix in another small bowl. Spread bean dip on a large shallow serving platter. Top with avocado mixture. Layer with sour cream mixture. Sprinkle with chopped onions, tomatoes, and olives. Cover with shredded cheese. Serve chilled or at room temperature with tortilla chips.

This recipe was given by friend, Kate.

Karen Obar, Watertown Day Lions Club
Watertown, CT, USA

Settle all accounts today, you can't bank on tomorrow.

❦ ❦ ❦

To get to heaven it's who you know that counts.

❦ ❦ ❦

Empathy is your pain in my heart.

❦ ❦ ❦

Gratitude should be a continuous attitude, not an occasional incident.

BEVERAGES

CRANBERRY PUNCH

4 c. cranberry juice
1½ c. sugar
4 c. pineapple juice

1 Tbsp. almond extract
2 qt. ginger ale

Combine first 4 ingredients. Stir until sugar is dissolved; chill. Add ginger ale just before serving.

Jo Anne Beavers, Bryan Lioness Club
Bryan, OH

PINK CHRISTMAS PUNCH

6 c. white grape juice
6 c. cranberry juice cocktail
2 (6 oz.) cans frozen pink
   lemonade, thawed

3 c. bottled soda water

Combine grape juice, cranberry cocktail, and lemonade. Refrigerate until needed. Put ice in punch bowl and add juices and soda water. Serves 30 to 35.

White grape juice is available in many grocery stores now.

Micheal and Ruth Bartolf, Oxbow and District Lions Club
Oxbow, Saskatchewan, Canada

HOT SPICE PUNCH

1 large can unsweetened
   pineapple juice

1 large can Hawaiian (red) Punch
4½ c. water

In top:

1½ c. brown sugar
4 or 5 cinnamon sticks, broken

1 tsp. whole cloves

Doris Smith, Brookhaven Alpha Lions Club
Brookhaven, MS

The smallest light is seen in the darkest night.

BANANA PUNCH
(Yellow)

8 c. water
4 c. sugar
2 (12 oz.) frozen orange juice
6 (12 oz.) water

2 (46 oz.) pineapple juice
½ c. fresh lemon juice
5 ripe bananas
2 (28 oz.) ginger ale

Bring water and sugar to boil. Allow to boil 15 minutes. Cool. Add juices and water. Place bananas in blender and liquefy. Add to juices. Mix well. Freeze for at least 3 hours. Freeze in plastic milk jugs.

Note: If frozen solid, remove from freezer 1 hour before serving. Beat punch frozen in plastic jugs with a hammer to break into a slush. Pour ginger ale in punch bowl and add frozen slush. Yield: 50 servings.

Lion Barbara Lane, Mount Airy Foothills Lions Club
Mount Airy, NC, USA

BANANA PINEAPPLE PUNCH

5 bananas, pureed
1 (46 oz.) can pineapple juice
1 (12 oz.) lemonade concentrate
2 (12 oz.) orange juice
    concentrate

4 c. sugar
6 c. water
2 (67 oz.) lemon-lime soda

Dissolve sugar in water. Add all but soda. Mix and freeze to be used later. Thaw mix part way and add soda.

Liz Birchen, O'Fallon Lions Club
O'Fallon, MO, USA

POWER PUNCH

½ half banana
½ c. 2% milk

½ c. plain yogurt
½ c. strawberries or blueberries

In blender or food processor, puree together all ingredients. Chill if desired.

Energize your whole family with this delicious, nutritious smoothie. Other fruits can be substituted for the berries but always include the banana for body.

Lion Micheal and Ruth (Sauskojus) Bartolf,
Oxbow and District Lions Club
Oxbow, Saskatchewan, Canada

DELICIOUS PUNCH

Mix:

6 pkg. jello (any flavor)
6 c. boiling water

4 c. sugar
6 c. cold water

Add:

3 large cans frozen orange juice
3 large cans lemonade (frozen)
3 large cans pineapple juice

3 qt. ginger ale
4 qt. sherbet (add sherbet when
you are getting ready to
serve)

This makes a lot of punch for party.

Olive Higinbotham, Bentleyville Lioness Club
Bentleyville, PA, USA

CHAMPAGNE SPARKLE PUNCH

1 (6 oz.) can frozen lemonade
concentrate, thawed
1 c. cognac
1 (⅘ qt.) bottle pink champagne,
chilled

64 oz. (2 qt.) lemon-lime
carbonated beverage (7-Up),
chilled
1 lime

Combine lemonade concentrate and cognac in punch bowl. Add champagne and slowly pour in lemon-lime carbonated beverage. Add ice and thin slices of lime. Makes 3½ quarts. *Excellent.*

Virginia Bayer, Franklin Park Lions Club
Park Ridge, IL, USA

PERFECT (SLUSH) PUNCH

1 (16 oz.) can frozen orange juice
1 (16 oz.) can water
1 (6 oz.) can frozen lemonade
1 (6 oz.) can water
1 (46 oz.) can pineapple juice

¼ c. fresh squeezed lemon juice
3 bananas
1 large box frozen strawberries
3½ c. sugar
Ginger ale

Mix 6 cups water and 3½ cups sugar; boil for 5 minutes. Completely cool. Blend bananas and strawberries. Mix all ingredients together and freeze. When ready to use, allow to partially thaw out and add 2 quarts of cold ginger ale. Keep punch slushy. Float strawberries on top.

Lion Mickey McConnell, Foley Lions Club
Foley, AL, USA

LEMONADE

1½ c. powdered lemonade
1 c. sugar

1 c. frozen lemonade
5 gal. water

Mix all ingredients and serve with ice.

We use this with our fund raisers.

O'Fallon Lions Club
O'Fallon, MO, USA

ORANGE JULIUS

⅔ c. orange juice concentrate
1 c. water
1 c. milk

½ tsp. vanilla
¼ c. powdered sugar
10 ice cubes

Pour all ingredients into blender and blend until smooth.

If using pre-mixed orange juice, use 1⅔ cups instead of concentrate and water.

A great cool treat for a hot day!

Diane Kemmerer, Green Lane-Marlboro Lioness Club
Green Lane, PA, USA

ICED RASPBERRY LEMONADE

4 lemons
2½ c. sugar
1½ c. raspberry syrup

3 c. lemon juice
1 pkg. (½ pt.) raspberries
10 c. ice water

Peel lemons with a vegetable peeler or a sharp knife, retaining as little of the white pith as possible. In medium saucepan over high heat, bring 1½ cups water to a boil with sugar and lemon peel; boil 5 minutes. Stir in raspberry syrup and lemon juice. Just before packing for picnic, stir raspberries, ice water, and cubes into chilled raspberry mixture. Makes 8 servings.

Note: Here's a tip to prevent your lemonade from getting watered down after a warm day in the park. Freeze cubes of the finished lemonade and stir in before packing for picnic. As the ice melts, it won't dilute your homemade beverage. For an extra-special surprise, place a single fresh raspberry or a sprig of mint in each cube before freezing.

Work time: 15 minutes. Total time: 1 hour and 15 minutes.

Per serving: 376 calories, 0 g protein, 96 g carbohydrate, 0 g fat, 0 mg cholesterol, 10 mg sodium.

Mrs. Lucy Aiken, Clarence Lions Club
Clarence Center, NY, USA

RASPBERRY CORDIAL
(Liqueur)

1½ c. sugar
1 c. vodka or gin

4 c. unsweetened raspberries

In a gallon container, stir together 1½ cups sugar and 1 cup vodka or gin till sugar dissolves. Gently stir in 4 cups unsweetened raspberries. Cover; set in cool place (not refrigerated) for 8 weeks. Invert jar once each week. Uncover jar and strain mixture through very fine cheesecloths. Pour into bottle and cap. Store in cool dry place. Makes 4 cups.

MELON MINT COCKTAILS

½ c. sugar
½ c. water
3 Tbsp. mint leaves
Juice of 1 lemon

Juice of 1 orange
Cantaloupe balls
Watermelon balls

Boil sugar and water for 5 minutes. Pour over mint leaves. Cool the syrup. Strain it. Add juice of lemon and orange; chill it. Prepare and chill cantaloupe and watermelon. Immediately before serving the cocktails, place the balls in cocktail glasses and pour the sirup on them. Garnish them with sprigs of mint.

Betty A. Birch, Bullhead City Lions Club
Bullhead City, AZ

MINT COOLER

1 gal. lemonade
2 (46 oz.) pineapple juice

10 oz. jar mint jelly
3 liters 7-Up, Sprite, or ginger ale

Follow directions on lemonade mix. Melt mint jelly in microwave and add to lemonade. Stir. Add pineapple juice and soda when ready to serve. Add ice. Makes 2 gallons.

Doris G. Brey, Upper Periomen Lioness Club
Harleysville, PA, USA

FRUITY SUMMER COOLER

6 to 8 ice cubes
½ c. cubed cantaloupe
½ c. pineapple chunks
½ c. cranberry juice
⅓ c. sliced banana

¼ c. pineapple juice
1 Tbsp. honey
¾ tsp. lemon juice
¼ tsp. grated lemon peel

Place all ingredients in a blender or food processor; cover and blend until smooth. Yield: 2 to 3 servings.

MOCHA MIX

1 (1 lb. 9.6 oz.) pkg. nonfat dry milk powder
1 (16 oz.) pkg. powdered sugar
1 (15 oz.) pkg. Nestle Quik

1 (11 oz.) jar non-dairy powdered creamer
½ c. cocoa
½ to 1 c. instant coffee granules

Combine all ingredients together. Stir until well mixed. Store in airtight containers. To serve, combine 6 ounces hot water to 3 tablespoons of mix.

To make a flavored mocha, add 1 to 2 teaspoons of flavored creamer. To make hot chocolate, omit coffee granules from the mix.

Judy Rannow, Arlington (SEA) Lions Club
Arlington, MN, USA

HOT MULLED CIDER

6 qt. apple cider or juice
¾ to 1 c. honey (depending on sweetness of cider)
4 lemons, sliced thin
4 cinnamon sticks, halved

2 Tbsp. minced fresh ginger
25 allspice berries
10 cardamom pods, crushed
5 lady apples or small apples
25 whole cloves

Place cider, honey, sliced lemons, cinnamon sticks, fresh ginger, allspice berries, and crushed cardamom pods in a large stock pot. Heat over medium-high heat, stirring occasionally, until it begins to simmer. Simmer for 15 minutes. Reduce heat to just below simmering. Place 5 cloves in each of 5 apples. Add whole apples to hot cider as a garnish; keep warm over low heat. When ready, serve hot with a ladle. Serves approximately 25.

Mrs. Lucy Aiken, Clarence Lions Club
Clarence Center, NY, USA

HOLIDAY NOG

This drink is a luscious alternative to eggnog. It tastes rich and delicious whether you make it with rum or rum flavoring.

2 pt. super-premium vanilla ice cream
½ c. milk

¼ tsp. rum extract or ¼ c. rum
¼ tsp. ground nutmeg

Place ice cream in a large bowl. Let stand until melted or place in a microwave on HIGH for 1 to 2 minutes, until ice cream becomes liquid. Whisk in the milk, rum extract (or rum), and nutmeg. Cover the mixture and refrigerate until well-chilled, about 30 minutes. Sprinkle each serving with additional dash of nutmeg. Makes 8 servings.

Per serving: 200 calories, 3 g protein, 12 g fat, 62 mg sodium, 17 g carbohydrate, 46 mg cholesterol.

Mrs. Mike Nowicki, Clarence Lions Club
Clarence Center, NY, USA

Salads

IRON FROM SOME COMMON FOOD SOURCES

Food	Amount	Iron (mg.)
Egg	1	1.1
Meat, lean	3 oz.	(approx.) 3.0
Mature beans and peas (legumes), nuts		
Almonds, Brazil nuts, cashew nuts, walnuts	¼ cup	(approx.) 1.5
Beans, common varieties, cooked, drained	1 cup	4.9
Lentils, cooked	1 cup	3.2
Peas, dry, cooked	1 cup	4.2
Vegetables		
Lima beans, immature, cooked	1 cup	4.3
Carrots, cauliflower, sweet corn	1 cup	(approx.) 1.0
Greens, cooked	1 cup	(approx.) 2.5
Peas, green, cooked	1 cup	2.9
Sweet potato	1 med. lg.	1.0
Tomato, cooked	1 cup	1.2
Fruits		
Apricots and peaches, dried, cooked	1 cup	5.1
Berries, fresh	1 cup	(approx.) 1.5
Dates, dry, cut	½ cup	2.6
Grape juice	1 cup	0.8
Prunes, dried, softened	4 medium	1.1
Prune juice, canned	1 cup	10.5
Raisins, dried	½ cup	2.8
Watermelon	Wedge 4x8 inch	2.1
Grain Products		
Bread, enriched	1 slice	(approx.) 0.6
Flour and meal, whole or enriched, dry	¼ cup	(approx.) 1.0
Spaghetti and macaroni, enriched, dry	⅓ cup	(approx.) 1.0
Wheat germ	¼ cup	1.8
Syrup, dark	1 Tbsp.	(approx.) 1.0
Sugar, brown	1 Tbsp.	.5

SALADS

SOUTHWESTERN CHICKEN PASTA SALAD

1 lb. boneless, skinless chicken breast, diced (cooking to follow)
1 lb. spinach and basil flavored rotellini (or favorite pasta), cooked, drained, and chilled
1 c. Ranch dressing
1 bunch green onion, diced
¼ c. fresh dill, crushed (may substitute dried dill weed to taste)

½ green pepper, diced
½ red pepper, diced
3 pepperoncini peppers, diced (optional)
¼ c. bacon bits
1 c. grated Cheddar cheese
2 Roma tomatoes, deseeded and diced
Salt and pepper to taste

For cooking chicken:

2 Tbsp. olive oil
¼ c. Worcestershire sauce

2 garlic cloves, crushed

Cut chicken in ½ inch strips. Combine olive oil, Worcestershire sauce, and garlic and pour over chicken. Let marinate in refrigerator a minimum of 1 hour.

Drain marinade into skillet and simmer on medium heat, then add chicken, stirring and turning occasionally, until chicken is cooked through, approximately 10 to 12 minutes. Remove from heat and drain chicken, discarding leftover sauce. Cut chicken in ½ inch cubes and refrigerate immediately. After chicken is completely chilled, combine with remaining ingredients and blend with spatula or by hand until thoroughly mixed. Salt and pepper to taste and serve. Serves approximately 4.

This salad is good for a variety of occasions or as a light summer meal by itself.

David L. Johnson, Princeton Lions Club
Princeton, IL, USA

Our rest day gives meaning to the rest of the week.

FRESH TOMATO-TUNA PASTA

3 lb. ripe plum tomatoes, cored,
  seeded, and diced
3 Tbsp. olive oil
¼ c. chopped fresh basil
1 large garlic clove, minced
¾ tsp. salt

½ tsp. cracked black pepper
8 oz. uncooked bow tie pasta
1 (6⅛ oz.) can solid white tuna
  (packed in canola oil),
  drained and flaked
Basil sprigs for garnish (optional)

In large serving bowl, stir together tomatoes, oil, basil, garlic, salt, and pepper; set aside at least 15 minutes to blend flavors.

Meanwhile, cook pasta in boiling salted water according to package directions; drain. Place in bowl with tomato mixture and tuna. Toss gently to combine. Garnish each plate, if desired, with basil sprig. Makes 4 servings.

Mrs. Lucy Aiken, Clarence Lions Club
Clarence Center, NY, USA

PASTA SALMON TOSS

3 eggs
1 clove garlic
1 scallion
14¾ oz. can salmon
Salt and pepper
¾ lb. spaghetti

¼ c. oil
4 Tbsp. butter (at room
  temperature)
2 Tbsp. chopped fresh parsley
1 Tbsp. lemon juice

Put the eggs in a saucepan, cover with cold water, and bring just to a boil. Cover, remove from heat, and let stand 12 minutes; drain. When cool enough to handle, peel and chop.

Meanwhile, mince the garlic. Cut the scallion into thin slices. Drain the salmon and flake. In a large pot of boiling salted water, cook the spaghetti. Drain. Return the pasta to the hot pot and stir in the oil, garlic, scallion, chopped eggs, salmon, butter, parsley, ¼ teaspoon pepper, and the lemon juice. Taste for seasoning and add salt and pepper if needed. Serve immediately. Makes 4 servings.

Per serving: 720 calories, 34 g protein, 35 g fat, 480 mg sodium, 65 g carbohydrate, 224 mg cholesterol.

Mrs. Lucy Aiken, Clarence Lions Club
Clarence Center, NY, USA

Honoring our parents is learned by example.

BLT PASTA SALAD

1 (7 oz.) pkg. elbow macaroni,
    cooked as pkg. directions and
    drained
8 slices bacon, cooked and
    crumbled
1 c. mayonnaise or salad dressing
⅓ c. chili sauce

¼ c. lemon juice
2 tsp. chicken flavor instant
    bouillon
2 tsp. sugar
1 large tomato, chopped
¼ c. sliced green onion
4 c. thinly sliced lettuce

In large bowl, combine mayonnaise, chili sauce, lemon juice, bouillon, and sugar. Stir in macaroni, tomato, and onion; cover and chill. Just before serving, stir in lettuce and bacon.

PASTA SALAD WITH CHEDDAR AND TOMATOES

Salt and pepper
½ lb. fusilli pasta
1 cucumber
¼ lb. extra-sharp Cheddar cheese
    (about 1 c. grated)

1 c. cherry tomatoes
¼ c. chopped red onion
½ c. plain yogurt
¼ c. sour cream

In a large pot of boiling salted water, cook pasta until tender. Drain and rinse under cool water. Score cucumber with a fork, cut in half lengthwise, and scoop out the seeds. Cut each half in half lengthwise and then cut crosswise into thin slices. Grate cheese. Halve tomatoes. Combine the pasta, cucumber, cheese, tomatoes, onion, yogurt, sour cream, ¼ teaspoon salt, and ¼ teaspoon pepper. Taste for seasoning and add salt and pepper if needed. Makes 4 servings.

Work time: 20 minutes. Total time: 30 minutes.

Per serving: 391 calories, 17 g protein, 14 g fat, 347 mg sodium, 49 g carbohydrate, 38 mg cholesterol.

Mrs. Lucy Aiken, Clarence Lions Club
Clarence Center, NY, USA

PASTA SALAD

1 lb. penne noodles
½ c. red onion
½ oz. fresh basil
½ c. sun-dried tomatoes
1 c. chopped artichoke
16 oz. fresh grated Parmesan
    cheese

½ c. fresh chopped parsley
⅓ c. fresh chopped asparagus
1 small can chopped black olives
¾ c. Girards Romano cheese
    salad dressing

Cook pasta and drain. Add all the rest of ingredients and toss with salad dressing. Serve.

Dee Asper, Southwest Lioness Club
South St. Paul, MN

PASTA SALAD

1 (16 oz.) pasta shells
1 (10 oz.) pkg. frozen peas
1 c. chopped celery
½ c. chopped onion

2 tsp. dill weed
1 tsp. garlic
2 c. Miracle Whip
1 large can tuna, drained

Cook pasta. Mix all ingredients. Chill before serving.

Mrs. Bill (Candy) McCartney, Elburn Lions Club
Elburn, IL, Kane County

PASTA SALAD

1 (16 oz.) pkg. pasta (corkscrew)
1 (16 oz.) pkg. frozen Birds Eye
    frozen vegetables (broccoli,
    peas, onion, red pepper), cut
    small

2 pkg. Good Seasons Italian
    dressing

Add:

1 c. green onions, chopped small
8 oz. ham strips (small)
8 oz. sharp Cheddar cheese,
    grated large

Salt and pepper to taste

Cook pasta and drain under cold water. Toss about 2 tablespoons oil in pasta. Add chopped vegetables. Mix "Good Seasons" dressing as directions on back of package. Toss up with pasta and vegetables. Add chopped green onions and cheese. Add salt and pepper to taste. Toss. Put some ham on top after it has been tossed. Make and refrigerate overnight. The next day, toss and put in bowl that it will be served in. Makes one gallon.

Mrs. Charlotte M. Garner, Pascagoula Evening Lions Club
Pascagoula, MS

BROCCOLI NOODLE SALAD

2 pkg. Ramen beef noodles
½ c. vinegar
½ c. oil

½ c. sugar
1 small pkg. sunflower seeds
1 pkg. broccoli slaw

Heat vinegar, oil, sugar, and beef flavor from Ramen noodles. Melt sugar. Remove from heat. Break up noodles. Add to liquid. Add sunflower seeds and broccoli slaw. Refrigerate - best if overnight.

Lion June Taylor, Foley Lions Club
Foley, AL, USA

CABBAGE NOODLE SALAD

½ head shredded cabbage
1 green pepper, chopped
1 red pepper, chopped
1 bunch green onions, chopped
⅔ c. sunflower seeds
⅔ c. peanuts or cashews
1 pkg. Ramen noodles, broken
    into small pieces

¼ c. oil
¼ c. water
1 Tbsp. sugar
1 Tbsp. vinegar
1 tsp. Tabasco
1 pkg. Ramen noodle seasoning

Mix together cabbage, peppers, onions, seeds, nuts, and noodles. Combine remaining ingredients and refrigerate 15 minutes. Pour over salad and serve immediately.

Mrs. Tim (Linda) Lyons, Elburn Lions Club
Batavia, IL, USA

ITALIAN SPAGHETTI SALAD

Cook 1 box vermicelli 7 minutes; rinse and drain.

Add:

1 pt. cherry tomatoes
1 large green pepper
3 stalks celery
1 bunch green onions
1 can sliced ripe olives

Durkee salad seasoning with
    cheese (spice jar size, dry)
1 large bottle Wish-Bone Italian
    salad dressing

Mix all ingredients in bowl. Add ½ jar Durkee salad seasoning with cheese (dry). Add large bottle Wish-Bone salad dressing and stir till all is mixed. Refrigerate.

From an Italian friend and it's so good.

Judy Hoffman, Southport Lions Club
Indianapolis, IN

MOSTACCIOLI SALAD

1 lb. mostaccioli, cooked, rinsed,
    and drained

2 thinly sliced cucumbers
2 thinly sliced onions

Mix:

1 c. vegetable oil
1½ c. vinegar
1¼ c. sugar

1 Tbsp. parsley flakes
1½ tsp. pepper
2 tsp. garlic salt

Pour over mostaccioli, cucumbers, and onions. Refrigerate and stir once in awhile.

This is a recipe that we served at my daughter's wedding dinner.

Kay Yelton, Mexico Morning Lions Club
Mexico, MO, USA

LINGUINE SALAD

1 lb. box linguine
3 medium tomatoes, diced
3 medium cucumbers, chopped
1 medium onion, chopped

1 (16 oz.) bottle Italian salad
  dressing
½ bottle salad seasoning

Break linguine into three to four inch pieces. Cook according to package (don't overcook). Drain and rinse with cool water. Mix linguine with all other ingredients. Cover and refrigerate overnight. Serves 12 to 14 people.

Lion Ida Rohrer, Moundbuilders Lions Club
Newark, OH, USA

MACARONI SALAD

1 lb. elbow macaroni
1 c. green pepper
1 c. onion
1 c. carrots
1 c. celery
1 c. Cheddar cheese, shredded

1 c. frozen peas
½ c. vinegar
1 c. sweetened condensed milk
1 c. sugar
2 c. mayonnaise or salad dressing
Salt and pepper to taste

Cook macaroni according to directions on the package. Drain. Chop or dice green pepper, onion, carrots, and celery. (I use the food processor.) Mix together macaroni, vegetables, cheese, and frozen peas.

For dressing mix vinegar, sweetened condensed milk, sugar, and mayonnaise until well blended, then add to salad mixture, then add salt and pepper to taste.

Dorothy Coon, Hutchinson Breakfast Lions Club
Hutchinson, KS, USA

TORTELLINI SALAD

½ c. olive oil
3 Tbsp. white wine vinegar
1 tsp. Worcestershire sauce
1½ Tbsp. Dijon mustard
½ tsp. black pepper
1 Tbsp. sugar
1¼ tsp. salt
1 small clove garlic
1 (7 oz.) pkg. cheese filled egg
  pasta tortellini

¼ c. snipped basil (fresh)
¾ c. chopped, unpeeled, seeded
  cucumber
½ c. celery, sliced diagonally
½ c. chopped green onions
¼ c. parsley (fresh)
1 (2 oz.) jar pimentos
1 (4 oz.) pkg. shredded Cheddar
  cheese

Combine first 9 ingredients. Cook pasta al dente 15 minutes. Toss dressing with warm pasta. Cool to lukewarm. Fold in remaining ingredients. Refrigerate. Makes 12½ cups.

Patty Geib, Arlington SEA Lions Club
Arlington, MN, USA

ACINI DE PEPE SALAD

1 box acini de pepe macaroni
3 eggs
1 Tbsp. cornstarch
2 cans pineapple, drained

8 oz. Cool Whip
1½ c. sugar
1¾ c. orange or pineapple juice
2 cans mandarin oranges, drained

Cook acini de pepe macaroni according to directions. In a saucepan, mix the sugar, eggs, and fruit juice together. Cook and cool. After the mixture has cooled, add the macaroni, pineapple, oranges, and Cool Whip. Mix thoroughly. Refrigerate.

Lion Theresa Hill, Hector Lions Club
Hector, MN

WATERMELON BOAT

1 c. lemon juice
1 c. sugar
2 tsp. all-purpose flour
2 eggs, beaten
1 c. whipping cream, whipped
1 large watermelon

1 large honeydew, cut into cubes
  or balls
1 large cantaloupe, cut into cubes
  or balls
2 pt. fresh strawberries, sliced
½ lb. green grapes

Combine lemon juice, sugar, and flour in a saucepan; bring to a boil. Reduce heat to low. Stir ¼ cup into eggs; return all to pan. Cook and stir for 15 minutes or until mixture coats a spoon (do not boil). Cool. Fold in whipped cream; cover and chill until serving.

For watermelon boat, cut a thin slice from bottom of melon with a sharp knife to allow it to sit flat. Mark a horizontal cutting line 2 inches above center of melon. With a long sharp knife, cut into melon along cutting line, making sure to cut all the way through. Gently pull off top section of rind. Remove fruit from both sections and cut into cubes or balls; set aside.

To cut decorative edge, place melon on its side. Position a 2½ inch 8 point star cookie cutter against inside edge of melon, allowing only half star to cut through rind. Use a mallet, if necessary, to help push cookie cutter through melon. Insert a toothpick into flat edge of removed piece. Attach piece onto melon edge where last cut ends. Repeat cutting and attaching pieces until entire melon edge is completed.

Combine honeydew, cantaloupe, strawberries, grapes, and watermelon; spoon into boat. Serve dressing on the side. Yield: 32 to 36 servings (about 2 cups dressing).

Note: Any star or petal cutter with an even number of points may be used. Or, serve this salad in an 8 quart serving bowl.

2075-99

VANILLA FRUIT SALAD

2 (16 oz.) cans pineapple chunks
1 (15 oz.) can peaches
1 (15 oz.) can pears
3 apples

2 c. seedless grapes
1 (1.4 oz.) box instant fat free
   sugar free vanilla pudding

Drain all juices from canned fruit, saving the juices. Cut up all fruit and put in large serving bowl. Sprinkle pudding on fruit and add about ¾ cup of juices until pudding forms. Makes about 10 cups.

Carol Hug, Bryan Lioness Club
Bryan, OH, USA

QUICK AND EASY FRUIT SALAD OR DESSERT

1 large Red Delicious apple,
   washed well
1 c. red seedless grapes, washed
   well
½ to 1 c. chopped (or broken)
   pecans

Fruit-Fresh
1 small container of your choice
   of fruit flavored yogurt

Cook pecans in microwave only slightly. Chop the unpeeled apple into bite-size pieces to suit your taste. Immediately sprinkle the apple liberally with Fruit-Fresh to avoid browning. Cut grapes in halves.

Mix apple, grapes, and yogurt for a refreshing salad or use for dessert.

Vivian Houser, Foley Lions Club
Foley, AL

FRUIT SALAD

1 large can fruit cocktail, drained
1 c. miniature marshmallows
1 small can grapes or 1 c. fresh
   grapes, halved
1 jar maraschino cherries,
   drained and halved

1 (8 oz.) pkg. cream cheese,
   softened
1 (8 oz.) container sour cream

Mix cream cheese and sour cream until well blended. Add drained fruit and mix well. Fold in marshmallows and refrigerate. Better if made several hours or overnight before serving.

Nettie Favara, Greenwood Lions Club
Greenwood, MS, USA

Anger is just one letter short of danger.

FESTIVE CURRIED FRUIT

1 (29 oz.) can pear halves
1 (29 oz.) can Freestone peach halves
1 (17 oz.) can Royal Anne light sweet cherries, pitted
1 (20 oz.) can pineapple chunks
1 (11 oz.) can mandarin orange sections
1 (17 oz.) can apricots (preferably peeled)

½ c. white raisins
¾ c. sugar
¼ tsp. salt
3 Tbsp. butter
3 Tbsp. flour
½ to 1 tsp. curry powder
½ c. white wine

Drain all fruit, reserving juice. Measure ¾ cup fruit juice and set aside. Soak raisins in hot water to cover for 10 minutes. Drain. Mix fruit juice with sugar, salt, butter, and flour. Heat, but do not boil. Stir until thick. Fold sauce into drained fruit and raisins. Add curry powder and wine. Let stand 3 hours. Cook 30 minutes at 350°F.

May be refrigerated and reheated next day. Improves with age. Serves 8 to 10.

Lion Carolyn Lambert, Brookhaven "Alpha" Lions Club
Brookhaven, MS

FRUIT SALAD

1 large can cocktail (undrained)
1 can pears, drained
1 can peaches, drained
1 can dark cherries

1 can crushed pineapple
1 jar maraschino cherries
3 or 4 bananas

Mix all together and add a little sugar.

Sue Bubb, Burnham Lions Club
McClure, PA

Nothing weakens the truth more than stretching it.

❧ ❧ ❧

Contentment is wanting what you have, not having everything you want.

COMPANY FRUIT SALAD

4 medium Golden Delicious
apples, diced
4 medium Red Delicious apples,
diced
2 c. seedless green grapes, halved

2 c. seedless red grapes, halved
1 (20 oz.) can pineapple chunks,
drained
1 (11 oz.) can mandarin oranges,
drained

Dressing:

1 (3 oz.) pkg. cream cheese,
softened
½ c. sour cream

½ c. mayonnaise
½ c. sugar

Combine all the fruit in a large bowl. In a mixing bowl, beat dressing ingredients until smooth. Pour over fruit; toss gently to coat. Serve immediately. Yield: 16 to 20 servings.

In the summer, this is one salad that really sets with everyone. We like to eat meals that are not too heavy.

Ruth Jones, Moorcroft Lions Club
Moorcroft, WY

CREAMY FRUIT FROST

1 (3 oz.) pkg. cream cheese,
softened
1 (12 oz.) non-dairy whipped
topping
1 (21 oz.) cherry fruit filling

1 (11 oz.) can mandarin oranges,
drained
1 (8 oz.) can pineapple chunks,
drained

Stir softened cream cheese into whipped topping. Gradually add cherry fruit filling, blending well. Fold drained mandarin oranges and pineapple chunks into cherry mixture. Refrigerate. Ready to serve immediately.

Could be used as a dessert.

Audrey Leisgang, Ashwaubenon Lioness Club
Green Bay, WI, USA

Trust God to move your mountain, but keep on digging.

FROZEN FRUIT SALAD

3 oz. soft cream cheese
⅓ c. mayonnaise
1 tsp. lemon juice
2 egg whites
1 c. whipped cream or Cool Whip
6 large marshmallows, cut up

¼ c. drained mandarin orange
   slices
1 lb. can fruit cocktail, drained
2 Tbsp. chopped maraschino
   cherries
1 Tbsp. chopped walnuts

Blend cream cheese, mayonnaise, and lemon juice. Beat egg whites until foamy. Beat in sugar, 1 tablespoon at a time, until soft peaks form. If using whipping cream, beat until smooth. Fold cream into egg whites. Fold into cheese mixture. Fold in rest of ingredients. Pour into 8 inch square pan or for individual servings, put cupcake papers in cupcake or muffin pan. Freeze.

Wonderful on hot days - very refreshing.

W.C. Murphey, Princeton Lions Club
Princeton, IL, USA

FROZEN FRUIT SALAD

1 ctn. sour cream
Buttermilk
2 Tbsp. lemon juice
2 Tbsp. chopped cherries
½ c. chopped nuts

1 c. crushed pineapple, drained
1 chopped banana
¾ c. sugar
Sour cream with enough butter to
   make 2 c.

Mix in order. Pour in muffin tin and freeze.

Has been in family many years.

Shirley Ward, Levelland Evening Lions Club
Levelland, TX

LEMON FRUIT SALAD

1 (20 oz.) can lemon pie filling
1 (20 oz.) can fruit cocktail
2 c. whipped topping

1 (20 oz.) can pineapple chunks
2 or 3 bananas, cut up (optional)

Thoroughly drain fruit cocktail and pineapple. Combine pie filling and whipped topping. Fold in fruit and other ingredients. Chill well and serve.

It's sweet and can be served as a dessert or a salad.

Amy Bromley, Iron City Lions Club
Iron City, TN, USA

Kindness is never out of season.

JOHN'S FAVORITE FRUIT SALAD

Cantaloupe, pared and diced
Kiwi, skinned and sliced

Strawberries
Blueberries

If a dressing is required, use plain yogurt, 1 teaspoon sugar, and 1 teaspoon poppy seeds.

Add cherries and/or grapes, halved.

Sarah Wehling, Bothell Lions Club
Bothell, WA, USA

AMBROSIA DELUXE

Oranges
Grapefruits
Tangerines
Sugar

Coconut
Bananas
Pineapple tidbits
Mandarin oranges

With a sharp knife, section oranges, grapefruits, and tangerines, removing membrane and seeds. Arrange fruit in layers, sprinkling each with a little fine, granulated, powdered, or confectioners sugar and grated fresh or packaged coconut. Other fruit, such as sliced bananas, sprinkled with lime or lemon juice, pineapple tidbits, or canned mandarin oranges can be added. Chill before serving.

Sarah Wehling, Bothell Lions Club
Bothell, WA, USA

PEACH CONGEALED SALAD

1 small can crushed pineapple
2 (3 oz.) pkg. peach jello
1 (15 oz.) can fruit cocktail

1 (8 oz.) cream cheese
2 c. water (boiling)

Do not drain fruits. Combine boiling water and jello. Dissolve. Add other ingredients. Put in greased mold or dish. Place in refrigerator, stirring several times till congealed.

Martha Daniel, Bellville Lions Club
Bellville, GA, USA

GINGER PEACH MOLDS

2 (3 oz.) boxes orange jello
2 c. hot water
2 (7 oz.) ginger ale

1 to 1½ c. thinly sliced peaches
1 c. heavy cream
1 tsp. ground ginger

Dissolve gelatin in hot water. Add ginger ale. Chill until slightly thickened. Add peaches and put into 1½ quart mold. Chill until firm. Unmold and serve with whipped cream flavored with ginger. Makes 6 to 8 servings.

This may also be served as a salad. Omit the whipped topping and use dairy sour cream flavored with ginger.

Sarah Wehling, Bothell Lions Club
Bothell, WA, USA

54

CRANBERRY-GLAZED PEARS

Make these well ahead of time so the cranberry juice has time to permeate the pears. They keep for days.

6 c. cranberry-juice cocktail
⅓ c. sugar
½ tsp. ground cinnamon

6 pears (about 2 lb.)
Ice cream (optional)

In a saucepan, combine juice, sugar, and cinnamon and bring to a boil over high heat. Meanwhile, peel pears. Cut in halves and use a melon baller to scoop out core. Put pears into the boiling juice mixture. Reduce heat to medium and simmer until pears are tender, about 15 minutes. Transfer pears and poaching liquid to a bowl and refrigerate at least 4 hours or overnight. Remove pears. Put poaching liquid in a saucepan and boil until reduced to about 1 cup of thick syrup, about 30 minutes. Cool. Spoon the poaching liquid over the pears and serve with a scoop of ice cream. Makes 6 servings.

Per serving: 269 calories, 1 g protein, 0 g fat, 5 mg sodium, 69 g carbohydrate, 0 mg cholesterol.

Mrs. Mike Nowicki, Clarence Lions Club
Clarence Center, NY, USA

CONGEALED PEAR SALAD

1 large (No. 2½) can pears
2 small (3 oz.) pkg. cream cheese
½ c. chopped pecans

1 small pkg. lime jello
1 ctn. Cool Whip

Drain 1 cup syrup from the pears. Bring to a boil and dissolve jello in it. Cool slightly. Mash pears. Blend pears and softened cream cheese with mixer. Fold in about 4 ounces of Cool Whip. Add nuts. Pour into an oblong Pyrex dish and chill until set. Serves 8 or more. Does not freeze.

Linda Fox, Saginaw Lions Club
Saginaw, TX

A wise man is like a pin, his head keeps him from going too far.

We show what we love by what we do with what we have.

APRICOT CREAM SALAD

1 (6 oz.) pkg. apricot or orange
   jello
2 (17 oz.) cans apricots (reserve
   liquid)

1 (6 oz.) can mandarin oranges,
   drained
2 c. small marshmallows

Topping:

1 (8 oz.) pkg. cream cheese,
   softened

1 (4 oz.) pkg. instant vanilla
   pudding

Dissolve jello in 1½ cups boiling apricot juice. If not enough juice, add water to make 1½ cups. Add fruits and marshmallows and pour into a 9x13 inch greased pan or glass dish. Let congeal.

For the topping, whip cream cheese and add milk and pudding. Beat until smooth. Spread mixture over congealed salad. Chill and cut into squares. Serves 10 to 12.

Janie Fox, Saginaw Lions Club
Saginaw, TX

STUFFED CANTALOUPE

1 cantaloupe (medium)
White or Rose wine
¼ lb. Blue cheese, crumbled
½ lb. Ricotta or Farmers cheese

¼ c. sour cream or heavy sweet
   cream
Salt and freshly ground pepper

Cut a slice off the top of the cantaloupe; scoop out the fruit with a melon-ball cutter. Marinate the melon balls in wine until time to serve.

In the meantime, blend together cheeses and cream. Season to taste with salt and pepper. Pile the cheese mixture lightly into the cantaloupe shell. If it does not fill the shell, lower the rim of the shell by cutting with knife in jagged edges to form a "basket edge."

To eat, spear melon balls with toothpicks and dip them into the cheese mixture for a very pretty, refreshingly different appetizer. Makes about 1 cup cheese mixture and about 20 melon balls.

Lion Micheal and Ruth (Sauskojus) Bartolf, Oxbow and District Lions
Club
Oxbow, Saskatchewan, Canada

FROZEN CHERRY SALAD

1 (16 oz.) can cherry pie filling
1 (14 oz.) can sweetened
   condensed milk

1 (14 oz.) can crushed pineapple
1 (13 oz.) ctn. Cool Whip

Mix all ingredients. Freeze in a 9x13 inch pan. Cut into squares and garnish with salad topping and strawberries.

Joe Phillips, Iron City Lions Club
Iron City, TN, USA

ROSE OF SHARON SALAD

1 large (6 oz.) pkg. raspberry jello
1 can cream of tomato soup
1½ c. shredded cabbage
½ c. large green pepper, chopped
½ c. large onion, chopped or
    grated

1 large cucumber (take out
    seeds), grated
1 clove garlic, grated
½ c. vinegar
⅓ c. water (mix with soup)
Salt and pepper to taste

Dissolve jello in *hot* tomato soup (and ⅓ cup water). Let cool for awhile, then add other ingredients. Mold until firm.

This recipe sounds awful, but it's really very good. A nice change from sweet congealed salads. *I* like a little extra vinegar in it.

Normanda Huffman, Shelbyville Lions Club
Shelbyville, TN, USA

HOLIDAY JELLO SALAD

1 (6 oz.) box raspberry jello
2 c. hot water
1 (20 oz.) can crushed pineapple
    (with juice)
1 (11 oz.) can mandarin oranges,
    cut in halves and drained

1 (16 oz.) can whole cranberry
    sauce
½ c. chopped nuts (optional)

Dissolve jello in hot water. Add remaining ingredients and stir well. Chill to set.

Kathy Simmons, Princeton Lions Club
Princeton, IL, USA

AUTUMN SALAD

1 (20 oz.) can crushed pineapple
    (undrained)
⅔ c. sugar
1 small (3 oz.) lemon jello
1 (8 oz.) cream cheese, softened

1 c. diced, unpeeled apples
1 c. chopped celery
1 c. whipped topping
Curly lettuce

In a small pan, combine pineapple and sugar. Bring to a boil for 3 minutes. Add gelatin; stir until mixture is dissolved. Add cream cheese; stir until mixture is thoroughly combined. Cool 5 minutes and fold in apples, nuts, celery, and whipped topping. Pour into casserole. Chill until firm. Cut into squares and serve on curly lettuce.

This is a recipe that will go over very big anytime served. Always a hit!

Lion JoAnn Jones, Mathews Lions Club
North, VA

RASPBERRY-APPLESAUCE SALAD

1 (3 oz.) pkg. raspberry jello
2/3 c. boiling water
1 pkg. frozen red raspberries
1 (16 oz.) can applesauce

1 (8 oz.) ctn. commercial sour cream
1 small pkg. miniature marshmallows

Combine jello in water, stirring until dissolved. Add frozen raspberries, breaking up with fork, then add applesauce. Pour into 9x13 inch baking dish. Let set until firm, then top with marshmallows, then sour cream.

Bert Morgan, Broken Bow Lions Club
Broken Bow, NE, Custer County

CHERRY SOUR CREAM JELLO SALAD

1 (3 oz.) pkg. cherry jello
1 c. boiling water
1 (10 oz.) pkg. frozen strawberries

1 c. crushed pineapple with juice
1 (8 oz.) ctn. sour cream

Dissolve jello in boiling water. Add strawberries and pineapple. Mix well. Pour half of jello mixture into a 3½ cup ring jello mold. When jello is set, cover with sour cream. Spoon remaining jello over sour cream. Put into a refrigerator until set and firm.

JEAN'S LEMON JELLO SALAD

1 (20 oz.) can crushed pineapple (undrained)
2/3 c. sugar
1 (3 oz.) pkg. lemon jello
1 (8 oz.) pkg. cream cheese, softened

1 c. diced, unpeeled apple
½ c. chopped nuts
1 c. chopped celery
1 c. Cool Whip

Boil sugar and pineapple. Add jello mix and stir. Add cream cheese and stir well. Cool. Fold in apples, nuts, celery, and Cool Whip. Chill. Serve on lettuce leaf.

Betty Rutledge, Bryan Lioness Club
Bryan, OH

GELATIN SALAD

1 small can pineapple
1 (6 oz.) pkg. jello

1 medium ctn. Cool Whip
2 c. buttermilk

Heat fruit and jello until it dissolves. Stir in the Cool Whip and the buttermilk. Cool the jello and fruit mixture, then add to Cool Whip mixture. Stir well. Store in the refrigerator in a flat container.

Martha C. Cox, Travelers Rest Lions Club
Travelers Rest, SC

CAROL'S PINEAPPLE SALAD

2 small pkg. lime jello
1 pt. sour cream
1 c. boiling water
½ tsp. salt
1 (15 oz.) can crushed pineapple
½ c. slivered almonds

Dissolve jello in boiling water. Cool. Add all ingredients and chill. *Enjoy!*

Lion Carol N. Kellner, Annapolis Lions Club
Annapolis, MD

PINEAPPLE NOEL SALAD

2 env. unflavored gelatin
2 Tbsp. sugar
¼ tsp. salt
3½ c. canned pineapple juice
2 Tbsp. lemon juice
1 (11 oz.) can mandarin oranges
3 bananas
½ c. thinly sliced celery
Pineapple slices for garnish
Salad greens

Mix gelatin, sugar, salt, and ½ cup pineapple juice. Place over low heat, stirring constantly, until gelatin is dissolved. Stir in remaining 3 cups juice and lemon juice. Cool until slightly thick. Fold well-drained oranges, sliced bananas, and finely chopped celery into thickened gelatin. Turn into 5 cup mold. Chill until firm. Unmold. Garnish with pineapple (sliced) and salad greens. Makes about 8 servings.

PDG James R. Schiebel, Hilton Lions Club
Hilton, NY, USA

CINNAMON SALAD

1 (3 oz.) pkg. cherry Jell-O
1 c. hot water
¼ c. red hots
½ c. boiling water
1 c. chopped apples
1 c. celery, cut fine
½ c. chopped nuts

Dissolve Jell-O in 1 cup hot water. Add red hots to the ½ cup boiling water and stir until dissolved. Add enough water to make 1 cup liquid. Add to Jell-O. Cool until partially set, then fold in other ingredients. Refrigerate until firm.

Janice Robison, Mexico Sunrise Lions Club
Benton City, MO, Audrain County

Be careful with your tongue. It's in a wet place and can easily slip.

2075-99

SUNSHINE SALAD

1 can Eagle Brand
½ c. lemon juice
1 can apricot pie filling
1 can mandarin oranges, drained
1 can pineapple tidbits, drained

1 c. small marshmallows
½ c. coconut
½ c. pecans
1 small (4 oz.) ctn. Cool Whip

Combine the Eagle Brand and lemon juice. Mix well. Add the rest of the ingredients. Let stand several hours or overnight in the refrigerator before serving.

Deryl Fox, Saginaw Lions Club
Saginaw, TX

RED DEVIL SALAD

2 pkg. lemon Jell-O
1 (18 oz.) can tomato juice
½ c. water
¼ c. vinegar
2 Tbsp. green onions

1 c. chopped celery
Salt and pepper to taste
1 avocado, chopped
½ to 1 lb. cooked shrimp
Dash of Tabasco

Boil tomato juice. Add Jell-O, stirring to dissolve. Add water and vinegar. Refrigerate until thickened slightly, then add onion, celery, salt, pepper, avocado, and shrimp. Add Tabasco and pour into mold.

Joanne Tuttle, Conroe Noon Lions Club
Conroe, TX, USA

TOMATO ASPIC

1 small pkg. lemon jello
1 (8 oz.) tomato sauce
1½ Tbsp. vinegar

½ tsp. salt
Dash of pepper
1¼ c. boiling water

Dissolve contents of 1 package of lemon jello in 1¼ cups boiling water. Add tomato sauce, vinegar, salt, and pepper. Chill in mold until firm.

For a large mold, double recipe.

I have added celery, carrots, onions, olives, shrimp or any other combination you wish.

This recipe is so easy and is much better than the more complicated recipes I've seen.

Mrs. Duane (Pam) Bennett, Mad River Lions Club
Riverside, OH, USA

Saving yourself for marriage will help to save your marriage.

HEAVENLY ORANGE FLUFF

Jell-O:

2 (3 oz.) boxes orange Jell-O
2 c. boiling water
1 (6 oz.) can frozen orange juice
2 (11 oz.) cans mandarin
    oranges, drained

1 (8 oz.) can crushed pineapple in
    juice (not drained)

Lemon Topping:

1 c. milk
1 (3¾ oz.) box instant lemon
    pudding

2 c. whipped topping

Jell-O: Dissolve Jell-O in boiling water. Add frozen orange juice, undiluted. Add orange sections and pineapple. Mix well and pour into a 9x13 inch glass pan which has been sprayed with Pam. When Jell-O is set, cover with Lemon Topping.

Lemon Topping: Add milk to pudding. Beat until thick. Fold whipped topping into pudding. Put on set Jell-O mixture. Cut into squares.

GRAPEFRUIT ASPIC SALAD

1 (3 oz.) pkg. lemon Jell-O
¾ c. boiling water
½ pkg. plain gelatin in 1 Tbsp.
    cold water
1 c. grapefruit juice

2 c. grapefruit sections
¼ tsp. salt
1 Tbsp. sugar
1 tsp. (or more) grated onion
½ c. slivered almonds

Mix ingredients as listed. Chill in refrigerator until set.

Betty Swope, Elizabethtown Lions Club
Elizabethtown, KY, USA

AVOCADO RING MOLD SALAD

1 (3 oz.) pkg. lemon gelatin
1 tsp. salt
1 c. mashed avocado
1 c. hot water

3 tsp. lemon juice
½ c. mayonnaise
⅔ c. heavy cream, whipped

Dissolve gelatin in hot water; chill until slightly thickened. Combine remaining ingredients and fold into gelatin mixture. Pour into a 1½ quart ring mold and chill until firm. Unmold on a large chilled plate and garnish with orange or grapefruit sections.

Zona Roberts, Bullhead City Lions Club
Bullhead City, AZ, USA

PEACHES AND CREAM SALAD

1 pkg. lemon gelatin
¾ c. boiling water
1 c. orange juice

1 env. whipped topping mix
1 (8 oz.) pkg. cream cheese
¼ c. pecans

Topping - Peach layer:

1 pkg. lemon gelatin
1 c. boiling water

1 (21 oz.) can peach pie filling

In a bowl, dissolve gelatin in boiling water. Add orange juice and refrigerate until partially set. Prepare whipped topping mix according to directions. In a mixing bowl, beat cream cheese until smooth. Fold in whipped topping and pecans, then fold in gelatin mixture. Pour into 8 inch square pan. Refrigerate until firm.

For peach layer, dissolve gelatin in boiling water. Stir in pie filling and chill until partially set. Carefully pour over creamy gelatin. Chill till firm.

Carol Hug, Bryan Lioness Club
Bryan, OH, USA

GREEN GRAPE SOUR-CREAM SWIRL

½ c. sour cream
½ c. plain yogurt
¼ c. fresh lime juice
½ tsp. grated lime rind
2 c. seedless green grapes, halved

¼ c. dark brown sugar
Extra grapes, sliced (for garnish)
Lime slices
Fresh mint

In a medium bowl, stir together the sour cream, yogurt, lime juice, and rind. In small glass dishes, alternate layers of grapes, sour cream mixture, and brown sugar, ending up with sour cream mixture. Refrigerate for at least 30 minutes to allow flavors to develop. Decorate with grape and lime slices and mint. Makes 4 servings.

Per serving: 191 calories, 3 g protein, 7 g fat, 36 mg sodium, 31 g carbohydrate, 16 mg cholesterol.

Low-fat swirl: Use nonfat yogurt in place of the sour cream and yogurt.

Per serving: 144 calories, 4 g protein, 0.5 g fat, 51 mg sodium, 33 g carbohydrate, 1 mg cholesterol.

Lion John J. Hess, Clarence Lions Club
Clarence Center, NY, USA

If you decide not to choose, you've already made the wrong choice.

GRAPE SALAD

8 oz. cream cheese
8 oz. sour cream
2½ lb. green grapes

⅓ c. sugar
2 tsp. vanilla

Wash grapes and pat dry. Mix cream cheese, sour cream, sugar, and vanilla together. Fold in the grapes. When ready to serve, sprinkle brown sugar over the top.

Eilene Moody, Bryan Lioness Club
Bryan, OH

CRANBERRY SALAD

1 can whole cranberries
3 to 4 bananas
3 to 4 apples

3 to 4 oranges
2 c. miniature marshmallows
¾ to 1 c. pecans, chopped

Set 12 hours.

Barb Tornes, Ave. of Pines Lions Club
Deer River, MN

CRANBERRY SALAD

1 large box cherry Jell-O
1 can crushed pineapple
1 can whole cranberry sauce

1 small jar applesauce
½ c. pecans, crushed
1 (8 oz.) Cool Whip

Dissolve Jell-O in 2 cups hot water, then add whole cranberry sauce. Mix well, then add applesauce and pecans and mix. This can go in a bowl or a 9x13 inch cake pan and be cut in squares. When jelled, top with Cool Whip.

A person of words and not of deeds is like a garden full of weeds.

Lion Jane McCune, Huffman Lions Club
Huffman, TX, USA

Work at building people up, not tearing them down.

Not all gifts are free, some have hidden price tags.

CRANBERRY SALAD

2 regular size cans whole
   cranberry sauce*
1 env. Knox gelatine
2 pkg. strawberry jello
1 grated apple

3 stalks diced celery
6 pecan halves
6 tsp. mayonnaise
6 leaves lettuce

Dissolve jello and gelatine in 2 cups of boiling water. Add 12 ice cubes and stir until ice melts. Add apple and celery. Stir in canned or cooked cranberry sauce. Pour mixture in jello mold (a Bundt cake pan works well) and allow to set 4 to 6 hours in fridge.

Line plate with lettuce. Dip mold *briefly* in warm water to loosen, then turn mold upside down on lettuce bed. Place teaspoons of mayo around top of the mold about an inch apart and top each spot with a pecan half.

* Or, use 1 pound bag of whole cranberries (cooked) and 2 packages Knox gelatine added to the hot water and cooked cranberries.

Liz Birchen, O'Fallon Lions Club
O'Fallon, MO, USA

CRANBERRY SALAD

1 bag fresh cranberries
1½ c. sugar
1 regular pkg. orange jello
1 c. water (or drain pineapple and
   use juice instead)

1 can crushed pineapple
1 c. semi-chopped walnuts

Grind cranberries (or use food processor). Dissolve gelatin in hot water or pineapple juice. Combine all ingredients and chill.

Lion Dan Clever, East Prospect Lions Club
East Prospect, PA, USA

CRANBERRY EGGNOG SALAD

28 oz. fruit cocktail, drained
1 env. plain gelatin
2 Tbsp. lemon juice
2 Tbsp. fruit cocktail juice
3 oz. cream cheese

¼ c. mayonnaise
Dash of salt
⅔ c. whipping cream, chilled
½ c. sugar
½ c. nuts, chopped

Soften unflavored gelatin in undrained pineapple and lime juice for 5 minutes. Heat gelatin mixture until gelatin dissolves. Cool. Stir in eggnog. Chill until firm. Heat cranberry juice to boiling; stir in the raspberry gelatin until dissolved. Chill until partially set. Fold in relish and celery. Carefully spoon atop eggnog mixture. Chill until firm. Cut into squares. Yield: 12 servings.

Author of "The Best of Mayberry" cookbook, honored in "America's Best" recipes by Oxmoor House, Inc.

Betty Conley Lyerly, Mount Airy Foothills Lions Club
Mount Airy, NC, USA

JELLIED RASPBERRY AND CRANBERRY SALAD

2 pkg. raspberry Jell-O
1½ c. boiling water
1 (10 oz.) pkg. frozen raspberries,
    thawed

1 (10 oz.) pkg. frozen cranberry
    relish, thawed
Grated rind and juice of 1 lemon
½ c. ginger ale

Dissolve Jell-O in water. Chill until partially thickened. Add remaining ingredients. Turn into quart mold and chill until firm. Serves 8.

Virginia Bayer, Franklin Park Lions Club
Park Ridge, IL

CRANBERRY SALAD

1 lb. cranberries, run through
    food chopper
1 c. sugar
½ pt. whipping cream

1 c. white grapes, chopped in
    halves
1 small pkg. marshmallows, cut
    into pieces

Put the sugar over the chopped cranberries and mix. Let stand at least 20 minutes. Add the grapes and marshmallows; whip the cream and fold into the first mixture. Place in refrigerator to set.

Linda Fox, Saginaw Lions Club
Saginaw, TX

CRANBERRY SALAD RING

4 (3 oz.) pkg. black raspberry
    gelatin
2 c. boiling water
½ c. fresh cranberries, ground (I
    use 1 pkg.)
2 oranges (unpeeled), cored and
    ground

1 (15¼ oz.) can crushed
    pineapple (undrained)
2 c. sugar
1 c. chopped pecans

Dissolve gelatin in boiling water. Add cold water and chill until consistency of unbeaten egg white. Combine next 6 ingredients; mix well. Fold fruit mixture into gelatin mixture. Pour into lightly oiled 10 cup ring mold; chill until set. Unmold on lettuce leaves. Serves about 15.

Optional: You may fill center of ring with mayonnaise and garnish with orange slices if desired. Very good with ham or turkey.

I got this recipe from a Lion friend. Very good.

Lion Dolly Muchow, Severn River Lions Club
Severna Park, MD

CRANBERRY MOUSSE

1 c. cranberry juice
1 (3 oz.) raspberry Jell-O
1 (16 oz.) can whole cranberry
sauce

1 Cool Whip (3 c.)

Heat cranberry juice; add Jell-O until dissolved. Stir in cranberry sauce. Chill until thickened. Fold in Cool Whip.

Lion Bev Wilkens, Plato Lions Club
Young America, MN, USA

WHITE SALAD

1 lb. marshmallows
½ c. milk
8 oz. cream cheese (room
temperature)

2 c. cottage cheese
1 (No. 2) can crushed pineapple
2 c. whipped topping

Melt marshmallows in milk on low heat and cool. Mix cream cheese with cottage cheese. Add well drained pineapple and whipped topping. Add to marshmallow mixture. Pour into 9x13 inch pan and set in refrigerator. *Keeps well several days.*

We call this the Funeral Salad because I have taken it to so many funeral dinners.

Lion Amy L. Kastle, Kirwin Lions Club
Kirwin, KS, USA

You can win more friends with your ears than with your mouth.

❧ ❧ ❧

Life's big turning point often hinges on little things.

❧ ❧ ❧

We won't have time to find fault with others if we are busy seeking wisdom.

WHITE JELLO

1 pkg. plus ¼ tsp. Knox
    unflavored gelatine
¾ c. sugar
1½ c. water

    Raspberry Sauce:

1 (10 oz.) pkg. frozen red
    raspberries, thawed
¼ c. red currant jelly or red
    raspberry jam

1 (16 oz.) sour cream
1 (8 oz.) Cool Whip, thawed
1½ tsp. almond extract

1 Tbsp. cornstarch

Boil Knox gelatine, sugar, and water, then let cool. Mix sour cream, Cool Whip, and almond extract together. When gelatine mixture is completely cool, fold in Cool Whip mixture. Pour into mold and let set overnight (for best results).

In a small saucepan, combine 10 ounce package of raspberries in syrup, jelly, and cornstarch. Cook, stirring often, till thick and clear. Cool. Makes about 1½ cups.

Spread on top of set gelatine and Cool Whip mixture. Extra sauce can be served on the side.

Very attractive when served in a goblet type bowl.

Mrs. Jan Callaghan, Elburn Lions Club
Elburn, IL, USA

SNICKERS SALAD

1 (8 oz.) cream cheese, softened
1 (12 oz.) Cool Whip, thawed
1 c. powdered sugar

1 (6 pack) Snickers bars
4 to 6 Granny Smith apples

Mix cream cheese, powdered sugar, and Cool Whip until smooth and creamy. Cut Snickers into desired size pieces and add to cream cheese mixture. Cut apples into chunks. Mix together and refrigerate at least 1 hour before serving.

Judy Rannow, Arlington (SEA) Lions Club
Arlington, MN, USA

Forgiveness is the glue that repairs broken relationships.

PRETZEL JELLO

Crust:

3 Tbsp. sugar
¾ c. margarine

2⅔ c. crushed pretzels

Filling:

8 oz. soft cream cheese
1 c. sugar

8 oz. Cool Whip

Topping:

6 oz. strawberry jello
16 oz. frozen strawberries,
    thawed

2 c. boiling water

Cream sugar and margarine. Add crushed pretzels. Press into a 9x13 inch dish. Bake at 350° for 10 minutes. Cool.

Mix the cream cheese, sugar, and Cool Whip thoroughly and spread over cooled crust.

Dissolve the jello in boiling water. Add the strawberries and allow to partially set. Pour over the filling. Refrigerate until firm.

Martha C. Cox, Travelers Rest Lions Club
Travelers Rest, SC

PRETZEL SALAD

Break 2 cups pretzels in small pieces. Melt 1 stick margarine in 9x12 inch pan. Add 4 tablespoons sugar. Add pretzel pieces. Bake 10 minutes at 350° and cool.

Mix:

1 (8 oz.) cream cheese
¾ c. sugar

1 (8 oz.) pkg. whipped topping

Pour over top of pretzel base. Refrigerate.

Top layer:

1 (6 oz.) pkg. strawberry jello
2 c. hot water

1 c. cold water
1 pkg. frozen strawberries

Chill until syrupy, then pour over cheese layer. Refrigerate till ready to use.

Delicious and enough for a crowd.

Judy Hoffman, Southport Lions Club
Indianapolis, IN

STRAWBERRY PRETZEL SALAD

2 c. crushed pretzels
3 Tbsp. sugar
¾ c. melted oleo or butter
1 (8 oz.) cream cheese
1 medium size tub Cool Whip

1 c. sugar
1 (20 oz.) bag unsweetened
  strawberries
2 c. boiling water
1 (6 oz.) strawberry Jell-O

Mix pretzels, sugar, and oleo together and put in 9x13 inch pan. Bake at 400° for 8 minutes.

Blend cream cheese, Cool Whip, and sugar with mixer. Place over cooled crust in 9x13 inch pan.

Blend Jell-O with hot water. Fold in strawberries and stir till it starts to jell. Pour over cream cheese mixture. Refrigerate.

Pat Wheeler, Green Lane-Marlboro Lioness Club
Green Lane, PA, USA

STRAWBERRY PRETZEL SALAD

¾ c. butter
3 Tbsp. sugar
1⅔ c. pretzels, broken up finely
1 (8 oz.) Cool Whip
1 (8 oz.) pkg. cream cheese

1 c. sugar
1 large pkg. strawberry jello
2 c. boiling water
1 pt. frozen strawberries, thawed

Cream butter and sugar; add pretzels. Press dough into a 9x13 inch pan. Bake 10 minutes at 350°F. Let cool.

Mix together Cool Whip, cream cheese, and sugar and spread on top of dough mixture that has cooled. Dissolve jello in water. Mix with strawberries when partially set. Spread on top of other two layers. Refrigerate till firm.

Elizabeth Maddock, Canaan Northwest Lions Club
Canaan, CT, USA

The best fathers not only give us life, but also teach us how to live.

❧ ❧ ❧

There is no limit to the good we can do if we don't care who gets the credit.

DEVILED EGG MOLD

1 env. Knox unflavored gelatine
½ c. cool water
¼ tsp. salt
2 Tbsp. lemon juice
¼ tsp. Worcestershire sauce
⅛ tsp. cayenne pepper

¾ c. mayonnaise
1½ tsp. grated onion
½ c. finely diced celery
¼ c. diced pimiento
4 to 5 hard-boiled eggs

Sprinkle gelatine over cool water to soften. Use a small saucepan and place over low heat. Bring to a soft boil or until gelatine looks clear. Remove from heat. Add salt, lemon juice, Worcestershire sauce, and cayenne pepper. Cool. Pour over mayonnaise and mix in bowl. Add other ingredients and blend well. Pour into 3 cup mold or glass loaf dish. Chill until firm. Garnish with fresh parsley and serve on lettuce.

This is a good way to use the extra hard-boiled eggs at Easter time.
Lion Ann K. Brumback, Silver Run-Union Mills Lions Club
Westminster, MD, USA

SAUERKRAUT SALAD

1 jar sauerkraut, washed and
    drained well (no taste left)
1 chopped green pepper

2 chopped onions
1 c. chopped celery

Bring to boil:

2 c. sugar

1 c. vinegar

Pour this over the sauerkraut. Refrigerate 6 hours.
Micheal and Ruth Bartolf, Oxbow and District Lions Club
Oxbow, Saskatchewan, Canada

RUTABAGA TERIYAKI

4 c. young rutabagas, peeled and
    thinly sliced
1 c. carrots, thinly sliced
1 Tbsp. low sodium soy sauce

½ c. vinegar
1 Tbsp. honey
1 tsp. fresh ginger root, grated

In a bowl, mix soy sauce, vinegar, and honey. Add vegetables and stir well. Chill in the refrigerator until serving. Just before serving, add ginger. Yields 6 servings.
Micheal and Ruth Bartolf, Oxbow and District Lions Club
Oxbow, Saskatchewan, Canada

Joy is a by-product of obedience.

PALLAS ATHENE SALAD

5 medium tomatoes, cut in
   wedges
1 tsp. oregano
Salt and pepper to taste
2 medium green sweet peppers

24 small Greek olives
Small curd cottage cheese
Sour cream

Cut the tomatoes into wedges and place in a bowl. Sprinkle with oregano, salt, and pepper. Toss lightly. Thinly slice and clean the peppers. Arrange tomatoes, peppers, and olives on a lettuce-lined serving dish. Spoon dollops of cottage cheese and sour cream on top.

Sarah Wehling, Bothell Lions Club
Bothell, WA, USA

BREAD SALAD WITH SALAMI

Day-old bread works best.

2 Tbsp. wine vinegar
Salt and pepper
1/3 c. + 1/4 c. olive oil
6 oz. French bread (about 5 c.
   cubed)
1/4 lb. sliced hard salami

1/4 lb. Provolone cheese (about 3/4
   c. cubed)
1 tomato (about 1/2 lb.)
1 scallion
1 clove garlic

In a small jar, combine the vinegar, 1/2 teaspoon salt, and 1/4 teaspoon pepper and shake until the salt dissolves. Add 1/3 cup of the oil and shake again to combine. Cut the bread into 3/4 inch cubes. Cut the salami into strips. Cut the cheese into cubes. Cut the tomato into chunks. Chop the scallion. Mince the garlic.

In a large frying pan, heat 1/4 cup oil over medium heat. Add the bread cubes and cook, stirring occasionally, until golden brown on all sides, 5 to 10 minutes. Add the garlic, stirring it into the bread, and cook until fragrant, about 30 seconds.

In a serving bowl, combine the fried bread with the salami, cheese, tomato, and scallion. Pour the dressing over the salad and refrigerate at least 30 minutes. Bring to room temperature before serving. Makes 4 servings.

Work time: 35 minutes. Total time: 1 hour and 5 minutes.

Per serving: 529 calories, 18 g protein, 39 g fat, 1316 mg sodium, 27 g carbohydrate, 42 mg cholesterol.

Mrs. Lucy Aiken, Clarence Lions Club
Clarence Center, NY, USA

BARLEY NUT SALAD

Time: 60 minutes.

1 c. uncooked barley
⅓ c. wheat berries
2⅔ c. spring water
½ c. fresh lemon juice
⅓ c. olive oil
½ tsp. sea salt

2 stalks celery, chopped
1 carrot, finely chopped
1 medium onion, finely chopped
½ c. minced fresh parsley
½ c. roasted nuts (almonds,
    walnuts, or hazelnuts)

Wash barley and wheat berries thoroughly. Combine with water in a 1½ to 2 quart saucepan and bring to a boil. Cover and simmer until all water is absorbed and the grains are tender (50 to 60 minutes). Allow to cool while preparing the dressing and vegetables. Wash and chop the celery, onion, and carrot. Mince parsley and chop nuts. Combine lemon, oil, and salt. Combine all ingredients and mix thoroughly. Check for seasoning and adjust if needed. Refrigerate for several hours before serving to blend flavors. Serves 3 to 4.

Can be served as is, on a bed of salad greens, or as filling for pita bread sandwich with sprouts.

PDG Jim Schiebel, Hilton Lions Club
Hilton, NY, USA

FENNEL AND ORANGE SALAD

3 oranges
Salt and pepper

2 Tbsp. oil
1 bulb fennel (about 1 lb.)

Squeeze 1 tablespoon juice from one of the oranges. In a small jar, combine the orange juice, ½ teaspoon salt, and a pinch of pepper and shake until the salt dissolves. Add the oil and shake again to combine. Trim the fennel and cut into thin slices. With a knife, peel the remaining oranges, cutting right down to the flesh and removing all the white pith. Slice oranges crosswise and cut each slice in half. Combine the fennel, the orange slices, and dressing. Makes 4 servings.

Per serving: 112 calories, 2 g protein, 7 g fat, 364 mg sodium, 12 g carbohydrate, 0 mg cholesterol.

Joanne M. Wetzler, Clarence Lions Club
Clarence Center, NY, USA

Gold can be a helpful servant, but a cruel master.

SWISS CHEESE SALAD

1 c. mayonnaise
3 Tbsp. milk
1 Tbsp. prepared mustard
1 tsp. horseradish
¼ tsp. salt
1 lb. Swiss cheese, cubed

2 large pears, cored and cubed
1 medium cucumber, cubed
1 c. diagonally sliced celery
1 c. California walnuts, coarsely
  chopped
Lettuce leaves

About 30 minutes before serving, in a large bowl, stir the first five ingredients with a fork until well mixed. Add cheese and remaining ingredients except lettuce. Toss gently and serve in lettuce leaves.

PED Doris J. Myers, Mexico Noon Club
Mexico, MO

MUSTARDY SALAD WITH RAISINS AND WALNUTS

1 Tbsp. Dijon mustard
2 tsp. wine vinegar
Salt and pepper
3 Tbsp. olive oil

8 leaves romaine lettuce (about 4
  c. torn leaves)
2 Tbsp. chopped walnuts
2 Tbsp. raisins

In a small jar, combine the mustard, vinegar, ¼ teaspoon salt, and ¼ teaspoon pepper and shake until the salt dissolves. Add the oil and shake again to combine. Tear the romaine into pieces. Combine romaine, the walnuts, and raisins. Just before serving, toss the salad with the mustard dressing. Makes 4 servings.

Per serving: 141 calories, 2 g protein, 13 g fat, 253 mg sodium, 60 g carbohydrate.

Lion John J. Hess, Clarence Lions Club
Clarence Center, NY, USA

WATERCRESS SALAD WITH CREAMY GARLIC DRESSING

⅓ c. mayonnaise
1 tsp. lemon juice
Salt and pepper
⅛ tsp. minced garlic

1 bunch watercress (about 6 oz.)
½ cucumber
1 carrot

Combine mayonnaise, 2 tablespoons of water, lemon juice, ¼ teaspoon salt, ⅛ teaspoon pepper, and garlic. Cut stems from watercress. Peel the cucumber. Cut in half lengthwise, remove the seeds, and cut into slices. Peel the carrot and grate it. Combine the watercress, cucumber slices, and grated carrot and pour the dressing on top. Makes 4 servings.

Per serving: 147 calories, 2 g protein, 14 g fat, 263 mg sodium, 4 g carbohydrate, 11 mg cholesterol.

Mrs. Mike Nowicki, Clarence Lions Club
Clarence Center, NY, USA

REUBEN SALAD

8 slices rye bread with caraway
2 tsp. olive oil
½ tsp. garlic salt
¾ lb. corned beef, sliced thin
½ lb. Swiss cheese, sliced thin

Sauerkraut, drained
½ c. Thousand Island dressing
6 to 8 leaves romaine lettuce,
   torn into 1 inch pieces

For croutons: Cut bread into ½ inch cubes. Heat olive oil in a large skillet over medium heat. Add croutons and sprinkle with garlic salt. Toss or coat all sides and brown lightly.

Julienne the corned beef slices and Swiss cheese. Place in large bowl; toss together with sauerkraut and croutons. Blend in Thousand Island dressing. Place torn lettuce in large bowl. Spoon salad mixture in center and serve. Makes 6 servings.

Mrs. Duane (Pam) Bennett, Mad River Lions Club
Riverside, OH, USA

CUCUMBER LIME SALAD

1 pkg. lime gelatin
¾ c. boiling water
Juice of 1 lemon (2 Tbsp.)
1 Tbsp. grated onion

1 c. grated, unpeeled cucumbers
   (European style), drained
½ c. mayonnaise
½ c. dairy sour cream

Dissolve gelatin in hot water. Add lemon juice and onion. Chill until slightly thickened. Add drained cucumber, mayonnaise, and sour cream. Blend well. Put into greased mold and chill. Serves 6. (Makes 4 individual molds.)

Easy and delicious - goes well with most meats and poultry.

Theresa Kromish, Community Lions Club
East Haddam, CT

MARINATED CUCUMBERS

6 cucumbers, thickly sliced
1 c. white vinegar
½ c. sugar

½ tsp. salt
1 Tbsp. chives
1 Tbsp. parsley, chopped

Combine last 5 ingredients and pour over cucumbers. Serves 10 to 12.

Agnes Williams, Alpha Lions Club
Brookhaven, MS, USA

Real help combines correction with compassion.

CREAMY CUCUMBERS

4 cucumbers, peeled and sliced
1 c. salad dressing (not mayo)
4 Tbsp. vinegar
½ tsp. salt
½ tsp. pepper
½ c. sugar

Mix together until cucumbers are covered. Can add cucumbers to the sauce all the time.

Lion Amy L. Kastle, Kirwin Lions Club
Kirwin, KS, USA

COOL CUCUMBER SURPRISE

1 (3 oz.) pkg. lemon jello
¼ tsp. salt
2 Tbsp. vinegar
1 (8 oz.) dairy sour cream
½ c. mayo or salad dressing
2 c. chopped, seeded cucumber
1 Tbsp. finely chopped onion
Lettuce leaves (optional)

Dissolve jello and salt in 1 cup boiling water. Stir in vinegar. Chill till partially set. Stir together sour cream, mayo, and a dash of pepper. Fold into jello mixture. Fold in cucumber and onion. Pour into 5 cup mold. Cover; chill till firm. Unmold onto a lettuce lined plate, if you like.

Ann Fisher, Findlay Lions Club

FRESH CUCUMBER SALAD

4 medium cucumbers (¹⁄₁₆ inch thick), peeled
1 Tbsp. salt
½ c. sugar
½ tsp. white pepper
½ c. white or wine vinegar

Peel and slice cucumbers. Place in a container with a tight lid. Mix salt, sugar, and white pepper and sprinkle over cukes. Add vinegar; stir and refrigerate 24 hours.

Emily Groover, Bellville Lions Club
Bellville, GA, USA

A good leader not only knows the way, but shows the way.

The more a diamond is cut, the more it sparkles.

RAMEN NOODLE BROCCOLI SLAW SALAD

Dressing:

½ c. oil
½ c. vinegar

½ c. sugar

Shake well. Refrigerate at least 2 hours.

Salad:

1 pkg. coleslaw mix
1 pkg. broccoli cole slaw mix
2 green onions
1 c. cashews

1 c. sunflower seeds
2 pkg. Ramen noodles (use
    chicken flavor or 1 chicken
    flavor and 1 oriental flavor)

Mix and refrigerate. Add dressing just before serving. Makes a large bowl.

Katheryn Thompson, Ave. of Pines Lions Club
Deer River, MN

WARM RED-PEPPER AND BROCCOLI SALAD

1 red bell pepper
1 bunch broccoli (about 1 lb.)
Salt and pepper

2 Tbsp. oil
¼ c. chopped pecans
1 tsp. wine vinegar

Cut red pepper into strips. Peel broccoli stems and cut into slices, about ¼ inch thick. Separate head into small florets. In a large pot of boiling salted water, cook broccoli until tender, about 5 minutes. Drain.

Meanwhile, in a large frying pan, heat 1 tablespoon of the oil over medium-high heat. Add pecans and cook until browned, about 1 minute. Remove nuts with a slotted spoon and reduce heat to low. Add red pepper strips and ½ teaspoon salt. Cover and cook until tender, 5 to 8 minutes. Add broccoli to the frying pan and heat through. Remove from heat; add vinegar, the remaining 1 tablespoon oil, and ⅛ teaspoon pepper and toss to coat. Sprinkle with pecans and serve. Makes 4 servings.

Per serving: 139 calories, 4 g protein, 12 g fat, 302 mg sodium, 8 g carbohydrate, 0 mg cholesterol.

Joann M. Brownell, Clarence Lions Club
Clarence Center, NY, USA

MARINATED SALAD

1 head cauliflower, chopped small
1 large bunch broccoli, chopped
    small
2 cucumbers, chopped small
2 peppers, chopped small

2 tomatoes, diced small
2 Tbsp. salad seasonings
1 (16 oz.) bottle Italian salad
    dressing

Mix all together well. Should set for 2 hours to marinate.

Lion Ida Rohrer, Moundbuilders Lions Club
Newark, OH, USA

BROCCOLI APPLE SALAD

½ c. raisins
1 c. broccoli, chopped

½ c. walnuts
½ c. diced apple

Mix above all together.

Add:

½ c. sugar
2 Tbsp. vinegar

1 c. mayo

Add together.

Debra James, Beckmantown Lions Club
West Chazy, NY

PEPPERONI AND BROCCOLI SALAD

1 (0.75 oz.) pkg. Italian salad
   dressing mix
1 (1 lb.) bunch broccoli
½ lb. fresh mushrooms, sliced

1 c. (4 oz.) diced Swiss cheese
1 (3½ oz.) pkg. sliced pepperoni
1 green pepper, chopped

Prepare dressing mix according to package directions. Use flowerets of broccoli. Break into small pieces. Reserve stalks for other recipes. Combine rest of ingredients in a large bowl. Pour dressing over salad. Toss gently. Cover and refrigerate 8 hours or overnight. Makes 6 to 8 servings.

I enjoy exchanging recipes. This recipe was given to me by my principal. Good salad.

Lion Dolly Muchow, Severn River Lions Club
Severna Park, MD

BROCCOLI-CAULIFLOWER SALAD

1 head broccoli, chopped
1 head cauliflower, chopped

1 red onion, chopped
1 lb. bacon, fried and crumbled

Dressing:

1 c. mayonnaise
½ c. sugar

2 Tbsp. vinegar

Toss ingredients with dressing. May be made the day before and stored in airtight container.

Recipe given to me by a friend. Very good!

Lion Dolly Muchow, Severn River Lions Club
Severna Park, MD

BROCCOLI SALAD

1 head fresh broccoli, cleaned
   and chopped
1 small onion, diced

½ lb. bacon, cooked and
   crumbled
1 c. grated Cheddar cheese
¾ c. sugar

Dressing:

½ c. sugar
2 Tbsp. vinegar

1 c. mayo or salad dressing

Mix well and pour over above ingredients. Refrigerate at least ½ hour.

Sue Bubb, Burnham Lions Club
McClure, PA

BROCCOLI SALAD

1 medium head broccoli
1 small onion
1 c. raisins
1 stalk celery
¼ c. cheese

6 slices bacon
½ c. mayonnaise
1 Tbsp. sugar
1 Tbsp. vinegar

Chop broccoli coarsely. Chop onion. Also chop celery. Shred cheese (use cheese of your choice). Fry bacon; drain on paper towels, then crumble. (You can use bacon bits.)

Mix mayonnaise, sugar, and vinegar until well blended, then add broccoli, onion, raisins, and celery. Mix until well coated. Cover and refrigerate for three hours, stirring occasionally. Add bacon just before serving.

Lion Donna Blake, Graysville-Proctor Lions Club
Glen Easton, WV, USA

CORN BREAD SALAD

1 recipe corn bread, crumbled
   (use ½)
½ lb. fried bacon, crumbled
2 medium green peppers,
   chopped
2 medium onions, chopped

3 to 4 tomatoes, chopped
½ c. sweet pickle, chopped
1 c. mayo
¼ c. sweet pickle juice
1 Tbsp. sugar

Layer corn bread, bacon, onions, green peppers, and tomatoes in that order. Sprinkle with salt, pepper, and sweet pickles, chopped. Combine mayo, pickle juice, and sugar. Drizzle over salad. Toss before serving.

Best made a day ahead. Will keep several days in refrigerator. Can be doubled.

Barbara Vaughn, Conroe Lioness Club
Montgomery County, Conroe, TX

CORNBREAD SALAD

1 box cornbread mix, baked,
  cooled, and crumbled
4 medium tomatoes, peeled and
  chopped
1 green pepper, chopped
1 medium onion, chopped

9 slices bacon, fried until crisp
  and crumbled
½ c. sweet pickles, chopped
1 c. mayonnaise
¼ c. sweet pickle juice

Combine tomatoes, pepper, onion, pickles, and bacon. Toss gently. Combine mayonnaise and pickle juice. Stir well and set aside. Mix mayonnaise mixture into vegetable mixture and cornbread in a larger glass bowl. Repeat layers. Cover and chill 2 hours. Toss before serving.

Melba Johnson, Brookhaven Alpha Lions Club
Brookhaven, MS

CORN SALAD

1 can white shoe peg corn
3 or 4 green onions, chopped
  small
1 tomato, cubed

½ green pepper, chopped small
Mayonnaise

Combine corn, onions, tomato, and pepper. Add enough mayonnaise to suit your taste (I use about ½ cup).

Lee Kerley, Biloxi Lions Club
Biloxi, MS

"COOL" CORN SALAD

¼ c. sour cream
¼ c. mayonnaise
1 Tbsp. prepared mustard
2 tsp. white vinegar
1 tsp. sugar
¼ tsp. salt

⅛ tsp. pepper
1 (17 oz.) can whole corn
1 (2 oz.) jar sliced pimentos
2 carrots, peeled and diced
½ c. diced onions

In medium sized bowl, make dressing by combining mayonnaise, mustard, vinegar, sugar, salt, and pepper. Add remaining ingredients and toss to blend. *Perfect picnic salad.*

Betty Lamphere, Lyons Muir Lions Club
Muir, MI, USA

It's better to swallow your pride than to eat your words.

CELEBRATION SALAD

Time: 30 minutes.

4 c. cooked brown rice or other grain of choice

2 c. vegetables, sliced (any combination of onions, broccoli, beans, radishes, parsnips, etc.)

1½ c. chopped kale or collards

1 c. toasted seed (sesame, sunflower or pumpkin)

1 dill pickle, diced

Salad dressing of choice

Boil vegetable slices 1 to 3 minutes in boiling water. Drain and save water for soup stock. Boil greens in fresh water for 3 to 6 minutes. Drain. Toss all ingredients together; add dressing and mix well. Garnish with more seeds, sprigs of watercress, parsley, or chopped scallions. Serve chilled in warm weather; serve warm in cold weather. Serves 4 to 6.

To boost protein level, add cooked beans or 1 pound of cubed tofu which has been lightly boiled. To boost nutrient levels, add wakame, kombu, or dulse (finely cut), cooked with the grain.

Use your choice of dressings or try either of these: ½ cup tahini with ½ cup umeboshi paste. Blend well. Or, use ½ cup tahini with ¾ to 1 cup umeboshi vinegar. Blend well.

Comments: Great for traveling.

PDG Jim Schiebel, Hilton Lions Club
Hilton, NY, USA

REFRESHING RHUBARB SALAD

4 c. diced fresh or frozen rhubarb

1½ c. water

½ c. sugar

1 (6 oz.) pkg. strawberry gelatin

1 c. orange juice

1 tsp. grated orange peel

1 c. sliced fresh strawberries

Mayonnaise, fresh mint, and additional strawberries (optional)

In saucepan over medium high heat, bring rhubarb, water, and sugar to a boil. Cook, uncovered, until rhubarb is tender, 6 to 8 minutes. Remove from heat; stir in gelatin until dissolved. Add orange juice and peel. Mix well. Chill until mixture begins to thicken. Fold in strawberries. Pour into a 2 quart bowl. Chill until set. If desired, serve with garnish of mayonnaise, mint, and strawberries.

I also added sliced bananas to leftover salad.

Eleanor McFadden, West Milford Lions Club
West Milford, WV, USA

Life's trials should make us better, not bitter.

CAULIFLOWER-PEA SALAD

1 c. chopped cauliflower
1 (10 oz.) pkg. frozen peas,
    thawed (not cooked)

1 c. chopped celery
¼ c. chopped onion
½ c. cashews

Dressing:

½ c. sour cream

1 c. Ranch salad dressing

Combine first 5 ingredients. Mix dressing and add. Garnish with 3 to 4 pieces of cooked, crumbled bacon. Chill before serving.

This recipe was shared by my daughter's sister-in-law and it is a favorite. Goes well at potluck dinners.

Lion Cheryl Kastle, Berthoud Lions Club
Berthoud, CO, USA

CRUNCHY PEA SALAD

1 (10 oz.) pkg. frozen peas,
    thawed
1 (8 oz.) can sliced water
    chestnuts, drained
1 c. thinly sliced celery

½ c. diced onions
¼ c. mayonnaise (lite)
¼ c. sour cream (no fat)
½ tsp. salt

Mix mayonnaise and sour cream together. Pour over pea mixture. Mix well. Chill. Serves 8.

Contains 60 calories, 1 mg cholesterol, trace of fat.

Lion Rae Hamilton, Graysville-Proctor Lions Club
Proctor, WV, USA

Oh, what a tangled web we weave when first we practice to deceive.

❦ ❦ ❦

You can't speak a kind word too soon for you never know how soon it will be too late.

❦ ❦ ❦

If you pause to think, you'll have cause to thank.

❦ ❦ ❦

It's better to lend a helping hand than to point an accusing finger.

BEET AND GREEN BEAN SALAD

1 lb. trimmed beets (2 large or 3
    medium)
½ lb. string beans
3 Tbsp. red-wine vinegar
2 tsp. Dijon mustard
¾ tsp. salt
¼ tsp. pepper
6 Tbsp. olive oil
1 small onion, thinly sliced

Put beets in pot of salted water to cover. Bring to a boil, reduce heat, and simmer until tender, about 30 minutes (for medium beets) or 55 minutes (for large). Drain. Put in a bowl of cold water to cool, about 10 minutes. Peel. While beets are cooking, add green beans to boiling salted water. Cook until tender, about 5 minutes. Drain.

Combine vinegar, mustard, salt, and pepper in a jar. Add oil and shake to combine. Cut beets lengthwise in thin wedges. Combine with onion in a bowl and toss with half the dressing.

In a separate bowl, combine beans with remaining dressing. Chill both mixtures. To serve, arrange beet mixture on platter. Arrange beans on top of the beets. Makes 4 servings.

Per serving: 235 calories, 2 g protein, 21 g fat, 520 mg sodium, 12 g carbohydrate, 0 mg cholesterol.

Mrs. Mike Nowicki, Clarence Lions Club
Clarence Center, NY, USA

SNAP SALAD

2 medium cucumbers, halved and
    thinly sliced
2 medium carrots, julienned
¼ c. diced onion
2 Tbsp. raisins
¾ c. water
¼ c. vinegar
2 Tbsp. sugar
½ tsp. salt
¼ tsp. pepper
¼ tsp. paprika

In a large bowl, combine cucumbers, carrots, onion, and raisins. Combine remaining ingredients; pour over the cucumber mixture. Cover and refrigerate for at least 6 hours. Serve with a slotted spoon. Yield: 6 servings.

Never put out the welcome mat for an evil thought.

MIXED VEGETABLE SALAD

1 pkg. frozen mixed vegetables
1 can kidney beans
½ c. celery
½ c. onions

½ c. green pepper
¾ c. sugar
½ c. vinegar
1 Tbsp. cornstarch

Cook mixed vegetables until tender. Drain. Place in bowl. Add kidney beans, celery, onion, and pepper. Bring sugar, vinegar, and cornstarch to a boil, stirring until thickened. Cool slightly and pour over vegetables; toss. Refrigerate until ready to serve.

Hazel Bailey, Iron City Lions Club
Iron City, TN, USA

VICTORY SALAD

1 can green beans, drained well
2 cans peas, drained well
1 can asparagus, drained well
6 sliced radishes
1 Tbsp. parsley
3 to 6 stalks celery, chopped
½ small head cabbage, grated

1 small chopped onion
¼ lb. American cheese, cubed
5 grated carrots
4 hard-boiled eggs, chopped
1 diced cucumber
3 or 4 tomatoes, cubed

Combine above ingredients.

Dressing:

1 pt. Miracle Whip
¼ c. vinegar

1 c. sugar
1 Tbsp. salt

Mix dressing and pour over vegetables shortly before serving.

Makes a very large salad - good for a large party.

Marriage works best when a couple has a single purpose.

❣ ❣ ❣

We pay a high price for cheap living.

❣ ❣ ❣

Christian homes don't just happen, they are built.

❣ ❣ ❣

When we live in the past, we tarnish the present and ignore the future.

TWO-TOMATO SALAD

1 lb. small new potatoes
⅛ tsp. salt
1 pt. cherry tomatoes, each cut
    into quarters
¼ c. sliced, drained sun-dried
    tomatoes (packed in oil)

3 Tbsp. olive oil
1 Tbsp. white-wine vinegar
2 Tbsp. chopped fresh basil
1 small garlic clove, minced
⅛ tsp. pepper

In a 2 quart saucepan, place potatoes with enough water to cover; bring to a boil over high heat. Add salt; reduce heat and cook until the potatoes are tender, about 15 minutes. Drain. When cool enough to handle, peel the potatoes and cut into quarters.

In a medium bowl, place the potatoes, cherry tomatoes, and sun-dried tomatoes. In a small bowl, whisk together the oil and vinegar, then add basil, garlic, and pepper. Pour over tomato mixture; toss well to coat. Makes 6 servings.

Per serving: 184 calories, 2 g protein, 12 g fat, 35 mg sodium, 18 g carbohydrate, 0 mg cholesterol.

Tip: Sun-dried tomatoes can also be purchased dry-packed without oil. Rehydrate in a small amount of hot water; drain before using or use liquid as called for in recipe.

Mrs. Mike Nowicki, Clarence Lions Club
Clarence Center, NY, USA

SLICED TOMATOES WITH CHUNKY OLIVE DRESSING

1 egg
3 Tbsp. mayonnaise
3 Tbsp. sour cream
⅓ c. chopped pimento-stuffed
    olives

¼ c. chopped onion
1 Tbsp. chopped fresh parsley
Salt and pepper
3 tomatoes (about 1½ lb.)

Put the egg in a saucepan of water and bring just to a boil. Cover the pan, remove from heat, and let stand 12 minutes; drain and cool. Peel and chop the egg. Combine the mayonnaise and the sour cream. Stir in the chopped egg, olives, onion, and parsley. Taste for seasoning and add salt and pepper if needed. Slice the tomatoes and serve with olive dressing. Makes 4 servings.

Per serving: 169 calories, 4 g protein, 14 g fat, 365 mg sodium, 10 g carbohydrate, 64 mg cholesterol.

Barbara Joy Hess, Clarence Lions Club
Clarence Center, NY, USA

The cost of obedience is nothing compared to the cost of disobedience.

TOMATO BASIL SALAD WITH GARLIC TOAST

2 cloves garlic
6 Tbsp. olive oil
1 Tbsp. red-wine vinegar
Salt and pepper

8 slices French bread, cut into ½ inch slices
2 tomatoes (about 1 lb.)
2 Tbsp. chopped fresh basil

Heat the broiler. Mince the garlic and combine with oil. In a small jar, combine the vinegar, ½ teaspoon salt, and ¼ teaspoon pepper and shake until the salt dissolves. Add 3 tablespoons of the garlic oil and shake again to combine. Brush bread on both sides with the remaining 3 tablespoons garlic oil. Put on a baking sheet and broil until toasted and lightly browned, about 1 minute on each side. Slice the tomatoes and sprinkle with the chopped basil. Pour the dressing over the tomatoes and serve with the garlic toast. Makes 4 servings.

Per serving: 246 calories, 2 g protein, 21 g fat, 370 mg sodium, 14 g carbohydrate, 0 mg cholesterol.

Mrs. Mike Nowicki, Clarence Lions Club
Clarence Center, NY, USA

CHINESE SALAD

3 c. carrots, sliced
1 (10 oz.) can mushroom pieces, drained
1 (10 oz.) can green beans, drained
1 (10 oz.) can yellow beans, drained

3 small onions, sliced
1 green pepper, cut in strips
1 red pepper, cut in strips

Dressing:

1 (10 oz.) can cream of tomato soup
½ soup can salad oil

¼ soup can vinegar
1 c. white sugar
1 tsp. dry mustard

Bring water to boil in saucepan and cook carrots for 3 minutes just crisp tender. Do not overcook. In a large bowl, mix all vegetables together; set aside. In a saucepan, mix tomato soup, salad oil, vinegar, sugar, and mustard. Bring to the boil over medium heat, stirring to melt sugar and prevent burning. Remove from heat and pour immediately over vegetables. Cover and refrigerate until ready to serve.

This salad can be kept covered in the refrigerator for up to two weeks.

Lion Violet Labelle, Lake of the Woods Lions Club
Kenora, Ontario, Canada

MARINATED CARROTS OR COPPER PENNY SALAD

Cut up 2 pounds carrots and slightly cook, about 5 minutes. Salt. Drain carrots. Add cut up green bell peppers and raw onions; mix with carrots.

Bring to a boil:

1 (10 oz.) can tomato soup
½ c. vinegar

1 (scant) c. sugar
1 tsp. ground mustard

Pour over carrots. Serve warm or cool for a salad side dish.

Micheal and Ruth Bartolf, Oxbow and District Lions Club
Oxbow, Saskatchewan, Canada

COPPER PENNIES

2 (14 oz.) cans sliced carrots
1 can tomato soup
¼ c. oil
½ c. vinegar
½ c. sugar

1 tsp. Worcestershire sauce
1 tsp. mustard
1 bell pepper
1 small onion

Drain carrots. Dice bell pepper. Cut onion in rings. Mix all ingredients together. Refrigerate overnight. Will keep 2 weeks.

We take this to picnics and tailgating at football games.

Dorothy Freeman, Travelers Rest Lions Club, District 32-A
Greenville, SC, USA

CARROT SALAD

2 lb. carrots
1 large onion

1 green pepper
3 stems celery

Dressing:

1 can tomato soup
½ c. salad oil
1 tsp. salt

1 c. sugar
½ c. vinegar
½ tsp. pepper

Cut carrots in desired shape and cook until soft, but holds shape. Cut onion, pepper, and celery fine and mix.

Mix dressing and bring to boil. Pour over carrot mixture. Let stand 2 days before using.

Clarissa Frey, Bullskin Township Lioness Club
Mt. Pleasant, PA

What we laugh at reveals our character.

FESTIVE RICE SALAD

3 c. rice, cooked
1 (5 oz.) can Bryan Vienna
    sausage, cut in ¼ inch slices
1 (8½ oz.) can peas and carrots,
    drained
1 (2 oz.) jar pimento, drained

2 hard-boiled eggs, chopped
½ c. chopped onion
½ c. chopped green pepper
½ c. mayonnaise
Salt and pepper to taste

    Mix well all ingredients in large bowl. Chill.

Agnes Williams, Alpha Lions Club
Brookhaven, MS, USA

BEET SALAD

1 pkg. strawberry jello
1 pkg. cherry jello
1 pkg. raspberry jello
4 c. boiling water

    Dressing:

1 c. mayonnaise
1 Tbsp. chopped green pepper

½ c. sweet pickle juice
1 (No. 303) can julienne beets (I
    cut sliced beets into strips)
1 (No. 2) can crushed pineapple

1 Tbsp. chopped green onions

    Dissolve all three kinds of jello in the boiling water. Drain beets and pineapple (save approximately 1½ cups liquid) and add liquid to pickle juice, then add this juice mixture to dissolved gelatin mixture. Chill. Serve in beets and pineapple and chill until firm. Serves 16.

    Optional: Prepare dressing in order given and add cream if the consistency needs it. Let stand several hours for the flavors to blend.

Agnes Williams, Alpha Lions Club
Brookhaven, MS, USA

CANNELLINI SALAD

1 (15.5 oz.) can cannellini beans,
    drained
¼ c. very thinly sliced or minced
    fresh red onion

1 Tbsp. extra virgin olive oil
¼ tsp. sea salt
Freshly ground black pepper

    Combine all ingredients and stir.

James R. Schiebel, Hilton Lions Club
Hilton, NY, USA

We can really live when we're ready to die.

OVERNIGHT VEGGIE SALAD

¾ c. vinegar
½ c. vegetable oil
1 tsp. salt
1 c. sugar
1 tsp. celery seed
1 tsp. ground pepper (through
    peppermill)
1 can French style green beans,
    drained

1 can tiny peas, drained
1 jar chopped pimento, drained
1 c. green pepper, chopped
1 can white whole kernel corn,
    drained
1 c. chopped celery
¼ c. green onion, chopped

Mix first six ingredients together in saucepan. Heat enough to dissolve the sugar. *Do not boil.* Cool. While liquid mixture is cooling, mix all the vegetables together in a large bowl. Once mixture has cooled, pour over vegetables. Mix well. Cover. Refrigerate overnight.

Lion Theresa Hill, Hector Lions Club
Hector, MN

CRUNCHY SALAD

1 can Ranch Style beans, drained
Onion or cucumber, sliced
Chopped bell pepper
Lettuce, shredded

Tomatoes, sliced
4 to 8 oz. Cheddar cheese
Crushed Fritos

Layer in order listed. Just before serving, pour Wish-Bone Italian dressing (large bottle) over top. Do not toss at this time. Let stand for 10 minutes, then toss and serve.

"If you wish to grow old gracefully, it is best to start young."

Lion Larry Chaudoir, Mandeville Lions Club
Mandeville, LA, USA

GERMAN POTATO SALAD

5 lb. red potatoes, cooked,
    peeled, and cubed
1 medium onion, chopped
1 lb. bacon

6 Tbsp. flour
1 c. sugar
1 c. vinegar
3 c. water

Dice bacon. Fry till brown. Remove bacon from drippings; add flour, sugar, vinegar, and water to drippings. Stir and boil till thick. Pour over potatoes, onion, and bacon. Salt and pepper to taste

Mrs. Gordon (Linn) Dierschow, Elburn Lions Club
Elburn, IL

NANNY'S POTATO SALAD

5 medium potatoes
½ c. celery, diced
2 Tbsp. mayonnaise (if needed)

½ c. onion, diced
¼ red or green pepper, diced
   (optional)

Boiled Dressing:

2 eggs, slightly beaten
¼ c. vinegar

½ c. sugar
1 stick margarine or butter

Dice, salt, and cook potatoes until tender; drain and cool.

Bring vinegar and butter to a boil in heavy pan. Mix eggs and sugar together and slowly add to liquid. Boil until thickened (about 5 minutes); remove from heat and *cool*. Mix first 4 ingredients; add cooked dressing and stir. If necessary, add enough mayonnaise to mix nicely. Refrigerate overnight if possible.

Note: If you double or triple the recipe, use less margarine - 1½ sticks for double recipe, 2 sticks for triple recipe.

Lioness Irene Frank, East Anne Arundel Lioness Club
Pasadena, MD, USA

PARTY POTATO SALAD

10 lb. potatoes, peeled and cubed
3 c. mayonnaise
3 c. sweet pickle relish
2 c. chopped onion

½ c. prepared mustard
1 Tbsp. salt
1 tsp. pepper
15 hard cooked eggs, chopped

Cook potatoes in boiling water until tender; drain. Combine mayonnaise, relish, onion, mustard, salt, and pepper; mix well. Add eggs and warm potatoes; toss gently. Cover and refrigerate. Yield: 60 (½ cup) servings.

Lion Sue Leidel, De Pere Lions Club
De Pere, WI

POTATO SALAD BY PAULETTE

10 medium size potatoes
2 celery stalks, diced
1 onion, diced (or more to taste)
Salt and pepper to taste
¼ c. apple cider vinegar

2 Tbsp. vegetable oil
6 hard-boiled eggs, chopped
1 c. mayonnaise (or enough to
   cover to make creamy)

Cook potatoes till done. Skin and cut in quarters. Add diced celery and onions; salt and pepper. Mix the vinegar and oil together. Pour over the potato mixture. Refrigerate overnight to let the ingredients flavor through. Chop the hard-boiled eggs and with the mayonnaise, toss all ingredients until covered and creamy.

Option: One-half teaspoon celery seed may be added for more flavor.

Nicki Florentine, Silver Run-Union Mills Lions Club
Westminster, MD, USA

DRESSING FOR POTATO SALAD

2 lb. potatoes, cooked and diced
2 eggs
2 Tbsp. sugar

2 Tbsp. vinegar
1 tsp. dry mustard
2 Tbsp. butter

Cook until thick. Add butter. Thin with cream or mayonnaise.

This comes from my grandmother.

Lion Bev Wilkens, Plato Lions Club
Young America, MN, USA

GRILLED-CHICKEN SALAD WITH BASIL VINAIGRETTE

2 red bell peppers
1 tsp. + 1 Tbsp. + ⅓ c. olive oil
4 boneless chicken breasts (about
    1¼ lb.)
Salt and pepper

2 Tbsp. wine vinegar
¼ c. chopped fresh basil
1 small head green-leaf lettuce
    (about 6 c. torn leaves)

Heat the grill. Cut peppers in halves and coat with 1 teaspoon of the oil. Grill until tender and slightly charred, 15 to 20 minutes. Put in a paper or plastic bag and set aside. When cool enough to handle, peel and cut into strips.

Meanwhile, coat the chicken with 1 tablespoon oil and sprinkle with salt and pepper. Grill until just springy to the touch, about 5 minutes per side.

In a small jar, combine the vinegar, ½ teaspoon salt, and ¼ teaspoon pepper and shake until the salt dissolves. Add ⅓ cup of the oil and the basil and shake again to combine.

Tear the lettuce into pieces and put in a bowl with the pepper strips. Add 2 tablespoons of the basil vinaigrette and toss. Cut the chicken breasts into diagonal slices. Divide lettuce mixture among four plates and top each serving with a sliced chicken breast. Spoon remaining basil vinaigrette over the chicken. Makes 4 servings.

Mrs. Lucy Aiken, Clarence Lions Club
Clarence Center, NY, USA

No one is unemployed who minds his own business.

❦ ❦ ❦

You may tremble on the rock of ages,
but the rock will never tremble under you.

❦ ❦ ❦

Our words have the power to build up or tear down.

CHINESE CHICKEN SALAD

3 c. chopped chicken (4 breasts)
1 medium cabbage or 1 pkg. cole slaw mix
1 bunch green onions (tops only)
2 pkg. chicken Ramen noodles
1 jar sesame seeds (8 Tbsp.)
2¼ oz. sliced almonds

3 Tbsp. oleo
1 c. salad oil
6 Tbsp. vinegar
1 tsp. salt
½ tsp. pepper
4 Tbsp. sugar

Cook chicken breasts. Cool and chop chicken, tops of onions, and cabbage. Mix together and set aside in a large bowl. Crush noodles in small pieces, then mix with sesame seeds and almonds. Brown in oleo, then mix flavor packets from noodles with sugar, oil, salt, pepper, and vinegar. Toss all together 20 to 30 minutes before serving.

This is a wonderful dish and makes a great dish to take for group socials.
Lion Ann Scotton, Foley Lions Club
Foley, AL

CHICKEN SALAD ON CANTALOUPE RINGS

2½ c. cubed, cooked chicken
1 c. thinly sliced celery
1 c. halved green grapes
2 Tbsp. minced fresh parsley
½ c. mayonnaise
1 Tbsp. lemon juice
1 Tbsp. cider vinegar

1½ tsp. prepared mustard
½ tsp. salt
½ tsp. sugar
⅛ tsp. pepper
4 cantaloupe rings
Toasted sliced almonds

In a large bowl, combine chicken, celery, grapes, and parsley. Combine the next seven ingredients; mix well. Pour over chicken mixture and toss. Chill for at least 1 hour. To serve, place 1 cup of chicken salad on each cantaloupe ring; sprinkle with almonds. Yield: 4 servings.

Don't reject anyone whom God has accepted.

If your mind goes blank, don't forget to turn off the sound.

2075-99

GREEN AND GOLD CHICKEN SALAD WITH ORANGE POPPY SEED DRESSING

6 to 8 c. assorted salad greens (Bibb, iceberg, romaine)
1½ to 2 c. chicken, cooked and cut in strips
3 to 4 oranges, peeled and sliced in half cartwheels

3 to 4 hard cooked eggs, cut in wedges
1 avocado, sliced
1 c. celery, cut diagonally
½ c. thinly sliced green onion

Orange Poppy Seed Dressing:

⅔ c. salad dressing
2 tsp. fresh grated orange peel
¼ c. orange juice
3 Tbsp. vinegar

1 Tbsp. poppy seeds
1 Tbsp. sugar
½ tsp. onion salt
½ tsp. salt

Makes 6 one cup servings.

Sarah Wehling, Bothell Lions Club
Bothell, WA, USA

CHICKEN AND ASPARAGUS SALAD

1 lb. asparagus
12 oz. frozen peas
1 roast chicken
4 hard cooked eggs
1 bunch parsley
4 slices canned pineapple

6 Tbsp. mayonnaise
3 Tbsp. whipping cream
¼ c. canned pineapple juice
1 tsp. lemon juice
Generous pinch of salt and sugar

Lightly peel lower part of asparagus stalks. Tie into 2 or 3 bundles with string. Cook asparagus; drain and cool. Cook peas as per package. Remove bones and chop chicken into pieces. Chop asparagus, egg, and pineapple.

In a small bowl, beat mayonnaise, cream, pineapple juice, lemon juice, salt, and sugar. Mix all. Garnish with chopped egg. Makes 4.

Sarah Wehling, Bothell Lions Club
Bothell, WA, USA

ORIENTAL SALAD WITH CHICKEN

3 c. diced, cooked chicken
1 (13½ oz.) drained pineapple
2 Tbsp. sliced green onions
1 (5 oz.) can water chestnuts, drained and sliced

¾ c. dairy sour cream
1 tsp. ground ginger
½ tsp. salt
Dash of pepper
¼ c. slivered almonds, toasted

Combine and chill first 4 ingredients. Blend next 4 and toss lightly. Sprinkle almonds and rechill. Serve on lettuce.

Sarah Wehling, Bothell Lions Club
Bothell, WA, USA

THAI BEEF SALAD

4 cloves garlic
4 tsp. oil
Salt and pepper
1 lb. beef top round (about 1 inch
thick)
1 cucumber
1 head iceberg lettuce (about 6 c.
cut up)

3 limes
2 hot red peppers
¼ c. rice-wine vinegar
¼ c. chopped fresh cilantro
½ tsp. sugar

Mince garlic. In a shallow bowl, combine garlic, oil, and ¼ teaspoon pepper. Add beef and turn to coat. Heat grill. Sprinkle beef with salt and grill, turning once, until done, about 20 minutes for medium-rare. Peel cucumber, cut in half lengthwise, and scoop out the seeds. Cut halves into thin slices. Cut lettuce into 1 inch strips. Squeeze ¼ cup juice from the limes. Mince peppers.

In a small jar, combine lime juice, peppers, vinegar, cilantro, sugar, and 1¼ teaspoons salt and shake until the salt dissolves. Cut meat into thin slices. Toss the lettuce with half the dressing and arrange on a platter. Just before serving, combine the cucumbers and meat with the remaining dressing and arrange on the lettuce. Makes 4 servings.

Work time: 30 minutes. Total time: 50 minutes.

Per serving: 256 calories, 26 g protein, 13 g fat, 750 mg sodium, 9 g carbohydrate, 69 mg cholesterol.

Mrs. Lucy Aiken, Clarence Lions Club
Clarence Center, NY, USA

DILLED CRAB SALAD

12 oz. imitation crab, sliced ½
inch thick
8 oz. snow peas, boiled 1 minute
and cooled
1 medium cucumber, sliced thin

1 small onion, chopped
⅓ c. fat free Ranch dressing
⅓ c. non fat sour cream
1½ Tbsp. dill weed

Mix all ingredients together when peas have cooled. Mix together dressing, sour cream, and dill weed. Pour over crab mixture. Mix gently. Refrigerate for 4 hours. Serve with rolls. *Enjoy.*

Very easy to make and is delicious.

Russell Larson, Hurley Lions Club
Hurley, WI

Choose your companions with care - you may become what they are.

HEAVENLY SHRIMP SALAD

1 (8 oz.) pkg. cream cheese,
   softened
1 c. chopped green onion
1 c. mayonnaise
1 c. chopped celery
1 (10 oz.) can cream of
   mushroom soup

1 Tbsp. Knox gelatine, dissolved
   in 3 Tbsp. water
2 cans small shrimp (you can
   substitute crabmeat)

Dissolve gelatine in water. Add to soup and heat until gelatine dissolves. Add remaining ingredients. Pour into oiled mold. Let sit overnight or 5 hours. Serve with crackers or toast rounds.

SHRIMP AND AVOCADO SALAD WITH LIME VINAIGRETTE

½ lb. medium shrimp
1 lime
Salt and pepper

2 Tbsp. oil
1 avocado
2 radishes

Bring enough salted water to a boil to cover the shrimp. Add the shrimp, return to a boil, and reduce heat. Cook the shrimp at a simmer until they turn pink, 2 to 3 minutes. Drain, cool, and peel.

Meanwhile, squeeze 1½ teaspoons juice from the lime. In a small jar, combine the lime juice, ¾ teaspoon salt, and a pinch of pepper. Shake until the salt dissolves. Add oil and shake again to combine. Slice the avocado and radishes and combine with the shrimp. Pour the lime dressing over the salad. Makes 4 servings.

Per serving: 191 calories, 10 g protein, 15 g fat, 486 mg sodium, 4 g carbohydrate, 71 mg cholesterol.

Mrs. Mike Nowicki, Clarence Lions Club
Clarence Center, NY, USA

SARAH'S SALMON SALAD

Jicama, peeled and chopped
1 can salmon, drained and
   chopped
Dill

Sunflower seeds
Mayonnaise
A bed of red rimmed lettuce

Toss first four ingredients. Lay lettuce in bowl to line it. Mound salad. Chill.

Sarah Wehling, Bothell Lions Club
Bothell, WA, USA

TEX-MEX CATFISH SALAD

1½ lb. catfish or halibut fillets
2 Tbsp. lime juice
2 Tbsp. olive oil
½ tsp. salt
1 red bell pepper
1 jalapeno pepper

4 large leaves green-leaf lettuce
Vegetable oil (for frying)
4 flour tortillas
¼ c. chopped red onion
½ c. chopped corn kernels
2 Tbsp. chopped fresh cilantro

In a large skillet, bring about ¼ inch lightly salted water to a simmer. Add fillets; cover and cook over low heat until done, 5 to 8 minutes. Drain fish and cut into small pieces. Wipe out skillet with a paper towel.

In a small jar, shake lime juice, olive oil, and a pinch of salt until combined. Set aside. Seed and dice bell pepper. Seed and mince jalapeno pepper. Shred lettuce. In same skillet, heat about 1 inch vegetable oil until hot. Add one tortilla and fry until brown and crisp, piercing tortilla with a fork and holding down, so it fries flat, about 2 minutes. Drain on paper towels and repeat with remaining tortillas.

In a large bowl, toss fish, bell and jalapeno peppers, lettuce, onion, corn, and cilantro with the lime dressing. Divide mixture among tortillas and serve. Makes 4 servings.

Work time: 30 minutes. Total time: 30 minutes.

Per serving: 610 calories, 34 g protein, 29 g fat, 714 mg sodium, 52 g carbohydrate, 56 mg cholesterol.

Joanne M. Wetzler, Clarence Lions Club
Clarence Center, NY, USA

LETTUCE WITH JAPANESE PEANUT SALAD DRESSING

¼ c. salad oil
3 Tbsp. rice vinegar
2 Tbsp. chopped dry roasted
  peanuts
2 Tbsp. sugar
2 Tbsp. toasted sesame seeds

3 scallions, thinly sliced (include
  green part)
1 tsp. salt
½ tsp. fresh ground black pepper
Torn or shredded iceberg lettuce

Any extra dressing can be kept several days in refrigerator.

Sarah Wehling, Bothell Lions Club
Bothell, WA, USA

Humor can make a serious difference.

CREAMY CAULIFLOWER LETTUCE SALAD

¾ c. Miracle Whip or light
   Miracle Whip dressing
½ c. Ranch dressing
¼ c. Parmesan cheese, grated
¼ c. sugar

1 finely chopped red onion
1 pkg. bacon, fried crisply and
   crumbled
1 head cauliflower, cut into pieces
6 c. torn romaine lettuce

    Mix dressings, cheese, and sugar in a large bowl. Add remaining ingredients. Mix lightly. Makes 8 servings.

LIME JELLO AND COTTAGE CHEESE SALAD

1 (3 oz.) pkg. lime Jell-O
1 c. cottage cheese
1 small head lettuce

1 (7 oz.) Reddi-Whip
1 (6 oz.) maraschino cherries (red
   or green)

    Prepare Jell-O as per instructions on package. When dissolved, add cheese and blend well. Put in refrigerator until solid. When ready to prepare, add lettuce to plate and add Jell-O mix on the lettuce. Add Reddi-Whip and cherries. Crushed nuts may also be used.

Clara Culbert, Scio Lions Club
Scio, NY, USA

To get out of a hard situation, try a soft answer.

❧ ❧ ❧

No man is poor who has a Godly mother.

❧ ❧ ❧

Worrying is paying interest on troubles that never come due.

❧ ❧ ❧

A watching Christian will be a working Christian.

GREEN SALAD WITH SHRIMP AND OLIVES

2 eggs
1 lb. medium-large shrimp (about 20)
Salt and pepper
1 lemon
¼ c. olive oil
1 head green-leaf lettuce (about 8 c. torn leaves)

½ c. chopped green olives (about 30)
½ c. chopped black olives (about 30)
2 Tbsp. chopped pimento
2 Tbsp. chopped fresh parsley
½ tsp. minced fresh garlic

Put the eggs in a saucepan, cover with cold water, and bring just to a boil. Cover, remove the pan from the heat, and let stand 15 minutes before draining.

Meanwhile, cook the shrimp in a large pot of boiling salted water until done, about 5 minutes. Drain. When cool enough to handle, peel the shrimp and chill. Peel and slice the eggs into wedges. Squeeze 1 tablespoon plus 2 teaspoons juice from the lemon.

In a small jar, combine the lemon juice, ½ teaspoon salt, and ¼ teaspoon pepper and shake until the salt dissolves. Add the oil and shake again to combine. Tear the lettuce into small pieces. Just before serving, combine the olives, pimento, parsley, and garlic and add to the lettuce with the eggs and the shrimp. Add the lemon dressing and toss to combine. Makes 4 servings.

Work time: 45 minutes. Total time: 45 minutes.

Per serving: 317 calories, 24 g protein, 22 g fat, 1008 mg sodium, 7 g carbohydrate, 246 mg cholesterol.

Mrs. Lucy Aiken, Clarence Lions Club
Clarence Center, NY, USA

OVERNIGHT LAYERED SALAD

1 head lettuce
1 (8 oz.) can water chestnuts, sliced
1 (16 oz.) pkg. frozen peas
1 tsp. seasoned salt
¼ tsp. garlic salt
½ lb. crisply fried bacon, crumbled
Tomato wedges

Green pepper rings
Sliced eggs
½ c. green onions
1 c. diced celery
½ c. grated Parmesan cheese
2 tsp. sugar
1½ c. mayonnaise

Shred lettuce into shallow serving dish (13x9 inches). Top with green onions, celery, water chestnuts, and peas. Spread mayonnaise evenly over top. Sprinkle with sugar, Parmesan cheese, season salt, and garlic salt. Cover with Saran Wrap and put in refrigerator as long as 24 hours. Decorate with tomato wedges, green pepper rings, and sliced eggs.

Lioness Catherine Violette, East Anne Arundel Lioness Club
Annapolis, MD, USA

DUNCAN'S GARLIC SALAD

1 medium head lettuce
½ head cabbage
1 large or 2 small carrots

2 c. mayonnaise
½ tsp. garlic powder
½ tsp. garlic salt

Wash and dry lettuce, cabbage, and carrots. Chop or grind very fine. Place in large bowl. Add mayonnaise and mix well. Add garlic powder and garlic salt; mix again. Sprinkle top of salad with paprika and Parmesan cheese if desired.

I often use Hidden Valley Ranch dressing or my own Ranch dressing in place of the mayonnaise.

Marty Clark, Hutchinson Breakfast Lions Club
Hutchinson, KS, USA

WILTED LETTUCE SALAD

1 bunch leaf lettuce, torn
6 to 8 radishes, thinly sliced

4 to 6 green onions with tops,
  thinly sliced

Dressing:

4 to 5 bacon strips
2 Tbsp. red wine vinegar
1 Tbsp. lemon juice

1 tsp. sugar
½ tsp. pepper

Toss lettuce, radishes, and onions in a large salad bowl; set aside. In a skillet, cook bacon until crisp. Remove to paper towels to drain. To the hot drippings, add vinegar, lemon juice, sugar, and pepper; stir well. Immediately pour dressing over salad; toss gently. Crumble the bacon and sprinkle on top. Yield: 6 to 8 servings.

WILTED GREEN SALAD WITH BACON DRESSING

4 c. salad greens (romaine,
  spinach, red leaf, green leaf,
  endive, etc.)
Sauteed bell pepper and onions
  (or whatever vegetables you
  choose)
8 slices bacon

1 medium onion, chopped
¼ c. red wine vinegar
¼ to ½ c. balsamic vinegar
¼ to ½ c. honey
3 to 4 Tbsp. Dijon mustard
2 to 3 cloves roasted garlic,
  chopped

In skillet, cook bacon until crisp. Take out of pan and drain. Drain most of grease out of pan and return to heat. Add in onion and garlic and saute until onions are clear. Deglaze pan with vinegars and cook down for a minute or two. Add remaining ingredients, more or less sweet and sour, according to taste. Crumble bacon into lettuce and add sauteed vegetables. Drizzle dressing over greens while hot. Serve immediately.

Lion Wanda Ramos, Foley Lions Club
Foley, AL

POPPY SEED SALAD

¾ c. Miracle Whip
⅓ c. sugar
¼ c. milk
2 Tbsp. vinegar

2 tsp. poppy seeds
1 head romaine lettuce
½ sweet purple onion
1 pt. strawberries

Mix dressing ingredients together. Toss with cut up lettuce, strawberries, and onion.

Patty Geib, Arlington Sea Lions Club
Arlington, MN

COBB SALAD

4 slices bacon
¼ c. vegetable oil
3 Tbsp. red-wine vinegar
⅛ tsp. salt
⅛ tsp. black pepper
1 head red-leaf lettuce, shredded

1 tomato, diced
1 red bell pepper, seeded and
   diced
1 green bell pepper, seeded and
   diced
¼ lb. Blue cheese, crumbled
   (about 1 c.)

In a 2 quart microwave-safe baking dish, arrange chicken breasts with thickest sides at the edge of dish. Add broth, onion, peppercorns, and parsley. Cover with plastic wrap and vent the side. Microwave on HIGH 10 to 12 minutes, until no longer pink. When cool enough to handle, cut chicken into ¼ inch dice; discard liquid and solids in dish.

In a large skillet, over medium heat, cook bacon until crisp; drain on paper towels and crumble.

In a small jar, shake oil, vinegar, salt, and pepper until blended. On a serving platter, toss lettuce with dressing. Arrange chicken, bacon, tomato, peppers, and cheese in bands across lettuce.

Work time: 15 minutes. Total time: 25 minutes.

Per serving: 451 calories, 43 g protein, 28 g fat, 693 mg sodium, 7 g carbohydrate, 110 mg cholesterol.

Mrs. Lucy Aiken, Clarence Lions Club
Clarence Center, NY, USA

He cannot speak well who cannot hold his tongue.

COBB SALAD

2 Tbsp. wine vinegar
Salt and pepper
⅓ c. oil
½ lb. bacon (about 10 strips)
¼ lb. Gruyere cheese (about 1 c. cubes)

1 lb. broccoli
3 carrots (about ½ lb.)
8 radishes
8 leaves romaine lettuce (about ½ lb.)

In a small jar, combine the vinegar, 1 teaspoon salt, and ¼ teaspoon pepper and shake until the salt dissolves. Add oil and shake again to combine. Cook bacon until crisp and drain on paper towels. Cut the cheese into small cubes. Separate broccoli tops into small florets; peel and dice the stems. Grate the carrots. Cut radishes into small cubes. Cut the romaine into strips. Put lettuce on a large platter and arrange bacon, cheese, broccoli, carrots, and radishes on top. Serve with dressing. Makes 4 servings.

Work time: 40 minutes. Total time: 40 minutes.

Per serving: 457 calories, 18 g protein, 38 g fat, 957 mg sodium, 14 g carbohydrate, 45 mg cholesterol.

Mrs. Lucy Aiken, Clarence Lions Club
Clarence Center, NY, USA

WESTERN WALDORF SALAD

1 head lettuce
1 red apple
½ c. diet mayonnaise
Walnut halves (optional)
1 (1 lb. 3 oz.) can peach slices, drained

1½ c. sliced celery
½ c. lemon juice
Maraschino cherries (optional)

Core, rinse, and thoroughly drain lettuce. Cut it horizontally into four slices, each about one inch thick. Place a lettuce slice on each individual plate. Reserve 20 of the peach slices and cut up the rest. Cut apple in half and remove core, but do not peel. Cut and reserve four thin slices; dice the rest. Combine the diced peach and apple with the celery, mayonnaise, and lemon juice. Spoon one fourth of the apple and peach mixture in the center of each lettuce raft. Surround with reserved peach slices and top with apple slices. Walnuts and maraschino cherries can be added as garnish for non-dieters or diced and added with apple and peach mixture. Makes 4 servings.

Contains 115 calories each.

Mary L. Coon, Hutchinson Breakfast Lions Club
Hutchinson, KS, USA

Will your memorial be a blessing or a blot?

CAESAR SALAD DRESSING

Hard boil 3 large or jumbo eggs for 30 minutes (no less). Separate the yolks from the whites. Run the yolks through a strainer. Add 3 fresh egg yolks to the boiled ones. Put the bowl under a mixer and gradually add ¾ cup of Italian olive oil (extra virgin is best). Run the boiled whites through a sieve and add to the bowl of yolks. Add a small can of chopped anchovies or 1.6 ounces anchovy paste and mix well. Add a tablespoon of chopped capers and mix well. Add a teaspoon of garlic powder (or to taste), oregano, summer savory, basil, Italian herbs (all dry), salt, black pepper, and MSG to taste. Mix well. Add a half bottle of Wish-Bone Italian dressing (4 ounces) and mix well.

You can add a few drops of Tabasco sauce if you like.

Victor L. Dreyer, Sr., Keizer Lions Club
Keizer, OR, USA

LINDA'S (RESTAURANT STYLE) CAESAR SALAD

1 large head rinsed and torn
    romaine
⅓ c. oil
3 minced cloves garlic
1 tsp. Dijon mustard
1 tsp. Worcestershire sauce
1 Tbsp. balsamic vinegar
1 Tbsp. lemon juice
4 oz. Egg Beaters (egg substitute)
1 c. croutons
¼ c. grated Parmesan cheese
Fresh ground pepper

To make dressing: In small bowl, mince garlic into oil. Blend mustard, Worcestershire sauce, vinegar, and lemon juice. Slowly pour the Egg Beaters into the oil while stirring or whisking until well blended. Pour dressing over romaine and croutons, sprinkle cheese and grind pepper, toss, and serve.

It's really good and no cholesterol!

Linda Uliana, Don Leisers daughter, Plainfield Township Lions Club
Nazareth, PA, Nothampton County

CAESAR SALAD

¼ lb. bread (about 3 c. cubes)
½ c. olive oil
4 anchovy fillets (optional)
1 clove garlic, minced
3 Tbsp. lemon juice
1 small head romaine lettuce
⅓ c. coarsely grated Parmesan
    cheese

Heat oven to 350°. Cut the bread into cubes. On a baking pan, toss bread cubes in ¼ cup of the oil until well-coated. Spread cubes evenly on pan and bake, turning occasionally, until golden brown, 8 to 12 minutes. In a serving bowl, mash anchovies with a fork. Stir in garlic and lemon juice. Whisk in remaining ¼ cup oil. Tear lettuce into bite-size pieces and add to dressing with the cheese. Toss to coat. Top with croutons. Makes 6 servings.

Per serving: 244 calories, 5 g protein, 20 g fat, 191 mg sodium, 12 g carbohydrate, 4 mg cholesterol.

Mrs. Mike Nowicki, Clarence Lions Club
Clarence Center, NY, USA

ORANGE AND BITTERS SALAD

6 oz. fresh spinach (about 4 c.
    cleaned and trimmed)
2 oranges
1½ tsp. bitters

Salt and pepper
3 Tbsp. oil
3 Tbsp. chopped red onion

Pull the stems from the spinach and discard them. Wash the leaves and tear them into bite-size pieces. Working over a bowl to catch the juice, peel the oranges with a paring knife, cutting right down to the flesh and removing all the white pith, then cut the sections away from the membrane. Measure 1½ tablespoons juice, squeezing more from the membranes if needed.

In a small jar, combine the orange juice, bitters, ½ teaspoon salt, and ⅛ teaspoon pepper and shake until the salt dissolves. Add the oil and shake again to combine. Combine the spinach, orange segments, and the red onion. Toss with the dressing just before serving. Makes 4 servings.

Work time: 20 minutes. Total time: 20 minutes.

Per serving: 139 calories, 2 g protein, 10 g fat, 298 mg sodium, 10 g carbohydrate, 0 mg cholesterol.

Barbara Joy Hess, Clarence Lions Club
Clarence Center, NY, USA

SPINACH SALAD

1 (1 lb.) pkg. fresh spinach
1 can drained bean sprouts
1 (6 oz.) can water chestnuts

3 to 4 hard-boiled eggs
½ lb. fried, drained, crumbled
    bacon

Add a few radishes and mushrooms.

Dressing - Mix together:

½ c. salad oil
½ c. sugar
½ c. catsup

1 tsp. salt
1 tsp. Worcestershire sauce
1 grated onion

Wash and dry spinach; tear into small pieces. Add drained bean sprouts and water chestnuts. Slice 3 to 4 hard-boiled eggs and ½ pound of fried, drained, crumbled bacon. Add radishes and mushrooms. *Toss* together.

Pour dressing over salad right before serving.

I have served this salad many times and always asked for the recipe. I got this recipe from a very good friend.

Lion Dolly Muchow, Severn River Lions Club
Severna Park, MD

MAUI-STYLE SPINACH SALAD

1 qt. shredded lettuce
1 (8 oz.) can water chestnuts,
    drained
2 c. chopped fresh broccoli
2 Tbsp. sugar
1 c. (4 oz.) shredded Cheddar
    cheese
8 slices bacon, crisply cooked and
    crumbled

1½ qt. torn spinach
1 c. red onion rings
1½ c. light salad dressing
2 Tbsp. vinegar
½ c. roasted sunflower seeds
    (optional)

Layer lettuce, spinach, water chestnuts, onions, and broccoli in a 4 quart serving bowl. Spread salad dressing, mixed with sugar and vinegar, over broccoli to edge of bowl. Sprinkle with cheese and cover. Refrigerate several hours or overnight. Sprinkle with bacon and sunflower seeds just before serving. Serves 10 to 12.

Use 2% shredded cheese, low-fat bacon, and have a guilt-free meal!
Mrs. Gloria D. Ball, Columbus (NE) Noon Lions Club
Columbus, NE

SPECIAL STRAWBERRY SPINACH SALAD

9 c. torn fresh spinach
1 pt. fresh strawberries, halved

½ c. slivered almonds, toasted

Dressing:

¼ c. vegetable oil
2 Tbsp. sugar
2 Tbsp. cider vinegar
1 Tbsp. chopped onion

1 tsp. poppy seeds
1 tsp. sesame seeds
¼ tsp. paprika
⅛ tsp. Worcestershire sauce

In a large bowl, combine the spinach, strawberries, and almonds. Place dressing ingredients in a blender; cover and process until combined. Pour over salad and toss to coat. Serve immediately. Yield: 6 to 8 servings.

SPINACH STRAWBERRY SALAD

1 bunch spinach leaves
Amount of your choice (fresh
    strawberries or mandarin
    oranges - drain oranges)
Sliced red onion to taste
½ c. sugar

⅓ c. white wine vinegar
1 c. oil
1 tsp. dry mustard
¼ c. Worcestershire sauce
2 Tbsp. poppy seed

Mix sugar and vinegar together. Add oil, mustard, Worcestershire sauce, and poppy seed. Toss salad greens with fruit and add dressing. Mix well and serve immediately.

Dee Asper, Southwest Lioness Club
South St. Paul, MN

SPINACH SALAD WITH MUSTARD DRESSING

1 medium onion
½ c. sugar
1 tsp. celery seed
1 tsp. salt
½ tsp. pepper

3 Tbsp. prepared mustard
⅓ c. white vinegar
1 c. salad oil
⅛ c. water

Blend all in food processor. Refrigerate 24 hours before using on spinach.

Patty Geib, Arlington Sea Lions Club
Arlington, MN

SPINACH SALAD

1 lb. fresh spinach
1 c. fresh strawberries, sliced
1 c. fresh bean sprouts

1 c. seedless grapes, cut in halves
¼ c. bacon bits

Wash spinach and towel dry. Tear into bite-size pieces. Add strawberries, sprouts, and grapes.

Sweet and Sour Sauce:

1 c. vegetable oil
1 medium onion, grated
1 tsp. salt

½ c. white vinegar
¾ c. sugar
1 tsp. Worcestershire

Mix and pour over salad just before serving. Add bacon bits.

Jan Moore, Sunrise Lions Club
Mexico, MO, Audrain County

SUPERSTAR SPINACH SALAD

1 cantaloupe half, seeded and
    peeled
7 c. torn fresh spinach

1½ c. cubed fully cooked ham
1 c. thinly sliced red onion
½ c. halved green grapes

Dressing:

3 Tbsp. sugar
2 Tbsp. orange juice
2 Tbsp. vinegar
1 Tbsp. chopped onion
1½ tsp. grated orange peel

Dash of pepper
⅓ c. vegetable oil
1 tsp. poppy seeds
⅓ c. chopped pecans, toasted

Cut melon half into ½ inch rings. Cut rings with a 1½ inch star-shaped cookie cutter or into 1 inch pieces; place in a bowl. Add spinach, ham, onion, and grapes. Chill for at least 2 hours. Place sugar, orange juice, vinegar, onion, orange peel, and pepper in a blender; cover and blend until smooth. With blender running, gradually add oil until slightly thickened. Stir in poppy seeds. Cover and chill. Just before serving, pour dressing over salad and toss. Top with pecans. Yield: 6 servings.

SPINACH SALAD WITH PECANS AND CROUTONS

4 slices whole-wheat bread, crusts
  removed
4½ Tbsp. olive oil
¼ c. pecan pieces
1 Tbsp. balsamic vinegar

¼ tsp. salt
⅛ tsp. pepper
½ lb. fresh spinach, cleaned and
  stems removed

Heat oven to 350°. Brush bread with oil, using 1½ tablespoons to coat both sides. Cut bread lengthwise into ½ inch batons. Spread in one layer on a cookie sheet. Bake until crisp and golden, about 8 minutes, turning once.

Meanwhile, in 9 inch pie pan or on baking sheet, dry roast pecans in oven until toasted, about 5 minutes. Set aside.

In large bowl, whisk together vinegar, salt, and pepper. Gradually whisk in remaining olive oil. Tear spinach into pieces; add to bowl along with the croutons and toss to coat with the dressing. Arrange salad on 4 plates and sprinkle with pecans before serving. Makes 4 servings.

Per serving: 259 calories, 5 g protein, 22 g fat, 338 mg sodium, 15 g carbohydrate, 0 mg cholesterol.

Joanne M. Wetzler, Clarence Lions Club
Clarence Center, NY, USA

ORIENTAL SALAD

2 bags coleslaw mix
6 green onions, chopped
¼ to ½ stick margarine or butter
½ c. chopped pecans
2 (3 oz.) Ramen noodles, finely
  crushed (no flavor packet)

1 c. sugar
½ c. vinegar
2 Tbsp. soy sauce
¼ c. oil

Mix coleslaw and onions in large bowl; set aside. Melt margarine or butter in skillet. Add peanuts and crushed Ramen noodles. Stir until mixture is browned. Drain on paper towel. Cool and add to coleslaw. Mix sugar, vinegar, and soy sauce until sugar is dissolved. Add oil and mix well. Add dressing sparingly to coleslaw-onion mix; toss and serve.

I have found once the salad has been combined it does not keep well, but will keep quite a while if the coleslaw and noodles and dressing are stored separately and mixed just before serving. Flavor is best if the coleslaw and onions are mixed the night before. I also prepare the dressing, noodles, and peanuts the night before.

Deb Fergeson, Kal Haven Trail Lions Club
Gobles, MI

Marriage is like a violin - after the music stops, the strings are still attached.

TEXAS CABBAGE SALAD

First mix:

1 head cabbage
8 to 10 green onions

1 medium bell pepper

Second:

2 pkg. Ramen noodles (chicken)
¾ c. sliced almonds

½ c. sunflower kernels

Prepare first mix as coleslaw and set aside in covered bowl. Second: Saute noodles, almonds, and sunflower kernels in 2 teaspoons margarine till lightly browned. Let cool. Add seasoning packets from noodles. Store first mixture and second mixture in separate containers to be mixed together just before serving.

Dressing:

1 c. oil
⅔ c. or less sugar

⅓ c. white wine vinegar
1 tsp. pepper and salt

Put dressing in separate container. Add before serving.

Barbara Vaughn, Conroe Lioness Club
Conroe, TX, Montgomery County

CHINESE PEANUT SALAD
(Makes large amount)

1½ bags coleslaw mix (or 1 head shredded cabbage plus some shredded carrots)
1 or 2 bunches green onions (optional)
2 Tbsp. slivered almonds (or more)

4 Tbsp. sesame seeds (or more)
1 c. cocktail peanuts (or more)
3 pkg. Top Ramen chicken flavored noodles, crushed (do not substitute)

Dressing:

3 pkg. flavoring from noodles
1 c. extra virgin olive oil

¾ c. rice wine vinegar
¾ c. sugar

Remove any large pieces from coleslaw mix. Toss salad ingredients together. Mix dressing in a jar and add to salad just before serving.

Gerry Fink, South Jefferson Lions Club
Adams, NY

No Jesus, No Peace. Know Jesus, Know Peace.

LAYERED SLAW

1 head cabbage, shredded
1 medium onion, cut in rings or
    strips
1 c. white vinegar
2 tsp. sugar
1 Tbsp. salt

1 large green pepper, cut in rings
    or strips
1 c. sugar
¾ c. oil
1 tsp. mustard

In large bowl, make a layer of cabbage, pepper, and onion. Pour 1 cup sugar over top. In saucepan, combine 1 cup vinegar, ¾ cup oil, 2 teaspoons sugar, 1 teaspoon mustard, and 1 tablespoon salt. Stir well and heat on medium heat till it comes to a full boil. Stirring, pour over slaw. Let cool and refrigerate. (Mix well before serving.)

Rayford Kimbrell, Iron City Lions Club
Iron City, TN, USA

DELI COLE SLAW

3 lb. cabbage, shredded
2 onions, chopped
1 green pepper, chopped or
    sliced
1 c. vinegar

1 c. safflower oil
1 Tbsp. celery seed
1 tsp. salt
1 c. sugar

In a saucepan, combine vinegar, oil, celery seed, and salt; bring to a boil. Stir in sugar. Combine cabbage, onion, and green pepper in a bowl. Pour dressing over and refrigerate up to 3 weeks if necessary. Serves 8 to 10.

Agnes Williams, Alpha Lions Club
Brookhaven, MS, USA

FREEZER COLE SLAW

1 medium head cabbage (about
    10 c. shredded)
1 carrot, shredded

1 green pepper, chopped
1 tsp. salt
1 sweet onion, chopped

Dressing:

1 c. white vinegar
2 c. sugar

1 tsp. celery seed
1 tsp. mustard seed

Combine vegetables in a large bowl. Add salt and let stand 1 hour. Mix dressing ingredients and bring to a boil for one minute. Let cool. Drain liquid off vegetables. Cover with dressing. May be stored in refrigerator for several days or placed in plastic containers and frozen.

This cole slaw is served at the chicken bar-b-qs put on by South Jefferson Lions Club.

Donald and Betty Whiteman, South Jefferson Lions Club
Adams, NY

LIONS COLD SLAW FOR 150

40 lb. cabbage
3 qt. vegetable oil
10 lb. sugar

2 large onions
½ gal. vinegar

Shred cabbage (fine). Divide oil, sugar, onion, vinegar, and onion in small amounts. Blend together until white; pour over cabbage.

Oil mixture will keep for 3 months in refrigerator.

Our Lions Club has used this salad every year with their pork chop dinner.

Elvera Trettin, Stewart Lions Club
Stewart, MN, USA

MEMPHIS-STYLE COLESLAW

2 c. mayonnaise
¼ c. sugar
¼ c. Dijon mustard
¼ c. cider vinegar
1½ to 2 Tbsp. celery seed
1 tsp. salt

⅛ tsp. pepper
1 medium cabbage, shredded
2 carrots, grated
1 green pepper, diced
2 Tbsp. grated onion

Stir together first 7 ingredients in a large bowl. Add cabbage and remaining ingredients, tossing gently. Cover and chill 3 to 4 hours; serve with a slotted spoon. Yields 12 servings.

Dressing will keep in refrigerator several days.

You can make a smaller bowl and keep the extra dressing for another bowl later. *Very good.*

Gloria Thompson, Bellville Lions Club
Bellville, GA, USA

RAINBOW COLESLAW

¾ lb. red cabbage, shredded
   (about 4 c.)
¾ lb. green cabbage, shredded
   (about 4 c.)
1 carrot, grated
2 Tbsp. cider vinegar
1 Tbsp. Dijon mustard

1 tsp. grated onion
1 Tbsp. sugar
1 tsp. caraway seeds
1 tsp. salt
¼ tsp. pepper
6 Tbsp. oil

In a large bowl, combine the shredded cabbages with the grated carrot. In a small bowl, whisk together the vinegar, mustard, onion, sugar, caraway seeds, salt, and pepper. Gradually whisk in the oil. Pour the dressing over the cabbage mixture and toss to coat well. Cover and chill at least 1 hour. Makes 6 servings.

Per serving: 162 calories, 1 g protein, 14 g fat, 447 mg sodium, 9 g carbohydrate, 0 mg cholesterol.

Lion John J. Hess, Clarence Lions Club
Clarence Center, NY, USA

WALDORF COLESLAW

4 c. coarsely shredded cabbage
2 c. chopped apples

1 c. sliced celery
1 c. chopped toasted walnuts

Dressing:

¼ c. bottled lemon juice or lime
    juice
3 Tbsp. honey
2 Tbsp. water

1 Tbsp. vegetable oil
1 tsp. Dijon-style mustard
1 tsp. garlic salt

Mix cabbage, apples, celery, and toasted walnuts. Mix remaining ingredients for dressing and add to cabbage mix. Cover and chill four hours to blend flavors.

Liz Birchen, O'Fallon Lions Club
O'Fallon, MO, USA

COLE SLAW DRESSING

1 c. Wesson oil

1 c. sugar

Add:

⅔ c. ketchup
½ c. vinegar
2 Tbsp. grated onion

1 tsp. salt
½ tsp. paprika

Put in mixer and beat for 15 minutes on medium speed. Put in tight container and leave overnight.

Can be kept in the refrigerator for some time.

Our church serves this on cole slaw for ham dinner. Everyone loves it.
Olive Higinbotham, Bentleyville Lioness Club
Bentleyville, PA, USA

COLD SLAW DRESSING

2 c. salad dressing
½ c. vinegar
½ c. oil
1⅓ c. sugar

2 tsp. mustard
½ tsp. celery seed
2 tsp. salt

Mix all together and blend well with blender or electric beaters. Makes 1 quart.

This is an excellent dressing for lettuce salad.
Eilene Moody, Bryan Lioness Club
Bryan, OH

HONEY-MUSTARD DIP OR SALAD DRESSING

In small bowl, with fork or whisk, mix:

¼ c. Dijon mustard
¼ c. honey
1 Tbsp. soy sauce

1 Tbsp. minced green onion
2 tsp. minced, peeled ginger root

Parmesan Dip - In small bowl, with fork:

1 c. mayonnaise
3 mashed anchovy fillets
2 Tbsp. grated Parmesan cheese

1 Tbsp. lemon juice
¼ tsp. black pepper

Sarah Wehling, Bothell Lions Club
Bothell, WA, USA

SALAD DRESSING MIX

½ c. dried parsley flakes
¼ c. freeze-dried chives
1 Tbsp. dill weed

¼ tsp. salt
⅛ tsp. pepper

Pour into spice jars or make packets, wrapping 2 tablespoons mix in plastic bags.

To use as dressing: Combine 2 tablespoons mix with 1 cup plain yogurt or sour cream.

To use as a dip with small quantities same ingredients. Chill at least 2 hours. Makes 1 cup dressing.

Sarah Wehling, Bothell Lions Club
Bothell, WA, USA

PEPPER SALAD DRESSING

6 qt. mayonnaise
2 qt. half & half cream
¾ c. coarsely ground pepper
⅓ c. thinly sliced green onions

¼ c. salt
2 Tbsp. white pepper
2 Tbsp. hot pepper sauce
1 Tbsp. Worcestershire sauce

Combine all ingredients in a large bowl; mix well. Transfer to jars or bottles; refrigerate. Yield: About 2 gallons.

To belittle is to be little.

SARAH'S FRENCH DRESSING

Whisk together:

1 c. oil (olive is good)
¼ c. cider vinegar
2 Tbsp. dry sherry

2 tsp. salt
¼ tsp. pepper

Toss with greens.

Sarah Wehling, Bothell Lions Club
Bothell, WA, USA

ROQUEFORT DRESSING

2 lb. Blue cheese (import)
3 gal. mayonnaise
6 qt. buttermilk
4 medium size onions
½ c. white pepper

2 c. lemon juice
1 c. salt
½ c. Accent (optional)
1 c. garlic powder
2 bunches parsley, stems
   removed

Grind onions, parsley, and Blue cheese together, then mix in other ingredients. Makes about 5 gallons.

J.V. Vandergrift, Fairmont East Grafton Road Lions Club
Fairmont, WV

TOMATO FRENCH DRESSING

1 (10¾ oz.) can zesty tomato
   soup
¼ c. vinegar
½ c. salad oil
1 Tbsp. minced onion
2 Tbsp. sugar

2 tsp. dry mustard
1 tsp. salt
¼ tsp. pepper
Parsley
1 garlic clove

Combine all ingredients in quart jar and shake.

Carol Hug, Bryan Lioness Club
Bryan, OH, USA

TANGY FRENCH DRESSING

Equal parts:

Vinegar
Oil

Sugar
Ketchup

Combine and store in refrigerator.

Mrs. Tim (Linda) Lyons, Elburn Lions Club
Batavia, IL, USA

SWEET AND SOUR SALAD DRESSING

1 small onion
1 tsp. salt
1 tsp. celery salt
1 tsp. dry mustard

½ c. vinegar
⅔ c. sugar
1 c. oil

Mix in blender. Add the oil last and a little at a time.

Lion Ida Rohrer, Moundbuilders Lions Club
Newark, OH, USA

SOUR CREAM VEGETABLE DRESSING

½ c. finely chopped cucumber, peeled
2 Tbsp. finely chopped green pepper
2 Tbsp. finely chopped red radishes

2 Tbsp. snipped green onions
1 c. light dairy sour cream
¼ tsp. salt
Dash of ground pepper

Combine cucumber, green pepper, radishes, and onions. Stir in sour cream, salt, and pepper. Mix well. Chill at least 4 hours.

Very good on cole slaw or can be used as a dip with crackers and vegetable sticks.

Carol Speicher, Columbus Lions Club
Columbus, NE, USA

GREENS AND WALNUT DRESSING

2 Tbsp. white wine vinegar
2 tsp. honey mustard
2 tsp. minced garlic
⅛ tsp. salt
½ c. walnut oil
2 Tbsp. minced shallots

1 c. coarsely chopped walnuts, toasted
2 (10 oz.) pkg. European stalia or French bread
Salad in a bag

Patty Geib, Arlington Sea Lions Club
Arlington, MN

APPLEBEE'S ORIENTAL CHICKEN SALAD DRESSING

3 Tbsp. honey
1½ Tbsp. white vinegar
4 tsp. mayonnaise

1 Tbsp. Grey Poupon
⅛ sesame oil

Combine all ingredients. *Enjoy.*

Patty Geib, Arlington Sea Lions Club
Arlington, MN

Soups,
Sandwiches
Sauces

A HANDY SPICE AND HERB GUIDE

ALLSPICE-a pea-sized fruit that grows in Mexico, Jamaica, Central and South America. Its delicate flavor resembles a blend of cloves, cinnamon, and nutmeg. USES: (Whole) Pickles, meats, boiled fish, gravies; (Ground) Puddings, relishes, fruit preserves, baking.

BASIL-the dried leaves and stems of an herb grown in the United States and North Mediterranean area. Has an aromatic, leafy flavor. USES: For flavoring tomato dishes and tomato paste, turtle soup; also use in cooked peas, squash, snap beans; sprinkle chopped over lamb chops and poultry.

BAY LEAVES-the dried leaves of an evergreen grown in the eastern Mediterranean countries. Has a sweet, herbaceous floral spice note. USES: For pickling, stews, for spicing sauces and soup. Also use with a variety of meats and fish.

CARAWAY-the seed of a plant grown in the Netherlands. Flavor that combines the tastes of anise and dill. USES: For the cordial Kummel, baking breads; often added to sauerkraut, noodles, cheese spreads. Also adds zest to French fried potatoes, liver, canned asparagus.

CURRY POWDER-a ground blend of ginger, turmeric, fenugreek seed, as many as 16 to 20 spices. USES: For all Indian curry recipes such as lamb, chicken, and rice, eggs, vegetables, and curry puffs.

DILL-the small, dark seed of the dill plant grown in India, having a clean, aromatic taste. USES: Dill is a predominant seasoning in pickling recipes; also adds pleasing flavor to sauerkraut, potato salad, cooked macaroni, and green apple pie.

MACE-the dried covering around the nutmeg seed. Its flavor is similar to nutmeg, but with a fragrant, delicate difference. USES: (Whole) For pickling, fish, fish sauce, stewed fruit. (Ground) Delicious in baked goods, pastries, and doughnuts, adds unusual flavor to chocolate desserts.

MARJORAM-an herb of the mint family, grown in France and Chile. Has a minty-sweet flavor. USES: In beverages, jellies, and to flavor soups, stews, fish, sauces. Also excellent to sprinkle on lamb while roasting.

MSG (MONOSODIUM GLUTAMATE)-a vegetable protein derivative for raising the effectiveness of natural food flavors. USES: Small amounts, adjusted to individual taste, can be added to steaks, roasts, chops, seafoods, stews, soups, chowder, chop suey, and cooked vegetables.

OREGANO-a plant of the mint family and a species of marjoram of which the dried leaves are used to make an herb seasoning. USES: An excellent flavoring for any tomato dish, especially pizza, chili con carne, and Italian specialties.

PAPRIKA-a mild, sweet red pepper growing in Spain, Central Europe, and the United States. Slightly aromatic and prized for brilliant red color. USES: A colorful garnish for pale foods, and for seasoning Chicken Paprika, Hungarian Goulash, salad dressings.

POPPY-the seed of a flower grown in Holland. Has a rich fragrance and crunchy, nut-like flavor. USES: Excellent as a topping for breads, rolls, and cookies. Also delicious in buttered noodles.

ROSEMARY-an herb (like a curved pine needle) grown in France, Spain, and Portugal, and having a sweet fresh taste. USES: In lamb dishes, in soups, stews, and to sprinkle on beef before roasting.

SAGE-the leaf of a shrub grown in Greece, Yugoslavia, and Albania. Flavor is camphoraceous and minty. USES: For meat and poultry stuffing, sausages, meat loaf, hamburgers, stews, and salads.

THYME-the leaves and stems of a shrub grown in France and Spain. Has a strong, distinctive flavor. USES: For poultry seasoning, croquettes, fricassees, and fish dishes. Also tasty on fresh sliced tomatoes.

TURMERIC-a root of the ginger family, grown in India, Haiti, Jamaica, and Peru, having a mild, ginger-pepper flavor. USES: As a flavoring and coloring in prepared mustard and in combination with mustard as a flavoring for meats, dressings, salads.

SOUPS, SANDWICHES, SAUCES
SOUPS

CHILI

1 lb. ground beef
1 medium onion, diced
½ c. green pepper, chopped
½ c. celery, chopped

2 (10¾ oz.) cans tomato soup
2 (16 oz.) cans tomatoes
1 (16 oz.) can kidney beans
1 to 1½ tsp. chili powder

Brown ground beef and onion. Drain off grease. Add remaining ingredients and simmer for 1 to 1½ hours, stirring often.

"WHO NEEDS COLD MEDICINE" CHILI

1 (16 oz.) jar *Pace* hot salsa
1 (15 oz.) can red kidney beans
1 (16 oz.) can chopped, peeled
   tomatoes
1 (7 oz.) can jalapenos, diced
1 white onion, chopped

2 lb. turkey, ground
1 c. water
1 (8 oz.) can tomato sauce
1 (4 oz.) *Carrol Shelby's Texas
   Brand chili mix (use
   everything)*

Fry and drain meat, onion, and jalapenos together. Dump everything in a large pot. Simmer on stove, stirring frequently. Jazz it up with shredded Cheddar cheese, sour cream, etc. If desired, serve with large amounts of ice water!

*Mike Hazzard
Littleton, CO*

TED MOHAN'S CHILI

1 lb. ground sausage
1 lb. ground beef
Green peppers, diced
Onions, diced
Fresh mushrooms, diced

Largest can kidney beans
Largest can baked beans
Largest can tomato juice
2 squirts of ketchup
Chili seasoning to taste

Brown sausage and ground beef. Add vegetables and saute until tender. Add remaining ingredients and heat thoroughly.

*Marge Sabin, Rootstown Township Lions Club 13-D
Rootstown, OH, USA*

Be unselfish, pray for others besides yourself.

TURKEY CHILI
(Mild)

2 Tbsp. vegetable oil
1 medium size onion, finely
    chopped (1 c.)
1 sweet green pepper, diced (1 c.)
3 cloves garlic, finely chopped
2 lb. ground turkey
3 Tbsp. chili powder
1½ tsp. ground cumin
2 Tbsp. tomato paste

1 tsp. oregano
1 (4 oz.) can mild green chilies
1 (16 oz.) can whole tomatoes
    (liquid), chopped
1 c. chicken broth
1 (16 oz.) can kidney beans,
    drained and rinsed
¼ tsp. salt

Heat oil in large saucepan over medium heat. Add onion, pepper, and garlic. Cook, stirring often, until onion is soft and transparent, 6 minutes. Add turkey and cook, stirring and breaking up meat with wooden spoon, until meat changes color. Add chili powder, cumin, and oregano; cook, stirring, 30 seconds. Add chilies, tomato, tomato paste, chicken broth, beans, and salt. Stir well to combine. Bring to boiling, lower heat, and simmer, uncovered, stirring occasionally, for 30 minutes.

Lion Glenda Conopask, Plymouth Lions Club
Terryville, CT, USA

SUMMER CHILI

2 onions
2 cloves garlic
1 lb. lean ground beef
1 Tbsp. oil
3 Tbsp. chili powder
1 tsp. ground cumin

Salt
16 oz. can tomatoes in juice
2 small zucchini (about ½ lb. in
    all)
2 small yellow squash (about ½
    lb. in all)
1 c. cooked kidney beans

Chop the onions. Mince the garlic. Brown the beef in a Dutch oven with the oil and onion. Add the garlic, chili powder, cumin, ½ teaspoon salt, and the tomatoes with their liquid, breaking them up with the side of a spoon. Cut the zucchini and yellow squash into quarters lengthwise and then crosswise into ¼ inch pieces. Add to chili and cook until tender, about 15 minutes. Stir in beans and cook another 5 minutes. Taste for seasoning and add more salt if necessary. Makes 4 servings.

Per serving: 464 calories, 27 g protein, 29 g fat, 599 mg sodium, 26 g carbohydrate, 85 mg cholesterol.

Lion John J. Hess, Clarence Lions Club
Clarence Center, NY, USA

STUFFED PEPPER SOUP

2 lb. ground beef or ground
   turkey
1 (28 oz.) can tomato sauce
1 (28 oz.) can diced tomatoes
   (undrained)
2 c. cooked long grain wild rice

2 c. chopped green pepper
2 beef bouillon cubes
¼ c. packed brown sugar
2 tsp. salt
1 tsp. pepper

In large pan, brown beef or turkey. Drain. Add remaining ingredients. Bring to a boil. Reduce heat; cover and simmer for 30 to 40 minutes or until peppers are soft. Makes 10 servings.

Sue Bubb, Burnham Lions Club
McClure, PA

HAMBURGER SOUP

1 lb. ground beef, browned and
   drained
6 bacon strips, chopped
½ c. celery
3 diced carrots
1 can beef bouillon

3 c. water
3 small diced potatoes
½ small onion
1 can tomatoes
1 can potato soup or cheese soup

Combine and simmer until vegetables are done. Add soup when almost done.

Jean Chestnut, Columbus Noon Lions Club
Columbus, NE, USA

Be thankful. Prayer is more than asking or receiving.

❧ ❧ ❧

It has been said lots of things are opened by mistake,
but none so often as the mouth.

❧ ❧ ❧

Maybe no two snowflakes are alike,
but most snow jobs seem pretty much the same.

❧ ❧ ❧

Good old days - when hamburger didn't need a helper.

REUNION SOUP

**5 lb. boneless beef, supplied by
the host**

Everyone else brings - 1 quart or pack of vegetables, cleaned, peeled, and cut up ready for cooking, such as:

Potatoes	Tomatoes
Onions	Cabbage
Celery	Limas
Carrots	More potatoes
Beans	More onions

Additional ingredients:

Salt to taste   **Water to cover**
Pepper to taste

We make this soup outdoors in a large lard kettle. Use the largest pot you can find. Start the beef boiling in water early in the day. As family members arrive, have them add the vegetables they bring. The longer the soup cooks and the more vegetables you add, the better it gets. Stir often.

We make this soup at camp-outs or reunions. It brings people together with a great tradition.

*Rootstown Historical Society, Rootstown Township Lions Club 13-D
Rootstown, OH*

SPICY CHEESEBURGER SOUP

1½ c. water
2 c. cubed, peeled potatoes
2 small carrots grated
1 small onion, chopped
¼ c. chopped green pepper
1 jalapeno pepper, seeded and
    chopped
1 garlic clove, minced
1 Tbsp. beef bouillon granules
½ tsp. salt

1 lb. ground beef, cooked and
    drained
2½ c. milk *divided*
3 Tbsp. all-purpose flour
8 oz. process American cheese,
    cubed
¼ to 1 tsp. cayenne pepper
    (optional)
½ lb. sliced bacon, cooked and
    crumbled

In a large saucepan, combine the first nine ingredients; bring to a boil. Reduce heat; cover and simmer for 15 to 20 minutes or until potatoes are tender. Stir in beef and 2 cups of milk; heat through. Combine flour and remaining milk until smooth; gradually stir into soup. Bring to a boil; cook and stir for 2 minutes or until thickened and bubbly. Reduce heat; stir in cheese until melted. Add cayenne if desired. Top with bacon just before serving. Yield: 6 to 8 servings (about 2 quarts).

When cutting or seeding hot peppers, use rubber or plastic gloves to protect your hands. Avoid touching your face.

QUICK BEEF AND VEGETABLE SOUP

1 onion
1 clove garlic
½ lb. ground beef
½ tsp. dried thyme
2 c. tomato juice
1¾ c. beef broth or canned stock

Salt
10 oz. pkg. frozen mixed
  vegetables
1 Tbsp. chopped fresh parsley
  (optional)

Chop the onion. Mince the garlic. In a soup pot, brown the ground beef with the onion over medium-high heat. Pour off the fat from the pan and discard. Add the garlic, thyme, tomato juice, broth, and ½ teaspoon salt. Cover and simmer 10 minutes. Add the vegetables and the parsley. Cover and cook until heated through, about 5 minutes. Makes 4 servings.

Per serving: 202 calories, 13 g protein, 9 g fat, 783 mg sodium, 17 g carbohydrate, 34 mg cholesterol.

Joanne M. Wetzler, Clarence Lions Club
Clarence Center, NY, USA

SMOKY VEGETABLE BARLEY SOUP

½ lb. carrots (about 4)
1 meaty ham hock (about 1½ lb.)
¾ c. barley
1 bay leaf
½ tsp. dried thyme
2 qt. chicken stock or canned
  broth
1 qt. water

1½ lb. potatoes (about 3)
3 c. canned tomatoes with their
  juice
Salt and pepper
3 Tbsp. chopped fresh parsley
  (optional)

Peel carrots and slice. Put in a soup pot with ham hock, barley, bay leaf, thyme, stock, and water over high heat. Cover and bring to a boil. Reduce heat and simmer until barley is tender, about 1 hour.

Meanwhile, peel potatoes and cut into approximately ½ inch cubes. Chop tomatoes and add to the pot along with their juice, potatoes, ¾ teaspoon salt, and ½ teaspoon pepper. Cook, uncovered, until potatoes are tender, 18 to 20 minutes. Remove meat from ham hock and cut into pieces. Return meat to pot and add parsley. Makes 8 servings.

Per serving: 224 calories, 12 g protein, 5 g fat, 795 mg sodium, 33 g carbohydrate, 16 mg cholesterol.

Mrs. Mike Nowicki, Clarence Lions Club
Clarence Center, NY, USA

WILD RICE SOUP

2 Tbsp. butter
½ to ¾ c. celery, chopped
1 bunch green onions, chopped
2 cloves garlic, minced
1 lb. very lean bacon, chopped
2 potatoes, chopped
8 oz. fresh mushrooms, sliced
2 c. raw wild rice

2 (10½ oz.) cans chicken broth
5 c. water
2 c. milk
1 pt. cream
¼ tsp. basil
½ tsp. parsley
Salt and pepper to taste

Soak wild rice for 1 hour in warm water. Drain and rinse. Saute celery, onions, garlic, bacon, potatoes, and mushrooms in the butter for 5 to 10 minutes. Add rice, chicken broth, water, and spices. Simmer (covered) on medium heat for ½ hour. Stir occasionally. Stir in cream and milk. Cook on low for 2 to 3 hours until rice is very tender and pops open. Stir occasionally while cooking.

Soup is very thick - if you want it thinner, add more water.

Judy Rannow, Arlington (SEA) Lions Club
Arlington, MN, USA

SOUP OF LAMB

1 lb. lamb (½ inch cubes)
¼ tsp. salt
2 carrots
1 leek
1 onion
¼ celery root

¼ cabbage
½ lb. potatoes
3 bay leaves
Parsley
Water to cover the meat

Bring the water, salt, meat, and bay leaves to boil. Cook for 45 minutes at low heat while skimming the soup. Add vegetables: Carrots, leek, onion, cabbage, sliced ⅛ inch potatoes, celery root, and bay leaves. Cook another 20 minutes. Add chopped parsley before serving. Serve with bread, rolls. Serves 4.

Lai Johnsen, Godthaab Lions Club
Nook, Greenland

Definition of a good day:
When the wheels of your shopping cart all go in the same direction.

An optimist is a person who sticks
on the stamp before addressing the envelope.

CHICKEN SOUP WITH MATZO BALLS

1 egg
1 Tbsp. melted chicken fat or oil
1 Tbsp. chopped parsley
1 tsp. salt
⅓ c. matzo meal
1 Tbsp. oil
1 carrot, diced

1 rib celery, diced
1 medium onion, chopped
1 clove garlic, minced
6 c. chicken broth or canned
   stock
Dash of pepper
¾ c. cooked skinless, boneless
   chicken, shredded

In a medium bowl, beat egg, chicken fat, parsley, 2 tablespoons water, and ½ teaspoon salt. Stir in the matzo meal and refrigerate 15 minutes.

Bring large pot of salted water to a boil. With wet hands, shape matzo meal mixture into 6 balls and drop them gently into the boiling water. Simmer, covered, until matzo balls are cooked through, 45 to 50 minutes.

While matzo balls cook, make soup. In a large saucepan, heat oil over medium-low heat. Add carrot, celery, onion, and garlic. Cover and cook until vegetables are just soft, about 5 minutes. Add broth, remaining salt, and the pepper and bring to a simmer. Cook, uncovered, until vegetables are very soft and soup is well-flavored, about 40 minutes.

With slotted spoon, transfer matzo balls to the soup. Stir in chicken and simmer 5 minutes longer. Makes 6 servings.

Work time: 35 minutes. Total time: 1 hour and 15 minutes.

Per serving: 169 calories, 8 g protein, 11 g fat, 391 mg sodium, 8 g carbohydrate, 54 mg cholesterol.

Mrs. Lucy Aiken, Clarence Lions Club
Clarence Center, NY, USA

Your true measure is determined by the way
you treat those who can't possibly do you any good.

❦ ❦ ❦

The three essentials of happiness are something to do,
someone to love, and something to hope for.

CHICKEN BROTH

2 Tbsp. oil
3½ lb. chicken, cut up
1 lb. chicken backs and necks,
    cut up
1 large onion, coarsely chopped

2 ribs celery, coarsely chopped
2 carrots, coarsely chopped
15 peppercorns
1 bay leaf

In a large pot, heat oil over medium-high heat. Add the chicken, making sure to leave room between pieces. (Cook in 2 batches if necessary.) Brown chicken on both sides, about 15 minutes. Remove chicken and drain off all but 1 tablespoon of fat. Reduce heat to low. Add onion, celery, and carrots to pot. Cook until just soft, about 5 minutes. Return chicken to pot. Add 8 cups cold water, the peppercorns, and bay leaf. Bring to a simmer. Cover and cook for 1 hour. Uncover pot and continue cooking 1½ hours longer. Strain broth, reserving the chicken. Cool broth, then refrigerate. Before using broth, remove layer of solidified fat that has risen to the top.

When chicken is cool enough to handle, remove skin and pull meat from bones. Discard skin and bones. Use meat in soups, salads, or sandwiches. Makes 6 cups.

Work time: 30 minutes. Total time: 4 hours.

Per serving: 45 calories, 1 g protein, 5 g fat, 2 mg sodium, 2 g carbohydrate, 2 mg cholesterol.

Note: To make your own *bouillon cubes*, place defatted broth in a pot and simmer until it has reduced to 1 cup, about 1 hour. Strain. Pour stock into 6 cubes of an ice cube tray and freeze. To use, dilute 1 cube of stock in 1 cup warm water.

Mrs. Lucy Aiken, Clarence Lions Club
Clarence Center, NY, USA

POTASSIUM BROTH

2 c. potato peelings
1 c. carrot peelings
1 c. chopped beets

2 c. onions and/or garlic
2 c. celery and dark greens
Water to cover

Put all ingredients in a large pot. Cover ingredients with water. Simmer on very low heat for 1 to 2 hours. Strain the veggies and drink only the broth.

Works great if you need a healing boost!

James R. Schiebel, Hilton Lions Club
Hilton, NY, USA

When you're over the hill, you pick up speed.

CHEESY BRAT STEW

6 Bratwurst
4 medium potatoes, cubed
1 small can green beans
1 small chopped onion

1 c. grated Cheddar or American
  cheese
1 can cream of mushroom soup
1 c. water

Precook Brats and cut them up into bit size pieces. Put in fry pan with onion. Saute for just a bit, then add the rest of the ingredients. Cover and cook over low heat for 30 minutes or until potatoes are done.

CHEDDAR CHEESE SOUP

4 to 5 medium boiling potatoes
1 can Campbell's Cheddar cheese
  soup
2 c. half & half or whole milk
1 stick butter
2 stalks celery, chopped

3 or 4 green onions, chopped
Dash of black pepper
6 slices bacon, cooked and
  crumbled
1 chicken bouillon cube

Peel and dice potatoes. Cover with water in saucepan and boil until tender. Drain. In large saucepan, combine Cheddar cheese soup, milk, butter, and chicken bouillon cube. Stir constantly over low heat until lumps are dissolved. Add celery, onions, black pepper, potatoes, and bacon. Simmer for 20 minutes. Can top with grated Cheddar cheese and toasted croutons if desired. Serves 4.

When I serve this soup with fresh made bread, there's not a drop left. Really tastes good on a cold day!

Lion Cheryl Kastle, Berthoud Lions Club
Berthoud, CO, USA

BROCCOLI CHEESE SOUP

½ c. butter, melted
3 heaping Tbsp. cornstarch
6 c. milk
2 inch chunk Velveeta cheese (or
  more)

1 bunch broccoli
1 small onion

Cook and chop broccoli. Saute butter and onions. Add cornstarch. Add milk and cheese and simmer until cheese is melted. (Add more cheese to taste.) Add cooked broccoli. Stir and serve. Makes 6 to 8 cups.

Deb Fergeson, Kal-Haven Trail Lions Club
Gobles, MI, USA

CHEESE SOUP

½ c. chopped onions
4 Tbsp. butter or margarine
⅓ c. flour
4 c. chicken stock

½ c. carrots, grated
½ c. celery, finely diced
4 c. milk
1½ c. grated American cheese

Saute onions in butter or margarine. Add flour, chicken stock, carrots, celery, and milk in order listed. Cook until bubbly. Add cheese. Heat until cheese melts.

Janie Fox, Saginaw Lions Club
Saginaw, TX

CREAM OF BROCCOLI AND CHEESE SOUP

2 c. chopped celery
1 c. finely chopped onion
1 (10 oz.) pkg. chopped broccoli
1 c. cottage cheese
2 c. whole milk

1 (10¾ oz.) can cream of chicken
  soup (undiluted)
½ tsp. salt (if desired)
⅛ tsp. white pepper

Cook celery, onion, and broccoli until tender. Set aside. Blend cottage cheese in blender until very smooth; slowly add milk while continuing to blend. Add chicken soup to cheese/milk mixture. Blend; add mixture to cooked vegetables. Heat through without boiling. Add salt and pepper. Yield: 6 servings.

A favorite at our house.

Lion June Taylor, Foley Lions Club
Foley, AL, USA

Once a man would spend a week patiently waiting if he missed a stage coach. Now he rages if he misses the first section of a revolving door.

❧ ❧ ❧

All people smile in the same language.

❧ ❧ ❧

There is no better tranquilizer in the world than a few kind words.

❧ ❧ ❧

Our duty is not to see through one another, but to see one another through.

CHEDDAR SOUP

1 small onion
1 small red bell pepper
¼ lb. green beans
½ lb. Cheddar cheese (about 2 c.), grated

4 Tbsp. butter
Salt and pepper
3 Tbsp. flour
2 c. chicken stock or canned broth
1 c. beer

Chop the onion. Seed and dice the pepper. Trim and dice the green beans. Grate the cheese. Melt butter in a soup pot over medium heat. Add onion, red pepper, beans, ¼ teaspoon salt, and ¼ teaspoon pepper. Cover and cook until the vegetables have softened, about 5 minutes. Reduce heat to low. Gradually stir in flour. Cook, stirring, 1 minute. Stir in stock and beer. Raise heat, bring to a boil, and cook 1 minute. Reduce heat and simmer about 5 minutes. Remove from heat, let cool slightly, and stir in the grated cheese. Taste soup for seasoning and add salt and pepper if needed. Makes 4 servings.

Work time: 25 minutes. Total time: 35 minutes.

Per serving: 407 calories, 17 g protein, 31 g fat, 521 mg sodium, 12 g carbohydrate, 91 mg cholesterol.

Mrs. Lucy Aiken, Clarence Lions Club
Clarence Center, NY, USA

BUTTERMILK SOUP

2 c. fresh buttermilk (do not use boughten buttermilk) or 8 Tbsp. dried buttermilk

2 c. water

Bring to a boil. Add oatmeal to thicken and cook until oatmeal is done. Sugar may be added or you can each add it to taste in individual servings. Some use rice instead of oatmeal.

Micheal and Ruth Bartolf, Oxbow and District Lions Club
Oxbow, Saskatchewan, Canada

MILK SOUP

4 c. milk
½ tsp. salt
1 Tbsp. sugar

1 egg
3 Tbsp. flour
Pinch of salt

Bring milk, sugar, and salt to boil, then make little dumplings by using 1 egg, 3 tablespoons flour, and a pinch of salt. Mix the egg with flour and salt. Spoon the mixture into the boiling milk, using ¼ teaspoon at a time. Cook in the milk for 3 to 4 minutes just before serving.

Micheal and Ruth Bartolf, Oxbow and District Lions Club
Oxbow, Saskatchewan, Canada

CREAMY POTATO SOUP

4 c. potatoes, peeled and cubed
1 c. celery (¾ inch slices)
1 c. onion, chopped
2 c. water
2 tsp. salt
1 c. milk

1 c. whipping cream
3 Tbsp. butter or margarine,
   melted
1 Tbsp. parsley flakes
½ tsp. caraway seeds
⅛ tsp. pepper

Combine potatoes, celery, onion, water, and salt in large Dutch oven. Simmer, covered, about 20 minutes or until potatoes are tender. Mash mixture once or twice with a potato masher, leaving some vegetable pieces whole. Stir in remaining ingredients; return to heat and cook, stirring constantly, until soup is thoroughly heated. Yield: 7 cups.

Lion Wilford Lyerly, PDG, Mount Airy Foothills Lions Club
Mount Airy, NC, USA

BERTHA REIMER'S POTATO SOUP

1 large potato
1 medium onion
5 whole allspice

1 bay leaf
Cream

Cut up potato and onion. Add spices and cover with water and boil until potatoes are done. Add a little cream, pepper, and salt to taste. Add hamburger meat or ham if you have some on hand. *Mennonite recipe.*

Veleta Young, Bellingham Harborview Lions Club
Bellingham, WA, USA

PLAIN POTATO SOUP

3 potatoes
1 Tbsp. butter
1 tsp. flour
1 small onion

Dash of paprika
1 qt. water
1 stalk celery
Salt to taste and white pepper

Peel potatoes and cut them in small cubes. Melt 1 tablespoon butter or fat. Add 1 teaspoon flour and blend well, then grate in 1 small onion. Fry gently until yellow. Add a dash of paprika. Pour over it 1 quart cold water gradually. Mix well and let it come to a boil. Add the potatoes, salt and a little white pepper, and one stalk of celery and boil gently for one hour, stirring occasionally. Garnish with 1 tablespoon finely chopped parsley. This soup is not supposed to be thick.

One of my mother's favorite Hungarian recipes.

Lion Evelyn M. Mongesku, Western Branch Lions Club
Chesapeake, VA, USA

BROCCOLI POTATO SOUP

2 c. broccoli florets
1 small onion, thinly sliced
1 Tbsp. butter or margarine
1 (10¾ oz.) can condensed cream
   of potato soup (undiluted)
1 c. milk

½ c. water
¾ tsp. minced fresh basil or ¼
   tsp. dried basil
¼ tsp. pepper
⅓ c. shredded Cheddar cheese

In a large saucepan, saute broccoli and onion in butter until tender. Stir in soup, milk, water, basil, and pepper; heat through. Add cheese; stir until melted. Yield: 4 servings.

Marge Sabin, Rootstown Township Lions Club 13-D
Rootstown, OH, USA

TACO SOUP

2 cans chili beans
2 cans whole kernel corn
2 cans tomato sauce
1 can Ro-Tel tomatoes
2 cans water

1 pkg. taco seasoning mix
1 pkg. Ranch dressing mix
1½ lb. ground chuck
1 onion, chopped

Brown ground chuck with onions until red is gone from meat and onions are transparent. Add remaining ingredients and cook over low heat for about 2 hours. Serve with shredded Monterey Jack cheese sprinkled on top and corn chips. Also, good with a dollop of sour cream. Freezes well.

Nettie Favara, Greenwood Lions Club
Greenwood, MS, USA

TACO SOUP

2 cans Ro-Tel tomatoes
2 cans stewed tomatoes
2 cans Mexican beans
2 cans shoe peg corn

2 pkg. taco seasoning
Large pkg. Ranch dressing
2 lb. hamburger meat
1 onion

Brown onion and ground meat. Drain. Add above. Heat and serve.

Doris Smith, Brookhaven Alpha Lions Club
Brookhaven, MS, USA

The future belongs to those who are willing to work for it.

TORTILLA SOUP

1 small fresh jalapeno, seeded
and chopped
1 c. chopped onion
Garlic powder
¼ c. vegetable oil
2 cans Ro-Tel tomatoes
2 cans chicken broth

2 cans beef broth
2 cans tomato soup
3 c. water
2 tsp. cumin
½ to 1 tsp. red pepper
1 c. shredded cheese

Saute the onion and garlic in the oil until tender. For a milder soup, use ½ to ¾ of a jalapeno. Add the rest of the ingredients except the cheese. Bring to a boil, cover, reduce heat, and simmer 30 minutes. Add the cheese. Simmer 5 minutes.

To serve, put tortilla chips in a bowl and pour soup over them. If preferred, cut flour tortillas into strips and add with the cheese and do not use the chips.

Janie Fox, Saginaw Lions Club
Saginaw, TX

LENTIL WIENER SOUP

½ lb. lentils
8 c. cold water
4 strips bacon
½ c. finely chopped celery
¼ c. finely chopped onion
2 Tbsp. flour

About 2 tsp. salt
¼ tsp. pepper
½ c. tomato paste
Pinch of soda
½ lb. best frankfurters

Cover lentils with plenty of cold water and let stand overnight. Drain. Add fresh water and cook slowly about 2 hours. Chop bacon fine and fry slowly several minutes. Add celery, onion, and flour. Cook several minutes more and add to lentils that have been cooked. Season with salt and pepper. Add tomato paste and soda. Cook all together for about 30 minutes more. Cut skinless frankfurters crosswise into ¼ inch slices and saute for a few minutes in butter. Add to soup. Let cook together about 15 minutes and serve hot.

I always double this recipe as my family loves it. If there are leftovers, they are delicious warmed up for lunch.

Virginia Bayer (Lion), Franklin Park Lions Club
Park Ridge, IL, USA

Blessed are those who give without remembering
and receive without forgetting.

INDIA CURRIED PARSNIP SOUP

Parsnips are naturally sweet and spicy, a perfect accompaniment for curry and other Indian seasonings.

1 Tbsp. butter
1 large onion, chopped
2 cloves garlic, minced
2 tsp. curry powder
½ tsp. turmeric
½ tsp. salt

¼ tsp. red-pepper flakes
1¾ c. chicken stock or broth
1 lb. parsnips (about 5 medium), peeled and cut into chunks
1 large potato (about ½ lb.), peeled and cut into chunks

In a medium frying pan, heat the butter over medium-low heat. Add onion and garlic and cook until soft, about 3 minutes. Add the curry, turmeric, salt, and red-pepper flakes and cook, stirring, 1 minute longer. Add the chicken stock, 1½ cups water, the parsnips, and potato. Simmer soup until the parsnips and potato are very tender, about 25 minutes.

Transfer 2 cups of the soup to a blender and puree. Return pureed mixture to the remaining soup. If desired, garnish with some red-pepper and scallion slices. Makes 4 servings.

Note: This soup thickens on standing, so add more water if necessary when reheating.

Mrs. Mike Nowicki, Clarence Lions Club
Clarence Center, NY, USA

PEANUT SOUP

3 c. chicken broth
1 c. peanut butter
⅛ tsp. celery salt
⅛ tsp. onion salt

⅛ tsp. sugar
1⅓ c. cream or 1 (13 oz.) can evaporated milk
Chopped peanuts

Heat chicken broth to boiling. Add peanut butter, stirring until smooth. Season to taste with salts. Add sugar. Stir in cream or milk. Heat; do not boil. Top with chopped peanuts. Makes 6 servings.

Sarah Wehling, Bothell Lions Club
Bothell, WA, USA

The time to make friends is before you need them.

Minds are like parachutes...they function only when open.

SAUERKRAUT SOUP

1 lb. sauerkraut
½ lb. smoked sausage
2 Tbsp. bacon drippings
2 Tbsp. flour

1 small onion, minced
1 Tbsp. paprika
3 Tbsp. sour cream
Salt (if needed)

Squeeze sauerkraut well and save juice. Cook sauerkraut in 2 quarts of water till it softens. Meantime, heat bacon drippings in pan. Add flour; stir and fry until the mixture is light beige, then add the onion and cook for another 5 minutes. Take off the heat; stir in paprika and immediately add 1 cup cold water. Whip until smooth. Pour reserved sauerkraut juice into a soup pot; add flour and onion mixture, sliced sausage, and the cooked sauerkraut. Cook 10 to 15 minutes. In soup tureen, mix the sour cream and a cup of the hot sauerkraut broth. Add salt if needed.

Micheal and Ruth Bartolf, Oxbow and District Lions Club
Oxbow, Saskatchewan, Canada

SUMMER SQUASH SOUP

Time: 30 minutes.

1 Tbsp. olive oil
1 medium size yellow squash
1 medium size zucchini squash
¾ c. celery leaves, packed
3 c. chicken broth or vegetable
   broth

¼ c. fresh basil
½ tsp. sea salt
¼ tsp. white pepper
Chopped chives or parsley for
   garnish

In large saucepan, saute onion in oil until limp. Dice squashes and add to mixture along with celery leaves and fresh basil. Add 1 cup of broth and simmer gently until vegetables are tender. Cool to room temperature and then blend in batches to a smooth thick consistency, adding more broth as needed. Return to saucepan and add seasonings. Taste and adjust to taste. Heat again to serve hot or refrigerate to serve cold. Soup should be rich and creamy, not watery. Garnish with chopped chives or parsley before serving. Serves 2 to 4.

Comments: Wonderful as a first course either hot or cold.

PDG Jim Schiebel, Hilton Lions Club
Hilton, NY, USA

We need some clouds in our life to have a beautiful sunset.

BROCCOLI SQUASH SOUP

2 c. chopped, peeled butternut or acorn squash
1 c. chopped, peeled broccoli stalks
1 medium tomato, peeled and seeded
3 c. chicken stock
2 c. small broccoli florets
1 tsp. cider vinegar
Dash of hot pepper sauce
2 tsp. sugar

In large saucepan over high heat, combine squash, broccoli, tomato, and 2 cups chicken stock; bring to boil. Cook for 7 to 10 minutes or until vegetables are tender. Let cool slightly. In food processor or blender, process squash mixture in batches until smooth. In same saucepan over high heat, heat the remaining 1 cup chicken stock until boiling. Add broccoli florets and cook for about 3 minutes until tender. Stir in vinegar, hot pepper sauce, and pureed squash mixture. Repeat. Stir in sugar just before serving. Serves 4.

Micheal and Ruth Bartolf, Oxbow and District Lions Club
Oxbow, Saskatchewan, Canada

CREAMY CARROT SOUP

Already-prepared frozen carrots and canned broth are the secrets to the speed of this heavenly soup.

1 small onion
1 Tbsp. oil
Salt and pepper
½ tsp. ground cumin
10 oz. pkg. frozen carrots
1½ c. chicken stock or canned broth
¼ c. heavy cream
1 Tbsp. chopped fresh parsley

Chop the onion. In a soup pot, heat the oil over medium-low heat. Add the onion and ¼ teaspoon salt. Cover and cook until tender, 5 minutes. Stir in the cumin. Add the carrots, stock, and ⅛ teaspoon pepper. Bring to a simmer. Cook until carrots are heated through, about 2 minutes. In a blender or food processor, puree the carrot mixture, in batches if necessary, until smooth. Return to pot. Stir in the cream and warm over low heat until soup is heated through. Taste for seasoning and add salt and pepper if needed. Sprinkle with parsley before serving. Makes 4 servings.

Per serving: 126 calories, 2 g protein, 10 g fat, 204 mg sodium, 8 g carbohydrate, 20 mg cholesterol.

Barbara Joy Hess, Clarence Lions Club
Clarence Center, NY, USA

The measure of a man is not how tall he is,
but how much his neighbors respect him.

ROYAL CARROT SOUP

3 c. chicken broth
2 c. fresh grapefruit juice
6 to 8 medium carrots (1 lb.),
    pared and cut in chunks

1 medium onion, cut in chunks
¾ tsp. cumin
½ tsp. cinnamon
1 c. plain low fat yogurt

In large saucepan, combine broth, grapefruit juice, carrots, onion, cumin, and cinnamon. Simmer 25 minutes or until carrots are tender. Puree vegetables and cooking liquid in blender. Return to saucepan. Heat and add yogurt. Serves 6.

Micheal and Ruth Bartolf, Oxbow and District Lions Club
Oxbow, Saskatchewan, Canada

LIMA BEAN SOUP

1 small onion
1 Tbsp. oil
28 oz. can tomatoes
16 oz. pork and beans
16 oz. frozen lima beans

1 Tbsp. brown sugar
¼ tsp. salt
16 oz. kidney beans
16 oz. Great Northern beans
Cheddar cheese (small amount)

Cook onion in oil. Add tomatoes, pork and beans, frozen lima beans, and brown sugar. Simmer till limas are tender. Add kidney and Great Northern beans. Heat till all is thoroughly hot. Serve in bowls. Sprinkle with Cheddar cheese.

I would like to dedicate this recipe to my mother, Grace Myers.

Doris Brewer, wife of Lion Guy Brewer,
Silver Run Union Mills Lions Club
Silver Run, MD, USA

PUMPKIN SOUP

4 c. chicken stock
2 c. diced pumpkin
½ tsp. cinnamon
½ tsp. nutmeg
½ tsp. coriander
Salt and pepper (to taste)

4 apples, peeled, cored, and
    diced
1 small onion
½ c. yogurt
1 c. apple cider
¼ c. chopped chives (optional)

In large pot, bring stock to boil. Add apples, pumpkin, onion, and spices. Simmer, partly covered, for 30 minutes. In small bowl, whisk together cider and yogurt till smooth. Stir into soup and reheat. Add salt and pepper to taste. Sprinkle servings with chives.

Micheal and Ruth Bartolf, Oxbow and District Lions Club
Oxbow, Saskatchewan, Canada

BEET, DILL, AND CARAWAY SOUP

1 onion
1 Tbsp. butter
Salt and pepper
5 beets (about 5 c. shredded)
1¾ c. chicken stock or canned
    broth

2 c. water
¼ tsp. caraway seeds
1 Tbsp. chopped fresh dill
Sour cream

Chop the onion. In a soup pot, melt the butter over medium-low heat. Add the onion and ½ teaspoon salt. Cover and cook until softened, about 5 minutes.

Meanwhile, peel and shred the beets. Add to the pot with the chicken stock, water, caraway seeds, and ¼ teaspoon pepper. Cover the pot and simmer until the beets are almost tender, about 10 minutes. Add the dill and continue cooking 5 minutes. Serve the soup garnished with a dollop of sour cream. Makes 4 servings.

Per serving: 122 calories, 4 g protein, 4 g fat, 420 mg sodium, 19 g carbohydrate, 8 mg cholesterol.

Barbara Joy Hess, Clarence Lions Club
Clarence Center, NY, USA

BEET SOUP

1 bunch small beets
1 qt. water
1 onion, chopped
Juice of a lemon

1 Tbsp. sugar
½ tsp. salt
1 pt. sour cream

Wash beets. Cut off greens one inch from tops. Cook 20 minutes or until tender, then skin. Grate with coarse grater or dice if preferred. Add remaining ingredients except sour cream. Boil 15 minutes. Chill thoroughly. Add sour cream to soup before serving. Serve heated. (Be careful to heat slowly, stirring constantly. Do not allow to boil.)

Micheal and Ruth Bartolf, Oxbow and District Lions Club
Oxbow, Saskatchewan, Canada

It doesn't do any good to sit up and take notice if you just keep on sitting.

❧ ❧ ❧

The easiest way to get to sleep is to
count your blessings instead of your problems.

CREAM OF ASPARAGUS SOUP

2 lb. fresh asparagus
4 Tbsp. butter or oleo
4 large shallots, chopped
6 Tbsp. Wondra flour
¼ tsp. saffron

6 c. chicken broth
2 egg yolks
1 c. half & half
White pepper to taste

Cut off tips of asparagus. Drop in boiling water for 30 seconds; drain and set aside. Cut remaining stalks into ½ inch lengths. Melt ½ of butter and saute the stalks for 5 minutes. Set aside.

In another pot, melt remaining butter and stir in flour. Cook 1 to 2 minutes, without browning. Add saffron, stock, and sauteed asparagus. Simmer 15 minutes. Pass through strainer or puree in blender. Cool slightly. Whisk egg yolks and half & half. Add to pureed mixture and cook over low heat for 5 minutes. Season with white pepper. Garnish with tips. Makes 6 to 8 servings.

Joanne Tuttle, Conroe Noon Lions Club
Conroe, TX, USA

FRESH TOMATO-ORANGE SOUP

3½ lb. plum tomatoes (about 20)
1 Tbsp. olive oil
2 carrots, diced
1 small onion, diced
1 garlic clove, minced
4 c. canned vegetable broth
1½ tsp. fresh chopped thyme or
    ½ tsp. dried

¼ tsp. salt
¼ tsp. pepper
½ tsp. grated orange peel
Orange peel and fresh thyme for
    garnish (optional)

In a large saucepot of boiling water, place tomatoes for 60 seconds. With slotted spoon, remove to a bowl of cold water for 1 minute, then peel off skins. Seed and dice tomatoes; set aside. Discard boiling water; dry pot. In the same saucepan, over medium-high heat, heat oil. Add carrots, onion, and garlic and saute about 10 minutes until carrot is softened. Add tomatoes, broth, thyme, salt, and pepper. Heat to boiling, then reduce heat to low, partially cover, and simmer 45 minutes, stirring occasionally.

In a blender container, in batches, pour the tomato mixture; puree. Pour into bowl, then stir in orange peel. Serve at room temperature or chill. Makes 6 servings.

Per serving: 104 calories, 3 g protein, 4 g fat, 796 mg sodium, 18 g carbohydrate, 0 mg cholesterol.

Mrs. Mike Nowicki, Clarence Lions Club
Clarence Center, NY, USA

TOMATO CHOWDER

½ c. diced side bacon
1 medium onion, minced
1 c. diced carrots
1 c. potatoes
1 c. diced celery
½ c. boiling water

2 c. canned tomatoes
4 Tbsp. flour
½ tsp. salt
¼ tsp. pepper
4 c. milk, scalded

Saute bacon until brown; add onion, carrot, potato, and celery and saute just until the onion begins to brown. Add boiling water; cover and cook until vegetables are tender. Add tomatoes and heat to boiling. In a separate pan, blend oil, flour, salt, and pepper; add milk gradually and cook until smooth. Add vegetable mixture to milk; heat and serve immediately. Do not boil. Makes 6 servings.

Micheal and Ruth Bartolf, Oxbow and District Lions Club
Oxbow, Saskatchewan, Canada

BUD'S BEAN SOUP

1 lb. dry navy beans, rinsed and
   picked over
10 c. water, divided
1 small ham hock or 1 lb. pork
   neck bones, spareribs, or
   country ribs
1 bay leaf
1 tsp. pepper

1 large onion, chopped
2 large ribs celery, chopped fine
¼ c. parsley
2 cloves garlic, minced
1 tsp. salt
1 tsp. oregano
1 tsp. basil
½ tsp. nutmeg

In large saucepan or Dutch oven, soak beans overnight in six cups water (or bring to boil, boil two minutes, and let stand, covered, one hour). Add remaining four cups water, the ham hock, bay leaf, and pepper. Bring to boil. Reduce heat, cover, and simmer 1¼ hours or until beans are almost tender. Stir in remaining ingredients, cover, and cook 20 to 30 minutes more until beans are tender. Discard bay leaf. Cut meat from bones and return to soup.

PDG Bud Myers, Guiding Lion, Sunrise Lions Club
(chartered June, 1999)
Mexico, MO

Some things are loved because they are valuable,
others are valuable because they are loved.

❧ ❧ ❧

If you think education is expensive, try ignorance.

2075-99

GRAIN, GREEN, AND BEAN SOUP

Time: 20 minutes.

1 Tbsp. olive oil
1 large carrot, chopped
1 celery stalk, chopped
1 small onion, chopped
3 c. vegetable stock
1 c. sliced, packed greens (kale or
  bok choy are good)

1 c. cooked garbanzo beans
1 c. cooked shell macaroni
Sea salt to taste
Shoyu to taste

In large saucepan, heat olive oil and saute carrot, celery, and onion for 5 minutes over medium heat until limp. Do not brown or burn. Add vegetable broth and chopped greens. Cover and simmer for 10 minutes. Add cooked beans and pasta; simmer until heated through. Season to taste with sea salt and shoyu and serve with garnish of chopped parsley or green scallions. Serves 4.

Comments: Easy to make and delicious to eat.

PDG Jim Schiebel, Hilton Lions Club
Hilton, NY, USA

SAUSAGE BEAN SOUP

¾ lb. bulk Italian sausage
½ c. chopped onion
1 garlic clove, minced
1 (15½ oz.) can butter beans,
  rinsed and drained
1 (15 oz.) can black beans, rinsed
  and drained

1 (14½ oz.) can diced tomatoes
  (undrained)
1 (14½ oz.) can beef broth
1 Tbsp. minced fresh basil or 1
  tsp. dried basil
2 Tbsp. shredded Parmesan
  cheese

In a large saucepan, cook sausage, onion, and garlic until the sausage is browned; drain. Add beans, tomatoes, broth, and basil. Cover and simmer for 10 minutes. Sprinkle each serving with Parmesan cheese. Yield: 4 to 6 servings.

CRABMEAT SOUP

1 stick margarine
1 onion, chopped
3 cans evaporated milk

2 cans cream of mushroom soup
1 can cream of celery soup
1 pkg. lump crabmeat

Saute onion in margarine. Add milk and soups. Add crabmeat. Simmer for 20 to 30 minutes. Stir occasionally, making sure all ingredients are blended well. Makes 4 to 6 servings.

This soup is delicious. Everyone usually asks for another bowl.

Lion Larry Chaudoir, Mandeville Lions Club
Mandeville, LA, USA

134

ROSARIO RESORT SEAFOOD SOUP - SOPA DEL MAR

Fish stock (about 2 to 3 qt.)
Clam juice
3 oz. Pernod
Cod
Broccoli
Fresh tomatoes
Onion
Parsley
Celery
Carrot
Saffron
Lemon juice
Pepper
Italian seasoning - oregano, basil

Sarah Wehling, Bothell Lions Club
Bothell, WA, USA

CHARLIE'S CLAM CHOWDER

1 lb. frozen minced clams
1½ pkg. frozen country-style
   hash browns
1 large can chopped tomatoes
1 qt. *Clamato* juice
4 large celery stalks, chopped
1 large yellow onion, chopped
4 slices crisp bacon, crumbled
Salt and pepper

Combine ingredients in large saucepan. Simmer over medium heat until done. Garnish with oyster crackers. Makes approximately 8 servings.

Charles Kaysner, Bothell Lions Club
Bothell, WA, USA

CORN AND SEAFOOD CHOWDER

1 Tbsp. butter
1 green bell pepper, chopped
1 clove garlic, minced
¾ tsp. cumin
¼ tsp. dried thyme
Salt
2 c. chicken stock or canned
   broth
1 c. clam juice
½ c. half & half
10 oz. pkg. frozen corn
½ tsp. hot-pepper sauce
6 oz. crabmeat (about 1½ c.)
Paprika (optional)

In a soup pot, melt the butter over medium-low heat. Add the green pepper. Cover and cook until tender, about 5 minutes. Stir in the garlic, cumin, thyme, and ½ teaspoon salt and cook about 1 minute. Add the chicken stock, clam juice, and 1 cup water. Bring to a simmer, reduce heat, and add the half & half, corn, hot-pepper sauce, and crabmeat. Continue cooking until heated through, about 5 minutes. Sprinkle with paprika if you like. Makes 6 servings.

Per serving: 130 calories, 9 g protein, 6 g fat, 387 mg sodium, 12 g carbohydrate, 41 mg cholesterol.

Mrs. Lucy Aiken, Clarence Lions Club
Clarence Center, NY, USA

OVEN STEW

1 lb. stew meat
1 c. carrots
½ c. celery
3 medium potatoes
1 medium onion

Salt and pepper
3 Tbsp. tapioca
1 tsp. sugar
1½ c. tomato juice

Put in casserole in this order. Bake at 300° for 5 hours.

J. Cozean, East Haddam Community Lions Club
Moodus, CT

5 HOUR STEW

2 lb. lean stew meat
2 onions, chopped
8 to 12 carrots, sliced
8 stalks celery, sliced
8 potatoes, cubed

1 tsp. salt
2 c. tomato juice
1 Tbsp. sugar
6 Tbsp. Minute tapioca

Mix all ingredients thoroughly in a casserole; cover. Bake at 250° for 5 hours.

Used unpeeled red potatoes. Slice celery and carrots about ¼ to ½ inch thick. Did not chop onions fine.

Virginia Bayer (Lion), Franklin Park Lions Club
Park Ridge, IL, USA

BRUNSWICK STEW

1 (6 to 7 lb.) hen
4 lb. fresh pork
Little chicken stock
3 medium onions, ground
3 Tbsp. mustard
Juice of 3 to 4 lemons

4 cans tomatoes
3 large cans white corn
1 qt. bottle catsup
½ tsp. red pepper
1 Tbsp. Tabasco sauce

Boil the hen in salted water and the pork in salted water. Remove all the meat from the bones and grind meat, onions, and tomatoes. Put in a large kettle and add other ingredients as well as salt and pepper to taste. Cook over low heat until thick, stirring often. *G-O-O-D!*

Lion John E. Chafin, Foley Lions Club
Foley, AL, USA

The best use of this life is to spend it for something that will outlast it.

OLD-FASHIONED BROWN BEEF STEW

2 lb. beef cubes
2 Tbsp. fat
4 c. boiling water
1 or 2 bay leaves
1 tsp. sugar
½ tsp. paprika
6 carrots, sliced
Celery (optional)

1 Tbsp. lemon juice
1 tsp. Worcestershire sauce
1 clove garlic
1 Tbsp. salt
½ tsp. pepper
Dash of allspice
1 lb. onions, sliced
4 to 6 potatoes, cubed

Brown meat; add water and other ingredients. Cover. Simmer 2 hours. Add vegetables. Makes 6 to 8 servings.

Lion Jerrie Jefferson, East Anne Arundel Lions Club
Pasadena, MD, USA

ROSALIE'S ARDENNES STEW

1½ lb. beef stew meat
3 Tbsp. flour
1½ tsp. salt
½ tsp. ground pepper
2 Tbsp. oil
2 c. hot water
½ c. diced onion

1 clove garlic, minced
4 carrots, thickly sliced
3 potatoes, quartered and sliced
1 can green beans (undrained)
1 Tbsp. catsup
1 tsp. Worcestershire sauce

Roll meat in flour, salt, and pepper. Brown in oil in large pot, stirring occasionally. When browned, stir in any remaining flour mixture. Add water, onion, and garlic. Cover and simmer until tender. Thirty minutes before cooking time is up, add carrots and potatoes. When vegetables are tender, add green beans, catsup, Worcestershire, and more water if necessary.

Carol Speicher, Columbus Lions Club
Columbus, NE, USA

CHICKEN STEW

3 lb. chicken, cut in 8 pieces
2 medium onions, chopped
1 medium bell pepper, chopped
3 cloves garlic, chopped

½ c. flour
Oil
Salt and pepper
Tabasco sauce

Cut up chicken; discard back and wing tips. Salt and pepper well. Heat oil ¾ inch deep in large, heavy pot. Brown chicken on all sides. Remove and reserve chicken. Add flour to make dark roux.

Chop 2 onions, 1 bell pepper, and 3 cloves garlic. Add to roux. Cook until wilted. Return chicken to pot. Cover with water. Cook, covered, for 3 hours over low heat. Check seasoning. Add salt, pepper, and Tabasco to taste. Serve over hot boiled rice or noodles.

John Hamner, Bellville Lions Club
Bellville, GA, USA

MOROCCAN CHICKEN STEW

1 Tbsp. vegetable oil
6 whole chicken legs (about 3 lb.), separated into thighs and drumsticks
1 large onion, chopped
1 clove garlic, minced
1 Tbsp. ground coriander
1½ tsp. ground cumin
1½ tsp. ground cinnamon
1 tsp. ground ginger

1 tsp. ground turmeric
½ tsp. salt
¼ tsp. crushed red-pepper flakes
14½ oz. can tomatoes
¾ lb. carrots, sliced diagonally into ¼ inch pieces (about 2 c.)
¼ c. toasted almonds
1½ tsp. confectioners sugar
Cooked rice or couscous
1 Tbsp. minced parsley

In a large frying pan, heat oil over medium-high heat. Add half the chicken pieces and brown well on both sides, about 10 minutes. Remove chicken and repeat with remaining pieces. Set aside. Pour off all but 2 tablespoons of the fat from pan. Add onion and garlic and cook 5 minutes, stirring frequently. Stir in coriander, cumin, 1 teaspoon of the cinnamon, the ginger, turmeric, salt, and crushed red-pepper flakes. Add the tomatoes with their juice and ¾ cup water. Break up tomatoes with a spoon and scrape up any brown bits from the bottom of the pan.

Return the chicken pieces to the pan and add the carrots. Bring stew to a boil, then reduce heat to low. Cover and simmer until the vegetables are tender and chicken is done, about 35 minutes.

Meanwhile, place the almonds, confectioners sugar, and the remaining ½ teaspoon cinnamon in the work bowl of a food processor or blender. Process until the mixture is finely chopped. Set aside.

Serve the stew over rice or couscous, sprinkled with the parsley. Pass the almond mixture to sprinkle on top. Makes 6 servings.

Work time: 25 minutes. Total time: 1 hour and 20 minutes.

Per serving: 426 calories, 33 g protein, 2 6 g fat, 408 mg sodium, 16 g carbohydrate, 109 mg cholesterol.

Mrs. Lucy Aiken, Clarence Lions Club
Clarence Center, NY, USA

Faith does not demand that we win, it does demand that we keep trying.

*Oh, to be half as wonderful as my children thought I was,
and only half as stupid as my teenagers think I am.*

FIREMEN'S STEW

1 pkg. beef franks
8 medium potatoes
6 large carrots

2 medium size onions
Salt
Pepper

Boil franks, potatoes, and carrots till done, then drain. Saute onions in about 1 tablespoon of oil until light brown. Drain. Save oil and make brown gravy. Cut franks and carrots into bite-size and potatoes. Put the brown gravy into a 2 quart stew pot and add franks, carrots, potatoes, and onions. Mix well. Salt and pepper to taste and simmer for 5 minutes. Serve with rice and homemade biscuits.

Lion Mary Clark, Foley Lions Club
Foley, AL, USA

FRANKFURTER GUMBO

6 to 12 franks, sliced ½ inch
   thick
1 can drained okra
1 can tomatoes
1 can tomato sauce
6 to 8 oz. glass tomato juice
1 or 2 onions

Diced garlic
Diced celery
Thyme spice
Cayenne pepper
Black pepper
Oregano spice

Slice franks, drain okra, and dice the garlic. Put about 6 tablespoons of grease in large saucepan and cook for a few minutes - not long enough to brown franks, then begin to add the rest of the ingredients. Make large or small amount. Put in ingredients accordingly and spice accordingly also. Let cook for about two hours for best results. If it starts to get too thick, add a little more tomato juice. Fix some 1 minute rice and place in soup bowls. Pour gumbo on top. *Delicious!*

Really, you just clean out your icebox. If you want to and have it, you can add some sliced fresh corn. It makes about 6 to 10 servings - all according to how much you want to fix.

This is so good to put on early on a Saturday, go to football game, come home, and have a big bowl. Especially on a *cold night!*

Barbara Vaughn, Conroe Lioness Club
Conroe, TX, Montgomery County

Joy shared is joy doubled. Sorrow shared is sorrow halved.

MARIE'S GUMBO

1 c. oil
1 c. flour
2 c. chopped celery
2 c. finely chopped onion
1 c. minced bell pepper
1 qt. water or chicken broth

1 hen (approx. 4 lb.), cut in
   serving pieces
1 qt. oysters and liquor
1 Tbsp. file powder (sassafras)
Salt to taste

Into heavy iron skillet, pour oil. Add flour, stirring until well mixed. Brown over medium heat, stirring constantly - it scorches easily. Into this roux, add the water or chicken broth and the hen pieces. Simmer until chicken is tender and falling off bones. Remove bones, skin, and skim off chicken fat. Add oysters and bring to boil, stirring, and boil 2 minutes. Add the file powder and salt to taste. Do not use pepper! Serve over hot, fluffy rice or plain. Makes about a gallon.

This is an authentic Weeks Bay (Baldwin County, Alabama) Creole Gumbo - it is not as dark nor as spicy as Cajun Gumbo.

Lion Jane Nelson, Foley Lions Club
Foley, AL, USA

Many hands make burdens lighter.

❦ ❦ ❦

Blessed are the flexible, for they shall not be bent out of shape.

❦ ❦ ❦

Don't go where the path leads.
Rather, go where there is no path and leave a trail.

❦ ❦ ❦

It's nice to be important, but it's more important to be nice.

CHICKEN, HAM, AND SHRIMP GUMBO

This recipe can easily be cut in half for a small party or leftovers can be frozen.

2 large onions
4 ribs celery
2 cloves garlic, minced
3½ tsp. salt
2 whole chickens (about 3 lb. each)
4 qt. water
1 red or green bell pepper
1 c. oil
8 oz. ham steak (1 piece), cut into ½ inch pieces

1 c. flour
1½ tsp. dried thyme
1½ tsp. dried oregano
½ tsp. cayenne pepper
½ tsp. black pepper
2 (9 oz.) pkg. frozen artichoke hearts, thawed
1 lb. medium shrimp, shelled and deveined
16 c. cooked long-grain rice

One day before serving: Cut one onion into quarters. Cut 2 ribs celery into 2 inch pieces. Make a stock by placing onion, celery, half the garlic, and 2 teaspoons of the salt in large stock pot with chickens and water. Bring to a boil, cover, and simmer until chicken meat falls off the bones, about 2 hours. Remove chicken and set aside; strain stock and discard vegetables. When chicken is cool enough to handle, discard skin, pull meat from bones, and cut into bite-size pieces.

While stock cooks, chop remaining onion, celery, and the bell pepper. In a large, heavy pot, heat oil until very hot. Add ham and cook, stirring constantly, until browned. Remove with slotted spoon and set aside. Stir flour into oil and cook, stirring constantly with a wooden spoon, until mixture is medium-brown, about 10 minutes. Add chopped vegetables, thyme, oregano, cayenne, black pepper, and remaining garlic and salt. Cook, stirring constantly, until flour mixture turns dark-brown, about 10 minutes. Take care not to burn.

Add 8 cups chicken stock (save remaining stock for other use). Bring to boil, reduce heat, and simmer, uncovered, 15 minutes or until vegetables are tender. Stir in chicken and ham. Remove from heat and let cool. Cover and refrigerate overnight.

Just before serving: In a heavy pot over medium-high heat, bring gumbo to a boil, stirring occasionally. Add artichoke hearts and shrimp and cook until shrimp is opaque, about 5 minutes. Serve over cooked rice. Makes 16 servings.

Work time: 1½ hours. Total time: 4 hours and 30 minutes.

Per serving: 444 calories, 27 g protein, 22 g fat, 829 mg sodium, 32 g carbohydrate, 92 mg cholesterol.

Lion John J. Hess, Clarence Lions Club
Clarence Center, NY, USA

HAMBURG CHOWDER OR VENISON CHOWDER

1 lb. hamburger or ground
    venison
½ c. ground onion
½ c. ground potatoes
½ c. ground carrots

1 qt. tomatoes
1 qt. boiling water
Salt to taste

Brown meat and add all ingredients; cook for a long time.

Venison hamburger is very good!
**Pauline and PDG Gerald Nuffer, South Jefferson Lions Club
Adams, NY**

BROCCOLI AND CHEESE SOUP

6 c. water
1 (10 oz.) pkg. frozen chopped
    broccoli
1 medium onion, chopped
1 (8 oz.) loaf Velveeta cheese
2 tsp. pepper
½ to ¾ tsp. salt

½ tsp. garlic powder
1 c. milk
1 c. half & half
¼ c. butter or margarine
½ c. flour
½ c. cold water

Bring water to a boil in a 3 quart Dutch oven; add broccoli and onion. Reduce heat and simmer, uncovered, 10 minutes. Add cheese and seasonings, stirring until cheese melts. Stir in milk, half & half, and butter; cook over low heat until thoroughly heated. Combine flour and water, stirring until smooth. Gradually add to broccoli mixture, stirring constantly; cook over medium heat until thickened, stirring occasionally. Yield: 2½ quarts.
**Pam Caldwell, Mexico Sunrise Lions Club
Mexico, MO**

*There is a light for you straight ahead,
but you have to keep your chin up to see it.*

❦ ❦ ❦

Don't talk unless you can improve the silence.

❦ ❦ ❦

*Wisdom is hardly understood in a few minutes,
and rarely learned in a lifetime.*

❦ ❦ ❦

When life gives you lemons, make lemonade.

SANDWICHES

BARBECUED TUNA SANDWICH

1 (7 oz.) can tuna
2 Tbsp. onions
½ c. chopped celery
⅓ c. catsup
1 tsp. mustard

1 Tbsp. sugar
1 Tbsp. vinegar
½ tsp. salt
6 hamburger buns or other choice

If tuna is packed in oil, use the oil to saute onions and celery till golden. Or, use olive oil. Add rest of the ingredients, breaking up the tuna last. Simmer about 3 minutes. Divide between 6 buns and serve warm.

Fish oil is not considered bad for our cholesterol.

Pat Worden, South Jefferson Lions Club
Adams, NY

HOT TUNA SALAD BUNS

1 c. cubed American cheese
3 hard cooked eggs, chopped
1 can tuna, flaked
2 Tbsp. diced celery
1 Tbsp. minced onion

2 Tbsp. sweet pickles, diced
1 Tbsp. lemon juice
½ c. Miracle Whip
Dash of salt
Pepper to taste

Combine all ingredients and put in buns. Wrap in foil (may put several in a packet). Heat in slow (300°) oven for 30 minutes on a cookie sheet.

Myra Franke, Plato Lions Club
Plato, MN, USA

SALMON-SALAD SANDWICHES

Crunchy apple bits are the surprise element in this nourishing sandwich.

1 lemon
½ apple
1 scallion
2 (7½ oz.) cans salmon

⅓ c. mayonnaise
Salt and pepper
8 slices whole-wheat bread

Squeeze 2 teaspoons juice from the lemon into a mixing bowl. Cut the apple into ¼ inch dice and toss with the lemon juice. Chop the scallion and add it to the bowl. Drain salmon and add with the mayonnaise, ¼ teaspoon salt, and ¼ teaspoon pepper. Taste for seasoning and add more salt or pepper if needed. Divide among 4 slices of bread. Top with remaining bread. Makes 4 servings.

Per serving: 380 calories, 24 g protein, 21 g fat, 962 mg sodium, 25 mg carbohydrate, 46 mg cholesterol.

Lion John J. Hess, Clarence Lions Club
Clarence Center, NY, USA

CRABMEAT SALAD

8 oz. crabmeat
4 oz. mayonnaise
1 small onion, chopped
½ green pepper, chopped

2 oz. pickled cucumbers, diced
2 Tbsp. fresh dill weed
1 dash of ketchup
Salt and pepper to taste

Cut crabmeat into small pieces and mix with the other ingredients. Serve on slices of toast topped with a lemon slice. Serves 4.

Lai Johnsen, Godthaab (Nook) Lions Club
Nook, Greenland

OLIVE-EGG SALAD FILLING

10 hard-boiled eggs, finely
   chopped
1 c. finely chopped pimento-
   stuffed olives

Salt to taste
¼ c. mayonnaise

Combine all. Chill. This makes 4½ cups.

Bread
1 (3 oz.) pkg. cream cheese,
   softened

½ Mustard-Mayonnaise Sauce

Mustard-Mayonnaise Sauce: Beat three ½ teaspoon dry mustard with 1¾ cups mayonnaise. Layer this with Pecan-Chicken filling on bread. Spread with cheese mix above.

Sarah Wehling, Bothell Lions Club
Bothell, WA, USA

Patience: The ability to idle your motor when
you feel like stripping your gears.

❦ ❦ ❦

If you worry, why pray? If you pray, why worry?

❦ ❦ ❦

If you aren't as close to God as you once were,
make no mistake about who moved.

TEA SANDWICHES

Use any bread - white, wheat, rye, raisin. Cut off crusts; cut any shape - round, triangle, or diamond. To keep, put on plates and cover with foil. Estimate 3 to 4 per person.

Fillings:

Cream cheese, minced cooked mushrooms, and ground nutmeg.

Chopped watercress, softened butter, and grated onion.

Strawberry marmalade, chopped pecans, and cream cheese.

Minced crab, mayonnaise, and ground turmeric.

Mashed avocado, fresh lemon juice, and hot pepper sauce.

Minced chicken, almonds, curry powder, and dairy sour cream.

Creamed Roquefort cheese, cream cheese, and sherry.

Sliced tomatoes, spread with smoked cheese.

Minced cucumbers, dairy sour cream, and capers.

Ginger marmalade and chopped walnuts.

Chopped cooked lobster, mushrooms, lemon juice, and mayonnaise.

Chopped walnuts, raisins, maraschino cherries, and cream cheese.

Chopped hard cooked eggs, crumbled bacon, minced sweet pickles, prepared mustard, and mayonnaise.

Minced clams, grated onion, and yogurt.

Chopped dried beef, hard cooked eggs, minced celery, and dairy sour cream.

Cottage cheese, chopped stuffed olives, onion juice, and salt.

Deviled ham, minced sweet pickle, and chili sauce.

Chopped dates, minced nuts, cream cheese, and pineapple juice.

Mashed salmon, fresh lemon juice, and mayonnaise.

Ground chicken, minced almonds, mayonnaise, and cayenne.

Chopped mint, chopped parsley, minced onion, mayonnaise, and paprika.

Guava jelly and cream cheese.

Sarah Wehling, Bothell Lions Club
Bothell, WA, USA

HOT SANDWICHES

1 can corned beef (remove fat)
4 hard cooked eggs
½ lb. Velveeta cheese
4 stalks celery
½ onion

½ c. Miracle Whip
2 Tbsp. sugar
2 Tbsp. vinegar
Salt and pepper to taste

Chop the first 5 ingredients. Combine the Miracle Whip, sugar, and vinegar. Fold all ingredients and dressing. Spread filling in each bun generously. Wrap each bun in foil and refrigerate. This makes 20 buns. When ready to serve, bake at 350°F. until heated through, about 30 to 45 minutes.

If used right away, refrigeration is not necessary.

My kids like it and their friends love it!

Mildred Weir, Bentley Lions Club

SNAPPY LUNCH'S WORLD FAMOUS PORK CHOP SANDWICH

Pork chops (boneless)

Batter:

2 c. plain flour
2 eggs, beaten
2 Tbsp. sugar

Salt to taste
About 1 c. milk

Place flour in mixing bowl; add sugar and salt. Add eggs and gradually add milk. Beat mixture until the batter is completely smooth, not lumpy or watery. The batter should run off the spoon without being watery and stick to the pork chop and not run off.

Remove the bone and fat from the pork chop. Pound the pork chop to tenderize. Wash pork and dry pork chop. Dip the *pork chop* in the *batter*. Place in greased hot skillet, but not too hot. The pork chop needs to cook done, brown, and not burn the batter. Turn, then brown on the other side. Yield: Enough batter for 12 large chops.

Note: For onion rings, slightly thin batter by adding more milk.

Author of "*The Best of Mayberry*" cookbook, honored in "America's Best" recipes by Oxmoor House, Inc.

Betty Conley Lyerly, Mount Airy Foothills Lions Club
Mount Airy, NC, USA

HOT CORNED BEEF SANDWICH

1 can corned beef
1 c. Velveeta cheese cubes
2 Tbsp. sliced green olives
2 Tbsp. chopped green peppers

1 Tbsp. chopped onion
½ c. catsup
1 tsp. Worcestershire sauce
6 hamburger buns

Mix all ingredients together and fill buns. Place in baking dish and cover with foil. Bake at 350° for about 20 minutes, just long enough to melt the cheese.

This is a husband's favorite!

Pat Worden, South Jefferson Lions Club
Adams, NY

WALDORF SANDWICHES

1 c. apples, peeled and chopped
1 rib celery, chopped
½ c. pecans, chopped
1 (8 oz.) pkg. cream cheese,
   softened

1 Tbsp. mayonnaise
2 Tbsp. sugar
1 tsp. lemon juice

Mix all ingredients 1 day before needed and refrigerate. Spread on raisin bread that has had crust cut. Cut sandwiches in halves and in halves again so that you have a triangular shaped sandwich. Makes enough spread for about 2 small loaves raisin bread.

Excellent for teas, showers, etc.

Nettie Favara, Greenwood Lions Club
Greenwood, MS, USA

BAGNA CAUDO

½ c. pure virgin olive oil
6 cloves garlic, minced
1 Italian Vienna bread

1 small can anchovy fillets
Fresh vegetables

Put oil in saucepan and add garlic. Saute over very low heat for 15 minutes. Add minced anchovies and stir until smooth. Keep hot over warmer.

Prepare raw fresh vegetables, such as broccoli, cauliflower, pepper strips, celery, curly cabbage, or whatever you have. Dip vegetables in hot sauce with fondue forks. When sauce reduces to almost a paste at the end, dip pieces of Vienna bread.

Linda Worrall, Canaan Northwest Lions Club
Canaan, CT, USA

MUFFULETTA

New Orleans' favorite sandwich is the muffuletta, invented at the Central Grocery and clearly of Italian lineage. The pungent olive-salad topping is sure to wake up your taste buds.

1 clove garlic
¾ c. chopped green olives
¾ c. chopped black olives
⅓ c. chopped pimento
¼ c. chopped parsley
¾ tsp. dried oregano

¼ tsp. pepper
⅓ c. + 1 Tbsp. oil
1 large round loaf crusty bread
½ lb. sliced hard salami
½ lb. sliced baked ham
¼ lb. sliced Provolone cheese

Mince garlic and combine with the olives, pimento, parsley, oregano, pepper, and ⅓ cup oil. Cut bread horizontally about 1 inch from the bottom. Pull out some of the center, leaving a 1 inch shell. Brush remaining 1 tablespoon oil on the bottom of the loaf. Cover with salami, ham, and cheese. Fill the top half of the bread with the olive salad. Put bottom piece on top and invert. Wrap and refrigerate about 8 hours or overnight. Bring to room temperature before cutting into wedges. Makes 6 sandwiches.

Work time: 25 minutes. Total time: 25 minutes plus marinating.

Joann M. Brownell, Clarence Lions Club
Clarence Center, NY, USA

VEGETARIAN FAJITAS

4 large soft corn tortilla shells
1 c. sliced portabello mushrooms
   (or favorite)
½ c. diced red onion
½ c. deseeded Roma tomato
½ c. finely chopped broccoli

2 Tbsp. olive oil
2 cloves fresh garlic, crushed and
   finely chopped
1 c. loosely packed Italian "six
   blend" cheese

Combine mushrooms, onions, tomatoes, broccoli, garlic, and olive oil in bowl and blend thoroughly. Heat skillet over medium heat and add mix. Stir periodically until vegetables are heated but still firm, approximately 5 to 7 minutes. Remove from heat and divide equally among shells. Sprinkle cheese in like amounts over mix and wrap shells tightly, using toothpicks if necessary. Place on baking sheet in oven preheated to 350°F. and bake until done and cheese melts, approximately 7 to 10 minutes. Serve with picante sauce and sour cream.

A quick and easy lunch or a great half time snack during the game!

David L. Johnson, Princeton Lions Club
Princeton, IL, USA

BLACK BEAN AND VEGGIE BURGER

1 c. shredded zucchini
½ c. shredded carrot
⅓ c. finely chopped onion
2 cloves garlic, minced
1 (15 oz.) can black beans,
    rinsed, drained, and coarsely
    mashed
½ c. brown rice, cooked
    according to pkg. directions

1 egg
2 Tbsp. plain bread crumbs
1 Tbsp. chopped fresh oregano
    or 1 tsp. dried
1 tsp. ground cumin
⅛ tsp. salt
⅛ tsp. pepper

Preheat grill or broiler. In bowl, combine first four ingredients. Blot with paper towels to absorb excess liquid. Add remaining ingredients; stir to combine. Shape into 8 burgers. Grease grill or rack set in broiler pan. Grill or broil 10 to 12 minutes, turning once. Serve 2 patties per person, tucked into a tortilla spread with honey mustard. Serve chilled with tomato slices and radish sprouts. Makes 4 servings.

Per serving: 424 calories, 15 g protein, 83 g carbohydrate, 9 g fat, 0 mg cholesterol, 824 mg sodium.

Mrs. Lucy Aiken, Clarence Lions Club
Clarence Center, NY, USA

CHEESY TURKEY BURGER

1 Tbsp. vegetable oil
1 red onion, sliced
1 tsp. sugar
⅛ tsp. salt
⅛ tsp. pepper
1½ lb. ground turkey
½ c. finely chopped green pepper

3 cloves garlic, minced
4 oz. smoked Gouda, cubed
3 Tbsp. chopped fresh dill or 1
    Tbsp. dried
1½ Tbsp. paprika
1 Tbsp. caraway seeds

Preheat grill or broiler. Heat oil in skillet over medium-high heat. Add onion; cook 5 minutes, stirring, until softened. Add next three ingredients. Cook 5 minutes, stirring, until onions are caramelized. Combine next four ingredients. Shape into 4 burgers. On waxed paper, combine remaining ingredients; coat burgers with spices. Grill or broil 16 minutes, turning once, until cooked through. Serve on kaiser rolls with spinach leaves and onions. Makes 4 servings.

Per serving: 566 calories, 41 g protein, 38 g carbohydrate, 28 g fat, 104 mg cholesterol, 675 mg sodium.

Mrs. Lucy Aiken, Clarence Lions Club
Clarence Center, NY, USA

MOROCCAN TURKEY BURGERS

Burgers:

⅓ c. couscous (about 1 c. cooked)
1 lb. ground turkey
1 small onion, grated (about ¼ c.)
1 small zucchini, grated (about ½ c.)
¼ red pepper, finely chopped (about ¼ c.)

2 Tbsp. chopped fresh parsley
1 Tbsp. chopped fresh mint
½ tsp. salt
¼ tsp. pepper
4 (6 inch) whole-wheat pita breads
Shredded lettuce for serving

Garlic-Mint Mayonnaise:

¼ c. mayonnaise
2 tsp. chopped fresh mint

1 small clove garlic, minced

Cook the couscous according to package directions. Fluff it with a fork and set aside to cool. Heat broiler or prepare outdoor grill. In a large bowl, combine the cooled couscous with the turkey, onion, zucchini, red pepper, parsley, mint, salt, and pepper. Divide the mixture in fourths, shaping each portion into a 1¼ inch thick patty.

Place the patties on the grill, broiler pan or a foil-lined cookie sheet and cook, turning once, until burgers are firm, 7 to 8 minutes per side. (Turkey burgers need to be cooked through completely.)

Meanwhile, in a small bowl, combine mayonnaise, mint, and garlic. Blend well. Place each burger in a warm whole-wheat pita lined with shredded lettuce. Top it with 1 tablespoon of the Garlic-Mint Mayonnaise. Makes 4 servings.

Mrs. Lucy Aiken, Clarence Lions Club
Clarence Center, NY, USA

Swallowing angry words is a lot easier than having to eat them.

❦ ❦ ❦

Anyone who doesn't cultivate a sense of humor
may grow weeds on his disposition.

❦ ❦ ❦

I'd rather work with a man than jog with a walkman.

MINTED LAMB BURGER

½ c. low-fat plain yogurt
⅓ c. chopped cucumber
⅓ c. chopped red pepper
½ tsp. ground cumin
⅛ tsp. plus ¾ tsp. salt, divided
⅛ tsp. plus ½ tsp. cracked black pepper, divided

1½ lb. ground lamb
2 to 3 cloves garlic, minced
3 Tbsp. chopped fresh mint or 1 Tbsp. dried
1 (12 oz.) jar roasted red peppers, well drained

Preheat grill or broiler. In bowl, stir together yogurt, cucumber, red pepper, cumin, and ⅛ teaspoon each salt and cracked black pepper; cover and chill. In bowl, combine lamb, garlic, mint, and remaining ¾ teaspoon salt and ½ teaspoon pepper. Shape into 4 burgers. Grill or broil 10 to 12 minutes, turning once, for medium. Serve burgers wrapped in pita pockets with roasted peppers, lettuce, tomato slices, and yogurt sauce. Makes 4 servings.

Food Note: When preparing burgers, don't overwork the mixture too much. The burgers will become tough and heavy.

Per serving: 591 calories, 44 g protein, 43 g carbohydrate, 27 g fat, 126 mg cholesterol, 930 mg sodium.

Mrs. Lucy Aiken, Clarence Lions Club
Clarence Center, NY, USA

If you're too busy to laugh, you're too busy.

❧ ❧ ❧

Only a fool tests the water with both feet.

❧ ❧ ❧

Success is relative. The more success, the more relatives!

❧ ❧ ❧

Personality has the power to open doors,
but it takes character to keep them open.

MEXICAN BURGERS

1 lb. ground beef
½ c. chunky-style salsa
4 scallions, finely chopped (about ⅓ c.)
1 large clove garlic, minced
1 tsp. ground cumin
½ tsp. ground coriander
1 tsp. salt

½ tsp. pepper
4 medium (10 to 12 inch) flour tortillas
2 oz. Cheddar cheese, shredded (about ½ c.)
Shredded lettuce (for serving)
Sliced avocado (optional)
Assorted olives (optional)

Heat broiler or prepare outdoor grill. In a large bowl, combine beef, salsa, scallions, garlic, cumin, coriander, salt, and pepper. Mix to blend well. Divide mixture in fourths, shaping each portion into a long oval patty, about 1¼ inches thick. Place patties on grill, broiler pan, or a foil-lined cookie sheet and cook until done (5 to 6 minutes per side for medium).

Meanwhile, wrap the tortillas in foil. Place them away from the heat on a cooler part of the grill or the bottom rack of oven to warm, 3 to 5 minutes.

To assemble, place patties on warmed tortillas and top each with 2 table-spoons cheese and some shredded lettuce. Serve with sliced avocado and olives if desired. Makes 4 servings.

Work time: 20 minutes. Total time: 35 minutes.

Per serving: 493 calories, 29 g protein, 27 g fat, 1131 mg sodium, 37 g carbohydrate, 91 mg cholesterol.

Lion John J. Hess, Clarence Lions Club
Clarence Center, NY, USA

In the midst of everything, take time to love and laugh and pray.
Then life will be worth living each and every day.

❦ ❦ ❦

If you want to feel rich, just count all the things money can't buy.

❦ ❦ ❦

There are two lasting things we give our children -
one is roots, the other wings.

MEATLESS MUSHROOM BURGERS

1 Tbsp. oil
8 oz. mushrooms, finely chopped (about ¾ c.)
1 medium zucchini, shredded into long strands (about 1 c.)
1 small onion, chopped (about ½ c.)
2 cloves garlic, minced
2 Tbsp. steak sauce
1 Tbsp. chopped fresh parsley
¼ tsp. dried basil
¼ tsp. dried oregano
¼ c. part-skim milk Ricotta cheese
1 egg
¾ c. wheat germ
½ c. quick-cooking oats
4 seeded kaiser rolls
4 leaves green leaf lettuce
1 tomato, cut into 4 slices

Heat the broiler (these are difficult to cook on an outdoor grill). In a medium frying pan, heat oil over high heat. Add mushrooms, zucchini, and onion and cook until the vegetables are softened and the liquid evaporates, 5 to 6 minutes. Add garlic and 1 tablespoon of the steak sauce and cook until the steak sauce begins to evaporate, 1 to 2 minutes. Stir in the parsley, basil, and oregano; remove pan from heat and allow mixture to cool.

in a large bowl, beat together the Ricotta cheese and egg until smooth. Add cooled vegetable mixture, wheat germ, oats, and remaining steak sauce. Mix to blend well. Divide mixture in fourths, shaping each portion into a 1¼ inch thick patty. Place patties on a foil-lined cookie sheet, cover with plastic wrap, and chill until firm, at least 1 hour.

Set patties on broiler pan or a foil-lined cookie sheet and cook, turning once, until done, 6 to 7 minutes per side. (The outside should be well browned and burgers should feel firm to the touch.) Split rolls and toast. Serve burgers in toasted rolls with lettuce and tomato. Makes 4 servings.

Work time: 20 minutes. Total time: 35 minutes + chilling.

Per serving: 370 calories, 16 g protein, 12 g fat, 420 mg sodium, 56 g carbohydrate, 58 mg cholesterol.

Lion John J. Hess, Clarence Lions Club
Clarence Center, NY, USA

HOT HAM HOAGIES

1 c. barbecue sauce
¾ tsp. ground mustard
¾ tsp. garlic salt
¼ tsp. ground cloves
1 lb. thinly sliced fully cooked ham
Lettuce leaves and sliced tomato, onion, and Swiss cheese
6 hoagie or submarine buns, split

In a saucepan over medium heat, combine the first five ingredients; bring to a boil. Reduce heat; cover and simmer for 15 minutes. Place lettuce, tomato, onion, and cheese on buns; top with ham mixture. Yield: 6 servings.

CHICKEN AND CHEDDAR GRILL

Cheddar or American cheese,
  sliced or shredded
French or Italian bread, sliced in
  half lengthwise

Chunky salsa
Sliced, cooked chicken breast

Layer bread halves with cheese, chicken, salsa, and additional cheese. Place on cookie sheet. Bake in preheated 350°F. oven for 8 to 10 minutes or until cheese is melted.

Lion John J. Hess, Clarence Lions Club
Clarence Center, NY, USA

SAUSAGE PITAS

1 c. chopped onion
1 green pepper, sliced
2 Tbsp. butter
1 lb. smoked sausage (bite-size
  pieces)

2 c. drained sauerkraut
1 c. sour cream or 8 oz.
  container
1 Tbsp. mustard (you can leave
  this out if you want)

Saute onion and green pepper in the 2 tablespoons butter. Add smoked sausage and sauerkraut; heat through. Mix in sour cream and mustard. Heat, but do not boil. Serve in pita breads.

HOMEMADE PIMENTO CHEESE SPREAD

8 oz. cream cheese
½ lb. mild Cheddar cheese,
  grated
1 small jar pimento, chopped

½ c. mayonnaise
Dash of sugar, salt, and pepper

In a large bowl, combine the cheeses and pimento with mayonnaise. Add salt, pepper, and sugar to taste. Blend on medium speed - should mixture be too stiff, add more mayonnaise to the consistency you would like for spreading.

Very good and will keep refrigerated for several days.

One of my old favorites.

Gloria Thompson, Bellville Lions Club
Bellville, GA, USA

When there's work to be done, turn up your sleeves, not your nose.

ITALIAN GRILLED CHEESE

4 slices Italian bread (1 inch
    thick)
4 slices Mozzarella or Provolone
    cheese
3 eggs

½ c. milk
¾ tsp. Italian seasoning
½ tsp. garlic salt
⅔ c. Italian-seasoned bread
    crumbs

Cut a 3 inch pocket in each slice of bread; place a slice of cheese in each pocket. In a bowl, beat eggs, milk, Italian seasoning, and garlic salt; soak bread for 2 minutes on each side. Coat with bread crumbs. Cook on a greased hot griddle until golden brown on both sides. Yield: 4 servings.

PIGS IN A BLANKET

1 (¼ oz.) pkg. active dry yeast
⅓ c. plus 1 tsp. sugar, *divided*
⅔ c. warm milk (110° to 115°)
⅓ c. warm water (110° to 115°)
1 egg, beaten
2 Tbsp. plus 2 tsp. shortening,
    melted

1 tsp. salt
3⅔ c. all-purpose flour
10 hot dogs
2 slices process American cheese

In a mixing bowl, dissolve yeast and 1 teaspoon sugar in milk and water; let stand for 5 minutes. Add egg, shortening, salt, remaining sugar, and enough flour to form a soft dough. Turn onto a floured surface; knead until smooth and elastic, about 8 to 10 minutes. Place in a greased bowl, turning once to grease top. Cover and let rise in a warm place until doubled, about 1 hour. Cut a ¼ inch deep lengthwise slit in each hot dog. Cut cheese slices into five strips; place one strip in the slit of each hot dog. Punch dough down; divide into 10 portions. Roll each into a 5 x 2½ inch rectangle and wrap around prepared hot dogs; pinch seam and ends to seal. Place, seam side down, on greased baking sheets; let rise for 30 minutes. Bake at 350° for 15 to 18 minutes or until golden brown. Yield: 10 servings.

Nothing should be prized more highly than the value of each day.

❦ ❦ ❦

A friend is a present you give yourself.

SUPER SLOPPY JOES

2 lb. ground beef
½ c. chopped onion
2 celery ribs with leaves, chopped
¼ c. chopped green pepper
1⅔ c. canned crushed tomatoes
¼ c. ketchup
2 Tbsp. brown sugar

1 Tbsp. vinegar
1 Tbsp. Worcestershire sauce
1 Tbsp. steak sauce
½ tsp. garlic salt
¼ tsp. ground mustard
¼ tsp. paprika
8 to 10 hamburger buns, split

In a Dutch oven over medium heat, cook beef, onion, celery, and green pepper until the meat is no longer pink and the vegetables are tender; drain. Add the next nine ingredients; mix well. Simmer, uncovered, for 35 to 40 minutes, stirring occasionally. Spoon ½ cup meat mixture onto each bun. Yield: 8 to 10 servings.

SOUPER BURGER

1 lb. ground beef
1 can cream of celery soup
1 Tbsp. mustard
6 hamburger rolls, toasted

1 medium onion, chopped
2 Tbsp. ketchup
⅛ tsp. pepper

In skillet, cook beef and onions until brown and onions are tender. Stir to separate meat; spoon off fat. Add soup, ketchup, and pepper and cook over low heat until all ingredients are heated through. Serve on rolls.

Lioness Carolee Hackmann, East Arundel Lioness Club
Pasadena, MD, USA

The minutes spent at the dinner table won't get you fat,
it's the seconds that do it.

❦ ❦ ❦

Good humor is goodness and wisdom combined.

❦ ❦ ❦

There is one art of which many should be master - the art of reflection.

❦ ❦ ❦

There are only three ages of man: youth, middle age,
and "you're looking well."

SAUCES

BAR-B-Q SAUCE

1½ lb. ground beef
1 (14 oz.) bottle ketchup
½ tsp. dry mustard
2 Tbsp. margarine
1 Tbsp. vinegar

2 onions, chopped
1 c. chopped celery
2 Tbsp. Worcestershire sauce
1 c. water
2 Tbsp. brown sugar

Brown beef in margarine. Drain. Add all other ingredients. Simmer slow until onions and celery are soft.

I usually double this recipe and freeze what is left for another meal.
Lioness Diane DeVincent, East Anne Arundel Lioness Club
Pasadena, MD, USA

EASY BARBECUE SAUCE

¾ c. corn syrup
½ c. ketchup
¼ c. Worcestershire sauce or low
    sodium soy sauce

¼ c. prepared mustard
2 tsp. ground ginger

Combine ingredients. When barbecuing or broiling meats or poultry, brush frequently with sauce during final 5 to 10 minutes. Keep handy in refrigerator. Makes 1½ cups.
Micheal and Ruth Bartolf, Oxbow and District Lions Club
Oxbow, Saskatchewan, Canada

BAR-B-QUE SAUCE

2 (14 oz.) bottles ketchup
1 (12 oz.) bottle chile sauce
⅓ c. prepared mustard
1 Tbsp. dry mustard
1½ c. firmly packed brown sugar
2 Tbsp. coarse freshly ground
    black pepper
1½ c. wine vinegar

1 c. fresh lemon juice
½ c. bottled thick steak sauce
Dash of Tabasco to taste
¼ c. Worcestershire sauce
1 Tbsp. soy sauce
2 Tbsp. salad oil
1 (12 oz.) can beer
Garlic (if desired)

Combine all ingredients, except garlic, and mix well. About an hour before using, add garlic if desired. Makes about 6 pints.

Best bar-b-q sauce in Texas!

Hugh Scott, Leakey Lions Club
Leakey, TX, USA

2075-99

EFFIE POWERS BARBECUE SAUCE

1 c. catsup
1 c. water
1 Tbsp. Worcestershire sauce
¼ c. cider vinegar
1 onion, minced

2 Tbsp. brown sugar
2 Tbsp. dry mustard
1 tsp. chili powder
1 Tbsp. liquid smoke

Combine all ingredients. Cook over low heat for 20 minutes.

Good on any kind of meat, especially on pork roast.

This is a very good sauce from a real good cook who passed away several years ago - try it.

Janie Phillips, Iron City Lions Club
Iron City, TN

SIMPLE BARBECUE SAUCE FOR CHICKEN

1 c. water
1 c. vinegar
¼ lb. butter or margarine

1 Tbsp. salt
1 Tbsp. Worcestershire sauce

Mix all ingredients and cook until it comes to a boil. It should be kept warm during the entire period of barbecuing.

The time required to barbecue chicken is approximately 45 minutes to 1 hour. The fire should not be too hot or the chicken will burn. Dip chicken in sauce and place, skin side up, on the grill. Each time the chicken is turned, the sauce should be brushed or sprayed on each piece.

PDG Gerald Ell, Southport Lions Club
Indianapolis, IN, USA

BLUEBERRY SAUCE SUPREME

½ c. sugar
¼ c. orange juice concentrate

2 Tbsp. cornstarch
3 c. fresh or frozen blueberries

In a saucepan, combine sugar, orange juice, and cornstarch. Stir until smooth. Add berries and bring to a boil. Boil for 2 minutes, stirring constantly. Use as a topping for pancakes, waffles, or pound cake.

Joyce A. Relihan, Plymouth Lions Club
Terryville, CT, USA

A child is a strange creature who wants to find out everything by asking questions no one can answer.

EASY CRANBERRY SAUCE

1 small pkg. raspberry Jell-O
1 c. boiling water
1 can whole cranberries

1 small can undrained crushed
    pineapple
1 orange, chopped fine

    Mix Jell-O and water. Add whole cranberries, crushed pineapple, and orange. Stir and let set. Refrigerate.

Lion Paul and Vale Welsh, East Prospect Lions Club
East Prospect, PA, USA

LIGHT ORIENTAL PLUM SAUCE

7¼ c. finely chopped plums (do
    not peel)
¾ c. finely chopped onion
2 Tbsp. mustard seed
1 to 2 jalapeno peppers, finely
    chopped
2 Tbsp. finely chopped fresh
    ginger

2 cloves garlic, finely chopped
¼ c. white vinegar
3 c. white sugar
2 c. lightly packed brown sugar
1 box *Certo Light* fruit pectin
    crystals

    Chop plums. Measure prepared fruit into a large saucepan. Add onion, mustard seed, jalapenos, ginger, garlic, and vinegar. Measure sugars and combine; set aside. Combine fruit pectin crystals with ¼ cup measured sugar. Stir pectin mixture into fruit. Place saucepan over high heat and stir until mixture comes to a full boil. Stir in remaining sugar. Continue to cook and stir over high heat until mixture comes to a full rolling boil. Boil hard 1 minute, stirring constantly. Remove from heat. Stir and skim foam for 5 minutes to prevent floating fruit. Pour quickly into warm, sterilized jars filling up to ¼ inch from rim. Seal while hot with sterilized 2 piece lids with new centers. Stir gently before serving.

Micheal and Ruth Bartolf, Oxbow and District Lions Club
Oxbow, Saskatchewan, Canada

OLD-FASHIONED LEMON SAUCE

½ c. butter or oleo
1 c. sugar
¼ c. water

1 well beaten egg
3 Tbsp. lemon juice
Grated rind of 1 lemon

    Cook over medium heat, stirring constantly, just until mixture comes to a boil. This is very good over angel food cake. Serve warm.

Pauline and PDG Gerald Nuffer, South Jefferson Lions Club
Adams, NY

The one thing worse than a quitter is the person who is afraid to begin.

GREEN HERB SAUCE

Any green herbs that you like the flavour of in combination can be made into a pesto sauce.

Try:

1 Tbsp. fresh chopped parsley
1 Tbsp. fresh chopped thyme
1 Tbsp. fresh chopped lemon
   thyme
1 Tbsp. fresh chopped lemon
   balm
1 Tbsp. fresh chopped tarragon

1 Tbsp. fresh chopped marjoram
3 to 4 cloves garlic
3 to 4 pats butter
3 to 4 Tbsp. herb vinegar (choose
   one of the flavours from
   above)

Put all in a blender with enough olive oil to make a marinade that can be scraped easily off the blender walls. Good on fish, chicken, pasta, and vegetables.

Sarah Wehling, Bothell Lions Club
Bothell, WA, USA

THAI FRUIT SALSA

Thai Fruit Salsa is a colorful tasty twist on traditional salsa that can be savored on its own or served with grilled main courses.

1½ c. seeded, diced tomatoes
1 c. diced mango
1 c. diced avocado
1 Tbsp. instant minced onion
1 Tbsp. lime juice

1 tsp. basil leaves, crushed
½ tsp. garlic salt
½ tsp. crushed red pepper
½ tsp. ground allspice

In a medium bowl, combine tomatoes, mango, avocado, onion, lime juice, basil leaves, garlic salt, crushed red pepper, and allspice. Sprinkle salsa with sweetened flaked coconut. Makes 3½ cups.

Micheal and Ruth Bartolf, Oxbow and District Lions Club
Oxbow, Saskatchewan, Canada

SALSA CALIENTE PARA LEGUMBRES

Hot sauce for vegetables
½ pt. table cream
¼ c. olive oil

½ lb. butter
2 (4 oz.) cans fillets of anchovies
6 cloves garlic, minced

Melt the butter in a saucepan on a slow fire. Add the minced garlic and anchovies. Crush them well with a strong fork while cooking. Add the olive oil and cream; stir well and let simmer for a few minutes. Pour into a chafing dish. Serve piping hot. Serve with hot or cold vegetables, salads, or on toasted sourdough bread.

Sarah Wehling, Bothell Lions Club
Bothell, WA, USA

160

RAISIN SAUCE

1 c. brown sugar
¼ tsp. salt
⅛ tsp. clove
1 c. water

1 Tbsp. vinegar
½ c. raisins
1 tsp. lemon juice
1 Tbsp. butter

Blend sugar, salt, cloves, and water. Cook slowly; thicken with cornstarch and water mixture. Blend in vinegar, raisins, lemon juice, and butter. Serve warm with ham.

Debra James, Beckmantown Lions Club
West Chazy, NY

RAISIN SAUCE

½ c. brown sugar
1½ tsp. dry mustard
1 Tbsp. cornstarch
1½ c. water

¼ c. vinegar
⅓ c. raisins
1 Tbsp. butter or margarine

Combine dry ingredients; slowly add water and vinegar. Add raisins. Cook over low heat, stirring constantly, till thickened. Cook 10 minutes longer to plump the raisins, then add butter.

This is wonderful with ham. I've used it for many holiday dinners.
Mrs. Duane (Pam) Bennett, Mad River Lions Club
Riverside, OH, USA

RED PEPPER PUREE

2 large or 3 small sweet peppers,
    chopped
½ c. chopped onion
1 minced clove garlic

2 Tbsp. olive oil
½ tsp. basil
¼ c. chicken broth
2 tsp. white wine vinegar

Saute peppers, onions, and garlic in olive oil until softened, 5 to 10 minutes. Add basil, chicken broth, and vinegar; cover and cook until peppers are tender and liquid has evaporated, 10 to 15 minutes.

Transfer mixture to a blender or food processor and blend until smooth. Serve while hot with pasta or cover and refrigerate, then reheat at serving time.
Marilyn Redifer, Whitehall Area Lions Club
Columbus, OH

By the time somebody decides to make a long story short,
it's already too late.

REFRESHING RHUBARB RELISH

2 c. diced rhubarb
½ c. hot water
1 (4 serving) pkg. Jell-O sugar
   free raspberry, strawberry, or
   lemon gelatin

1 c. cold water
1 c. chopped, unpeeled apple
   (approx. 2 small)
¼ c. raisins
⅓ c. chopped nuts

In a medium saucepan, cook rhubarb in hot water until soft, about 10 minutes. Dissolve gelatin in hot rhubarb; add cold water and stir well. Blend in apples, raisins, and nuts. Mix gently to combine. Pour into 8x8 inch dish. Refrigerate until set, about 4 hours. Serves 6.

Wonderful with grilled pork chops or chicken and great for potlucks.

Joyce A. Relihan, Plymouth Lions Club
Terryville, CT, USA

ZUCCHINI RELISH

12 c. zucchini, grated or ground
4 c. onions, finely chopped or
   ground

1 sweet pepper, ground
1 large branch celery, ground

Mix the above together and sprinkle with ½ cup salt. Allow to sit 1 hour, then drain well. Add 1½ cups vinegar that is mixed with ½ cup water.

Add:

4 c. white sugar
½ tsp. pepper
1 tsp. nutmeg

1 tsp. turmeric
2 Tbsp. cornstarch

Boil 8 to 10 minutes. Can and seal.

This is the very best relish! You now know what to do with all that summer zucchini.

A. Keister Brumback (of Littlestown, PA),
Silver Run Union Mills Lions Club
Westminster, MD, USA

Be cautious. Opportunity does the knocking for temptation too.

No brook is too little to seek the sea.

PEPPER RELISH

12 green peppers
12 red sweet peppers or yellow
    sweet
15 onions

½ c. salt
3 c. sugar
2 pt. apple cider vinegar
2 tsp. celery seed

I use a food processor to dice peppers and onions. Cover with the salt. Pour hot boiling water over the mixture. After cooled, place in a large strainer, let drain, and squeeze out any excess moisture. I use a wooden spoon to press down which helps remove the moisture. Return to large pot. Add the sugar, vinegar, and celery seed. Boil 15 minutes. Transfer to pint size canning jars. Wipe off jar mouth and place hot canning lid, covering top. Tighten with ring and let seal.

The variety of colored peppers make the relish attractive for gift giving. Our Lions Club requested this relish over store brand when we sell hot dogs and hamburgers.

Nicki Florentine, Silver Run-Union Mills Lions Club
Westminster, MD, USA

ZUCCHINI RELISH

I. Relish:

10 c. grated zucchini
1 c. carrots, grated
3 sweet red peppers
1 c. celery, diced

4 c. minced onion
3 green peppers, minced
5 Tbsp. salt

Wash zucchini; leave skins on. Grate and place in large container. Add salt. Place in refrigerator overnight. Rinse grated zucchini in cold water. Press out water by placing bowl on top of large colander - not too dry.

II. Brine:

4½ c. sugar
1 Tbsp. dried mustard
4½ c. sugar
3 Tbsp. cornstarch
½ tsp. black pepper

2 tsp. turmeric
3 Tbsp. celery seed
4½ c. white vinegar
1 Tbsp. nutmeg
½ tsp. black pepper

In large enamel pot, combine above ingredients.

Add all ingredients, plus vegetables. Bring to a boil; simmer 1 hour. Ladle relish into hot sterilized jars and seal. Makes 5 to 6 pints.

Lioness Carole Hackmann, East Anne Arundel Lioness Club
Pasadena, MD, USA

BEET RELISH

2 c. coarsely shredded, cooked
   beets
2 Tbsp. chopped red onion
2 Tbsp. red wine vinegar

1 tsp. sugar
2 Tbsp. Dijon mustard
3 Tbsp. olive oil
Salt and pepper to taste

Combine all ingredients in a small bowl and blend well. Chill thoroughly. Yields about 2 cups.

Keeps well stored in the refrigerator for up to one week.

Lion Ann K. Brumback, Silver Run-Union Mills Lions Club
Westminster, MD, USA

SWEET-ONION AND CARROT RELISH

Relish is good with any grilled meat and it's the best thing to happen to hot dogs since mustard.

1 large sweet onion (about ¾ lb.
   or 4 c. sliced)
1 Tbsp. red-wine vinegar
Salt and pepper
3 Tbsp. oil

2 carrots (about ⅓ lb. or 1 c.
   grated)
¼ tsp. caraway seeds
1 Tbsp. chopped fresh parsley

Cut the onion into slices and push apart into rings. Put the onion rings in a bowl and cover with cold water. In a small jar, combine the vinegar, ½ teaspoon salt, and ¼ teaspoon pepper and shake until the salt dissolves. Add the oil and shake again to combine. Grate the carrots. Dice the onion slices and pat dry. Combine the onion, carrots, caraway seeds, parsley, and dressing and toss until well coated. Makes 3½ cups.

Per ¼ cup serving: 43 calories, 1 g protein, 3 g fat, 86 mg sodium, 4 g carbohydrate, 0 mg cholesterol.

Mrs. Lucy Aiken, Clarence Lions Club
Clarence Center, NY, USA

Your work is a commentary on your character.

Joy is not in what we own ... it's in what we are.

ONION AND RED PEPPER RELISH
(Fat free)

1 medium red onion, finely
    chopped (about 2 c.)
1 clove garlic, minced
¼ c. sugar
3 Tbsp. rice-wine vinegar
1 tsp. salt

1 tsp. mustard seeds
½ tsp. black pepper
Pinch of ground cloves
1 medium red pepper, finely
    chopped (about 1 c.)

In a medium frying pan over medium-high heat, combine the red onion, garlic, sugar, vinegar, salt, mustard seeds, black pepper, cloves, and 2 tablespoons of water. Bring the mixture to a simmer and cook 5 minutes. Add the red pepper and cook until vegetables are tender-crisp, 7 to 9 minutes. Cover and chill. Serve with burgers, hot dogs, or sandwiches. Makes about 2 cups.

Per 2 tablespoon serving: 22 calories, 0 g protein, 0 g fat, 34 mg sodium, 5 g carbohydrate, 0 mg cholesterol.

Lion John J. Hess, Clarence Lions Club
Clarence Center, NY, USA

GREEN TOMATO RELISH

3 lb. (10 medium) green tomatoes
4 medium red apples
3 red sweet peppers
4 onions
4½ tsp. salt

1½ tsp. cinnamon
¾ tsp. ground cloves
2½ c. sugar
2 c. white vinegar

Wash and remove stem ends from tomatoes. Core apples (do not peel). Remove cores and seeds from peppers. Force apples and all vegetables through food chopper. Combine remaining ingredients and bring to a boil in a kettle. Add vegetables and simmer for 30 minutes or until thick, stirring occasionally. Pack in 4 or 5 hot jars and seal.

Eric and Karen Dutton, South Jefferson Lions Club
Adams, NY

CUCUMBER RELISH

12 cucumbers
3 red sweet peppers
3 green sweet peppers
12 good size onions
1 cabbage
Salt

1½ qt. cider vinegar
5 c. white sugar
½ oz. celery seed
½ c. flour
3 tsp. dry mustard
1 tsp. turmeric powder

Grind vegetables through food chopper; sprinkle with salt. Let stand overnight. Squeeze out in morning and throw juice away. Make paste of flour, dry mustard, and turmeric. Mix with vinegar and cook 10 minutes or until thickened and seal in jars.

Eric and Karen Dutton, South Jefferson Lions Club
Adams, NY

TOFU MAYONNAISE

Time: 15 minutes.

½ cake soft tofu
½ c. spring water
1 Tbsp. brown rice vinegar or
    umeboshi vinegar

1 Tbsp. fresh lemon juice
1 Tbsp. olive oil
¼ tsp. dried mustard
½ tsp. sea salt (or to taste)

Combine all ingredients and blend until thick and creamy. Can be refrigerated for several days. If mixture separates, stir well before using. Serves 4 to 5.

Comments: Use as you would any mayonnaise, can be refrigerated several days.

PDG Jim Schiebel, Hilton Lions Club
Hilton, NY, USA

GRANDMA'S MAYONNAISE

1 tsp. mustard (dry)
½ tsp. salt
1 c. sugar
2 tsp. flour

⅛ tsp. paprika
2 eggs, beaten
½ c. milk
½ c. vinegar

In saucepan, combine mustard, salt, sugar, flour, and paprika. Blend well. Add 2 beaten eggs. Mix until smooth. Add milk. Mix well. Add vinegar. Mix well. Cook over medium heat until it thickens (comes to a boil). Add 1 tablespoon of butter if desired.

If being used for potato salad, increase sugar to 1 cup.

Grandma's from Pennsylvania Dutch country.

Mildred Weir, Bentleyville Lioness Club
Bentleyville, PA

DUTCH HONEY

1 c. white sugar
1 c. brown sugar

1 c. cream
1 c. white syrup

Combine all ingredients in heavy saucepan; boil until it begins to thicken. Watch carefully, so it doesn't burn.

Oh, so good on hot pancakes, biscuits, or ice cream.

Bert Morgan, Broken Bow Lions Club
Broken Bow, NE, Custer County

Education is ... hanging around until you've caught on.

FREEZER - TOMATO SAUCE

6 c. chopped Bermuda onions
6 cloves garlic, crushed
6 green peppers, chopped
8 lb. tomatoes, peeled and diced

3 (6 oz.) cans tomato paste
4 tsp. salt
½ tsp. pepper
2 Tbsp. brown sugar

Saute onion, garlic, and green peppers in ½ cup of oil in large container until tender. Stir in tomatoes, tomato paste, salt, pepper, and brown sugar. Simmer, uncovered, until tender at least one hour. Cool. Freeze in containers. Makes 4½ quarts.

Very delicious in hot dishes, chili, etc.

Joyce Wise, Randall-Cushing Little Elk Lions Club
Randall, MN, USA

ONION GRAVY

Time: 25 minutes.

2 large onions, sliced thinly
1 tsp. oil
2 c. spring water

2 tsp. tamari (or to taste)
1½ Tbsp. kuzu
Dash of sea salt (if desired)

Slice onions thinly and saute in skillet with the oil. Cook at very low temperature until onions become very brown and bottom of pan is well browned. Add water and simmer for 10 to 15 minutes. Combine tamari and kuzu with enough cold water to dissolve. Add to onion and water mixture; stir over medium heat until thick and clear. Taste and adjust seasonings. Serves 4.

Comments: Serve over millet mashed potatoes and any grain burger or croquette.

PDG Jim Schiebel, Hilton Lions Club
Hilton, NY, USA

CONEY SAUCE

½ lb. ground beef
¼ c. chopped onion
1 c. seasoned tomato sauce
½ tsp. monosodium glutamate

¼ c. water
1 clove garlic, minced
½ to ¾ tsp. chili powder
½ tsp. salt

Brown beef slowly but thoroughly, breaking with a fork till fine. Add remaining ingredients; simmer, uncovered, 10 minutes. Serve in bowl to ladle over hot franks in heated coney buns. Makes enough sauce for 12 Coney Islands.

Mike Hazzard
Littleton, CO

2075-99

Notes

Pancakes and sausage - for batter, for wurst.

Vegetables

TO QUICK-FREEZE VEGETABLES

Vegetables for freezing are prepared as for cooking, then blanched (scalded) and packed dry or with the brine. The dry pack is less trouble and is satisfactory for all vegetables except green peppers.

Blanching vegetables is important because it minimizes loss of flavor and color. To blanch in boiling water, put about one pound of vegetables in a fine-mesh wire basket with a wire cover to hold food under the water and lower into rapidly boiling water, enough to cover food. Cover the kettle and then COUNT THE TIME RECOMMENDED FOR EACH vegetable. After blanching, chill quickly and thoroughly, plunge the vegetables into ice water, or hold under cold running water. When completely chilled, remove and drain, and PACK AT ONCE.

VEGETABLE	HOW PREPARED	BLANCHING
ASPARAGUS	Wash, cut, sort into groups according to thickness of stalk. Blanch, chill, pack.	3 to 4 minutes in boiling water, depending on size.
BEANS, GREEN AND WAX	Wash, stem, slice, cut or leave whole. Blanch, chill, pack.	Cut: 2 minutes in boiling water. Whole: 2½ minutes in boiling water.
BEANS, LIMA	Shell, wash, blanch, chill. Remove white beans, which may be used for cooking. Pack.	1 to 2 minutes in boiling water, depending on size.
CARROTS	Remove tops, wash, scrape. Slice lengthwise or crosswise as preferred, or leave small carrots whole.	Whole: 4½ minutes in boiling water. Sliced: 3 minutes in boiling water.
CAULIFLOWER	Break heads into flowerets about 1 inch across. Wash, blanch, chill, pack.	3 to 4 minutes in boiling water.
CORN, ON COB	Husk, trim away silk and spots. Wash, blanch, chill, pack.	7 minutes in boiling water for slender ears, 9 for medium, 11 for large.
CORN, KERNELS	Same as corn on cob. After chilling, cut off kernels and pack.	
GREENS Beet, Chard, Kale, Mustard, Spinach, Collards, etc.	Wash, discard bad leaves, tough stems. Blanch, chill, pack.	2 minutes in boiling water.
PEAS	Shell, sort, blanch, chill, pack.	1 to 2 minutes in boiling water, depending on size.
PEPPERS, GREEN	Wash, cut away seeds, slice. Blanch, pack in brine of 1 tsp. salt to 1 c. cold water.	3 minutes in boiling water.

VEGETABLES

OVEN-ROASTED SWEET POTATOES

2 lb. sweet potatoes
1/3 c. oil

Salt and pepper

Heat oven to 400°. Cut the sweet potatoes into spears, about 1 inch long and 1/2 inch wide. Put the sweet potatoes on a baking sheet in a single layer and toss with the oil, 1 teaspoon salt, and 1/4 teaspoon pepper. Bake, turning occasionally, until the sweet potatoes are tender and golden brown, 40 to 45 minutes. Makes 4 servings.

Per serving: 398 calories, 4 g protein, 19 g fat, 580 mg sodium, 55 g carbohydrate, 0 mg cholesterol.

Lion John J. Hess, Clarence Lions Club
Clarence Center, NY, USA

CANDIED SWEET POTATOES

2 medium sized sweet potatoes,
    peeled and quartered
1 c. sugar
1 tsp. salt
1/2 tsp. black pepper

1 tsp. nutmeg
2 tsp. cornstarch
1/2 stick margarine
1 1/2 to 2 c. water

Place potatoes in deep dish casserole. Sprinkle with sugar, salt, pepper, and nutmeg. Dot with margarine. Mix cornstarch with about 1 cup of the water. Pour over other ingredients and enough of remaining water to cover potatoes. Place in 350° oven and cook until potatoes are tender and sauce is thickened.

Nettie Favara, Greenwood Lions Club
Greenwood, MS, USA

SALLY'S SWEET POTATO CASSEROLE

5 c. mashed sweet potatoes
1 c. sugar
1/4 c. milk
2 eggs

1 tsp. vanilla
1/2 c. melted margarine
1 c. coconut

Topping:

1 c. pecans
1 c. brown sugar

1/2 c. margarine
1/2 c. flour

Cook potatoes. Mash potatoes and combine with other ingredients. Pour into greased 13x9 inch pan. Spread with topping. Bake at 350° for 20 minutes.

Martha C. Cox, Travelers Rest Lions Club
Travelers Rest, SC

APRICOT SWEET POTATOES

2 Tbsp. margarine
1 (18 oz.) can sweet potatoes or
    yams, drained and cut into ½
    inch thick slices
1 c. firmly packed brown sugar
1½ Tbsp. cornstarch

1 tsp. grated orange peel
¼ tsp. salt
⅛ tsp. cinnamon
1 (15 oz.) can apricot halves (save
    nectar - use 5½ oz.)
½ c. pecan halves

Heat oven to 375°. Grease 1½ quart casserole dish. Place sweet potatoes in dish. Mix sugar, cornstarch, peel, salt, and cinnamon in saucepan. Stir in 5½ ounces nectar plus ⅓ cup water. Cook and stir till comes to a rolling boil. Remove and add 2 tablespoons margarine and apricots (cut in fourths). Pour over potatoes. Sprinkle with pecans. Bake, uncovered, 25 minutes or until hot and bubbly. Makes 6 to 8 servings.

Family loves this at holiday time.

Bonnie Smith, Princeton Lions Club
Princeton, IL

SWEET POTATO WITH APPLES
(No sugar)

2 lb. sweet potatoes, sliced thin
3 apples, cored and sliced (can be
    peeled - Golden Delicious
    apples)

4 Tbsp. melted butter
⅓ c. apple juice
Sprinkle of cinnamon

Layer potatoes and apples. Pour apple juice and butter over top, then sprinkle with cinnamon. Bake at 350° covered for one hour and 15 minutes uncovered. *No sugar recipe.*

Arlene H. Wall, Past President, Biloxi Lions Club
Biloxi, MS, USA

SWEET POTATOES CASSEROLE

1 large and 1 small can sweet
    potatoes (pour all in a big
    boiler)

1 stick butter
1 or 1½ c. sugar
1 inch stem or fry sausage

Pour all potatoes in big boiler and add 1½ cups sugar and stick butter. Mash up real good. Pour in a greased 9x12 inch long casserole dish. Cut sausage in 1 inch size and fry in a little grease for a little bit and put sausages in sweet potatoes. Pour grease over top of potatoes. Bake at 350° for 30 to 40 minutes.

Lion Carolyn Lambert, Brookhaven "Alpha" Lions Club
Brookhaven, MS

CREAMY POTATO STICKS

¼ c. all-purpose flour
½ tsp. salt
1½ c. milk
1 (10¾ oz.) can condensed cream
    of celery soup (undiluted)
½ lb. process American cheese,
    cubed

5 to 6 large baking potatoes,
    peeled
1 c. chopped onion
Paprika

In a saucepan, combine flour and salt; gradually whisk in milk until smooth. Bring to a boil; cook and stir for 2 minutes. Remove from the heat; whisk in soup and cheese until smooth. Set aside.

Cut potatoes into 4 x ½ x ½ inch sticks; place in a greased 13 x 9 x 2 inch baking dish. Sprinkle with onion. Top with cheese sauce. Bake, uncovered, at 350° for 55 to 60 minutes or until potatoes are tender. Sprinkle with paprika. Yield: 6 servings.

BACON HASH BROWN BAKE

4 c. grated, cooked potatoes
12 bacon strips, cooked and
    crumbled
½ c. milk
⅓ c. chopped onion
½ tsp. salt

¼ tsp. pepper
¼ tsp. garlic powder
1 Tbsp. butter or margarine,
    melted
½ tsp. paprika

In a bowl, combine the first seven ingredients. Transfer to a greased 9 inch pie plate. Drizzle with butter; sprinkle with paprika. Bake at 350° for 35 to 45 minutes or until lightly browned. Yield: 6 to 8 servings.

POTATOES DELUXE

2 lb. pkg. frozen hash brown
    potatoes, thawed for 30
    minutes
1 medium onion, finely chopped
1 stick oleo (⅔ stick melted, ⅓
    stick to dot top with)
1 c. sour cream

1 tsp. salt
½ tsp. pepper
8 to 10 oz. grated sharp Cheddar
    cheese
2 cans cream of chicken soup
2 c. crushed corn flakes

Grease well a 9x13 inch pan. In large bowl, mix all ingredients except corn flakes and ⅓ stick oleo. Place ingredients in greased pan. Top with crushed corn flakes and dot with oleo. Bake in 350° oven for 50 minutes or until bubbly.

Marge Sabin, Rootstown Township Lions Club 13-D
Rootstown, OH, USA

TEXAS POTATOES

2 lb. pkg. hash browns, thawed
½ c. butter, melted
1 tsp. pepper
2 tsp. salt
½ c. chopped onion

1 can chicken soup (creamed)
1 small ctn. sour cream
¼ c. butter
2 c. crushed corn flakes

Mix all ingredients except last 2. Put in 9x13 inch baking dish. Top with corn flakes and butter. Bake at 350° for 45 minutes.

Barbara Vaughn, Conroe Lioness Club
Conroe, TX

TEXAS POTATOES

2 lb. frozen hash browns
½ c. chopped onions
1 tsp. salt
1 can creamed chicken soup
10 oz. Cheddar cheese, grated

½ c. melted butter or margarine
¼ tsp. pepper
1 pt. sour cream
2 c. crushed corn flakes

Mix all above, then put crushed corn flakes on top. Use a well greased 9x13 inch pan. Bake 1 hour at 350°.

Rosalie Hoffman, East Haddam Community Lions Club
East Haddam, CT, Middlesex

PARTY POTATOES

8 to 10 medium sized potatoes
1 (8 oz.) cream cheese, softened
1 (8 oz.) sour cream

4 Tbsp. margarine
⅓ c. chopped chives (optional)
Salt and pepper to taste

Boil peeled potatoes until tender. Beat the sour cream and cheese together. Add hot potatoes and beat until smooth. Add margarine and salt and pepper to taste. Add optional chives. Pour into a well greased 2 quart casserole. Bake at 350° for 25 minutes. Does not freeze.

Janie Fox, Saginaw Lions Club
Saginaw, TX

A grandmother is a mother who has been given a second chance.

❦ ❦ ❦

There are hundreds of languages in the world, but a smile speaks all of them.

GOURMET POTATOES

8 medium potatoes, boiled with
   skin on
2 c. grated Cheddar cheese
10 Tbsp. butter, divided
1½ c. sour cream (at room
   temperature)
½ c. chopped green onions plus
   tops

1 tsp. salt
½ tsp. pepper
1 c. crushed potato chips
2 Tbsp. butter
½ c. grated cheese

Peel and cut potatoes. Combine cheese and 8 tablespoons butter in large saucepan. Cook over low heat until almost melted. Remove from heat and stir in sour cream, onions, salt, and pepper. Fold in potatoes and put in greased 2 quart baking dish. Dot with remaining butter.

Melt 2 tablespoons butter and add the cheese and potato chips. Put on top of the potato casserole. Bake at 350° for 25 minutes or until heated through.

Lion Ida Rohrer, Moundbuilders Lions Club
Newark, OH, USA

QUICK (BUT TASTY) SCALLOPED POTATOES

3 medium potatoes
1 large onion, diced
Salt and pepper

1 c. scalded milk
1 c. grated cheese (Cheddar,
   Mozzarella, or Colby)

Preheat oven to 350°F. Peel and shred potatoes. Spread in a greased casserole. Add diced onion. Season to taste. Add milk and ⅔ of the cheese. Mix. Bake in covered casserole for one hour. The last 15 minutes, spread remaining cheese over top and return to oven to finish baking. Yield: 4 servings.

Lion Ann Frechette, Lake of the Woods Lions Club
Kenora, Ontario, Canada

SUSAN'S POTATO-BACON CHOWDER

8 slices cut-up bacon
2 c. cubed potato
1 can cream of chicken soup
1¾ c. milk
Dash of pepper

1 c. chopped onion
1 c. water
½ c. sour cream
½ tsp. salt
2 Tbsp. parsley (optional)

Fry bacon crisp. Add onion and saute 2 to 3 minutes. Pour off fat. Add potatoes and water. Bring to a boil; cover and simmer 10 to 15 minutes, until potatoes are tender. Stir in soup and cream. Gradually add milk. Add salt and pepper (and parsley). Heat to serving temperature. *Do not boil!* Serves 4.

Judy Brasgalla, Cass Lake Lions and Lioness Club
Cass Lake, MN

QUICK AND EASY PIEROGI

1 box giant shells
4 to 5 medium onions, diced
1¼ to 1½ lb. Longhorn cheese

½ lb. extra sharp Cheddar cheese
5 to 7 medium potatoes
3 sticks oleo

Brown onions in 1 to 1½ sticks oleo; set aside. Cut and boil potatoes until soft. Cube the cheese in small pieces. Cook and drain the shells; set aside. Mash the potatoes and add the cheese; mix well. Add onions, then fill the cooked shells. Melt remaining butter and pour over shells. Bake at 350° for 15 to 20 minutes.

You can use this as a main dish or a side dish.

Maria Gaso, Bentleyville Lioness Club
Bentleyville, PA, USA

FAIR POTATOES

1 egg, beaten
2 c. milk
1 c. grated Swiss cheese
1 to 2 tsp. salt (I use 1 tsp.)
¼ tsp. ground pepper

Dash of nutmeg
Garlic powder to taste (I use ⅛
    tsp. garlic powder)
5 c. coarsely grated potatoes
2 Tbsp. butter

Mix beaten egg, milk, seasonings, and ¾ cup cheese. Mix well with potatoes and pour into well-buttered 1½ quart dish. Cut 1 tablespoon butter in small pieces and push into potatoes. Cut other tablespoon butter in pieces and distribute over top. Sprinkle with remaining cheese. Bake at 350° for 1 hour and 15 minutes. Makes 6 servings.

Mrs. Duane (Pam) Bennett, Mad River Lions Club
Riverside, OH, USA

To think too long about doing something often because its undoing.

❧ ❧ ❧

Not only is a woman's work never done, but the definition keeps changing.

❧ ❧ ❧

If you ask of life, "What have you to offer me?",
the answer is, "What do you have to give?"

EASY, CREAMY POTATOES

2 lb. (1 kg) diced frozen hash
    brown potatoes, thawed
2 c. (500 ml) sour cream
2 (10 oz. - 284 ml) cream of
    mushroom soup
½ c. (250 ml) melted butter or
    margarine
1¾ c. (500 ml) grated Cheddar
    cheese
¼ c. (50 ml) Miracle Whip salad
    dressing
¼ tsp. (1 ml) basil

¼ tsp. (1 ml) parsley
¼ tsp. (1 ml) dill weed
½ tsp. (2 ml) salt (or to taste)
½ tsp. (2 ml) pepper (or to taste)
1 medium onion, finely chopped
1 stalk celery, finely chopped
6 slices crisp cooked, crumbled
    bacon (optional)
1 (10 oz. - 284 ml) mushroom
    stems and pieces, drained,
    rinsed, and chopped fine
    (optional)

Topping:

1 c. (250 ml) soft bread crumbs
1 Tbsp. (15 ml) melted butter or
    margarine

¼ c. (50 ml) grated Cheddar
    cheese

Preheat oven to 325°F. In a large bowl, cream together thoroughly sour cream, soup, and Miracle Whip. Add Cheddar cheese, onions, celery, mushroom pieces, and bacon (if using) and thawed potatoes. Crush basil and parsley and add all spices to mixture. Add melted butter and mix well. Spread evenly into 9x13 inch cake pan. Mix together bread crumbs, melted butter, and cheese. Spread over top of potatoes, pat down, and bake for one to one and a half hours until bubbly and top golden.

To make smaller casseroles, use two cake pans. Eat one, freeze one. Freezes well for up to one month, double wrapped tightly in Saran Wrap. Serve with make ahead egg casserole printed elsewhere in this cookbook.

Lion Lillian Marchant, Lake of the Woods Lions Club
Kenora, Ontario, Canada

THYME AU GRATIN POTATOES

6 medium potatoes, peeled and
    diced
1 c. sour cream
1 can cream of celery soup

2 green onions, chopped
⅛ tsp. pepper
½ tsp. dried thyme
1½ c. shredded Cheddar cheese

Combine all ingredients in casserole and bake at 350° for 45 minutes.

Anne Tibbetts, South Jefferson Lions Club
Adams, NY

If you can look back on life without regrets,
you have one of life's most precious gifts - a selective memory.

POTATO CASSEROLE

32 oz. frozen hash brown
   potatoes, thawed
1 c. chopped onion
1 stick margarine

1½ tsp. salt and pepper
1 can cream of celery soup
   (undiluted)
1 pt. sour cream

Mix all ingredients together. Bake, uncovered, at 350° for 1 hour. Remove from oven, cover with shredded cheese, and sprinkle crushed corn flakes on top. Return to oven until cheese melts and corn flakes brown.

Diana Risha, Conroe Noon Lions Club
Conroe, TX

POTATO CASSEROLE

2 lb. hash browns (frozen)
1 can cream of chicken soup
1 stick margarine
1 c. (½ pt.) sour cream

½ c. chopped onions
2 c. shredded cheese
1 tsp. salt
2 c. buttered corn flakes

Combine all ingredients except corn flakes. Place mixture into a casserole dish. Top mixture with the corn flakes. Bake at 350° for 1 hour.

Lion Martha Joyce, Foothills of Mount Airy Lions Club
Mount Airy, NC, USA

POTATOES MASHED LIKE THE AMISH DO

5 lb. potatoes
Salt

½ lb. butter
½ c. sour cream

Peel potatoes and cover with water in pan. Add salt the size of a hickory nut. Boil until tender pricked with a fork. Drain. Mash with masher. Add ½ pound butter; whip. Add ½ cup sour cream. Whip with fork. Keep hot till served. When the potatoes are in the bowl, brown ½ pound butter in a pan till it's light brown. Pour over top.

These are served in Amish and Mennonite homes and restaurants. We make them on holidays for a large crowd and keep them hot in the crock-pot. We also use an electric beater to whip them. I use 5 pounds potatoes for 20 people.

We live near Sugar-Creek and Holmes Co., a large Amish settlement in Ohio. Good cookin!

Shirley Riemenschneider,
Rootstown Township Lions Club 13-D
Lions Club
Rootstown, OH

A bigger fool than the fellow who knows it all is the one who will argue him.

MOCK MASHED POTATOES

Time: 30 minutes.

1 c. millet
½ small cauliflower, sliced thinly

2½ c. spring water
Pinch of sea salt

Wash millet and drain well. Bring water and sea salt to a boil. Thinly slice the cauliflower. Combine all ingredients and bring to boil, reduce heat, and simmer for 25 minutes. May be pressure cooked if preferred. Remove from heat and mash well with a potato masher. Add a little hot water if too thick. Serves 3 to 4.

Comments: Serve with onion gravy for a real treat.

PDG Jim Schiebel, Hilton Lions Club
Hilton, NY, USA

SMASHING MASHED POTATOES

2¼ c. mashed potatoes
1 c. sour cream
¼ c. milk

½ tsp. garlic powder
1 c. (4 oz.) shredded Cheddar
cheese

Preheat oven to 350°. Combine mashed potatoes, sour cream, milk, and garlic powder in a large bowl. Mix well. Spoon half the mixture into a greased 2 quart baking dish. Sprinkle with ⅔ cup French fried onions and ¼ cup cheese. Top with remaining potato mixture. Bake 30 minutes or until heated through. Sprinkle with remaining ⅔ cup onions and ½ cup cheese. Bake 5 more minutes until onions are golden.

If you like cheese, you'll love this!

JoAnn Jones, Mathews Lions Club
North, VA

POTATOES IN FOIL

4 to 5 baking potatoes, peeled
and salted
Coarse ground pepper
5 slices bacon, fried crisp

1 large onion, sliced
8 oz. sharp cheese, cubed
½ c. butter

Heat oven to 375° (1 hour). Slice potatoes in a large piece of foil. Season with salt and pepper. Crumble bacon over potatoes; add onion and cheese. Slice butter over all. Bring foil up around the potato mixture and seal it well, so that the steam cooks everything well done in about 45 minutes. If you do this on a grill, turn it a few times. Serves 6.

This really is a tasty potato dish and very simple.

Mrs. Duane (Pam) Bennett, Mad River Lions Club
Riverside, OH, USA

GERMAN BAKED POTATOES

5 large potatoes, grated
1 onion, grated
2 tsp. salt
1 pinch of black pepper
3 eggs, beaten
1 c. hot milk
6 Tbsp. melted margarine

Mix all ingredients. Bake in a casserole, which has been sprayed with Pam, at 350° for 1 hour and 15 minutes or until potatoes are tender.

OVEN-ROASTED POTATOES

4 medium potatoes
1 medium red bell pepper, seeded
2 tsp. rosemary, crumbled
4 cloves garlic, minced
½ tsp. salt
¼ tsp. pepper
2 Tbsp. olive oil

Cut potatoes into ½ inch wedges. Cut pepper into 1 inch squares. Preheat oven. Place potatoes and remaining ingredients onto a greased baking sheet with sides. Toss well. Arrange in single layer. Bake until potatoes are tender and lightly browned. Toss two or three times during baking. Bake at 475° for 30 to 35 minutes. Yield: 4 servings.

Lion Bill Townsend, Mount Airy Foothills Lions Club
Mount Airy, NC, USA

POTATO LOAF

6 medium potatoes, cooked in
   jackets
4 Tbsp. butter
3 Tbsp. flour
1½ tsp. salt
¼ tsp. pepper
1½ c. milk (more if needed)
1 Tbsp. parsley flakes
1 tsp. onion, chopped fine
1 c. sharp cheese, cut up

Cool potatoes; peel and cut into cubes. Melt butter; blend in flour. Add salt and pepper. Add milk and cool. If mixture is too thick, use additional milk, 1 teaspoon at a time. Stir in parsley and onion. Mix with potatoes. Pour into buttered loaf pan. Place in refrigerator and chill.* Bake 45 minutes in 350° oven. Sprinkle with cheese. Return to oven for 15 minutes.

This recipe goes well with meatloaf, roasts, etc., as it can be put into oven and cooked along with other dishes. Serves about 12; good for potlucks, too.

* May be chilled overnight to be cooked the following day.

Margaret Wooden, Princeton Lions Club
Princeton, IL, USA

MICROWAVE RED POTATOES AND ONIONS

5 medium red potatoes, thinly
   sliced
1 large onion (sweet or Vidalia),
   thinly sliced

1 tsp. Italian seasoning
3 Tbsp. melted margarine
Dash of salt

In ungreased 3 quart microwave-safe baking dish, layer 1 thinly sliced potato and layer of onion. Sprinkle with Italian seasoning and pepper. Drizzle butter on top. Continue layering till all ingredients have been used. Cover with vented plastic wrap. Microwave on HIGH 12 minutes or until tender.

Jill Morefield, Western Branch Lions Club
Portsmouth, VA

AUNT HELEN'S BAKED BEANS

2 lb. Northern navy beans
1 large can V-8 juice
1 lb. bacon

1 large onion
1 c. sugar

Wash beans and soak overnight. Save ⅓ of bean water. Chop onion and bacon. Add all ingredients to crock pot and cook on HIGH all night.

Great for potluck dinners. Enjoy.

Lioness Diane DeVincent, East Anne Arundel Lioness Club
Pasadena, MD, USA

BAKED BEANS

3 (1 lb. 12 oz.) cans pork and
   beans
1 medium onion, chopped
1 tsp. prepared mustard

¾ c. plus 1 Tbsp. ketchup
1½ c. firmly packed brown sugar
5 slices bacon, diced

Mix all together. Put in 3 quart baking dish. Cover. Bake at 300° for 3½ to 4 hours. Remove the cover and bake 30 minutes longer. Stir 2 or 3 times during baking.

Cindy Bamburg, Biloxi Lions Club
Biloxi, MS, USA

You make more friends by being interested in them
than by trying to get them interested in you.

❦ ❦ ❦

Doubt your doubts instead of your beliefs.

2075-99

BAKED BEAN CASSEROLE

1 can kidney beans (red)
1 small can lima beans (green)
1 can cut green beans

1 can Italian cut green beans
1 (22 oz.) jar "B&M baked beans"

Sauce:

1 Tbsp. Worcestershire sauce
3 Tbsp. vinegar
½ c. brown sugar
1 tsp. salt

1 small onion, chopped
8 to 10 slices bacon
¾ c. catsup

Drain liquid from all beans except the "B&M baked beans" and combine all in a buttered roaster or casserole dish. Mix the sauce ingredients, with the exception of bacon slices, and pour over the beans. Mix well. Cut up bacon slices into bits (uncooked) and sprinkle on top. Bake, uncovered, at 325° for one hour.

They will be back for seconds on this one!

Lion John H. Johnson, Glendive Noon Lions Club
Glendive, MT, Dawson County

LIZ'S CROCK POT BAKED BEANS

4 c. dried beans (mix of at least 3 kinds)
1 c. BBQ sauce (I use Silver Dollar City)
1 c. honey
1 Tbsp. dry onion flakes

1 or 2 stalks celery, diced
¼ red pepper, diced
¼ green pepper, diced
4 strips bacon
1½ tsp. salt
1 tsp. pepper

Put beans in 2½ quart crock pot and fill with water. Set on LOW and cook overnight. Drain water off. Cut bacon in small pieces and fry. Add bacon and grease to beans. Add all other ingredients. Add water as needed. Cook at least 5 hours more.

Liz Birchen, O'Fallon Lions Club
O'Fallon, MO, USA

The biggest problem with perfection is what to do with all the unused erasers.

❧ ❧ ❧

Gossip: Letting the chat out of the bag.

BAKED BEANS

2 lb. navy beans
1 large onion, chopped fine
¾ c. table molasses
1 tsp. dry mustard

½ c. firmly packed brown sugar
1 tsp. salt
½ lb. lean salt pork

Wash beans thoroughly in several waters. Place beans in large Dutch oven and cover with cold water. Make sure water is clear and beans clean because this water is used to cook beans. Let stand overnight. Add minced onion to beans and water and bring to a boil. Cover and simmer about 30 minutes or until skins begin to crack when you blow on them. Remove from heat and mix in remainder of ingredients except salt pork. Cut rind from salt pork and cube. Place rind in bottom of bean pot. Using slotted spoon, fill pot with beans, layering with salt pork. Pour enough liquid into bean pot to cover contents.

There may be too much beans for your bean pot, so you may want to divide salt pork. Use an ovenproof casserole dish with tight lid for remaining beans and salt pork. Pour liquid over to cover. Keep remaining liquid for use as beans are baking. Place bean pot and casserole dish on large cookie sheet (to catch any spillage) and bake in a 350°F. oven until juices come to a boil, about 1 hour. Turn oven down to 250°F., put lids on dishes, and bake for 8 to 10 hours, or until beans are tender, but not mushy. Mix periodically, adding remaining juices as needed. Beans should be evenly browned.

These beans are a great side dish with barbequed pork chops or ribs and baked potatoes. Beans freeze well in tightly covered containers for up to four months.

Lion Bob Marchant, Kenora Lions Club
Kenora, Ontario, Canada

HECTOR LIONS BAKED BEANS

8 lb. pinto beans
1 (50 oz.) can tomato soup
3 c. ketchup
1 (24 oz.) bottle molasses
2 medium onions

2 lb. diced ham
2 lb. brown sugar
½ tsp. pepper
1 Tbsp. chili powder
1 Tbsp. garlic salt

Soak beans in large electric roaster overnight. Cook beans next day until soft to bite. Drain liquid to just below level of beans. Add other ingredients. Heat thoroughly until ham and beans are tender.

We always use these beans for our large fundraisers - they are really good and economical.

Hector Lions Club
Hector, MO

BAKED BEANS

1 (No. 303) can pork and beans
½ c. chopped onion
2 Tbsp. prepared bar-b-q sauce
3 slices bacon (uncooked)

½ c. chopped sweet pepper
  (optional)
½ c. tomato catsup
2 Tbsp. molasses (optional)

Mix all ingredients, except bacon, and pour in baking dish. Place the uncooked bacon on top. Bake in 350° oven for 1 to 1½ hours.

Terry Kelly, Iron City Lions Club
Iron City, TN, USA

BEAN AND CHEESE ROAST

2 c. cooked white (navy) beans
1½ c. grated medium Cheddar
  cheese
1 small onion, finely chopped
¼ c. celery or apple, finely
  chopped

1 tsp. chopped parsley
½ to 1 tsp. salt
Pepper to taste
1 egg
2 Tbsp. fat
2 c. soft, stale bread crumbs

Mash drained beans; add cheese, onion, celery or apple, parsley, salt, and pepper. Beat egg and add to bean mixture, mixing thoroughly. Melt fat in a saucepan and in it, cook the bread crumbs until slightly browned. Add sufficient crumbs to bean-cheese mixture to produce consistency needed to shape into a loaf. Roll the loaf in remaining crumbs. Bake in 350°F. oven until heated well through and nicely browned (20 to 30 minutes). Serve hot with tomato sauce. Serves 6.

Micheal and Ruth Bartolf, Oxbow and District Lions Club
Oxbow, Saskatchewan, Canada

Status quo: That's Latin for the mess we're in.

❦ ❦ ❦

Pick your friends, but not to pieces.

❦ ❦ ❦

Truth has only to change hands a few times to become fiction.

❦ ❦ ❦

Always behave like a duck - keep calm and unruffled on the surface,
but paddle like the dickens underneath.

182

BLACK BEAN TORTILLA PIE

1 pkg. Pillsbury All-Ready pie
  crusts
3 Tbsp. oil
½ c. chopped green pepper
1 c. chopped onions
1 (15 oz.) can black beans,
  drained and rinsed
¾ c. salsa

2 Tbsp. minced jalapeno peppers
  (optional)
½ tsp. chili powder
½ tsp. cayenne pepper
8 oz. (2 c.) shredded Cheddar
  cheese
3 (8 inch) flour tortillas
½ c. sour cream

Prepare pie crusts according to directions for a 2 crust pie, using a 9 or 10 inch deep dish pie pan. Heat oven to 350°. Heat oil in large skillet over medium heat until hot. Add onions and bell pepper; cook and stir until tender. Add beans, salsa, jalapenos, chili powder, and cayenne; simmer about 10 minutes, stirring occasionally.

Spoon about ½ cup bean mixture into crust-lined pan. Sprinkle with ½ cup cheese and top with 1 tortilla. Repeat layers twice, sprinkling remaining cheese on top. Top with second crust and seal edges. Cut slits in top crust to vent steam. Bake 40 to 50 minutes until golden brown. Let stand 10 minutes before serving. Serve with sour cream. Serves 6 to 8.

John Simpson, Stafford-Missouri City Lions Club
Stafford-Missouri City, TX, USA

DILLY BEANS

2 c. vinegar
2 c. water
¼ c. salt
Fresh dill weed

Garlic
Raw green beans
Small red peppers

Bring vinegar, water, and salt to a boil. Keep hot on stove. In each canning jar, put some dill, garlic, raw green beans, and a small red pepper. Process in hot water bath 10 to 15 minutes (half-pints) and 20 minutes (quart). Begin timing when water starts to boil.

Sarah Wehling, Bothell Lions Club
Bothell, WA, USA

If opportunity doesn't knock, build a door.
Milton Berle

Footprints in the sands of time are not made sitting down.

GREEN BEANS WITH SAGE

1 lb. green beans
Salt and pepper

2 Tbsp. butter
¾ tsp. rubbed sage

Trim the green beans. Cook the beans in boiling salted water until they are tender, about 10 minutes. Drain. In the hot pot, melt the butter with ¼ teaspoon salt, ¼ teaspoon pepper, and the sage. Add the green beans and toss to coat. Makes 4 servings.

Per serving: 82 calories, 2 g protein, 6 g fat, 142 mg sodium, 782 g carbohydrate, 16 mg cholesterol.

Ahead-of-time tip: You can boil the green beans hours, or even days, in advance and reheat in the sage butter when you're ready to serve.

Barbara Joy Hess, Clarence Lions Club
Clarence Center, NY, USA

INDIA CURRY ROASTED GREEN BEANS

1 lb. green beans, trimmed
2 Tbsp. butter
1 tsp. curry powder
½ tsp. ground turmeric

½ tsp. ground coriander
¼ tsp. salt
¼ tsp. red-pepper flakes

Heat the oven to 425°. Put the beans in a large bowl. In a small pan over low heat, melt the butter with the curry powder, turmeric, coriander, salt, and red-pepper flakes. Pour the spice mixture over the beans and toss until they are well coated. Transfer the beans to a shallow roasting pan or jellyroll pan and bake until some of the beans begin to brown slightly, but are still crisp, approximately 15 minutes. Makes 4 servings.

Work time: 10 minutes. Total time: 30 minutes.

Per serving: 87 calories, 2 g protein, 6 g fat, 188 mg sodium, 8 g carbohydrate, 16 mg cholesterol.

Mrs. Mike Nowicki, Clarence Lions Club
Clarence Center, NY, USA

Every man carries with him the world in which he must live.

❦ ❦ ❦

The man who makes hard things easier is the educator.

GREEN BEAN CASSEROLE

2 cans seasoned, French cut
   green beans
1 can cream of mushroom soup
1 can French fried onion rings

1 slice process cheese
1 tsp. black pepper
1 Tbsp. bacon drippings

Cook green beans with bacon drippings until most of liquid is absorbed. Layer ingredients as follows: Green beans, soup, cheese, and onion rings. Repeat layers except for onion rings. Sprinkle last layer of soup with pepper. Bake at 350° for 30 to 45 minutes or until bubbly. During last 5 minutes of cooking, sprinkle with remainder of onion rings.

For variation, almonds or water chestnuts may be layered.

Nettie Favara, Greenwood Lions Club
Greenwood, MS, USA

GREEN BEAN AND POTATO CASSEROLE

1 qt. green beans, drained
4 medium potatoes, peeled and
   diced (precook)
1 (4 oz.) can mushrooms, drained
1 can celery soup

1 c. grated Cheddar cheese
1 small onion, diced
Salt and pepper to taste
1 can dried onion rings

Spread green beans in bottom of casserole dish. Next, add potatoes, which have been cooked. Mix together the celery soup, mushrooms, and onions. Add a small amount of milk if it is too thick. Pour over the potatoes. Spread the Cheddar cheese on top and bake in 350° oven until hot and bubbles. Before removing from oven, add the dried onion rings and bake 5 minutes longer or until brown.

Janet Colbert, Bullskin Township Lioness Club
Mt. Pleasant, PA

CABBAGE-GREEN BEANS

4 slices bacon, cut in small pieces
½ c. vinegar
¼ c. sugar
3 Tbsp. chopped onion
3 c. shredded cabbage

½ tsp. salt
¼ tsp. pepper
1 lb. can French-style green
   beans, drained

Cook bacon till crisp; remove and drain. Add vinegar, sugar, onion, cabbage, salt, and pepper to remaining fat in skillet. Cover and simmer 5 minutes more. Stir in bacon and serve.

Good warmed over, so you can make ahead.

Jo Anne Beavers, Bryan Lioness Club
Bryan, OH

SAUTEED FRESH CORN WITH SCALLIONS

4 ears corn (about 3 c. kernels)
3 scallions
1 Tbsp. butter
1 Tbsp. oil

Salt and pepper
1/8 tsp. mace
1/8 tsp. celery seed

Scrape the kernels from the ears of corn. Chop the white part of the scallion and slice the green part. In a frying pan, melt the butter in the oil over medium heat. Add the white part of the scallion and cook until tender, about 2 minutes. Add the corn, scallion tops, 1/2 teaspoon salt, 1/4 teaspoon pepper, the mace, and celery seed. Cover and cook, stirring occasionally, until the corn is tender, about 10 minutes. Makes 4 servings.

Per serving: 160 calories, 4 g protein, 8 g fat, 293 mg sodium, 23 g carbohydrate, 8 mg cholesterol.

Mrs. Mike Nowicki, Clarence Lions Club
Clarence Center, NY, USA

MICROWAVE CORN

Corn on the cob

Butter

Shuck and clean corn. Butter corn completely. Lay on microwave plate or wax paper in microwave. Cover with wax paper. Microwave on HIGH 10 to 15 minutes or until tender. *Delicious and easy.*

Virginia Bayer, Franklin Park Lions Club
Park Ridge, IL

CREAM STYLE CORN
(Southern style - Microwave)

8 to 10 ears tender corn (or 1
  can cream corn)
1/3 c. butter or bacon drippings
1/2 c. water

1/2 c. milk
2 Tbsp. cornstarch
Salt and pepper to taste

Cut corn from the cob halfway through kernels, then scrape remaining corn from each ear, catching all the corn juice. Add the water and butter or bacon drippings and place mixture in baking dish, covering tightly with plastic wrap. Microwave at HIGH power 7 to 9 minutes, stirring once. Add cornstarch to milk and blend. Add blended mixture to corn, stirring well. Cook at 70% power for 3 to 5 minutes, stirring once. Salt and pepper to taste.

Enjoy a taste delight - without all the stirring required in conventional cooking to prevent sticking.

Agnes Williams, Alpha Lions Club
Brookhaven, MS

FRESH CORN PUDDING

4 ears fresh corn, husked
3 oz. lean baked ham, diced
2 Tbsp. margarine or butter
½ c. chopped scallions
2 Tbsp. all-purpose flour
1 c. low-fat (1%) milk
½ tsp. dried thyme

½ tsp. salt
¼ tsp. pepper
2 egg yolks
5 egg whites
2 (7 oz.) jars roasted red peppers, drained
¼ to ½ tsp. hot red-pepper sauce

Preheat oven to 400°F. Spray a 12x8 inch baking dish with vegetable cooking spray. Cut kernels from each corn ear to yield about 4 cups. Place kernels into medium bowl with ham; toss lightly, then set aside.

In 2 quart saucepan, over medium heat, melt margarine. Add scallions and cook 2 minutes, stirring occasionally. Add flour; cook 1 minute, stirring frequently. Whisk in milk, thyme, salt, and pepper. Cook until mixture thickens, stirring occasionally.

In small bowl, beat egg yolks slightly. Stir some hot-milk mixture into yolks. Return yolk mixture to saucepan. Reduce heat to low; cook 2 minutes, stirring frequently. Remove from heat; stir in corn mixture and set aside.

In large bowl, with electric mixer at high speed, beat egg whites until stiff peaks form. Stir ¼ of the egg whites into corn mixture; fold in remaining egg whites. Spoon mixture into prepared dish. Place dish in oven. Reduce oven temperature to 350°F. Bake 30 minutes or until knife inserted into center comes out clean.

Meanwhile, in food processor or blender, process peppers until almost pureed. Remove to serving bowl; stir in hot pepper sauce. Serve sauce with corn pudding. Makes 6 servings.

Work time: 15 minutes. Total time: 45 minutes.

Per serving: 203 calories, 12 g protein, 8 g fat, 497 mg sodium, 23 g carbohydrate, 82 mg cholesterol.

Mrs. Lucy Aiken, Clarence Lions Club
Clarence Center, NY, USA

CORN CASSEROLE

1 can cream style corn
1 can whole kernel corn
¾ c. sour cream
1 stick oleo, melted
1 egg

Chopped onion (to taste)
Chopped green pepper (to taste)
Salt and pepper
1 pkg. Jiffy corn muffin mix
1 c. grated yellow cheese

Mix together all ingredients except muffin mix and cheese. Place in greased 9x13 inch pan or casserole dish. Stir in dry muffin mix and cheese. Bake 40 to 50 minutes at 350°.

P. Diane Baldwin, Broken Bow Lions Club
Broken Bow, NE, USA

CHEESY CHILI CORN CASSEROLE

2 (16 oz.) pkg. frozen sweet corn, thawed and drained
2 (8 oz.) pkg. Velveeta, shredded and divided
1¼ c. milk

1¼ c. coarsely chopped corn chips, divided
1 c. chopped red bell peppers
1 (4 oz.) can chopped green chilies, drained

Heat oven to 350°. Mix corn, 3½ cups Velveeta, milk, ½ cup corn chips, peppers, and green chilies until well blended. Spoon into greased 12x17 inch baking dish. Sprinkle with remaining ½ cup Velveeta cheese and balance of corn chips on top. Bake 50 minutes and continue baking maybe 5 more minutes until all cheeses look melted. Let stand 5 minutes before serving. Makes 10 to 12 servings.

This is kind of a southwestern dish. It will be a hit when served. Not really "hot" at all - just really tasty!

JoAnn Jones, Mathews Lions Club
North, VA

BAKED CORN CASSEROLE

2 cans whole corn, drained
1 can creamed crushed corn
1 egg, beaten
2 Tbsp. butter

½ tsp. salt
¼ tsp. pepper
2 Tbsp. flour
½ Tbsp. chopped parsley

Mix together. Pour into a buttered casserole. Top with butter and French fried onion rings. Bake at 350° for 25 minutes.

Evelyn Herschberger, Bullskin Township Lioness Club
Mt. Pleasant, PA

SCALLOPED CORN

1 can whole kernel corn
1 can creamed style corn
1 box Jiffy corn bread mix

8 oz. sour cream
1 stick melted margarine

Mix together. Bake at 350° for 45 minutes.

Lion Ida Rohrer, Moundbuilders Lions Club
Newark, OH, USA

CORN CASSEROLE

1 (16 oz.) can whole-kernel corn
1 (16 oz.) can cream-style corn
½ stick margarine or butter

1 c. process cheese, diced
1 c. small elbow macaroni
¼ c. diced onions

Butter a casserole dish. Combine undrained corns, margarine, cheese, macaroni, and onions. Bake, covered, at 375° for 30 minutes. Remove cover and continue to bake another 30 minutes.

Nancy Lansky, Tuscola Lions Club
Tuscola, IL, USA

CORN BREAD CASSEROLE

1 pkg. Jiffy corn bread mix
1 can whole (kernel) corn with
   juice
1 can creamed corn

1 stick margarine
2 eggs
1 c. sour cream or yogurt

    Preheat oven to 350°F. In a large bowl, mix together eggs, margarine, and sour cream. Add the corn one can at a time and mix. Add Jiffy corn bread mix. Make sure well blended together. Pour into 8x12 inch baking dish and bake for about 45 minutes. Let cool for five minutes; cut into squares and serve.

    This dish is easily doubled for a large crowd and is delicious with any main course.

Lion Nancy Smith, Lake of the Woods Lions Club
Kenora, Ontario, Canada

CORN PUDDING

1 can Del Monte cream style corn
1 can Del Monte kernel corn
2 c. milk
2 eggs

Salt and pepper to taste
1½ c. Ritz cracker crumbs or
   about ¾ of 1 sleeve
½ c. butter

    Make no substitutions! Whip milk and eggs till foamy. Add corn, seasonings, and crackers. Melt butter and pour into center of pudding. Stir lightly until butter comes around edges. Bake at 350° for 45 minutes to 1 hour. It may be brown around edges and when shaken, will be slightly firm in center.

    This is a 4 generation family recipe which is not usually shared!

Anne Tibbetts, South Jefferson Lions Club
Adams, NY

Children are like wet cement, whatever falls on them makes an impression.

❧ ❧ ❧

Diplomacy is the art of letting other people have your way.

❧ ❧ ❧

Failure is one thing than can be achieved without effort.

❧ ❧ ❧

The less you talk, the more you are listened to.

CORN-OYSTER BAKE

2 cans oyster stew
1 (1 lb. 1 oz.) can cream style
   corn
1 (1 lb. 1 oz.) can whole-kernel
   corn, drained
1¼ c. crushed soda cracker
   crumbs
1 egg, slightly beaten
½ tsp. salt

Dash of pepper
2 Tbsp. pimiento, chopped
¼ c. onion, chopped
1 tsp. parsley, chopped
¼ tsp. ground sage
2 Tbsp. butter, melted
½ c. cracker crumbs

Combine stew, cream corn, whole-kernel corn, 1¼ cups crackers, egg, seasoning, pimiento, and onion. Pour into greased 2 quart casserole. Combine melted butter and ½ cup cracker crumbs; sprinkle on top of corn mixture. Bake in 350° oven for 1 hour or until knife inserted comes out clean. Serves 8 to 10.

Optional: Add 1 or 2 small cans oysters to mix.

This dish is a must in our family at Thanksgiving/Christmas. Good anytime. Wow them at your next potluck supper.

Lois Shinkle, First Female President (1999 to 2000),
Elizabethtown Lions Club
Elizabethtown, KY, USA

SWEET-AND-SOUR RED CABBAGE

2 Tbsp. olive oil
¼ c. packed brown sugar
3 Tbsp. vinegar
1 c. water

¼ tsp. salt
A dash of pepper
¼ tsp. caraway seeds
4 c. peeled and sliced cabbage

In a large skillet, combine oil, brown sugar, vinegar, water, salt, and pepper. Cook for 2 to 3 minutes. Add caraway seeds and stir. Add cabbage; cover and cook for 10 minutes over medium low heat, stirring occasionally. Add apples; cook, uncovered, for about 10 minutes more or until tender, stirring occasionally. Yields 6 to 8 servings.

This keeps well when frozen in an airtight container.

Ann K. Brumback, Silver Run Union Mills Lions Club
Westminster, MD, USA

Happiness can be thought, taught, and caught - but not bought.

❦ ❦ ❦

You will never get experience on the easy-payment plan.

ZUCCHINI PILAF

2 zucchini, sliced
2 Tbsp. olive oil
2 cloves garlic
1 c. long-grain rice
2 Tbsp. butter

1½ c. chicken stock
½ c. dry white wine
Salt to taste
Fresh grated Parmesan or
Romano cheese

Saute the zucchini in the oil and garlic. Remove from pan. Add the rice and brown it in the butter. Place the rice in a saucepan and add the chicken broth and white wine. Bring to a boil without lid. Add salt. Place the zucchini on top of the rice. Do not stir. Cover and simmer until rice is tender (about 20 minutes). Stir in cheese before serving.

Betty Rutledge, Bryan Lioness Club
Bryan, OH

GARDEN BOUNTY MEDLEY

4 c. thickly sliced zucchini
  (unpeeled)
4 tomatoes, sliced
2 medium onions, sliced
1 tsp. salt (or to taste)
¼ tsp. pepper (or to taste)

1 tsp. garlic powder
¼ c. fresh chopped basil
¼ c. fresh chopped oregano
1½ c. American cheese, grated
4 slices bacon (uncooked)

Preheat oven to 350°F. Place zucchini in a 9x13 inch baking dish. Season with salt, pepper, garlic powder, fresh basil, and fresh oregano. Top with layer of sliced tomatoes, sliced onions, and grated American cheese. Cut bacon into pieces and place over cheese. Bake for 45 to 60 minutes.

Tastes even better next day when reheated.

Note: If fresh basil and oregano are not available, 1 teaspoon dried basil and 1 teaspoon dried oregano can be substituted, but will not be quite as flavorful.

Lion Joan Shores, St. Charles Lions Club
St. Charles, MO, USA

If you cannot get people to listen any other way, tell them it's confidential.

❦ ❦ ❦

People can't change truth, but truth can change people.

❦ ❦ ❦

Life is tragic for the person who has plenty to live on,
but nothing to live for.

2075-99

191

ZUCCHINI CRESCENT PIE

4 c. thinly sliced, unpeeled
    zucchini
1 c. coarsely chopped onion
¼ c. margarine
½ c. chopped parsley or flakes
½ tsp. salt
½ tsp. pepper
¼ tsp. garlic powder

¼ tsp. basil
¼ tsp. oregano leaves
2 eggs, well beaten
8 oz. Mozzarella cheese
8 oz. can quick crescent frozen
    dinner rolls
2 tsp. Dijon or prepared mustard

Heat oven to 375°. In fry pan, cook zucchini and onion in the margarine until tender, about 10 minutes. Stir in parsley and seasonings. In large bowl, blend cheese and eggs. Stir in vegetables. Separate dough into 8 triangles. Place in 10 inch pie tin or 12x8 inch baking dish; press over bottom and up sides to form a crust. Pour vegetable mix. Bake at 375° for 18 to 20 minutes or until a knife in center comes clean. Let stand a few minutes before cutting in wedges.

Have lots of zucchini? You'll love this.

Betty Lamphere, Lyons Muir Lions Club
Muir, MI, USA

ZUCCHINI BOATS

1 large zucchini
1 lb. bulk sausage
1 egg
Parmesan cheese
Progresso bread crumbs
2 toes garlic, minced

1 can stewed tomatoes
Herbs to taste - parsley, sage,
    oregano
Pepper to taste
Tomato sauce

Wash 1 large zucchini. Cut in half lengthwise. Microwave on HIGH until crisp-tender, 5 to 10 minutes, depending on size of zucchini. Scoop out the "meat" of the zucchini, leaving about ½ inch thickness remaining. Place cooked zucchini in large bowl and set aside. Saute sausage and garlic over medium heat till cooked thoroughly. Drain. Place sausage in bowl with zucchini "meat." Add egg, Parmesan cheese to taste, Progresso bread crumbs to taste, stewed tomatoes, salt (optional), and pepper and herbs to taste. Mix thoroughly by hand. Stuff zucchini shells with sausage mixture. Pour tomato sauce over entire stuffed zucchini and bake at 350° for 20 minutes or until thoroughly heated.

May also be placed in microwave on HIGH for 10 minutes.

Elaine Germont, Glendale Evening Lions Club
Glendale, AZ, USA

A different world cannot be built by indifferent people.

SQUASH GRATIN

3 Tbsp. butter
1 large clove garlic, minced
½ tsp. dried thyme
½ tsp. salt

¼ tsp. pepper
2 lb. butternut or Hubbard squash
⅓ c. dry bread crumbs

Heat oven to 400°. Melt butter. Combine 1 tablespoon butter with the garlic, thyme, salt, and half the pepper. Halve squash lengthwise and cut into ½ inch slices. Peel each slice with a paring knife and halve the slices. Put squash in a 1½ quart baking dish. Pour butter mixture over and toss to combine. Combine remaining 2 tablespoons melted butter, bread crumbs, and remaining pepper. Sprinkle crumb mixture over squash. Bake until squash is tender and top is golden brown, about 40 minutes. Makes 4 servings.

Per serving: 187 calories, 3 g protein, 9 g fat, 407 mg sodium, 26 g carbohydrate, 24 mg cholesterol.

Mrs. Mike Nowicki, Clarence Lions Club
Clarence Center, NY, USA

MINTED SQUASH GRATIN

1 lb. yellow squash (about 2)
1 lb. zucchini (about 3)
2 Tbsp. olive oil
Salt and pepper

¾ tsp. dried thyme
2 Tbsp. butter
⅓ c. dried bread crumbs
2 tsp. chopped fresh mint

Butter a 1½ quart gratin or baking dish. Slice squash and zucchini lengthwise into pieces about ¼ inch thick. In a large frying pan, heat oil over medium-high heat. Add squash and zucchini and sprinkle with 1 teaspoon salt. Cover and cook 5 minutes. Remove cover and continue cooking until tender and the liquid has evaporated, 5 to 10 minutes. Stir in thyme and ¼ teaspoon pepper. Remove slices and drain on paper towels. Heat broiler. Arrange squash in dish. Melt butter and combine with the crumbs, ⅛ teaspoon salt, and ⅛ teaspoon pepper. Sprinkle over the squash and zucchini. Broil until top is browned, about 1 minute. Sprinkle with the mint. Makes 4 servings.

Per serving: 184 calories, 4 g protein, 13 g fat, 702 mg sodium, 15 g carbohydrate, 15 mg cholesterol.

Joanne M. Wetzler, Clarence Lions Club
Clarence Center, NY, USA

To teach is to learn twice.

WINTER-VEGETABLE SAUTE

1 butternut squash (about 2 lb.)
1 onion
1 clove garlic
2 Tbsp. oil
¾ tsp. dried thyme
Salt

½ lb. green cabbage (about 4 c.
　shredded)
½ lb. red cabbage (about 4 c.
　shredded)
1 Tbsp. wine vinegar
1 Tbsp. butter

Peel and seed squash. Cut into pieces, about ½ x ¾ inch. Chop onion. Mince garlic. In a large frying pan, heat 1 tablespoon oil over medium heat. Add onion and garlic. Cover and cook until tender, about 3 minutes. Add remaining 1 tablespoon oil, squash, thyme, and ½ teaspoon salt. Cover, reduce heat, and cook until squash is tender, about 15 minutes.

Meanwhile, shred cabbages. Toss red cabbage with the vinegar. Add butter and cabbages to pan, cover, and cook until cabbage is very tender, about 30 minutes. Taste and add salt if needed. Makes 6 servings.

Mrs. Mike Nowicki, Clarence Lions Club
Clarence Center, NY, USA

BUTTERNUT SQUASH BAKE

⅓ c. butter
¾ c. sugar
2 eggs

1 (5 oz.) can evaporated milk
1 tsp. vanilla
2 c. mashed, cooked squash

Topping:

½ c. crisp rice cereal
¼ c. packed brown sugar

¼ c. chopped pecans
2 Tbsp. melted butter

In a mixing bowl, cream butter and sugar. Beat in eggs, milk, and vanilla. Stir in squash (mixture will be thin). Pour into a greased 11x7 inch baking pan. Bake, uncovered, at 350° for 45 minutes. Combine topping ingredients; sprinkle over casserole. Bake for 5 to 10 minutes.

Deb Fergeson, Kal-Haven Trail Lions Club
Gobles, MI

Anyone who isn't pulling his weight is pushing his luck.

❦ ❦ ❦

Income Tax Advice - Pay It!

SPINACH PIE

Pie shell (frozen or otherwise)
1 lb. Ricotta cheese
4 beaten eggs
1 (10 oz.) box chopped spinach
1 small diced onion
3 Tbsp. flour
½ c. grated sharp or Mozzarella
    cheese

¼ tsp. salt
½ tsp. dill weed (dry)
Black pepper
Butter for sauteed onions
1 c. sour cream
Dash of nutmeg

Use large deep dish pie pan. Chill pie shell. Saute onion in butter. Add salt and pepper; set aside. Beat eggs. Mix in Ricotta cheese, sour cream, and flour. Fold in cooked, drained spinach, sauteed onions, and grated cheese. You may use both sharp and Mozzarella or one cheese. Add dill weed and blend well. Pour into pie shell. Dash nutmeg on top and add extra cheese and black pepper if you wish. Bake at 350° for 1 hour. Allow to cool 15 minutes after it is baked before serving.

In honor of all Lion Tamers past and present.
Lion Ann K. Brumback of Littlestown, PA,
Silver Run Union Mills Lions Club
Westminster, MD, USA

SPINACH STRATA

54 Ritz crackers
2 (10 oz.) pkg. frozen chopped
    spinach, thawed and well-
    drained
10 oz. Muenster cheese, grated

2 Tbsp. Dijon mustard
5 eggs
2½ c. milk
½ tsp. liquid hot pepper
    seasoning
2 cloves garlic, minced

In 2 quart shallow baking dish, arrange 18 Ritz crackers in 3 long rows. Combine spinach and 2 cups grated cheese; sprinkle half of mixture over crackers. Repeat layers. Top with remaining crackers and sprinkle with remaining cheese.

In medium bowl, beat together milk, eggs, mustard, liquid hot pepper seasoning, and garlic. Pour evenly over mixture in baking dish. Refrigerate for one hour. Bake at 350° for 1 hour, until puffed and golden. Cut into squares.
Agnes Williams, Alpha Lions Club
Brookhaven, MS, USA

Poor indeed is the man who cannot enjoy the simple things of life.

FRESH SPINACH CASSEROLE

2½ lb. spinach
1½ tsp. salt
2 Tbsp. margarine
2 eggs, slightly beaten

1 c. milk
⅛ tsp. pepper
1 tsp. finely grated onion
½ c. shredded Swiss cheese

Trim stems from spinach and wash leaves well. Put into a large pan or Dutch oven. Add 1 teaspoon salt; cover and cook quickly in the water that clings to the leaves until tender and bright green (about 3 minutes). Drain well in a colander, pressing out water lightly with the back of a spoon; chop finely.

In a bowl, gently mix the spinach, remaining ½ teaspoon salt, butter, eggs, milk, pepper, onion, and cheese. Pour into a shallow 1 quart baking dish. (Cover and refrigerate if done ahead.) Uncover and bake in a 325° oven until set (about 30 minutes, 45 minutes if refrigerated). Serve immediately. Makes 6 servings.

Sarah Wehling, Bothell Lions Club
Bothell, WA, USA

SPINACH CASSEROLE

14 oz. pkg. frozen chopped
    spinach
2 Tbsp. chopped onion
2 beaten eggs
½ c. milk (or some of spinach
    juice)

½ c. shredded sharp Cheddar
    cheese
½ c. buttered soft bread crumbs
¼ tsp. salt
¼ tsp. pepper

Cook and drain the spinach. Mix all ingredients, except bread crumbs, and put in 1½ quart casserole. Top with bread crumbs. Bake at 350° for 20 minutes.

Liz Birchen, O'Fallon Lions Club
O'Fallon, MO, USA

SAUTEED FENNEL AND SPINACH

1 bulb fennel
2 Tbsp. oil
Salt and pepper

1 Tbsp. lemon juice
10 oz. pkg. cleaned spinach

Trim the fennel and cut it into thin slices. In a large frying pan, heat the oil over medium-high heat. Add the fennel and ½ teaspoon salt. Cover and reduce the heat to medium-low. Cook until the fennel has softened, 8 to 10 minutes. Stir in the lemon juice. Add the spinach, ¼ teaspoon salt, and ¼ teaspoon pepper and stir just until the spinach begins to wilt. Taste for seasoning and add more salt and pepper if needed. Makes 4 servings.

Per serving: 94 calories, 3 g protein, 7 g fat, 571 mg sodium, 6 g carbohydrate, 0 mg cholesterol.

Joann M. Brownell, Clarence Lions Club
Clarence Center, NY, USA

BEST BROCCOLI CASSEROLE

1 c. water
½ tsp. salt
1 c. instant rice
¼ c. butter or margarine
¼ c. chopped onion
¼ c. chopped celery
1 (10¾ oz.) can condensed cream
of mushroom soup (undiluted)

1 (10¾ oz.) can condensed cream
of celery soup (undiluted)
1 (10 oz.) pkg. frozen chopped
broccoli, thawed
½ c. diced process American
cheese

In a saucepan, bring water and salt to a boil. Stir in rice; cover and remove from the heat. Let stand for 5 minutes. In a skillet, saute onion and celery in butter until tender. Add to rice. Add soup, broccoli, and cheese. Transfer to a greased 1½ quart baking dish. Bake at 350° for 1 hour. Yield: 6 servings.

BROCCOLI CASSEROLE

2 (10 oz.) boxes broccoli cuts
1 stack Ritz cracker crumbs
1 small jar Cheez Whiz

½ to ⅓ c. milk
½ stick butter or margarine

Mix Cheez Whiz and milk. Start with layer of broccoli in a greased baking dish, then a layer of cracker crumbs, then layer of broccoli. Put cheese sauce over, then end with a layer of cracker crumbs. Melt butter and pour on top. Bake at 350° for 20 minutes or until brown on top.

Sue Bubb, Burnham Lions Club
McClure, PA, Miffin

CHEEZY BROCCOLI BAKE

1 (10 oz.) broccoli (frozen or
fresh)
1 (10 oz.) can Cheddar cheese
soup
1 (5 oz.) can ham or chicken (any
brand)

1 c. cooked rice
½ c. sour cream
½ c. bread crumbs

Stir soup and cream together. Add broccoli, ham or chicken, and cooked rice. Mix well and put in ½ quart casserole. Sprinkle bread crumbs on top. Bake at 350°.

"A pessimist sees the difficulty in every opportunity; an optimist sees the opportunity in every difficulty." Sir Winston Churchill.

Denny Culbert, Scio Lions Club
Scio, NY, USA

WARM BROCCOLI WITH PARMESAN

2 Tbsp. olive oil
1 Tbsp. red-wine vinegar
½ tsp. salt
⅛ tsp. pepper

1 head broccoli (about 1 lb.)
1 oz. Parmesan cheese, shaved
  with vegetable peeler (about
  ¾ c.) or grated (about 2
  Tbsp.)

In a small bowl, combine olive oil, vinegar, salt, and pepper. Steam broccoli until just tender, about 5 minutes. Remove broccoli from pan and discard steaming liquid. Return broccoli to pan and cook until most of the water is evaporated, 30 to 60 seconds. Add oil mixture and cook over high heat until almost evaporated, about 1 minute longer. Allow to cool slightly, then top with Parmesan and serve. Makes 4 servings.

Per serving: 96 calories, 4 g protein, 8 g fat, 338 mg sodium, 5 g carbohydrate, 2 mg cholesterol.

Joanne M. Wetzler, Clarence Lions Club
Clarence Center, NY, USA

BROCCOLI PESTO CHEESE RAVIOLI

10 oz. pkg. frozen chopped
  broccoli, thawed
3 Tbsp. olive oil
2 Tbsp. grated Parmesan cheese
1½ tsp. fresh lemon juice

¼ tsp. minced garlic
¼ tsp. salt
⅛ tsp. black pepper
2 Tbsp. walnut pieces
1 lb. cheese ravioli

In a blender or processor, combine half of broccoli, the oil, cheese, lemon juice, garlic, salt, and pepper and blend until the mixture is smooth. Add walnuts and then pulse machine until nuts are just chopped. Set aside.

Cook the ravioli in a large pot of boiling salted water until just tender. During the last minute of cooking, add the remaining broccoli to the pot to heat through. Drain ravioli and broccoli and return to the warm pot. Stir in the broccoli mixture until well coated. Serve with extra cheese alongside. Makes 4 servings.

Work time: 25 minutes. Total time: 25 minutes.

Per serving: 505 calories, 21 g protein, 28 g fat, 680 mg sodium, 44 g carbohydrate, 102 mg cholesterol.

Lion John J. Hess, Clarence Lions Club
Clarence Center, NY, USA

Love is a hammer that will break the hardest heart.

SAUTEED FENNEL AND BROCCOLI

1 bunch broccoli (about 1½ lb.)
1 bulb fennel (about ½ lb.)
2 cloves garlic
Salt

1 Tbsp. butter
1 Tbsp. oil
1 Tbsp. lemon juice
⅛ tsp. red-pepper flakes
  (optional)

Cut broccoli into small florets. Cut the fennel into thin slices. Mince garlic. In a large frying pan filled with about ¼ inch boiling salted water, cook broccoli until tender, 3 to 5 minutes. Drain and set aside.

In the same pan, combine the butter and oil over medium-high heat. When butter has melted, add fennel, garlic, and ½ teaspoon salt. Cover, reduce heat to low, and cook, stirring occasionally, until fennel is tender, about 8 minutes. Stir in broccoli, lemon juice, and pepper flakes. Cook the vegetables until heated through, about 2 minutes. Makes 4 servings.

Per serving: 115 calories, 6 g protein, 7 g fat, 372 mg sodium, 11 g carbohydrate, 8 mg cholesterol.

Mrs. Mike Nowicki, Clarence Lions Club
Clarence Center, NY, USA

We are responsible for not only what we say, but also for how we say it.

❧ ❧ ❧

If you want to leave footprints in the sands of time, wear work shoes.

❧ ❧ ❧

Your words may hide your thoughts, but your actions will reveal them.

❧ ❧ ❧

Achievers are not born, they are made.

PEPPER AND ONION FRITTATA

2 tsp. olive oil
1 small green bell pepper, seeded and cut into ½ inch pieces
1 small red bell pepper, seeded and cut into ½ inch pieces
1 small yellow bell pepper, seeded and cut into ½ inch pieces
1 medium onion, cut into thin wedges

10 egg whites
½ c. nonfat Ricotta cheese
1¼ tsp. minced fresh thyme
¼ tsp. salt
¼ tsp. pepper
8 pitted oil-cured or ripe olives, each cut in half

Preheat oven to 375°F. In a 10 inch nonstick skillet, with oven-safe handle (or wrap a non-oven-safe handle with double thickness of foil before oven use), over medium heat, heat oil. Add peppers and onions and cook, stirring frequently, until vegetables are just tender, about 7 minutes.

In large bowl with wire whisk, beat egg whites, cheese, thyme, salt, and pepper until frothy. Pour egg white mixture into skillet. Cook 2 to 3 minutes until mixture begins to set. With a plastic spatula, gently pull and push egg mixture, allowing some of the uncooked egg mixture to flow to bottom of pan. Sprinkle top of frittata with olives; place pan in oven. Bake 10 minutes or until set and top is lightly browned. Makes 4 servings.

Work time: 10 minutes. Total time: 20 minutes.

Per serving: 129 calories, 14 g protein, 5 g fat, 383 mg sodium, 7 g carbohydrate, 0 mg cholesterol, 169 mg calcium.

Mrs. Lucy Aiken, Clarence Lions Club
Clarence Center, NY, USA

HEAVENLY ONIONS

4 large sweet onions, sliced
½ lb. fresh mushrooms
¼ c. margarine
1 can cream of chicken soup
½ c. milk

3 Tbsp. soy sauce
Salt and pepper
10 slices French bread
¾ c. shredded Swiss cheese

Saute onions and mushrooms in margarine. Mix together chicken soup, milk, soy sauce, salt, and pepper. Layer the two mixtures in 9x13 inch pan with the onion mixture on the bottom and the soup mixture on top. Butter the bread on both sides and lay on top of casserole. Sprinkle with Swiss cheese. Cover pan tightly with foil and refrigerate overnight. Bake, uncovered, at 350° for about 40 minutes.

Betty Rutledge, Bryan Lioness Club
Bryan, OH

BAKED VIDALIA ONION

Salt
Pepper
Parmesan cheese

Butter
Large Vidalia onion

Cut off top and bottom of a large Vidalia onion; cut in half. Sprinkle each half with salt, pepper, and Parmesan cheese. Dot with butter. Bake 5 minutes in microwave oven on HIGH.

Lioness Edith Ramsay, East Anne Arundel Lioness Club, District 22A
Pasadena, MD, USA

SICILIAN BAKED ONIONS

Hot, they are eaten with butter, salt, and pepper. Cold, they are eaten with salt, pepper, a little olive oil, and a squeeze of lemon juice. The onions must be unpeeled. Bake 1 to 1½ hours, then the skins come off.

Sarah Wehling, Bothell Lions Club
Bothell, WA, USA

CARROT CASSEROLE

5 c. carrot rounds
5 c. diced, unpeeled red apples
½ c. flour
⅓ c. white sugar

¼ c. brown sugar
6 or 8 Tbsp. oleo, melted
1 c. frozen orange juice
   (undiluted)

Partially cook carrots. Layer carrots, then apples, carrots, and apples. Combine remaining ingredients and pour over carrots and apples. Bake in 350° oven for 1 hour.

Jean Chestnut, Columbus Noon Lions Club
Columbus, NE, USA

CHEESY CARROT RICE CASSEROLE

2 c. cooked Minute rice
2 c. grated carrot
1 c. grated old Cheddar cheese
½ c. Miracle Whip salad dressing
   or Miracle Whip light
   dressing
¼ c. milk

1 egg, beaten
1 Tbsp. onion, minced
½ tsp. salt
Little pepper
Chopped parsley

Preheat oven to 350°F. Combine ingredients, mixing lightly. Pour into 4 cup casserole. Cover and bake for 35 minutes. Serves 6.

Micheal and Ruth Bartolf, Oxbow and District Lions Club
Oxbow, Saskatchewan, Canada

HONEYED CARROTS

12 carrots, cooked and cut up in large pieces
1 (No. 2) can small onions
¼ lb. oleo
¼ c. honey
1 tsp. oregano
¼ c. ketchup
¼ c. brown sugar
¼ c. fresh chopped parsley

Melt oleo. Add brown sugar and remaining sauce ingredients. Pour over carrots and onions in lightly greased casserole. Bake 40 minutes at 350°.

Joanne Tuttle, Conroe Noon Lions Club
Conroe, TX, USA

ASPARAGUS CASSEROLE

3 c. fresh or 2 pkg. frozen asparagus
3 Tbsp. margarine
3 Tbsp. flour
1 c. asparagus liquid or milk
½ tsp. salt
½ c. grated American cheese
2 c. large pulled bread crumbs

Cook asparagus until just tender. Add ½ teaspoon salt towards end. Drain well, saving liquid. Place drained asparagus in greased round baking dish that measures 10 x 1½ inches.

Prepare sauce: Melt margarine; add flour, then liquid, a little at a time, stirring constantly. Cook until thick. Add salt and grated cheese. Continue to cook until cheese is fully melted. If sauce is too thick, add more liquid. Pour over asparagus. Top with crumbs and drizzle with melted butter. Bake at 325° for 30 minutes.

Supporter of Lions, Princeton Lions Club
Princeton, IL, USA

ASPARAGUS CASSEROLE

1 can asparagus
1 small jar pimento
1 can mushroom soup
Grated cheese

Place ½ can of asparagus in a buttered baking dish. Sprinkle ½ of the pimento over this. Spread ½ of the soup over the pimento. Repeat with asparagus, pimento, and soup. Sprinkle with grated cheese. Cook at 350° for 20 minutes.

Table Grace

"We thank you God for happy hearts,
For rain and sunny weather.
We thank you God for this our food,
And that we are together."

Rayford Kimbrell, Iron City Lions Club
Iron City, TN, USA

202

ASPARAGUS PATTIES

10 oz. frozen chopped asparagus
3 eggs, beaten
¼ c. bread crumbs
¼ c. cheese, grated

Salt to taste
Pepper to taste
Oil or butter

Combine all the ingredients except the oil. Drop by tablespoon into hot oil. Fry on both sides until golden brown.

Joan Katz, Stafford-Missouri City Lions Club
Stafford, TX, USA

ITALIAN FRITTATA

1 lb. thin asparagus
Salt
2 Tbsp. extra-virgin olive oil
3 medium shallots, minced
6 large eggs

½ c. freshly grated Parmesan
    cheese
¼ c. shredded basil leaves
Fresh ground black pepper

Bring several quarts of water to a boil. Snap and discard tough ends from the asparagus. Slice asparagus diagonally into 1 inch long pieces. Add asparagus to the boiling water. Salt to taste. Cook until almost tender, about 1.5 minutes. Drain and set aside.

Preheat broiler. Heat oil in a nonstick skillet with an ovenproof handle. Swirl the oil to coat the bottom of the pan evenly. Add the shallots and saute over medium heat until translucent, about 3 minutes. Add asparagus and cook about 30 seconds. Use a fork to lightly beat the eggs, cheese, and basil. Salt and pepper to taste. Add egg mixture to pan and stir gently. Cook over medium-low heat, occasionally sliding a spatula around the edges of the pan to loosen the frittata as it sets. Continue cooking until frittata is set, except for the top, about 8 minutes.

Place the pan under the broiler and cook just until the top is golden brown and set, about 1 to 2 minutes. Do not burn. Invert the frittata on a large dish and cut into wedges. Yield: 4 servings.

Lonnie Morse, Spokane-Southeast Lions Club
Otis Orchards, WA

Cooperation is doing with a smile what you have to do anyway.

❧ ❧ ❧

An ounce of accomplishment is worth a ton or more of good intentions.

TOMATO-EGGPLANT BAKE

¼ c. olive oil
1 small garlic clove, minced
1 Tbsp. chopped fresh sage or 1
   tsp. dried

1 small eggplant, sliced thin
10 small plum tomatoes, sliced
½ tsp. salt
¼ tsp. pepper

Preheat broiler. Adjust rack to setting closest to heating element. In a cup, combine oil, garlic, and sage; set aside. In a 10 inch cast-iron or heavy-bottom skillet with ovenproof handle (or wrap non-ovenproof skillet handle with double thickness of aluminum foil), arrange eggplant in overlapping fashion to fit. Brush with half the oil mixture. Broil about 10 minutes, just until tender. Remove from the oven and arrange tomato slices over the eggplant. Drizzle with the remaining oil mixture. Sprinkle with salt and pepper. Broil 8 minutes, until the tomatoes are soft and lightly browned. Makes 6 servings.

Per serving: 106 calories, 1 g protein, 9 g fat, 189 mg sodium, 6 g carbohydrate, 0 mg cholesterol.

Tip: For best flavor and texture, do not refrigerate tomatoes. They will turn mealy when stored below 55°F.

Mrs. Mike Nowicki, Clarence Lions Club
Clarence Center, NY, USA

EGGPLANT CASSEROLE

1 very large or 2 small eggplants
¼ stick margarine or butter
2 tsp. Worcestershire sauce
1 diced onion

1 diced green pepper
1 can cream of mushroom soup
1½ c. buttered cracker crumbs

Peel, cube, and boil eggplant until barely tender, approximately 10 to 15 minutes. Drain well and mash. Set aside.

To make bread crumbs, melt several tablespoons margarine or butter in skillet and stir in crumbs until coated. Set aside.

Melt ¼ stick of margarine or butter in skillet. Add one diced onion and one diced green pepper. Cook until tender. Remove from heat and add one can cream of mushroom soup, 2 teaspoons Worcestershire sauce, one cup buttered cracker crumbs, and the mashed eggplant. Pour into a buttered casserole dish and cover with the balance of the buttered cracker crumbs. Bake at 350° until bubbly and lightly browned.

Vivian Houser, Foley Lions Club
Foley, AL

No one is rich enough to do without a neighbor.

MIXED VEGETABLE DELITE

2 pkg. (10 oz.) mixed vegetables
1 c. celery
1 c. mayonnaise
¾ c. onions

1½ c. sharp cheese, grated
1 roll Ritz crackers
1 stick margarine, melted

Mix mixed vegetables (thawed), celery, mayonnaise, and onions. Stir in ¾ cup grated cheese into vegetable mixture. Put in casserole. Spread balance of grated cheese over all vegetables. Crush Ritz crackers and spread over all ingredients. Drizzle melted margarine over mixture and bake at 350° for 30 minutes.

JoAnn Jones, Mathews Lions Club
North, VA

MIXED VEGETABLE CASSEROLE

1 can mixed vegetables
1 c. chopped onions
1 can water chestnuts, chopped
¾ c. mayonnaise

1 c. Cheddar cheese, shredded
½ roll Ritz crackers
½ stick oleo or butter

Mix first five ingredients together and pour into buttered one quart casserole. Top with crushed Ritz crackers and cover top with thinly sliced pats of butter. Bake, uncovered, in preheated 325° oven for 30 minutes.

I take this to the monthly Shriners dinner and have been told "don't leave home without it!!"

Jeannie Angelone, Marlin Evening Lions Club
Marlin, TX

VEGETABLE MEDLEY

6 ears sweet corn
2 cucumbers
2 c. shredded cabbage

1 onion, diced
2 Tbsp. butter or margarine

Clean corn; cut off cob. Peel cucumbers; dice. Shred cabbage to make 2 cups. Dice 1 medium onion or 4 green onions (tops also). Saute all of the above in 2 tablespoons butter. May add more butter as needed. Cook on low to medium heat until vegetables are just starting to soften. Don't overcook. Take off stove. Add salt and pepper and serve.

Ann Fisher, Findlay Lions Club
Findlay, OH

Keep your words soft and sweet just in case you have to eat them.

GOLDEN RUTABAGA AND CARROTS

¼ c. Zesty Italian dressing
1 small onion, finely chopped
2 c. carrots (in julienne strips)

2 c. rutabaga (in julienne strips)
½ c. chicken broth or water
2 Tbsp. crumbled, cooked bacon

In a large frypan, cook onions in salad dressing to soften. Stir in carrots, rutabaga, and broth. Over medium heat, cook, uncovered, for 20 minutes, stirring occasionally, until vegetables are tender-crisp. Sprinkle with bacon. Serves four.

Micheal and Ruth Bartolf, Oxbow and District Lions Club
Oxbow, Saskatchewan, Canada

SAVOURY RUTABAGA

1 medium rutabaga, cut into ½
   inch cubes
1 tsp. salt
½ tsp. caraway seeds
1 small onion, finely chopped

¼ c. Miracle Whip salad dressing
   or Miracle Whip light
   dressing
3 green onions, sliced
Pepper to taste

Cook rutabaga with salt and caraway seeds in boiling water until almost tender, about 10 minutes. Drain well through a fine sieve, reserving rutabaga and caraway seeds. Saute white onions in 1 tablespoon of the salad dressing to soften. Add rutabaga mixture, remaining salad dressing, and green onions. Cook and stir until rutabaga is tender. Add pepper to taste. Serves 6.

Micheal and Ruth Bartolf, Oxbow and District Lions Club
Oxbow, Saskatchewan, Canada

COLCANNON
(Means potatoes, cabbage, and onions)

1 lb. Chinese cabbage
3 large potatoes, peeled and
   halved
½ medium onion, sliced

⅔ c. evaporated milk
Freshly ground pepper to taste

Cover potatoes with water in large Dutch oven or pot; boil until tender, about 20 minutes. While potatoes cook, trim and slice cabbage. Add to pan, adding more water as necessary. Combine onion and evaporated milk in medium saucepan and simmer over medium heat until onion is soft, about 15 minutes. When potatoes and cabbage are tender, drain water from pan. Spoon potatoes into bowl and mash. Add cabbage and milk-onion mixture; season with pepper to taste and serve. Serves 8.

Micheal and Ruth Bartolf, Oxbow and District Lions Club
Oxbow, Saskatchewan, Canada

LEEKS

Clean 8 leeks and steam until tender. Boil 2 large tomatoes 10 seconds, then plunge into cold water, then peel. Cut in halves, remove seeds, and chop.

¼ c. Greek olives, chopped and pitted
1 piece or 2 prosciutto, chopped
2 Tbsp. lemon juice

⅓ c. olive oil
Zest of 2 lemons
Fresh thyme

Serve at room temperature.

Sarah Wehling, Bothell Lions Club
Bothell, WA, USA

WILD GREENS

Time: 15 minutes.

2 qt. fresh dandelion greens
1 c. boiling water
¼ tsp. sea salt (optional)

Chopped chives and/or fresh parsley (make a nice garnish)

Same recipe can be used for lambs quarters, nettles, and other wild vegetables. Dandelion can also be used raw in salads or added to soups.

Wash greens in cold water and cut into small pieces. Bring water and salt to a boil in large pan and add greens. Cover and cook until greens turn a bright green. Drain well. Save liquid for soups or as a vegetable drink. Garnish with chives and/or parsley and serve hot. Serves 3 to 4.

Comments: Wild greens are strengthening and fun to obtain yourself.

PDG Jim Schiebel, Hilton Lions Club
Hilton, NY, USA

MEDITERRANEAN GREENS AND BEANS

Time: 15 minutes.

½ Tbsp. olive oil
1 clove garlic, minced
1 small bunch kale
½ c. cooked garbanzo beans

Pinch of sea salt (optional)
3 Tbsp. spring water
Tamari sauce to taste

Heat oil in a large skillet. Add minced garlic and saute briefly. Do not let brown. Add chopped kale and saute for 2 to 3 minutes. Add cooked beans and water. Cover and cook just until greens are tender. Add tamari sauce to taste and serve. Serves 2 to 4.

Comments: Also good with other hearty greens.

PDG Jim Schiebel, Hilton Lions Club
Hilton, NY, USA

SIMPLE MILLET WITH VEGETABLES

Time: 30 minutes.

1 c. millet
2½ c. spring water
⅓ c. sunflower or pumpkin seeds
2 carrots

1 parsnip
2 scallions or small onion
Pinch of sea salt

Wash millet and drain well. Combine with water and sea salt in large saucepan or pressure cooker and place over high heat. Slice or chop vegetables and add to mixture. Add sunflower or pumpkin seeds to mixture. Cover and cook for 20 to 30 minutes. If using pressure cooker, bring to pressure first before you start timing cooking period. Stir well and check for seasoning before serving. Can be garnished with green scallions or chopped parsley. Serves 4.

Comments: Easy and delicious.

PDG Jim Schiebel, Hilton Lions Club
Hilton, NY, USA

ARTICHOKES WITH TARRAGON

½ c. wine vinegar
Salt and pepper
½ c. plus 1 Tbsp. oil

1 Tbsp. chopped fresh or 1 tsp.
    dried tarragon
4 medium artichokes

In a small jar, shake together 3 tablespoons of the vinegar, 1 teaspoon salt, and ¼ teaspoon pepper until the salt dissolves. Add the oil and shake again to combine. Stir in the tarragon. Trim the stems from the artichokes. Trim the pointed ends of the artichoke leaves, if you like. Add the remaining vinegar to a large pot of boiling salted water. Add the artichokes and cook until tender, about 25 minutes. Drain upside down. Remove inner core of small leaves and scrape out the choke. Serve the artichokes warm or at room temperature with the tarragon vinaigrette spooned into the hollow left by the choke. Makes 4 servings.

Per serving: 342 calories, 6 g protein, 7 g fat, 201 mg sodium, 17 g carbohydrate, 95 mg cholesterol.

Barbara Joy Hess, Clarence Lions Club
Clarence Center, NY, USA

If there is no love, nothing is possible.

❦ ❦ ❦

It's never too late - in fiction or in life - to revise.

PEPPERS, ROMAN FASHION

4 large peppers (green, yellow, red)
1 Tbsp. lard
1 Tbsp. olive oil
1 small onion, diced
3 large tomatoes, peeled and chopped

½ tsp. salt
¼ tsp. pepper
¼ tsp. basil (optional)

Place peppers over high heat directly on burners and roast until skin is black and blistered. Using your fingers under cold water, trim peppers and free membranes and seeds. Cut into strips. Dry thoroughly.

In heavy saucepan, combine lard and onion. Cook until onion is soft. Add tomatoes and cook about 5 minutes. Add peppers, salt, pepper, and basil. Simmer for 10 to 15 minutes or until peppers are tender. If too thick, add a little hot water.

Sarah Wehling, Bothell Lions Club
Bothell, WA, USA

PEPPERS PICADELLO

2 medium green peppers, chopped
8 oz. ground hamburger
1 tsp. cumin
¼ tsp. cayenne pepper
½ tsp. ground cinnamon

1 c. instant rice
1½ c. tomato salsa
1 c. water
¼ c. raisins (optional)

Brown meat with cumin, cayenne pepper, and cinnamon. Add remaining ingredients. Bring to a boil. Reduce heat, cover, and simmer 10 to 12 minutes until rice is tender. Bake at 375° for 25 minutes or until peppers are tender.

Lion Dan Clever, East Prospect Lions Club
East Prospect, PA, USA

The harder you work, the luckier you get.

❧ ❧ ❧

If your life is free of failures, you're not taking enough risks.

❧ ❧ ❧

It's not hard to make decisions when you know what your values are.

BAKED VEGETABLE FRITTATA

2 Tbsp. unsalted butter
1 onion, finely chopped
1 clove garlic, minced
1 green pepper, diced
¼ c. chopped fresh or frozen
    parsley
1 (19 oz.) can tomatoes or
    equivalent fresh, chopped
    and drained

5 eggs
½ c. fresh bread crumbs
1 tsp. salt
¼ tsp. freshly ground pepper
1 tsp. Worcestershire sauce
2 c. shredded Swiss cheese

In skillet, melt butter over medium heat. Cook onion and garlic until tender. Add diced green pepper and parsley and cook for 1 minute longer. Remove from heat. Add tomatoes.

In large mixing bowl, beat eggs until well mixed. Stir in bread crumbs, salt, pepper, Worcestershire sauce, and cheese; gently stir in vegetables. Pour mixture into 9 inch round dish, buttered. Bake in 350° oven for 30 to 35 minutes or until top is golden and mixture is firm in the center. Let stand 5 minutes before serving. Serves 6.

This frittata is delicious served hot for brunch or cold as an appetizer or addition to a salad plate.

Lion Micheal and Ruth (Sauskojus) Bartolf,
Oxbow and District Lions Club
Oxbow, Saskatchewan, Canada

SWISS CHARD WITH DRESSING

40 or so Swiss chard leaves
2 tsp. flour
½ tsp. salt
3 Tbsp. milk
1 egg, beaten

⅓ c. sugar
⅓ c. vinegar
3 Tbsp. milk
3 slices bacon or 3 Tbsp. Bac-Os

Wash Swiss chard and cut in 1½ inch pieces. Put in Dutch oven (or large kettle) with 1 cup water. Steam for 8 to 10 minutes; drain in colander.

Dressing: Combine flour, salt, and milk. Add and mix beaten egg until smooth. Add sugar, vinegar, and remaining milk. Add broken bacon pieces. Stir over heat until mixture thickens. Combine sauce with drained Swiss chard. Stir through and serve. *A family favorite.*

Mildred Weir, Bentleyville Lioness Club
Bentleyville, PA

SUMMERTIME FRIED TOMATOES

⅓ c. flour
½ tsp. salt
¼ tsp. pepper
4 medium green tomatoes, sliced

¼ c. margarine
1 can condensed cream of
  mushroom soup
⅓ c. milk

Combine flour, salt, and pepper. Dip tomatoes in flour mixture. Fry in margarine over low heat until lightly browned on both sides. Remove to heated platter. Stir soup and milk into skillet. Heat, stirring occasionally. Pour over tomatoes. Yield: 4 to 6 servings.

Lion Adron Groves Martin, Mount Airy Foothills Lions Club
Mount Airy, NC, USA

TEXAS CAVIAR

1 can black beans, drained
1 can whole kernel corn, drained
1 small can diced black olives
½ clove garlic
Juice from ½ lemon
1 can black-eyed peas, drained

2 medium tomatoes, diced
1 small bunch cilantro, chopped
Juice from ½ lime
1 avocado, diced
Havarti or similar cheese
  (optional)

Combine all ingredients in a bowl. Drizzle with Italian dressing. Let marinate in refrigerator at least 2 hours, but longer is better. Top with cheese before serving if desired. Serve on romaine lettuce as a salad or with tortilla chips as an appetizer.

Jacquelin Borth, Montezuma Lions Club
Montezuma, KS, USA

CUCUMBER WEDGES

1 (8 oz.) pkg. cream cheese,
  softened
2 Tbsp. Italian salad dressing mix
1 loaf Jewish rye bread, cut
  round

1 to 2 medium cucumbers, sliced
  ⅛ inch
Lemon-pepper seasoning

Mix softened cream cheese with salad dressing. Mix. Spread on bread. Place cucumber on top and sprinkle lemon-pepper seasoning on top.

This is a big hit for office party, wedding reception, teas, or coffees. It is great!

JoAnn Smith, Brookhaven Alpha Lions Club
Bogue Chitto, MS

TURNIP PUFF

3 lb. turnip
¼ c. butter or margarine
½ c. brown sugar, packed
Salt and pepper to taste
3 eggs
½ c. applesauce

1 c. soft bread crumbs
1½ tsp. lemon juice
¼ c. fine bread crumbs
1 Tbsp. butter, melted
¼ tsp. ground nutmeg (optional)

Preheat oven to 350°F. Wash and cut up turnip in small pieces. Bring to boil in covered saucepan; cook until tender. Drain well. Mash turnip very well and add butter, brown sugar, salt, and pepper, mixing thoroughly. In separate bowl, beat eggs until frothy. Fold into turnip mixture with applesauce, crumbs, and lemon juice. Mix together fine bread crumbs with butter and nutmeg (if using) and spread evenly over top. Bake, uncovered, for 45 to 50 minutes, or until set.

This vegetable casserole is a nice accompaniment to roast turkey or chicken. Bread crumb topping can be substituted with finely crushed Ritz or soda crackers.

Lion Lillian Marchant, Lake of the Woods Lions Club
Kenora, Ontario, Canada

STUFFED EGGPLANT

1 large eggplant
1 lb. lean ground beef
1 egg
Parmesan cheese
Progresso bread crumbs
2 toes garlic, minced

1 can stewed tomatoes
Salt and pepper to taste
Herbs to taste - parsley, oregano
½ c. cooked rice
tomato sauce

Wash 1 large eggplant. Cut in half lengthwise. Microwave on HIGH until crisp-tender, approximately 10 minutes, depending on size of eggplant. Scoop out the "meat" of the eggplant, leaving about ½ inch thickness remaining in the eggplant. Place cooked eggplant "meat" in large bowl; set aside. Saute ground beef and garlic over medium heat till cooked thoroughly. Drain. Place ground beef in bowl with eggplant "meat." To this mixture, add egg, Parmesan cheese to taste, bread crumbs to taste, cooked rice, stewed tomatoes, herbs to taste, and salt and pepper to taste. Mix thoroughly by hand. Stuff eggplant shells with ground beef mixture. Pour tomato sauce over entire stuffed eggplant and bake at 350° for 30 minutes or until thoroughly heated.

May also be placed in microwave on HIGH for 15 minutes.

Elaine Germont, Glendale Evening Lions Club
Glendale, AZ, USA

CREAMED GREENS

1 lb. fresh greens (kale, collards, spinach, Swiss chard, or others)
1 small onion or shallot
1 Tbsp. olive oil
1½ Tbsp. oat flour
¼ tsp. sea salt
Dash of nutmeg
¾ c. hot vegetable stock or spring water*

Wash greens and chop finely. Steam briefly until bright green and wilted. Drain thoroughly in mesh strainer. Press firmly to extract as much liquid as possible. Set aside while you prepare cream sauce. Peel and mince onion or shallot.

In a 1 quart saucepan, heat oil and saute onion or shallot until transparent. Add oat flour, sea salt, and nutmeg and mix well. Add hot stock gradually while stirring to avoid lumping until mixture comes to a boil. Simmer for 1 to 2 minutes, then add chopped greens and cook over low heat until greens are hot. Serve immediately.

People will eat greens this way that never did before.

* Can use ¼ teaspoon Herbamare seasoning if using water in place of stock.

James R. Schiebel, Hilton Lions Club
Hilton, NY, USA

CAULIFLOWER WITH QUICK TOMATO SAUCE

1 small onion
1 clove garlic
1 Tbsp. oil
14 oz. can tomatoes in juice (about 1½ c.)
¾ tsp. dried marjoram
Salt and pepper
1 tsp. sugar
1 head cauliflower (about 2 lb.)

Chop onion. Mince garlic. In a saucepan, heat oil over medium-low heat. Add the onion and garlic; cover and cook until tender, about 5 minutes. Add the tomatoes with their juice, the marjoram, 1 teaspoon salt, ¼ teaspoon pepper, and the sugar. Chop up the tomatoes with the side of a spoon. Cook, partially covered, until the sauce is thick and flavorful, about 20 minutes.

Meanwhile, cut the cauliflower into small florets. Cook in boiling salted water until tender, about 5 minutes. Drain. Taste the tomato sauce for seasoning and add salt and pepper if needed. Serve the cauliflower with the sauce. Makes 6 servings.

Per serving: 54 calories, 2 g protein, 3 g fat, 484 mg sodium, 7 g carbohydrate, 0 mg cholesterol.

Mrs. Mike Nowicki, Clarence Lions Club
Clarence Center, NY, USA

HARVARD BEETS

Scant ½ c. white vinegar
½ c. sugar
1 tsp. salt
1 Tbsp. butter or margarine

1 Tbsp. corn starch
4 medium red beets, boiled with
  skin removed

Measure ingredients, except beets (which you have already cooked), into large saucepan. Simmer until thickens, about 5 to 7 minutes, stirring constantly. Slice peeled beets into sauce and cook until beets are warm. Makes 4 to 6 servings.

Frances Blount, Saginaw Lions Club
Saginaw, TX, USA

CREAMED PEAS

5 lb. peas (frozen)
Water to cover

1 Tbsp. salt
2 qt. cream sauce

Prepare cream sauce. Thaw and place the peas in a saucepan with boiling water. Add the salt and simmer until tender, then drain thoroughly. Blend in the hot cream sauce. Adjust the seasonings and serve.

Mike Nowicki, Clarence Lions Club
Clarence Center, NY, USA

FLORENTINE MUSHROOMS

1 lb. mushrooms
3 Tbsp. olive oil
1 clove garlic
Salt
Pepper

1 Tbsp. butter
4 anchovies, chopped
2 Tbsp. chopped parsley
Juice of ½ lemon

Slice mushrooms thinly. Heat olive oil in large skillet and brown garlic. Remove garlic. Add mushrooms, salt, and pepper and cook over high heat until all mushroom liquid has evaporated. Add butter, anchovy fillets, and parsley and cook over medium heat 5 minutes longer. Remove from fire. Add lemon juice and serve very hot.

Sarah Wehling, Bothell Lions Club
Bothell, WA, USA

VEGETABLES VINAIGRETTE

Arrange 1 cup cooked tiny beets, 1 cup cooked green beans, and 1 cup cooked carrot circles on a bed of lettuce. Sprinkle with 1 tablespoon tarragon vinegar, 2 tablespoons salad oil, and salt and pepper to taste. Chill for at least 1 hour. Makes 6 servings.

Sarah Wehling, Bothell Lions Club
Bothell, WA, USA

CORN CASSEROLE

3 eggs, beaten
¾ c. yellow corn meal
2 cans creamed corn
6 Tbsp. oil or butter

1 tsp. garlic salt
3 c. grated Cheddar cheese
3 medium cans Ortega chillies, finely chopped

Mix well; bake in casserole dish for one hour at 350° or until knife inserted in center comes out clean.

Pam Caldwell, Mexico Sunrise Lions Club
Mexico, MO

Always assume the electric fence is on before you step over it.

If you think you left the water on in the barn, you did.

Save money for a sunny day too.

The only thing you should worry about your neighbors criticizing is your lack of neighborliness.

Try to get your kids to laugh at least once a day.

Notes

Some people go anywhere for dinner - except the kitchen.

MEAT ROASTING GUIDE

Cut	Weight Pounds	Approx. Time (Hours) (325° oven)	Internal Temperature
BEEF			
Standing rib roast			
(10 inch) ribs	4	1¾	140° (rare)
(If using shorter cut (8-inch)		2	160° (medium)
ribs, allow 30 min. longer)		2½	170° (well done)
	8	2½	140° (rare)
		3	160° (medium)
		4½	170° (well done)
Rolled ribs	4	2	140° (rare)
		2½	160° (medium)
		3	170° (well done)
	6	3	140° (rare)
		3¼	160° (medium)
		4	170° (well done)
Rolled rump	5	2¼	140° (rare)
(Roast only if high quality.		3	160° (medium)
Otherwise, braise.)		3¼	170° (well done)
Sirloin tip	3	1½	140° (rare)
(Roast only if high quality.		2	160° (medium)
Otherwise, braise.)		2¼	170° (well done)
LAMB			
Leg	6	3	175° (medium)
		3½	180° (well done)
	8	4	175° (medium)
		4½	180° (well done)
VEAL			
Leg (piece)	5	2½ to 3	170° (well done)
Shoulder	6	3½	170° (well done)
Rolled shoulder	3 to 5	3 to 3½	170° (well done)

POULTRY ROASTING GUIDE

Type of Poultry	Ready-To-Cook Weight	Oven Temperature	Approx. Total Roasting Time
TURKEY	6 to 8 lb.	325°	2½ to 3 hr.
	8 to 12 lb.	325°	3 to 3½ hr.
	12 to 16 lb.	325°	3½ to 4 hr.
	16 to 20 lb.	325°	4 to 4½ hr.
	20 to 24 lb.	300°	5 to 6 hr.
CHICKEN	2 to 2½ lb.	400°	1 to 1½ hr.
(Unstuffed)	2½ to 4 lb.	400°	1½ to 2½ hr.
	4 to 8 lb.	325°	3 to 5 hr.
DUCK	3 to 5 lb.	325°	2½ to 3 hr.
(Unstuffed)			

NOTE: Small chickens are roasted at 400° so that they brown well in the short cooking time. They may also be done at 325° but will take longer and will not be as brown. Increase cooking time 15 to 20 minutes for stuffed chicken and duck.

MEAT, SEAFOOD, POULTRY
MEAT

BEEF STROGANOFF

1 to 2 lb. sirloin steak, cut in
    cubes
2 Tbsp. shortening
¼ c. flour
1 tsp. salt
⅛ tsp. pepper
1 large onion, chopped

1 c. sliced mushrooms
1 Tbsp. Worcestershire sauce
1 can tomato soup
1 c. sour cream
Cooked noodles

Combine flour, salt, and pepper in a bag. Shake meat pieces until coated. Melt shortening in large skillet. Brown meat and onion. Add Worcestershire, mushrooms, and soup and cook on low until meat is tender (45 minutes). Add water if needed. Remove from heat. Add sour cream and serve over cooked, drained noodles. Serves 6 to 8.

Supporter of Lions, Princeton Lions Club
Princeton, IL, USA

SHORT CUT BEEF STROGANOFF

2 lb. stewing beef
2 Tbsp. cooking oil
Flour
Salt and pepper
Garlic powder

1 can cream of mushroom soup
½ c. white wine
1 medium onion
1 can mushrooms
1 can water chestnuts

Preheat oven to 300°F. Dredge beef in flour and seasonings. Add 2 tablespoons oil to skillet and brown beef. Place brown beef in ovenproof baking dish. In a separate bowl, mix remaining ingredients together until well blended. Pour over beef and bake for 3 to 4 hours, until meat is tender. Serve with fettuccini noodles.

Lion Helen Oneschuk, Lake of the Woods Lions Club
Kenora, Ontario, Canada

BEEF STROGANOFF

2 lb. cubed sirloin or tenderloin
1 can celery soup
1 can mushroom soup

Fresh onions and mushrooms (as
    much as you like), sliced

Mix all ingredients in a casserole; cover and bake for 2 hours at 350°. Uncover the last hour. Last ½ hour, add ¼ cup red wine and ½ cup sour cream. Serve over cooked noodles. (Bake 3 hours at 350°.)

Mrs. Gordon (Linn) Dierschow, Elburn Lions Club
Elburn, IL

JOE'S SPECIAL

1 lb. ground beef
1 small onion, chopped
1 tsp. seasoned salt
½ tsp. garlic powder
¼ tsp. pepper

½ tsp. oregano
1 pkg. frozen spinach, thawed
   and drained
4 eggs

Saute beef in a large skillet, breaking it up as it cooks. Mix in onion and seasonings. Add spinach and cook about 10 minutes, until spinach is cooked. Add eggs. Cook, stirring, over low heat, until eggs set. Sprinkle with Parmesan or Romano cheese. Makes 4 servings.

Nancy Poole, Bend Lions Club
Bend, OR

BARBECUE BEEF

3 lb. chuck roast
1 large onion
½ c. celery
2 Tbsp. butter
2 Tbsp. brown sugar

2 Tbsp. vinegar
4 Tbsp. lemon juice
3 Tbsp. Worcestershire sauce
1 c. catsup
1½ c. water

Roast meat about 3 hours or until tender. Saute onion and celery in butter. Mix next six ingredients together. Shred meat when cooked. Place in pan. Add sauce. Simmer. Add one cup of gravy made from drippings. Makes barbecue smooth and thick.

If in a hurry: Place beef in roaster. Put onion and celery on top of meat. Combine remaining ingredients and pour over beef. Cover and bake at 350° about 3 hours. Remove fat and bones; shred. Return to sauce. Salt and pepper if desired. Simmer on stove. Thicken if desired with 1 cup gravy made from some of the sauce or flour and water.

Smile - God loves you and so do your fellow Lions.

Lois Shinkle, First Female President (1999 to 2000),
Elizabethtown Lions Club
Elizabethtown, KY, USA

The time to put out rat poison is when you don't see rats.

Don't swat at a fly at an auction.

KOREAN BARBECUED BEEF STRIPS

2 lb. top round steak, cut ¾ inch
    thick
½ c. Japanese soy sauce (shoyu)
½ c. saki
2 Tbsp. sesame oil
1 tsp. brown sugar

2 tsp. garlic powder
½ tsp. MSG
¼ tsp. cayenne
1 c. uncooked white rice
1 (12 oz.) jar kim chee

Slice steak cross grain into 3 x ¾ x ⅛ inch strips. Combine soy sauce, sake, sesame oil, brown sugar, garlic powder, MSG, and cayenne in bowl. Add steak strips and marinate overnight or at least 4 hours. Prepare rice according to package directions. Drain marinade from meat. Heat marinade in saucepan. Broil steak strips 6 inches from heat, basting with heated marinade. Serve with white rice and kim chee. Use remaining marinade as dipping sauce.

Victor L. Dreyer, Sr., Keizer Lions Club
Salem, OR

BEEF KEBABS WITH SCALLION AVOCADO SAUCE

1 scallion
½ California avocados (such as
    Haas)
1½ tsp. wine vinegar

Salt
1 clove garlic
1 lb. ground beef
1 Tbsp. chopped fresh parsley

Mince the white part of the scallion and cut the green part into pieces. Put the scallion greens, peeled avocado, vinegar, ½ cup water, and ½ teaspoon salt in a food processor or blender and whirl until smooth. Taste for seasoning and add salt and pepper if needed. If not using immediately, cover with plastic wrap pressed directly onto the surface of the sauce to prevent it from browning. Heat the broiler. Mince the garlic. Combine the garlic and minced scallion with the ground beef, the chopped parsley, and ¾ teaspoon salt.

Shape into 16 balls and thread on 4 skewers. Put on a rack in a broiler pan and set the pan about 6 inches from the heat source. Broil the meat until it has cooked through, about 4 minutes per side. Serve the room temperature avocado sauce with the hot meatballs. Makes 4 servings.

Work time: 30 minutes. Total time: 30 minutes.

Per serving: 289 calories, 21 g protein, 21 g fat, 486 mg sodium, 3 g carbohydrate, 77 mg cholesterol.

Mrs. Lucy Aiken, Clarence Lions Club
Clarence Center, NY, USA

Choose a tractor and a spouse with great deliberation.
They should both last a long time.

EASY BEEF TIPS

1½ lb. stew meat
2 (15 oz.) cans beef broth
1 can cream of celery soup

1 onion, chopped
1 (8 oz.) can sliced mushrooms

Mix all ingredients together (do not brown meat). Place in large casserole in 350° oven, uncovered, for 5 hours. Add water at end if beef seems dry (usually isn't). Put over noodles or rice.

This is a no standing over stove meal, easy, and with noodles/rice, almost a complete meal with vegetables and salad.

Kathy Dunn, Rootstown Township Lions Club 13-D
Rootstown, OH, Portage

BEEF TENDERLOIN

2 Tbsp. garlic salt
2 Tbsp. celery salt
2 Tbsp. onion salt
1½ tsp. red pepper

1½ tsp. black pepper
1½ tsp. paprika
Beef tenderloin

Mix seasoning. Sprinkle on meat. Rub in. Place in foil boat. Do not cover. Place in baking pan. Cook at 500° for 7 minutes per pound. Turn oven off. Leave in oven 2 hours without opening oven. If medium rare is preferred, cook 6 minutes per pound.

Christine Gibson, Brookhaven Alpha Lions Club
Brookhaven, MS

KOREAN SHORT RIBS

Cut 2 pounds meaty beef short ribs into serving pieces.

Sauce - Mix together:

½ c. brown sugar
½ tsp. salt (or omit)
1 clove garlic, minced
2 stalks green onion, chopped

⅔ c. light soy sauce
1 Tbsp. grated fresh ginger root
1 Tbsp. sesame oil
2 Tbsp. sesame seeds, toasted

Marinate ribs for several hours or overnight, turning at least once. Broil or barbecue on grill for 5 minutes; baste with sauce, then turn and cook until desired doneness. Makes 4 servings.

In Hawaii, they serve ribs with rice or macaroni salad, kim chee, and coleslaw. Ono! (Delicious!)

Mrs. Gloria D. Ball, Columbus Noon Lions Club
Columbus, NE

SLOW-ROASTED SHORT RIBS

With this roasting method, the fat drips out, leaving the meat crisp on the outside, still juicy within.

6 lb. beef short ribs   **Salt and pepper**

Heat the oven to 500°. Pour about 1 cup of water into a roasting pan. Put the short ribs, fat side up, on a rack in the roasting pan and sprinkle them with salt and pepper. Roast 20 minutes. Reduce the oven temperature to 300° and continue roasting until the short ribs are tender, about 2 hours and 30 minutes longer. Makes 8 servings.

Work time: 10 minutes. Total time: 3 hours.

Per serving: 802 calories, 37 g protein, 71 g fat, 85 mg sodium, 0 g carbohydrate, 160 mg cholesterol.

Barbara Joy Hess, Clarence Lions Club
Clarence Center, NY, USA

CAJUN GRILLED SHORT RIBS

2 tsp. dried thyme   **Salt and pepper**
¼ tsp. cayenne   **4 lb. beef short ribs**

Prepare the grill for very low indirect heat. Combine the thyme, cayenne, 1½ teaspoons salt, and 1 teaspoon pepper. Rub this spice mixture all over the ribs. Grill, covered, until the ribs are very tender, 2 to 3 hours. Turn occasionally for even browning. Makes 4 servings.

Per serving: 365 calories, 38 g protein, 22 g fat, 895 mg sodium, 1 g carbohydrate, 114 mg cholesterol.

Mrs. Lucy Aiken, Clarence Lions Club
Clarence Center, NY, USA

GLAZED BRISKET

4 to 5 lb. boneless beef brisket
Dill pickle juice (enough to
   marinate roast)

Glaze:

½ c. brown sugar   **½ tsp. Worcestershire sauce**
2 Tbsp. prepared mustard

Marinate roast in pickle juice for 48 hours in refrigerator. Drain off juice and place in baking pan. Cover and bake at 325° for 3 hours. Uncover roast. Combine glaze ingredients and put on roast. Return roast to oven and bake 1 hour. Baste occasionally. Roast will be tender and nice and brown. Yield: 5 to 7 servings.

Great dish for the holidays.

Louis Katz, Stafford-Missouri City Lions Club
Stafford, TX, USA

BEEF BRISKET

1 (6 lb. approx.) brisket of beef
2 tsp. salt
1 tsp. pepper

2 tsp. dry mustard
1 env. dry onion soup mix

Preheat oven to 350°. Rub brisket with salt, pepper, and dry mustard mixture. Place brisket, fat side up, on large sheet of heavy-duty aluminum foil. Sprinkle with dry onion soup mix. Fold foil tightly, leaving air space. Place in shallow baking dish. Bake 3 to 4 hours. Pour off broth for gravy. Let cool in foil for about 15 minutes before slicing. May be frozen and reheated.

Shirley J. Hoyt, Hutchinson Breakfast Lions Club
Hutchinson, KS, USA

BAVARIAN BEEF POT ROAST

1 (4 to 5 lb.) boneless roast (rump
   or round)
2 Tbsp. vegetable oil
1 Tbsp. sugar
3 tsp. salt
2 tsp. caraway seed
½ tsp. ground cardamon

1 c. chopped onion
1 c. chopped carrots
1 c. chopped celery
½ c. fresh chopped parsley
1 c. dry red wine
2 Tbsp. flour, mixed in ¼ c.
   water

Brown roast slowly in oil in a Dutch oven or electric skillet. Stir in sugar, salt, caraway seeds, cardamon, onion, carrot, celery, parsley, and wine; heat to boiling. Cover and simmer, turning meat once or twice, 3 hours, or until very tender. Remove roast to a heated serving platter; keep warm while making gravy. Spoon remaining vegetables and liquid into an electric blender container. Cover and beat until smooth. (Or, strain into a bowl, pressing vegetables through sieve into liquid.) Return liquid to cooking pan and reheat just to boiling. Stir in flour-water mixture and cook until gravy thickens, stirring constantly. Carve roast into ¼ inch thick slices. Serve with gravy.

Lion Joan Shores, St. Charles Lions Club
St. Charles, MO, USA

Expect some things to go right. That guy Murphy didn't know everything.

❦ ❦ ❦

The shiniest trucks do the least work.

❦ ❦ ❦

Consideration for others can mean taking a wing instead of a drumstick.

GARLICKY BEEF ROAST WITH GRILLED PEPPERS

8 cloves garlic
4 to 5 lb. beef rump roast
Salt and pepper
1 tsp. dried thyme

2 green bell peppers
2 red bell peppers
1 large onion (about 1 lb.)
¼ c. oil

Prepare the grill with coals surrounding a drip pan for very low, indirect heat. Put about 1 inch water in the drip pan. Sliver the garlic. Cut the roast horizontally almost all the way through the middle so it opens like a book. Open and sprinkle with salt, pepper, thyme, and half the garlic. Close and tie. Put on grill directly over the drip pan. Cover grill and cook until meat is very tender, 5 to 6 hours.

Meanwhile, cut peppers and onion into thick rings. Toss with the oil, remaining garlic, ½ teaspoon salt, and ¼ teaspoon pepper and spread on a large sheet of heavy-duty foil. After meat has cooked about 2 hours, put sheet of vegetables on the grill. Cover the grill and continue cooking, stirring the vegetables occasionally, until very soft, about 3 hours. Cut meat into thin slices and serve with the pepper mixture. Makes 10 servings.

Work time: 25 minutes. Total time: 6 hours.

Per serving: 452 calories, 41 g protein, 28 g fat, 207 mg sodium, 7 g carbohydrate, 120 mg cholesterol.

Mrs. Mike Nowicki, Clarence Lions Club
Clarence Center, NY, USA

SIRLOIN-TIP ROAST WITH ONION SAUCE

2 lb. onions
1 Tbsp. butter
2 Tbsp. oil

Salt and pepper
3 lb. sirloin-tip roast

Heat oven to 325°. Slice onions. Melt butter with oil in a large frying pan over medium heat. Add onions, 1½ teaspoons salt, and ½ teaspoon pepper. Cook, stirring occasionally, until onions are golden brown, 25 to 30 minutes. Transfer to a roasting pan. Add ½ cup water. Sprinkle meat with salt and pepper and put on top of onions. Roast until meat is medium rare (135°) for 1 hour and 45 minutes to 2 hours. Add water to pan as needed, ½ cup at a time, to keep the onions from burning. Let stand 10 to 20 minutes before carving into very thin slices. Makes 8 servings.

Work time: 20 minutes. Total time: 2 hours and 45 minutes.

Per serving: 451 calories, 34 g protein, 31 g fat, 505 mg sodium, 8 g carbohydrate, 118 mg cholesterol.

Lion John J. Hess, Clarence Lions Club
Clarence Center, NY, USA

ITALIAN POT ROAST

1 onion
1 carrot
1 rib celery
1 Tbsp. oil
3½ lb. chuck roast

Salt and pepper
14½ oz. can tomatoes
¼ c. chopped fresh parsley
1 tsp. dried oregano
½ tsp. dried thyme

Chop onion, carrot, and celery. In a Dutch oven, heat oil over medium-high heat. Sprinkle meat with salt and pepper and brown well, about 5 minutes. Remove meat, reduce heat to low, and add onion, carrot, celery, 1 teaspoon salt, and ¼ teaspoon pepper. Cover and cook until softened, about 5 minutes. Add tomatoes with their juice, the parsley, oregano, and thyme. Break up tomatoes with the side of a large spoon. Return meat to pot, cover, and simmer until tender, about 2½ hours. Remove meat from pot and cover to keep warm. Bring cooking juices to a boil and cook until thickened, about 5 minutes. Slice meat and serve with the sauce. Makes 8 servings.

Per serving: 540 calories, 35 g protein, 42 g fat, 501 mg sodium, 5 g carbohydrate, 143 mg cholesterol.

Joann M. Brownell, Clarence Lions Club
Clarence Center, NY, USA

STEAK CASSEROLE

¼ c. flour
2 tsp. paprika

2 tsp. salt
½ tsp. pepper

Mix together and roll the steak, which has been cut in small pieces, in this mixture.

1 lb. round steak
2 large onions
½ c. oil

½ c. uncooked rice
2 c. tomatoes
2 c. hot water

Brown onions in oil. Remove onions from pan and set aside. Brown steak in same oil. Place browned steak and onions in 3 quart casserole dish. Add uncooked rice and tomatoes on top. Add rest of flour mixture to oil in pan and make a gravy, using the 2 cups of hot water. Pour gravy over the rest of ingredients. Bake at 350° for 1½ hours.

Jill Morefield, Western Branch Lions Club
Portsmouth, VA

It's an extra-special occasion these days if
it's celebrated by staying home for dinner.

ROUND STEAK HOTDISH

2 lb. round steak, cubed
2 cans cream of mushroom soup
6 to 8 stalks celery
Minced onion to taste
4 cans water (including liquid
 from browned meat)

1 c. converted rice
2 cans cream of chicken soup
1 small jar chopped pimento
Salt and pepper to taste

Brown steaks and add some water; simmer until tender. Cook celery until tender. Add the rest of the ingredients and meat. Stir until well mixed. Pour into 9x13 inch cake pan. Bake at 375° for 1½ hours. Serve over rice or egg noodles. May flavor with soy sauce.

Lion Theresa Hill, Hector Lions Club
Hector, MN

MINUTE STEAK BAKE

6 minute steaks
½ can cream of mushroom soup
1 soup can water
Butter

Salt and pepper to taste
½ can cream of celery soup
1 medium onion, chopped

Season steaks with salt and pepper. Place steaks in casserole; cover with soups and water. Add onion and dot with butter. Bake at 350° for 2 hours. Serves 6.

"It's better to be small than not to be at all!"

Amy Bromley, Iron City Lions Club
Iron City, TN, USA

OVEN-BARBECUED STEAKS

3 lb. round steak, cut ¾ inch
 thick
2 Tbsp. vegetable oil
¼ c. chopped onions
¾ c. catsup
½ c. vinegar
¾ c. water

1 Tbsp. brown sugar
1 Tbsp. prepared mustard
1 Tbsp. Worcestershire sauce
½ tsp. salt
⅛ tsp. black pepper

Heat oven to 350°. Cut steak into 10 equal portions. Pour oil into skillet. Brown each piece of steak on both sides. Transfer steaks to roasting pan. Add rest of ingredients to skillet and simmer the sauce 5 minutes. Pour sauce over steaks and bake about 1 hour or till done.

Janette Greene, South Jefferson Lions Club
Adams, NY

STEAK PETRUSSE

2 lb. tenderized round steak
3 Tbsp. flour
1 tsp. salt, fresh ground pepper
1 small onion, chopped

½ lb. fresh mushrooms, sliced
1 (16 oz.) can tomatoes
1 (6 oz.) can tomato paste
1 paste-can Moselle wine

Mix flour, salt, and pepper and coat meat. Place meat in greased 9x13 inch baking dish. Mix together onion, undrained tomatoes, mushrooms, tomato paste, and wine. Pour over meat. Cover tightly. Bake at 350° for 2½ hours or until meat is fork-tender. Serves 6.

This is excellent served with parslied new potatoes.

Carol Speicher, Columbus Lions Club
Columbus, NE, USA

LONDON BROIL

1 flank steak (not tenderized)

Marinating Sauce:

1 clove garlic, sliced
1 c. Mazola or other salad oil
½ c. vinegar
1 tsp. salt
¼ tsp. pepper (fresh ground)

2 tsp. dry mustard
2 tsp. Worcestershire sauce
Dash of cayenne
Few drops of Tabasco

Mix all marinade ingredients in shallow glass pan until well blended. Add steak, which has been scored about ⅛ inch deep on both sides. Marinate 3 hours to overnight in refrigerator.

When ready to cook: Remove meat from marinade. Discard marinade. Cook meat over hot coals for rare. Slice on diagonal against the grain.

Martin Findling, Princeton Lions Club
Princeton, IL, USA

SWEET GEORGE'S FLANK STEAK

2½ lb. butter
1 c. parsley
¼ c. garlic

½ c. vermouth (dry)
1 flank steak

Slice flank steak thin. Place in sauce 4 to 5 minutes.

Mark Doennebrink, Bothell Lions Club
Bothell, WA, USA

Anybody who knows everything should be told a thing or two.

STEAK

Water   Pepper
Salt   Flour

Rinse off with water. While still damp, sprinkle with salt, pepper, and flour on each side until covered. Put in fry pan ¼ inch deep in oil or shortening. Take casserole dish and cover bottom with water. When steaks are brown, put in casserole.

Make gravy. In same grease you browned steaks, add 2 tablespoons flour and a little salt and pepper. Brown mixture. Add 2 cups of water. Let thicken a little. Pour over steaks and cover with foil. Cook in oven at 400° until tender, approximately 1 hour or more. Check often. If gravy cooks away or too thick, add more water.

Lion Carolyn Lamburt, Brookhaven "Alpha" Lions Club
Brookhaven, MS

PASTA AND STEAK WITH FRESH TOMATO SAUCE

1 tomato   2 Tbsp. olive oil
1 clove garlic   1 lb. boneless sirloin steak
Salt and pepper   ½ lb. linguine
1 tsp. vinegar   ⅓ c. chopped fresh parsley

Prepare fire in grill or heat broiler. Seed and dice tomato. Mince garlic and combine with tomato, ¾ teaspoon salt, ¾ teaspoon pepper, vinegar, and oil. Sprinkle steak with salt and pepper and grill over hot coals or broil, turning once, about 15 minutes for medium rare. In a large pot of boiling salted water, cook linguine until done. Drain. Return pasta to pot. Add parsley and ¾ of the tomato mixture. Toss to combine. Cut steak diagonally into thin slices. Top pasta with slices of steak and remaining tomato mixture. Makes 4 servings.

Per serving: 481 calories, 29 g protein, 20 g fat, 471 mg sodium, 46 g carbohydrate, 68 mg cholesterol.

Joann M. Brownell, Clarence Lions Club
Clarence Center, NY, USA

MUSHROOM STEAK

¼ c. flour   2 Tbsp. shortening
Dash of pepper   1 can (Campbell's) mushroom
1½ lb. round steak   soup
                         ½ soup can water

Combine flour and pepper; flour steak and pound with meat hammer or use the edge of heavy saucer. In large skillet, add shortening, then add floured steak and brown on both sides. When the steak is brown, add the soup and water. Cover. Cook over low heat about 45 minutes or until tender. Stir now and then.

Lion Roger VanScyor, Graysville-Proctor Lions Club
Glen Gaston, WV, USA

VIOLET'S EASY ROUND STEAK

Round steak, cut into serving pieces

1 can cream of mushroom soup

In a baking pan, mix can of mushroom soup with ½ can of water. Put in pieces of round steak. Cover with foil. Bake 2 hours at 350°. I use a large baking pan so the steak lays in the soup.

A friend of mine gave me this recipe and my whole family makes it a lot because other cream soups can be used giving it a different flavor.

Virginia Bayer (Lion), Franklin Park Lions Club
Park Ridge, IL, USA

SLOW-COOKED PEPPER STEAK

1½ to 2 lb. beef round steak
2 Tbsp. cooking oil
¼ c. soy sauce
1 c. chopped onion
1 garlic clove, minced
1 tsp. sugar
½ tsp. salt
¼ tsp. pepper
¼ tsp. ground ginger

4 tomatoes, cut into eighths, or 1 (16 oz.) can tomatoes with liquid, cut up
2 large green peppers, cut into strips
½ c. cold water
1 Tbsp. cornstarch
Cooked noodles or rice

Cut beef into 3x1 inch strips; brown in oil in a skillet. Transfer to a slow cooker. Combine the next seven ingredients; pour over beef. Cover and cook on LOW for 5 to 6 hours or until meat is tender. Add tomatoes and green peppers; cook on LOW for 1 hour longer. Combine the cold water and cornstarch to make a paste; stir into liquid in slow cooker and cook on HIGH until thickened. Serve over noodles or rice. Yield: 6 to 8 servings.

SIMPLE SALISBURY STEAK

1 can cream of mushroom soup, divided
1 lb. lean ground beef
⅓ c. dry bread crumbs

1 egg, beaten
¼ c. minced onion
1 (7 oz.) can sliced mushrooms

Beat egg in bowl; add ¼ cup soup, onion, crumbs, and meat. Mix thoroughly and shape firmly into 6 oval patties. In skillet over high heat, in 1 tablespoon hot oil, cook patties until browned on both sides; drain, if necessary, and remove from skillet. Stir in remaining soup and mushrooms; return patties to skillet. Cover; simmer 20 minutes or until done, turning occasionally.

I rinse soup can with approximately ¼ cup water to thin sauce slightly and serve with egg noodles.

Barbara Rohrbaugh, Plainfield Township Lions Club
Nazareth, PA, USA

BROILED STEAK WITH BLUE CHEESE

2 lb. sirloin steak (about 1½
   inches thick)
2 cloves garlic, cut in halves
   lengthwise

½ tsp. salt
¼ tsp. pepper
4 oz. Blue cheese (about 1¼ c.
   crumbled)

Heat broiler. Flavor steak by rubbing all over with the cut side of garlic cloves. Discard garlic. Sprinkle meat with salt and pepper and arrange on a broiler rack. Broil steak, turning once, until cooked to desired doneness, about 12 minutes for medium-rare. Sprinkle the meat with crumbled cheese and return to broiler. Cook until cheese melts, about 1 minute longer. Cut in diagonal slices and serve. Makes 6 servings.

Per serving: 321 calories, 27 g protein, 23 g fat, 499 mg sodium, 0 g carbohydrate, 89 mg cholesterol.

Joanne M. Wetzler, Clarence Lions Club
Clarence Center, NY, USA

POTATO BURGERS

1 medium onion, grated
1 tsp. salt
1 (No. 2½) can tomatoes

2 large potatoes, grated
1½ lb. ground beef

Mix onion and potatoes; add salt and ground beef. Mix well. Shape into patties. Brown on one side in heavy skillet. Turn; pour tomatoes over patties. Cover and continue cooking on low heat for 35 to 40 minutes or till done. Yield: 4 to 6 servings.

Rayford Kimbrell, Iron City Lions Club
Iron City, TN, USA

Age is not important unless you're a cheese.

Giving does not drain our resources, but provides a space for us to refill.

*It's hard to convince a child that in meeting the day's requirement
for vegetables, carrot cake doesn't count.*

Good character, like good soap, is usually homemade.

HAMBURGER STEAKS IN A MUSTARD CRUST

1½ lb. ground beef
1 Tbsp. whole mustard seeds
1 Tbsp. coarse-grind pepper
Salt

1 Tbsp. butter
1 Tbsp. oil
1 c. beef stock or canned broth

Shape the ground beef into 4 ovals. Combine the mustard seeds and the pepper. Press this mixture onto both sides of each patty and sprinkle with salt. In a large frying pan, melt the butter with the oil over medium heat. Cook the hamburgers, about 6 minutes on each side for medium-rare, and remove. Add the beef stock to the pan. Bring to a boil over high heat, scraping up any browned bits from the bottom of the pan. Boil for 5 minutes. Taste for seasoning and add salt and pepper if needed. Pour the reduced stock over the hamburgers and serve. Makes 4 servings.

Work time: 30 minutes. Total time: 30 minutes.

Per serving: 603 calories, 29 g protein, 52 g fat, 118 mg sodium, 2 g carbohydrate, 152 mg cholesterol.

Mrs. Lucy Aiken, Clarence Lions Club
Clarence Center, NY, USA

BLUE PLATE BEEF PATTIES

1 egg
2 green onions with tops, sliced
¼ c. seasoned bread crumbs
1 Tbsp. prepared mustard
1½ lb. ground beef

1 (12 oz.) jar beef gravy
½ c. water
2 to 3 tsp. prepared horseradish
½ lb. fresh mushrooms, sliced

In a bowl, beat the egg; stir in onions, bread crumbs, and mustard. Add beef and mix well. Shape into four ½ inch thick patties. In an ungreased skillet, cook patties for 4 to 5 minutes on each side or until meat is no longer pink; drain.

In a small bowl, combine gravy, water, and horseradish; add mushrooms. Pour over patties. Cook, uncovered, for 5 minutes or until mushrooms are tender and heated through. Yield: 4 servings.

Face powder may win a husband, but it takes baking powder to hold him.

MEXICAN MEAT BALLS

1 lb. hamburger meat
2 Tbsp. chopped onions
½ c. corn meal
1 tsp. chili powder
½ tsp. dry mustard
1 tsp. salt

½ c. milk
1 egg, beaten
2 Tbsp. chopped green pepper
½ tsp. pepper
½ c. bread crumbs
3 Tbsp. butter

Mix meat with all ingredients except bread crumbs and butter. Form into balls. Roll with bread crumbs. Fry in butter and serve with tomato sauce.

Hint - For washing woodwork:

¼ c. baking soda
1 c. ammonia

½ c. vinegar
1 gal. hot water

No rinse necessary.

Clara Culbert, Scio Lions Club
Scio, NY, USA

BARBECUED MEAT BALLS

3 lb. hamburger
2 c. quick oatmeal
1 c. chopped onion
2 tsp. salt
2 tsp. chili powder

2 eggs, beaten
1 (13 oz.) evaporated milk
½ tsp. garlic powder
½ tsp. pepper

Sauce:

2 c. catsup
2 Tbsp. liquid smoke
½ c. chopped onion

1½ c. brown sugar
½ tsp. garlic powder

Mix hamburger, oatmeal, onion, salt, chili powder, eggs, milk, garlic, and pepper together. Shape into balls. Place single layer into a 9x13 inch pan. Cover with sauce. Bake 1 hour at 350°.

Carol Chrisp, Sargent Lions Club
Sargent, NE, USA

The trouble with common sense is that it is so uncommon.

SPEEDY MEATBALLS AND GRAVY

1 lb. ground chuck
1 egg
½ c. fine dry bread crumbs
3 Tbsp. fresh parsley or 1 tsp.
  parsley flakes

¼ tsp. salt
⅛ tsp. pepper
⅛ tsp. onion flakes
1 (10 oz.) jar (good brand) beef
  gravy

Recipe can be doubled.

Mix all ingredients and form into balls. Put in slow cooker. Pour gravy over balls. Cook until meatballs are done. Serve over mashed potatoes or noodles.

Good for two people.

Mrs. Don (Marge) Zahn, Elburn Lions Club
Elburn, IL, USA

TERIYAKI-MEATBALL KEBABS WITH MUSTARD SAUCE

Serve with rice and whatever vegetable your family likes best.

1 scallion
6 Tbsp. teriyaki sauce
3 Tbsp. ketchup
1 egg

¼ c. dry bread crumbs
1 lb. ground beef
¼ c. Dijon mustard

Heat oven to 400°. Chop the white bulb and half the green top of the scallion. Combine chopped scallion, 2 tablespoons teriyaki sauce, 1 tablespoon ketchup, the egg, bread crumbs, and the beef. Shape into 24 balls. Combine the remaining 4 tablespoons teriyaki sauce and 2 tablespoons ketchup. Coat the meatballs in the teriyaki mixture. Thread on skewers. Put in a shallow pan. Bake until done, turning once, about 15 minutes. Stir ¼ cup water into the mustard to thin. Serve as a sauce with the meatballs. Makes 4 servings.

Per serving: 388 calories, 23 g protein, 26 g fat, 1745 mg sodium, 14 g carbohydrate, 136 mg cholesterol.

Mrs. Mike Nowicki, Clarence Lions Club
Clarence Center, NY, USA

Some people think a balanced diet is a burger in each hand.

❦ ❦ ❦

Prayer should be the key to the day and the lock of the night.

MEATBALLS WITH CREAM SAUCE

1 egg, lightly beaten
¼ c. milk
2 Tbsp. ketchup
1 tsp. Worcestershire sauce
¾ c. quick-cooking oats
¼ c. finely chopped onion

¼ c. minced fresh parsley
1 tsp. salt
¼ tsp. pepper
1½ lb. lean ground beef
3 Tbsp. all-purpose flour

Cream Sauce:

2 Tbsp. butter or margarine
2 Tbsp. all-purpose flour
¼ tsp. dried thyme
Salt and pepper to taste

1 (14 oz.) can chicken broth
⅔ c. whipping cream
2 Tbsp. minced fresh parsley

In a bowl, combine the first nine ingredients. Add beef and mix well. Shape into 1½ inch balls. Roll in flour, shaking off excess. Place 1 inch apart on greased 15x10x1 inch baking pans. Bake, uncovered, at 400° for 10 minutes. Turn meatballs; bake 12 to 15 minutes longer or until meat is no longer pink.

Meanwhile, for sauce, melt butter in a saucepan over medium heat. Stir in flour, thyme, salt, and pepper until smooth. Gradually add broth and cream; bring to a boil. Cook and stir for 2 minutes or until thickened and bubbly. Drain meatballs on paper towels; transfer to a serving dish. Top with sauce; sprinkle with parsley. Yield: 6 servings.

MARVELOUS MEAT LOAF

1½ lb. ground beef
1 egg
½ c. dry bread crumbs
⅓ c. catsup
⅓ c. finely chopped onion

2 Tbsp. milk or water
1 tsp. Worcestershire sauce
½ tsp. salt
¼ tsp. pepper

Combine all ingredients. Place in 9x5x3 inch loaf pan. Microwave on MEDIUM 20 to 24 minutes. Drain liquid occasionally. Let stand, covered, 5 minutes before serving. Makes 6 servings. *Very good.*

My daughter-in-law gave me this recipe.
Betty J. Kaniper, Plainfield Township Lions Club
Stockertown, PA, USA

Advice is like cooking - you should try it before you feed it to others.

MEAT LOAF EXTRAORDINAIRE

2 c. fresh bread crumbs
¾ c. minced onion
¼ c. minced green pepper
2 eggs
2 lb. ground beef (lean)

2 Tbsp. horseradish sauce
2½ tsp. salt
1 tsp. dry mustard
¼ c. evaporated milk
¾ c. catsup

Heat oven to 400°. Have bread crumbs and onion ready. In large bowl, beat eggs. Lightly mix in beef, then crumbs, onion, and pepper. Add horseradish, salt, mustard, milk, and ¼ cup catsup. Mix lightly but well. Form into loaf and place in 9x13 inch pan. The remaining catsup is spread on top.

A dear friend, a lawyer, said I could pay him his "fee" with this meat loaf.
Edith C. Rich (Dee), Bullhead City Lions Club
Bullhead City, AZ, USA

MEAT LOAF FROM MINNESOTA

2 lb. ground beef hamburger
2 eggs

1 can Campbell's onion soup
1 box Stove Top dressing

Mix together. Put in 9x11 inch greased pan and bake for 30 minutes at 350°F. You may top it with catsup and brown sugar before baking.

Our church has made this in large batches for fundraisers.
Elvera Trettin, Stewart Lions Club
Stewart, MN, USA

NEW ENGLAND MEAT LOAF

16 oz. whole cranberry sauce
1½ lb. lean ground beef
1 c. bread crumbs
1 egg, well beaten

3 Tbsp. onion, chopped
3 Tbsp. green pepper, chopped
½ c. carrot, chopped
Salt and pepper to taste

Spread cranberry sauce in bottom of baking dish. Mix remaining ingredients and place on top of cranberry sauce mixture. Bake at 350° for 1 hour. Slice and serve with sauce in pan. Yield: 1 meat loaf.
Lion Geneva Gee, Mount Airy Foothills Lions Club
Mount Airy, NC, USA

Government regulation is a lot like ketchup -
you either get none or more than you want.

SWEET-AND-SOUR MEATLOAF

1½ lb. ground beef
1 c. dry bread crumbs
1 tsp. salt
¼ tsp. pepper

2 eggs
1 tsp. instant minced onion
1 (15 oz.) can tomato sauce or 2
    small cans

Topping:

2 Tbsp. brown sugar
2 Tbsp. vinegar

½ c. white sugar
2 tsp. mustard

Mix together beef, bread crumbs, salt, pepper, and eggs. Add onion and one-half the tomato sauce. Form into loaf in 9x5x3 inch pan. Bake at 350° for 50 minutes.

In saucepan, combine topping ingredients; bring to boil. Pour over and bake 10 minutes more. Let stand a few minutes before cutting.

Janet Johnson, Treasurer, Princeton Lions Club
Princeton, IL, USA

EASY ITALIAN MEATLOAF

1 egg
¼ c. chopped fresh parsley
½ tsp. dried oregano
Salt and pepper

½ c. spaghetti sauce
½ c. dry bread crumbs
1½ lb. ground beef or meatloaf
    mixture

Heat the oven to 350°. Beat the egg to mix. Stir in the parsley, oregano, 1 teaspoon salt, ½ teaspoon pepper, ¼ cup of the spaghetti sauce, and the bread crumbs. Crumble in the meat and mix thoroughly. Pack the mixture into a 9x5 inch loaf pan. Spread the remaining ¼ cup spaghetti sauce on top. Bake the meatloaf until browned, about 1 hour and 15 minutes. Let stand 10 minutes before slicing. Makes 12 slices.

Per slice: 149 calories, 10 g protein, 9 g fat, 295 mg sodium, 5 g carbohydrate, 52 mg cholesterol.

Barbara Joy Hess, Clarence Lions Club
Clarence Center, NY, USA

Friends are the chocolate chips in the cookie of life.

❧ ❧ ❧

Promises are like snowballs - easy to make but hard to keep.

SKILLET MEAT LOAF

2 eggs, beaten
½ c. ketchup
1 Tbsp. Worcestershire sauce
1 tsp. prepared mustard
¼ tsp. salt
¼ tsp. pepper
2 c. crushed saltines (about 40
   crackers)

1 small onion, chopped
½ c. thinly sliced celery
½ c. thinly sliced carrot
2 lb. lean ground beef
Additional ketchup and mustard
   (optional)

In a large bowl, combine the first six ingredients. Add saltines, onion, celery, and carrot. Add beef and mix well. Pat into a 10 inch skillet. Top with ketchup and mustard if desired. Cover and cook over medium heat for 8 minutes. Reduce heat to low; cook and cook 15 to 20 minutes longer or until meat is no longer pink and a meat thermometer reads 160°. Drain. Let stand a few minutes before serving. Yield: 8 servings.

Meat loaf that cooks in less than half an hour!!! It's fast and great with mashed potatoes.

Barbara K. Hugus, West Milford Lions Club
West Milford, WV, USA

LI'L CHEDDAR MEAT LOAVES

1 egg
¾ c. milk
1 c. (4 oz.) shredded Cheddar
   cheese
½ c. quick-cooking oats
½ c. chopped onion

1 tsp. salt
1 lb. lean ground beef
⅔ c. ketchup
½ c. packed brown sugar
1½ tsp. prepared mustard

In a bowl, beat the egg and milk. Stir in cheese, oats, onion, and salt. Add beef and mix well. Shape into eight loaves; place in a greased 13x9x2 inch baking dish. Combine ketchup, brown sugar, and mustard; spoon over loaves. Bake, uncovered, at 350° for 45 minutes or until the meat is no longer pink and a meat thermometer reads 160°. Yield: 8 servings.

To check your resistance, stop at a doughnut shop and only order coffee.

❧ ❧ ❧

Let God have your life; He can do with it more than you can.

BAKED PORK CHOPS WITH DRESSING

Flour
Salt to taste
Pepper to taste
4 c. bread cubes
2 Tbsp. chopped onion
¼ c. melted butter

¼ c. chicken stock
¼ tsp. poultry seasoning
12 oz. sour cream
12 oz. cream of mushroom soup
   (undiluted)

Coat pork chops in flour, salt, and pepper. Brown. While chops are browning, mix bread cubes, onion, butter, poultry seasoning, and chicken stock. Place in bottom of baking dish. Place browned pork chops on top. Mix together sour cream and mushroom soup. Spread over chops and dressing. Cover with foil or lid and bake at 350° for 1 hour or until chops are tender.

Connie Nagengast, Columbus Noon Lions Club
Columbus, NE, USA

PORK CHOP CASSEROLE

4 pork chops
1 large onion
1 c. cooked tomatoes
2 tsp. salt

Pepper
½ c. uncooked rice
2 c. hot water
1 green pepper

Put chops in bottom of baking dish; place rice over them. Slice onion and green pepper over rice and pour in hot water and tomatoes. Add salt and pepper. Cover and bake 1 hour in medium oven until rice is cooked and chops are tender.

Lion Glenda Conopask, Plymouth Lions Club
Terryville, CT, USA

PORK CHOPS WITH LEMON AND ROSEMARY

1 lemon
4 (1 inch thick) pork chops (about
   2 lb.)

2 cloves garlic
1½ tsp. dried rosemary
Salt and pepper

Squeeze 1 tablespoon juice form the lemon and sprinkle the juice over the pork chops. Crush the garlic and rub it over the chops. Crush the rosemary between your fingers and sprinkle it over the chops with ¾ teaspoon pepper. Let the chops stand while preparing the grill for direct heat. Sprinkle the pork chops with salt and grill until just slightly pink near bone, 5 to 7 minutes per side. Makes 4 servings.

Per serving: 418 calories, 36 g protein, 29 g fat, 93 mg sodium, 1 g carbohydrate, 127 mg cholesterol.

Joanne M. Wetzler, Clarence Lions Club
Clarence Center, NY, USA

2075-99

MUSHROOM ORANGE CHOP

1 butterfly pork chop (¾ inch thick)
2 tsp. vegetable oil
2 green onions, thinly sliced
2 fresh mushrooms, chopped

1 garlic clove, minced
2 Tbsp. orange marmalade
1 tsp. soy sauce
1 Tbsp. sunflower kernels (optional)

In a skillet over medium heat, brown pork chop in oil on both sides. Continue cooking until a meat thermometer reads 160° to 170°, about 6 minutes. Remove and keep warm. In the same skillet, saute onions, mushrooms, and garlic until tender. Add marmalade and soy sauce; cook and stir until heated through. Pour over chop. Sprinkle with sunflower kernels if desired. Yield: 1 serving.

PORK CHOP HOTDISH

1 c. raw rice
1½ cans water
1 env. Lipton onion soup

6 pork chops
1 can cream of mushroom soup

Pour rice in 9x13 inch pan. Place pork chops on top of rice. Mix last three ingredients in bowl. Pour over pork chops. Bake at 350° for 1 to 1½ hours, depending on the thickness of cut. Remove from oven. *Enjoy.*

Lion Theresa Hill, Hector Lions Club
Hector, MN

PORK TENDERLOIN WITH FENNEL AND PEPPER CRUST

Though this roast could not be simpler, it's fit for the fanciest dinner party. It's even good cold.

2 tsp. fennel seeds
½ tsp. whole black peppercorns
¾ tsp. salt

1 Tbsp. Dijon mustard
1 lb. pork tenderloin
1 Tbsp. oil

Heat oven to 350°. Crush fennel seeds and peppercorns. Combine with salt. Spread spice mixture out on a plate. Stir 1 tablespoon water into the mustard and brush the thinned mustard over the pork. Roll the pork in spice mixture. Smear 1½ teaspoons of the oil in a roasting pan. Put pork on top of the oil and drizzle the remaining 1½ teaspoons oil over the pork. Roast under the pork is done (160°), 35 to 40 minutes. Makes 4 servings.

Per serving: 166 calories, 24 g protein, 7 g fat, 581 mg sodium, 1 g carbohydrate, 74 mg cholesterol.

Mrs. Mike Nowicki, Clarence Lions Club
Clarence Center, NY, USA

SAUTEED PORK WITH WHISKY SAUCE

1 scallion
1 lb. pork tenderloin
Salt and pepper

1 Tbsp. butter
1 Tbsp. oil
¾ c. Scotch whisky

Chop scallion. Cut pork diagonally into 8 slices and sprinkle with salt and pepper. In a large frying pan, heat butter and oil over medium-high heat. Add pork and cook until browned, 3 to 5 minutes per side. Remove pork and keep warm. Reduce heat to medium. Add scallion to pan. Stir and cook 1 minute. Add whisky, ½ teaspoon salt, and ¼ teaspoon pepper. Bring to a boil and cook, stirring with a wooden spoon, to dislodge all the brown bits on the bottom of pan, until liquid is reduced to about ⅓ cup, about 2 minutes. Serve pork with the whisky sauce. Makes 4 servings.

Per serving: 184 calories, 24 g protein, 9 g fat, 230 mg sodium, 0 g carbohydrate, 82 mg cholesterol.

Barbara Joy Hess, Clarence Lions Club
Clarence Center, NY, USA

GLAZED PORK TENDERLOIN

1 orange
¼ c. soy sauce

1 tsp. minced fresh ginger
1 lb. pork tenderloin

Heat oven to 325°. Grate 1 teaspoon of the colored zest from the orange and squeeze ¼ cup of juice. Combine the zest, juice, soy sauce, and ginger in a saucepan. Boil until liquid is reduced to about 2 tablespoons, 3 to 4 minutes. Brush this glaze over the pork. Put in a roasting pan and roast until cooked through, about 40 minutes (160°). Cover with foil after 20 minutes if the pork is getting too browned. Let rest 5 minutes before slicing. Makes 4 servings.

Work time: 15 minutes. Total time: 55 minutes.

Per serving: 166 calories, 27 g protein, 4 g fat, 1089 mg sodium, 3 g carbohydrate, 83 mg cholesterol.

Mrs. Lucy Aiken, Clarence Lions Club
Clarence Center, NY, USA

Housework is like stringing beads without a knot in the end of the string.

Worry is the misuse of the imagination.

CRANBERRY PORK ROAST

1 (2½ to 3 lb.) boneless rolled
    pork loin roast
1 (16 oz.) can jellied cranberry
    sauce
½ c. sugar
½ c. cranberry juice

1 tsp. dry mustard
¼ tsp. ground cloves
2 Tbsp. cornstarch
2 Tbsp. cold water
Salt to taste

Place pork roast in a slow cooker. In a medium bowl, mash cranberry sauce; stir in sugar, cranberry juice, mustard, and cloves. Pour over roast. Cover and cook on LOW for 6 to 8 hours or until meat is tender. Remove roast and keep warm. Skim fat from juices; measure 2 cups, adding water, if necessary, and pour into a saucepan. Bring to a boil over medium-high heat. Combine the cornstarch and cold water to make a paste; stir into gravy. Cook and stir until thickened. Season with salt. Serve with sliced pork. Yield: 4 to 6 servings.

VERY FIRST RIBS

4 lb. lean meaty pork back ribs
Water to cover
1 c. water
½ c. chopped onion
¾ c. white vinegar
2 Tbsp. Worcestershire sauce

½ c. white sugar
1 tsp. dry mustard
1½ tsp. salt
¼ tsp. pepper
⅛ tsp. ground cloves
5½ oz. tomato paste

Cut ribs into 2 rib servings. Place in large pot. Add water; cover and bring to a boil. Boil for 30 minutes. Drain. Measure remaining ingredients into saucepan. Heat, stirring frequently, until it simmers. Simmer gently until onion is soft. Using tongs, transfer ribs to roaster. Pour sauce over top. Cover and bake in 350° oven for 1 hour. Makes 8 servings.

Lion Micheal and Ruth (Sauskojus) Bartolf,
Oxbow and District Lions Club
Oxbow, Saskatchewan, Canada

A weed is a plant with nine lives.

❦ ❦ ❦

Always do right. This will gratify some people, and astonish the rest.

❦ ❦ ❦

Bigotry creates enemies. Tolerance makes friends.

GARLIC RIBS

2½ lb. spareribs, cut as for sweet
   and sour
2 Tbsp. minced onion
2 tsp. salt
2 tsp. ground ginger
1 beef bouillon cube or packet
¾ c. boiling water
2 Tbsp. corn starch

¼ c. vinegar (cider or white)
¾ c. brown sugar
2 Tbsp. soya sauce
½ tsp. ground ginger
½ tsp. garlic powder
½ tsp. curry powder
¼ tsp. ground cloves

Place spareribs in Dutch oven. Cover with cold water. Mix minced onion, salt, and ginger in water and bring to a boil. Let ribs simmer for about 30 minutes. Do not allow meat to come away from bones. At this stage, ribs can be cooled, covered, and refrigerated until ready to bake. Preheat oven to 325°F. Cut ribs between each bone and place in roaster sprayed with nonstick coating. Dissolve bouillon in water and set aside.

In a microwave-safe bowl, mix corn starch with brown sugar and spices until smooth and corn starch has no lumps. Stir in vinegar, soya sauce, and bouillon mixture. Microwave on HIGH for 5 or 6 minutes, stirring two or three times until thickened and clear. If using stove top, heat until thick, stirring constantly. If sauce is too thick, add water to desired consistency. Pour sauce over ribs, making sure meat is coated. Bake, covered, in oven for 45 minutes, basting often so glaze is evenly distributed.

These ribs are delicious. Serve with steamed rice and stir-fry vegetables.
Lion Lillian Marchant, Lake of the Woods Lions Club
Kenora, Ontario, Canada

RIBS WITH PLUM SAUCE

5 to 6 lb. pork spareribs
¾ c. soy sauce
¾ c. plum jam or apricot
   preserves

¾ c. honey
2 to 3 garlic cloves, minced

Cut ribs into serving-size pieces; place with bone side down on a rack in a shallow roasting pan. Cover and bake at 350° for 1 hour or until ribs are tender; drain. Combine remaining ingredients; brush some of the sauce over ribs. Bake at 350° or grill over medium coals, uncovered, for 30 minutes, brushing occasionally with sauce. Yield: 6 servings.

Memory is the power to gather roses in winter.

BAR-B-Q PORK

1 (3 to 4 lb.) rolled pork roast
5 c. chopped celery
1 large onion, chopped

1 (14 oz.) bottle ketchup
1 bottle chili sauce

Remove string from roast. Place in large pan or roaster. Pour ingredients over roast. Cover pan and roast at 250° for 5 hours.

This can be served as the main dish or on rolls as sandwiches.

Mrs. Don (Marge) Zahn, Elburn Lions Club
Elburn, IL, USA

HAM LOAF

1½ lb. ham, ground
1½ lb. unseasoned pork, ground
1 c. milk

2 c. bread crumbs
2 eggs (unbeaten)

Sauce:

½ c. brown sugar
½ tsp. dry mustard

¼ c. cider vinegar
¼ c. water

Mix ground ham and pork, bread crumbs, and eggs as for meatloaf. Shape into balls or individual loaves. Place in sprayed 9x13 inch pan.

Sauce: Mix sugar, mustard, vinegar, and water. Pour over loaves. Bake 1½ hours at 325° in open pan. Baste often, about every 20 minutes.

I make individual loaves, about 1½ x 3 inches.

Gloria Hansen, Princeton Lions Club
Princeton, IL, USA

HONEY BAKED HAM

1 ham
1 c. Pepsi
½ c. brown sugar

½ tsp. dry mustard
½ c. pineapple juice
1 Tbsp. whole cloves

Baste the ham with half the Pepsi. Stick whole cloves around on ham. Bake 1 hour at 325°. Remove from the oven. Make a paste of the remaining ingredients. Spread over the ham. Return to the oven and continue baking until the recommended time for the size ham.

Martha C. Cox, Travelers Rest Lions Club
Travelers Rest, SC

When your outgo exceeds your income, your upkeep will be your downfall.

HAM STEAK WITH SPICY ONION SAUCE

1 small onion
1 lb. ham steak (about ½ inch
   thick)
About 1 Tbsp. oil
½ c. sour cream

1 Tbsp. whole-grain mustard
2 tsp. cider vinegar
1 tsp. prepared horseradish
½ tsp. dry mustard
Pepper

Mince the onion. In a large frying pan, cook the ham over medium-high heat, turning once, until browned, about 8 minutes. Remove and keep warm. If necessary, add enough oil to the pan drippings to equal about 1 tablespoon of fat. Add the onion and cook until lightly browned, about 5 minutes.

Combine sour cream, mustard, vinegar, horseradish, dry mustard, and ¼ teaspoon pepper and stir into the cooked onion until heated through. Serve the ham steak with the mustard sauce. Makes 4 servings.

Per serving: 285 calories, 21 g protein, 18 g fat, 1,550 mg sodium, 8 g carbohydrate, 77 mg cholesterol.

Mrs. Mike Nowicki, Clarence Lions Club
Clarence Center, NY, USA

HAM ROLLS

1¼ lb. ground ham
1 lb. pork, ground
½ lb. ground beef
1½ c. graham cracker crumbs
2 eggs

1 c. milk
1 can tomato soup
1 c. brown sugar
2 Tbsp. vinegar
1 Tbsp. dry mustard

Mix meat with cracker crumbs, eggs, and milk. Blend well. Make into balls the size of eggs. Place in baking pan and cover with sauce made from tomato soup and other ingredients. Bake 1¼ hours at 350°.

Alberta Oliver, Rivesville Lions Club
Rivesville, WV, USA

A smile is a passport that will take you anywhere you want to go.

❦ ❦ ❦

Winning isn't everything - wanting to win is.

❦ ❦ ❦

A child is one who can take apart in a few minutes
the toy it took an adult 2 hours to put together.

LAMB, EGGPLANT, AND PEPPER KEBABS

1 eggplant (about 1 lb.)
1 green bell pepper
3 cloves garlic
⅓ c. lemon juice
½ c. oil

1½ tsp. dried oregano
Salt and pepper
2 lb. boneless leg of lamb, cut
   into 2x1 inch chunks

Heat oven to 400°. Halve eggplant lengthwise and then cut crosswise into slices, about ½ inch thick. Cut pepper into chunks. Mince garlic. In a stainless-steel or glass bowl, combine garlic, lemon juice, oil, oregano, 1½ teaspoons salt, and ¾ teaspoon pepper. Add vegetables. Toss to coat. Remove and put on a baking sheet in a single layer. Add lamb and garlic mixture and set aside to marinate. Roast vegetables, stirring once, until tender, about 15 minutes. When ready to eat, heat grill. Thread vegetables and lamb on skewers. Grill, turning once, until lamb is done, about 10 minutes for medium-rare. Makes 6 servings.

Barbara Joy Hess, Clarence Lions Club
Clarence Center, NY, USA

LAMB SHANKS IN TOMATO SAUCE

1 onion
3 cloves garlic
2 Tbsp. flour
Salt and pepper
4 lamb shanks (about 3 lb.)
2 Tbsp. oil

28 oz. can tomatoes with juice
   (about 3 c.)
2 tsp. dried marjoram
¾ tsp. ground allspice
1 Tbsp. chopped fresh parsley

Chop the onion. Mince the garlic. Combine the flour, 1 teaspoon salt, and ¼ teaspoon pepper. Dredge the lamb shanks in the seasoned flour. In a Dutch oven, heat the oil over medium-high heat. Brown the lamb shanks on all sides, about 8 minutes. Remove the shanks and reduce the heat. Add the onion; cover and cook 2 minutes. Stir in the garlic, tomatoes with their juice, the marjoram, allspice, and 1 teaspoon salt. Return the lamb shanks to the pot. Cover and simmer over low heat until tender, 2 to 2½ hours. Sprinkle with the parsley. Makes 4 servings.

Per serving: 583 calories, 45 g protein, 38 g fat, 1555 mg sodium, 14 g carbohydrate, 152 mg cholesterol.

Barbara Joy Hess, Clarence Lions Club
Clarence Center, NY, USA

Vacation makes you feel good enough to go back
to work and poor enough to have to.

ROSEMARY-BRAISED LAMB SHANKS

1 onion
1 carrot
2 cloves garlic
1 Tbsp. oil

4 lamb shanks (about 3 lb. total)
1 tsp. dried rosemary
Salt and pepper

Heat oven to 350°. Chop onion and carrot. Mince garlic. In a Dutch oven, heat oil over medium-high heat. Brown lamb shanks well on all sides and remove. Discard all but 1 tablespoon drippings. Reduce heat to low. Add onion, carrot, and garlic. Cover and cook until tender, about 3 minutes. Stir in 1 cup water, the rosemary, 1 teaspoon salt, and ¼ teaspoon pepper. Return shanks to pot, cover, and bring to simmer. Put in oven and cook until lamb is very tender, about 1 hour and 45 minutes. Remove the shanks and keep warm. Skim the fat from the pan juices. Bring to a boil over high heat and cook until reduced to about 1 cup and slightly thickened. Serve the reserved juices with the lamb shanks. Makes 4 servings.

Per serving: 328 calories, 49 g protein, 12 g fat, 701 mg sodium, 4 g carbohydrate, 150 mg cholesterol.

Mrs. Mike Nowicki, Clarence Lions Club
Clarence Center, NY, USA

LAMB OR BEEF KEBABS

3 lb. lamb or beef, cut in 1½ inch
    cubes
1 jar small white onions
1 large green pepper (optional)
½ c. water
⅓ c. cider vinegar
⅓ c. tomato catsup
1 tsp. seasoning salt

18 whole mushrooms (or 1
    medium can)
Cherry tomatoes
1 (No. 2) can pineapple chunks
2 tsp. soy sauce
½ tsp. Worcestershire sauce
½ c. brown sugar
1 tsp. ground ginger

Drain pineapple; add water to syrup to make 1 cup. Combine with vinegar, catsup, brown sugar, salt, ginger, and sauces. Pour this marinade over meat. Cover and refrigerate 12 hours or overnight.

Thread meat, alternating with vegetables, on skewers. Place each kebab on sheet of heavy Reynolds Wrap. Brush liberally with marinade. Bring up foil and seal sides and ends with double fold. Place packets on grill about 3 inches over very hot coals or in 325° oven for 20 to 25 minutes, turning several times. *Enjoy.*

Lioness Catherine Violette, East Anne Arundel Lioness Club
Annapolis, MD, USA

Happiness isn't so much environmental as mental.

LAMB KEBABS

1 large onion
1 red bell pepper
1 small eggplant (about ¾ lb.)
1 zucchini (about ½ lb.)
½ c. olive oil
Salt and pepper

½ lb. ground lamb
½ lb. ground beef
1 tsp. ground cumin
½ tsp. ground cinnamon
3 Tbsp. chopped fresh mint or 1
  Tbsp. + 1 tsp. dried

Heat oven to 400°. Cut onion into wedges. Cut the bell pepper and eggplant into approximately 1 inch chunks. Slice zucchini in half lengthwise, then cut halves into ½ inch slices. Combine oil, 1½ teaspoons salt, and ¾ teaspoon pepper in a baking pan. Add vegetables and toss to coat. Roast vegetables, stirring once, until just tender, about 15 minutes.

Meanwhile, combine lamb, beef, cumin, cinnamon, ½ teaspoon salt, ¼ teaspoon pepper, and the mint. Shape into 16 balls. Heat grill. Thread meatballs and vegetables on skewers. Cook directly over the hot coals, turning twice, until meatballs are done, about 10 minutes. Makes 4 servings.

Per serving: 515 calories, 21 g protein, 43 g fat, 1,171 mg sodium, 13 g carbohydrate, 71 mg cholesterol.

Mrs. Mike Nowicki, Clarence Lions Club
Clarence Center, NY, USA

SARAH'S LEG OF LAMB

4 to 5 lb. leg of lamb

Salt, pepper, and dill outside of meat. Stuff leg with many cloves of garlic. Add 1 cup red wine and baste as lamb cooks. Add 1 tablespoon butter. Use meat thermometer.

Sarah Wehling, Bothell Lions Club
Bothell, WA, USA

VENISON MEAT LOAF

2½ lb. ground venison
2 tsp. salt
¼ tsp. pepper
¾ c. dry bread crumbs

2 eggs, slightly beaten
¾ c. milk
½ small onion, chopped

Preheat oven to 350°F. Combine all ingredients in a bowl and mix well. Press into a greased loaf pan, 9x5x3 inches. Bake for 2½ hours.

Beef suet or salt pork may be ground in with venison if it seems dry.

Lion Ann Frechette, Lake of the Woods Lions Club
Kenora, Ontario, Canada

VEAL MADELEINE

2 lb. boneless veal, cubed
2 Tbsp. flour
1 tsp. salt
¼ tsp. pepper

4 Tbsp. butter, melted
2 (1 inch) wide strips lemon peel
1 c. boiling water
1 c. heavy cream

Cook veal with seasoned flour. Brown in melted butter. Add lemon peel and water. Cover and simmer until tender, about 1½ hours. Remove peel and stir in cream. Yield: 6 servings.

Lion Jo Townsend, Mount Airy Foothills Lions Club
Mount Airy, NC, USA

LIVER AND SAUSAGE CASSEROLE

1 lb. pork sausage
1 lb. beef liver
Flour for dredging and thickening

1 medium onion, chopped
Water for gravy
Salt and pepper (sparingly)

Brown sausage in hot skillet. Remove sausage to casserole or baking dish. Cook onion slightly in sausage drippings and add to casserole. Cut liver slices into strips and dredge with flour. Brown liver strips and distribute with sausage in dish. Pour off fat from skillet, leaving about 2 tablespoons. Brown 2 tablespoons flour in hot fat. Blend in about a cup of water to make gravy to cover meats, adding salt and pepper to taste. Place a lid or piece of foil over dish and bake at 350° for 35 minutes.

Lion Micheal and Ruth (Sauskojus) Bartolf,
Oxbow and District Lions Club
Oxbow, Saskatchewan, Canada

BARBECUE WIENERS

36 wieners
3 cans tomato soup

6 slices bacon
1 medium onion, chopped

Cut bacon into small pieces. Fry until crisp with the onion. Combine this with the tomato soup. Put wieners in pan and pour mixture over. Bake at 275° for 2 hours. Serve on wiener buns.

Easy party recipe that can be doubled or tripled and served with baked beans and potato salad.

JoAnn Hansen, Two Rivers Lioness Club
Two Rivers, WI, USA

Kindness is something the blind can see and the deaf can hear.

BAR B.Q WIENERS

1 (8 oz.) can tomato sauce
¼ c. chopped onion
Black pepper (to taste)

¼ c. sweet pickle relish
¼ tsp. chili powder
1 lb. wieners, cut in chunks

Combine all ingredients but wieners. Mix well. Add wieners and simmer 15 to 20 minutes. *The sauce is delicious!*

Doris (Cricket) Kimbrell, Iron City Lions Club
Iron City, TN, USA

FRIED RICE WITH CURRIED MEATBALLS

1 c. rice
Salt
1 lb. ground pork
3 Tbsp. dry bread crumbs
5 tsp. curry powder
2 Tbsp. oil

2 carrots, halved lengthwise and sliced
1 zucchini, halved lengthwise and sliced
2 cloves garlic, minced
2 scallions, cut into 1 inch pieces

Cook rice in boiling salted water until tender. Drain. Combine ground pork, bread crumbs, 1 teaspoon of the curry powder, and ¾ teaspoon salt. Roll into 1 inch balls. In a large frying pan, heat 1 tablespoon of the oil over medium-high heat. Add meatballs and brown well, about 5 minutes. Add carrots, cover, and cook 5 minutes. Stir in zucchini, garlic, scallions, and ¾ teaspoon salt. Cook until tender, about 10 minutes. Push vegetables and meatballs to side of pan. Add remaining 1 tablespoon oil. Stir in remaining 4 teaspoons curry powder. Add rice. Cook, stirring, until rice is heated through, about 5 minutes. Makes 4 servings.

Per serving: 598 calories, 23 g protein, 34 g fat, 943 mg sodium, 48 g carbohydrate, 83 mg cholesterol.

Barbara Joy Hess, Clarence Lions Club
Clarence Center, NY, USA

I am not afraid of tomorrow for I have seen yesterday and I love today.

If you have to keep reminding yourself of a thing, perhaps it isn't so.

Life is the garment we continually alter, but which never seems to fit.

SEAFOOD

SESAME SALMON FILLET

1 (1½ to 2 lb.) salmon fillet
2 Tbsp. cider vinegar
2 Tbsp. soy sauce
1 Tbsp. honey
1 tsp. vegetable oil

1 tsp. spicy brown or horseradish
    mustard
⅛ to ¼ tsp. ground ginger
2 Tbsp. sesame seeds, toasted
3 green onions, sliced

Place salmon in a shallow dish. Combine vinegar, soy sauce, honey, oil, mustard, and ginger; pour over salmon. Cover and refrigerate for 1 hour, turning once. Drain and discard marinade. Broil the salmon or grill, covered, over medium-high heat for 15 to 20 minutes or until the fish flakes easily with a fork. Sprinkle with sesame seeds and onions. Yield: 4 servings.

ASIAN SALMON BURGER

1 (14¾ oz.) can red salmon,
    drained and bones and skin
    removed
3 slices firm white bread, torn
    into small pieces
⅓ c. chopped fresh cilantro
2 eggs, lightly beaten

¼ tsp. pepper
½ c. bottled Italian dressing
2 Tbsp. reduced-sodium soy
    sauce
½ lb. mesclun or spring salad mix
¼ lb. snow peas, steamed
1 pt. cherry tomatoes, cut in
    halves
1 (3½ oz.) pkg. enoki mushrooms

Preheat grill or broiler. In bowl, combine salmon, bread, cilantro, eggs, and pepper, stirring to break up salmon. Shape into 4 burgers. Grease grill or rack set in broiler pan. Grill or broil 8 to 10 minutes, turning once.

In small bowl, combine dressing and soy sauce. Arrange vegetables on 4 serving plates. Top each with salmon burger. Serve with dressing. Makes 4 servings.

Per serving: 395 calories, 24 g protein, 20 g carbohydrate, 30 g fat, 107 mg cholesterol, 1080 mg sodium..

Mrs. Lucy Aiken, Clarence Lions Club
Clarence Center, NY, USA

May your days be filled with the gift of dreams ...
and may your heart be full of the courage to follow them.

MUSTARD SALMON PUFF

2 eggs
⅔ c. milk
½ c. sour cream
¾ c. dry bread crumbs
1 tsp. seafood seasoning
½ tsp. lemon-pepper seasoning

¼ tsp. dill weed
3 c. cooked, flaked salmon
3 Tbsp. chopped celery
2 Tbsp. chopped onion
4½ tsp. lemon juice

Topping:

1⅓ c. mayonnaise*
1 Tbsp. prepared mustard

1 egg white
2 Tbsp. minced parsley

In a bowl, stir eggs, milk, and sour cream until smooth. Add bread crumbs, seafood seasoning, lemon pepper, and dill. Add salmon, celery, onion, and lemon juice; mix well. Transfer to a greased 11x7x2 inch baking dish. Bake at 350° for 25 to 30 minutes or until a knife inserted near the center comes out clean.

Meanwhile, combine mayonnaise and mustard in a bowl. In a mixing bowl, beat egg white until stiff peaks form; fold into mayonnaise mixture. Spread over salmon mixture. Bake 10 to 15 minutes longer or until lightly browned. Sprinkle with parsley. Yield: 8 servings.

* Do not use light or fat-free mayonnaise.

SALMON TARTLETS

½ c. butter, softened
1 (3 oz.) pkg. cream cheese, softened

1 c. all-purpose flour

Filling:

2 eggs
½ c. milk
1 Tbsp. butter, melted
1 tsp. lemon juice
½ c. dry bread crumbs
1½ tsp. dried parsley flakes

½ tsp. rubbed sage
½ tsp. salt
¼ tsp. pepper
1 (14¾ oz.) can salmon, drained
    and bones removed
1 green onion, sliced

In a mixing bowl, beat butter, cream cheese, and flour until smooth. Shape tablespoonfuls of dough into balls; press onto the bottom and up the sides of greased miniature muffin cups. In a bowl, combine eggs, milk, butter, and lemon juice. Stir in crumbs, parsley, sage, salt, and pepper. Fold in salmon and onion. Spoon into shells. Bake at 350° for 30 to 35 minutes or until browned. Yield: 2 dozen.

GINGER SALMON CAKES

1 lemon
2½ tsp. grated fresh ginger
Salt and pepper
5 Tbsp. oil
6 c. watercress leaves (about 2 bunches)

1 egg
15½ oz. can salmon
1 scallion, chopped
2 Tbsp. chopped fresh parsley
½ c. + 3 Tbsp. dry bread crumbs

Squeeze 1½ tablespoons juice from lemon. In a small jar, shake together lemon juice, ½ teaspoon ginger, ¾ teaspoon salt, and ¼ teaspoon pepper until salt dissolves. Add 3 tablespoons oil and shake to combine. Remove tough stems from watercress and divide leaves among 4 plates. In a large bowl, beat egg. Drain salmon and add to egg with the remaining 2 teaspoons ginger, the scallion, parsley, ½ cup bread crumbs, ½ teaspoon salt, and ¼ teaspoon pepper. Mix well and shape into 8 patties.

In a large nonstick frying pan, heat remaining 2 tablespoons oil over medium heat. Coat salmon patties with remaining 3 tablespoons crumbs and cook until golden brown on both sides, 3 to 5 minutes. Put 2 cakes on each plate. Shake dressing again and pour over salmon and watercress. Makes 4 servings.

Per serving: 399 calories, 27 g protein, 26 g fat, 1458 mg sodium, 15 g carbohydrate, 54 mg cholesterol.

Barbara Joy Hess, Clarence Lions Club
Clarence Center, NY, USA

PAN-STEAMED SALMON WITH HORSERADISH CHIVE CREAM

1 c. heavy cream
Salt and pepper
1 Tbsp. prepared horseradish

2 tsp. chopped fresh chives or scallion tops
4 salmon fillets (about 1½ lb. in all)

Combine cream, ½ teaspoon salt, and ⅛ teaspoon pepper in a saucepan and bring to a boil over medium-high heat. Reduce heat and simmer until cream has reduced to ½ cup, about 5 minutes. Remove from heat and stir in horseradish and chives. Cover and keep warm while preparing fish.

Heat a nonstick frying pan until very hot. Put fish in pan, skin side up. Sear until browned, about 2 minutes. Turn fish over and sear other side, about 2 minutes. Reduce heat to low; add 2 tablespoons water and immediately cover pan. Let steam until fish is done, about 5 minutes. Serve with the sauce. Makes 4 servings.

Work time: 20 minutes. Total time: 20 minutes.

Per serving: 449 calories, 35 g protein, 33 g fat, 375 mg sodium, 2 g carbohydrate, 175 mg cholesterol.

Mrs. Lucy Aiken, Clarence Lions Club
Clarence Center, NY, USA

SMOKED SALMON WITH HORSERADISH SPREAD

4 Tbsp. butter (at room
   temperature)
4 Tbsp. cream cheese (at room
   temperature)
1 Tbsp. prepared horseradish,
   drained

2 cucumbers
6 oz. smoked salmon
Thinly-sliced rye bread

Combine butter, cream cheese, and horseradish until smooth. Score cucumbers with a fork. Cut into thin slices. Cut salmon into pieces. Cut each slice of bread into 4 triangles. Arrange on a platter. Makes about 3 dozen pieces.

Work time: 30 minutes. Total time: 30 minutes.

Per piece: 39 calories, 2 g protein, 2 mg fat, 77 mg sodium, 4 mg carbohydrate, 6 mg cholesterol.

Lion John J. Hess, Clarence Lions Club
Clarence Center, NY, USA

SALMON STUFFED SHELLS

12 jumbo pasta shells
1 egg, beaten
1 c. part-skim Ricotta cheese
2 Tbsp. chopped onion
2 Tbsp. snipped parsley

$1/4$ tsp. finely grated lemon peel
1 c. canned salmon, drained and
   flaked
1 tsp. seafood seasoning
$1/2$ c. evaporated milk (skim)

Dill Sauce:

1 Tbsp. margarine
1 Tbsp. flour
$1/4$ tsp. salt
$1/8$ tsp. pepper

$1\frac{1}{2}$ c. skim milk
3 Tbsp. finely snipped fresh dill
   or 2 tsp. dried dill weed
1 Tbsp. lemon juice

Preheat oven to 350°. Cook pasta according to package directions; drain well and cool on waxed paper or aluminum foil to keep shells from sticking together. Combine egg, Ricotta, onion, parsley, lemon peel, salmon, and seafood seasoning. Pour evaporated skim milk into lightly buttered 9 inch square baking dish. Fill each pasta shell with heaping tablespoon of filling. Arrange shells in baking dish and cover with foil. Bake 30 to 35 minutes or until hot and bubbly.

While shells are baking, melt margarine in small pan over medium heat; stir in flour, salt, and pepper. Remove pan from heat. Gradually add skim milk, stirring until mixture is smooth. Return to medium heat; bring to boiling, stirring constantly. Reduce heat; stir in dill and lemon juice. Remove dish from oven; arrange shells on serving platter. Serve with dill sauce over baked shells.

In honor of my father, Lion John T. Keister.
Lion Ann K. Brumback, Silver Run-Union Mills Lions Club
Westminster, MD, USA

EASY BAR-B-QUE SHRIMP

2 lb. medium-large shrimp (heads off - in shell)
1 stick butter or margarine
1 (16 oz.) bottle Wish-Bone Italian salad dressing (oil base)

1 Tbsp. fresh ground black pepper (to taste)
1 loaf French bread

Heat oven to 375°. Melt butter in 9x13 inch pan. Rinse shrimp and place in pan with butter. Top with Wish-Bone dressing and pepper. Bake 25 to 30 minutes, stirring once, until all are pink. Serve small bowls of the sauce on the side to dip shrimp and bread into.

Pepper can be adjusted to taste.

Lion Connie Hughes, Foley Lions Club
Foley, AL, USA

SHRIMP AND MUSHROOM SAUTE

1 lb. medium shrimp, peeled and deveined
Creole seafood seasoning (recipe on file)
Flour
1 stick unsalted butter
1 c. onion, diced fine

4 cloves garlic, minced
1 Tbsp. parsley, minced
2 c. fresh mushrooms, chopped
1 tsp. Creole seafood seasoning
1 tsp. flour
1 c. dry white wine

Peel and devein shrimp. Sprinkle with seafood seasoning and barely dust with flour. Melt butter in a large saute pan; add shrimp, onions, garlic, parsley, mushrooms, and 1 teaspoon each seafood seasoning and flour. Gradually stir in wine and cook, stirring gently, until shrimp are just done, 3 to 5 minutes. Serve over cooked rice or buttered toast points.

Do not soak shrimp before cooking. It leaches out the flavor.

John Hamner, Bellville Lions Club
Bellville, GA, USA

Happiness is contagious - infect a friend.

❧ ❧ ❧

Knowledge is power, but enthusiasm pulls the switch.

SHRIMP WITH LIME MAYONNAISE

16 large shrimp (about ¾ lb.)
½ c. mayonnaise
2 Tbsp. lime juice

1 tsp. lime zest
2 scallions, finely chopped
Cayenne pepper

Devein shrimp by snipping backs with a scissors, leaving the shells on. Cook shrimp in salted boiling water for 2 to 3 minutes. Chill in refrigerator. Shell the shrimp. In a small bowl, combine the mayonnaise, lime juice and zest, scallions, and cayenne pepper to taste. Whisk to blend well. Serve shrimp with the mayonnaise. Makes 4 servings.

Per serving: 232 calories, 6 g protein, 22 g fat, 200 mg sodium, 2 g carbohydrate, 60 mg cholesterol.

Mrs. Mike Nowicki, Clarence Lions Club
Clarence Center, NY, USA

GRILLED SHRIMP

⅓ c. chili sauce
¼ c. orange juice
2 jalapeno peppers, minced

1 medium clove garlic, minced
1 tsp. prepared mustard
24 jumbo shrimp (about 1½ lb.)

Heat grill. If using wooden skewers, soak eight of them in cold water for about 30 minutes and drain before using. While grill is heating, make barbecue sauce. In a small bowl, combine chili sauce, orange juice, jalapeno peppers, garlic, and mustard. Mix to combine and set aside.

Put three shrimp on each skewer. Brush shrimp with some of the sauce and place on the grill. Cook, turning once and brushing with additional sauce, until shells turn pink, about 2 minutes on each side. Serve with remaining sauce. Makes 4 servings.

Work time: 15 minutes. Total time: 15 minutes + soaking.

Per serving: 183 calories, 29 g protein, 3 g fat, 528 mg sodium, 10 g carbohydrate, 215 mg cholesterol.

Joanne M. Wetzler, Clarence Lions Club
Clarence Center, NY, USA

Some people think it's holding on that makes one strong ...
sometimes it's letting go.

Don't let life discourage you.
Everyone who got where he is had to begin where he was.

GRILLED SHRIMP WITH GARLIC SAUCE

1 clove garlic
2 Tbsp. chopped fresh parsley
1/4 c. light sour cream
1/4 c. reduced-fat, cholesterol-free
    mayonnaise dressing

1 Tbsp. lime juice
1 1/2 lb. large shrimp
Salt and pepper

Heat the grill. Mince garlic and combine with the parsley, sour cream, and mayonnaise. Set aside. Toss the shrimp with the lime juice and sprinkle with salt and pepper. Grill shrimp over hot coals until done, 4 to 5 minutes per side. Makes 4 servings.

Barbara Joy Hess, Clarence Lions Club
Clarence Center, NY, USA

SHRIMP SCAMPI

6 cloves garlic
1 1/2 lb. large shrimp
1 Tbsp. butter
3 Tbsp. oil

Salt and pepper
1 Tbsp. lemon juice
2 Tbsp. chopped fresh parsley

Mince garlic. Shell and devein shrimp, leaving tails on. In a large frying pan, melt the butter in the oil over medium-high heat. Add shrimp and cook, stirring occasionally, until just cooked through, about 5 minutes. Stir in garlic and cook about 30 seconds. Remove from heat; add 1/2 teaspoon salt, 1/4 teaspoon pepper, lemon juice, and parsley and toss until the shrimp are coated. Serve immediately. Makes 4 servings.

Work time: 30 minutes. Total time: 30 minutes.

Per serving: 271 calories, 28 g protein, 16 g fat, 481 mg sodium, 3 g carbohydrate, 218 mg cholesterol.

Mrs. Mike Nowicki, Clarence Lions Club
Clarence Center, NY, USA

SHRIMP NEW ORLEANS

2 Tbsp. butter or margarine
1 c. chopped onion
2 Tbsp. flour
2 c. water
1/4 tsp. pepper

2 tsp. salt
1/3 c. canned tomato paste
2 lb. raw shrimp, shelled and
    cleaned

Melt butter in skillet. Saute onions until limp. Stir in flour. Combine water, tomato paste, pepper, and salt. Stir into onions. Add shrimp to the skillet and simmer for thirty (30) minutes. Add chopped parsley, if desired, for color and flavor. Serves six.

Lioness Carolyn Kellner, East Anne Arundel Lioness Club
Glen Burnie, MD, USA

SHRIMP CREOLE

2 lb. medium shrimp, peeled and deveined
2 medium chopped bell peppers
1 large onion, chopped
½ c. celery, chopped
1 Zatarain's crab boil (in mesh bag)
Salt and pepper to taste

1 large jar Prego/Ragu spaghetti sauce (chunky vegetable - no meat or mushrooms)
1 large (14.5 oz.) can crushed tomatoes
⅓ c. cooking oil
Cooked white rice

Over medium heat, cook onions and celery in oil till onions are clear. Add bell pepper and cook till tender, stirring frequently. Drain oil and pour vegetables in a large saucepan. Add tomatoes, Ragu sauce, salt, pepper, and crab boil and cover. Cook over medium heat approximately 1 hour, stirring occasionally. Fifteen minutes before serving, add shrimp, stirring frequently. Do not tear crab boil bag. Cook about 15 minutes on low heat. Prior to serving, remove bag, squeeze juice from bag, and discard. Pour Creole over white rice. Serves 8 to 10 generously.

Emily Groover, Bellville Lions Club
Bellville, GA

SHRIMP CREOLE

1 c. uncooked rice
1 c. chopped onion
1 c. chopped celery
4 Tbsp. cooking oil
2 Tbsp. flour
1 tsp. salt
⅛ tsp. pepper

2 tsp. chili powder
2 c. water
3 c. diced tomatoes
1 (10 oz.) pkg. frozen English peas
1½ Tbsp. vinegar
2 tsp. sugar
1 lb. shelled shrimp

Cook rice in boiling water until tender; drain. Saute onion and celery in cooking oil until soft. Blend in flour and seasonings. Add water slowly, stirring constantly. Simmer 15 minutes, covered. Add remaining ingredients and continue cooking 15 to 20 minutes until shrimp is done. Serve over hot rice. Serves 6.

Rose Scanlin, Stafford-Missouri City Lions Club
Missouri City, TX, USA

A college student is one who has learned to
write home for money in three or four languages.

STIR-FRIED SPICED SHRIMP

4 cloves garlic
2 jalapeno peppers
2 Tbsp. minced fresh ginger
Salt

½ c. oil
2 lb. shrimp (in the shell)
3 Tbsp. minced scallion (optional)

Mince garlic and jalapenos and combine with ginger, 2 teaspoons salt, and 6 tablespoons of the oil. With a sharp knife or scissors, slit open the back of each shrimp shell so it is easier to peel later. Add shrimp to garlic mixture and toss to coat. In a wok or large frying pan, heat 1 tablespoon oil over high heat until smoking hot. Add half the shrimp and stir-fry until pink, 4 to 5 minutes. Transfer to serving platter. Repeat with remaining 1 tablespoon oil and shrimp. Sprinkle shrimp with scallions and serve. Makes 70 shrimp.

Work time: 30 minutes. Total time: 30 minutes.

Per shrimp: 5 calories, 1 g protein, 1 g fat, 19 mg sodium, 0 g carbohydrate, 4 mg cholesterol.

Mrs. Lucy Aiken, Clarence Lions Club
Clarence Center, NY, USA

SHRIMP AND CHEESE SAUCE CASSEROLE

8 Tbsp. butter
4 Tbsp. flour
2 c. milk
8 oz. grated Cheddar cheese

1 qt. boiled and peeled shrimp
Salt
Ritz crackers

Boil shrimp in salted water until barely done. (*Do not overcook - you will complete this recipe by later baking in the oven.*) Cool, peel, and set aside.

Butter a casserole dish and line with only one layer of Ritz crackers. (Avoid too many crackers which will absorb the cheese sauce.)

To make cheese sauce, melt butter in saucepan and stir in flour. Stir out all lumps. Gradually add milk, then grated cheese. Cook until cheese melts, stirring constantly. Combine cheese sauce and cooked shrimp. Carefully pour the cheese sauce and shrimp mixture over the Ritz crackers and bake in a 350° oven for 15 to 20 minutes, or until thoroughly hot.

Vivian Houser, Foley Lions Club
Foley, AL

Be grateful for the doors of opportunity -
and for the friends who oil the hinges.

SHRIMP OVER RICE

4 lb. shrimp
¼ lb. butter
2 tsp. Old Bay seasoning
4 cans cream of celery soup or 4
    cans cream of shrimp soup or
    2 cans soup and 2 c. stock or
    2 cans cream of celery soup
    and 2 cans shrimp soup

    Boil shells in water (2 cups to make stock). Fry shrimp in butter until tender; sprinkle Bay seasoning. Pour soup or soup and stock over shrimp and let cook. Serve over rice. Do in frying pan or wok.

Lioness Ruth Metallo, East Anne Arundel Lioness Club
Pasadena, MD, USA

ROMMIE'S SHRIMP-CRAB CASSEROLE

2 c. chopped onions
3 Tbsp. butter
1 tsp. salt
¼ tsp. pepper
5 c. heavy whipping cream
¾ c. all-purpose flour

1 lb. grated mild Cheddar cheese
1 can cream of celery soup
1 lb. crabmeat
1 lb. cooked shrimp
½ c. butter

    Saute onions and crabmeat in 3 tablespoons butter; add salt and pepper. Bring milk to boil. Add ½ cup butter and flour. Add soup and cheese. Cook till cheese is melted and sauce is thickened. Add cooked shrimp and crab-onion mixture. Mix together and put in large greased casserole dish. Heat until bubbly and brown in 300° oven.

    Crushed Ritz crackers makes a nice topping.

Gloria Thompson, Bellville Lions Club
Bellville, GA, USA

So often our listening is only in part;
what we need is a hearing aid for the heart.

What the future has in store for you depends on
what you have stored for the future.

LINGUINE-N-SEAFOOD
(Yummy!)

½ box linguine
1 lb. large steamed and seasoned
  shrimp
1 can chopped clams, drained

1 pkg. Knorr herb and garlic
  sauce
3 medium sized squash, chopped
3 medium sized zucchini,
  chopped

Chop cooked shrimp into chunks. Chop squash and zucchini into chunks. Follow directions on package of sauce. Cook or steam squash and zucchini until almost soft. Cook linguine.

When sauce is done, add shrimp and drained clams to sauce. Cook low heat, uncovered, 3 to 4 minutes. Add cooked veggies (well drained) to linguine. Pour sauce over veggies and linguine. Toss to mix well. Sprinkle with Parmesan cheese.

This is great to impress company - have tossed salad and Italian bread to accompany. *Enjoy!*

Melissa Berdick Borum, Western Branch Lions Club
Portsmouth, VA

BAKED COD WITH TOMATO ZUCCHINI SALSA

2 tomatoes (about 1 lb.)
1 small zucchini (about ¼ lb.)
1 clove garlic
3 Tbsp. oil

2 Tbsp. chopped fresh basil
  (optional)
Salt and pepper to taste
1½ lb. cod fillet

Have the tomatoes horizontally and remove the seeds. Chop the tomatoes and the zucchini. Mince the garlic. Combine the tomatoes, zucchini, garlic, 2 tablespoons oil, the basil, 1 teaspoon salt, and ¼ teaspoon pepper. Heat the oven to 350°. Lightly brush a roasting pan with oil. Cut the cod fillet into 4 pieces, put in the pan, and brush with remaining 1 tablespoon oil. Sprinkle with salt and pepper. Bake until the fish is opaque throughout, 10 to 15 minutes. Serve the cod with the tomato-zucchini salsa. Makes 4 servings.

Per serving: 320 calories, 32 g protein, 18 g fat, 653 mg sodium, 7 g carbohydrate, 73 mg cholesterol.

Barbara Joy Hess, Clarence Lions Club
Clarence Center, NY, USA

If it weren't for the last minute, a lot of things wouldn't get done.

CRISP CODFISH GRATIN

3 Tbsp. butter
½ tsp. minced garlic
1 Tbsp. lemon juice
2 Tbsp. chopped fresh parsley
   (optional)
1 tsp. Dijon mustard

Salt and pepper
1½ lb. codfish
1 Tbsp. olive oil
1 c. fresh bread crumbs (from
   about 3 slices bread)

Heat oven to 425°. Melt the butter. Combine 2 tablespoons of the melted butter, the garlic, lemon juice, parsley, mustard, ¾ teaspoon salt, and ¼ teaspoon pepper. Cut the fish into 2 inch pieces. Add to the butter mixture and toss to coat. Coat a 1 quart gratin or baking dish with oil and sprinkle ½ cup of the bread crumbs in the dish. Put the fish and any leftover butter mixture in dish. Combine the remaining 1 tablespoon melted butter with the remaining ½ cup bread crumbs and sprinkle over the fish. Bake until the fish is opaque and the crumb topping is browned, 15 to 20 minutes. Makes 4 servings.

Per serving: 280 calories, 31 g protein, 14 g fat, 599 mg sodium, 6 g carbohydrate, 97 mg cholesterol.

Mrs. Mike Nowicki, Clarence Lions Club
Clarence Center, NY, USA

SEAFOOD THERMIDOR

1 lb. fresh or frozen cod fillets
1 small onion, quartered
1 lemon slice
1 can condensed cream of shrimp
   soup*
3 Tbsp. flour
¼ c. milk

¼ c. dry white wine
¼ c. shredded Mozzarella cheese
2 Tbsp. snipped parsley
½ c. bread crumbs
2 Tbsp. grated Parmesan cheese
1 tsp. butter or margarine
½ tsp. paprika

Thaw frozen fish and cut into ½ inch cubes. Place fish, onion, and lemon in greased skillet. Add water to cover. Bring to boiling, reduce heat, and simmer, covered, for 5 to 6 minutes, or until fish flakes easily.

Meanwhile, in a saucepan, blend soup and flour; gradually stir in milk and wine. Cook until thickened and bubbly. Stir in Mozzarella and parsley and heat through. Carefully drain fish well, fold into sauce, and spoon into 4 coquille shells or ovenproof dishes. Combine bread crumbs, Parmesan, butter, and paprika. Sprinkle over sauce. Broil one or two minutes. Makes 4 servings.

* Available in the United States.

Lion Lily Borden, Lake of the Woods Lions Club
Kenora, Ontario, Canada

POOR MAN'S LOBSTER

1 lb. fresh or frozen cod fillets
1 small onion, quartered
Lemon slice
1 can condensed cream of shrimp
    soup
3 Tbsp. flour
1/4 c. milk

1/4 c. (1 oz.) shredded Mozzarella
    cheese
2 Tbsp. snipped parsley
1/2 c. soft bread crumbs
2 Tbsp. grated Parmesan cheese
2 tsp. butter or margarine
1/2 tsp. paprika

Thaw frozen fish and skin if necessary. Cut into 1/2 inch cubes. Place fish, onion, and lemon in greased skillet. Add water to cover. Bring to boiling; reduce heat and simmer, covered, 5 to 6 minutes or until fish flakes easily.

Meanwhile, in a small saucepan, blend soup and flour; gradually stir in milk and wine. Cook and stir till thickened and bubbly. Stir in the Mozzarella and parsley. Heat through. Carefully drain fish well. Fold in sauce. Spoon into 4 coquille shells or small baking dish. Combine bread crumbs, Parmesan, butter or margarine, and paprika. Sprinkle over sauce. Broil 1 to 2 minutes. Makes 4 servings.

This taste is just as good as using the real thing (lobster).
Margaret Anderson, Bedford Breakfast Lions Club
Bedford, VA

CRAB CAKES WITH THREE-PEPPER MAYONNAISE

1/2 c. + 2 Tbsp. mayonnaise
2 Tbsp. finely chopped green
    pepper
1/4 tsp. paprika
Salt and pepper
1 lemon
1 egg

1 lb. lump crabmeat
2 Tbsp. chopped chives or
    scallion green
2 Tbsp. + 1/2 c. dry bread crumbs
1/4 tsp. hot-pepper sauce
Vegetable oil

Combine 1/2 cup mayonnaise, green pepper, paprika, and 1/2 teaspoon pepper and set aside. Squeeze 2 tablespoons juice from lemon. Beat egg and stir in crabmeat, chives, lemon juice, 2 tablespoons bread crumbs, hot-pepper sauce, 1/2 teaspoon salt, and 1/4 teaspoon pepper. Shape into 8 patties. Coat with remaining 1/2 cup bread crumbs. In a frying pan, heat about 2 tablespoons oil over medium heat. Add crab cakes and fry until golden brown, about 1 minute per side. Serve with the mayonnaise. Makes 4 servings.

Per serving: 507 calories, 27 g protein, 38 g fat, 925 mg sodium, 14 g carbohydrate, 188 mg cholesterol.
Joann M. Brownell, Clarence Lions Club
Clarence Center, NY, USA

BACON-WRAPPED SCALLOPS ON SPINACH

12 strips bacon
2 Tbsp. wine vinegar
Salt and pepper
¼ c. oil

4 c. spinach leaves (about ¼ lb.)
¼ red onion
1 lb. sea scallops

Heat broiler. Cook bacon until it has rendered some fat but is still soft, about 1 minute. Drain on paper towels. In a small jar, combine vinegar, ½ teaspoon salt, and ¼ teaspoon pepper and shake until salt dissolves. Add oil and shake again to combine. Pull stems from spinach, wash leaves, and tear into pieces. Cut onion into thin slices. Thread scallops and bacon on skewers. Put on a rack in a broiling pan. Cook until done, about 3 minutes per side. Toss spinach and onion together with dressing. Divide among 4 plates. Top each with 2 skewers. Makes 4 servings.

Per serving: 307 calories, 24 g protein, 21 g fat, 693 mg sodium, 6 g carbohydrate, 48 mg cholesterol.

Barbara Joy Hess, Clarence Lions Club
Clarence Center, NY, USA

TUNA PIE

1 unbaked pie shell (bake for 10
   minutes at 375°)
2 small cans or 1 large can tuna,
   drained
1 c. Swiss, yellow, or Cheddar
   cheese

½ c. green pepper, finely
   chopped
½ c. onion, finely chopped
3 eggs
1 c. salad dressing
½ c. milk

Combine tuna, cheese, pepper, and onion. Beat eggs, salad dressing, and milk together. Combine all ingredients and bake in pie shell for 50 minutes.

Lioness Carolyn Kellner, East Anne Arundel Lioness Club
Glen Burnie, MD, USA

Memories bloom forever in the garden of the heart.

❧ ❧ ❧

May it matter not that we are stars, but that we twinkle.

❧ ❧ ❧

Looking for the bad in others will make you sad ...
looking for the good will bring happiness.

SEAFOOD CAKES

1 (12½ oz.) can tuna in water,
  drained
½ c. Miracle Whip or Miracle
  Whip Light dressing
¼ c. Dijon mustard
¼ c. finely chopped celery
¼ c. finely chopped green onions

¼ c. finely chopped green pepper
1 (2 oz.) jar chopped pimiento,
  drained
½ tsp. salt
½ tsp. black pepper
1¼ c. dry bread crumbs, divided
Oil

Mix tuna, dressing, mustard, vegetables, pimiento, seasonings, and ½ cup of the bread crumbs. Shape mixture into 15 (2 inch) balls. Roll in remaining ¾ cup bread crumbs, coating well. Flatten balls into small patties. Refrigerate 30 minutes. Heat ½ cup oil in large skillet over medium-high heat. Add tuna patties. Cook 5 minutes on each side or until golden brown, adding additional oil as needed. Remove from skillet; drain on paper towels. Makes 8 servings.

Mrs. Mike Nowicki, Clarence Lions Club
Clarence Center, NY, USA

EASY BAKED TROUT

¼ c. mayonnaise
1 Tbsp. minced scallions

2 tsp. Dijon mustard with seeds
4 trout fillets

Heat broiler. In a small bowl, combine mayonnaise, scallions, and Dijon mustard. Arrange the fish fillets on a rack in broiling pan. Sprinkle fillets with salt and pepper. Spread the mayonnaise mixture over the top of each fillet. Broil until the fish is just opaque, 5 to 8 minutes. Makes 4 servings.

Per serving: 263 calories, 28 g protein, 16 g fat, 189 mg sodium, 1 g carbohydrate, 86 mg cholesterol.

Lion John J. Hess, Clarence Lions Club
Clarence Center, NY, USA

FISH BATTER

1½ c. flour
1½ tsp. baking powder
½ tsp. salt
1 Tbsp. sugar

2 eggs
2 c. beer
2 Tbsp. vegetable oil

In a large bowl, mix dry ingredients in order given. Make a well and add eggs, beer, and oil, mixing well to blend. Let stand for one half hour before using. Pat fish dry, dip into batter, and deep-fry in hot oil.

Lion Rolf Anderson, Kenora Lions Club
Kenora, Ontario, Canada

PARMESAN FISH

6 pan dressed catfish or 2 lb.
   small filets
¾ c. Parmesan cheese
¼ c. flour
½ tsp. salt

½ tsp. pepper
1 tsp. paprika
1 egg, beaten
1 Tbsp. milk
¼ c. margarine, melted

Combine cheese, flour, salt, pepper, and paprika in bowl. Mix egg and milk. Dip fish in egg mixture and then in cheese mixture to coat well. Place aluminum foil in 13x9x2 inch baking dish and place fish on foil. Pour margarine over fish and bake at 350° until golden brown. *Southern and sassy!!*

Doris Wirborne, Brookhaven Alpha Lions Club
Brookhaven, MS, USA

CURRIED FISH WITH CUCUMBER

½ cucumber
Salt
¼ tsp. ground cumin
1 c. plain yogurt
⅓ c. flour
2 Tbsp. curry powder

1½ lb. cod fillet
1 Tbsp. oil
1 Tbsp. butter
Chopped fresh cilantro or parsley
   (optional)

Peel and seed cucumber and chop into small pieces. Combine cucumber, ¾ teaspoon salt, cumin, and yogurt. Chill. Combine flour, curry powder, and 1 teaspoon salt. Cut cod into 4 pieces. Dredge cod in flour mixture. In large frying pan, heat oil and butter over medium-high heat. Add fish and reduce heat to medium. Cook until fish is golden brown on both sides, 3 to 4 minutes per side. Serve with cucumber mixture. Sprinkle with cilantro or parsley if desired. Makes 4 servings.

Per serving: 283 calories, 35 g protein, 9 g fat, 1098 mg sodium, 15 g carbohydrate, 84 mg cholesterol.

Mrs. Mike Nowicki, Clarence Lions Club
Clarence Center, NY, USA

A key chain is something that lets you lose all your keys at the same time.

❧ ❧ ❧

Kindness is like snow - it will make beautiful anything it covers.

FISH AND LEEKS IN PARCHMENT

1 lemon
4 leeks, washed, trimmed, and
   sliced thin
½ tsp. salt
¼ tsp. pepper

4 flounder fillets (about 1 lb.)
8 oz. peeled and deveined shrimp
2 Tbsp. chopped fresh dill
4 tsp. margarine or butter, melted
¼ c. dry white wine

Preheat oven to 400°F. Grate zest from lemon; squeeze juice. Using parchment paper, cut out four 12 inch circles. Scatter leeks over one side of each circle. Sprinkle with lemon zest, salt, and pepper. Place one fish fillet over each circle of leeks; top each with shrimp and dill. Stir together margarine, wine, and lemon juice; pour over each packet, then fold other half circle over top and roll edge to seal. Put packets on baking sheet; bake 12 to 15 minutes until fish flakes easily when tested with a fork. Put packets on dinner plates; cut away parchment. Makes 4 servings.

Per serving: 281 calories, 35 g protein, 6 g fat, 518 mg sodium, 18 g carbohydrate, 141 mg cholesterol.

Barbara Joy Hess, Clarence Lions Club
Clarence Center, NY, USA

Keep your fears to yourself, but share your kindness with others.

❦ ❦ ❦

Talking to yourself is a good way to stay out of arguments.

❦ ❦ ❦

A day without sunshine is like, well, night.

❦ ❦ ❦

On the other hand, you have different fingers.

POULTRY

BEER BUTT CHICKEN

1 whole chicken
Fajita seasoning
Mustard

Salt and pepper to taste
1 can beer

Clean chicken. Rub fajita seasoning, salt, and pepper inside and out. Smear entire chicken with regular mustard. Close neck area with a toothpick. Open 1 can of beer; empty half of beer from can. Place chicken on top of can of beer and put all on your bar-b-que pit. Cook 2 to 2½ hours or until done.

Miles Dyess, Huffman Lions Club
Huffman, TX, USA

MUSTARD-GLAZED ROAST CHICKEN

1 scallion, chopped
1 Tbsp. chopped parsley
¼ c. Dijon mustard

½ tsp. salt
¼ tsp. pepper
3 lb. chicken, cut into quarters

Heat oven to 400°. Combine the scallion, parsley, mustard, salt, and pepper. Spread mixture over chicken. Put in a shallow roasting pan, skin side up. Roast until skin is golden and juices run clear, about 45 minutes. Makes 4 servings.

Per serving: 372 calories, 40 g protein, 21 g fat, 834 mg sodium, 1 g carbohydrate, 130 mg cholesterol.

Mrs. Mike Nowicki, Clarence Lions Club
Clarence Center, NY, USA

I just got lost in thought. It was unfamiliar territory.

I feel like I'm diagonally parked in a parallel universe.

Ever wonder how much deeper the ocean would be without sponges?

ROASTED CHICKEN AND VEGETABLES

1 lb. parsnips (about 4)
¾ lb. carrots (about 4)
Salt and pepper
1½ lb. boiling potatoes (about 6)
1 onion

2 cloves
1½ tsp. dried thyme
2 Tbsp. oil
1 (3 lb.) chicken

Heat oven to 425°. Peel parsnips and carrots and slice about ¾ inch thick. Cook in boiling salted water until just tender, about 5 minutes. Drain. Peel potatoes and cut into chunks. Slice onion and garlic.

In a roasting pan, combine parsnips, carrots, potatoes, onion, garlic, 1 teaspoon thyme, 1¾ teaspoons salt, ¼ teaspoon pepper, and 1 tablespoon oil. Remove backbone from chicken. Spread chicken out and press down on breastbone to flatten. Put on top of the vegetables. Brush chicken with remaining 1 tablespoon oil and sprinkle with remaining ½ teaspoon thyme and salt and pepper to taste. Roast, stirring vegetables occasionally, until chicken is done, 50 to 55 minutes. Makes 4 servings.

Per serving: 774 calories, 48 g protein, 42 g fat, 1169 mg sodium, 50 g carbohydrate, 174 mg cholesterol.

Mrs. Mike Nowicki, Clarence Lions Club
Clarence Center, NY, USA

CAJUN ROAST CHICKEN

2 Tbsp. butter
2 cloves
Salt
½ tsp. paprika

½ tsp. dried basil
½ tsp. dried thyme
½ tsp. cayenne pepper
3 lb. chicken

Heat the oven to 400°. Melt the butter. Mince the garlic. Combine the melted butter, the garlic, 2 teaspoons salt, the paprika, basil, thyme, and cayenne. Brush the entire chicken with the butter mixture and put it in a roasting pan. Roast until done (170°), about 1 hour and 15 minutes. Tent with foil if the chicken starts to brown too much. Let stand for 15 minutes before carving. Serve with the pan juices. Makes 4 servings.

Per serving: 553 calories, 43 g protein, 41 g fat, 1264 mg sodium, 1 g carbohydrate, 189 mg cholesterol.

Barbara Joy Hess, Clarence Lions Club
Clarence Center, NY, USA

Honk if love peace and quiet.

HONEY FRIED CHICKEN

½ c. honey
2 Tbsp. wine vinegar
3 to 3½ lb. chicken, cut into
    serving pieces
½ c. all-purpose flour

2 Tbsp. whole-wheat flour
2 tsp. cayenne
Oil for frying
Salt and pepper

In a glass or stainless-steel bowl, combine honey, vinegar, and chicken pieces. Toss to coat. Marinate at least 2 hours. Combine the flours and the cayenne. In a large frying pan, heat about ¼ inch oil over medium-high heat to 325°. Remove chicken from the marinade and drain on paper towels. Sprinkle chicken with salt and pepper and dredge in the flour mixture. Put legs and thighs in the hot oil and fry about 10 minutes. Add breast pieces and continue cooking the chicken, turning twice, until well browned and tender, 20 to 25 minutes total for the legs and thighs and about 15 minutes for the breasts. Makes 4 servings.

Work time: 40 minutes. Total time: 40 minutes plus marinating.

Per serving: 561 calories, 50 g protein, 26 g fat, 145 mg sodium, 31 g carbohydrate, 153 mg cholesterol.

Mrs. Lucy Aiken, Clarence Lions Club
Clarence Center, NY, USA

BUTTERMILK FRIED CHICKEN WITH GRAVY

1 (2½ to 3 lb.) broiler-fryer
    chicken, cut up
1 c. buttermilk
1 c. all-purpose flour

1½ tsp. salt
½ tsp. pepper
Cooking oil for frying

Gravy:

3 Tbsp. all-purpose flour
1 c. milk

1½ to 2 c. water
Salt and pepper to taste

Place chicken in a large flat dish. Pour buttermilk over; refrigerate 1 hour. Combine flour, salt, and pepper in a double-strength paper bag. Drain chicken; toss pieces, one at a time, in flour mixture. Shake off excess; place on waxed paper for 15 minutes.

Heat ⅛ to ¼ inch of oil in a skillet; fry chicken until browned on all sides. Cover and simmer, turning occasionally, for 40 to 45 minutes, or until juices run clear. Uncover and cook 5 minutes longer. Remove chicken and keep warm. Drain all but ¼ cup drippings; stir in flour until bubbly. Add milk and 1½ cups water; cook and stir until thickened and bubbly. Cook 1 minute more. Add remaining water if needed. Season with salt and pepper. Serve with chicken. Yield: 4 to 6 servings.

JAMAICAN CHICKEN WINGS

¼ c. molasses
2 Tbsp. rum
Salt
¼ tsp. ground allspice

⅛ tsp. cinnamon
⅛ tsp. nutmeg
1 Tbsp. oil
12 chicken wings (about 2 lb.)

Make a marinade by combining the molasses, rum, 1½ teaspoons salt, the allspice, cinnamon, nutmeg, and oil. Remove the wing tips and discard. Cut the wings at the joint into 2 pieces. Add to the marinade. Let marinate, refrigerated, at least 4 hours. Heat the oven to 400°. Remove the wings from the marinade and put on a rack in a broiler pan. Bake until browned and cooked through, turning and brushing with marinade halfway through, about 30 minutes. Makes 24 pieces.

Work time: 15 minutes. Total time: 45 minutes + chilling.

Per piece: 55 calories, 4 g protein, 3 g fat, 150 mg sodium, 2 g carbohydrate, 12 mg cholesterol.

Mrs. Lucy Aiken, Clarence Lions Club
Clarence Center, NY, USA

JAPANESE CHICKEN WINGS

3 lb. chicken wings
1 beaten egg

1 c. flour
1 c. butter

Sauce:

3 Tbsp. low sodium soy sauce
1 c. sugar (white)
1 tsp. salt

3 Tbsp. water
½ c. vinegar

Cut wings in halves. Dip in slightly beaten egg and then flour. Fry in butter until deep brown and crisp. Put in shallow roasting pan and pour sauce over wings. Bake at 350°F. for ½ hour. Spoon sauce over chicken during cooking.

This dish freezes well. Other pieces of chicken may be used.

Micheal and Ruth Bartolf, Oxbow and District Lions Club
Oxbow, Saskatchewan, Canada

Remember - half the people you know are below average.

Despite the cost of living, have you noticed how popular it remains?

Nothing is foolproof to a talented fool.

OVEN CRISP CHICKEN

½ pt. sour cream
2 tsp. lemon juice
2 Tbsp. Worcestershire sauce
1 tsp. celery salt
1 tsp. paprika
½ tsp. salt

½ tsp. garlic salt
Dash of pepper
2½ to 3 lb. chicken
1 pkg. prepared herb seasoned
  stuffing

Mix sour cream, lemon juice, Worcestershire sauce, celery salt, and paprika. Dip chicken pieces in shallow baking dish. Dip covered chicken in herb stuffing and brush with melted butter. Bake, uncovered, in a 350° oven for 1 hour or until chicken is tender and a crusty brown.

Teresa White, Graysville-Proctor Lions Club
Proctor, WV, USA

HUNGARIAN BAKED CHICKEN

½ stick butter
1 cut up chicken (3 lb.)
1 small head cabbage, cored and
  cut into ½ inch pieces
Salt and pepper
2 red cooking apples, cored and
  sliced

1 medium onion, sliced thin
1 Tbsp. grated lemon peel
2 tsp. caraway seeds
1 tsp. sugar
1½ c. shredded Swiss cheese

Melt butter in skillet with cover. Dust chicken lightly with paprika. Brown chicken on all sides. Reduce heat and cook 30 minutes. Preheat oven to 375°. Place cabbage on bottom of buttered 9x13 inch pan. Salt and pepper. Cover with foil and bake 20 minutes until cabbage is tender. Remove from oven. Place apples and onions over cabbage. Sprinkle with lemon peel, caraway seed, and sugar. Place chicken on top. Cover with foil and bake 25 to 30 minutes. Remove from oven. Sprinkle cheese on top and bake until melted.

Ila Harrington, Bryan Lioness Club
Bryan, OH, USA

TERRIFIC BAKED CHICKEN

Boneless chicken breasts
Sliced mushrooms (optional)
Grated cheese (Swiss or
  Mozzarella)
Cream of chicken soup

¼ c. water
Stove top stuffing mix (round box)
Oleo/butter

Lay chicken in bottom of pan. Top with sliced mushrooms and grated cheese. Combine cream of chicken soup and water; spread over chicken. Dump box of Stove Top stuffing mix over top. Place 6 to 8 pats of oleo/butter on top. Cover with foil. Bake 1½ hours at 350°. Remove foil towards end of cooking.

Marge Sabin, Rootstown Township Lions Club 13-D
Rootstown, OH, USA

270

BARBECUED CHICKEN

2 cloves garlic
⅔ c. ketchup
2 Tbsp. cider vinegar
1 Tbsp. Worcestershire sauce

2 tsp. brown sugar
2 Tbsp. liquid smoke (optional)
4 chicken breasts on the bone
(about 2 lb. in all)

Heat grill. Mince garlic. Combine ketchup, vinegar, Worcestershire sauce, brown sugar, garlic, and liquid smoke, if using. Set aside about half this sauce. Remove skin from the chicken and brush the breasts with some of the remaining sauce. Brown the chicken on both sides over medium-hot coals. Cover the grill and cook, brushing occasionally with the sauce, until the chicken is done, about 10 minutes per side. Heat the remaining sauce and serve with the chicken. Makes 4 servings.

Per serving: 219 calories, 24 g protein, 6 g fat, 595 mg sodium, 15 g carbohydrate, 73 mg cholesterol.

Joanne M. Wetzler, Clarence Lions Club
Clarence Center, NY, USA

CURRIED CHICKEN BREASTS WITH GARLIC YOGURT SAUCE

½ c. plain yogurt
¼ tsp. minced garlic
1½ tsp. fresh chopped mint or ½
tsp. dried
Salt

2 tsp. curry powder
1 tsp. ground cumin
4 boneless chicken breasts (about
1 lb.)
2 Tbsp. oil

Combine yogurt, garlic, mint, and ⅛ teaspoon salt and set aside. Combine curry powder, cumin, and 1 teaspoon salt and rub all over the chicken breasts. In a large frying pan, heat oil over medium-high heat. When hot, add chicken and brown, about 1 minute per side. Reduce heat to medium-low and continue cooking until chicken is springy to the touch, 6 to 8 minutes. Serve with yogurt sauce. Makes 4 servings.

Work time: 25 minutes. Total time: 25 minutes.

Per serving: 209 calories, 28 g protein, 9 g fat, 714 mg sodium, 3 g carbohydrate, 68 mg cholesterol.

Joann M. Brownell, Clarence Lions Club
Clarence Center, NY, USA

He who laughs last thinks slowest.

2075-99

PEPPERED CHICKEN BREASTS

4 boneless chicken breasts (about
   1 lb. in all)
Salt
1 tsp. coarse-grind pepper

1 Tbsp. oil
1/3 c. white wine
1 Tbsp. butter

Sprinkle the chicken breasts with salt and pepper. In a large frying pan, heat the oil over medium-high heat. Brown the chicken breasts 1 minute per side. Reduce heat to medium-low and continue cooking until just springy to the touch, 6 to 8 minutes. Remove the chicken breasts and cover to keep warm.

Increase the heat to high. Add the wine and 1/4 teaspoon salt to the hot pan. Bring to a boil and cook until reduced to about 3 tablespoons. Remove from heat. Stir in the butter until it softens and thickens the liquid, but doesn't melt completely. Pour over the chicken. Makes 4 servings.

Per serving: 195 calories, 26 g protein, 8 g fat, 210 mg sodium, 0 g carbohydrate, 74 mg cholesterol.

Mrs. Lucy Aiken, Clarence Lions Club
Clarence Center, NY, USA

CHICKEN BREASTS IN VINEGAR SAUCE

2 scallions
2 Tbsp. butter, chilled
2 Tbsp. oil
4 boneless, skinless chicken
   breasts (about 1 1/4 lb. in all)

Salt and pepper
1/3 c. wine vinegar

Chop scallions, keeping white and green parts separate. In a frying pan, melt 1 tablespoon butter in the oil over medium-high heat. Sprinkle chicken with salt and pepper; add to pan and reduce heat to medium. Cook until just done, about 10 minutes. Remove chicken and keep warm. Reduce heat. Pour off all but 1 tablespoon of the pan drippings. Add white part of scallions and cook until softened, about 2 minutes. Increase heat to high; add vinegar and boil until reduced to about 3 tablespoons, about 2 minutes. Remove from heat. Cut remaining 1 tablespoon butter into pieces. Add to pan with 1/4 teaspoon salt and a pinch of pepper. Stir until butter has softened and combined with vinegar to form a sauce, but not completely melted. Pour over chicken and sprinkle with scallion greens. Makes 4 servings.

Per serving: 272 calories, 33 g protein, 14 g fat, 233 mg sodium, 1 g carbohydrate, 98 mg cholesterol.

Joann M. Brownell, Clarence Lions Club
Clarence Center, NY, USA

STUFFED CHICKEN BREASTS

4 large chicken breast halves,
  skinned and boned
½ c. chopped onion
5 Tbsp. chopped green peppers
1 small clove garlic, minced
1½ c. herb seasoned stuffing mix
⅔ c. water
¼ tsp. salt

¼ tsp. pepper
4 Tbsp. butter or margarine,
  melted
1⅓ c. cream of chicken soup
  (undiluted)
3 Tbsp. dry wine
Balance of stuffing (4 to 5 Tbsp.)

Place each piece of chicken between 2 sheets of wax paper; flatten to ¼ inch thickness, using a meat mallet or rolling pin. Set aside.

Saute onion, green pepper, and garlic into 3 tablespoons of butter. Stir in 1½ cups of stuffing, water, salt, and pepper.

Spread stuffing mixture on each chicken breast, leaving a ½ inch margin on all sides. Fold short ends of chicken over stuffing. Roll up and secure with wooden toothpicks. Brown chicken in 2 tablespoons butter. Place in 9x13 inch dish.

Combine soup and wine; pour over chicken. Sprinkle with 4 to 5 table-spoons dressing. Cover with aluminum foil. Bake at 325° for 50 to 55 minutes. Makes 4 servings.

Delicious always. A dish that can be done ahead for the busy woman.
JoAnn Jones, Mathews Lions Club
North, VA

BREADED PARMESAN CHICKEN BREASTS

4 chicken breasts, halved

1 beaten egg

Breading Mixture:

2 c. cracker crumbs
¾ c. Parmesan cheese
½ tsp. salt

½ tsp. pepper
2 Tbsp. dried parsley

Preheat oven to 350°F. Flatten chicken breasts for even cooking. Dip breasts into beaten egg and then into breading mixture. Brown in skillet, using olive oil to prevent sticking. Transfer to baking sheet and bake for about 20 minutes until chicken is cooked.

Serve with potatoes and vegetable of your choice. Also, great with pastas.
Lion Joan Burrows, Lake of the Woods Lions Club
Kenora, Ontario, Canada

SHRIMP STUFFED CHICKEN BREASTS WITH FETTUCCINI

4 boneless, skinless chicken breasts
8 oz. basil and garlic flavored fettuccini
8 medium shrimp, shelled and deveined
1 c. shiitake mushrooms (or favorite), chopped
1 bunch green onions, diced
2 Roma tomatoes, deseeded (1 diced, 1 quartered lengthwise)

¼ c. + 3 Tbsp. olive oil
1 Tbsp. cracked black pepper (may substitute 1 tsp. ground pepper)
⅛ c. teriyaki sauce
2 cloves fresh garlic, crushed and finely chopped

In a covered bowl, combine shrimp, mushrooms, green onions, diced tomato, ¼ cup olive oil, pepper, teriyaki sauce, and garlic. Baste shrimp thoroughly, then cover bowl tightly and refrigerate a minimum of 2 hours.

Add 1 tablespoon olive oil to 4 quarts water and bring to rolling boil, then add fettuccini and cook "al dente" (cooked but still firm). Drain and set aside. Heat remaining 2 tablespoons olive oil in skillet on high heat and add chicken breasts, pan searing them (approximately 5 minutes each side). Remove from heat and cut slits lengthwise to form a pocket and set aside.

In same skillet, add shrimp (without marinade!) and pan sear until pink, approximately 2 minutes each side. Remove shrimp and stuff 2 inside each breast. Bake in oven preheated to 350°F. until done, about 15 minutes.

While chicken is baking, add marinade to skillet and cook until vegetables are tender, then reserve on low heat. When chicken is done, secure wedges of tomato to breasts with a toothpick (skin side up) and return to oven. Set to broil. Broil until tomato skin begins to crack and peel, approximately 5 minutes, then remove. Place chicken breasts on equally divided beds of fettuccini and pour marinade over all. (Note: Pasta may be buttered if desired.) Serve immediately.

Although this recipe may sound complex at first, it is very easy to prepare and your guests will marvel at your culinary skills.

David L. Johnson, Princeton Lions Club
Princeton, IL, USA

Depression is merely anger without enthusiasm.

Eagles may soar, but weasels don't get sucked into jet engines.

CHICKEN BREASTS WITH TOMATO BUTTER

4 Tbsp. butter (at room
   temperature)
¼ tsp. minced garlic
1 tsp. tomato paste
1 tsp. chopped fresh parsley

¼ c. flour
Salt and pepper
4 boneless, skinless chicken
   breasts (about 1 ¼ lb. in all)
2 Tbsp. oil

Combine 3 tablespoons of the butter with the garlic, tomato paste, and parsley. Scrape onto a piece of plastic wrap and use the wrap to help form the butter into a cylinder. Wrap tightly and chill. Combine flour, ½ teaspoon salt, and ¼ teaspoon pepper. Dredge chicken in the flour mixture. In a large frying pan, melt remaining 1 tablespoon butter in the oil over medium-high heat. Add chicken and reduce heat to medium. Cook, turning once, until chicken is just done, about 10 minutes. Top hot chicken with slices of the butter. Makes 4 servings.

Per serving: 348 calories, 34 g protein, 20 g fat, 378 mg sodium, 6 g carbohydrate, 113 mg cholesterol.

Joanne M. Wetzler, Clarence Lions Club
Clarence Center, NY, USA

ALOHA CHICKEN

4 boneless chicken breasts
1 Tbsp. flour
2 (8 oz.) cans pineapple chunks

1 Tbsp. cornstarch
1 Tbsp. honey
1 Tbsp. teriyaki and pepper

Pound chicken breasts with 1 tablespoon flour. Brown in skillet and set aside. Drain pineapple, reserving ¼ cup of liquid. Mix liquid with cornstarch. Stir in honey, teriyaki, and pepper. Boil for 30 seconds in skillet until it thickens. Add chicken and pineapple. Cook until heated through. Serve over rice.

Carol Hug, Bryan Lioness Club
Bryan, OH, USA

The early bird may get the worm, but the second mouse gets the cheese.

❦ ❦ ❦

I intend to live forever - so far, so good.

❦ ❦ ❦

Borrow money from a pessimist - they don't expect it back.

18-MINUTE CHICKEN

4 (12x18 inch) sheets Reynolds
   Wrap heavy-duty aluminum
   foil
1 medium onion
4 skinless, boneless chicken
   breast halves
Dijon mustard
2 medium zucchini or yellow
   squash, sliced

2 medium carrots
½ lb. fresh mushrooms, sliced
4 Tbsp. margarine or butter
Basil leaves
Garlic powder
Paprika

Preheat oven to 450°. Center ¼ of onion and chicken on each foil sheet. Spread chicken with mustard. Top with squash, carrots, and mushrooms. Dot with margarine; sprinkle with basil, garlic powder, and paprika. Wrap and seal to form four packets, leaving room for heat to circulate inside packets. Bake 18 to 22 minutes on a cookie sheet. Makes four servings.

Lion Ethel Harbaugh, Tuscola Lions Club
Tuscola, IL, USA

CHICKEN EN PAPILLOTE

4 skinless, boneless chicken
   breasts (about 1 lb.)
2 scallions, chopped
1 medium carrot, sliced
   diagonally
1 small zucchini, cut lengthwise in
   half, then crosswise into ½
   inch pieces

1 tsp. dried tarragon
½ tsp. grated orange zest

Heat oven to 400° (425° if you're using foil). Cut four 2 foot lengths of parchment paper or foil and fold each in half to make a 1 foot square. Sprinkle chicken breasts with salt and pepper. Place a breast slightly below the middle of each square of paper.

In a small bowl, combine the scallions, carrot, zucchini, tarragon, and orange zest. Spoon ¼ of vegetable mixture over each chicken breast. Fold the parchment of foil over chicken, crimp edges together tightly, and bake for 20 minutes. Makes 4 servings.

Work time: 15 minutes. Total time: 35 minutes.

Per serving: 173 calories, 34 g protein, 2 g fat, 233 mg sodium, 4 g carbohydrate, 82 mg cholesterol.

Mrs. Lucy Aiken, Clarence Lions Club
Clarence Center, NY, USA

CORNMEAL CHICKEN WITH CUMIN CREAM

3 Tbsp. cornmeal
Salt and pepper
4 boneless, skinless chicken
    breasts (about 1¼ lb. in all)

1 Tbsp. butter
1 Tbsp. oil
¾ c. heavy cream
¾ tsp. cumin

Combine cornmeal, 1 teaspoon salt, and ¼ teaspoon pepper. Coat breasts with cornmeal mixture. In a large frying pan, melt butter in oil over medium-high heat. Add chicken. Cook until golden brown, about 4 minutes per side. Remove to a warm plate. Reduce heat to low. Add cream, cumin, and ⅛ teaspoon salt to pan. Bring to a boil, scraping up all the browned bits with a wooden spoon, and boil until reduced to a scant ½ cup, about 5 minutes. Serve chicken with the cream sauce. Makes 4 servings.

Per serving: 430 calories, 25 g protein, 33 g fat, 775 mg sodium, 6 g carbohydrate, 142 mg cholesterol.

Joann M. Brownell, Clarence Lions Club
Clarence Center, NY, USA

CHICKEN PAPRIKA

1 pkg. chicken breasts
Oil
1 onion, chopped
3 Tbsp. or less paprika
2 Tbsp. dill
1 Tbsp. parsley

1 pt. sour cream
¼ c. flour
Chicken stock
Salt
Pepper

Saute onion in oil. Cut up chicken. Add to onion and brown slightly. Add enough stock to cover. Add paprika, dill, and parsley. Mix sour cream and flour. Slowly add to stock and simmer. Add salt and pepper to taste. Serve over noodles.

Risa Hughes, Bullskin Township Lioness Club
Mt. Pleasant, PA

CHICKEN DIVAN

1 can cream of celery soup
½ pt. whipping cream, whipped
½ c. mayonnaise

½ tsp. Worcestershire sauce
⅛ tsp. nutmeg

Mix all together. Cook chicken breast and debone. Cook 2 packages broccoli. Put broccoli in pan with chicken on top of broccoli; pour cream mixture over top. Sprinkle with Romano cheese and paprika. Bake 30 minutes at 350°.

Debbie Wilson, Bullskin Township Lioness Club
Mt. Pleasant, PA

EVERYDAY BROCCOLI CHEESE CHICKEN

1 Tbsp. margarine
4 skinless, boneless chicken
   breast halves
1 can Campbell's broccoli cheese
   soup

⅓ c. milk
⅛ tsp. pepper
2 c. broccoli flowerets

In skillet over medium heat, in hot margarine, cook chicken until browned. Stir in soup, water, and pepper. Heat to boiling. Add broccoli. Reduce heat to low. Cover and simmer until chicken is tender and broccoli is done.

Shirley Bennett, Plainfield Township Lions Club
Nazareth, PA, USA

CHICKEN CONTINENTAL

3 skinless chicken breasts
8 oz. sliced mushrooms
1½ c. uncooked rice
12 oz. French style green beans
15 oz. fat free chicken broth
¼ tsp. celery seed

½ tsp. basil leaves
4 cloves garlic, finely chopped
1 medium bell pepper, coarsely
   chopped
½ white onion, coarsely chopped

Cook chicken breasts until tender, then cut into bite-size cubes. Combine celery seed, basil, and green beans in chicken broth in separate bowl. Saute onion, bell pepper, and mushrooms in large skillet, which has been Pam coated. Add chicken cubes and cook until onion is tender.

In separate skillet, cook broth mix until boiling, then add rice and cover until boiling. Add sauteed mix to broth mix and bring back to boiling. Remove from heat and set aside for 5 minutes, then uncover until ready to serve.

Lion Joseph V. Morrisey, Southport Lions Club
Marion County, Indianapolis, IN

CHEESE CHICKEN CASSEROLE

4 chicken breasts
2 (10½ oz.) cans cream of
   chicken soup (undiluted)
1½ (10½ oz.) cans cream of
   celery soup (undiluted)

1½ c. Cheddar cheese, grated
4 green onions
1 chopped onion

Paprika the chicken breasts well and add a small amount of salt and pepper. Place chicken in large casserole, bone-side down. Do not stack. Put onions all over the top. Sprinkle cheese all over the top. Mix the soups and spoon over the onions, cheese, and chicken. Bake at 325° for 1½ hours. Serve over rice (chicken flavor Rice-A-Roni).

Cara Sauer, Ogallala Lions Club
Ogallala, NE

CHICKEN REUBEN BAKE

6 chicken breasts (skinless), boned
1 can sauerkraut

1 c. Thousand Island dressing
6 slices Swiss cheese

Place breasts in baking dish; pour can of sauerkraut over them. Place Swiss on top of sauerkraut; pour Thousand Island dressing over all. Bake at 350° for 1 to 1½ hours or until chicken is tender.

This is a different type of Reuben.

Maria Gaso, Bentleyville Lioness Club
Bentleyville, PA, USA

EASY GRILLED CHICKEN WRAPS

¼ lb. American or sharp cheese
4 chicken breasts, skinned, boned, and cut in halves (8)

16 slices bacon
¼ c. barbecue sauce

Cut cheese into ½ to 1 x 1 inch cubes. Make a vertical slit in each chicken breast to form a pocket. Put cheese chunks in pocket. Roll chicken into a bundle. Wrap crisscross with 2 slices bacon. Hold together with wooden toothpick. Grill about 6 inches above hot coals for 30 to 40 minutes or until tender, turning every 15 minutes. Move chicken wraps over direct heat last 10 minutes to crisp bacon. Turn 3 or 4 times, brushing with barbecue sauce. Serves 8.

May be made ahead of time and chilled (wrapped and refrigerated).

As a newlywed, I have used the other 2 cookbooks (Volumes I and II) to keep my "honey" well fed and happy!

Melissa Berdick Borum, Western Branch Lions Club
Portsmouth, VA

CHICKEN WITH POPPY SEEDS

2 chicken breasts (skinless and boneless)
Salt and pepper to taste
2 Tbsp. butter
1 (8 oz.) can sliced mushrooms

1 (14 oz.) can artichoke hearts, quartered and drained
¼ c. poppy seeds
1 (8 oz.) sour cream
½ pt. light cream

Saute in butter chicken, cut into bite-size pieces, 4 or 5 minutes. Season with salt and pepper. Add mushrooms and artichokes until warm, then add poppy seeds, sour cream, and cream to warm. Serve over whole wheat pasta. *No sugar recipe.*

Arlene Wall, Past President, Biloxi Lions Club
Biloxi, MS, USA

2075-99

RUSSIAN CHICKEN

5 lb. boneless chicken breasts
8 oz. apricot jam
8 oz. Russian dressing

1 pkg. dry onion soup mix
1 pkg. egg noodles, cooked

Place chicken breasts in 13x9 inch pan. Mix remaining ingredients, except noodles, in a bowl and pour over chicken. Bake at 350° for 1 hour. Serve over cooked noodles. Serves 6.

Elaine (Pepin) Howes, Northfield Lions Club
Northfield, MA

TEX-MEX CHICKEN AND PEPPERS

2 Tbsp. plus 1½ tsp. vegetable
   oil
1 lb. boneless, skinless chicken
   breasts, cut into thin strips
2 red peppers, cut into thin strips
1 large clove garlic, sliced thinly
1 medium onion, cut into thin
   wedges
1 tsp. dried oregano

1 tsp. salt
1½ c. bottled salsa
15 oz. can black beans, drained
   and rinsed
2 Tbsp. minced coriander
Flour tortillas or tortilla chips
   (optional)

In a medium frying pan, heat 2 tablespoons of the oil over high heat. Add chicken and cook, stirring frequently, until no longer pink, about 5 minutes. With a slotted spoon, remove the chicken to a plate. Add remaining oil to the pan. Add the peppers, garlic, onion, oregano, and salt. Cook, stirring frequently, until the vegetables are tender-crisp, about 5 minutes. Return the chicken to the frying pan. Add salsa and black beans and heat through. Sprinkle with coriander. Garnish with tortilla chips if desired. Alternatively, serve rolled up inside soft tortillas or over rice. Makes 6 servings.

Work time: 15 minutes. Total time: 30 minutes.

Per serving: 203 calories, 22 g protein, 6 g fat, 971 mg sodium, 19 g carbohydrate, 44 mg cholesterol.

Mrs. Lucy Aiken, Clarence Lions Club
Clarence Center, NY, USA

If Barbie is so popular, why do you have to buy her friends?

🌶 🌶 🌶

Quantum mechanics: The dreams stuff is made of.

CHICKEN RATATOUILLE

2 Tbsp. olive oil, divided
1 medium onion, chopped
1 medium green bell pepper,
    seeded and sliced
2 small zucchini, sliced
2 medium tomatoes, each cut into
    wedges
2 medium garlic cloves, minced
1 lb. skinless, boneless chicken
    breasts, cut crosswise into
    strips

3 Tbsp. chopped fresh basil
1 Tbsp. chopped fresh oregano
    or 1½ tsp. dried oregano
½ tsp. salt
¼ tsp. black pepper
2 Tbsp. lemon juice
Oregano sprigs for garnish
    (optional)

In a large skillet, over medium-high heat, heat 1 tablespoon of the oil. Add onion and bell pepper and cook until soft, about 3 minutes. Add zucchini and cook until it begins to brown, about 3 minutes. Add tomatoes and garlic and cook until soft, about 3 minutes. Push vegetables to one side and add remaining 1 tablespoon oil and the chicken strips. Cook, stirring, until chicken begins to brown, about 2 minutes. Stir in basil, oregano, salt, and pepper; continue cooking until chicken is cooked thorough and liquid has evaporated, about 5 minutes. Just before serving, stir in lemon juice. Garnish with oregano. Makes 4 servings.

Work time: 30 minutes. Total time: 30 minutes.

Per serving: 234 calories, 28 g protein, 9 g fat, 358 mg sodium, 11 g carbohydrate, 66 mg cholesterol.

Mrs. Lucy Aiken, Clarence Lions Club
Clarence Center, NY, USA

The only substitute for good manners is fast reflexes.

❦ ❦ ❦

When everything's coming your way,
you're in the wrong lane and going the wrong way.

❦ ❦ ❦

If at first you don't succeed, destroy all evidence that you tried.

2075-99

CHICKEN TANGIER

1 onion
2 cloves garlic
1 acorn squash (about 1¼ lb.)
1 green bell pepper
1 Tbsp. oil
2 lb. chicken thighs
2 tsp. minced fresh ginger
2 tsp. cumin

2 tsp. coriander
¼ tsp. turmeric
1¾ c. chicken stock or canned
   broth
Salt and pepper
1 c. instant couscous
1 Tbsp. chopped fresh parsley
⅛ tsp. red-pepper flakes

Chop the onion. Mince the garlic. Peel the squash and cut into approximately 1 inch chunks. Cut the bell pepper into approximately 1 inch squares. In a large frying pan, heat the oil over medium-high heat. Add the chicken thighs and brown well on both sides, about 8 minutes in all. Remove the chicken. Pour off all but 1 tablespoon fat from the pan and reduce heat to low. Add the chopped onion and cook until tender, about 5 minutes. Stir in the minced garlic, ginger, cumin, coriander, and turmeric. Add ¼ cup of the stock and the bell pepper. Put the chicken thighs on top and sprinkle with 1 teaspoon salt and ½ teaspoon pepper. Cover and simmer 15 minutes. Remove the chicken, stir in the squash, and replace the chicken. Cover and cook until the vegetables are tender and the chicken is done, 15 to 20 minutes.

Meanwhile, combine the remaining 1½ cups stock with ¼ teaspoon salt and ⅛ teaspoon pepper in a saucepan and bring to a boil. Stir in the couscous, cover, and remove from heat. Let stand 5 minutes. Fluff the couscous with a fork. Serve the chicken and vegetables over the couscous, sprinkled with the parsley and the red-pepper flakes. Makes 4 servings.

Mrs. Lucy Aiken, Clarence Lions Club
Clarence Center, NY, USA

A conclusion is the place where you got tired of thinking.

Experience is something you don't get until just after you need it.

For every action there is an equal and opposite criticism.

CHICKEN PAPRIKA WITH
MUSHROOMS AND PEARL ONIONS

2 strips bacon (about 2 oz.), cut
   in ¼ inch pieces
2 Tbsp. oil
3½ lb. chicken, cut into 8 pieces
½ lb. pearl onions, peeled

¾ lb. mushrooms, cut in quarters
1 Tbsp. paprika
¾ tsp. salt
¼ tsp. pepper
¾ c. sour cream

Heat a large frying pan over medium-high heat. Add bacon and cook until fat is rendered. With a slotted spoon, transfer bacon to paper towels. Discard bacon fat. Return pan to stove and add oil. Over medium-high heat, brown chicken, about 10 minutes. Remove pieces as they're done and set aside. Add onions to the pan and brown well, about 5 minutes. Add 2 tablespoons water and scrape up any brown bits. Return chicken to pan and add mushrooms, paprika, salt, and pepper. Cover, reduce heat to low, and cook until chicken is done, about 25 minutes. Stir in sour cream and cook over very low heat 1 minute longer, taking care not to boil. Sprinkle reserved bacon over chicken and serve. Makes 6 servings.

Work time: 35 minutes. Total time: 1 hour and 10 minutes.

Per serving: 436 calories, 34 g protein, 30 g fat, 412 mg sodium, 8 g carbohydrate, 116 mg cholesterol.

Mrs. Lucy Aiken, Clarence Lions Club
Clarence Center, NY, USA

CHICKEN MOLE

1 Tbsp. oil
3 lb. chicken, cut into 8 pieces
Salt
2 cloves garlic, minced
1 onion, chopped
1 corn tortilla, chopped
1 Tbsp. raisins

1 Tbsp. slivered almonds
2 Tbsp. chili powder
¼ tsp. ground cinnamon
1 tsp. ground cumin
1 c. tomato puree
¾ c. chicken stock or canned
   broth
1 oz. semi-sweet chocolate

In a large frying pan, heat oil over medium-high heat. Sprinkle chicken with salt and cook until well browned, about 10 minutes. Remove chicken from pan. Reduce heat to low. Add garlic, onion, and 1½ teaspoons salt to pan. Cover and cook until tender, about 5 minutes. In a food processor or blender, puree onion mixture, tortilla, raisins, almonds, chili powder, cinnamon, cumin, tomato puree, and stock until smooth. Return to pan. Add chocolate and stir over low heat until melted. Add chicken, cover, and simmer until done, 30 to 35 minutes. Makes 4 servings.

Per serving: 655 calories, 47 g protein, 43 g fat, 1299 mg sodium, 21 g carbohydrate, 174 mg cholesterol.

Barbara Joy Hess, Clarence Lions Club
Clarence Center, NY, USA

LEMON-LIME GARLIC CHICKEN

10 cloves garlic
3 lb. chicken, cut into 8 pieces
Salt and pepper
1 Tbsp. butter
1 Tbsp. oil

1 c. water
1 Tbsp. lemon juice
1 Tbsp. lime juice
3 Tbsp. chopped chives or
   scallion greens

Cut garlic into slivers. Sprinkle chicken with salt and pepper. In a large frying pan, melt butter with oil over medium-high heat. Add chicken. Brown well on all sides, about 10 minutes. Remove from pan. Reduce heat. Stir in garlic, water, ½ teaspoon salt, and ¼ teaspoon pepper, scraping up browned bits. Cover pan and cook 5 minutes. Add chicken, cover, and cook over low heat until cooked through, about 25 minutes. Remove chicken and cover to keep warm. Bring pan juices to a boil and cook until slightly thickened, about 3 minutes. Stir in lemon and lime juices. Pour over chicken and sprinkle with chives. Makes 4 servings.

Work time: 30 minutes. Total time: 1 hour.

Per serving: 267 calories, 44 g protein, 41 g fat, 439 mg sodium, 3 g carbohydrate, 181 mg cholesterol.

Mrs. Mike Nowicki, Clarence Lions Club
Clarence Center, NY, USA

CHICKEN TORTILLAS

4 boneless breasts of chicken
½ can cream of chicken soup
8 oz. sour cream
1 small can jalapeno peppers,
   chopped

Small amount of sliced black
   olives
1 pkg. flour tortillas
1 pkg. Monterey Jack cheese

Cook chicken 4 minutes on one side and 3 minutes on other in microwave, then cut up in bite-size pieces. Mix together all of the above ingredients (using *half of sour cream*). Fill tortillas (1 tablespoon or more to each of above mixture); roll up.

Spray Pam on bottom of rectangular dish or melt small amount of butter in bottom of dish; place tortillas, side by side, in pan, seam side down. Mix remainder of soup and sour cream together and spread on top of rolled tortillas. Place slices of Monterey Jack cheese on top. Bake at 350° for 20 to 25 minutes until brown. Serve with salad.

Working with Lioness/Lions Clubs is very fulfilling, especially with peace posters. Also, the camaraderie is wonderful.

Lioness Catherine Violette, East Anne Arundel Lioness Club
Annapolis, MD, USA

SWEET 'N SOUR CHICKEN

½ c. brown sugar
1 tsp. salt
1½ c. pineapple juice
½ c. vinegar
2 Tbsp. soy sauce

1 c. crushed pineapple
2 c. cooked, cut up chicken
3 c. cooked rice
¼ c. green peppers

Combine brown sugar and salt. Stir in pineapple juice, vinegar, and soy sauce. Bring to a boil. Thicken with cornstarch and water mixture. Take off stove. Add chicken, pineapple, and peppers. Stir well and serve on bed of rice.

Debra James, Beckmantown Lions Club
West Chazy, NY

SWEET AND SPICY CHICKEN

1 lb. boneless, skinless chicken
   breast, cut into ½ inch cubes
3 Tbsp. taco seasoning

1 to 2 Tbsp. vegetable oil
1 (11 oz.) jar chunky salsa
½ c. peach preserves

Place chicken in a large resealable plastic bag. Add taco seasoning and toss to coat. In a skillet, brown chicken in oil. Combine salsa and preserves. Stir into skillet. Cover and simmer 2 to 3 minutes. Serve over rice.

Fast, easy, and different and delicious.

W.C. Murphey, Princeton Lions Club
Princeton, IL, USA

HAWAIIAN CHICKEN

1 chicken, cut up
20 oz. pineapple chunks
11 oz. mandarin oranges
10 oz. sweet and sour sauce
1 can Chinese vegetables, drained

Coconut or shaved almonds
   (optional)
Season salt
Garlic powder

Brown chicken pieces in skillet, seasoning with season salt and garlic. Put Chinese vegetables in casserole dish, spreading evenly over the bottom. Place browned chicken on top of vegetables. Drain half of juice from pineapple and oranges. Pour remaining contents of cans over the chicken. Pour sweet and sour over the chicken. Bake at 350° for about 1 hour.

Optional: Ten minutes before end of cooking time, sprinkle coconut or almonds over mixture. Serve over long grain or brown rice.

What's for you, won't go by you.

John H. Maury, Kal Haven Trail Lions Club
Gobles, MI, USA

CHICKEN PARMESAN

Chicken fillets, cut up in small
    pieces

2 eggs, beaten

Place in shallow dish. Add chicken filet. Place in refrigerator for 1 hour. Take chicken from egg mixture and roll in Italian style bread crumbs, then brown in skillet. Put in a baking dish and sprinkle 1 cup Parmesan cheese on top of everything. Bake at 350° for 1½ to 2 hours.

Linda Colbert, Bullskin Township Lioness Club
Mt. Pleasant, PA

CHICKEN-WALNUT STIR-FRY

2 whole large chicken breasts
1 c. walnuts
2 Tbsp. salad oil
⅛ c. sugar
1 c. celery
1 green pepper
3 tsp. salt
¼ tsp. ginger

½ lb. snow pea pods
½ lb. bean sprouts
6 oz. water chestnuts
1 c. chicken broth
2 tsp. cornstarch
2 Tbsp. soy sauce
¾ c. water
3 c. rice

Cut boneless chicken into ¼ inch strips. Slice celery, green pepper, and water chestnuts into thin pieces. Cook 3 cups rice as directed on package. Heat salad oil in large skillet and add green pepper, walnuts, salt, and ginger, stirring continuously, for about 3 minutes or until vegetables are slightly crisp. Use slotted spoon to take vegetables and nuts from the oil and place on heated platter. Cover to keep warm.

Drop chicken slices in remaining oil in skillet and stir for about 5 minutes. Add chicken broth, water, sugar, cornstarch, soy sauce, snow pea pods, bean sprouts, and water chestnuts to skillet and spoon in previously heated vegetables. Continue to cook until the sauce thickens, adding cornstarch (¼ teaspoon at a time) if necessary. Spoon over prepared rice and serve immediately.

Betty Rutledge, Bryan Lioness Club
Bryan, OH

SCALLOPED CHICKEN

1 chicken or 1 large can
    shredded chicken

1 large box soda crackers
1 stick butter

Cook chicken and take the meat off the bones; save the broth. Break half of the crackers in the bottom of a cake pan, 13x9 inches. Spread the chicken over the crackers and top with the other half of crackers. Cut the butter over the crackers and add enough water to moisten all of the crackers. Bake for 45 minutes at 350°.

Lion Ida Rohrer, Moundbuilders Lions Club
Newark, OH, USA

CHICKEN ALFREDO

4 to 4½ lb. chicken or turkey, cooked and cut into bite-sized pieces
1 c. half & half
1 c. Romano cheese (fresh or grated)
½ stick butter
1 Tbsp. garlic powder
1 Tbsp. Italian seasoning
1 tsp. salt
Black pepper to taste
8 or 10 oz. frozen chopped vegetables
5 to 6 oz. mushrooms, sauteed in butter
16 oz. fettucini, broken into 2 inch lengths

Heat together in pan over stove the half & half, cheese, butter, garlic powder, Italian seasonings, salt, and pepper. Stir well. If sauce is too thick, add more milk or cream.

Thaw vegetables and add to sauce. Saute mushrooms and add to mixture. Add chicken or turkey pieces. Boil fettucini until done. Place in bowls and top with sauce.

Vic L. Dreyer, Sr., Keizer Lions Club
Salem, OR

CHICKEN IN A BISCUIT

8 oz. cream cheese
¼ tsp. pepper
2 Tbsp. milk
1 Tbsp. dried onion flakes
2 c. cooked and cubed chicken
Chives or parsley flakes (1 tsp. optional)
1 (8 oz.) can crescent rolls

Mix all together *except* crescent rolls. Unroll crescent rolls. Pinch seams of two crescent rolls together and roll out slightly to form a square. Put ¼ of chicken mixture in center of each square. Bring 4 corners of rolls to top; pinch and seal edges. Place on cookie sheet that has had the bottom brushed with melted butter or margarine. Brush tops of rolls with melted butter. Sprinkle tops of rolls with bread crumbs (optional). Bake at 350° for about 25 minutes. Serves 4.

Brows may wrinkle, hair grow gray -
But friendship never knows decay.

Debby Chaudoir, Mandeville Lions Club
Mandeville, LA, USA

Bills travel through the mail at twice the speed of checks.

CHICKEN DOLORES

1 cut up frying chicken
4 Tbsp. oil
1 pkg. Spanish Rice-A-Roni
2 c. hot water

1 env. seasoning mix
1 lb. can tomatoes
1 (3¼ oz.) pitted olives (black)
1 dash of Tabasco sauce

Brown cut up chicken in oil. Cook slowly until tender (about 45 minutes). Set aside. Brown 1 package Spanish Rice-A-Roni. Stir in hot water, seasoning envelope, and tomatoes. Add drained olives and a dash of Tabasco sauce. Arrange chicken on top of rice mixture; cover and simmer 15 minutes.

Hazel Bailey, Iron City Lions Club
Iron City, TN, USA

CHICKEN WITH DUMPLINS

"Stewed chicken"

Dumplins:

1 c. sifted all-purpose flour
2 tsp. baking powder
½ tsp. salt

2 Tbsp. salad oil
Enough milk to make dough

Sift together flour, baking powder, and salt. Add oil and milk. Roll out on floured surface and cut into thin strips. Drop into boiling broth. Cook on low heat 12 to 15 minutes. Increase amount of ingredients to make more dumplins.

This is a recipe from a good friend of mine, Pat Weaver, who passed away on March 24, 1992.

Janie Phillips, Iron City Lions Club
Iron City, TN

CHICKEN PIE

3 c. diced, cooked chicken
1 can cream of chicken soup

1 c. chicken broth

Place chicken in a 2½ to 3 quart baking dish. Combine the chicken broth and soup in a saucepan. Bring to a boil.

Batter:

1 c. self-rising flour
1 stick melted margarine

1 c. buttermilk

Combine to make a batter. Dip batter over chicken. Bake 30 to 40 minutes at 350°.

Janie Fox, Saginaw Lions Club
Saginaw, TX

CHICKEN OR TURKEY UPSIDE-DOWN CAKE

6 Tbsp. oleo
1¾ c. flour
1 c. milk

2 tsp. baking powder
½ tsp. salt
2 eggs, beaten

Beat oleo until soft. Add eggs. Mix flour with baking powder and salt. Add alternately with milk, beginning and ending with flour. Mix well 4 cups chicken or turkey (cubed) and 4 cups Chicken Cream Sauce. Mix chicken or turkey with sauce. Pour in 9x13 inch pan. Pour batter over chicken/turkey sauce. Bake at 375° for 45 minutes.

Chicken Cream Sauce:

½ c. oleo
1 c. flour

6 c. chicken stock or broth
Salt and pepper to taste

Melt oleo; stir in flour, stirring constantly to prevent sticking. Add chicken stock to above, slowly stirring while cooking for 10 minutes to thicken. Season to taste. Makes 6 cups.

TASTY GARLIC TURKEY LEGS

1 Tbsp. oil
4 turkey legs (about 3 lb. total)
Salt and pepper
1 head garlic
1 carrot
1 parsnip

1 rib celery
¼ c. chopped fresh parsley
¾ tsp. dried thyme
1⅔ c. chicken stock or canned
broth

In a Dutch oven, heat oil over medium-high heat. Sprinkle turkey with salt and brown well on all sides, about 10 minutes.

Meanwhile, peel garlic. Chop carrot, parsnip, and celery. Remove legs and reduce heat to low. Add garlic, carrot, parsnip, celery, parsley, and 1 teaspoon salt. Cover and cook until mixture starts to soften, about 5 minutes. Add thyme, ¼ teaspoon pepper, and stock. Cover and simmer, turning occasionally, for 1 hour. Uncover and continue cooking until legs are tender, about 30 minutes. Remove legs and boil remaining liquid until reduced to 1 cup. Serve legs with reduced braising liquid. Makes 4 servings.

Per serving: 494 calories, 57 g protein, 23 g fat, 802 mg sodium, 11 g carbohydrate, 201 mg cholesterol.

Barbara Joy Hess, Clarence Lions Club
Clarence Center, NY, USA

MICROWAVE TURKEY BREAST

6 lb. turkey breast
Brown-n-Bag
1 stick margarine

1 pkg. Italian dressing mix
1 pkg. Lipton onion soup mix

Melt margarine and mix in dressing mix and soup mix. Brush on turkey in bag. Microwave on HIGH for 1 hour. (Make sure bag has a few slits in it.) If smaller size of breast, cook 10 minutes per pound (4 pounds for 40 minutes, 2½ pounds for 25 minutes). Don't overcook, but let stand a minute or two before opening to slice.

Can be cooked in a regular oven (cooking time according to directions on the turkey breast).

Deryl Fox, Saginaw Lions Club
Saginaw, TX

MARINADE FOR TURKEY

¾ c. ReaLemon juice
¼ c. noniodized salt
1 Tbsp. Tabasco sauce

1 c. warm water
1 Tbsp. clear garlic juice

Dissolve salt in warm water and combine with rest of ingredients. Inject into a 14 pound turkey. Use a large hypodermic needle and inject juices under skin of turkey. Let stand overnight in refrigerator on a glass or plastic container. Barbecue the next day on an oven grill.

Lion Reverend Craig Bowyer, Foley Lions Club
Foley, AL, USA

Never do a card trick for the group you play poker with.

❦ ❦ ❦

No one is listening until you make a mistake.

❦ ❦ ❦

Success always occurs in private. Failure occurs in full view.

❦ ❦ ❦

The colder the x-ray table, the more of your body is required on it.

ORIENTAL TURKEY ROLL-UPS

2 cloves garlic
1 scallion
1 Tbsp. minced fresh ginger
2 Tbsp. hoisin sauce
3 Tbsp. rice-wine vinegar
1 tsp. soy sauce

Salt
4 Tbsp. oil
1 lb. ground turkey
1 tomato (about ½ lb.)
8 leaves Boston lettuce
4 tsp. toasted sesame seeds

Mince garlic. Chop white part of the scallion and slice the green top. Combine garlic, white part of the scallion, and the ginger. Combine hoisin sauce, 2 tablespoons vinegar, soy sauce, and ¼ teaspoon salt. In a large frying pan, heat 1 tablespoon oil over medium heat. Add garlic mixture and cook, stirring, until mixture starts to brown, about 30 seconds. Crumble in turkey and cook, stirring, until cooked through. Stir in hoisin-sauce mixture and cook 1 minute. Put meat mixture in a bowl and cool to room temperature. Cut tomato into ½ inch dice.

In a small jar, combine remaining 1 tablespoon vinegar and ½ teaspoon salt and shake until salt dissolves. Add remaining 3 tablespoons oil and shake again to combine.

To serve: Fill a lettuce leaf with some of the turkey mixture. Top with tomatoes, scallion greens, and sesame seeds and pour some of the dressing over all. Makes 4 servings.

Mrs. Lucy Aiken, Clarence Lions Club
Clarence Center, NY, USA

The hardness of butter is directly proportional to the softness of the bread.

❧ ❧ ❧

The severity of the itch is universally proportional to the ability to reach it.

❧ ❧ ❧

To steal ideas from one person is plagiarism; to steal from many is research.

❧ ❧ ❧

Monday is an awful way to spend ⅟₇ of your life.

BISTRO TURKEY BURGERS

Burgers:

1 Tbsp. oil
2 medium carrots, finely chopped
  (about ¾ c.)
3 ribs celery, finely chopped
  (about ½ c.)
1 medium onion, chopped (about
  1 c.)
8 oz. mushrooms, coarsely
  chopped (about 2 c.)
1 large clove garlic, minced

2 tsp. dried thyme
1 tsp. tomato paste
½ c. red wine
1 lb. ground turkey
1 c. dried bread crumbs
1 tsp. salt
½ tsp. pepper
1 loaf French bread (about 22
  inches long)

Carrot Topping:

2 large carrots, finely grated
  (about 1½ c.)
3 Tbsp. chopped fresh parsley

2 Tbsp. red-wine vinegar
1 small clove garlic, minced

Heat the broiler or prepare outdoor grill. In a large nonstick frying pan, heat the oil over high heat. Add carrots and celery and cook, stirring occasionally, until they begin to soften, 3 to 4 minutes. Stir in onion and mushrooms and continue cooking until vegetables are soft and most of their juices have evaporated. Blend in garlic, thyme, and tomato paste. Continue cooking until tomato paste colors the mixture, about 3 minutes longer. Add red wine and cook until liquid has evaporated, about 3 minutes. Set aside to cool.

In a large bowl, combine the cooled vegetable mixture with the turkey, bread crumbs, salt, and pepper. Mix until well blended. Divide in fourths, shaping each portion into 1¼ inch thick patty. If grilling, refrigerate uncooked patties at least 20 minutes to firm them. Set patties on grill, broiler pan or a foil-lined cookie sheet and cook, turning once, until well browned and firm to the touch, 7 to 8 minutes per side. (Turkey burgers need to be cooked through completely.)

Meanwhile, in a small bowl, mix together grated carrots, parsley, vinegar, and garlic. Set aside. Cut off the ends of the French bread and slice the loaf into 5 inch lengths. Split each length in half and grill or toast. Place each burger on toasted French bread and top with carrot salad. Makes 4 servings.

Work time: 20 minutes. Total time: 50 minutes + chilling time if burgers are grilled.

Per serving: 649 calories, 35 g protein, 20 g fat, 1336 mg sodium, 80 g carbohydrate, 60 mg cholesterol.

Mrs. Mike Nowicki, Clarence Lions Club
Clarence Center, NY, USA

TURKEY STUFFING

1 c. bread crumbs
4 c. chopped onions
2 eggs
1 c. unpopped popcorn

1 c. water
1 Tbsp. sage
Salt and pepper to taste

Mix all dry ingredients in a bowl. Add beaten eggs and water. Blend thoroughly. After stuffing turkey, roast at 325° in oven. The bird will be done when the popcorn blows the end off the turkey.

Lion Eleanor Reuter, Landisville Lions Club
Landisville, PA, USA

BREAD STUFFING

¾ c. onion, finely chopped
1½ c. celery with leaves, chopped
1½ tsp. dried sage leaves
1 tsp. dried thyme leaves

1 c. margarine or butter
9 c. soft bread cubes
2 tsp. salt
½ tsp. pepper

Cook and stir onion and celery in margarine in 10 inch skillet until onion is tender. Stir in about ⅓ of the bread cubes. Turn into deep bowl. Add remaining ingredients; toss. Stuff turkey just before roasting.

Mike suggests that a package of 12 King Soopers' Hawaiian Honey and Wheat rolls can be substituted for the bread cubes.

Allow ¾ cup stuffing for each pound of ready-to-cook chicken or turkey. A 1 to 1¼ pound Rock Cornish hen requires about 1 cup stuffing. Allow ¼ to ⅓ cup stuffing for each rib pork chop and about ½ cup per pound of dressed fish. This recipe makes enough for a 12 pound turkey.

Mike Hazzard
Littleton, CO

RICE DRESSING

Turkey or chicken giblets
1 lb. pork sausage (prefer Owens)
1 lb. ground round
2 cloves garlic

1 whole head celery
2 bunches green onions
3 or 4 c. raw rice
Salt, pepper, and broth

Boil giblets (amount desired). Fry sausage until very brown. Add ground round and fry until done. Add diced celery, finely chopped onions (including green parts), and garlic. Fry. Salt and pepper to taste. Cover with broth. Place lid on pot and simmer until dry. If desired, chop giblets and add. In separate pot, steam rice. Add steamed rice to meat mixture; mix well and serve.

May be served with baked turkey or chicken or served as casserole along with desired vegetables.

Mildred Court, Stafford-Missouri City Lions Club
Stafford, TX, USA

2075-99

FRIED GAME HENS

Just like chicken, only littler.

Vegetable oil (for frying)
2 Cornish game hens (about 3½ lb.)

1½ c. flour
1 Tbsp. salt
1 tsp. pepper

Fill a large frying pan about ⅓ full with the oil and heat over medium-high heat. The ideal temperature is about 375°. Cut hens into individual pieces - legs, thighs, breasts, and wings - and put them into a bowl of water. Combine the flour, 1 tablespoon salt, and 1 teaspoon pepper in a paper or plastic bag. Lift the hen pieces out of the water and immediately add to the flour mixture. Shake to coat well. Let stand while oil heats. Just before frying, shake the hen pieces in the flour mixture again. Fry in the hot oil until golden brown, 8 to 10 minutes. Drain on paper towels. Makes 4 servings.

Per serving: 596 calories, 49 g protein, 38 g fat, 694 mg sodium, 12 g carbohydrate, 154 mg cholesterol.

Lion John J. Hess, Clarence Lions Club
Clarence Center, NY, USA

CORNISH HENS WITH PEACHES

2 Cornish hens (about 1¾ lb. each)
1 onion
6 peaches (about 1 lb.)
2 Tbsp. oil

Salt and pepper
½ c. wine vinegar
½ c. chicken stock or canned broth

Split hens in halves. Chop onion. Peel peaches and slice. In a large frying pan, heat oil over medium-high heat. Sprinkle hens with salt and pepper; brown in the hot oil and remove. Put peaches in the pan and cook, stirring, until softened, about 3 minutes. Remove. Put vinegar, onion, 1 teaspoon salt, and ¼ teaspoon pepper in the pan. Cook, stirring constantly and scraping up any browned bits, until vinegar is reduced to about ¼ cup. Reduce heat to low and add stock and the hens. Cover and cook until hens are done, 25 to 30 minutes. Remove hens and keep warm. Bring pan juices to a boil and cook to thicken slightly. Add peaches and cook until heated through. Pour over the hens and serve. Makes 4 servings.

Barbara Joy Hess, Clarence Lions Club
Clarence Center, NY, USA

Two wrongs are only the beginning.

Casseroles,
Main Dishes,
Breakfasts

FREEZING CASSEROLES

Casserole cookery can mean carefree cooking when the dish can be prepared in large batches for more than one use. This will also be quite economical since you will be able to take advantage of less expensive vegetables when they are at peak seasons and meats on special sale.

Since many casseroles require time-consuming chopping and measuring, it is wise to fix an extra portion that can be cooked and frozen — to be used in the future when there isn't enough time to prepare a family meal or when unexpected guests arrive.

If you feel that you can't spare having the casserole dish in the freezer and out of daily use, just line the dish with heavy duty aluminum foil. Pour the mixture into the foil-lined dish and freeze solid. After the food is frozen, remove the foil from the casserole dish, peel off the food, wrap in freezer paper, fold tightly, seal with freezer tape and return to freezer.

DOs & DON'Ts

* DO label each container with the contents and the date it was put into the freezer. Always use frozen cooked foods within one to two months.

* DO avoid freezing a large recipe of casserole mixture until you try freezing a small amount. Some flavors tend to change during freezing.

* DO cook large turkeys and roasts. Remove large portions of meat from the bone and freeze for casseroles.

* DON'T overcook foods that are to be frozen. Food will finish cooking while being reheated.

* DON'T use too much salt and other seasonings. Some flavors tend to fade while others get stronger. It is better to add more seasonings later if necessary.

* DON'T freeze spaghetti, macaroni, or noodle mixtures. These tend to lose texture and become too soft when reheated.

* DON'T freeze potatoes. Don't freeze fried poultry or meats. Don't freeze cooked egg white.

* DON'T re-freeze thawed meats and poultry. Use thawed meat or poultry within twenty-four hours.

CASSEROLES, MAIN DISHES, BREAKFASTS
CASSEROLES

HAM AND BROCCOLI QUICHE

1 (15 oz.) pkg. refrigerated pie
    crusts

    Filling:

1½ c. cubed, cooked ham
6 oz. (1½ c.) shredded Swiss
    cheese
1 c. frozen 100% broccoli florets,
    thawed and drained
    thoroughly on paper towel

4 eggs
1 c. milk
½ tsp. salt
½ tsp. dry mustard
½ tsp. pepper

Heat oven to 375°F. Prepare pie crust as directed on package for one-crust filled pie, using 9 inch glass pie pan. (Refrigerate remaining crust for later use.)

Layer ham, cheese, and broccoli in crust. In medium bowl, combine remaining ingredients. Beat well. Pour over broccoli. Bake at 375°F. for 35 to 45 minutes or until knife inserted in center comes out clean. Let stand 5 minutes before serving. Makes 6 servings.

Lion Marie Ceasar, Mount Airy Foothills Lions Club
Mount Airy, NC, USA

HAM AND BROCCOLI BAKE

1 (20 oz.) pkg. frozen cut broccoli
½ c. chopped onion
⅛ c. margarine
1 (10¾ oz.) can cream of
    mushroom soup
1 (10¾ oz.) can cream of celery
    soup

1 soup can milk
1 c. shredded sharp American
    cheese
3 c. cubed fully cooked ham
2 c. quick-cooking rice
½ Tbsp. Worcestershire sauce

Cook frozen broccoli according to package directions; drain well. In sauce-pan, cook onion in margarine till tender, but not brown.

In a large mixing bowl, stir together mushroom soup, celery soup, milk, and cheese. Add drained broccoli, cooked onion, ham, uncooked rice, and Worcestershire sauce; mix well. Place in 2½ quart casserole that has been sprayed with Pam. Bake, covered, at 350° till rice is done, 45 to 50 minutes.

2075-99

CAULIFLOWER HAM BAKE

16 oz. pkg. cut cauliflower
10¾ oz. can Cheddar cheese
  soup
1 c. sour cream
¼ tsp. prepared mustard

1½ c. cubed ham
½ c. dry bread crumbs
2 Tbsp. butter

Heat oven to 350°. Cook cauliflower to package directions; drain. Cut cauliflower into bite-size pieces. In 2 quart casserole, combine soup, sour cream, and mustard. Stir in cauliflower and ham. Combine bread crumbs and butter; sprinkle over casserole. Bake 25 to 30 minutes or until heated through.

SAVORY CREAMED HAM AND VEGETABLES

2 c. diced cooked ham or chicken
1 (10¾ oz.) can condensed cream
  of mushroom soup
⅓ c. milk
1 Tbsp. Dijon mustard

1 (15¼ oz.) can whole kernel
  corn, drained
1 (8¼ oz.) can sliced carrots,
  drained

Combine ham, soup, milk, and mustard in large skillet. Stir in vegetables and cook 6 to 8 minutes or until hot. Serve over rice, noodles, or baked puff pastry shells if desired. Makes 4 to 6 servings.

Mrs. Rodger Sands, Rootstown Township Lions Club 13-D
Rootstown, OH, USA

EMERGENCY CASSEROLE

2 c. sliced potatoes
½ tsp. salt
½ tsp. pepper
2 onions, sliced
1 can chopped ham

2 Tbsp. butter or margarine
1 can corn
⅓ c. evaporated milk
½ c. bread crumbs

In a 2 or 3 quart casserole, place a layer of sliced onions. Add salt and pepper. Add a layer of ham and cold corn, butter, and milk. Top with bread crumbs and bake at 350°F. for about 20 to 30 minutes.

Barbara Kelly, Iron City Lions Club
Iron City, TN, USA

The problems with the gene pool is that there is no lifeguard.

CHEEZY HAM CASSEROLE

1½ c. rotini (corkscrew) noodles
2 c. frozen broccoli, thawed (chop up larger pieces)
1½ c. shredded Cheddar cheese
1½ c. cubed ham
½ c. chopped peppers (red and/or green)
¼ c. finely chopped onion
¼ c. finely chopped celery

1 (10 oz.) tin cream soup (mushroom, chicken, or celery)
½ c. milk
¼ c. Miracle Whip salad dressing
Salt and pepper to taste
¼ tsp. basil
¼ tsp. cilantro
¼ tsp. parsley
1 c. croutons, crushed (any flavour)

Preheat oven to 350°F. Cook noodles in rapidly boiling water for 6 to 8 minutes. Add frozen broccoli to boiling water for last couple of minutes if not thawed. Do not overcook. Drain and set aside.

In a large bowl, mix together thoroughly soup, milk, Miracle Whip, and seasonings. Add noodles and broccoli and mix well. Stir in one cup shredded cheese, ham, peppers, onions, and celery. Pour into 9x13 inch cake dish. Sprinkle with remaining cheese and croutons. Bake, uncovered, for 30 to 45 minutes until bubbly.

This dish is also great with leftover turkey or chicken. If using cream of celery soup, omit chopped celery. Fine bread crumbs (seasoned with garlic powder) or finely crushed potato chips can also be used in place of croutons.

Lion Lillian Marchant, Lake of the Woods Lions Club
Kenora, Ontario, Canada

HAM AND NOODLES CASSEROLE

1 lb. cheese, grated or sliced
½ c. margarine
½ c. flour
1 can cream of celery soup

1 Tbsp. prepared mustard
1 qt. milk
12 oz. dry wide noodles
2 lb. ground ham

Combine cheese, margarine, flour, soup, mustard, and milk. Heat only until cheese is melted. Cook noodles according to package directions. In a greased 9x13 inch pan, put drained noodles. Top with ham. Pour sauce over top and mix slightly. Bake at 350° for 1 to 1½ hours. Serves 15.

Large recipe, travels, and keeps well.

P. Diane Baldwin, Broken Bow Lions Club
Broken Bow, NE, USA

The sooner you fall behind, the more time you'll have to catch up.

HAM AND POTATO CASSEROLE

2 pkg. potatoes au gratin
1 c. cubed ham

1 can French fried onion rings
Paprika

Thaw potatoes au gratin. In casserole, mix potatoes and ham, which has been lightly browned in a skillet. Bake at 350° for 15 minutes. Top with the onion rings. Sprinkle with paprika and bake 10 minutes more.

Use this for leftover ham.

Virginia Bayer, Franklin Park Lions Club
Part Ridge, IL, USA

HAM POT PIE
(Pennsylvania)

2 ham hocks
4 c. water
2 medium size potatoes

1 Tbsp. chopped onion (optional)
2 Tbsp. parsley, chopped
(optional)

Dough:

2½ c. all-purpose flour
2 Tbsp. shortening

1 egg
Water (as needed)

Slowly boil ham hocks in 4 cups water until meat is tender. Remove hocks from the water (broth) and let cool enough to remove meat from the bone.

To make dough: Mix flour, shortening, and egg, adding enough water to be able to roll dough to a very thin sheet. Cut into diamond shape, 1½ to 2 inch pieces.

Peel and slice potatoes ¼ inch thick. Add onion and parsley to the broth and bring to a boil. Add dough, one piece at a time, to prevent sticking together. Add sliced potatoes (alternating with the dough) along with the ham from the ham hocks. Cook on medium or low heat till potatoes are tender, approximately 15 to 20 minutes. *Enjoy.*

Lois Leber, East Prospect Lions Club
East Prospect, PA, USA

ONE DISH MEAL

4 or 5 medium potatoes
1 small head cabbage

3 or 4 slices ham

Peel potatoes and cut in quarters. Clean cabbage and cut in wedges. Put potatoes, then cabbage wedge, then ham in pot. Cover with water and cook till potatoes and cabbage are done. You can salt and pepper to taste.

Lion Denny Van Scyoc, Graysville-Proctor Lions Club
Glen Easton, WV, USA

LEFTOVER CASSEROLE

Leftover chicken, turkey, or tuna
Cooked pasta, drained

Chopped zucchini and
   mushrooms
Cooked chopped broccoli

Mix all with some mayonnaise and 1 can cream of celery or chicken soup, undiluted. Top with almonds and grated medium Cheddar cheese. Heat at 350° for 30 to 45 minutes.

Sarah Wehling, Bothell Lions Club
Bothell, WA, USA

CHICKEN ARTICHOKE CASSEROLE

1 lb. boneless, skinless chicken
   breasts, cut into 2 inch cubes
4 Tbsp. butter or margarine,
   divided
Salt and pepper to taste
1 (9 oz.) pkg. frozen artichoke
   hearts, thawed, or 1 (14 oz.)
   can water-packed artichoke
   hearts, drained and halved
¼ c. all-purpose flour

⅛ tsp. ground nutmeg
2 c. chicken broth
1 c. (4 oz.) shredded Cheddar
   cheese
¼ c. dry bread crumbs
1 Tbsp. minced fresh savory or 1
   tsp. dried savory
1 Tbsp. minced fresh thyme or 1
   tsp. dried thyme
Hot cooked noodles or rice

In a skillet, saute chicken in 1 tablespoon butter until no longer pink. Season with salt and pepper. Place chicken and artichokes in a greased 11x7x2 inch baking dish; set aside. In a saucepan, melt remaining butter; stir in flour and nutmeg until smooth. Gradually add broth. Bring to a boil; cook and stir for 2 minutes or until thickened and bubbly. Stir in cheese until melted; spoon over chicken. Combine bread crumbs, savory, and thyme; sprinkle over chicken. Bake, uncovered, at 350° for 25 to 35 minutes or until golden brown. Serve over noodles or rice. Yield: 4 to 6 servings.

A clear conscience is usually the sign of a bad memory.

Change is inevitable. Well, except from vending machines.

CHICKEN AND SAUSAGE JAMBALAYA

1 tsp. oil
½ lb. hot Italian sausage, cut into
    ½ inch slices
1 lb. boneless, skinless chicken
    breasts, cut into bite-size
    pieces
1 onion, chopped
1 rib celery, chopped
2 cloves garlic, minced

16 oz. can plum tomatoes
1 c. rice
1 tsp. dried oregano
1 tsp. black pepper
½ tsp. dried thyme
½ tsp. cayenne pepper
1½ c. (approx.) chicken broth
10 oz. pkg. frozen okra, thawed

Heat oil in a large frying pan over medium heat. Add sausage and cook 5 minutes. Add chicken; sear on both sides and remove mixture to a plate. Add onion and celery to pan and cook 5 minutes. Add garlic and cook 1 minute. Drain the tomatoes, reserving the liquid, and add to the pan. Break up tomatoes with a fork. Stir in the rice, oregano, black pepper, thyme, and cayenne. Measure reserved tomato juice and add enough broth to equal 2 cups liquid. Add liquid to pan along with the chicken-sausage mixture. Bring to a boil over medium-high heat. Lower heat, cover, and simmer 10 minutes. Add okra. Cover pan again and cook until the rice is tender, about 10 minutes. Makes 4 servings.

Work time: 30 minutes. Total time: 45 minutes.

Per serving: 570 calories, 41 g protein, 22 g fat, 708 mg sodium, 51 g carbohydrate, 109 mg cholesterol.

Joanne M. Wetzler, Clarence Lions Club
Clarence Center, NY, USA

CHINESE CHICKEN

3 c. cooked chicken or turkey,
    cubed
1 c. celery, diced
1 c. rice, cooked
¾ c. mayonnaise
1 c. mushrooms, sliced
1 tsp. onion, chopped
1 tsp. salt

1 can cream of chicken soup
    (undiluted)
4 oz. water chestnuts, drained
    and sliced
½ c. butter
½ c. slivered almonds
1 c. crushed corn flakes

Preheat oven to 350°. Mix all ingredients except butter, almonds, and corn flakes. Put in a 1 quart casserole. Melt butter. Add almonds and corn flakes. Sprinkle on top of casserole. Bake 35 minutes or until bubbly. Serves 8 or 10. Also freezes well!

JoAnn Jones, Mathews Lions Club
North, VA

300

CHICKEN CASSEROLE

1 chicken, boiled and boned (save broth
1 (16 oz.) pkg. Pepperidge Farm cornbread stuffing mix
1 can cream of mushroom soup (do not dilute)

1 can cream of chicken soup (do not dilute)
2 soup cans broth
1 stick margarine

Melt margarine and mix with stuffing mix. Mix soups and broth together. Break chicken into smaller pieces. Put a layer of dressing mix, then a layer of chicken, then a layer of soup mix. Repeat, ending with dressing. Bake at 350° for 40 minutes.

Our son will drive 3 hours home from college if I tell him we're having this for supper.

Janet Brown, Covington Lions Club
Covington, GA, USA

CHICKEN AND DRESSING CASSEROLE

1 can cream of celery soup
1 can cream of chicken soup
1 can clear chicken broth

1 box Stove Top dressing
2 c. cooked, cubed chicken

Place chicken in bottom of dish. Mix soups and stuffing; add broth. Place mixture on top of chicken. Bake at 350° for 25 to 35 minutes (optional). Add ½ cup chopped celery and ½ cup chopped onion.

Cheryl Forkel, Elberfeld Lions Club
Haubstadt, IN

Get a new car for your spouse - it'll be a great trade!

❦ ❦ ❦

From now on, plan to be spontaneous.

❦ ❦ ❦

Always try to be modest and be proud of it!

CLASSIC POT PIE

1 (15 oz.) pkg. Pillsbury refrigerated pie crust

Filling:

⅓ c. margarine or butter
⅓ c. chopped onion
⅓ c. all-purpose flour
½ tsp. salt
¼ tsp. pepper
1½ c. chicken broth

⅔ c. milk
2½ to 3 c. shredded, cooked chicken or turkey
2 c. frozen mixed vegetables, thawed

Heat oven to 425°F. Prepare pie crust as directed on package for two-crust pie, using 9 inch pie pan.

In medium saucepan, melt margarine over medium heat. Add onion; cook 2 minutes. Stir in flour, salt, and pepper until blended. Gradually stir in broth and milk; cook, stirring constantly, until bubbly and thickened. Add chicken and mixed vegetables. Remove from heat. Spoon chicken mixture into pie crust. Top with second crust and flute; cut slits in several places. Bake at 425°F. for 30 to 40 minutes or until crust is golden brown. Let stand 5 minutes before serving. Serves 6.

Lion Robert Blake, Mount Airy Foothills Lions Club
Mount Airy, NC, USA

SWISS CHICKEN CASSEROLE

6 skinless, boneless chicken breasts
6 slices Swiss cheese
1 can cream of chicken soup (undiluted)

¼ c. milk

Place chicken in greased casserole. Top with cheese. Mix soup and milk; stir well. Spoon over chicken and cover. Bake 1 hour at 350°. So easy!

Mrs. Duane (Pam) Bennett, Mad River Lions Club
Riverside, OH, USA

If you think nobody cares, try missing a couple of payments.

How many of you believe in telekinesis? Raise my hand ...

BROCCOLI-CHICKEN CASSEROLE

2 (10 oz.) pkg. frozen broccoli,
   chopped
2 c. cooked chicken or turkey, cut
   in chunks
1 c. mayonnaise
1 c. shredded sharp Cheddar
   cheese

2 eggs
1 (10 oz.) can cream of
   mushroom soup
Pepperidge Farm herb dressing

Cook broccoli and drain real good. Spread in bottom of casserole dish. Place chicken on top. Combine rest of ingredients except dressing. Pour over chicken. Sprinkle with cheese and herb dressing. Bake at 350° for 30 minutes.

This can be made without chicken for a vegetable dish. It's delicious either way.

Dorothy Freeman, Travelers Rest Lions Club, District 32-A
Travelers Rest, SC, USA

SAUSAGE CASSEROLE

2½ c. herb croutons
2 c. shredded American cheese
2 lb. sausage
5 eggs

¾ tsp. dry mustard
2½ c. milk
1 can cream of mushroom soup
½ can milk

Spread croutons on bottom of 9x13 inch bake dish. Top with cheese. Brown sausage; drain and spread over cheese. Beat eggs; add mustard and 2¼ cups milk. Pour over above ingredients. Cover and refrigerate overnight.

Before baking, dilute soup with ¼ can of milk and pour over casserole. Bake 1¼ hours at 300°.

Bert Morgan, Broken Bow Lions Club
Broken Bow, NE, Custer County

CLASSIC BAKED PENNE RIGATE

1 lb. box penne rigate (uncooked)
1 lb. bulk Italian sausage or lean
   ground beef
2 (26 oz.) jars tomato and basil
   pasta sauce

4 c. (1 lb.) Mozzarella cheese,
   shredded

Preheat oven to 350°. Prepare penne rigate as package directs. Cook and drain meat. In large bowl, combine penne rigate, meat, pasta sauce, and 2 cups cheese. Mix well. Turn into greased 13x9 inch baking dish; cover. Bake 45 minutes or until hot and bubbly. Uncover and top with remaining 2 cups cheese. Bake 10 minutes longer. Refrigerate leftovers.

Carolyn Hale, Eliot Lions Club
Eliot, ME, USA

CORNED BEEF AND NOODLES

1 can corned beef
½ (16 oz.) pkg. noodles, cooked and drained
1 c. milk

½ c. chopped onion
¼ lb. American cheese, cubed
1 can cream of mushroom soup
¾ c. bread crumbs

Mix all ingredients together. Place in casserole. Cover with buttered bread crumbs. Bake 1 hour.

Olive Higinbotham, Bentleyville Lioness Club
Bentleyville, PA, USA

HUNGRY JACK BEEF CASSEROLE

1 lb. ground beef
1 tsp. salt
1 (16 oz.) can pork and beans
¾ c. barbecue sauce
1 Tbsp. brown sugar

1 Tbsp. instant minced onion
1 can Hungry Jack biscuits
1 c. shredded Cracker Barrel Cheddar cheese

Brown ground beef and drain. Stir in next 5 ingredients and heat till bubbly. Pour into 2 quart casserole dish. Cut biscuits in halves to form half circles. Place, cut side down, around edge of casserole. Sprinkle with cheese. Bake at 375° for 25 to 30 minutes.

Alberta Oliver, Rivesville Lions Club
Rivesville, WV, USA

SPINACH BEEF BISCUIT BAKE

2 (7½ oz.) tubes refrigerated buttermilk biscuits
1½ lb. ground beef
½ c. finely chopped onion
2 eggs
1 (10 oz.) pkg. frozen chopped spinach, thawed and squeezed dry
1 (4 oz.) can mushroom stems and pieces, drained

4 oz. crumbled Feta or shredded Monterey Jack cheese
¼ c. grated Parmesan cheese
1½ tsp. garlic powder
Salt and pepper to taste
1 to 2 Tbsp. butter or margarine, melted

Press and flatten biscuits onto the bottom and up the sides of a greased 11x7x2 inch baking dish; set aside. In a skillet over medium heat, cook beef and onion until meat is no longer pink; drain. In a bowl, beat eggs. Add spinach and mushrooms; mix well. Stir in the cheeses, garlic powder, salt, pepper, and beef mixture; mix well. Spoon into prepared crust. Drizzle with butter. Bake, uncovered, at 375° for 25 to 30 minutes or until crust is lightly browned. Yield: 6 servings.

RICE CASSEROLE

Brown 1 pound hamburger, then add 1 large onion (chopped fine), ½ green pepper (chopped fine), and a few pieces of diced celery. Add a can of undiluted cream of chicken soup, a can of undiluted cream of mushroom soup, 4 tablespoons low sodium soy sauce, and very little salt. Put in 1 cup long grain (uncooked) rice. Stir together and bake in 300° to 350° oven for about 2 hours. Add a little water from time to time and stir.

Micheal and Ruth Bartolf, Oxbow and District Lions Club
Oxbow, Saskatchewan, Canada

MACARONI SUPREME

1 lb. ground beef
1 green pepper
2 stalks celery
1 small onion

Cheese slices (as many as you like)
1 c. uncooked macaroni
1 can tomato soup

Brown ground beef, green pepper, celery, and onion. Season to taste, using salt and pepper. Drain macaroni and place in casserole dish. Add cooked macaroni. On top of macaroni mixture, add slices of American cheese. Spread undiluted tomato soup on top. Bake at 350° for 20 minutes or until completed heated.

Marie Alicie, North Tazewell Lions Club
North Tazewell, VA

CORNBREAD BAKE

1 lb. ground meat cooked until color changes and drained

½ lb. cheese, grated

Mix:

1 c. meal
1 Tbsp. flour
1 tsp. soda
¾ tsp. salt
1 can cream corn

2 eggs
1 c. sweet milk
1 chopped onion
1 chopped bell pepper

Pour half batter in iron skillet or Pyrex pan with ¼ cup bacon grease. Spread meat and cheese, then pour rest of batter on. Bake 35 to 40 minutes or until done at 350° or 375°.

Barbara Vaughn, Conroe Lioness Club
Conroe, TX, Montgomery County

Love may be blind, but marriage is a real eye-opener.

PIZZA HOT DISH

1 to 1½ lb. hamburger
½ c. chopped green pepper
3 oz. chopped onion
3 c. tomato sauce (no sugar)
½ tsp. garlic salt
½ tsp. oregano
½ tsp. onion salt
½ tsp. pepper
4 oz. grated Cheddar cheese
2 oz. Parmesan cheese
½ c. canned mushrooms
3 c. noodles, cooked

Brown meat. Combine meat, pepper, onion, and spices with tomato sauce. Simmer about 15 minutes over low heat. Cook noodles; drain. Place noodles in bottom of 9x13 inch nonstick pan, sprayed. Pour meat sauce over noodles. Sprinkle cheeses evenly on top. Arrange mushrooms on top. Cover with foil. Bake at 350° for 35 to 40 minutes. Cool a little and cut into squares. Freezes well.

MASHED POTATO BEEF CASSEROLE

2 bacon strips, diced
1 lb. ground beef
1 large onion, finely chopped
¼ lb. fresh mushrooms, sliced
1 large carrot, finely chopped
1 celery rib, finely chopped
3 Tbsp. all-purpose flour
1 c. beef broth
1 Tbsp. Worcestershire sauce
1 tsp. dried tarragon
¼ tsp. pepper
3 c. hot mashed potatoes
¾ c. shredded Cheddar cheese, divided
Paprika

In a skillet, cook bacon until crisp; drain, reserving 1 teaspoon drippings. Set bacon aside. Cook beef in drippings over medium heat until no longer pink.; drain. Toss onion, mushrooms, carrot, and celery in flour; add to skillet with the broth, Worcestershire sauce, tarragon, and pepper. Bring to a boil; reduce heat. Simmer, uncovered, for 15 to 20 minutes or until the vegetables are tender. Add bacon; transfer to a greased 2 quart baking dish. Combine potatoes and ½ cup of cheese; spread over beef mixture. Sprinkle with paprika and remaining cheese. Bake, uncovered, at 350° for 20 to 25 minutes or until heated through. Broil 4 inches from the heat for 5 minutes, until bubbly. Yield: 4 to 6 servings.

If at first you don't succeed, then skydiving is not for you.

❧ ❧ ❧

This life is a test; it is only a test. If it were a real life,
you would receive instructions on where to go and what to do.

WESTERN-STYLE BEEF 'N' BEANS

3 lb. ground beef
2 medium onions, chopped
2 celery ribs, chopped
2 tsp. beef bouillon granules
2/3 c. boiling water
2 (28 oz.) cans baked beans with molasses

1 1/2 c. ketchup
1/4 c. prepared mustard
3 garlic cloves, minced
1 1/2 tsp. salt
1/2 tsp. pepper
1/2 lb. sliced bacon, cooked and crumbled

In a Dutch oven over medium heat, cook beef, onions, and celery until meat is no longer pink and vegetables are tender; drain. Dissolve bouillon in water; stir into beef mixture. Add the beans, ketchup, mustard, garlic, salt, and pepper; mix well. Cover and bake at 375° for 60 to 70 minutes or until bubbly; stir. Top with bacon. Yield: 12 servings.

RANCH-STYLE HASH

Brown 1 pound ground beef.

Add:

3 1/2 c. canned tomatoes
1 c. chopped green pepper

1/2 c. chopped onion
1/2 c. uncooked rice

Season with:

1/4 tsp. basil
1/2 tsp. salt

Dash of pepper

Cover and simmer 25 minutes. Top with slices of Velveeta cheese and heat until nicely melted.

Jo Anne Beavers, Bryan Lioness Club
Bryan, OH

TATER-TOT CASSEROLE

2 lb. hamburger
1 large bag tater tots
1 can mushroom soup

1 can celery soup
1 onion

In a 9x13 inch pan, flatten hamburger on the bottom of the pan. Slice the onion and make onion rings. Place them on top of the hamburger. Mix the two cans of soup together and spread over the onions. Put the tater tots in rows across the top. Bake one hour in 350° oven.

Leftovers can be frozen and warmed up on MEDIUM heat in microwave.

This is an ideal recipe for company. If you don't know if they like onions, I only put them on half the pan. The end that doesn't have onions, I put the first row of tater tots lengthways across the top.

Eilene Moody, Bryan Lioness Club
Bryan, OH

"RICE CALIENTE"

1 lb. lean ground beef
1 c. chopped onions
1 tsp. salt
1 tsp. garlic salt

1 c. tomatoes with green chilies
3 c. cooked rice
½ c. sour cream
1 c. grated Monterey Jack cheese

Grease skillet lightly with oil; saute ground beef, onions, and seasoning until meat turns colors and onions are tender. Drain off fat. Add tomatoes and chilies, rice, and sour cream. Pour into buttered 1½ quart casserole. Sprinkle with grated cheese and bake at 350° for 20 minutes. Serves 6 to 8 people.

Barbara Vaughn, Conroe Lioness Club
Montgomery County, Conroe, TX

HUNGRY BOY

1 lb. hamburger
1 can Great Northern beans
1 can pork and beans
1 (6 oz.) can tomato paste
1 small onion

1 c. chopped celery
¼ tsp. garlic powder
1 pkg. refrigerated biscuits
6 to 8 oz. water
Salt and pepper

Fry hamburg, onions, and celery; drain. Put mixture in casserole dish. Add beans, seasonings, and tomato paste. Add enough water that the mixture is not real thick. Top casserole with biscuits. Bake at 400° about 35 minutes or until biscuits are brown.

Lion Nelson Bonager, East Prospect Lions Club
East Prospect, PA, USA

HAMBURGER DELIGHT

1 lb. hamburger
3 Tbsp. vegetable oil
1 medium onion
1 c. celery

8 oz. (1 c.) noodles
1 can baked beans
1 c. tomato catsup

Brown hamburger, onion, and celery in fat. Cook noodles in 1 quart of water. Add drained noodles, baked beans, and catsup to browned mixture. Pour into a 9x13 inch baking dish and bake in a 350° oven for 1 hour. Serve hot.

Dorothy Coon, Hutchinson Breakfast Lions Club
Hutchinson, KS, USA

"Striving for excellence motivates you;
striving for perfection is demoralizing."

Harriet Braiker

GROUND MEAT CASSEROLE

1 lb. ground meat
1 can green beans or corn
1 can cream of chicken soup

Tater tots
Velveeta cheese

Grease casserole dish and pat meat in bottom. Drain beans or corn and spread over meat. Put sliced cheese on top. Pour soup over everything and place tater tots on top. Bake at 350° for 1½ hours, uncovered.

Dorothy Hankins, Bullskin Township Lioness Club
Mt. Pleasant, PA

BEEF CASSEROLE

3 or 4 potatoes, sliced thin
1 or 2 onions, sliced thin
1 lb. ground beef, browned

½ c. uncooked Minute rice
1 can diced tomatoes

Grease casserole and place ingredients into it in order given. Sprinkle with salt and pepper. Bake, covered, 1½ hours at 350°.

I got this recipe from my mother-in-law and it has become a family favorite.

Janet Brown, Covington Lions Club
Covington, GA, USA

7 LAYER DINNER

4 c. sliced potatoes
Salt and pepper
¾ c. rice
2 lb. ground beef, browned

3 large onions, chopped fine
2 green peppers, chopped fine
1 can tomatoes
2 c. grated Cheddar cheese

Place potatoes in casserole; season with salt and pepper. Add layer of rice and layer of ground beef. Season. Cover with onions and green peppers. Pour tomatoes over top; top with grated cheese. Cover and bake at 350° for 1½ hours.

This is a great blizzard dinner.

Sandy Holva, Plainfield Township Lions Club
Bangor, PA

"Mothers, food, love, and career - the four major guilt groups."
Cathy Guisewife

IRISH CASSEROLE

2 qt. cubed squash or zucchini or
    5 to 6 medium potatoes
1 c. frozen peas
1 medium onion, quartered
½ tsp. salt
¾ lb. ground lean chuck
¾ tsp. salt

¼ c. chopped onion
1 can cream of mushroom soup
1 small can mushroom pieces
¼ lb. American cheese, cut in
    small pieces
⅓ c. milk

Combine first 4 ingredients in saucepan and cook for 10 minutes. If using potatoes, cook 15 minutes. Drain in colander. Brown meat and onion in skillet; add salt. When browned, add remaining 4 ingredients. Stir until cheese is melted. Combine drained vegetables into skillet. Transfer to a casserole and put in microwave on HIGH for 7 minutes. Serve.

Can be finished in regular oven at 350°F. for 30 minutes.

Popular at tureen dinners, funeral dinners, and at home.

Mildred Weir, Bentleyville Lioness Club
Bentleyville, PA

PINTO BEAN CASSEROLE

1 lb. ground chuck
1 c. chopped onions
1 can condensed tomato soup
    (undiluted)
1 (No. 3) can pintos (1 pt. cooked
    pintos)

1 tsp. chili powder
¼ tsp. Worcestershire sauce
1 Tbsp. cooking oil

Cornbread Topping:

1 c. self-rising cornmeal
1 egg

½ c. milk

Brown hamburger and onions in the oil. Drain. Add tomato soup, pintos, chili powder, and Worcestershire sauce. Mix. Place in casserole dish.

Mix Cornbread Topping. Pour cornbread mixture over pinto mixture. Cook at 350° for 30 minutes.

Lion Geneva Gee, Foothills of Mount Airy Lions Club
Mount Airy, NC, USA

"Anything which parents have not learned from experience
they can now learn from their children."

CHINESE HASH

1 lb. hamburger
1 c. chopped onion
½ c. chopped celery
1½ c. Minute rice or 1 c. regular
   rice

1 can cream of mushroom soup
1 can cream of chicken soup
4 c. water
2 Tbsp. soy sauce
Salt and pepper to taste

Brown hamburger, then add rest of ingredients. Bake at 450° for ½ hour, then turn to 325° for 1½ hours. Top with chow mein noodles the last ½ hour.

Mary Ann Corbett, South-West Lioness Club
So. St. Paul, MN

CONFETTI CASSEROLE

2 lb. ground beef
½ c. chopped onions
2 tsp. salt (or less)
1 (8 oz.) pkg. cream cheese
2 (10 oz.) pkg. frozen mixed
   vegetables

¼ tsp. pepper
½ tsp. dry mustard
2 Tbsp. brown sugar
2 (8 oz.) cans tomato sauce

Brown meat in skillet; add onions and cook until tender. Add seasonings, sugar, and cream cheese. Stir until cheese melts. Add tomato sauce and defrosted vegetables. Turn into 3 quart casserole. Sprinkle crushed corn chips over top. Cover and bake at 375° for 40 minutes. Uncover and bake 10 minutes more. Makes 10 to 12 servings.

Geraldine Fink, South Jefferson Lions Club
Adams, NY

MEXI GETTI

1 lb. ground beef
1 can kidney beans, drained and
   rinsed
2 c. macaroni or spaghetti

1 qt. tomato juice
2 tsp. chilli powder
1 medium onion, chopped

Stir all ingredients together (raw) and bake 1 hour at 325° to 350°.

Bert Morgan, Broken Bow Lions Club
Broken Bow, NE, Custer County

"I know God won't give me anything I can't handle.
I just wish that He didn't trust me so much."
Mother Theresa

BAKED CHILI

1 lb. ground beef
1 large onion, chopped
1 large green pepper, chopped
1 (16 oz.) can kidney beans,
   rinsed and drained
1 (15¼ oz.) can whole kernel
   corn, drained
1 (15 oz.) can tomato sauce

1 (14½ oz.) can diced tomatoes
   (undrained)
1 (4 oz.) can chopped green
   chilies
2 tsp. chili powder
1 tsp. salt
1 tsp. ground cumin
½ tsp. sugar
½ tsp. garlic powder

Corn Bread Biscuits:

1 c. all-purpose flour
1 c. cornmeal
2 tsp. baking powder
⅛ tsp. salt

1 egg
½ c. milk
½ c. sour cream

In a Dutch oven over medium heat, cook beef, onion, and green pepper until meat is no longer pink; drain. Add remaining ingredients; bring to a boil, stirring occasionally. Reduce heat; cover and simmer for 10 minutes.

Meanwhile, combine flour, cornmeal, baking powder, and salt in a bowl. Beat egg, milk, and sour cream until smooth; stir into dry ingredients just until moistened. Transfer chili to an ungreased 13x9x2 inch baking dish. Drop batter by heaping teaspoonfuls onto hot chili. Bake, uncovered, at 400° for 15 to 17 minutes or until biscuits are lightly browned. Yield: 8 servings.

BAKED CHILI

1½ lb. ground beef
1 medium onion, chopped
1 (8 oz.) pkg. spaghetti, cooked
   as directed

1 can chili beans
1 can tomatoes
3 Tbsp. chili powder (or to taste)

Brown together beef and onion; drain off grease. Add cooked spaghetti, beans, tomatoes, and chili powder. Mix well. Place in 9x13 inch casserole and bake at 350° for 1 hour.

Lion Wilma Ell, Southport Lions Club
Indianapolis, IN, USA

"You cannot plow a field by turning it over in your mind.
You have to get off your butt and do something."
Dail C. West

CRAB CASSEROLE

1 can crabmeat
1 c. celery, diced
1 medium green pepper, diced
1 medium onion, diced
1 c. mayonnaise

1 c. buttered bread crumbs
1 Tbsp. Worcestershire sauce
1 tsp. (Old Bay) seafood
  seasoning
Salt and pepper to taste

Mix all ingredients until well blended. Bake in baking dish at 350°F. for 30 minutes.

For all Maryland and Pennsylvania Lions who are never "crabby."

A.K. Brumback, Silver Run Union Mills Lions Club
Westminster, MD, USA

SALMON-RICE-OLIVE CASSEROLE

½ c. sliced celery
½ small onion, chopped
2 Tbsp. butter/margarine
1 can cream of celery soup
1½ c. water

⅓ c. sliced stuffed green olives
1 tsp. lemon juice
1½ c. instant (uncooked) rice
1 (16 oz.) can salmon, boned and
  flaked

In large skillet, saute celery and onion in butter until soft. Add can of soup and water. Bring to boil, stirring. Add olives and lemon juice. Pour half into lightly greased 1½ quart casserole. In separate layers, add rice, then the salmon and remainder of sauce. Bake, covered, at 375° for 10 minutes. Stir well to mix the layers. Cover and bake 10 more minutes.

Can garnish the center with whole olives.

Colorful and delicious - a hit even with kids.

Candace Wellman, Bellingham Harborview Lions Club
Bellingham, WA, USA

TUNA CASSEROLE

1 (6 oz.) can tuna
1 can peas or corn, drained
1 can evaporated milk

1 large pkg. potato chips
1 can cream of mushroom soup
  (undiluted)

In a two quart casserole dish, put layer of chips in casserole. Add some of the vegetable, then flake some of the tuna over the vegetable. Spoon some of the soup over this. Repeat these layers until all ingredients are used. Always end up with chips on top of the casserole. Pour the can of milk over this. Heat in the oven at 350° until bubbly and chips are brown.

Alberta Oliver, Rivesville Lions Club
Rivesville, WV, USA

TUNA MUSHROOM CASSEROLE

1 (12 oz.) pkg. wide noodles,
cooked and drained
2 (6 oz.) cans tuna, drained
1 (4 oz.) can mushroom stems
and pieces, drained
1 (10¾ oz.) can condensed cream
of mushroom soup (undiluted)
1⅓ c. milk

½ tsp. salt
¼ tsp. pepper
½ c. crushed saltines
3 Tbsp. butter or margarine,
melted
Paprika, tomato slices, and fresh
thyme (optional)

In a large bowl, combine noodles, tuna, and mushrooms. Combine soup, milk, salt, and pepper; pour over noodle mixture and mix well. Pour into a greased 2½ quart baking dish. Combine saltines and butter; sprinkle over noodles. Bake, uncovered, at 350° for 35 to 45 minutes or until heated through. If desired, sprinkle with paprika and garnish with tomato and thyme. Yield: 6 servings.

MUSHROOM QUICHE

1 unbaked pastry shell (9 inches)
4 c. sliced fresh mushrooms
1 Tbsp. butter or margarine
1 c. (4 oz.) shredded Swiss cheese
2 Tbsp. all-purpose flour
3 eggs, lightly beaten

1¼ c. milk
1 Tbsp. minced fresh savory or 1
tsp. dried savory
½ tsp. salt
¼ tsp. pepper

Line unpricked pastry shell with a double thickness of heavy-duty foil. Bake at 425° for 10 minutes or until edges begin to brown. Remove foil; set the crust aside. In a skillet, saute mushrooms in butter. Remove with a slotted spoon; set aside. In a bowl, toss cheese with flour; add eggs, milk, savory, salt, and pepper. Stir in mushrooms. Pour into crust. Bake at 350° for 1 hour or until a knife inserted near the center comes out clean. Let stand 10 minutes before cutting. Yield: 6 to 8 servings.

FULL OF BOLOGNEY

2 c. cubed raw potatoes
2 Tbsp. minced green pepper
¼ tsp. salt
3 Tbsp. butter

1½ c. cut-up bologna
6 Tbsp. flour
¼ tsp. pepper
2 c. milk

Heat oven to 350°. Arrange potatoes, bologna, green pepper, flour, and seasonings in layers in a 1½ quart baking dish. Dot each layer with butter. Pour milk over and bake 1 hour and 15 minutes.

You don't stop laughing because you grow old. You grow old because you stop laughing.

Doris (Cricket) Kimbrell, Iron City Lions Club
Iron City, TN, USA

CURRIED FRUIT BAKE

2 cans *chunky* fruit cocktail
½ c. brown sugar
2 Tbsp. corn starch
1 tsp. (or less) curry powder

1 c. black pitted cherries (canned)
6 to 8 *firm* bananas
½ c. melted margarine

Drain canned fruit for several hours or overnight. Peel and cut bananas into salad-size pieces. Lightly toss bananas with other fruit. Add margarine and mix lightly. Put into lightly buttered casserole dish. Combine sugar, corn starch, and curry powder. Sprinkle generously over fruit. Bake 40 minutes at 350°. Serve hot. Makes 8 servings.

This dish is excellent as a side dish with chicken or fish entrees.

Debby Chaudoir, Mandeville Lions Club
Mandeville, LA, USA

BEANS 'N WIENERS WAIKIKI

2 Tbsp. butter or margarine
¼ c. chopped onion
⅓ c. green peppers, coarsely
   chopped
1 (2 oz.) can pineapple rings,
   drained (reserve juice)
1 pkg. wieners, cut into chunks

2 Tbsp. vinegar
1 Tbsp. soy sauce
⅓ c. catsup
⅓ c. brown sugar, packed firm
1 (31 oz.) can Van Camp's pork
   and beans
1 can chow mein noodles
   (optional)

Cut pineapple into chunks, reserving 3 or 4 rings for garnish. Saute green pepper, onion, pineapple, and wiener chunks in margarine. Simmer 5 minutes. Add pineapple juice, vinegar, soy sauce, catsup, and brown sugar. Heat until bubbly. Pour pork and beans into baking dish. Add pineapple mixture. Stir gently to blend. Place halved rings on top of casserole. Bake in moderate (350°) oven for 30 minutes. Serve with chow mien noodles (optional). Serves 6 generously.

Zona Roberts, Bullhead Lions Club
Bullhead City, AZ, USA

"Love doesn't make the world go 'round.
Love is what makes the ride worthwhile."
Franklin P. Jones

BLACK-EYED PEA CASSEROLE

1 gal. can black-eyed peas
1½ to 2 lb. hamburger meat,
    browned and drained
1½ c. cooked rice

1 c. onion, 2 large bell peppers,
    and ¼ c. garlic, sauteed
2 (No. 303) cans Ro-Tel tomatoes

Mix all ingredients and put in refrigerator the night before serving so flavors will blend. Heat in crock pot to a simmer for about 1 hour. Top with 1 to 1½ cups mild Cheddar cheese (in crock pot).

Oh-oo-o so good! Goes well with cornbread. This will serve about 20 people.

Gossip is like the wind. One doesn't know where it comes from or where it goes. It biteth like a serpent and singeth like an adder leaving scars that surgery cannot remove.

Ruth T. Mullen, Brookhaven Alpha Lions Club
Brookhaven, MS, USA

PINEAPPLE CASSEROLE

2 cans chunk pineapple, drained
    (reserve juice)
6 Tbsp. flour
1 c. sugar

6 Tbsp. reserved juice
1 stick margarine, melted
1½ stacks Ritz crackers, crushed
1½ c. shredded Cheddar cheese

Layer pineapple chunks in bottom of a lightly greased casserole dish (9x13 inches). Mix juice, flour, and sugar and pour over pineapple. Sprinkle cheese evenly over mixture. Bake at 350° for about 30 minutes. During last 5 minutes of cooking, sprinkle cracker crumbs that have been mixed with margarine evenly over top.

Nettie Favara, Greenwood Lions Club
Greenwood, MS, USA

SCALLOPED PINEAPPLE

1 (20 oz.) can pineapple tidbits
1 c. sugar
6 slices white toast, cut in 1 inch
    cubes

2 eggs, beaten
⅓ c. melted margarine
½ c. milk

Mix all ingredients together. Place in 1 quart casserole. Sprinkle with brown sugar and cinnamon. Bake at 350° for 45 to 60 minutes. Serves 6. *Very easy - so good.*

Bonnie Smith, Princeton Lions Club
Princeton, IL

CASSOULET

1 lb. dried white or Great
    Northern beans or 6 c.
    canned beans
2 whole cloves
2 onions
½ tsp. dried thyme
3 parsley sprigs
1 bay leaf
Salt and pepper
2 cloves garlic

½ lb. smoked sausage
2 Tbsp. oil
1 lb. lamb or pork stew meat, cut
    into approx. 1 inch chunks
1 c. chicken stock
1 lb. can tomato sauce
4 Tbsp. butter
3 c. fresh crumbs from firm bread
½ c. chopped fresh parsley

The beans: If using dried beans, add water to cover by about 2 inches and let soak overnight. Drain. Put in a large pot with water to cover by 2 inches. Stick cloves into 1 of the onions and add to the beans with the thyme, parsley sprigs, and the bay leaf. Bring to a boil, then reduce the heat and simmer, partially covered, until tender, about 1½ hours.

The meat: Meanwhile, chop remaining onion. Mince garlic. Cut sausage into thick slices. Heat oil in a Dutch oven over medium high heat. Brown the sausage slices and remove. Add lamb and brown in batches if necessary. Reduce heat to medium and add chopped onion, garlic, and 1 teaspoon salt. Cover and cook until softened, about 5 minutes. Stir in chicken stock, scraping up browned bits. Add tomato sauce and cook until lamb is tender, about 1½ hours.

Assembling the dish: Drain beans, reserving the liquid. Discard the onion and parsley. Add 1 teaspoon salt and ¼ teaspoon pepper. Heat oven to 350°. Stir excess sauce from lamb into beans. Put half the beans in a 3½ quart baking dish. Top with lamb and remaining sauce. Add sausage. Cover with remaining beans. Add reserved bean liquid if needed so liquid almost reaches top of beans. Bake 45 minutes.

Meanwhile, melt butter. Combine bread crumbs with the chopped parsley and the melted butter. Sprinkle on top of beans and continue baking until crumbs are golden brown, about 45 minutes longer. Makes 6 servings.

Work time: 1 hour. Total time: 4 hours and 45 minutes.

Per serving: 897 calories, 47 g protein 3 g fat, 1779 mg sodium, 67 g carbohydrate, 160 mg cholesterol.

Mrs. Lucy Aiken, Clarence Lions Club
Clarence Center, NY, USA

"Many a man has fallen in love with a girl
in a light so dim he would not have chosen a suit by it."
Maurice Chevalier

RICE PILAF
(Judy Winkler)

3 Tbsp. olive oil
3 Tbsp. onions, chopped
1 c. rice (raw)

½ tsp. salt
¼ tsp. pepper
2 c. broth

Heat oil. Add onion and cook until soft. Add rice. Cook over low heat 3 minutes. Add salt, pepper, and broth. Cover and cook 20 minutes or bake, covered, 1 hour at 350°. Add sauteed fresh mushrooms. Serve hot.

Sarah Wehling, Bothell Lions Club
Bothell, WA, USA

ORIENTAL WILD RICE

¾ c. wild rice
1½ c. water
1 lb. ground beef
¼ c. chopped green pepper
¼ c. chopped onion
1 can cream of mushroom soup

1 (4 oz.) can mushrooms with juice
¼ c. soy sauce
1 (8 oz.) can sliced water chestnuts, drained
1 (8 oz.) can bamboo shoots, drained

Gently cook wild rice in water, covered, about 45 minutes or until the degree of doneness you desire. Drain if necessary. Brown ground beef and then saute together the green pepper, celery, and onion. In a large bowl, mix soup, mushrooms with juice, and soy sauce. Add rice, meat, sauteed vegetables, water chestnuts, and bamboo shoots. Bake in a 2 quart casserole or a 9x13 inch pan, covered, at 350° for 45 minutes. Do not add salt. Serves 6. *Very good!*

Lion Doris Schrupp, Plato Lions Club
Plato, MN, USA

WILD RICE CASSEROLE

1 c. wild rice
6 c. boiling water
Salt
1 c. grated Cheddar cheese
½ c. butter

1 medium onion, chopped
Fresh or canned mushrooms, sliced
Salt and pepper to taste
2½ c. canned tomatoes

Wash the wild rice. Boil for 5 minutes in 3 cups of the boiling water. Cover and let stand off of the element for 1 hour. Drain rice. Add the remaining 3 cups boiling water with a little salt and cook for 25 to 30 minutes. Drain. Add the cheese. Heat the butter and saute the onion and mushrooms (the more, the better). Add to the rice and cheese along with the salt, pepper, and tomatoes. Cover and bake at 350°F. for 1 hour.

Micheal and Ruth Bartolf, Oxbow and District Lions Club
Oxbow, Saskatchewan, Canada

318

SPANISH RICE

4 slices bacon, cut up
¼ c. chopped green pepper
2 c. canned tomatoes
⅛ tsp. pepper

¼ c. finely chopped onion
3 c. cooked rice (it's 1 c. uncooked)
1½ tsp. salt
¼ c. grated cheese

Heat oven to 400° (moderate heat). Fry bacon till crisp; remove to 1½ quart casserole and whisk bacon around to grease casserole. Add onion and green pepper to bacon fat; cook till onion is yellow. Combine all ingredients in casserole. Sprinkle cheese on top. Bake 25 to 30 minutes. Makes 4 to 6 servings.

People who wait for their ship to come in usually find it a hardship.

Rayford Kimbrell, Iron City Lions Club
Iron City, TN, USA

SPANISH RICE

1 tsp. cooking oil
1 c. rice (regular, not instant)
¼ onion, diced
2 or 3 garlic cloves, mashed

3 slices bell pepper
1 or 2 beef bouillon cubes
3 c. water

Brown the rice in the oil. Dissolve the bouillon cubes in one cup of the water. Add the rest of the ingredients and cook, covered, 15 minutes.

Deryl Fox, Saginaw Lions Club

ONION RICE CASSEROLE

1½ c. rice (regular), washed
2 cans Campbell's onion soup

½ c. oleo
2 small cans mushroom pieces

Place the rice and onion soup in a greased casserole. Slice the oleo on the mixture. Sprinkle the mushrooms (drained) on top. Bake 1 hour, uncovered, at 350°.

Jean Chestnut, Columbus Noon Lions Club
Columbus, NE

OVEN RICE

1 stick margarine, melted
1 c. rice (long grain, not Minute)

1 can onion soup
1 can beef consomme

Mix together and put in a covered dish. Bake in the oven for 1 hour at 350°.

Janie Fox, Saginaw Lions Club
Saginaw, TX

PEROGIE HOTDISH

9 to 12 lasagne noodles, cooked and drained
½ tsp. onion salt, mixed in sour cream
1 c. cubed Velveeta cheese (add to potatoes)
1 diced onion, sauteed in 1 c. butter
16 oz. sour cream
3 c. instant mashed potatoes, prepared
1½ lb. cut, fried, drained bacon

Layer in 9x13 inch pan: Noodles, sour cream, and potato mixture. You should have enough for three layers. Pour onion and butter over top, then sprinkle with bacon. Bake ½ hour at 350°.

Judy Brasgalla, VDG, Cass Lake Lions and Lioness Club
Cass Lake, MN, USA

SPAGHETTI CASSEROLE

¾ lb. spaghetti, cooked
1 large jar spaghetti sauce
1 small onion, chopped
½ c. milk
1 lb. ground beef, browned
1 green pepper, cleaned and chopped
8 oz. cream cheese
Parmesan cheese

Mix ground beef and spaghetti sauce together. Mix green pepper, onion, cream cheese, and milk together. Layer as follows: ½ spaghetti, ½ meat mixture, all of cream cheese mixture, ½ of spaghetti, and ½ of meat mixture. Bake at 350° for 30 to 45 minutes till bubbly and heated through. Sprinkle with Parmesan cheese.

This is a large recipe and freezes well. Go ahead and add the Parmesan cheese before freezing, then bake when needed.

P. Diane Baldwin, Broken Bow Lions Club
Broken Bow, NE, USA

NITA'S SPAGHETTI CASSEROLE

1 box spaghetti
1 can tomato soup
1 (8 oz.) can tomato sauce
2 lb. ground beef
1 jar chopped olives
1 can condensed cream of mushroom soup
1 bell pepper, chopped
¾ c. grated Cheddar cheese

In large casserole dish, place a layer of spaghetti. Brown ground beef and spread over spaghetti. Combine tomato soup and tomato sauce and pour half over the spaghetti and ground beef. Sprinkle with cheese. Repeat the process. Layer the top of the casserole with mushroom soup, olives, and bell pepper. Cover with aluminum foil and bake at 200° for 2 hours.

Martha C. Cox, Travelers Rest Lions Club
Travelers Rest, SC

CHICKEN SPAGHETTI

1 hen or 2 fryers
1 stick margarine
1 large bunch green onions,
   chopped, or 1 medium white
   onion, chopped
1 large bell pepper

1 can Ro-Tel tomatoes
1½ lb. Velveeta cheese
1 (4 oz.) can pimentos
1 c. chicken broth
1 lb. spaghetti

Boil the chicken and remove the meat from the bones. Saute the onions and bell pepper in the margarine until soft. Cook the spaghetti and drain. Add the broth to the spaghetti. Cut up the Velveeta and let melt with the broth and spaghetti. Add the onion mixture and stir until all ingredients are well mixed. Add the Ro-Tel tomatoes and pimento. Pour into casserole dishes that have been oiled. Place in 350° oven until the cheese is bubbly. Freezes well.

Janie Fox, Saginaw Lions Club
Saginaw, TX

BAKED MACARONI AND CHEESE CASSEROLE

"This is a nice and rich baked mac and cheese that I added a few extras to. Serve with a salad for a great meatless dinner."

8 oz. dried macaroni
¼ c. butter
3 Tbsp. all-purpose flour
3 c. milk
2 c. grated extra sharp Cheddar
   cheese

½ c. grated Parmesan cheese
Toasted bread crumbs
Paprika

Cook macaroni according to package directions and drain. Melt the butter over medium heat and stir in the flour to form a thick paste. Cook until mixture begins to bubble. Add the milk to roux slowly, stirring constantly. Add cheeses and cook over low heat until cheese is melted and sauce is a little thick.

Put macaroni in large casserole dish and pour sauce over macaroni. Stir well. Sprinkle toasted bread crumbs over the top of the macaroni and cheese to cover. Sprinkle with a little paprika. Bake in a preheated 325°F. (165°C.) oven for 30 minutes. Makes 2 to 4 servings.

Barbara K. Hugus, West Milford Lions Club
West Milford, WV, USA

What does "proverb" mean? It is the wit of one and the wisdom of many.

MAIN DISHES

CHICKEN-AND-SAUSAGE GUMBO

1 lb. hot smoked sausage, cut
    into ¼ inch slices
4 chicken breast halves, skinned
¼ to ⅓ c. vegetable oil
¾ c. all-purpose flour
1 c. chopped onion
½ c. chopped green pepper
½ c. sliced celery
2 qt. hot water
3 cloves garlic, minced

2 bay leaves
2 tsp. Creole seasoning
½ tsp. dried whole thyme
1 Tbsp. Worcestershire sauce
½ to 1 tsp. hot sauce
½ c. sliced green onions
¼ tsp. salt (optional)
Hot cooked rice
Gumbo file (optional)

Brown sausage in a Dutch oven over medium heat. Remove to paper towels, leaving drippings in Dutch oven. Brown chicken in drippings; remove to paper towels, reserving drippings.

Measure drippings, adding enough vegetable oil to measure ½ cup. Heat in Dutch oven over medium heat until hot. Add flour to hot oil; cook, stirring constantly, until roux is the color of chocolate (about 30 minutes). Add onion, green pepper, and celery; cook until vegetables are tender, stirring often. Gradually stir in water; bring to a boil. Return chicken breasts to Dutch oven; add garlic and next 5 minutes. Reduce heat; simmer, uncovered, 30 minutes. Stir in green onions; cook, uncovered, an additional 30 minutes. Add salt if desired. Bone chicken breasts and cut into strips. Add gumbo and cook until thoroughly heated. Remove bay leaves; serve gumbo over rice. Sprinkle with gumbo file if desired. Yield: 8 servings.

Lion Lucille Caruso, wife of P.D.G. James (Jim) Caruso,
Delta Lions Club, District 8-S
Metairie, LA, USA

Advise is advise when it is asked for.
When unasked for, it is generally meddling.

❦ ❦ ❦

To find his place and then to fill it is success for a man.

❦ ❦ ❦

Aimless talk, speaking without thinking, is like shooting without taking aim.

SUMMER RISOTTO

2 Tbsp. olive oil divided
1 small onion, chopped fine
1 c. uncooked Arborio rice
¼ c. dry white wine
2 c. reduced-sodium chicken
 broth
1 medium carrot, cut into
 matchstick pieces
4 oz. small white mushrooms,
 sliced thin
1 small zucchini, cut into
 matchstick pieces

1 small yellow squash, cut into
 matchstick pieces
1 Tbsp. chopped fresh parsley
1 tsp. chopped fresh rosemary
⅓ c. freshly grated Parmesan
 cheese
Shaved Parmesan (optional)
Rosemary sprigs for garnish
 (optional)

In 2 quart saucepan over medium-high heat, heat 1 tablespoon olive oil. Add onion; cook until tender. Stir in rice; cook, stirring frequently, until rice turns opaque. Stir in wine; cook until wine is almost evaporated. Stir in chicken broth. Over high heat, bring to a boil. Reduce heat to low and simmer about 15 minutes, stirring occasionally.

Meanwhile, in nonstick skillet, over medium-high heat, heat remaining 1 tablespoon olive oil; add carrots and cook until just tender. Add mushrooms, zucchini, and yellow squash; cook until vegetables are tender-crisp. Remove rice mixture from heat; stir in cooked vegetables, parsley, rosemary, and grated cheese until blended. If desired, serve with shaved Parmesan and garnish with rosemary. Makes 4 servings.

Work time: 10 minutes. Total time: 40 minutes.

Per serving: 194 calories, 8 g protein, 11 g fat, 518 mg sodium, 18 g carbohydrate, 8 mg cholesterol, 5,376IU vitamin A.

Mrs. Lucy Aiken, Clarence Lions Club
Clarence Center, NY, USA

TURKEY CHOW MEIN

1 green pepper, cut in strips
2 c. celery, chopped
1 c. sliced onion
1 c. mushroom pieces
4 Tbsp. butter
2 c. turkey stock
1 tsp. salt

2 Tbsp. corn starch
3 c. turkey, cooked and cubed
3 Tbsp. soya sauce
1 can bean sprouts
2 cans chow mein noodles
 (optional)

Saute green pepper, celery, onion, and mushrooms in butter. Add broth, salt, and pepper; bring to a boil. Mix corn starch with small amount of water to form paste. Add to liquid and stir until thickened. Add turkey, soya sauce, and bean sprouts. Heat thoroughly and serve over noodles if desired.

Tasty way to use up leftover turkey.

Lion Joan Brinkhurst, Lake of the Woods Lions Club
Kenora, Ontario, Canada

FRIED RICE WITH CURRRIED MEATBALLS

1 c. uncooked rice
½ lb. ground pork
½ lb. ground turkey
3 Tbsp. dry bread crumbs
5 tsp. curry powder, divided
½ tsp. salt
2 Tbsp. vegetable oil, divided

2 medium carrots, halved
  lengthwise and sliced
1 small zucchini, halved
  lengthwise and sliced
2 medium garlic cloves, minced
2 medium scallions, cut into 1
  inch pieces

Cook rice in boiling salted water according to package directions until tender.

Meanwhile, in a large bowl, combine ground pork and turkey, the bread crumbs, 1 teaspoon curry powder, and the salt. Shape mixture into 1 inch balls. In a large nonstick skillet, over medium-high heat, heat 1 tablespoon oil. Add meatballs and brown well. Add carrots; cover and cook 5 minutes. Stir in zucchini, garlic, and scallions and cook until tender, about 10 minutes. Push vegetables and meatballs to one side of pan. Add remaining 1 tablespoon oil to pan and stir in remaining 4 teaspoons curry powder. Add rice and cook, stirring, until heated through, about 5 minutes. Makes 4 servings.

Work time: 30 minutes. Total time: 30 minutes.

Per serving: 511 calories, 25 g protein, 24 g fat, 421 mg sodium, 48 g carbohydrate, 82 mg cholesterol.

Mrs. Lucy Aiken, Clarence Lions Club
Clarence Center, NY, USA

TURKEY-STUFFED SPUDS

2 slices lean bacon
4 baking potatoes (each about 8
  oz.), scrubbed
1 c. plain low-fat yogurt
1½ Tbsp. Dijon-style mustard

3 Tbsp. chopped fresh chives
¼ tsp. pepper
8 oz. piece smoked turkey breast,
  diced

Place bacon on paper towel-lined microwave-safe plate; cover with another paper towel. Place plate in microwave. Cook on HIGH about 3 minutes or until crisp; chop bacon and set aside. Prick potatoes with fork. Cook on HIGH 12 to 14 minutes until tender, turning once during cooking.

Meanwhile, in large bowl, stir yogurt, mustard, chives, and pepper. Add turkey and scooped-out flesh of each potato; mix well. Pile mixture back into potato shells. Serve at once. Makes 4 servings.

Per serving: 283 calories, 20 g protein, 4 g fat, 841 mg sodium, 44 g carbohydrate, 30 mg cholesterol.

Food note: For variety, substitute leftover cooked chicken, pork, lamb, or beef for turkey.

Barbara Joy Hess, Clarence Lions Club
Clarence Center, NY, USA

HEARTY HOLIDAY PIE

1 (7.5 oz.) pkg. refrigerated
    buttermilk biscuits
½ c. celery slices
¼ c. chopped red or green
    pepper
3 c. chopped and cooked turkey
    or chicken or ham

2 Tbsp. margarine
½ c. slivered almonds, toasted
1 c. sour cream
1 c. (4 oz.) shredded sharp
    natural cheese

Press biscuits onto sides and bottom of greased 9 inch pie plate. Bake at 450° for 8 minutes or until lightly browned. Saute vegetables in margarine. Add turkey and almonds; heat thoroughly, stirring occasionally. Stir in ¾ cup sour cream and cheese. Heat until cheese is melted. Spoon mixture into shell. Top with remaining sour cream. Makes 6 to 8 servings.

This is great when you want to use leftover chicken or ham or turkey.

Lion Louise K. Berdick, Western Branch Lions Club
Chesapeake, VA

TURKEY PIE

Pastry for 9 inch two-crust pie
¾ c. chicken broth or ¾ c. water
    and 1 chicken bouillon cube
2 Tbsp. butter
¾ c. light cream
2 c. cubed turkey

1 c. cooked carrots, sliced
⅔ c. frozen peas
2 Tbsp. flour
⅛ tsp. pepper
⅛ tsp. thyme
1 c. diced onion

Melt butter; blend in flour, salt, pepper, and thyme. Cook until mixture is bubbly and smooth. Stir in chicken broth and cream. Heat to boiling, stirring. Stir in turkey and vegetables. Pour into pie crust. Bake at 425° for 35 to 40 minutes.

Judy Brasgalla, VDG, Cass Lake Lions and Lioness Club
Cass Lake, MN, USA

Did you ever stop to think that it takes more thought
on how to be bad than how to be good.

Boogy: "Who was more patient than Job, wiser than Socrates,
braver than Lancelot, and more handsome than Apollo?"
Woogy: "Oh, so you knew my wife's first husband?"

RED BEANS

1 lb. dried kidney beans
1 ham bone or leftover ham
6 c. water
2 lb. link sausage, cut in 1 inch
    pieces
1 tsp. salt

½ tsp. hot pepper sauce
1 tsp. Worcestershire sauce
1 tsp. onion powder
1 bay leaf
3 c. cooked rice

Soak beans overnight. Drain. In a large Dutch oven or kettle, add all ingredients (except rice) and bring to a boil, stirring frequently to prevent sticking. Reduce heat to low and cook slowly for several hours,* stirring occasionally. If necessary, add water if beans are not tender. If you prefer a thick gravy, mash a few beans and cook longer.* Serve over rice. Serves 6.

* Your personal taste will determine exactly how long the beans should cook.

Cindy Bamburg, Biloxi Lions Club
Biloxi, MS, USA

STIR-FRIED CORNED-BEEF AND CABBAGE

1 onion
1 lb. cabbage (about 6 c.
    shredded)
¾ lb. cooked corned beef (about
    3 c.)
1 Tbsp. oil

Salt and pepper
½ tsp. caraway seeds
½ c. beer
2 tsp. drained prepared
    horseradish

Chop onion. Shred cabbage. Cut corned beef into strips. In a wok or large frying pan, heat oil over medium heat. Add onion; cover and cook until tender, about 5 minutes. Add cabbage, ½ teaspoon salt, ¼ teaspoon pepper, the caraway seeds, and beer. Cover and cook until almost tender, about 5 minutes. Uncover and continue cooking until the cabbage is tender and the liquid has evaporated, about 5 minutes. Stir in the corned beef and the horseradish. Cook until just heated through, 1 to 2 minutes. Makes 4 servings.

Per serving: 286 calories, 17 g protein, 20 g fat, 1264 mg sodium, 10 g carbohydrate, 83 mg cholesterol.

Mrs. Mike Nowicki, Clarence Lions Club
Clarence Center, NY, USA

The best way to get even is to forget.

Utilize the power of love, not the love of power.

STIR-FRIED BEEF

½ c. beef stock or canned broth
2 Tbsp. soy sauce
4 tsp. rice-wine vinegar
Salt
1 Tbsp. cornstarch
2 Tbsp. oil
¾ lb. mushrooms, sliced

½ lb. snow peas, trimmed
1 lb. flank steak, cut into ¼ inch
   slices
2 cloves garlic, minced
1 Tbsp. minced fresh ginger
4 scallions, cut into 1 inch pieces
8 oz. can sliced water chestnuts

Combine stock, soy sauce, vinegar, and ½ teaspoon salt. Mix cornstarch with 1 tablespoon water. In a large frying pan, heat 1 tablespoon oil. Add mushrooms and cook about 3 minutes. Stir in snow peas and cook 1 minute. Remove vegetables and any liquid. Heat remaining 1 tablespoon oil. Add meat and sear, about 3 minutes. Stir in garlic, ginger, and stock mixture. Bring to a boil. Stir in cornstarch. Cook briefly to thicken. Stir in mushrooms, snow peas, scallions, and water chestnuts and serve. Makes 4 servings.

Per serving: 361 calories, 27 g protein, 19 g fat, 883 mg sodium, 20 g carbohydrate, 59 mg cholesterol.

Lion John J. Hess, Clarence Lions Club
Clarence Center, NY, USA

STIR-FRY BEEF

3 Tbsp. reduced-sodium soy
   sauce
1 Tbsp. honey
1 garlic clove, minced
2 tsp. grated fresh ginger root
½ tsp. crushed red-pepper flakes
1 lb. lean beef, cut into ½ inch
   cubes

8 oz. uncooked vermicelli
1 tsp. sesame seed
1 Tbsp. canola oil
4 c. shredded savoy cabbage
1 c. bean sprouts
2 scallions, chopped

In medium bowl, stir first five ingredients. Add beef; let stand 15 minutes. Cook vermicelli as package directs; drain. Return to pot; toss with sesame oil. In wok or large nonstick skillet, over medium-high heat, heat canola oil; add beef, reserving marinade. Stir-fry 5 to 6 minutes until well browned. Add cabbage, sprouts, and scallions; stir-fry 1 minute. Add noodles and reserved marinade. Cook until heated through, about 1 minute. Makes 4 servings.

Per serving: 462 calories, 35 g protein, 11 g fat, 735 mg sodium, 55 g carbohydrate, 66 mg cholesterol.

Barbara Joy Hess, Clarence Lions Club
Clarence Center, NY, USA

BEEF AND PEPPER STIR-FRY

2 Tbsp. cornstarch, *divided*
4 Tbsp. beef broth or dry sherry, *divided*
4 Tbsp. soy sauce, *divided*
1 garlic clove, minced
½ to 1 tsp. crushed red pepper flakes
1 lb. top sirloin, thinly sliced into ¼ inch strips
½ c. water
3 Tbsp. vegetable oil, *divided*
1 green pepper, cut into strips
1 sweet red pepper, cut into strips
Chow mein noodles or hot cooked rice

In a medium bowl, combine 1 tablespoon cornstarch, 2 tablespoons broth or sherry, 2 tablespoons soy sauce, garlic, and red pepper flakes. Add beef and toss to coat; set aside. In a small bowl, combine water with remaining cornstarch, broth, and soy sauce; set aside. In a wok or skillet, heat 1 tablespoon oil over medium-high. Add green and red peppers; stir-fry for 1 minute or until crisp-tender. Remove peppers to a platter. Add remaining oil and half of the beef to the pan; stir-fry for 1 to 2 minutes or until beef is no longer pink. Remove to platter. Stir-fry the remaining beef. Return peppers and beef to pan. Stir cornstarch mixture and add to pan; bring to a boil, stirring constantly until thickened. Cook 1 minute longer. Serve immediately over chow mein noodles or rice. Yield: 4 to 6 servings.

THAI BEEF WITH NOODLES
(30 minutes)

1 lb. boneless beef top sirloin, cut 1 inch thick
¼ c. dry sherry
1½ Tbsp. reduced-sodium soy sauce
1 tsp. grated fresh ginger
1 tsp. minced ginger
1 tsp. oriental dark roasted sesame oil
¼ to ½ tsp. crushed red pepper pods
2 c. cooked Ramen noodles or linguine
¼ c. chopped green onion tops or fresh cilantro

Combine sherry, soy sauce, ginger, garlic, sesame oil, and pepper pods. Place beef steak in plastic bag; add marinade. Close bag securely and marinate 15 minutes. Pour off marinade; reserve. Heat nonstick skillet over medium heat 5 minutes. Add steak and cook 12 to 15 minutes for rare (140°F.) to medium (160°F.), turning once. Remove steak; keep warm.

Dissolve 2 teaspoons cornstarch in reserved marinade and ¼ cup water; add to skillet. Bring to a boil, stirring constantly. Stir in noodles. Carve steak into thin slices and serve over noodles. Sprinkle with green onion. Makes 4 servings.

Barbara Joy Hess, Clarence Lions Club
Clarence Center, NY, USA

HAMBURGER GOULASH

1 to 2 small onions
1 lb. hamburger

Ketchup

Brown 1 large or 2 small onions that have been cut up into small pieces in a little oil. Add a pound of hamburger and brown. Add enough ketchup to make very moist. Simmer a short time. Serve over fluffy white rice. Very easy.

Glenn E. Bunch, Jr., PDG 31-H, Snow Hill Lions Club
Snow Hill, NC, USA

YAKISODE

1 lb. ground beef or turkey
1 chopped onion
3 c. water
2 carrots, thinly sliced

1 pkg. noodles or angel hair
   pasta
½ medium sized head cabbage,
   chopped
1 Tbsp. soy sauce

Brown ground beef and onions. Add water and carrots; cover and cook until tender. Add noodles and cabbage and cook until tender. After all ingredients are tender, add soy sauce.

Can use chicken broth instead of water when using ground turkey.

Jean Lemley, Fairmont East Grafton Road Lions Club
Fairmont, WV

"PEPPERS WITH A PUNCH"

2 lb. ground beef
6 to 8 green peppers
1 Tbsp. red pepper seasoning
¼ c. Worcestershire sauce
Couple drops of hot sauce

Lots of garlic powder (spice it up)
1 Tbsp. black pepper
1 tsp. basil
¼ c. bbq sauce
1 jar your favorite spaghetti sauce

Clean and boil peppers for about 10 minutes. Add all ingredients to ground beef except spaghetti sauce. Fill peppers and put in glass casserole pan. Cover with spaghetti sauce. Bake at 350° for 1 hour or until done as you like.

Hint: If you pour a little sauce on bottom of casserole before putting peppers in, they won't stick to bottom!

Tammy Wintermute, Plainfield Township Lions Club
Palmer Township, Easton, PA

Love people and use things - not love things and use people.

CRAWFISH MONIQUE

1 lb. preferably fresh pasta (linguine, fettucine, spinach fettucine, egg noodles or spaghetti)
1 stick butter or ¼ lb. crawfish butter (see recipe below)

¾ c. chopped green onions
1 lb. crawfish tails, peeled (see note)
1 Tbsp. name-brand seafood seasoning (Cajun style product)
1 pt. half & half

This recipe does not mention salt and pepper - add to taste if necessary.

Cook pasta according to package directions. Drain and chill by running under cold water. Drain thoroughly. Melt butter in large saucepan and saute onions for two or three minutes. Add seasoning and crawfish tails. (Note: If you peel your own crawfish, I would definitely add the crawfish fat for extra flavor.) Saute one minute. Add half & half and cook for five to ten minutes over medium heat until sauce thickens. Add pasta to pan and toss well. Serve immediately. Makes four servings.

Lion Lucille Caruso, wife of P.D.G. James "Jim" Caruso,
Delta Lions Club, District 8-S
Metairie, LA, USA

SHRIMP AND CELERY STIR-FRY

⅓ c. chicken broth
3 Tbsp. rice-wine vinegar
2 Tbsp. reduced-sodium soy sauce
1½ Tbsp. cornstarch
¼ c. slivered almonds
1 Tbsp. vegetable oil
1½ lb. peeled and deveined medium shrimp

1 c. sliced celery
1 head bok choy (about 1½ lb.), trimmed and cut into strips (about 6 c.)
1 tsp. fennel seeds
1 tsp. grated fresh ginger
3 medium scallions (green parts only), chopped

In a cup, stir together broth, vinegar, soy sauce, and cornstarch. Set aside. Heat a wok or large skillet over medium heat. Add almonds and stir until golden, about 30 seconds. Remove to a plate and set aside. Add oil to wok. When oil is hot, add shrimp and stir-fry until shrimp are just pink, 2 to 3 minutes. Remove to another plate. Add celery, bok choy, fennel seeds, ginger, and half of broth mixture to wok. Cover and cook until vegetables are soft, 3 to 5 minutes. Return shrimp to wok along with remaining cornstarch mixture and scallions. Cook until thickened, stirring, about 2 minutes. Just before serving, sprinkle with almonds. Makes 4 servings.

Work time: 30 minutes. Total time: 30 minutes.

Per serving: 309 calories 40 g protein, 11 g fat, 922 mg sodium, 12 g carbohydrate, 259 mg cholesterol.

Mrs. Lucy Aiken, Clarence Lions Club
Clarence Center, NY, USA

TUNA TOMATO HASH

2 large baking potatoes (about 1 lb.)
¼ c. plus 1 Tbsp. oil
Salt and pepper

1 large onion
4 canned tomatoes
½ tsp. thyme
2 (6½ oz.) cans tuna (packed in oil)

Peel potatoes and cut into ¼ inch dice. In a nonstick frying pan, heat ¼ cup of the oil over medium-high heat. Add potatoes; sprinkle with ½ teaspoon salt and cook, stirring occasionally, until golden and crisp, about 15 minutes. Chop onion. Drain and chop tomatoes. When potatoes are done, remove from pan and set aside.

Add remaining 1 tablespoon oil to pan and heat over medium heat. Add onion and cook until soft, about 5 minutes. Add tomatoes, thyme, ¼ teaspoon salt, and ⅛ teaspoon pepper and cook until juices thicken, about 5 minutes. Add tuna with its oil and potatoes. Cook, stirring, until heated through, about 1 minute. Taste for seasoning and add salt and pepper if needed. Makes 4 servings.

Per serving: 511 calories, 25 g protein, 36 g fat, 976 mg sodium, 21 g carbohydrate, 51 mg cholesterol.

Joanne M. Wetzler, Clarence Lions Club
Clarence Center, NY, USA

PASTA AND TUNA AND ARTICHOKES

2 cloves garlic
9 oz. pkg. frozen artichoke hearts, thawed
2 (6½ oz.) cans tuna in oil
3 Tbsp. oil

Salt and pepper
3 Tbsp. butter
½ lb. spaghetti
1 Tbsp. chopped fresh parsley

Mince garlic. Cut artichokes hearts in halves. Drain tuna, pouring the oil into a saucepan. Heat the tuna oil with the additional 3 tablespoons oil over medium heat. Add garlic and cook 1 minute. Add the artichokes and cook 5 minutes. Remove from heat. Flake the tuna and add along with ¾ teaspoon salt, ¼ teaspoon pepper, and the butter. In a large pot of boiling salted water, cook the spaghetti until just done. Drain and return to the hot pot. Add tuna and artichoke mixture; toss, taste for seasoning, and salt and pepper if needed. Sprinkle with the parsley and serve. Makes 4 servings.

Per serving: 670 calories, 31 g protein, 39 g fat, 1185 mg sodium, 48 g carbohydrate, 74 mg cholesterol.

Joann M. Brownell, Clarence Lions Club
Clarence Center, NY, USA

CLASSIC CABBAGE ROLLS

1 medium head cabbage, cored
1½ c. chopped onion, *divided*
1 Tbsp. butter
2 (14½ oz.) cans Italian stewed
   tomatoes
4 garlic cloves, minced
2 Tbsp. brown sugar
1½ tsp. salt, *divided*

1 c. cooked rice
¼ c. ketchup
2 Tbsp. Worcestershire sauce
¼ tsp. pepper
1 lb. lean ground beef
¼ lb. bulk Italian sausage
½ c. V-8 juice (optional)

In a Dutch oven, cook cabbage in boiling water for 10 minutes or until outer leaves are tender; drain. Rinse in cold water; drain. Remove eight large outer leaves (refrigerate remaining cabbage for another use); set aside. In a saucepan, saute 1 cup onion in butter until tender. Add tomatoes, garlic, brown sugar, and ½ teaspoon salt. Simmer for 15 minutes, stirring occasionally.

Meanwhile, in a bowl, combine rice, ketchup, Worcestershire sauce, pepper, remaining onion, and salt. Add beef and sausage; mix well. Remove thick vein from cabbage leaves for easier rolling. Place about ½ cup meat mixture on each leaf; fold in sides. Starting at an unfolded edge, roll up leaf to completely enclose filling. Place, seam side down, in a skillet. Top with the sauce. Cover and cook over medium-low heat for 1 hour. Add V-8 juice if desired. Reduce heat to low; cook 20 minutes longer or until rolls are heated through and meat is no longer pink. Yield: 4 servings.

CANADIAN CHEDDAR AND ONION TARTS

Sufficient pastry for double crust
   9 inch pie (may substitute for
   frozen tart shells)
1 lb. extra old Cheddar cheese
2 Tbsp. butter
1 c. finely chopped onions

1 Tbsp. flour
½ tsp. dry mustard
2 eggs
1 c. light cream
1 tsp. Worcestershire sauce
Grated Parmesan cheese

Roll out pastry and line 24 tart shells. Cut Cheddar cheese into ¼ inch cubes. Divide cheese evenly among tart shells. Melt butter in medium frypan; saute onions until tender. Remove from heat. Add flour and dry mustard; toss to coat. Beat eggs; stir in cream and Worcestershire sauce. Blend in onion mixture. Divide egg-onion mixture evenly among tart shells (shells will be very full). Sprinkle each tart lightly with Parmesan cheese. Bake in 350°F. oven for 20 to 25 minutes or until set. Garnish as desired. Serve warm. Makes 2 dozen tarts.

Micheal and Ruth Bartolf, Oxbow and District Lions Club
Oxbow, Saskatchewan, Canada

PASTA WITH GREENS AND BEANS

Time: 30 minutes.

½ lb. whole wheat pasta shells or
  flats
3 tsp. olive oil
3 cloves garlic
1 large bunch leafy greens or
  bunch of broccoli

½ c. water
Pinch of sea salt
½ tsp. dried marjoram (optional)
1½ c. cooked chickpeas or white
  beans, well drained

Cook pasta al dente; drain and toss while still warm with 1 teaspoon of olive oil. While pasta is cooking, saute garlic in 2 teaspoons olive oil, using low heat for 1 minute. Add chopped greens or broccoli floret; saute briefly, then add water and seasonings if desired. Cover and cook for 4 to 5 minutes. Add the beans and simmer gently for 3 to 5 minutes longer until greens are tender and beans are heated through. Toss the pasta and vegetable bean mixture together. Check for seasonings and serve to 3 hungry people.

Comments: Good way to get those greens and beans into your diet.
PDG Jim Schiebel, Hilton Lions Club
Hilton, NY, USA

OATMEAL WALNUT PATTIES

2 eggs
1 c. ground walnuts
1 medium minced onion
1 Tbsp. soy sauce

1 c. rolled oats
¼ c. evaporated milk
1 tsp. salt
Sage (if desired)

Mix together. Let mixture stand for a few hours or overnight. Combine all ingredients. Drop by spoonful and brown in hot oil. Cover with a gravy, such as cream of mushroom soup thinned with ½ cup of water or tomato sauce. Simmer ½ hour or bake at 350° in oven until bubbly.

Bertha Vandergrift, Fairmont East Grafton Road Lions Club
Fairmont, WV

"The only limits are, as always, those of vision."
James Broughton

"I wash everything on the gentle cycle. It's much more humane."

"In three words I can sum up everything I've learned about life. It goes on."
Robert Frost

COLD SPICY PEANUT NOODLES

8 oz. uncooked linguini
5 Tbsp. reduced-fat peanut butter
3 Tbsp. rice-wine vinegar
1 Tbsp. reduced-sodium soy
   sauce
1 tsp. sesame oil

½ c. diced red bell pepper
¼ c. chopped fresh cilantro
½ tsp. crushed red-pepper flakes
1 head broccoli
1 tsp. sesame seeds, toasted

In a large saucepot of boiling salted water, cook linguini according to package directions until just *al dente*.

Meanwhile, in a 1 cup glass measuring cup, place the peanut butter, ¼ cup water, the vinegar, soy sauce, and oil. Place cup in microwave and cook on HIGH 20 to 30 seconds until peanut butter is softened; stir. Drain linguini. Toss with peanut mixture, peppers, cilantro, and pepper flakes; chill. Cut the broccoli into florets; cut stems into pieces. In 10 inch nonstick skillet, place broccoli; add ¼ cup water. Cover; place over medium heat and steam about 10 minutes, until crisp-tender or until desired doneness. Drain and toss with the toasted sesame seeds. Season to taste. Makes 4 servings.

Work time: 10 minutes. Total time: 30 minutes.

Per serving: 372 calories, 15 g protein, 10 g fat, 264 mg sodium, 57 g carbohydrate, 0 mg cholesterol.

Mrs. Lucy Aiken, Clarence Lions Club
Clarence Center, NY, USA

AUTUMN APPLE RICE PILAF

Time: 50 minutes.

1 c. water
1 c. apple juice
1 c. short grain brown rice
1 tsp. oil
1 tsp. rice syrup

Pinch of sea salt
2 medium sized red apples
½ c. thinly sliced celery
⅓ c. chopped walnuts

Wash rice. Bring apple juice, water, rice syrup, oil, and salt to a boil and add rice. Reduce heat, cover tightly, and cook over low heat until all liquid is absorbed (approximately 50 minutes). Chop nuts, slice celery, and prepare apples by quartering, removing core and chopping coarsely. When rice is cooked, add the apple, celery, and nuts and heat thoroughly. Apples and celery may be blanched before adding to rice if less chewy dish is preferred. Serves 4 to 6.

Comments: Serve with baked squash and dark green vegetables.

PDG Jim Schiebel, Hilton Lions Club
Hilton, NY, USA

PARMESAN RICE CAKES

1 onion
3 Tbsp. butter
1 c. rice
2 c. chicken stock or canned
    broth
1½ oz. Parmesan cheese (about
    ½ c. grated)

1 slice whole-wheat toast
3 eggs
Salt and pepper
2 Tbsp. oil

Chop onion. In a large frying pan, melt 1 tablespoon butter over medium heat. Add onion and cook until softened, about 5 minutes. Stir in rice and cook 2 minutes. Add stock and bring to a boil. Cover, reduce heat, and simmer until rice is tender, about 20 minutes; cool slightly.

Meanwhile, grate cheese. Crumble toast and add to rice with eggs, cheese, ½ teaspoon salt, and ¼ teaspoon pepper. Shape the rice mixture into 8 patties. In a large frying pan, melt 1 tablespoon butter with 1 tablespoon oil over medium-high heat. Fry 4 patties, turning once, until golden brown, about 5 minutes. Remove from pan and keep warm. Melt the remaining 1 tablespoon butter with the remaining 1 tablespoon oil and fry the remaining patties. Makes 8 servings.

Per serving: 220 calories, 7 g protein, 12 g fat, 279 mg sodium, 21 g carbohydrate, 95 mg cholesterol.

Barbara Joy Hess, Clarence Lions Club
Clarence Center, NY, USA

TEX-MEX PIZZA

3 Tbsp. oil
1 onion, sliced
½ c. chopped green pepper
Salt
6 oz. sharp Cheddar cheese
    (about 1½ c. grated)

10 oz. pkg. refrigerated pizza
    dough
2 tsp. chili powder
1 c. spaghetti sauce
½ c. corn kernels
¼ lb. sliced pepperoni

Heat oven to 425°. In a frying pan, heat 2 tablespoons oil over medium heat. Add onion. Cook until softened, about 15 minutes. Add peppers and ¼ teaspoon salt. Cook 5 minutes, stirring occasionally. Grate cheese. Brush ½ tablespoon oil in a 15x10 inch cookie pan with sides. Press dough into pan. Bake until lightly browned, 7 to 8 minutes. Brush edge of crust with remaining ½ tablespoon oil. Stir chili powder into spaghetti sauce and spread over crust. Top with onion mixture, corn, cheese, and pepperoni. Bake until cheese has melted, about 8 minutes. Makes 8 slices.

Per slice: 340 calories, 13 g protein, 21 g fat, 827 mg sodium, 25 g carbohydrate, 34 mg cholesterol.

Joanne M. Wetzler, Clarence Lions Club
Clarence Center, NY, USA

2075-99

GRILLED PIZZA

1 large tomato (about 10 oz.)
Salt and pepper
4 oz. Mozzarella cheese (about 1 c. shredded)

½ clove garlic
10 oz. roll refrigerated pizza dough
¼ c. olive oil
1 Tbsp. chopped fresh basil

Cut the tomato in half, discard the seeds, and chop the flesh. Combine the chopped tomato with ½ teaspoon salt and let stand. Heat grill. Shred cheese. Mince garlic. Drain juice from chopped tomato and add garlic and ⅛ teaspoon pepper. On a lightly floured work surface, shape the dough into a rectangle, approximately 13x9 inches. Brush with 1 tablespoon oil and put oil-side down on the hot grill. Cook until dough starts to brown, about 3 minutes. Brush surface with 1 tablespoon oil and turn the dough over. Lower grill heat or move crust to a cooler part of grill. Spread tomato mixture on top of crust. Drizzle with remaining 2 tablespoons oil. Sprinkle cheese on top. Cover grill and cook until cheese has melted, 3 to 5 minutes. Sprinkle with the basil and serve. Makes 6 slices.

Per slice: 262 calories, 8 g protein, 15 g fat, 428 mg sodium, 24 g carbohydrate, 15 mg cholesterol.

Joanne M. Wetzler, Clarence Lions Club
Clarence Center, NY, USA

BEEF TORTILLA PIZZA
(27 minutes)

1 lb. lean ground beef
1 medium onion, chopped
1 tsp. dried oregano leaves
1 tsp. salt
4 large (10 inch) flour tortillas

1 medium tomato, chopped
1 Tbsp. thinly sliced fresh basil leaves
1 c. shredded Mozzarella cheese
¼ c. grated Parmesan cheese

Brown ground beef and onion in skillet over medium heat 8 to 10 minutes or until beef is no longer pink. Pour off drippings. Stir oregano and salt into beef. Lightly brush tortillas with oil. Bake tortillas on 2 baking sheets in preheated 400°F. oven for 3 minutes. Spoon beef mixture evenly over top of each tortilla; top with an equal amount of tomato. Sprinkle with basil and cheeses. Return to oven and bake 12 to 14 minutes or until lightly browned. Makes 4 servings.

Mrs. Mike Nowicki, Clarence Lions Club
Clarence Center, NY, USA

"There is a time in the life of every problem when
it is big enough to see, yet small enough to solve."
Mike Leavitt

SICILIAN-STYLE PIZZA

12 ripe tomatoes (about 5 lb.)
1 large onion, chopped
2 garlic cloves, minced
2 Tbsp. olive oil
2½ tsp. dried oregano, divided
¼ tsp. salt
¼ tsp. pepper

1 (2 lb.) pkg. frozen pizza or
   bread dough, thawed
1 (15 oz.) container part-skim
   Ricotta cheese
½ c. shredded Mozzarella cheese
2 Tbsp. grated Parmesan cheese

Preheat oven to 450°F. Reserve two tomatoes; seed and coarsely chop the remainder. In a large skillet, saute onion and garlic in oil until soft. Add the chopped tomatoes, 2 teaspoons oregano, salt, and pepper; bring to a boil, then simmer until thickened, about 20 minutes.

Spray two baking sheets with nonstick cooking spray. With floured hands, stretch and pat dough into two 10 inch rounds; place on baking sheets. Spoon the sauce over each round, then spread on the Ricotta. Slice the remaining two tomatoes; place over the Ricotta, then sprinkle the Mozzarella, Parmesan, and remaining oregano over the tomatoes. Bake 20 minutes or until the crust is golden-brown on the bottom and the topping is bubbly. Makes 12 slices.

Per slice: 321 calories, 14 g protein, 9 g fat, 510 mg sodium, 47 g carbohydrate, 15 mg cholesterol.

Mrs. Mike Nowicki, Clarence Lions Club
Clarence Center, NY, USA

SALAMI AND ARTICHOKE PIZZA

Vegetable oil
Cornmeal
2 tomatoes
Salt and pepper
4 canned artichoke hearts
¾ oz. Parmesan cheese (about ¼
   c. grated)

3 oz. Mozzarella cheese
1 lb. frozen pizza dough, thawed
¼ c. tomato paste
¼ tsp. dried basil
¼ tsp. dried oregano
10 slices salami (about 2 oz.)
¼ c. black olives

Heat oven to 450°. Oil 2 large baking pans and sprinkle with cornmeal. Slice tomatoes and sprinkle with salt and pepper. Halve artichoke hearts. Grate Parmesan. Slice Mozzarella. Divide dough in half. Shape into two approximately 10 inch circles. Put on baking sheets. Spread tomato paste over each and sprinkle with basil and oregano. Top with salami, tomatoes, Mozzarella, artichoke, olives, and Parmesan. Bake until golden brown, about 20 minutes. Makes 16 servings.

Per serving: 127 calories, 5 protein, 4 g fat, 302 mg sodium, 16 g carbohydrate, 8 mg cholesterol.

Joann M. Brownell, Clarence Lions Club
Clarence Center, NY, USA

BASIC PIZZA DOUGH

1 c. hot water
1 tsp. sugar
1 env. active dry yeast

1 tsp. salt
2 to 4 Tbsp. oil
2½ c. flour

Measure water into large mixing bowl; stir in sugar. When lukewarm, sprinkle with yeast. Let stand 10 minutes. Stir well. Stir in salt, oil, and 1½ cups flour. Beat until smooth. Stir in additional flour. You may need a little extra flour to be able to gather dough into a slightly sticky ball. On floured board, knead dough for about 5 minutes or until smooth and elastic. Form into a ball, cover with waxed paper, and let rest for 10 minutes.

To make two 15 inch pizzas, cut dough in half. On lightly floured board, roll out one piece into a circle, 15 to 18 inches across. Place on greased pizza pan. Carefully stretch and pull dough with fingers to fit pan. Repeat with second piece of dough. Let rest for 15 minutes before adding toppings. For slightly thicker crust, let dough rise for about 30 minutes. Add the toppings just before baking. Top with whatever your heart desires. Bake at 450° for 10 minutes, then 350° for 10 to 15 minutes more.

Micheal and Ruth Bartolf, Oxbow and District Lions Club
Oxbow, Saskatchewan, Canada

EASY LASAGNA

8 oz. lasagna noodles
3 c. shredded Mozzarella cheese
1 lb. cottage cheese
1 (32 oz.) jar spaghetti sauce

1 lb. ground beef
¼ to ¾ c. water
1 tsp. salt
¼ c. Parmesan cheese

Brown ground beef and drain fat. Add spaghetti sauce, salt, and water. Boil for several minutes. In a 9x13 inch pan, layer the sauce, ½ of the uncooked noodles, 1 cup of cottage cheese, and ⅓ cup of the Mozzarella and Parmesan cheeses. Cover with foil. Bake at 350° for 55 to 60 minutes. Remove foil and let stand for ten minutes before serving.

Deryl Fox, Saginaw Lions Club

MICROWAVE LASAGNA

8 oz. lasagna noodles (not
    cooked)
1 lb. hamburger
1 qt. Hunt's spaghetti sauce

3 c. Mozzarella cheese
2 c. cottage cheese
½ c. Parmesan cheese

Cook meat and drain. Add sauce to meat with ½ cup water. Cover and cook till it bubbles. In 9x13 inch dish, place 3 large spoons of sauce in dish, then layer of noodles, cheeses, and end with sauce. Cover with plastic. Cook on FULL power for 30 minutes. Leave set 10 minutes before serving.

Lion Ida Rohrer, Moundbuilders Lions Club
Newark, OH, USA

MIRACLE LASAGNA

1 (28 oz.) jar spaghetti sauce
6 dry lasagna noodles
1 (15 oz.) ctn. Ricotta cheese

2 c. shredded Mozzarella cheese
¼ c. grated Parmesan cheese

In 2 quart baking dish (11x7 inches), spread 1 cup sauce. Top with 3 dry noodles, Ricotta cheese, Parmesan cheese, 1 cup Mozzarella cheese, and 1 cup sauce. Top with remaining dry noodles and sauce. Cover; bake at 375° for 1 hour. Top with remaining cheese. Place in oven about 5 minutes. Let stand 5 minutes.

This is also very good with browned hamburg in layer 2.

Lion Gloria Bonager, East Prospect Lions Club
East Prospect, PA, USA

"Accept that some days you're the pigeon, and some days you're the statue."
Roger C. Anderson

"All the things I really like to do are either immoral, illegal, or fattening."
Alexander Woollcott

"To get something done a committee should consist of no more than three people, two of whom are absent."
Robert Copeland

"A consultant is someone who saves his client almost enough to pay his fee."
Arnold Glasgow

LASAGNA

2 onions
1 carrot
1 rib celery
3 cloves garlic
1 lb. ground beef
Salt and pepper
2 tsp. dried oregano
¾ tsp. dried thyme
2 bay leaves
4½ c. canned crushed tomatoes

½ lb. Mozzarella cheese (about 2 c. shredded)
2 oz. Parmesan cheese (about ⅔ c. grated)
1 egg
1 lb. 6 oz. Ricotta cheese (about 2½ c.)
¼ c. chopped fresh parsley
Pinch of nutmeg
10 oz. lasagna noodles

Chop the onion, the carrot, and the celery. Mince the garlic. In a large frying pan, cook the ground beef, onion, carrot, and celery over medium-high heat until the meat is browned. Stir in the garlic, 2½ teaspoons salt, ½ teaspoon pepper, the oregano, thyme, bay leaves, tomatoes, and 1½ cups water. Cook, uncovered, stirring occasionally, until thick, 45 to 50 minutes. Shred the Mozzarella. Grate the Parmesan. Beat the egg and stir in the Ricotta, parsley, ½ cup Parmesan, the nutmeg, ½ teaspoon salt, and ¼ teaspoon pepper. Cook the lasagna noodles in boiling salted water, in batches if necessary, until almost tender, but not entirely cooked through, about 10 minutes. Drain.

Assembly and cooking: Heat the oven to 375°. Spread ⅕ of the sauce in a 13x9 inch pan. Top with ¼ of the noodles. Spread with ½ of the Ricotta mixture and ⅕ of the remaining sauce. Top with another ¼ of the noodles. Spread with ⅕ of the sauce and sprinkle with ½ of the Mozzarella. Top with another ¼ of the noodles and the remaining Ricotta mixture. Spread with another ⅕ of the sauce. Top with the remaining noodles and sauce. Sprinkle with the remaining Mozzarella and Parmesan. Bake until browned and bubbling, about 35 minutes. Let stand 10 minutes before cutting. Makes 8 servings.

Work time: 55 minutes. Total time: 2 hours.

Per serving: 580 calories, 34 g protein, 31 g fat, 1437 mg sodium, 41 g carbohydrate, 127 mg cholesterol.

Barbara Joy Hess, Clarence Lions Club
Clarence Center, NY, USA

"Everybody should believe in something; I believe I'll have another drink."

❧ ❧ ❧

"The absolute fundamental aim is to make money out of satisfying customers."

Sir John Egan

LASAGNE

1½ lb. ground beef
½ c. chopped onion
1 lb. can tomatoes
16 oz. can tomato paste
⅓ c. water
1 clove garlic, minced (I use garlic salt)

1 tsp. pepper (salt slightly)
½ lb. lasagne noodles, cooked
2 (6 oz.) pkg. Mozzarella cheese
½ lb. Velveeta cheese
½ c. Parmesan cheese

Brown ground beef and onion in large skillet. Drain off excess liquid. Add tomatoes, tomato paste, water, garlic, and seasonings. Cook lasagne noodles by package directions. In greased 9x13 inch baking dish, layer noodles and meat mixture, then top with ½ cup Parmesan cheese. Bake at 350° for 30 minutes.

Pam Caldwell, Mexico Sunrise Lions Club
Mexico, MO

FIVE-CHEESE LASAGNA

6 (16 oz.) pkg. lasagna noodles
10 lb. bulk Italian sausage
10 medium onions, chopped
30 garlic cloves, minced
11 (29 oz.) cans tomato sauce
⅔ c. dried basil
3 Tbsp. ground nutmeg
2 Tbsp. fennel seed, crushed
1 Tbsp. salt
1 Tbsp. pepper

6 (32 oz.) ctn. Ricotta cheese
10 lb. shredded Mozzarella cheese
4 (8 oz.) ctn. grated Parmesan cheese
5 (5 oz.) blocks Romano cheese, grated
10 (6 oz.) pkg. sliced Provolone cheese, cut into strips
1 c. minced fresh parsley

Cook noodles in boiling water for 5 minutes; rinse in cold water and drain. Cook sausage, onions, and garlic until meat is no longer pink; drain. Add the tomato sauce and seasonings; bring to a boil. Reduce heat; simmer, uncovered, for 50 to 60 minutes.

Grease ten 13x9x2 inch baking dishes. In each dish, layer about 1½ cups tomato sauce, four noodles, about 1¼ cups Ricotta, 1½ cups Mozzarella, about ⅓ cup Parmesan, ¼ cup Romano, and three slices Provolone. Repeat layers. Top with four noodles, about 1½ cups of tomato sauce, 1 cup Mozzarella, and about 1 tablespoon parsley. Bake, uncovered, at 375° for 40 to 50 minutes or until browned and bubbly. Let stand 10 to 15 minutes before serving. Yield: 120 to 150 servings.

"I wear my wife's eyeglasses because she wants me to see things her way."
Jayson Feinburg

MEXICAN LASAGNA

1 lb. lean ground beef
1 (16 oz.) can refried beans
2 tsp. dried oregano
1 tsp. ground cumin
¾ tsp. garlic powder
12 uncooked lasagna noodles
2½ c. water

2½ c. picante sauce or salsa
¾ c. sliced green onion
2 c. sour cream
1 (2.2 oz.) can sliced black olives, drained
1 c. shredded Monterey Jack cheese

Combine beef, beans, oregano, cumin, and garlic. Place four of uncooked noodles on bottom of 9x13 inch pan. Spread ½ the beef mixture over the noodles. Top with more noodles and remaining beef mixture. Cover with remaining noodles. Combine water and salsa. Pour over all. Cover tightly with foil. Bake at 350° for 1½ hours or until noodles are tender.

Combine sour cream, onions, and olives. Spoon over casserole; top with cheese. Bake, uncovered, until cheese is melted, about 5 minutes. Yield: 12 servings.

Mexican-Italian - very tasty!!

Edith C. Rich, Bullhead City Lions Club
Bullhead City, AZ, USA

SEAFOOD LASAGNE

8 lasagne noodles
2 Tbsp. butter or margarine
1 c. chopped onion
1 (8 oz.) pkg. cream cheese
1½ c. creamed cottage cheese
1 beaten egg
2 tsp. basil
½ tsp. salt
⅛ tsp. pepper
2 (10 oz.) tins cream of mushroom soup

⅓ c. milk
⅓ c. dry white wine or dry vermouth
1 (5 oz.) tin crab
1 lb. shelled, deveined, cooked shrimp or pickerel
¼ c. grated Parmesan cheese
½ c. shredded sharp Cheddar cheese

Preheat oven to 350°F. Cook noodles according to package directions. Drain. Place 4 in a buttered 9x13 inch cake pan. In a skillet over medium heat, cook onion in butter. Add cream cheese, cottage cheese, beaten egg, basil, salt, and pepper to skillet and mix well. Spread half the mixture over noodles. Combine soup, milk, and wine. Stir in crab and shrimp. Spoon half of mixture over cheese layer. Repeat all layers. Sprinkle the Parmesan cheese over top and bake, uncovered, for 45 minutes. Remove from oven and sprinkle with sharp Cheddar cheese. Place under broiler, watching closely until browned and bubbly. Let stand 15 minutes, cut into squares, and serve.

This dish is great as a main course accompanied with a green salad and garlic toast.

Lion Diane Milliard, Lake of the Woods Lions Club
Kenora, Ontario, Canada

CHICKEN LASAGNE

3 c. fresh mushrooms
2 c. chopped onion
2 pkg. Knorr Hollandaise sauce
1 lb. (oven ready) lasagne noodles
2 lb. cooked, sliced chicken
  breasts (about 6 chicken
  breasts)
Salt and pepper to taste

2 (12 oz.) cans asparagus tips
1 tsp. basil
1 tsp. oregano
1 tsp. garlic powder
3 c. Mozzarella cheese
1 c. fresh grated Parmesan
  cheese

Preheat oven to 350°F. Saute mushrooms, onions, chicken, and spices until tender. Cook Hollandaise sauce according to package directions. Spread a small amount of Hollandaise sauce in pan. Place a layer of noodles, half of the chicken mixture, salt and pepper to taste, and cheese sauce. Layer asparagus. Repeat layers of cheese sauce, noodles, chicken, and Parmesan until all used, ending with Parmesan. Bake in a 10x13 inch baking dish for 35 minutes.

Oven ready lasagne noodles can be used right out of the package.

Lion Donna Walsh, Lake of the Woods Lions Club
Kenora, Ontario, Canada

LASAGNA SAUCE

½ c. olive oil
1 lb. sausage
2 lb. ground beef
3 Tbsp. garlic, chopped
1½ c. onions, chopped
¾ c. green pepper, chopped
4 cans Hunt's tomato sauce with
  tomato bits
2 c. water
¼ c. chopped parsley
1 c. burgundy wine

½ c. chopped pepperoncini (a
  pepper sold in jars)
2 tsp. savory seasoning
2 tsp. basil
2 bay leaves
2 tsp. oregano
2 tsp. marjoram
1 Tbsp. salt
1 Tbsp. black pepper
Lasagna noodles
¾ lb. mushrooms, sauteed in
  butter

Cook meat until it loses its red color. Add remaining ingredients, except for noodles and mushrooms, and simmer for 3 hours.

Place some of the sauce in 13x9x2 and 8x8x2 inch baking dishes. Put in a row of lasagna noodles. Put a pint of Ricotta cheese, cut with ½ cup warm milk, over the noodles. Add another row of noodles and cover with sauteed mushrooms and more sauce. Add more noodles and cover with a blend of Cheddar, Jack, and American shredded cheeses and more sauce. Add more noodles and top with sauce, a blend of Parmesan and Romano cheeses, and garlic powder. Cover with foil and bake at 350°F. until hot and bubbly, about 30 minutes.

Victor L. Dreyer, Sr., Keizer Lions Club
Salem, OR

SAUSAGE LASAGNA WRAPS

6 lasagna noodles
½ lb. sliced Mozzarella cheese
16 oz. spaghetti sauce

Parmesan cheese
1 lb. smoked sausage (kielbasa is
   good too)

Cook and drain the lasagna noodles. Divide the smoked sausage into 6 pieces. Split lengthwise and stuff with ½ slice of Mozzarella cheese. Wrap each piece in a noodle. Place in baking dish and cover with spaghetti sauce. Sprinkle with Parmesan cheese. Bake at 350° for 30 minutes or microwave on HIGH for 15 minutes.

Lion Susan E. Shaffer, Connumach Lions Club
Davidsville, PA, USA

TEX-MEX SPAGHETTI

1 onion
2 cloves garlic
1 lb. ground beef
Salt
14½ oz. can tomatoes (about 1¾
   c.)

8 oz. can tomato sauce (about 1
   c.)
1 Tbsp. wine vinegar
2 tsp. chili powder
2 tsp. ground cumin
¼ tsp. ground cinnamon
½ lb. spaghetti

Chop onion. Mince garlic. In a frying pan, cook ground beef over medium-high heat until no longer pink. Reduce heat to low. Add onion, garlic, and 1¾ teaspoons salt. Cook until onion is tender, about 5 minutes. Add tomatoes with their juice, the tomato sauce, vinegar, chili powder, cumin, and cinnamon. Break up tomatoes with the side of a spoon. Continue simmering until thick and flavorful, about 20 minutes.

Meanwhile, cook spaghetti in a large pot of boiling salted water until done. Drain. Serve with the sauce. Makes 4 servings.

Per serving: 618 calories, 28 g protein, 32 g fat, 1569 mg sodium, 54 g carbohydrate, 96 mg cholesterol.

Barbara Joy Hess, Clarence Lions Club
Clarence Center, NY, USA

CHICKEN SPAGHETTI

1 can cream of chicken soup
1 can cream of mushroom soup
1 can water
1 box spaghetti

1 whole chicken, cooked (I use
   canned white chicken breast)
Shredded cheese

Cook spaghetti and drain. Boil chicken and tear into pieces. Warm soups and water. Layer spaghetti, chicken, soup, and cheese. Bake at 350° for 20 minutes or until bubbly.

Pam Caldwell, Mexico Sunrise Lions Club
Mexico, MO

SPAGHETTI WITH SMOTHERED ONIONS

1½ Tbsp. bacon drippings
1½ lb. onions, thinly sliced
½ tsp. salt
½ tsp. freshly ground pepper
½ c. dry white wine

8 oz. spaghetti, cooked
2 Tbsp. chopped fresh parsley
⅓ c. freshly grated Parmesan
cheese

Heat drippings in a heavy skillet over medium high heat; add onion. Cover and reduce heat to low and cook 45 minutes. Uncover and cook over medium heat, stirring often, until onion browns and liquid evaporates. Add salt, pepper, and wine. Cook until wine evaporates. Toss with pasta, parsley, and cheese. Makes four side dish servings.

PDG Doris J. Myers, Mexico Noon Lions Club
Mexico, MO

SPAGHETTI AND SAUCE

1 lb. ground round steak
3 large onions, chopped fine
⅓ c. vegetable oil
½ c. Crisco
1 small can peeled green chillies
    or 3 green peppers, diced
3 cloves garlic, minced
1 qt. tomato juice

1 tsp. salt
½ tsp. pepper
1 small can sliced mushrooms
1 c. olives, chopped
1 bay leaf
½ lb. grated Parmesan or
    American cheese
2 lb. spaghetti

Brown onions and steak in fat and oil, then add chillies, minced garlic, tomato juice, salt, and pepper and simmer slowly for two hours. During the last half hour, add mushrooms and olives. The tomato liquid should be allowed to evaporate to make the sauce thick and rich.

Cook spaghetti with bay leaf in boiling salted water. When tender, drain and remove bay leaf. Pile on large platter; cover with cheese. Pour over the sauce and let stand in hot oven for a few minutes. Serves 6.

Lion Wilma Ell, Southport Lions Club
Indianapolis, IN, USA

"The government deficit is the difference between the amount of money the government spends and the amount it has the nerve to collect."
Sam Ewing

"Good friends are good for your health."
Irwin Sarason

SPAGHETTI SAUCE WITH MEATBALLS

Sauce:

5 cloves garlic, crushed
1¼ c. olive oil
10 medium tomatoes
5 small cans tomato sauce
5 small cans tomato paste
1¼ qt. water

1⅔ Tbsp. basil
⅔ c. parsley, chopped
3⅓ Tbsp. salt
1¼ tsp. pepper
2½ c. onion, chopped
4 medium bay leaves

Meatballs:

2½ c. Parmesan cheese, grated
⅓ c. parsley, chopped
5 cloves garlic, crushed
2½ c. milk
10 medium eggs, beaten

2½ Tbsp. salt
⅔ tsp. black pepper
5 lb. ground beef
1¼ qt. bread crumbs

Sauce: Saute onions and garlic in oil until onions are transparent and wilted. Add tomatoes, water, and spices. Bring to simmer and cook, covered, for 4 to 5 hours.

Meatballs: Combine all ingredients in mixer bowl; mix at medium speed until well blended. Form 1 inch meatballs and fry in oil at 375° until well browned. Transfer to cooking sauce. Serve over hot cooked spaghetti or vermicelli. Makes 30 servings.

John Hamner, Bellville Lions Club
Bellville, GA, USA

"Wealth is something you acquire so you can share it, not keep it."
LaDonna Harris

"Without music, life is a journey through a desert."
Pat Conroy

"Think big thoughts, but relish small pleasures."
H. Jackson Brown, Jr.

SPAGHETTI AND MEAT BALLS

Sauce:

2 Tbsp. cooking oil
1 large onion, chopped
3 large cloves garlic, chopped
2 (15 oz.) cans tomato paste

¼ c. sugar
3 tsp. salt
1 tsp. black pepper
8 c. boiling water

Meat Balls:

3 lb. ground round
3 cloves garlic
2 eggs
1 Tbsp. salt

½ tsp. black pepper
3 Tbsp. bread crumbs
2 Tbsp. grated Parmesan cheese

Saute finely chopped onion and garlic in cooking oil. Add tomato paste and rinse cans with one can of water. Add sugar, salt, and pepper and continue to fry slowly for 10 or 15 minutes. Add boiling water; cover and cook slowly 3 hours. Mix all meat ball ingredients well and shape into meat balls. Bake in 375° oven for about 30 minutes. Add to sauce and cook. Makes about 10 large or 24 small meatballs.

To cook spaghetti: Bring 5 or 6 quarts of water to boil in large pot. Add spaghetti or macaroni and cook according to package directions. Use about 2 pounds long spaghetti, broken in halves, or 1 cup of macaroni per person. Drain cooked spaghetti. Put in large container and cover with sauce. Top each serving with sauce. Sprinkle with Parmesan cheese and serve.

Mildred Court, Stafford-Missouri City Lions Club
Stafford, TX, USA

SPAGHETTI WITH CHERRY-TOMATO SAUCE

Salt
1 clove garlic
1 pt. cherry tomatoes
1 scallion

2 Tbsp. olive oil
8 oz. spaghetti
2 Tbsp. butter
¼ c. grated Parmesan cheese

Bring a large pot of salted water to a boil. Mince the garlic. Cut the tomatoes into quarters. Chop the white part of the scallion and slice the green tops. In a frying pan, heat the oil over low heat. Add the garlic and the white part of the scallion. Cook, stirring, until fragrant, about 30 seconds. Add the tomatoes and ½ teaspoon salt. Cook until slightly softened, 2 to 3 minutes. Set aside. Cook the spaghetti in the boiling water until just done. Drain and return to the warm pot. Toss with the butter and the tomato mixture. Serve sprinkled with Parmesan cheese and the scallion tops. Makes 4 servings.

Per serving: 356 calories, 10 g protein, 15 g fat, 570 mg sodium, 45 mg carbohydrate, 19 mg cholesterol.

Mrs. Lucy Aiken, Clarence Lions Club
Clarence Center, NY, USA

DAD'S TWENTY MINUTE SPAGHETTI SAUCE

1 (12 oz.) can tomato paste
3 c. water
2 Tbsp. dry minced onion
1 Tbsp. grated Parmesan cheese
1 Tbsp. sugar (you can use a
  sugar substitute, such as
  Sweet 'N Low or Equal)

1 tsp. Italian herb seasoning
½ tsp. garlic powder
⅛ tsp. pepper
1 beef bouillon cube
½ tsp. salt (may be omitted)

Combine all ingredients in a heavy saucepan. Cover and simmer 20 minutes. Stir occasionally. Makes 4 cups of sauce that tastes like you cooked it all day!!!

Dad's Italian Meatballs:

4 slices bread
½ c. water
2 eggs
1 lb. ground beef
¼ c. Parmesan cheese

2 Tbsp. parsley
¼ tsp. oregano
Dash of pepper
1 tsp. salt (optional)

Soak slices of bread in ½ cup water for 2 or 3 minutes. Add eggs and mix well. Mix with ground beef, Parmesan cheese, parsley, oregano, pepper, and salt. With wet hands, form the mixture into small meatballs (about 24, depending on size). Brown slowly in 2 tablespoons hot oil. (You can use nonstick spray instead.) Carefully turn them to brown all over. Add to a double batch of the sauce above. Will serve 6 or 8.

Serve with your favorite pasta and garlic bread.

Porter Schoff, PID, Portsmouth Lions Club
Portsmouth, NH, USA

SPAGHETTI SAUCE

2 lb. ground beef
1 lb. pork sausage
¼ c. olive oil
2 large onions, chopped
2 large green peppers, chopped
2 Tbsp. garlic, chopped
4 cans Hunt's tomato sauce with
  tomato bits
1 c. burgundy wine

½ c. water
1 Tbsp. Italian herbs
1 tsp. basil
1 tsp. savory seasoning
½ tsp. cayenne
Salt and pepper to taste
¾ lb. chopped mushrooms
MSG (optional)

Cook meat until it loses its red color. Add onions, green peppers, and garlic. Cook until vegetables are tender. Add remaining ingredients, except mushrooms, and simmer for three hours. Saute mushrooms in butter and add to sauce. If desired, add MSG before serving. Serve sauce over hot cooked spaghetti.

Victor L. Dreyer, Sr., Keizer Lions Club
Salem, OR

FETTUCINE WITH CREAM, BASIL, ROMANO

2 Tbsp. butter
4 green onions, chopped
½ c. whipping cream
½ c. freshly ground Romano or
  Parmesan or ¼ c. each (I use
  each) cheese

⅓ c. chopped fresh basil
½ lb. fettuccine
Salt and fresh ground pepper
Additional cheese

Melt butter in medium skillet over medium heat until beginning to brown. Add green onions and stir until softened, about 1 minute. Add cream and simmer until beginning to thicken, about 1 minute. Mix in ½ cup (¼) of cheese and chopped fresh basil.

Meanwhile, cook fettuccine in large pot of boiling salted water until just tender, but still firm to bite, stirring occasionally. Drain well. Return to hot pot. Add sauce and stir to coat. Season with salt and pepper. Serve immediately. Sprinkle with additional cheese.

Sarah Wehling, Bothell Lions Club
Bothell, WA, USA

CURRIED NOODLES AND SHRIMP

8 oz. spaghetti or Chinese egg
  noodles
Salt
2 Tbsp. oil
1 green pepper
2 carrots
2 scallions
1 clove garlic

¼ c. salted peanuts
1 Tbsp. minced fresh ginger
1 Tbsp. curry powder
½ tsp. cumin
1 Tbsp. soy sauce
8 oz. can tomato sauce
1 lb. cooked medium shrimp

Cook spaghetti in a large pot of boiling salted water until done. Drain and toss with 1 tablespoon oil. Meanwhile, cut pepper into approximately 1 inch pieces. Grate carrots. Cut scallion into piece about 1 inch long. Mince garlic. Chop peanuts.

In a large frying pan, heat remaining 1 tablespoon oil over medium-high heat. Add green pepper; cover and reduce heat to low. Cook 5 minutes. Add carrots and scallion. Cover and cook until tender, about 5 minutes. Push vegetables aside and add garlic, ginger, curry powder, and cumin to the pan. Cook 1 minute. Increase heat to medium and stir in soy sauce, ½ cup water, the tomato sauce, and ¼ teaspoon salt. Cover and let simmer 1 minute. Stir in spaghetti and shrimp. Cook, stirring occasionally, until heated through, about 3 minutes. Sprinkle with peanuts before serving. Makes 4 servings.

Work time: 30 minutes. Total time: 30 minutes.

Per serving: 487 calories, 35 g protein, 14 g fat, 1083 mg sodium, 56 g carbohydrate, 221 mg cholesterol.

Mrs. Mike Nowicki, Clarence Lions Club
Clarence Center, NY, USA

BUCKWHEAT NOODLES WITH SCALLOPS

Time: 30 minutes.

1 c. water
1 Tbsp. lemon juice
½ lb. bay scallops
1 tsp. grated ginger root
1 Tbsp. rice vinegar
1 tsp. barley malt syrup

1 Tbsp. olive oil
1 Tbsp. tamari sauce
1 Tbsp. mirin
6 oz. buckwheat noodles
2 Tbsp. chopped chives

Bring water and lemon juice to a boil; add scallops. Reduce heat and simmer 2 to 3 minutes. Drain and place in large salad bowl. Combine the ginger root, vinegar, oil, tamari sauce, and mirin in a small jar and shake well. Set aside. Cook 6 ounces of soba noodles according to the package directions. Drain and cool until lukewarm. Add to scallops. Pour on dressing and toss gently; add the chopped chives and toss again. Serve at room temperature. Serves 2 to 3.

Comments: Wonderful late summer dinner with fresh vegetables.

PDG Jim Schiebel, Hilton Lions Club
Hilton, NY, USA

MACARONI AND CHEESE

1 c. raw macaroni
½ tsp. salt
½ tsp. black pepper

2 c. sharp cheese
¼ c. butter
2 c. milk

Melt butter in a saucepan. Pour the milk in with the butter and heat until warm, while stirring. Mix all of the dry ingredients together. Spray a 1¾ quart casserole dish with Pam. Put dry ingredients in casserole dish and pour butter and milk over it. Place in 350° oven for 1 hour, covered.

What makes this so good is you don't have to cook the macaroni first.

Janet Brown, Covington Lions Club
Covington, GA, USA

"Heredity is what sets the parents of a teenager wondering about each other."
Laurence J. Peter

"Success is how high you bounce when you hit bottom."
Gen. George Patton

"The reputation of a thousand years may be
determined by the conduct of one hour."
Japanese proverb

MACRO MACARONI AND CHEESE

Time: 30 minutes.

½ lb. whole wheat macaroni,
cooked and drained

Sauce:

1 lb. pkg. silky or soft tofu
4 Tbsp. tahini butter
3 Tbsp. white miso

1 Tbsp. fresh lemon juice
¼ to ½ c. spring water or more
to create a thin sauce

Preheat oven to 350°F. Combine all sauce ingredients and blend well. Sauce should be quite thin for baking. Combine macaroni with sauce and place in an oiled casserole. Bake in 350°F. oven in covered casserole for 20 minutes. Remove cover and bake for 10 to 15 minutes longer to brown top. Serve while still hot. Makes 4 servings.

Comments: Tastes great! You'll never miss the dairy cheese - kids love it.
PDG Jim Schiebel, Hilton Lions Club
Hilton, NY, USA

MOSTACCIOLI

Mostaccioli is a hollow, macaroni-like pasta that is sometimes difficult to find in stores. But it's generally available at Albertson's.

1½ lb. ground beef
½ lb. sausage
½ c. chopped green pepper
1½ c. chopped celery
1½ c. chopped onions
1 c. burgundy wine
1 c. water
3 Tbsp. chopped garlic
1 tsp. black pepper
1 tsp. salt
1 tsp. marjoram
1 tsp. oregano

1 tsp. savory seasoning
1 tsp. basil
1 tsp. Italian herbs
½ tsp. MSG (optional)
3 cans Hunt's tomato sauce with
tomato bits
½ c. saki
1 tsp. sugar
Dash of Tabasco
½ lb. mushrooms, sliced
½ lb. mostaccioli
1 (15 oz.) can marinara sauce

Brown ground beef and sausage in ⅓ cup olive oil. Add green pepper, celery, and onions and cook until onions are soft. Add burgundy wine, water, garlic, seasonings, MSG, tomato sauce, saki, sugar, and Tabasco sauce. Cook for several hours. Saute mushrooms in butter and salt and pepper; add to rest of mixture. Cook mostaccioli in salted, boiling water until half done. Add to sauce mixture.

Pour half of mixture in baking dish and spread with a combination of shredded Cheddar, Jack, and American cheeses. Pour in other half of sauce and cover with marinara sauce. Top with a blend of Parmesan and Romano cheeses. Cover with foil and bake at 300°F. for 30 minutes or until bubbly.

Victor L. Dreyer, Sr., Keizer Lions Club
Salem, OR

2075-99

STUFFED MANICOTTI

1½ lb. ground round
1 lb. hot pork sausage
1 c. chopped onions
1 c. chopped green peppers
½ c. olive oil
½ stick butter
1 tsp. salt
1 tsp. pepper
1 tsp. oregano
1 tsp. garlic powder
1 tsp. savory
1 tsp. basil
1 pkg. rontoni manicotti (14 tubes)

Combine and cook all above ingredients, except manicotti, on medium heat until meat turns brown. When it has cooled a little, run mixture through your food chopper or other equipment on its finest blade. Boil manicotti no more than 7 minutes. Drain hot water off and fill pan with cold water. Using a cake decorating tube with a large opening, place the filling in the bag and stuff the manicotti with it. Place in a baking pan and cover with sauce below.

Manicotti Sauce:

1 c. chopped onions
1 c. chopped green peppers
5 large garlic cloves, chopped
2 c. diced mushrooms
½ c. olive oil
½ stick butter
1 (26 oz.) can spaghetti sauce
1 (29 oz.) can tomato sauce
Salt, pepper, garlic powder,
oregano, and savory to taste

Cook first six ingredients in a pan until vegetables are limp. Stir in tomato and spaghetti sauces. Add salt, pepper, garlic powder, oregano, and savory to taste. Simmer for one hour, stirring often. Pour over stuffed manicotti and bake at 300° until it is soft when pricked with a toothpick.

Vic L. Dreyer, Sr., Keizer Lions Club
Salem, OR

MUSTARD PENNE AND CHEESE

½ lb. extra-sharp Cheddar cheese
(about 2 c. grated)
2 Tbsp. butter
3 Tbsp. flour
4½ tsp. dry mustard
1½ c. milk
Salt and pepper
¾ tsp. Worcestershire sauce
½ lb. penne or other hollow
pasta

Heat broiler. Butter a 2 quart baking dish. Grate cheese. In a saucepan, melt the 2 tablespoons butter over medium-low heat. Stir flour and mustard into butter and cook until it bubbles. Gradually stir in milk. Add ½ teaspoon salt. Bring to a boil, stirring, and cook 1 minute. Reduce heat and stir in ¼ teaspoon pepper, the Worcestershire sauce, and cheese until cheese melts. Cook penne in a large pot of boiling salted water until tender. Drain, combine with sauce, and put in prepared dish. Broil until top browns, about 5 minutes. Makes 4 servings.

Per serving: 578 calories, 26 g protein, 29 g fat, 685 mg sodium, 52 g carbohydrate, 88 mg cholesterol.

Joann M. Brownell, Clarence Lions Club
Clarence Center, NY, USA

PASTA SALVI - PASTA CROQUETTES

1 (8 oz.) pkg. noodles
6 Tbsp. butter or margarine
3 Tbsp. chopped green onions
6 Tbsp. flour
1/4 tsp. salt
1/8 tsp. white pepper
2 c. milk

1/2 c. Parmesan cheese
1 egg, beaten
Flour
2 eggs, beaten with 2 Tbsp. water
Fine dry bread crumbs
Vegetable oil for deep-frying
Red Pepper Puree

Cook noodles according to package directions. Drain well. Meanwhile, melt butter in medium saucepan. Add green onions and saute until softened. Stir in flour, salt, and white pepper and cook until bubbly. Stir in milk and cook, stirring constantly, until thickened and bubbly. Stir in Parmesan cheese until melted, then stir a little of the mixture into the beaten egg. Add egg mixture back into the pan and bring just to a boiling point. Add sauce to drained noodles; mix thoroughly.

Press mixture into a well greased 9 inch square pan. Place a square of aluminum foil over the top, pressing down on it to pack noodles. Chill until cold, several hours or overnight.

Before serving, place flour, egg-water mixture, and bread crumbs into separate shallow dishes. Heat oil to 375°.

Cut chilled noodle mixture into squares. Coat with flour, then with egg mixture, then with bread crumbs, covering all sides thoroughly. Fry squares in hot oil, 1 to 2 at a time, until golden brown and heated through, 2 to 3 minutes. Drain on paper towel.

Serve hot with Red Pepper Puree if desired. Makes 12 appetizer or side dish servings or 9 main-dish servings.

Marilyn Redifer, Whitehall Area Lions Club
Columbus, OH

"The manner in which it is given is worth more than the gift."
Pierre Corneille

"If only God would give me a clear sign!
Like making a large deposit in my name at a Swiss bank."
Woody Allen

"If you want to test your memory, try to remember
what you were worrying about one year ago today."
E. Joseph Cossman

PASTA WITH FOUR CHEESES

2 oz. Fontina cheese (about ½ c. grated)
2 oz. Mozzarella cheese (about ½ c. grated)
2 oz. Provolone cheese (about ½ c. grated)
2 oz. Parmesan cheese (about 1 c. grated)
¾ lb. tricolored radiatori or other macaroni
2 Tbsp. butter
½ c. heavy cream
Salt and pepper
2 Tbsp. chopped fresh parsley

Grate the Fontina, Mozzarella, and Provolone on the coarse side of the grater. Grate the Parmesan fine. Cook the pasta in boiling salted water until just done. Drain the pasta and return it to the hot pot. Add butter and cream and toss. Stir in all the grated Fontina, Mozzarella, and Provolone, half of the Parmesan, and ¼ teaspoon pepper. Don't overmix or the cheeses will get stringy. Taste the pasta for seasoning and add salt and pepper if needed. Serve immediately, sprinkled with parsley and remaining Parmesan. Makes 4 servings.

Work time: 20 minutes. Total time: 30 minutes.

Per serving: 667 calories, 27 g protein, 27 g fat, 567 mg sodium, 66 g carbohydrate, 103 mg cholesterol.

Mrs. Lucy Aiken, Clarence Lions Club
Clarence Center, NY, USA

VEGETARIAN PASTA

½ lb. spaghetti
Salt
3 Tbsp. oil
2 zucchini (about ¾ lb.)
2 scallions
2 cloves garlic, minced
½ lb. carrots (about 3), chopped
1 green pepper, cut into ¼ inch dice
5 tsp. soy sauce
Grated zest from 1 lime and 1 Tbsp. juice
½ c. chopped roasted cashews

In a pot of boiling salted water, cook spaghetti; drain and toss with 1 tablespoon oil. Quarter zucchini lengthwise and cut crosswise into ¼ inch slices. Chop white part of scallion and slice green tops. In a large frying pan, heat 2 tablespoons oil over medium-high heat. Add zucchini; reduce heat to low and cook until starting to brown, about 5 minutes. Add garlic, white part of scallion, carrots, green pepper, and ½ teaspoon salt. Cover and cook until softened, 5 to 8 minutes. Stir in soy sauce; add spaghetti and heat through. Stir in lime juice, zest, and scallion tops. Sprinkle with cashews. Makes 4 servings.

Per serving: 436 calories, 12 g protein, 18 g fat, 734 mg sodium, 59 g carbohydrate, 0 mg cholesterol.

Joanne M. Wetzler, Clarence Lions Club
Clarence Center, NY, USA

CHEESE FILLED JUMBO SHELLS

1 (12 oz.) box jumbo shells
4 c. (2 lb.) Ricotta cheese
2 c. (8 oz.) shredded Mozzarella
   cheese
¾ c. grated Parmesan cheese
3 eggs
1 Tbsp. chopped fresh parsley
¾ tsp. oregano
½ tsp. salt
¼ tsp. pepper
3½ c. (32 oz. jar) spaghetti sauce

Cook shells according to package instructions; drain and cool. Cool in single layer on wax paper or foil. Combine cheese, eggs, parsley, oregano, salt, and pepper. Fill each shell with 1½ tablespoons cheese mixture.

Spread a thin layer of sauce on bottom of 13x9 inch baking dish or pan. Place shells in pan. Cover with remaining space. Sprinkle with more shredded and Parmesan cheese for cheesier taste. Cover with foil. Bake at 350° for 35 minutes till hot and bubbly. Fills about 36 shells. Makes 10 to 12 servings.

A great family favorite for many years served with garlic bread.

Judy Hoffman, Southport Lions Club
Indianapolis, IN

PASTA WITH BROCCOLI RABE

¼ c. oil
1 red onion (about ½ lb.), sliced
1 bunch broccoli rabe (about 1
   lb.), trimmed, washed, and
   cut into 1½ inch pieces
Salt and pepper
½ lb. spaghetti
2 Tbsp. butter, cut into small
   pieces
¼ c. grated Parmesan cheese

Heat the oil in a large frying pan over medium-high heat. Add the onion and cook until softened, about 5 minutes. Add the broccoli rabe, 1 teaspoon salt, and ½ teaspoon pepper. Cook, stirring constantly, until broccoli rabe is bright green, about 3 minutes. Cover and continue cooking, stirring occasionally, until broccoli rabe is tender, about 10 minutes.

Meanwhile, in a large pot of boiling salted water, cook spaghetti until done. To serve, drain spaghetti, put in serving bowl, and toss with broccoli-rabe mixture, butter, and cheese. Serve with additional cheese if you like. Makes 4 servings.

Per serving: 457 calories, 14 g protein, 22 g fat, 714 mg sodium, 53 g carbohydrate, 19 mg cholesterol.

Lion John J. Hess, Clarence Lions Club
Clarence Center, NY, USA

"Budget: A mathematical confirmation of your suspicions."
A.A. Latimer

TACORITOS

2 lb. ground beef
1 large can refried beans
2 Tbsp. chili powder
1 Tbsp. garlic powder
2 cans cream of chicken soup
1 can water
1 tsp. oregano

1 tsp. sage
1 tsp. cumin
Chopped onions
10 large flour tortillas
16 oz. shredded Cheddar cheese
Sour cream, lettuce, tomato to
  garnish

Brown meat and onions. Drain grease. Add refried beans and 1 cup sauce to meat. Heat through.

Sauce: Mix soup, water, chili powder, garlic powder, oregano, sage, and cumin. Heat through.

Place large spoonful of meat in center of tortilla. Sprinkle with cheese. Roll and place, seam side down, in large baking dish. Pour sauce over all. Sprinkle with any remaining cheese. Bake at 350° for 15 minutes.

Can top with sour cream, lettuce, and tomato if desired.

Connie Clayton, Dixon Sunrise Lions Club
Dixon, IL, USA

TURKEY AND WALNUT TACOS

1 tsp. vegetable oil
1 small onion, chopped
½ c. chopped walnuts
2 c. diced, cooked turkey
4 oz. cream cheese, cut into small
  pieces

¼ c. raisins
¼ tsp. ground cinnamon
8 taco shells
Shredded lettuce, chopped
  scallions, and halved cherry
  tomatoes

In a large nonstick skillet, over medium-low heat, heat oil. Add onion; cover and cook until tender, about 5 minutes. Uncover, add walnuts, and cook until toasted, 1 to 2 minutes. Stir in turkey, cream cheese, raisins, and cinnamon. Stir until cheese has melted. Divide mixture among taco shells. Top each taco with some lettuce, scallions, and tomatoes. Serve immediately. Makes 8 tacos.

Work time: 25 minutes. Total time: 30 minutes.

Per taco: 231 calories, 14 g protein, 12 g fat, 213 mg sodium, 17 g carbohydrate, 34 mg cholesterol.

Joann M. Brownell, Clarence Lions Club
Clarence Center, NY, USA

"If it weren't for the last minute, a lot of things wouldn't get done."
Michael S. Traylor

RED ENCHILADAS

1 can tomato soup (no water)
1 can red enchilada sauce
Lettuce, shredded
Onion, chopped (optional)

12 corn tortillas
4 eggs
Cooking oil (Wesson)
Cheese (Cheddar), grated

Mix tomato soup with red enchilada sauce in saucepan. Warm on low heat and keep warm. Put oil in skillet. Place corn tortillas, one at a time, into hot oil and fry till crisp. Drain on paper towel. Do it quickly.

To assemble, put on individual plates. Start with lettuce, onion, and cheese. Dip tortillas, one at a time, in sauce mix. Coat well and place on top of lettuce, cheese, and onions. Repeat in a stack three times. In a small skillet, fry one egg at a time, basting to desired degree of choice. Put on top of stack and serve. Yields four servings.

A big hit in my family - my youngest son's favorite meal.

Carol J. Judy, Berthoud Lions Club
Berthoud, CO, USA

CRAB ENCHILADAS

¾ lb. crab or imitation crab
6 green onions, finely chopped
½ c. chopped dill
8 tortillas

1 jar green salsa or green taco
sauce
½ lb. grated Mozzarella cheese

Lightly grease 9x13 inch pan. Combine onions and dill. Prepare each tortilla with layer of crabmeat sprinkled with onion and dill mixture. Roll to form an enchilada. Cover all enchiladas with salsa or taco sauce. Sprinkle grated cheese on top. Bake at 350° for about 15 minutes until cheese is melted and lightly browned.

Green salsa or taco sauce is needed! Red does not provide the right flavor. Recipe created by Carmen Daugherty.

Marjorie A. Crutchfield, Manhattan Beach Lions Club
Manhattan Beach, CA, USA

"Once you get people laughing, they're listening
and you can tell them almost anything."
Herb Gardner

"I never learn anything talking. I only learn things when I ask questions."
Lou Holtz

2075-99

GARLIC BEEF ENCHILADAS

1 lb. ground beef
1 medium onion, chopped
2 Tbsp. all-purpose flour
1 Tbsp. chili powder
1 tsp. salt

1 tsp. garlic powder
½ tsp. ground cumin
¼ tsp. rubbed sage
1 (14½ oz.) can stewed tomatoes

Sauce:

4 to 6 garlic cloves, minced
⅓ c. butter or margarine
½ c. all-purpose flour
1 (14½ oz.) can beef broth
1 (15 oz.) can tomato sauce
1 to 2 Tbsp. chili powder

1 to 2 tsp. ground cumin
1 to 2 tsp. rubbed sage
½ tsp. salt
10 flour tortillas (7 inches)
2 c. (8 oz.) shredded Co-Jack
   cheese

In a saucepan over medium heat, cook beef and onion until meat is no longer pink; drain. Add flour and seasonings; mix well. Stir in tomatoes; bring to a boil. Reduce heat; cover and simmer for 15 minutes.

Meanwhile, in another saucepan, saute garlic in butter until tender. Stir in flour until blended. Gradually stir in broth; bring to a boil. Cook and stir for 2 minutes or until bubbly. Stir in tomato sauce and seasonings; heat through.

Pour about 1½ cups sauce into an ungreased 13x9x2 inch baking dish. Spread about ¼ cup beef mixture down the center of each tortilla; top with 1 to 2 tablespoons cheese. Roll up tightly; place, seam side down, over sauce. Top with the remaining sauce. Cover and bake at 350° for 30 to 35 minutes. Sprinkle with remaining cheese. Bake, uncovered, 10 to 15 minutes longer or until the cheese is melted. Yield: 4 to 6 servings.

"Learn a new language and get a new soul."
Czech proverb

*"A man's greatest strength develops at the point
where he overcomes his greatest weakness."*
Elmer G. Letterman

*"It's hard to detect good luck -
it looks so much like something you've earned."*
Fred A. Clark

BURRITO

Brown the following:

1 lb. hamburger
½ medium onion
½ medium green pepper

1 clove garlic
½ Anaheim pepper

Add:

1¼ tsp. cayenne pepper

2 tsp. cumin

Combine with:

1 c. cooked rice

2 c. cooked pinto beans

Use ¼ to ⅓ cup of above mixture in each tortilla. Top with ⅛ cup Monterey Jack cheese and roll into burrito. Wrap each burrito in foil. Bake at 350° for 10 minutes.

To serve:

Shredded lettuce

Also, the following:

1 c. sour cream
1 c. diced tomatoes
½ Anaheim pepper, diced

½ medium onion
½ medium green pepper

Makes 12 to 15 burritos.

Lion Dan Clever, East Prospect Lions Club
East Prospect, PA, USA

MEXICAN BUILD-UPS

1 lb. ground beef
1 small onion
8 oz. tomato sauce
6 oz. tomato paste
1 (10 oz.) tomatoes
3 cans water in tomato paste can
1 small can green chillies (mild)

1 tsp. salt
1 c. rice (uncooked)
2 tsp. sugar
1 tsp. oregano
1 tsp. chili powder
1 tsp. cumin seed
1 clove garlic

First layer: Fritos, meat sauce, and grated cheese, then add any of all: Chopped tomatoes, green salad olives, sour cream, avocado, taco sauce, lettuce, green onions.

Mrs. Tom Reynolds (Ethel), Elburn Lions Club
Elburn, IL, USA

CHEESY CHICKEN-TORTILLA STACK

½ c. vegetable oil
6 (8 inch) flour tortillas
1 (8 oz.) ctn. commercial sour cream
½ tsp. seasoned salt
½ tsp. hot sauce
2½ c. shredded, cooked chicken
2½ c. (10 oz.) shredded Monterey Jack cheese
1¼ c. (5 oz.) shredded Longhorn cheese
½ c. plus 2 Tbsp. minced green onions
1½ Tbsp. butter or margarine, melted
⅓ c. shredded lettuce
¼ c. chopped tomato

Heat oil to 375° in a 10 inch skillet. Fry tortillas, one at a time, in hot oil 3 to 5 seconds on each side or until tortillas hold their shape and begin to crisp. Drain well on paper towels; set aside.

Combine sour cream, salt, and hot sauce. Place 1 tortilla on a lightly greased baking sheet; spread about 1 tablespoon sour cream mixture over tortilla. Sprinkle with ½ cup shredded chicken, ½ cup Monterey Jack cheese, and 2 tablespoons green onions. Repeat all layers 4 times. Top with remaining tortilla. Reserve remaining sour cream mixture. Brush top tortilla and sides of tortillas with melted butter.

Cover with foil; bake at 400° for 25 minutes. Immediately remove foil after baking; place tortilla stack on serving plate. Spread remaining sour cream mixture on top tortilla; sprinkle with lettuce and tomato. Cut into wedges and serve immediately. Yield: 4 servings.

Sarah Wehling, Bothell Lions Club
Bothell, WA, USA

MEXICAN STACK

Put 2 chicken breasts in boiling water for 20 minutes; debone and then dice. Put chicken in bowl. Add 8 ounces sour cream. Add 5 drops of hot pepper sauce. I use "Durkee" red hot sauce.

Meanwhile, separately fry 5 flour tortillas and drain on paper towels. Spread the mixture on four of the tortillas. Last tortilla is the topper. Cover with foil. Bake 35 to 40 minutes at 350°F.

Sarah Wehling, Bothell Lions Club
Bothell, WA, USA

"Babies are always more trouble than you thought - and more wonderful."
Charles Osgood

MEXICAN SHELLS

12 jumbo shells
1 lb. ground beef
1 (12 oz.) picante sauce
1 (4 oz.) green chile peppers
1 (8 oz.) tomato sauce

1 can Durkee fried onions
1 c. shredded Monterey Jack
  cheese
½ c. water

Cook shells. Brown ground beef and drain. Mix picante sauce, water, and tomato sauce. Set aside. Stir ½ cup mixture, ground beef, chile peppers, ½ cup cheese, and ½ can Durkee onions; mix well.

Pour ½ cup sauce in bottom of baking dish. Stuff shells with meat mixture. Place in dish. Cover with remaining sauce. Bake at 350° for 30 minutes. Sprinkle remaining cheese and onions on top. Bake for 5 minutes.

MADGE'S MEXICAN LUNCHEON

2 lb. pork sausage
1 c. diced onion
1 c. green pepper, chopped fine
1 (16 oz.) can tomatoes
2 c. sour cream

2 c. uncooked elbow macaroni
2 Tbsp. sugar
2 Tbsp. chili powder
1 tsp. salt

Brown pork; add onion and green peppers. Stir well. Add sugar, chili powder, and salt. Stir well. Add tomatoes and stir well. Add sour cream and macaroni. Stir well. Place in casserole dish. Cove and cook slowly until macaroni is done. Bake at 250° to 275° for about 1½ hours. Stir often.

PDG Doris J. Myers, Mexico Noon Lions Club
Mexico, MO

Your friend is the person who knows all about you, and still likes you.

❧ ❧ ❧

"The nice thing about meditation is that it makes
doing nothing quite respectable."
Paul Dean

❧ ❧ ❧

"The best bridge between despair and hope is a good night's sleep."
E. Joseph Cossman

2075-99

BREAKFASTS

AMISH BAKED OATMEAL

1½ c. quick cooking oats
½ c. sugar
½ c. milk
1 tsp. vanilla extract

1 egg
¼ c. butter or margarine, melted
1 tsp. baking powder
¾ tsp. salt

Preheat oven to 350°F. Combine all ingredients and mix well. Spread evenly in a greased 9x13 inch baking dish. Bake for 25 to 30 minutes, or until edges are golden brown. Immediately spoon into bowls. Serve with warm milk and top with fruit and brown sugar if desired.

Lion Joan Shores, St. Charles Lions Club
St. Charles, MO, USA

CHEESE STRATA

12 slices whole wheat bread
(about 12 oz.)
½ lb. Cheddar cheese (about 2 c.
shredded)
2 c. milk

3 eggs
3 scallions, sliced
½ tsp. salt
¼ tsp. cayenne pepper

Heat oven to 350°. Butter a 1½ quart baking dish. Cut each slice of bread in half crosswise. Shred cheese. In small bowl, combine milk, eggs, scallions, salt, and pepper. Line dish with the bottom halves of the bread slices, then top with half the cheese. Make a second layer with the top halves of the slices, overlapping them slightly to completely cover the first layer. Top with remaining shredded cheese. Pour egg mixture over the slices. Bake until strata is set in the center, 30 to 40 minutes. Makes 6 servings.

Per serving: 368 calories, 20 g protein, 20 g fat, 833 mg sodium, 30 g carbohydrate, 155 mg cholesterol.

Lion John J. Hess, Clarence Lions Club
Clarence Center, NY, USA

"Between two evils, I always pick the one I never tried before."
Mae West

"Those who agree with us may not be right, but we admire their astuteness."
Cullen Hightower

EGGS ALA GOLDENROD

4 hard-boiled eggs
1 pt. half & half
Pat of butter
½ tsp. Tabasco sauce

Salt and pepper to taste
2 Tbsp. corn starch
1 Tbsp. milk
4 slices bread

Hard boil eggs for at least 30 minutes. Peel, then slice whites into ½ inch pieces. Crush yolks in a bowl. Bring half & half to a boil on the stove. Add pat of butter, Tabasco, salt, and pepper. In a separate bowl or cup, stir and dissolve corn starch in milk. Slowly add to the half & half mixture until well dissolved and thickened. Add egg white pieces. Toast bread slices, then cover them with the egg white sauce. Sprinkle with yolks and serve with bacon or sausage. Serves 2 people.

Victor L. Dreyer, Sr., Keizer Lions Club
Salem, OR

GRANOLA

5 c. oatmeal
1 c. wheat germ
1 c. almonds, chopped
1 c. sesame seeds
1 c. soy flour (optional)

1 c. coconut
1 c. sunflower seeds
1 c. non-fat dry milk
1 c. honey
1 c. vegetable oil

Mix wet ingredients together (honey too). Add liquid to dry ingredients which have been placed in a cast iron kettle. Bake in a 300° oven for 1 hour. Stir every 15 minutes. Done when very *light* brown. Don't let it get too dark or it will have a burnt taste. Store in closed container.

Optional: Add ½ cup peanut butter to honey, 1 cup cracked wheat to dry ingredients. Can also add raisins after baked. If you don't mix wet ingredients together first, granola becomes lumpy.

Liz Birchen, O'Fallon Lions Club
O'Fallon, MO, USA

"What the world really needs is more love and less paperwork."
Pearl Bailey

"A cloudy day is no match for a sunny disposition."
William Ward

"If Noah had been truly wise, he would have swatted those two flies."
Helen Castle

EGG FOO YONG

1 c. chicken stock or broth
1 Tbsp. cornstarch
3 Tbsp. soy sauce
2 tsp. sugar
2 tsp. oil
1 carrot, finely chopped

3 scallions, finely chopped
¼ lb. bean sprouts
2 Tbsp. flour
5 eggs, beaten
¼ tsp. pepper

Combine ¼ cup chicken stock with cornstarch. Bring remaining ¾ cup stock, 2 tablespoons soy sauce, and sugar to a boil. Stir in cornstarch mixture. Simmer until thick, about 2 minutes. Reserve. Heat 1 teaspoon oil in large nonstick frying pan. Add carrot; cover and cook until liquid evaporates, 5 minutes. Add 1 tablespoon scallions and sprouts. Cook until tender, 3 to 5 minutes. Remove and combine with 1 tablespoon soy sauce, flour, eggs, and pepper. Heat 1 teaspoon oil in pan.

For pancakes, fry 2 tablespoons egg mixture until brown on bottom, about 1 minute. Turn and cook 30 to 60 seconds. Sprinkle with scallions. Serve with sauce. Makes 4 servings.

Per serving: 117 calories, 11 g protein, 9 g fat, 1052 mg sodium, 13 g carbohydrate, 267 mg cholesterol.

Lion John J. Hess, Clarence Lions Club
Clarence Center, NY, USA

I LOVE YOU BREAKFAST

Toss together:

¼ c. flaked almonds
½ c. sunflower seeds
1 c. wheat germ
½ c. banana chips

2 c. oats
1 c. raisins
1 c. Grape-Nuts

Use ½ cup of above mixture. Layer with sliced fruit (strawberries, kiwi, blueberry). Drizzle with honey. Add ⅔ cup plain yogurt. Top with more fruit and again drizzle with honey.

Lion Sandy Clever, East Prospect Lions Club
East Prospect, PA, USA

"If you want to truly understand something, try to change it."
Kurt Lewis

HASH BROWN BRUNCH BREAKFAST

24 oz. hash browns, thawed
2 lb. sausage or ham, cooked
½ c. butter (or margarine)
2 c. Mozzarella cheese

2 c. Cheddar, shredded
8 eggs
½ tsp. seasoned salt
1 c. milk

Spread hash browns in 13x9 inch pan or baking dish. Pour melted butter over them. Pat down, then bake at 425° for 25 minutes. Sprinkle (cooked) sausage over hash browns. Add shredded cheese. Beat eggs, milk, and salt together. Pour over everything. Bake at 350° for 40 minutes more.

Delicious Christmas morning breakfast with fruit and drink.

Judy Hoffman, Southport Lions Club
Indianapolis, IN

BACHELOR'S DELIGHT

¼ lb. bacon
2 c. hash brown potatoes
4 medium eggs

½ c. kernel corn
Seasonings to taste

Cut bacon into ½ to 1 inch strips and fry. Add hash browns to frying pan and brown. Add eggs and cook until eggs are almost cooked. Add corn and finish cooking. Add seasonings to taste - salt, pepper, chopped parsley, chopped green onion, etc. Serve with side order of toast and a large glass of milk.

Variation: May add half a can of hot, undiluted tomato soup to finished product.

Micheal and Ruth Bartolf, Oxbow and District Lions Club
Oxbow, Saskatchewan, Canada

BROCCOLI QUICHE

8 slices cooked bacon
4 oz. Swiss cheese
4 oz. Cheddar cheese
1 (10 oz.) box broccoli (frozen,
    but needs to be cooked and
    drained)

4 Tbsp. flour
2 c. milk
4 eggs
½ tsp. salt
¼ c. margarine or butter

Melt butter. Blend with flour. Add milk, cheese, cooked broccoli, bacon, eggs, and salt. Line quiche pan with pie crust (your recipe). Bake at 350° for 45 minutes. Sprinkle with nutmeg before cooking.

My husband, Al, is Vice District Governor of our club now.

Anita J. Anderson, Kenmore Lions Club
Kenmore, NY

BREAKFAST QUICHE

1 unbaked pastry shell (9 inches)
12 bacon strips, cooked and
    crumbled
½ c. shredded pepper Jack or
    Monterey Jack cheese
½ c. shredded sharp Cheddar
    cheese
⅓ c. finely chopped onion
4 eggs
2 c. whipping cream
¾ tsp. salt
¼ tsp. sugar
⅛ tsp. cayenne pepper

Line unpricked pastry shell with a double thickness of heavy-duty foil. Bake at 450° for 5 minutes; remove foil. Bake 5 minutes longer; remove from the oven and let cool. Reduce heat to 425°. Sprinkle bacon, cheeses, and onion over the crust. In a bowl, beat eggs, cream, salt, sugar, and cayenne; pour into the crust. Bake for 15 minutes. Reduce heat to 300°; bake 30 minutes longer or until a knife inserted near center comes out clean. Yield: 6 to 8 servings.

FRENCH SPINACH CHEESE QUICHE

Pastry:

¾ c. all-purpose flour
3 Tbsp. butter, cut into small
    pieces
¼ tsp. salt
2 Tbsp. ice water

Mix flour and salt; cut in margarine until mixture resembles small peas. Sprinkle with water and toss with fork until pastry clumps together. Pat evenly on bottom only of greased pie pan. Bake 7 minutes at 425°. Reduce heat to 375°.

6 large eggs
½ c. milk
½ tsp. salt
¼ tsp. pepper
1 (10 oz.) box frozen chopped
    spinach, thawed and
    squeezed dry
3 oz. Swiss cheese (¾ c.),
    shredded
¾ c. diced kielbasa (4 oz.)

Lightly whisk eggs, milk, salt, and pepper. Layer spinach, ½ the cheese, and kielbasa over crust. Pour on egg mixture. Bake 10 minutes at 375°. Sprinkle with remaining cheese. Bake 15 to 20 minutes until set and top is golden.

Lion Dan Clever, East Prospect Lions Club
East Prospect, PA, USA

"A stumble may prevent a fall."
English proverb

OVERNIGHT BREAKFAST CASSEROLE

8 slices bread, cubed
2 c. grated cheese
6 eggs
½ tsp. salt

1½ lb. sausage, browned
1 small can mushrooms
1 tsp. dry mustard
2½ c. milk

Layer bread, sausage, grated cheese, and mushrooms in a 9x13 inch pan. Combine eggs, mustard, salt, and milk and pour over layers. Refrigerate· overnight. Bake at 300° for 1½ hours.

Christine Gibson, Brookhaven Alpha Lions Club
Brookhaven, MS

SCRAMBLED EGG CASSEROLE

½ c. butter, divided
2 Tbsp. all-purpose flour
½ tsp. salt
⅛ tsp. pepper
2 c. milk
1 c. shredded process American cheese

1 c. cubed fully cooked ham
¼ c. sliced green onions
12 eggs, beaten
1 (4 oz.) can sliced mushrooms, drained
1½ c. soft bread crumbs

In medium saucepan, melt 2 tablespoons butter. Add flour, salt, and pepper; cook and stir until mixture begins to bubble. Gradually stir in milk; cook until thickened and bubbly, stirring constantly. Remove from the heat. Add cheese; mix well and set aside. In a large skillet, saute ham and onions in 3 tablespoons butter until onions are tender. Add eggs; cook and stir until they begin to set. Add the mushrooms and cheese sauce; mix well. Pour into greased 11x7x2 inch baking dish. Melt remaining butter; toss with bread crumbs. Sprinkle over top of casserole. Cover and refrigerate for 2 to 3 hours or overnight. Bake, uncovered, at 350° for 25 to 30 minutes or until top is golden brown. Serves 6 to 8.

Diana Risha, Diana McHugh, Conroe Noon Lions Club
Conroe, TX

BRUNCH EGG CASSEROLE

1 box seasoned croutons
1½ c. grated Cheddar cheese
1 c. pepper cheese or Monterey Jack cheese
1 lb. shredded ham or bacon, cooked

8 eggs
1 pt. half & half
1½ c. milk
1½ tsp. prepared French's mustard
Salt and pepper

In a 9x13x2 inch casserole pan, spread seasoned croutons. Spread ham or bacon over croutons. Spread cheese over ham. Mix eggs, milk, half & half, mustard, and salt and pepper to taste; pour this mixture over cheese, etc. Cover with plastic wrap and refrigerate overnight. Bake at 325° for 45 minutes.

Frances Blount, Saginaw Lions Club
Saginaw, TX, USA

EASY BREAKFAST EGG CASSEROLE

16 to 18 slices white bread with crusts removed
16 slices crisp cooked, crumbled bacon or cubed, cooked ham
16 to 18 slices cheese*
6 eggs
½ tsp. salt (or to taste)
½ tsp. pepper (or to taste)
1 tsp. dry mustard
½ c. finely chopped onion
½ c. finely chopped red or green pepper
½ c. finely chopped celery (optional)
1 to 2 tsp. Worcestershire sauce
3 c. milk
Dash of red pepper sauce (Tabasco)
¼ lb. butter or margarine
½ c. crushed Special K or corn flakes**

Preheat oven to 350°F. In a 9x13 inch buttered baking dish, cover bottom with bread slices, cut to fit. Sprinkle meat and vegetables over bread and layer cheese slices. Place rest of bread slices over cheese slices so it makes a sandwich. In a large bowl, using wire whip, beat eggs until frothy. Add salt, pepper, mustard, Worcestershire, red pepper sauce, and milk. Mix well. Pour over sandwich. Cover tightly with plastic wrap and refrigerate overnight. Remove from refrigerator and let stand to room temperature. Melt butter and pour over casserole. Top with crushed corn flakes. Bake, uncovered, one hour. Let stand 10 minutes, cut into squares, and serve.

This casserole is great for a buffet brunch.

* I've used various and combination of cheeses: Kraft slices, shredded medium and old Cheddar cheese, or Swiss cheese.

** Soft bread crumbs can also be used.

Lion Lillian Marchant, Lake of the Woods Lions Club
Kenora, Ontario, Canada

BREAKFAST PIZZA

8 slices bread, cubed
8 eggs
2 tsp. ground mustard
Salt and pepper to taste
1½ c. milk
1 lb. sausage
8 oz. Cheddar cheese

Grease oblong pan (9x13 inch). Line pan with bread cubes. Layer shredded cheese. Cook and drain sausage; layer on. Mix salt, pepper, milk, mustard, and eggs; pour on. Bake 30 to 45 minutes at 350°.

You can mix this up the night before, refrigerate, and bake in the morning.

Lion Ida Rohrer, Moundbuilders Lions Club
Newark, OH, USA

BREAKFAST PIZZA

6 eggs
2 c. milk
1 tsp. salt
1 Tbsp. dry mustard

1 c. Cheddar cheese, grated
1 lb. hot sausage
1 lb. mild sausage
6 slices bread

Beat eggs with milk, salt, and mustard. Brown sausage and drain. Place bread slices in a 9x13 inch pan, then the sausage and the cheese. Pour egg mixture over the above ingredients. Refrigerate overnight. Bake at 350° for 45 to 55 minutes. Serves 8 to 10.

Janice Robison, Mexico Sunrise Lions Club
Benton City, MO, Audrain County

LEMON POPPY SEED WAFFLES

2 c. flour
2 tsp. baking powder
1 tsp. salt
1 Tbsp. sugar
2 c. milk

2 eggs
2 Tbsp. melted butter or oil
2 tsp. lemon extract
3 Tbsp. poppy seeds

Combine milk, eggs, oil, and extract in a bowl and mix well. Sift dry ingredients into liquid and mix until it forms a smooth batter. Stir in poppy seeds. Cook according to your waffle iron directions. Serve with butter and powdered sugar.

Batter keeps well in the fridge for several days or make waffles and freeze. Thaw waffles out in toaster for a fast breakfast.

Judy Rannow, Arlington (SEA) Lions Club
Arlington, MN, USA

PEANUT BUTTER AND JELLY FRENCH TOAST

12 slices bread
¾ c. peanut butter
6 Tbsp. jelly or jam
3 eggs

¾ c. milk
¼ tsp. salt
2 Tbsp. butter or margarine

Spread peanut butter on six slices of bread; spread jelly on other six slices of bread. Put one slice of each together to form sandwiches. In mixing bowl, lightly beat eggs; add milk and salt and mix together. Melt butter in a large skillet over medium heat. Dip sandwiches in egg mixture, coating well. Place in skillet and brown both sides. Serve immediately. Yield: 6 servings.

"The moment of victory is much too short to live for that and nothing else."
Martina Navratilova

PAIN PERDU

4 thick (½ inch) slices good egg
    bread
1 egg
5 Tbsp. butter or margarine
    (unsalted)
3 Tbsp. white sugar

Pinch of salt
½ tsp. ground cinnamon
Pinch of ground nutmeg
⅓ c. all-purpose flour
¾ c. milk
¾ tsp. vanilla extract

Cut the bread and place on a wire rack to dry out a little as you prepare the batter. Whisk the egg to blend. Melt 3 tablespoons of the butter in a saucepan or on the stove top and allow to cool slightly. Whisk the sugar, salt, and spices into the egg. When the butter has cooled slightly, slowly drizzle it into the egg, whisking all the time. A little at a time, add the flour to the egg mixture to make a smooth thick paste. After it is all added, slowly blend in the milk and finally the vanilla. Whisk until just smooth and set aside.

Heat the remaining butter in a large skillet over medium heat. Dip a slice of the bread in the batter and allow to soak for 30 seconds, no more. Remove from the batter and allow the excess to drip off back into the bowl. Place the battered slice in the skillet. Repeat with the remaining slices. Cook until golden on one side and then flip to brown the other. Serve immediately - a fresh squeeze of lemon juice and a good dusting of powdered sugar is traditional. Makes 4 servings.

Yes, this is French toast, but a superior one. Unlike normal French toast, this batter cooks into a custardy, crispy coating that leaves the bread creamy and oh so good. The use of good egg bread is a must here. Homemade is best, however store bought (such as Hawaiian bread) will work in a pinch.

Barbara K. Hugus, West Milford Lions Club
West Milford, WV, USA

NUTMEG FRENCH TOAST

3 eggs
¾ c. milk
¼ tsp. nutmeg

¼ tsp. vanilla extract
3 Tbsp. butter
8 slices Italian bread

Heat oven to 250°. Beat the eggs, milk, nutmeg, and vanilla. In a large frying pan, melt 1½ tablespoons of the butter over medium-high heat. Dip half of the bread slices in the egg mixture and let the excess drip off. Fry the bread in the hot butter until golden-brown on both sides, about 5 minutes in all. Transfer to a heatproof platter and put in the oven to keep warm. Melt the remaining 1½ tablespoons butter in the pan and dip and fry the remaining bread. Makes 8 servings.

Per serving: 159 calories, 6 g protein, 7 g fat, 201 mg sodium, 17 g carbohydrate, 95 mg cholesterol.

Barbara Joy Hess, Clarence Lions Club
Clarence Center, NY, USA

RASPBERRY PANCAKES

1 box raspberry "Jiffy" muffin
  mix
1 egg

¼ c. milk (sour milk if possible)

Mix night before. Make it thin. Let stand overnight.

Delores Wilkerson, Bellville Lions Club
Bellville, GA, USA

POTATO PANCAKES

Boil potatoes with skins for 20 minutes. Skin and mash well. Cook pancheta, diced, till almost crisp and add to potatoes. Salt and pepper to taste. Place in a skillet with small amount of oil and pack down to cover all of skillet. Cook on medium heat. When one side is brown, turn over and cook other side until brown.

Victor L. Dreyer, Sr., Keizer Lions Club
Keizer, OR, USA

SWEDISH PANCAKES

1 c. milk
2 Tbsp. butter
2 eggs, beaten

½ c. flour
1 tsp. baking powder
½ tsp. salt

Heat milk and butter in saucepan. Let cool. After it is cooled, beat eggs in and add dry ingredients. Bake on hot skillet.

Sarah Wehling, Bothell Lions Club
Bothell, WA, USA

"Whoever says that money can't buy you happiness
doesn't know where to shop."
Telegraph Magazine

"Money is better than poverty, if only for financial reasons.
Woody Allen

"Perseverance is not a long race; it is many short races one after another."
Walter Elliott

BAKED PEAR PANCAKE

2 pears
3 Tbsp. butter
3 Tbsp. granulated sugar
3 eggs
½ c. milk

½ c. flour
¼ tsp. salt
⅛ tsp. nutmeg
⅛ tsp. cinnamon
Confectioners sugar

Heat oven to 425°. Peel, core, and slice pears. In large ovenproof frying pan, melt 1 tablespoon butter over medium-high heat. Add pears and sprinkle with sugar. Cook until tender and golden brown, about 10 minutes. Remove pears and any juices from pan. Wipe pan clean. Add remaining 2 tablespoons butter to pan and melt. Briefly beat eggs with milk, flour, salt, nutmeg, and cinnamon until almost smooth. Leave some lumps. When butter in pan is hot, pour in batter. Arrange pears in center of batter and pour juices over. Bake until puffed and golden brown, 15 to 20 minutes. Sprinkle with confectioners sugar. Makes 4 servings.

Per serving: 293 calories, 8 g protein, 14 g fat, 199 mg sodium, 36 g carbohydrate, 187 mg cholesterol.

Mrs. Mike Nowicki, Clarence Lions Club
Clarence Center, NY, USA

HONEY PANCAKES WITH STRAWBERRIES

1 pt. strawberries
1 Tbsp. sugar
3 Tbsp. butter
1¼ c. flour
¾ tsp. baking powder
½ tsp. baking soda

½ tsp. salt
1¼ c. milk
1 Tbsp. lemon juice
1 egg
6 Tbsp. honey
Vegetable oil

Slice strawberries; sprinkle with sugar and let stand. Melt butter; cool. Combine flour, baking powder, soda, and salt. Beat together milk, lemon juice, egg, 2 tablespoons honey, and the cooled butter. With a few quick strokes, combine wet and dry ingredients. Heat a large frying pan, brushed with oil, over medium-high heat. Pour batter by scant ¼ cupfuls into hot pan. Cook until bubbles burst. Flip and cook until golden. Remove from pan and repeat with remaining butter, brushing pan with oil as needed. Serve pancakes with strawberries and drizzle with remaining honey. Makes 12 pancakes.

Per pancake: 149 calories, 3 g protein, 5 g fat, 171 mg sodium, 23 g carbohydrate, 29 mg cholesterol.

Barbara Joy Hess, Clarence Lions Club
Clarence Center, NY, USA

YOGURT PANCAKES

⅓ c. orange juice
¾ c. plain yogurt
1 egg
2 Tbsp. butter or margarine
1 c. flour
1 tsp. baking powder

½ tsp. salt
½ tsp. baking soda
2 c. blueberries
½ c. sugar
¼ c. water
Cornstarch

Measure flour, baking powder, baking soda, and salt into a bowl and mix well together. Make a well and mix in egg, juice, and yogurt, blending well. Melt butter. Let cool slightly and blend into pancake mixture. Cook as usual. Set aside to keep warm.

Topping: Bring blueberries, sugar, and water to a boil. Thicken to desired consistency with cornstarch. Serve over pancakes.

As an alternative to blueberries, try serving with additional yogurt (plain or flavoured) and your favourite fresh fruit.

Lion Nancy Smith, Lake of the Woods Lions Club
Kenora, Ontario, Canada

CRISP CORNMEAL PANCAKES

1 c. corn meal
½ c. flour
1 Tbsp. baking powder
1 Tbsp. sugar

¾ tsp. salt
1 c. milk
1 egg
Vegetable oil

Combine cornmeal, flour, baking powder, sugar, and salt. Combine milk, egg, and 1 tablespoon oil. Stir milk mixture into dry ingredients until just smooth. Pour about ¼ inch of oil into a large frying pan over medium heat. When hot, spoon batter into pan by heaping tablespoonfuls. Spread out slightly. Cook until brown. Turn and cook until brown and crisp on the other side. Continue with rest of batter, thinning with milk or water if it becomes too thick. Makes 16 pancakes.

Variations -

Blueberry: Stir ½ cup fresh or frozen blueberries into batter.

Raspberry: Stir ½ cup fresh or frozen raspberries (thawed and drained if in syrup) into batter.

Banana Pecan: Stir ¾ teaspoon ground nutmeg or cinnamon into flour mixture. Slice one banana and stir into batter with ½ cup chopped pecans.

Work time: 20 minutes. Total time: 20 minutes.

Per pancake: 81 calories, 2 g protein, 3 g fat, 195 mg sodium, 11 g carbohydrate, 15 mg cholesterol.

Lion John J. Hess, Clarence Lions Club
Clarence Center, NY, USA

GERMAN PANCAKES

4 eggs
¾ c. milk
¾ c. flour
½ tsp. salt

¼ c. butter
2 apples, thinly sliced
1 tsp. cinnamon
¼ c. sugar

Beat eggs. Add flour, milk, and salt. Beat. In 2 round cake pans, divide butter and coat both pans with the butter, then divide batter into the 2 pans. Arrange thinly sliced apples in a circular pattern on top of the batter. Top with sugar, then cinnamon. Bake at 400° for approximately 25 minutes or until the edges peak and turn an even golden brown. Serve immediately. Serves 2 hearty appetites.

Kevin Bishop, Mayfield Lions Club
Mayfield, KY, USA

BEST BUTTERMILK PANCAKES

2 Tbsp. butter
1 c. flour
2 Tbsp. sugar
½ tsp. baking powder
½ tsp. baking soda

½ tsp. salt
1 c. buttermilk
1 egg
Vegetable oil

Melt butter. Combine flour, sugar, baking powder, soda, and salt. Combine buttermilk, egg, and the melted butter. Stir buttermilk mixture into dry ingredients until just smooth. Heat a large frying pan over medium heat. Brush with oil. Pour batter into pan by scant ¼ cupfuls. Spread each slightly with spatula. Cook until batter bubbles. Turn and cook until golden. Continue with rest of batter, thinning with water if it becomes too thick. Makes 8 pancakes.

Work time: 20 minutes. Total time: 20 minutes.

Per pancake: 127 calories, 3 g protein, 5 g fat, 247 mg sodium, 17 g carbohydrate, 9 mg cholesterol.

Lion John J. Hess, Clarence Lions Club
Clarence Center, NY, USA

"A porch is the only real reward you need after a long summer's day."
Shwan Sell

"In the absence of certainty, instinct is all you can follow."
Jonathan Cainer

SESAME-SEED PANCAKES

¼ c. all-purpose flour
¼ c. whole wheat flour
2 Tbsp. wheat germ
¾ tsp. salt
½ tsp. baking soda
1 tsp. baking powder
4 tsp. brown sugar

2 eggs
4 tsp. vegetable oil
1 c. milk
3 Tbsp. sesame seeds, lightly
   toasted
4 tsp. sunflower seeds

In a medium bowl, combine the flours, wheat germ, salt, baking soda, baking powder, and sugar. Whisk in eggs, oil, and milk just until blended. Gently fold in sesame and sunflower seeds. Spray a large frying pan with nonstick spray and place over medium-high heat. Pour about 2 tablespoons batter per pancake into pan and cook until bubbles burst, about 2 minutes. Flip over and cook until underside is golden. If desired, serve with jam and extra sesame seeds. Makes 4 servings.

Per serving: 254 calories, 10 g protein, 14 g fat, 639 mg sodium, 23 g carbohydrate, 115 mg cholesterol.

Lion John J. Hess, Clarence Lions Club
Clarence Center, NY, USA

CHOKE CHERRY SYRUP

3 or 3½ c. juice
1 c. white corn syrup

1 pkg. pectin

Bring to a boil and add 3½ cups sugar. Bring to a boil again; boil for 2 minutes. Pour into hot sterilized jars and seal. *Very good on pancakes.*

Micheal and Ruth Bartolf, Oxbow and District Lions Club
Oxbow, Saskatchewan, Canada

"Humility comes from understanding that
the obstacles in front of you are not going to go away."
Sarah Ferguson

❧ ❧ ❧

"Thinking is what a great many people think they are doing
when they are merely rearranging their prejudices."
William James

❧ ❧ ❧

"Cooperation isn't the absence of conflict but a means of managing conflict."
Deborah Tannen

Notes

Breads,
Rolls

EQUIVALENT CHART

3 tsp. .... 1 Tbsp.	¼ lb. crumbled Bleu cheese...................... 1 c.
2 Tbsp. .... ⅛ c.	1 lemon .... 3 Tbsp. juice
4 Tbsp. .... ¼ c.	1 orange.................................... ⅓ c. juice
8 Tbsp. .... ½ c.	1 lb. unshelled walnuts ..... 1½ to 1¾ c. shelled
16 Tbsp. .... 1 c.	2 c. fat .... 1 lb.
5 Tbsp. + 1 tsp. .... ⅓ c.	1 lb. butter..................... 2 c. or 4 sticks
12 Tbsp. .... ¾ c.	2 c. granulated sugar.......................... 1 lb.
4 oz. .... ½ c.	3½-4 c. unsifted powdered sugar.............. 1 lb.
8 oz. .... 1 c.	2¼ c. packed brown sugar...................... 1 lb.
16 oz. .... 1 lb.	4 c. sifted flour................................. 1 lb.
1 oz. .... 2 Tbsp. fat or liquid	4½ c. cake flour.............................. 1 lb.
2 c. .... 1 pt.	3½ c. unsifted whole wheat flour .... 1 lb.
2 pt. .... 1 qt.	4 oz. (1 to 1¼ c.) uncooked
1 qt. .... 4 c.	macaroni.................................. 2¼ c. cooked
⅝ c. ....½ c. + 2 Tbsp.	7 oz. spaghetti .... 4 c. cooked
⅞ c. ....¾ c. + 2 Tbsp.	4 oz. (1½ to 2 c.) uncooked
1 jigger ....1½ fl. oz. (3 Tbsp.)	noodles.......................... 2 c. cooked
8 to 10 egg whites .... 1 c.	28 saltine crackers.......................... 1 c. crumbs
12 to 14 egg yolks .... 1 c.	4 slices bread .... 1 c. crumbs
1 c. unwhipped cream .... 2 c. whipped	14 square graham crackers........... 1 c. crumbs
1 lb. shredded American cheese................ 4 c.	22 vanilla wafers........................... 1 c. crumbs

SUBSTITUTIONS FOR A MISSING INGREDIENT

1 square **chocolate** (1 ounce) = 3 or 4 tablespoons cocoa plus ½ tablespoon fat
1 tablespoon **cornstarch** (for thickening) = 2 tablespoons flour
1 cup sifted **all-purpose flour** = 1 cup plus 2 tablespoons sifted cake flour
1 cup sifted **cake flour** = 1 cup minus 2 tablespoons sifted all-purpose flour
1 teaspoon **baking powder** = ¼ teaspoon baking soda plus ½ teaspoon cream of tartar
1 cup **sour milk** = 1 cup sweet milk into which 1 tablespoon vinegar or lemon juice has been stirred
1 cup **sweet milk** = 1 cup sour milk or buttermilk plus ½ teaspoon baking soda
¾ cup **cracker crumbs** = 1 cup bread crumbs
1 cup **cream, sour, heavy** = ⅓ cup butter and ⅔ cup milk in any sour milk recipe
1 teaspoon **dried herbs** = 1 tablespoon fresh herbs
1 cup **whole milk** = ½ cup evaporated milk and ½ cup water or 1 cup reconstituted nonfat dry milk and 1 tablespoon butter
2 ounces **compressed yeast** = 3 (¼ ounce) packets of dry yeast
1 tablespoon **instant minced onion, rehydrated** = 1 small fresh onion
1 tablespoon **prepared mustard** = 1 teaspoon dry mustard
⅛ teaspoon **garlic powder** = 1 small pressed clove of garlic
1 lb. **whole dates** = 1½ cups, pitted and cut
3 medium **bananas** = 1 cup mashed
3 cups **dry corn flakes** = 1 cup crushed
10 **miniature marshmallows** = 1 large marshmallow

GENERAL OVEN CHART

Very slow oven	250° to 300°F.
Slow oven.............................	300° to 325°F.
Moderate oven	325° to 375°F.
Medium hot oven...................	375° to 400°F.
Hot oven	400° to 450°F.
Very hot oven	450° to 500°F.

CONTENTS OF CANS

Of the different sizes of cans used by commercial canners, the most common are:

Size:	Average Contents
8 oz.	1 cup
Picnic	1¼ cups
No. 300	1¾ cups
No. 1 tall	2 cups
No. 303	2 cups
No. 2	2½ cups
No. 2½	3½ cups
No. 3	4 cups
No. 10	12 to 13 cups

BREADS, ROLLS
BREADS

HONEY WHEAT BREAD
(For bread machine)

1 c. water
1½ Tbsp. honey
2 Tbsp. butter
2½ c. white bread flour
½ c. whole wheat flour

1½ Tbsp. dry milk
1½ tsp. salt
1½ tsp. fast rise yeast or active
dry yeast

Add ingredients to bread machine in order listed. Bake using white, rapid, or delay bake cycles.

Judy Rannow, Arlington (SEA) Lions Club
Arlington, MN, USA

BAKED POTATO BREAD
(For the bread machine)

¾ c. water
½ c. sour cream
1½ Tbsp. dried onion flakes
3 c. white bread flour
1½ Tbsp. dry milk
1½ Tbsp. sugar

1½ tsp. salt
3 Tbsp. potato flakes
1½ Tbsp. dried chives
2 tsp. fast rise yeast or 3 tsp.
active dry yeast

Put ingredients in bread machine pan in order above. Bake using white or rapid bake cycles.

For a different flavor, add 2 tablespoons bacon bits.

Judy Rannow, Arlington (SEA) Lions Club
Arlington, MN, USA

ALOHA LOAF

½ c. margarine
1 c. sugar
2 eggs
1 large ripe banana, mashed
2 c. flour
1 tsp. baking powder

½ tsp. baking soda
½ tsp. salt
½ c. shredded coconut
1 (7 oz.) can crushed pineapple
1 c. chopped nuts

Cream margarine and sugar. Add eggs. Beat well. Stir in mashed banana. Sift dry ingredients together and add to creamed mixture. Fold in undrained pineapple, coconut, and nuts. Bake in well-greased loaf pan about 1 hour at 350° (until center tests done).

Zona Roberts, Bullhead City Lions Club
Bullhead City, AZ, USA

2075-99

MAMIE'S BREAD

5 lb. flour (and a little more)
1 qt. 1 pt. warm water
3 pkg. yeast or 4 Tbsp. loose
    yeast

Small handful sugar
Much salt
1 Tbsp. full Crisco

Mix all together. Let rise. Knead it down and put in pan. Let rise again, then bake at 425° to 450° till done.

Sue Bubb, Burnham Lions Club
McClure, PA, Mifflin

HOT HERB BREAD

½ c. soft butter
¼ tsp. dill seed
¼ tsp. oregano
Grated Parmesan cheese (little or
    lots)

1 loaf French bread
1 tsp. parsley flakes
¼ tsp. garlic salt

Melt butter and herbs in a saucepan. Brush on bread. Sprinkle with the cheese. Wrap in foil. Bake for 10 minutes at 400°.

Sarah Wehling, Bothell Lions Club
Bothell, WA, USA

SALLY LUNN BREAD

1 Tbsp. dry yeast
1 c. lukewarm milk
½ c. butter, softened
⅓ c. sugar

3 medium eggs, beaten
1 tsp. salt
4 c. flour

Preheat oven to 350°. Adjust oven rack to middle position. Dissolve yeast in warm milk. Cream butter and sugar until well blended. Add eggs to butter mixture. Mix well. Add salt to flour; mix well and add alternately with yeast mixture to batter, blending well. Let rise until doubled in bulk. Beat down. Pour into 2 well-greased loaf pans. Let rise, covered lightly, until ¾ way up the side of the pan. Bake for 25 to 30 minutes until done. Cool on a wire rack.

John Hamner, Bellville Lions Club
Bellville, GA, USA

"Buying stock is exactly the same thing as going to a casino,
only with no cocktail service."

Ted Allen

DILLY BREAD

1 pkg. dry yeast
¼ c. warm water
1 c. creamed cottage cheese
2 Tbsp. sugar
1 Tbsp. instant onion (minced)
1 Tbsp. butter or margarine

2 tsp. dill seed
1 tsp. salt
¼ tsp. baking soda
1 egg
2¼ to 2½ c. flour

Sprinkle yeast over warm (110°) water. Heat cottage cheese to lukewarm. Combine in mixing bowl with sugar, onion, butter, dill, salt, soda, beaten egg, and yeast mixture. Add flour to form a stiff dough, beating well after each addition. Cover and let rise in warm place until double, about 1 hour. Stir down dough. Turn into well-greased 1½ quart casserole. Let rise in warm place until light, 30 to 40 minutes. Bake at 300° about 45 minutes. Brush with melted butter and sprinkle with salt.

Bonnie Smith, Princeton Lions Club
Princeton, IL, USA

DILLY BREAD

1 pkg. yeast in ½ c. lukewarm
    water
1 tsp. sugar
1 c. creamed cottage cheese
    (lukewarm)
2 Tbsp. sugar
1 Tbsp. onion flakes

1 tsp. salt
1 egg
2 tsp. dill seeds
½ tsp. soda
1 Tbsp. butter
1 tsp. dill weed
2½ c. flour

Blend above first 11 ingredients with electric mixer, then the 2½ cup flour is added by using wooden spoon. Cover and let rise in warm place until double in size and dough is light. Divide into 2 parts and knead with a little flour for 6 to 8 minutes. Place in 2 small loaf pans or 2 coffee cans. Let rise until double in size. Bake 40 minutes at 350°F. Brush with butter after baking.

Ann K. Brumback of Littlestown, PA,
Silver Run Union Mills Lions Club
Westminster, MD, USA

"In a conversation, keep in mind that you're more interested in what you have to say than anyone else is."
Andy Rooney

"Discipline without freedom is tyranny; freedom without discipline is chaos."
Cullen Hightower

TRADITIONAL SODA BREAD
(Ireland)

900 g (2 lb.) plain flour
2 tsp. cream of tartar
600 ml (1 pt.) milk

1 tsp. salt
1 tsp. bread soda

Use fairly hot oven (205°C.). Sieve flour, salt, soda, and cream of tartar into a mixing bowl. Make a well in the centre and pour in the milk. Mix with a knife until most of the flour is taken up. Knead with floured hands, adding more milk if necessary. The dough should be soft. Shape the dough into a 22 cm (9 inch) round flattish cake and place on a floured baking tin. Cut a cross on top to allow for rising and bake in a fairly hot oven (205°C.) for an hour or more. Cover with foil about halfway through cooking time so that it does not get too brown.

In Ireland, we'd ate fresh homemade (this was one of their recipes) bread at every meal. Real good. Sela Head Farm B & B Dingle, Kerry, Ireland.

Doris L. Mahalak, Biloxi Lions Club
Biloxi, MS

SWEDISH RYE BREAD

No. 1:

2 c. water
1 tsp. salt
1 tsp. caraway seed

1 tsp. anise
½ c. brown sugar
1 Tbsp. lard

No. 2:

½ c. molasses
¼ oz. yeast

2 c. white flour
2 c. rye flour

Boil No. 1 ingredients for 3 minutes. Pour over ½ cup molasses. Dissolve yeast in ½ cup of warm water. Stir the flour into the mixture. Set in warm place and let rise until double in size. Bake at 350° for approximately 50 minutes. Brush with mixture of water and molasses.

Alyce Reinking, Princeton Lions Club
Princeton, IL, USA

"Your dreams can be realities.
They are the stuff that leads us through life toward great happiness."
Deborah Norville

HONEY BEAR BREAD

1½ c. flour (bread or unbleached flour)
1 pkg. Fleischmann's RapidRise yeast
1 tsp. salt
1½ c. warm water (125°F. to 130°F.)
2 Tbsp. honey
1 Tbsp. oil or margarine
1½ c. whole wheat flour

Mix together 1½ cups flour, 1 package RapidRise yeast, and salt. Add 1½ cups water, 2 tablespoons honey, and oil. Stir vigorously about 2 minutes, then stir in 1½ cups whole wheat flour. Whole grain bread should not pull away from sides of the bowl and ball up at this stage. If it does, add a little water.

Resting: Sprinkle ½ cup whole wheat flour over dough. Do not stir. Let dough rest for 5 minutes, then scrape sides of bowl with up and down motion. Tilt bowl and scrape bottom several times to coat dough with dry flour. Do not stir. Dust counter/table with flour and dump dough out onto the counter. Knead dough 8 to 10 minutes by turning, folding, and stretching dough. If and when dough gets sticky, add a little flour. Knead dough until smooth and elastic. Dough will spring back quickly when lightly punched. Cut dough in half. Smooth each lump into a round ball. Cover with clean kitchen towel and allow dough to rest 20 minutes. After 20 minutes, punch each lump of dough into a flat circle. Press dough firmly to squeeze out air bubbles.

Fold over two edges of each circle to form a triangle. Starting at the point, roll up like a jelly roll. Pinch edges and bottom seam to seal. Place loaves seam side down in 2 greased loaf pans (8x4 inches). Place pans in warm place until dough doubles in size, about an hour.

Bake bread at 375°F. for 35 to 40 minutes. To test for doneness, remove bread from pan and tap on bottom and sides. Baked bread will sound hollow. Cool bread on wire rack. "Warm fresh homemade bread lifts the spirit and warms the heart."

This is in honor of John Stuffle, who was our Treasurer for 20 years. He is a real *honey* and loved by all. Thanks, John.

Lion Ann Brumback of Littlestown, PA,
Silver Run Union Mills Lions Club
Westminster, MD, USA

"There's no cap on success. The jury stays out till you take your last breath."
Judy Sheindlin

"Invest yourself in everything you do. There's fun in being serious."
Wynton Marsalis

LION ANN'S COCONUT BREAD

¾ c. sugar
1 large egg
2 Tbsp. peanut oil
1 c. coconut milk
1 tsp. coconut extract

½ c. coconut flakes
3 c. flour
1 Tbsp. baking powder
⅛ tsp. salt

Mix together first 6 ingredients with electric mixer. In separate bowl, sift together dry ingredients - flour, baking powder, and salt. Add dry ingredients to milk/egg mixture and stir by hand until well blended. Pour into greased large bread pan or 2 medium bread pans. Bake at 325° for 50 to 55 minutes.

In honor of Lion Nicki Florentine, Secretary of Silver Run Union Mills Lions Club, Westminster, Maryland.

Ann K. Brumback of Littlestown, PA,
Silver Run Union Mills Lions Club
Westminster, MD

SWEET POTATO BREAD

4 eggs
3 c. sugar
⅔ c. water
2 c. sweet potatoes, mashed
1 small can crushed pineapple
3½ c. flour
1 c. Wesson oil

2 tsp. salt
2 tsp. soda
3 tsp. cinnamon
2 tsp. nutmeg
2 c. pecans
1 c. chopped dates or raisins

Mix all ingredients together and divide batter into two loaf pans or into a tube pan. Bake at 350° for one hour.

Lion Jane McCune, Huffman Lioness Club
Huffman, TX

RHUBARB BREAD

1 c. brown sugar, packed
½ c. sugar
⅔ c. oil
2 eggs
1 c. sour milk
1 tsp. salt

1½ tsp. vanilla
2½ c. flour
1½ c. diced rhubarb
1 tsp. soda
½ c. chopped nuts

Combine all ingredients except rhubarb and nuts. Mix well, then add rhubarb and nuts. Pour into 2 greased 9x5 inch pans. Before baking, top each loaf with 2 teaspoons melted oleo, then sprinkle 1 tablespoon sugar over each loaf. Bake at 350° for 1 hour.

Thelma Hoke, Bullskin Township Lioness Club
Mt. Pleasant, PA

ONION SESAME BREAD

⅓ c. very warm water
2 pkg. yeast
10½ oz. condensed onion soup
   (undiluted)

4 c. biscuit mix
¼ c. melted butter or margarine
2 tsp. sesame seeds
¼ c. Cheddar cheese, grated

Into very warm water, in small bowl, sprinkle yeast and stir until it is dissolved. Add onion soup. Stir into biscuit mix in bowl until well blended. Pour butter or margarine into a 12x8x2 inch baking dish; sprinkle with 1 teaspoon sesame seeds. Cool. Spread batter evenly over butter. Sprinkle with cheese and 1 teaspoon sesame seeds. Cover with towel and let rise in warm place about ½ hour or until double. Preheat oven to 400°. Bake until done, 25 minutes. Yield: 6 buns.

May be served as hot bread or split as buns for hamburgers.

Lion Barbara Lane, Mount Airy Foothills Lions Club
Mount Airy, NC, USA

ONION BREAD

2 onions (about ½ lb.)
1 Tbsp. butter
1 egg

¾ c. sour cream
Salt and pepper
1 lb. frozen bread dough, thawed

Heat the oven to 425°. Slice the onions. Melt the butter. With a wooden spoon, combine the egg and sour cream until just mixed. Stir in the melted butter, 1 teaspoon salt, and ½ teaspoon pepper. Add the onions and stir to coat. Divide the bread dough into 6 pieces. On a lightly floured work surface, roll or pat the dough into approximately 5 inch circles. Put about 2 inches apart on ungreased baking sheets. Top with the onion mixture. Bake until golden, about 20 minutes. Makes 6 servings.

Work time: 20 minutes. Total time: 40 minutes.

Per serving: 273 calories, 8 g protein, 10 g fat, 833 mg sodium, 37 g carbohydrate, 53 mg cholesterol.

Mrs. Lucy Aiken, Clarence Lions Club
Clarence Center, NY, USA

"If you have but one wish, let it be for an idea."
Percy Sutton

❧ ❧ ❧

"Half of the harm that is done in the world is due
to people who want to feel important."
T.S. Eliot

SAVORY CARROT QUICK BREAD

3 c. flour
4 tsp. baking powder
1½ tsp. salt
5 scallions
1 c. walnuts

4 carrots (about 2 c. grated)
6 Tbsp. chopped parsley
2 eggs
1½ c. milk
½ c. oil

Heat oven to 350°. Butter a 9 inch square cake pan. Combine the flour, baking powder, and salt. Chop the scallions and walnuts. Grate the carrots. Add the scallions, walnuts, carrots, and parsley to the flour mixture. Beat eggs, milk, and oil. Stir into the flour mixture until just combined. Spread in pan and smooth top. Bake until toothpick inserted in the center comes out clean, about 1¼ hours. Makes 12 servings.

Per serving: 291 calories, 7 g protein, 17 g fat, 398 mg sodium, 30 g carbohydrate, 40 mg cholesterol.

Lion John J. Hess, Clarence Lions Club
Clarence Center, NY, USA

OLD-FASHIONED DATE NUT BREAD

1 c. chopped dates
2 c. flour
1 tsp. baking soda
½ tsp. salt
6 Tbsp. unsalted butter (at room
    temperature)

½ c. brown sugar
½ tsp. vanilla extract
2 eggs
½ c. chopped walnuts

Pour 1 cup boiling water over the dates and let cool. Heat oven to 350°. Butter an 8½ x 4½ inch loaf pan. Combine the flour, soda, and salt. With an electric mixer set at medium-low speed, beat the butter, sugar, and vanilla until creamy. Beat in the eggs, one at a time, beating well after each addition. Reduce speed to low and beat in flour mixture in thirds, alternating with the date mixture. Stir in the walnuts. Pour batter into prepared pan. Bake until a toothpick stuck in the center comes out clean, about 1 hour. Cool 10 minutes. Remove from the pan and cool completely before slicing. Makes 20 slices.

Per slice: 150 calories, 3 g protein, 6 g fat, 105 mg sodium, 22 g carbohydrate, 31 mg cholesterol.

Mrs. Mike Nowicki, Clarence Lions Club
Clarence Center, NY, USA

"Beauty isn't worth thinking about; what's important is your mind.
You don't want a fifty-dollar haircut on a fifty-cent head."
Garrison Keillor

BANANA NUT BREAD

1¼ c. sugar
½ c. butter (or half shortening)
2 eggs
¼ c. sour milk

1 tsp. soda
2¼ c. flour
2 bananas, mashed
½ c. chopped nuts

Cream sugar and shortening; add bananas, beaten eggs, and nuts. Add flour and soda alternately with milk until all is used. Bake at 350° for 50 to 60 minutes in a loaf pan until tested done with a toothpick. Toothpick will come out of cake clean. Makes one loaf.

This recipe was a favorite of my mother's - she always used it when she had several "tired" bananas.

Barbara J. Pedersen, Othello Lions Club
Othello, WA, USA

BANANA BREAD

¾ c. white sugar
4 Tbsp. softened oleo (½ stick)

⅓ tsp. salt
3 eggs

Beat all together.

2 c. flour
1 tsp. baking soda
7 Tbsp. sour milk (sour with
    vinegar)

½ to 1 c. raisins (through food
    grinder)
½ c. walnuts, cut up
3 mashed bananas

May add ½ cup chopped dried apricots if desired.

Mix together and beat sugar, oleo, salt, and eggs. Add soda to flour; pour in sour milk. Stir. Add raisins and walnuts. Gently mix in 3 mashed bananas by hand. Bake in 2 individual well greased loaf pans 35 to 40 minutes at 350°.

Rita Maiers, Stewart Lions Club
Stewart, MN, USA

"Nobody minds having what is too good for them."
Jane Austen

"Money brings some happiness.
But after a certain point, it just brings more money.
Neil Simon

An ego trip is a trip that never gets you anywhere.

BANANA BREAD WITH BUTTERMILK

1¾ c. flour
1½ c. sugar
1 tsp. baking soda
½ tsp. salt
2 eggs

3 ripe bananas, mashed (1 c.)
½ c. vegetable oil
¼ c. plus 1 Tbsp. buttermilk
1 tsp. vanilla
1 c. nuts

Mix in order given. Pour in a 9x5x3 inch greased loaf pan. Bake at 325° for 1 hour and 20 minutes. Serves 6.

Note: No buttermilk - use ½ cup milk plus 1 teaspoon white vinegar or lemon juice and let sit 5 minutes. Measure amount for your recipe and continue.

Note: When bananas are ripe, but you do not have time to make bread, peel and smash 3 bananas (about 1 cup), place in freezer bag, and place in freezer. When you are ready to make bread, remove smashed bananas from freezer, partly thaw, and use as fresh. Bananas may be brown, but still okay to use.

Elaine (Pepin) Howes, Northfield Lions Club
Northfield, MA

NEVER FAIL BANANA BREAD

½ c. margarine
1 c. sugar
1 c. very ripe bananas (about 3)
2 eggs
2 c. flour

½ c. sour milk with 1 tsp. baking
    soda added
½ c. walnuts, chopped
1 tsp. vanilla

Mix margarine and sugar till creamy. Add bananas, eggs, flour, sour milk, and vanilla. Mix, then stir in nuts. Pour into 1 to 2 large loaf pans or 3 to 4 small loaf pans. Bake in 350° oven for 1 hour for large pans or 35 to 45 minutes for small pans. Test with toothpick for doneness.

P. Diane Baldwin, Broken Bow Lions Club
Broken Bow, NE, USA

"The only person who listens to both sides of an argument is the fellow in the next apartment."

Ruth Brown

"Naps are nature's way of reminding you that life is nice - like a beautiful, softly swinging hammock strung between birth and infinity."

Reggy Noonan

BANANA NUT BREAD

⅓ c. shortening
½ c. sugar
2 medium eggs
1¾ c. flour
1 tsp. baking powder

½ tsp. baking soda
½ tsp. salt
1 c. ripe bananas, mashed
½ c. walnuts or pecans, chopped

Place shortening and sugar in mixer bowl; beat at high speed for 1 minute. Scrape down and beat another minute. Reduce to medium speed. Add eggs and beat 30 seconds. Scrape down and beat at high speed for 1½ minutes.

Stir together flour, baking powder, baking soda, and salt in a separate bowl. Add half the flour mixture and half the bananas to the mixer bowl; mix for 30 seconds. Add remaining flour and bananas; mix for 30 seconds. Scrape down. Add nuts and mix well. Pour batter into greased and floured large loaf pan. Bake at 350° for 40 to 45 minutes. Cool on wire rack.

Annette Hamner, Bellville Lions Club
Bellville, GA, USA

BANANA NUT BREAD

½ c. margarine
1½ c. sugar
2 beaten eggs
1 tsp. vanilla
2 c. cake flour, measured after
  sifting

½ tsp. salt
½ tsp. baking soda
¼ c. milk
3 small or 2 large bananas,
  mashed to a pulp
1 c. chopped pecans

Cream margarine and sugar. Add eggs and vanilla. Beat until fluffy. Add sifted dry ingredients alternately with milk, bananas, and nuts. Beat well after each addition. Bake in waxed paper lined 6½ x 10½ inch pan in a 350° oven for 50 minutes or until brown and an inserted toothpick comes out clean.

This bread keeps well in plastic wrap and also freezes well.

Cindy Bamburg, Biloxi Lions Club
Biloxi, MS, USA

"Growth demands a temporary surrender of security."
Gail Sheehy

"When you don't know what you want,
you often end up where you don't want to be."
Bob Greene

"The art of being wise is the art of knowing what to overlook."
William James

2075-99

TROPICAL-FRUIT BREAD

2 large ripe bananas (about 1 c. mashed)
8 oz. can pineapple chunks
1½ c. flour
¾ c. sugar
1 tsp. baking powder

1 tsp. baking soda
½ tsp. salt
2 eggs
¼ lb. butter (at room temperature)
½ c. + 1 Tbsp. flaked coconut

Heat oven to 350°. Butter an 8½ x 4½ inch loaf pan. Mash bananas. Drain pineapple; chop and pat dry. With an electric mixer set at low speed, beat flour, sugar, baking powder, soda, salt, eggs, bananas, and butter until blended. Increase speed to medium and beat 2 minutes. Stir in pineapple and ½ cup coconut. Pour into prepared pan and sprinkle with the remaining 1 tablespoon coconut. Bake until a toothpick stuck in the center comes out clean, about 1 hour. Cool on wire rack 10 minutes. Remove from pan and cool completely. Makes 12 slices.

Work time: 15 minutes. Total time: 1 hour and 15 minutes.

Per slice: 33 calories, 3 g protein, 10 g fat, 217 mg sodium, 34 g carbohydrate, 57 mg cholesterol.

Mrs. Lucy Aiken, Clarence Lions Club
Clarence Center, NY, USA

WHOLE-WHEAT BLUEBERRY BREAD

1⅓ c. flour
⅔ c. whole-wheat flour
1½ tsp. baking powder
¼ tsp. baking soda
½ tsp. salt
½ tsp. cinnamon

2 oranges
⅓ c. milk
¼ lb. butter
¾ c. sugar
1 egg
1 c. blueberries

Heat oven to 350°. Butter an 8x4 inch loaf pan. Combine flours, baking powder, soda, salt, and cinnamon. Grate ¾ teaspoon zest from oranges and squeeze ⅓ cup juice. Combine juice and milk. Beat zest, butter, and sugar until fluffy. Beat in egg. Stir in flour mixture in thirds, alternating with milk mixture. Stir in blueberries. Put in pan. Bake until a toothpick stuck in the center comes out clean, about 1 hour. Makes 16 slices.

Per slice: 157 calories, 2 g protein, 6 g fat, 129 mg sodium, 23 g carbohydrate, 30 mg cholesterol.

Joann M. Brownell, Clarence Lions Club
Clarence Center, NY, USA

"Fear is just excitement in need of an attitude adjustment."
Russ Quaglia

RAISIN BREAD

1 c. milk
1 c. water
5½ c. flour
2 tsp. vanilla
¼ lb. butter or margarine
2 c. sugar

3 eggs
5 tsp. baking powder
¼ tsp. nutmeg
1 lb. raisins
1 tsp. lemon extract
1 tsp. grated lemon rind

Preheat oven to 350°. Take ¼ cup flour and mix with raisins. Cream butter or margarine with sugar. Fold in eggs and beat until fluffy. Add dry ingredients. Gradually add milk and water and mix well. Put raisins in and mix well. Divide into 2 well-greased and floured loaf pans. Bake 1 hour until done. Cool in pans. This bread freezes well.

Lioness Diane DeVincent, East Anne Arundel Lioness Club
Pasadena, MD, USA

BROCCOLI BREAD

10 oz. frozen chopped broccoli
4 eggs
1 c. cheese
1 stick butter

1 medium onion, chopped
1 box Jiffy cornbread mix
Salt

Mix all ingredients and bake as directed on package. An iron skillet works best.

Kitty Plyler, Bellville Lions Club
Claxton, GA, USA

LEMON BREAD

½ c. butter
1⅓ c. sugar
2 eggs, beaten
½ c. milk
Juice and grated rind of 1 lemon

1½ c. flour
1 tsp. baking powder
½ tsp. salt
¾ c. chopped walnuts or pecans
   (optional)

Cream butter and 1 cup sugar. Add eggs, milk, and lemon rind. Mix flour with baking powder and salt, then add to creamed mixture. Mix well. Add nuts if using. Spoon batter into well greased loaf pan (9x5x2 inches). Bake at 350° for 1 hour and 5 minutes. Pour mixture of remaining sugar and lemon juice over loaf immediately. Cool bread in pan.

Lion Micheal and Ruth (Sauskojus) Bartolf,
Oxbow and District Lions Club
Oxbow, Saskatchewan, Canada

BLUEBERRY GINGERBREAD

½ c. shortening
1 egg
½ tsp. ginger
½ tsp. salt
1 tsp. baking soda
3 Tbsp. molasses

3 Tbsp. sugar
1 c. sugar
2 c. flour
1 tsp. cinnamon
1 c. sour milk
1 c. blueberries

Cream shortening and sugar. Add egg and mix well. Mix dry ingredients and add to creamed mixture alternately with milk into which the soda has been dissolved. Add molasses last. Stir in berries. Pour into greased and floured 9x9x2 inch baking pan. Sprinkle 3 tablespoons sugar over batter. Bake at 350° for 50 minutes.

Carolyn Hale, Eliot Lions Club
Eliot, ME, USA

APPLE SPICE BREAD

Beat the following together until smooth and creamy:

½ c. butter
½ c. honey
2 eggs
2 Tbsp. buttermilk

1 tsp. vanilla
½ tsp. nutmeg
½ tsp. cinnamon

Mix together briefly and combine with above:

½ tsp. salt
1 tsp. baking powder

½ tsp. baking soda
Scant ¼ c. vinegar

Add 2 cups whole wheat flour and mix until just incorporated.

Stir in:

2 c. coarsely chopped, peeled
   apples

½ c. nuts

Bake at 350° for 50 to 60 minutes in a greased 9x5 inch pan. Bake until well browned and toothpick comes out clean. Let cool in pan 15 minutes before removing to cool on a rack.

Lion Sandy Clever, East Prospect Lions Club
East Prospect, PA, USA

"It says something about our times that we rarely use the word sinful, except to describe a really good dessert."
Williard Ferrell

PUMPKIN BREAD

2½ c. all-purpose flour
2 c. granulated sugar
½ c. packed brown sugar
1 tsp. baking soda
½ tsp. salt
1 tsp. nutmeg
1 tsp. cinnamon

1 tsp. cloves
1 (16 oz.) can pumpkin
¾ c. cooking oil
⅓ c. orange juice
3 large eggs, beaten
1 c. chopped walnuts
1 c. raisins (uncooked)

Combine flour, granulated sugar, brown sugar, baking soda, salt, nutmeg, cinnamon, and cloves. In another mixing bowl, combine pumpkin, oil, orange juice, and beaten eggs. Add to the flour mixture, stirring just until combined. Stir nuts into batter. Pour batter into 2 greased and floured 8x4x2 inch loaf pans. Bake in a 350° oven for 1 hour. Cool in pans for 10 minutes. Remove; cool thoroughly on wire racks. Wrap and store overnight before slicing. Spread slices with cream cheese if desired. Makes 2 loaves.

Dorothy Coon, Hutchinson Breakfast Lions Club
Hutchinson, KS, USA

PUMPKIN BREAD

1 pkg. yellow cake mix
⅓ c. Grandma's molasses (gold label)
4 eggs
1 can pumpkin (2 c.)

1 tsp. cinnamon
1 tsp. nutmeg
⅓ c. chopped nuts
⅓ c. raisins

Preheat oven to 350°. Grease one 9x5 inch or two 8x4 inch size loaf pans. Combine all ingredients in a large bowl and blend. Beat at medium speed for 2 minutes. Pour into pans and bake (approximately 1 hour and 10 minutes for one 9x5 inch loaf or 45 minutes for two 8x4 inch loaves or until toothpick inserted in center comes out clean). Serve with cream cheese, preserves, or ice cream.

Joyce A. Relihan, Plymouth Lions Club
Terryville, CT

"If you accept the expectations of others, especially the negative ones, then you never will change the outcome."
Michael Jordan

"Only two kinds of people can talk without inhibitions - strangers or lovers. Everyone in between is just negotiating."
James Grippando

HARVEST LOAF

½ c. butter
1 c. sugar
2 eggs
¾ c. pumpkin
¾ c. semi-sweet chocolate chips
¾ c. walnuts, chopped fine
½ c. frosting or glaze

1¾ c. flour (all-purpose)
1 tsp. baking soda
1 tsp. cinnamon
½ tsp. salt
½ tsp. nutmeg
¼ tsp. ginger
¼ tsp. ground cloves

Mix butter and sugar until creamy. Add eggs and pumpkin; blend well. Add flour, soda, cinnamon, salt, nutmeg, ginger, and ground cloves and blend well. Add ½ cup walnuts and the chocolate chips. Blend well. Pour batter into greased pan (or line pan with wax paper, then grease and flour wax paper and ends of pan). Bake in 350° oven for 65 to 75 minutes. Test for doneness. Cool on wire rack. (Remove wax paper immediately if used.) When cool, glaze and sprinkle with remaining walnuts.

My family likes this instead of fruitcake at Christmas. Can be used as dessert or bread with coffee.

ZUCCHINI BREAD

3 eggs
1¾ c. sugar
1 c. salad oil (I use olive oil)
3 tsp. vanilla or maple flavoring
2½ c. zucchini, seeded and
    shredded
1 c. sifted white flour

1 c. whole wheat flour
1 tsp. salt
1 tsp. baking soda
1 tsp. baking powder
1 c. chopped nuts
1 c. raisins (optional)

Beat eggs until light and fluffy. Add sugar and beat well, then stir in salad oil and vanilla or maple flavor. Add all dry ingredients that have been premeasured and mixed together. Add chopped nuts and raisins last. Mix well. Pour into two greased bread/loaf pans. Bake at 325° for 50 to 60 minutes or until inserted toothpick comes out clean.

In honor of Jacob B. Brumback who always enjoys home cooking. Jake is a good cook.

Lion Ann K. Brumback, Silver Run Union Mills Lions Club
Westminster, MD

"You don't need to take a person's advice to make him feel good - just ask for it."
Laurence J. Peter

ZUCCHINI BREAD

2 c. grated zucchini
2 c. sugar
3 eggs
1 c. oil
½ c. raisins
½ c. crushed pineapple
¼ c. maraschino cherries

1 tsp. salt
1 tsp. vanilla
1 tsp. soda
1 tsp. baking powder
3 c. flour
¼ c. nuts
1 tsp. cinnamon

Preheat oven to 325°. Grease regular bread pans. Mix all above ingredients together well. Pour into pans. Bake 1 hour till brown. This bread can be frozen.

This is a great substitute for fruit cake! A family favorite.

Dianna L. Reed, Junior Lions Club
Junior, WV

ZUCCHINI BREAD

4 eggs
2 tsp. vanilla
1 c. oil

1½ c. sugar
½ c. brown sugar
2 c. grated zucchini

Mix in separate bowl:

4 c. flour
1 tsp. baking soda
½ tsp. baking powder

1 tsp. salt
1 Tbsp. cinnamon

Beat eggs until foamy. Add the next 4 ingredients. Blend well. Add flour mixture; blend well. Pour into 2 greased loaf pans. Bake approximately 1 hour at 325°.

Mrs. Ron (Lyn) Alms
Elburn, IL, USA

ZUCCHINI CARROT BREAD

3 eggs
1½ c. brown sugar, packed
1 c. grated carrots
2 tsp. vanilla
½ c. bran cereal
1 tsp. baking powder
3 tsp. cinnamon

1 c. salad oil
1 c. grated zucchini, squeezed
    and tightly packed
2½ c. all-purpose flour
1 tsp. baking soda
1 tsp. salt
1 c. chopped nuts

Preheat oven to 350°. Use 2 well-greased 8½ x 4½ inch loaf pans. Mix in large bowl the eggs and oil, then stir in sugar, zucchini, carrots, and vanilla. Stir in flour, baking soda, baking powder, salt, and cinnamon. Finally, add bran cereal, then nuts. Bake for 50 to 55 minutes.

Lioness Carolee Hackmann, East Arundel Lioness Club
Pasadena, MD, USA

ZUCCHINI BREAD

3 eggs
1 c. brown sugar
1 c. sugar
2 tsp. vanilla
1 c. vegetable oil
2 c. grated zucchini
2 tsp. baking soda

1 tsp. baking powder
1 tsp. salt
3 tsp. cinnamon
2½ c. flour
½ c. wheat germ
1 c. chopped walnuts or pecans
   (optional)

Preheat oven to 350°. Grease and flour 2 (8½ x 4½ inch) loaf pans. In large bowl, beat eggs. Add the two sugars, vanilla, oil, zucchini, baking soda and powder, salt, and cinnamon. Mix well. Add flour and wheat germ. Stir in nuts. Bake at 350° for 50 minutes to 1 hour or until toothpick comes out clean.

This recipe is requested in my family a lot!

Maria Gaso, Bentleyville Lioness Club
Bentleyville, PA, USA

ZUCCHINI BREAD

3 eggs
1¾ c. sugar
1 c. salad oil (½ olive oil)
3 tsp. flavoring (vanilla and/or
   maple)
2½ c. zucchini, seeded and
   shredded
1 c. sifted white flour

1 c. whole-wheat flour
1 tsp. salt
1 tsp. baking soda
1 tsp. baking powder
2 tsp. cinnamon
1 c. chopped walnuts
½ box raisins (optional)

Beat eggs until light and fluffy. Add sugar and beat well, then stir in oil, flavoring, and zucchini. Add white and wheat flours, salt, soda, and baking powder. Blend and then add cinnamon, nuts, and raisins. Mix well. Pour into 2 greased bread pans. Bake at 325° for 50 to 60 minutes. Test for doneness.

In honor of all creative zucchini fans.

Ann K. Brumback, of Littlestown, PA,
Silver Run Union Mills Lions Club
Westminster, MD, USA

GRANDMA'S DUMPLINGS

5 c. flour
5 eggs

1 soft stick butter
1½ c. milk (or half & half)

Mix together. Use enough milk to make a stiff dough. Roll out on floured surface. Roll very thin. Cut into desired size and drop into boiling broth. Cover and cook approximately 20 minutes.

Grandma used 1 can Pet milk or just sent the nearest child standing around to go milk the cow. She always had a house full.

Cynthia Hall, Huffman Lions Club
Huffman, TX, USA

MEXICAN SPOON BREAD

For 9x9 inch square pan.

1 (No. 1) can cream style corn	½ tsp. soda
¾ c. milk	1 tsp. salt
⅓ c. melted shortening or oil	1 (4 oz.) can green chiles
2 eggs, slightly beaten	1½ c. shredded Cheddar cheese
1 c. cornmeal	

Mix all ingredients, except chiles and cheese, in order given above. Wet ingredients first and the dry ingredients in bowl. Pour ½ batter into a greased 9x9 inch pan. Spread with green chiles, which have been split open and seeds removed, then spread one-half the shredded cheese over top. Pour rest of batter on top and rest of cheese over all. Bake at 400° for 45 minutes. Let stand a short time for better cutting. Serves 8 to 10.

For baking in 9x13 inch pan, double recipe.

Goldie Fultz, Bullhead City Lions Club
Bullhead City, AZ, USA

PIKELETS

Are similar to pancakes, but they are smaller and make delicious and nutritious snacks.

½ c. whole wheat flour	1 tsp. grated lemon rind
½ c. white flour	Squeeze of lemon juice
1 Tbsp. baking powder	Enough milk to make a
1 ripe banana, mashed	consistent, dropping batter

Combine dry ingredients, then stir in banana and milk, preferably low-fat milk. Drop spoonfuls of mixture onto a heated, lightly greased, nonstick skillet. As bubbles appear on top of each pikelet, turn over so the other side browns. Remove from pan and serve topped with slices of fresh bananas. Recipe makes 12 pikelets.

John and Fran Stahl, Charlton Lions Club
Charlton, Victoria, Australia

CHEESY-GARLIC BREAD

1 loaf French bread, split lengthwise	2 c. shredded Mozzarella cheese
½ c. mayo	½ lb. margarine
	1 tsp. garlic salt

Mix topping ingredients and spread on bread. Bake in 400° oven to melt and brown topping. *Nummy good - so easy!*

P. Diane Baldwin, Broken Bow Lions Club
Broken Bow, NE, USA

CHRISTMAS STOLLEN

1 c. scalded milk
1 (2 oz.) cake compressed yeast
1 c. butter
4 c. bread flour
1 tsp. sugar

½ c. sugar
3 egg yolks
½ tsp. salt
¼ tsp. nutmeg

Scald milk. Allow to cool to lukewarm. Mix yeast with 1 teaspoon sugar until liquid. Add to milk. Add part of the flour. Beat until smooth. Cream butter and ½ cup sugar. Add to above mixture with beaten egg yolks, salt, nutmeg, and remainder of flour. Knead until smooth and elastic, using about ½ cup flour on canvas. Place in buttered bowl in warm place to rise until double in bulk (about 3½ hours). When dough has doubled in bulk, divide into 3 equal parts. Roll each piece into a triangle, ½ inch thick. Brush with melted butter.

Cover with the following filling:

1 lb. pitted dates, cut in pieces
½ c. nutmeats, chopped

1 c. maraschino cherries, cut small
1 slice candied pineapple, cut small

Roll dough (like jelly roll), starting with wide end. Shape into a crescent. Place on cookie sheets. Let rise until light (about 1½ hours). Bake at 375° about 30 to 40 minutes. Frost and decorate with cherries and fruit. Makes 3 stollens.

Yeast substitutes: 2 ounce cake equals three ¼ ounce packages of dry yeast or 6 + ¾ teaspoons of dry yeast.

My grandmother made this recipe every Christmas. She died in 1983 at age 92.

Lion Diane Pfotenhauer, DePere Lions Club
DePere, WI, USA

CORN BREAD

1 c. corn meal
1 c. flour
3 Tbsp. sugar
1 Tbsp. baking powder

1 tsp. salt
2 eggs
2½ Tbsp. bacon drippings
Milk

Mix all the ingredients and add only enough milk to make the batter consistency.

Lion Ida Rohrer, Moundbuilders Lions Club
Newark, OH, USA

"Life isn't a science; we make it up as we go along."
Al Hirschfeld

QUICK AND EASY CORNBREAD
(Very moist)

1½ c. mayonnaise
2 eggs

1 (16 oz.) cream style corn
1 (12 oz.) pkg. corn muffin mix

Combine mayonnaise, eggs, and cream style corn; mix together, then add 12 ounces of corn muffin mix. Mix well until thoroughly all mixed. Grease a 9x13 inch pan and pour into dish.

This is the most moist cornbread your lips will ever touch.

JoAnn Jones, Mathews Lions Club
North, VA

ANGEL CORN STICKS

1½ c. corn meal
1 c. flour
1 pkg. yeast
1 Tbsp. sugar
1 tsp. salt
1½ tsp. baking powder

½ tsp. baking soda
Sage to taste
2 eggs, beaten
2 c. buttermilk
½ c. vegetable oil

Combine dry ingredients in a large bowl. Combine eggs, buttermilk, and oil; add to dry ingredients, stirring until smooth. Spoon the batter into well greased cast iron corn stick pans, filling half full. Bake 12 to 15 minutes at 450°. Yield: 3 dozen.

Lion Benny Warde, Mount Airy Foothills Lions Club
Mount Airy, NC, USA

CORN LIGHT BREAD

2 c. self-rising meal
¾ c. sugar
2 c. buttermilk

1 c. self-rising flour
½ c. Wesson oil

Mix all ingredients and bake in a greased loaf pan for 1 hour at 350°.

Terry Kelly, Iron City Lions Club
Iron City, TN, USA

"Some of God's greatest gifts are unanswered prayers."
"Unanswered Prayers" by Garth Brooks

MEXICAN CORN BREAD

1½ c. corn meal
½ c. flour
1 Tbsp. baking powder
1 tsp. salt
1 c. milk
½ c. vegetable oil
2 eggs, beaten
1 c. whole corn, drained, or 1 c. creamed corn

6 to 30 jalapeno peppers (as many as you can stand), chopped
5 to 6 green onions, chopped (also use the tops)
1½ c. shredded sharp Cheddar cheese
½ c. green pepper, chopped
1 lb. sausage (hot or mild), cooked and crumbled (drain off fat)

Mix all together until well blended. Place in a 9x13 inch pan and bake at 350° for 30 to 35 minutes or until done.

Lion Robert Ell, Southport Lions Club
Indianapolis, IN, USA

MEXICAN CORN BREAD

1½ c. self-rising cornmeal
1 c. plain flour
1 can Del Monte low salt cream corn
8 oz. sour cream

1 c. shredded Cheddar cheese
2 eggs
½ c. canola oil
1 tsp. mild jalapeno salsa

Mix all ingredients. Pour into pan. Bake at 350° for 30 minutes.

Dorothy Freeman, Travelers Rest Lions Club, District 32-A
Travelers Rest, SC, USA

"If you're truly serious about preparing your child for the future, don't teach him to subtract - teach him to deduct."
Fran Lebowitz

❧ ❧ ❧

Opportunities are like sunrises. If you wait too long, you miss them.
William Arthur Ward

❧ ❧ ❧

People who keep stiff upper lips find that it is really hard to smile.

CHEESE-TOPPED CORN BREAD

2 c. flour
2 c. yellow cornmeal
¼ c. sugar
4 tsp. baking powder
1½ tsp. salt
½ tsp. baking soda

2 c. buttermilk
8 oz. unsalted butter, melted
2 eggs
¼ c. shredded sharp Cheddar
  cheese

Heat oven to 350°. Butter a 13x9 inch baking pan. In a large bowl, combine flour, cornmeal, sugar, baking powder, salt, and soda. In small bowl, combine buttermilk, ½ cup water, butter, and eggs. Make a well in center of flour mixture and stir in buttermilk mixture until just blended. Spread in prepared pan, sprinkle with cheese, and bake until a toothpick inserted in center comes out clean, 25 to 30 minutes. Makes 16 servings.

Work time: 15 minutes. Total time: 45 minutes.

Per serving: 205 calories, 5 g protein, 8 g fat, 403 mg sodium, 29 g carbohydrate, 45 mg cholesterol.

Lion John J. Hess, Clarence Lions Club
Clarence Center, NY, USA

SAGE AND PARMESAN CORN BREAD

2 Tbsp. unsalted butter
1 c. cornmeal
1 c. flour
⅓ c. + 1 Tbsp. grated Parmesan
  cheese
2 Tbsp. sugar

1 Tbsp. baking powder
1 tsp. salt
1 tsp. sage
1 c. milk
1 egg

Heat oven to 425°. Butter a 9 inch square baking pan. Melt the 2 table-spoons butter and let cool. In a mixing bowl, combine cornmeal, flour, ⅓ cup of the Parmesan, the sugar, baking powder, salt, and sage. Combine milk and egg and stir into the cornmeal mixture with the melted butter until all the ingredients are just moistened. Pour into the prepared pan and sprinkle with the remaining Parmesan. Bake until edges start to brown and pull away from the sides of the pan, 15 to 20 minutes. Cool to room temperature before cutting. Makes 12 squares.

Per square: 144 calories, 5 g protein, 5 g fat, 391 mg sodium, 20 g carbohydrate, 30 mg cholesterol.

Joann M. Wetzler, Clarence Lions Club
Clarence Center, NY, USA

"Dreams are really important. You can't do it unless you imagine it."
George Lucas

MONKEY BREAD

3 tubes roll dough
1 tsp. cinnamon

1 c. sugar

Boil together:

1 c. sugar
1 tsp. cinnamon

1 stick margarine

Cut rolls in 4 pieces and drop in cinnamon and sugar mixture. Shake to cover and put in a greased Bundt pan, then pour the boiled mixture over top. Bake at 350° for 30 minutes, then pick a piece off at a time and enjoy. *Kids really love this.*

DANISH COFFEE CAKE

1 c. flour
½ c. butter
2 Tbsp. cold water
½ c. butter
1 c. water

1 tsp. almond, lemon, or rum
    flavoring
1 c. flour
¼ tsp. salt
3 eggs

Measure 1 cup flour into bowl. Cut in butter and sprinkle with 2 tablespoons water. Mix with fork and round into ball. Divide in half, then pat into two long strips on greased cookie sheet. Bring to boil ½ cup butter, 1 cup water, and flavoring. Remove from heat, then add one cup of flour all at once; add salt and stir. Add each egg separately and stir until smooth. After each, spoon evenly onto each strip of pastry. Bake for 60 minutes at 350°. Serves 8.

May be baked day before use. Frost with a powdered sugar frosting and flavoring.

Several years ago, I won a local baking contest with this recipe.

Barbara J. Pedersen, Othello Lions Club
Othello, WA, USA

*"We come to love not by finding a perfect person,
but by learning to see an imperfect person perfectly."*
Sam Keen

*"There's nothing so dangerous for manipulators
as people who think for themselves."*
Meg Greenfield

SOUR CREAM COFFEE CAKE

1 c. butter or margarine
1¾ c. sugar
2 eggs
2 tsp. vanilla
1 tsp. baking powder
½ tsp. salt

2 c. flour
1 c. sour cream
½ c. chopped nuts
½ c. brown sugar
1 tsp. cinnamon

Cream butter, sugar, eggs, and vanilla. Add baking powder, salt, and flour. Fold in the sour cream last. Put half of the batter in pan and sprinkle half of topping over, then repeat. Top with nuts, brown sugar, and cinnamon mixture. Bake at 300° for one hour.

It may be necessary to leave in oven a few minutes longer, but this is supposed to be a moist cake. This cake is better if baked in a Bundt pan.

Lion Ida Rohrer, Moundbuilders Lions Club
Newark, OH, USA

PARTY COFFEE CAKE

3 Tbsp. sugar
2 tsp. cinnamon
½ c. chopped nuts
1 yellow cake mix

½ c. sugar
¾ c. oil
1 c. commercial sour cream
4 eggs

Step 1: Mix 3 tablespoons sugar, cinnamon, and chopped nuts; set aside.

Step 2: Mix in large bowl 1 yellow cake mix, ½ cup sugar, ¾ cup Wesson oil, and 1 cup commercial sour cream. Add 4 eggs, one at a time, and beat. Grease and flour Bundt pan. Pour half of batter into pan and sprinkle nut mixture, then add remaining batter. Bake 1 hour at 350°.

Glaze:

1 c. powdered sugar
½ tsp. vanilla

2 Tbsp. milk or cream

Can put on glaze after removed from pan.

A nice cake for a brunch.

Leola C. Jurrens, Downtown Bartlesville Lions Club
Bartlesville, OK, USA

"Souvenirs are perishable; fortunately, memories are not."

Susan Spano

EASY COFFEE CAKE

1¾ c. flour
1½ tsp. baking powder
½ tsp. baking soda
¼ tsp. salt
½ tsp. cinnamon
⅓ + ½ c. brown sugar
½ lb. unsalted butter (at room temperature)

½ c. granulated sugar
½ tsp. grated lemon zest
1 tsp. vanilla extract
2 eggs
¾ c. sour cream
⅓ c. chopped pecans

Heat oven to 350°. Butter a 9 inch pan. Combine flour, baking powder, soda, and salt. Combine cinnamon and ⅓ cup brown sugar. Beat ½ cup brown sugar, the butter, granulated sugar, and zest. Beat in vanilla and eggs. Beat in half flour mixture, then sour cream and then remaining flour mixture. Spread half the batter in pan. Sprinkle with half the cinnamon-sugar. Spoon on remaining batter. Sprinkle with cinnamon-sugar and nuts. Bake until done, 35 to 40 minutes. Makes 9 servings.

Per serving: 388 calories, 5 g protein, 19 g fat, 209 mg sodium, 51 g carbohydrate, 84 mg cholesterol.

Joann M. Brownell, Clarence Lions Club
Clarence Center, NY, USA

SNICKERDOODLE COFFEE CAKE

1 c. sugar
½ c. butter
1 egg
1 c. milk

2¼ c. flour
2 tsp. baking powder
Pinch of salt
1 c. raisins

Topping:

Sugar
Cinnamon

Chopped nuts

Mix and pour into greased 9 inch pan. Sprinkle with sugar, cinnamon, and chopped nuts. Bake 25 to 30 minutes in 350° oven.

P. Diane Baldwin, Broken Bow Lions Club
Broken Bow, NE, USA

"Morality is truth in full bloom."

Victor Hugo

ROLLS

PUFF PILLOW BUNS

1 pkg. active dry yeast
¼ c. warm water
½ c. scalded milk
⅓ c. butter
¼ c. sugar
1 tsp. salt

1 tsp. grated lemon peel
2 beaten eggs and 1 egg yolk
2 (3 oz.) cream cheese
½ tsp. vanilla
3 c. sifted flour (add more if
    dough clings to hands)

Stir till butter melts. Cool to lukewarm. Add 2 beaten eggs, 1 teaspoon grated lemon peel, and 1 cup sifted all-purpose flour; beat well. Stir in the softened yeast. Add two cups sifted all-purpose flour, mixing well. Cover bowl with damp cloth and refrigerate dough at least four hours or overnight.

When ready to shape dough, prepare cream cheese filling. Blend 2 (3 ounce) packages softened cream cheese, one tablespoon sugar, one slightly beaten egg yolk, and ½ teaspoon vanilla. Divide dough in fourths. (Refrigerate unused dough.)

On generously floured surface, roll each portion into 12x8 inch rectangle. With floured knife, cut in six 4 inch squares or roll up. Place about two tablespoons of filling in center (can be filled with jam). Bring opposite corners to the center and pinch to seal. Place on greased bake sheet. Let rise, uncovered, till large; bake 20 to 30 minutes at 400°.

Everyone seems to like seconds when I bake this recipe.

Lion Evelyn M. Mongesku, Western Branch Lions Club
Chesapeake, VA, USA

"Virtually every important action in life involves educated guesswork. Too few chances reliably translate into too few victories."
Thomas W. Hazlett

"There's too much said for the sake of argument and too little said for the sake of agreement."
Cullen Hightower

"Today is always here. Tomorrow, never."
Toni Morrison

OVERNIGHT BUNS

1 pkg. yeast (traditional)
1 c. white sugar
1 Tbsp. salt
4 c. lukewarm milk

1 c. cooking oil (Crisco)
12½ c. flour
1 egg

Dissolve yeast in ¼ cup water with 1 teaspoon sugar and let rise about 15 minutes. Beat together egg, sugar, oil, and salt. Add 4 cups of lukewarm water and the dissolved yeast mixture and beat until foamy. Make a well in the flour and add the above mixture. Mix and knead until soft and smooth. Knead on flat surface with a little oil. Do not add more flour after dough is mixed. Let rise in a covered greased bowl for 2½ hours. Punch down and let rise again for 1 hour. Form into buns and place on greased cookie sheets or muffin tins. Cover and let rise overnight. In the morning, preheat oven to 375°F. and bake buns for 20 minutes. If oven is hotter, bake at 350°F. for 20 minutes.

I also make these into hamburger buns using deeper cookie sheet, 3 across. Muffin tins make a nice size dinner roll.

Let buns rise in a *cool* place overnight. I always use oil on my hands to shape, *never flour.*

Lion Ann Bishop, Lake of the Woods Lions Club
Kenora, Ontario, Canada

MARTHA'S ROLLS

2 c. water
1 stick margarine
Pinch of salt
½ c. sugar

1 pkg. RapidRise yeast
Gold Medal bread flour (yellow
bag - about 6 c.)

In a large pan, put water, margarine, and salt. Heat until margarine melts. Add sugar. Cool. Dissolve yeast in ½ cup warm water. Add to water mixture. Stir in flour (not all at once - may not need quite all). Cover with waxed paper sprayed with Pam. Let rise until double in size. Roll out and shape as desired. Butter tops. Refrigerate until 1½ hours before serving. Let rise. Bake 10 to 15 minutes at 375° until lightly browned.

I make these the day before and store in refrigerator.

Martha C. Daniel, Bellville Lions Club
Bellville, GA, Evans County, USA

"What is a vision? It is a compelling image of an achievable future."
Laura Berman Fortgang

90 MINUTE ROLLS

5¾ c. flour
½ c. warm water
2 pkg. active dry yeast
1½ c. lukewarm water

3 Tbsp. sugar
1½ tsp. salt
½ c. shortening (I use canola oil)

Spoon flour into dry measuring cup; level off and set aside. Soak yeast in the ½ cup warm water for 5 minutes. Combine lukewarm milk, sugar, and salt in large mixing bowl; stir to dissolve. Beat in shortening, yeast mixture, and 2 cups of flour (not sifted) until smooth. Add remaining flour and mix until dough leaves sides of bowl. Turn onto lightly floured board; knead until dough becomes smooth, elastic, and no longer sticky. Set in warm place to raise about 30 to 40 minutes. Punch down at once. Make into rolls and place on greased baking sheet. Let rise 30 minutes. Bake at 425° for 12 to 15 minutes.

Teresa White, Graysville-Proctor Lions Club
Proctor, WV, USA

GRANDMA'S ROLLS

Mix together:

2 c. warm water
½ c. sugar

2 Tbsp. yeast

Add:

½ c. oil
1 egg

1 tsp. salt
5½ c. flour (more if needed)

Mix thoroughly and knead until the mixture is not doughy, yet remains a soft dough. Let raise. Reknead, roll out, and put butter, brown sugar, cinnamon, and/or chocolate chips or raisins on top. Roll up and slice approximately one inch thick. Place the rolls in a pan with 1 cup sugar (brown or white) and ¾ cup half & half or condensed milk. Let raise again and bake at 350° for 25 minutes or until light brown on top.

P. Diane Baldwin, Broken Bow Lions Club
Broken Bow, NE, USA

"Most people have a desire to look at the exception instead of the desire to become exceptional."
John C. Maxwell

"Ideas matter in American politics, but results matter more."
Dan Balz and Ronald Brownstein

ICEBOX ROLLS

1 qt. sweet milk
1 c. sugar
3 env. dry yeast
1 c. shortening (Crisco)

2 tsp. salt
1 tsp. baking powder
1 tsp. soda
8 c. plain flour

For more rolls:

1½ qt. sweet milk
1½ c. sugar
4½ env. dry yeast
1½ c. shortening (Crisco)

3 (plus 1½ times) salt
2 plus ½ tsp. baking powder
2 plus ½ tsp. baking soda
12 c. plain flour

Mix milk, sugar, and shortening; heat well (but do not boil). Let cool. Soak yeast until dissolved in lukewarm water. Add yeast to milk mixture. Add 4 cups flour; mix well and let set for 1 hour. Add other 4 cups of flour, soda, salt, and baking powder. *Knead well.* Put in container at least twice size of dough. Cover with damp cloth. Place in refrigerator. Let rise. When ready to cook, make rolls and let rise 2 hours before baking. Will keep in refrigerator for many days. Dampen cloth cover occasionally.

Lion Carolyn Lambert, Brookhaven "Alpha" Lions Club
Brookhaven, MS

DINNER ROLLS

1 Tbsp. yeast
1 c. water
3 c. flour
¼ c. sugar
1 Tbsp. sugar

¼ c. dried milk
¼ c. shortening
¼ tsp. salt
1 egg, well beaten

Dissolve yeast and 1 tablespoon sugar in lukewarm water. Add dried milk and 1¼ cups flour to make a sponge. Beat until smooth. Cover and let rise in warm place until light, about 1 hour. Cream shortening, sugar, and salt; add to yeast mixture. Add egg and remaining 1¾ cups flour. Knead until smooth and elastic (very important for light rolls). Cover and let rise until double in bulk. Shape into rolls; place in pans sprayed with Pam (or equivalent). Let rise until light. Bake approximately 20 minutes at 350°.

Carrie Tyler, President, Montezuma Lions Club
Copeland, KS

"Thanksgiving dinner is truly a magical meal. It keeps reappearing for days."
Linda Perret

SESAME CUMIN BOW TIES

2 tsp. cumin
¾ tsp. salt
2 Tbsp. sesame seeds

1 sheet frozen puff pastry (half a
17¼ oz. pkg.), thawed
1 egg white

Heat oven to 375°. Combine cumin and salt. Sprinkle half this salt mixture and 1 tablespoon of the sesame seeds over a lightly floured work surface and lay the pastry on top. Sprinkle with remaining salt mixture and sesame seeds. Roll pastry to an approximately 11x14 inch rectangle, pressing the sesame seeds into dough with the rolling pin. With a sharp knife, cut pastry crosswise into approximately 1 inch wide strips and cut each long strip crosswise into 4 shorter ones. Twist each and pinch the center to form a bow tie. Put about 1 inch apart on ungreased baking sheet. Beat egg white with 1 tablespoon water and brush over the tops of the bow ties. Bake until puffed and golden, about 10 minutes. Serve warm or room temperature.

Work time: 15 minutes. Total time: 25 minutes.

Per piece: 23 calories, 0 g protein, 1 g fat, 55 mg sodium, 2 g carbohydrate, 0 mg cholesterol.

Lion John J. Hess, Clarence Lions Club
Clarence Center, NY, USA

CORNMEAL DINNER ROLLS

⅓ c. cornmeal
½ c. sugar
2 tsp. salt
½ c. shortening
2 c. milk
1 (¼ oz.) pkg. active dry yeast

¼ c. warm water (110° to 115°)
2 eggs, lightly beaten
4 c. all-purpose flour
Melted butter
Additional cornmeal

Combine cornmeal, sugar, salt, shortening, and milk in medium saucepan; cook until thickened. Cool to lukewarm. Dissolve yeast in water; add to cornmeal mixture. Add eggs; beat thoroughly. Add flour to form a soft dough. Knead well on a lightly floured surface. Place in a bowl; cover and let rise. Punch down. On lightly floured surface, roll out to 1 inch thickness; cut into 1½ inch circles. Place on greased baking sheet. Brush with melted butter; sprinkle with cornmeal. Cover and let rise. Bake at 375° for 15 minutes.

"Should you shield the canyons from the windstorms,
you would never see the beauty of their carvings."
Elisabeth Kubler-Ross

REFRIGERATOR BRAN MUFFINS

2 c. 100% All Bran
2 c. boiling water
1 c. cooking oil
3 c. sugar
4 eggs, beaten
1 qt. buttermilk

5 c. flour
3 Tbsp. baking soda
1 Tbsp. salt
4 c. bran flakes
1 c. raisins

Pour boiling water over 100% All Bran and set aside. Cream together oil, sugar, eggs, buttermilk, and All Bran. Sift flour, baking soda, and salt and add to buttermilk mixture. Add bran flakes and mix just until combined. Add raisins that have been coated with flour. Chill in refrigerator for one day before baking. Fill muffin tins to ¾ and bake for 15 to 20 minutes at 400°F.

This muffin mixture will keep in refrigerator for 4 to 6 weeks.

Lion Rita Bollenbach, Lake of the Woods Lions Club
Kenora, Ontario, Canada

BASIC OAT BRAN MUFFINS

Time: 25 minutes.

1 c. oat bran
1 c. whole wheat pastry flour
3 tsp. baking powder
1½ tsp. cinnamon
¼ c. vegetable oil

¼ c. honey, maple syrup, rice
    syrup, or barley malt
Sweetener
1 c. soymilk or apple juice

Preheat oven to 350°F. Combine all dry ingredients in a large mixing bowl. Combine all liquid ingredients in a 2 cup measure. Prepare muffin tins. Combine wet ingredients with dry ingredients and stir just until moistened. Do not beat. Divide batter between the 12 muffin cups. Bake at 350°F. for 15 minutes. Serves 6.

Comments: Up to ½ cup of nuts, raisins, blueberries, or chopped fresh apples can be added if desired.

PDG Jim Schiebel, Hilton Lions Club
Hilton, NY, USA

"Reverence for the past is important, but so is regard for the future."
Brad Herzog

"Resentment is like taking poison and waiting for the other person to die."
Malachy McCourt

BRAN MUFFINS

6 c. 100% bran cereal
2 c. boiling water
1 c. shortening (cooking oil)
3 c. sugar
2 tsp. salt

5 c. flour
4 eggs
1 qt. buttermilk
5 tsp. soda

Combine water, shortening, and 2 cups bran. Let cool. Beat sugar and eggs together. Add remaining ingredients, including the remaining bran cereal. Nuts and raisins may be added if desired. (I use 1 box raisins and the whole box of bran.) Grease tins. Bake at 350° for 20 minutes. Batter may be stored in refrigerator in tightly closed container for as long as six weeks.

Lion Paul and Vale Welsh, East Prospect Lions Club
East Prospect, PA, USA

OATMEAL MUFFINS

Soak together for 1 hour:

1 c. rolled oats

1 c. buttermilk

Mix together:

⅓ c. soft shortening
½ c. brown sugar

1 egg

Sift:

1 c. flour
1 tsp. baking powder

½ tsp. soda
1 tsp. salt

Optional:

Raisins

Nuts

Stir in alternately with oatmeal mixture. Fill greased muffin cup ⅔ full and bake until golden brown. Bake at 400° for 20 to 25 minutes. Yields 12 medium-sized muffins.

Janice Eldred, Urbana Lions Club
Urbana, IA

"Life does not have to be perfect to be wonderful."
Annette Funicello

ENGLISH MUFFIN LOAVES

5½ to 6 c. flour*
2 pkg. Fleishmann's active dry
   yeast
1 Tbsp. sugar
2 tsp. salt

¼ tsp. baking soda
2 c. milk
½ c. water
Cornmeal

Combine 3 cups flour, yeast, sugar, salt, and soda. Heat liquids until very warm (120°F. to 130°F.). Add to dry mixture; beat well. Stir in enough more flour to make a stiff batter. Spoon into two 8½ x 4½ inch pans that have been greased and sprinkled with cornmeal. Sprinkle tops with cornmeal. Cover; let rise in warm place for 25 minutes. Bake at 400°F. for 45 minutes. Remove from pans immediately and cool. Makes 2 loaves.

Microwave oven directions: Reduce flour by 1 cup. Mix and let rise as directed above. Microwave each loaf on HIGH power 6½ minutes (no longer). Surface of loaf will be moist, flat, and pale. Allow to rest 5 minutes before removing from pans.

To serve: Slice and toast. Makes 16 slices.

* Measure by spooning flour lightly into cup.

Lion Robert Monaghan, Foley Lions Club
Foley, AL, USA

ENGLISH MUFFINS

1 c. milk
2 Tbsp. sugar
1 tsp. salt
¼ c. (½ stick) butter/oleo

1 c. warm water
1 pkg. dry yeast
5½ c. unsifted flour (about)
Cornmeal

Scald milk; add sugar, salt, and butter. Cool to lukewarm. Sprinkle yeast into warm water in large bowl and stir in milk mixture. Add 3 cups flour and beat until smooth. Add enough additional flour to make a soft dough. Turn out onto lightly floured board and knead until smooth and elastic, about 8 to 10 minutes.

Place in greased bowl, turning to grease top. Cover and let rise until doubled in bulk, about 1 hour. Punch down and divide in half.

On board heavily sprinkled with cornmeal, roll each piece to ½ inch thick and cut into circles with 3 inch cutter. Cover and let rest 30 minutes. Place on medium hot griddle, cornmeal side down, and bake until well browned, about 15 minutes. Turn and bake about 15 minutes longer.

My blue ribbon winner from 4-H days!

Carol Worden, South Jefferson Lions Club
Adams, NY

CINNAMON APPLE MUFFINS

2⅓ c. flour
¼ c. brown sugar
½ tsp. cinnamon
Salt
9 Tbsp. butter
1 large apple (about ½ lb.)

⅓ c. granulated sugar
1 Tbsp. baking powder
1 egg
1 c. milk
1 tsp. vanilla extract

Heat oven to 375°. Butter two 6 cup muffin pans, including tops. Combine ⅓ cup flour, the brown sugar, cinnamon, and a pinch of salt. Cut in 3 tablespoons butter until mixture resembles large crumbs. Set aside. Melt remaining 6 tablespoons butter. Quarter, core, and peel apple. Cut into small pieces. Combine remaining 2 cups flour, the granulated sugar, baking powder, and ½ teaspoon salt. Mix together egg, milk, vanilla, and melted butter. Stir egg mixture into flour mixture until just combined. Stir in apple. Spoon into prepared pans. Top with crumb mixture. Bake until a toothpick stuck in the center comes out clean, about 25 minutes. Immediately remove from pans. Serve warm or cooled. Makes 12 muffins.

Work time: 25 minutes. Total time: 50 minutes.

Per muffin: 242 calories, 4 g protein, 11 g fat, 125 mg sodium, 32 g carbohydrate, 46 mg cholesterol.

Mrs. Lucy Aiken, Clarence Lions Club
Clarence Center, NY, USA

CARROT PINEAPPLE MUFFINS

1¾ c. flour
1 tsp. baking powder
1 tsp. baking soda
½ tsp. salt
½ tsp. ground cinnamon
¼ tsp. ground nutmeg
½ lb. carrots (about 1 c. grated)

2 eggs
⅔ c. vegetable oil
⅔ c. brown sugar
¼ c. water
½ c. crushed pineapple, drained
½ c. chopped pecans

Heat oven to 350°. Butter 12 cup muffin tin. Combine flour, baking powder, soda, salt, cinnamon, and nutmeg. Grate carrots. In a bowl, stir together eggs, oil, sugar, and the water until smooth. Add to dry ingredients with pineapple, carrots, and pecans. Stir until just combined. Spoon into muffin cups. Bake until tops spring back when lightly touched, 20 to 25 minutes. Makes 12 muffins.

Per muffin: 286 calories, 4 g protein, 17 g fat, 217 mg sodium, 30 g carbohydrate, 38 mg cholesterol.

Joanne M. Wetzler, Clarence Lions Club
Clarence Center, NY, USA

BANANA MUFFINS

1½ c. flour
⅓ tsp. baking powder
½ tsp. salt
¾ c. sugar
1 tsp. baking soda

1 egg, beaten
½ c. crushed pineapple
½ c. oil
½ c. bananas, mashed
1 tsp. vanilla

Preheat oven to 375°. Mix dry ingredients in a large bowl. Mix egg, pineapple, oil, bananas, and vanilla. Add to dry ingredients and stir only until flour is moistened. Spoon batter into paper lined muffin tins ⅔ full. Bake for 20 minutes.

Serve warm or cold. Muffins freeze well.

BLUEBERRY MUFFINS

2 c. plain flour
¼ c. sugar
1 egg
1 c. milk
¼ c. vegetable oil

1 Tbsp. baking powder
½ tsp. salt
1 tsp. lemon peel
¼ tsp. nutmeg
1 c. blueberries

Heat oven to 425°. Combine dry ingredients. Beat the egg. Stir milk and oil into beaten egg. Add the dry ingredients and stir until well blended. Spoon into muffin tins and bake at 425° for 20 to 25 minutes.

Martha C. Cox, Travelers Rest Lions Club
Travelers Rest, SC

BERRY PICKERS REWARD MUFFINS

2 c. flour
1 tsp. baking powder
½ tsp. baking soda
¼ tsp. salt1/2 c. butter, softened
1¼ c. sugar
2 eggs
1 (8 oz.) sour cream

1 tsp. vanilla
1 c. fresh or frozen raspberries,
   thawed and drained
2 Tbsp. sugar
¼ tsp. ground cinnamon
¼ tsp. nutmeg

Line 24 muffin cups with paper baking cups or spray with cooking spray. In medium bowl, stir together flour, baking powder, soda, and salt. In a large bowl, beat butter with an electric mixer on medium speed for 30 seconds. Add 1¼ cups sugar and beat with electric mixer on medium speed till combined. Beat in eggs, sour cream, and vanilla till combined. With spoon, stir the dry ingredients into the beaten mixture till moistened. Fold in raspberries. Spoon into cups, filling ¾ full.

For topping: In small bowl, stir together the 2 tablespoons sugar, cinnamon, and nutmeg. Sprinkle on batter. Bake at 400° for 18 to 20 minutes. Serve warm.

Eleanor McFadden, West Milford Lions Club
West Milford, WV, USA

TEX-MEX BISCUITS

2 c. biscuit mix
1 (4 oz.) can chopped green
   chilies, drained

1 c. finely shredded Cheddar
   cheese
⅔ c. milk

In a bowl, combine biscuit mix and milk till a soft dough forms. Stir in cheese and chilies. Turn onto a floured surface; knead 10 times. Roll out to ½ inch thick. Cut with a 2½ inch biscuit cutter. Place on ungreased baking sheet. Bake at 450° for 8 to 10 minutes or till golden brown. Serve warm. Makes about 1 dozen.

Volunteers are underpaid, not because they are worthless, but because they are priceless.

Doris (Cricket) Kimbrell, Iron City Lions Club
Iron City, TN, USA

ANZAC BISCUITS

1 c. rolled oats
1 c. white flour, sifted
1 c. sugar
¾ c. shredded coconut
4 oz. butter or margarine

2 Tbsp. light-colored pancake
   syrup, molasses, or treacle
½ tsp. baking soda
1 Tbsp. boiling water

Combine oats, sifted flour, sugar, and coconut. Combine butter/margarine with syrup in saucepan; stir over low heat until melted and thoroughly blended. Mix baking soda with boiling water and add to butter and syrup mixture. Stir liquid mixture into dry ingredients until batter is formed. Place teaspoons of batter onto greased cookie sheet, about 3 inches apart, to allow for spreading. Bake in 350° oven for 20 minutes. Place biscuits on rack to cool.

John and Fran Stahl, Charlton Lions Club
Charlton, Victoria, Australia

SWEET POTATO BISCUITS

1 lb. cooked sweet potatoes,
   steamed or boiled
1 c. light brown sugar

¼ c. water
2¼ c. Bisquick (or any other
   biscuit mix)

Cool and peel sweet potatoes. Mix together sweet potatoes, brown sugar, Bisquick mix, and water. Combine ingredients thoroughly. (The mixture will be moister than regular biscuits.) Flour table. Roll biscuit mix to ½ inch thickness. Cut with a 2½ inch cutter. Place on greased sheet pan. Bake in a preheated oven at 350° for 16 to 17 minutes. The moist mixture does not allow the biscuits to rise a great deal. A mindful eye should be kept on the biscuits so they do not overcook.

Very delicious and easy to make for anytime!

JoAnn Jones, Mathews Lions Club
North, VA

ANGEL FLAKE BISCUITS

5 c. plain flour
1 tsp. salt
1 tsp. baking soda
3 tsp. baking powder
¼ c. sugar

1 pkg. dry yeast
2 Tbsp. hot water
2 c. buttermilk
1 c. shortening

Sift dry ingredients. Put the yeast in a warm cup and add the water. Set aside. Add the shortening to the dry ingredients and blend with a pastry blender. Mix with the milk and yeast mixture. Cover and refrigerate. Pinch off and form rolls as needed. Bake at 400° until brown. Mixture will keep in the refrigerator up to two weeks.

Martha C. Cox, Travelers Rest Lions Club
Travelers Rest, SC

HERBED BISCUITS

Seasoning Mix:

2 Tbsp. dried oregano
2 Tbsp. dried marjoram
2 Tbsp. dried basil

4 tsp. dried savory
2 tsp. dried rosemary, crushed
2 tsp. rubbed sage

Biscuits:

¼ c. chopped onion
2 Tbsp. butter or margarine,
   divided
1½ c. all-purpose flour
2 tsp. baking powder
½ tsp. salt

¼ c. shortening
1 egg
⅓ c. milk
2 Tbsp. grated Parmesan or
   Romano cheese

Combine seasoning mix ingredients. Store in an airtight container in a cool dry place. For biscuits, saute 1 tablespoon mix and onion in 1 tablespoon butter in a skillet until onion is tender; set aside.

In a bowl, combine flour, baking powder, and salt. Cut in shortening until crumbly. Combine egg, milk, and onion mixture; stir into dry ingredients just until moistened. Turn onto a floured surface; knead 10 to 15 times. Roll to ¾ inch thickness; cut with a 2½ inch biscuit cutter. Place on an ungreased baking sheet. Melt remaining butter; brush over biscuits. Sprinkle with cheese. Bake at 450° for 10 to 14 minutes or until golden brown. Yield: 6 biscuits (½ cup seasoning mix).

Seasoning mix is enough for eight batches of biscuits. It may also be used on chicken, pork, beef, and steamed vegetables.

MOM'S BUTTERMILK BISCUITS

2 c. all-purpose flour
2 tsp. baking powder
½ tsp. baking soda

½ tsp. salt
¼ c. shortening
¾ c. buttermilk

In a bowl, combine the flour, baking powder, baking soda, and salt; cut in shortening until the mixture resembles coarse crumbs. Stir in buttermilk; knead dough gently. Roll out to ½ inch thickness. Cut with a 2½ inch biscuit cutter and place on a lightly greased baking sheet. Bake at 450° for 10 to 15 minutes or until golden brown. Yield: 10 biscuits.

BISCUITS FOR SHORTCAKE

2 c. flour (all-purpose - level)
4 tsp. baking powder
3 Tbsp. sugar
1 tsp. salt

4 Tbsp. rounded shortening
   (Crisco)
¾ c. milk

Mix dry ingredients. Add shortening. Cut with knife to reduce to chunks, then crumble with hands until "pebbles" form. Add the milk. Mix until all holds together. Add tablespoon or more milk if needed. Turn onto floured surface. Knead gently (10 times) until all dough holds. Pat out with hand or use rolling pin, until thickness of cutter (¾ inch). Cut. Place on ungreased baking pan. Bake at 425° for 15 minutes. If crowded very close together, they will rise for a very inviting biscuit! Makes 8 to 10 biscuits.

This recipe passed on by Corabelle Lounsberry, one of the creators of Scio Strawberry Festival, to the Lions Club when they assumed the activity. Anyone wishing amounts for 100 servings contact the Club.

Marian Towner, Scio Lions Club
Scio, NY, USA

QUICK CARAMEL ROLLS

¼ c. butter
½ c. chopped pecans

1 c. caramel ice cream topping
2 tubes refrigerated crescent rolls

Place butter in a 13x9x2 inch baking pan. Heat in a 375° oven until melted. Sprinkle with pecans. Add ice cream topping and mix well. Remove dough from tubes (do not unroll). Cut each section of dough into 6 rolls. Arrange rolls in prepared pans, cut side down. Bake at 375° for 20 to 25 minutes. Immediately invert onto serving plate. Makes 2 dozen.

Eleanor McFadden, West Milford Lions Club
West Milford, WV, USA

NO-KNEAD CINNAMON ROLLS

3 Tbsp. shortening
3 Tbsp. sugar
1½ tsp. salt
½ c. scalded milk

1 egg, slightly beaten
1 pkg. yeast
3¼ c. flour, sifted

Combine ½ cup scalded milk with shortening, sugar, and salt. Cool to lukewarm by adding ¼ cup water. Add 1 package yeast, dissolved in ¼ cup warm water. Blend in one egg. Gradually add flour. Cover and let stand 15 minutes. Roll out to 18x12 inch rectangle. Spread with butter, sugar, and cinnamon. Roll as for jelly roll and cut into 1 inch slices.

Place in well greased pan. Let rise in warm place until double in bulk (about 1 hour). Bake at 375° for 20 to 25 minutes. Glaze with confectioners sugar frosting.

This recipe was given to me by a neighbor many years ago and has been a most favorite with the family surpassing my other sweet roll recipes. I double the recipe and make 2 pans. They freeze well! *Quick and simple!*

Betty Goers, Princeton Lions Club
Princeton, IL

CINNAMON ROLLS

1½ c. warm water
1 pack dry yeast
¼ c. sugar
1⅓ sticks margarine

¼ c. oil
1 egg
½ tsp. salt
About 2 lb. plain flour

Icing:

1½ sticks margarine
¼ c. brown sugar

About ½ to ¾ lb. powdered
    sugar

Mix water, yeast, sugar, margarine, oil, egg, salt, and flour in a mixing bowl. Mix the flour until stiff enough to roll out. Let set in warm place until about double in size, about 45 minutes, then roll out rather thin. Brush with melted butter. Mix 1 part cinnamon and 3 parts of white sugar and sprinkle on rolled out dough. Roll dough up and cut in ¾ inch parts. Let set 30 minutes and bake at 400° for about 10 minutes or until done.

Icing: Mix margarine and brown sugar together and bring to a boil. Take off burner and use mixer to mix in powdered sugar until a little stiff, then spread over rolls.

Edwin Young, Elizabethtown Lions Club
Elizabethtown, KY, USA

QUICK BREAKFAST ROLLS

4 cans refrigerated biscuits
1 c. butter or margarine
1 c. vanilla ice cream

1 c. brown sugar
¾ c. sugar
2 tsp. cinnamon

Cut each biscuit in four pieces. Coat in the mixture of ¾ cup sugar and cinnamon. Place in ungreased 9x13 inch pan. In the microwave, bring the butter, ice cream, and brown sugar to a boil. Immediately pour over biscuits. Bake in a preheated oven at 350° for 20 minutes.

This is a favorite of our grandchildren and great-grandchildren.

Lion Amy L. Kastle, Kirwin Lions Club
Kirwin, KS, USA

STICKY CINNAMON ROLLS

1¼ c. confectioners sugar
½ c. whipping cream
1 c. coarsely chopped pecans
2 (1 lb.) loaves frozen white bread
    dough, thawed

3 Tbsp. butter or margarine,
    melted
½ c. packed brown sugar
1 tsp. ground cinnamon
¾ c. raisins (optional)

In a small bowl, combine confectioners sugar and cream. Divide evenly between two greased 9 inch square baking pans. Sprinkle with pecans; set aside. On a floured surface, roll each loaf of bread dough into a 12x8 inch rectangle; brush with butter. Combine brown sugar and cinnamon; sprinkle over butter. Top with raisins if desired. Roll up from a long side; pinch seam to seal. Cut each roll into 12 slices; place with cut side down in prepared pans. Cover and refrigerate overnight. Remove from the refrigerator; cover and let rise until doubled, about 2 hours. Cover loosely with foil. Bake at 375° for 10 minutes. Uncover and bake 8 to 10 minutes longer or until golden brown. Yield: 2 dozen.

"There's nothing like a good family when you're really up a tree."
Carolyn Hax

"The best method of overcoming obstacles is the team method."
Colin L. Powell

"Too many people overvalue what they are not
and undervalue what they are."
Malcom S. Forbes

ORANGE ROLLS

Use your favorite sweet roll recipe until ready to shape.

Orange Mixture:

¾ c. sugar   Grated rind of 2 oranges

Frosting:

1 c. confectioners sugar   ¼ c. orange juice

Roll out a portion of the recipe into a rectangle, about ¼ inch thick. Spread with melted butter or oleo. Spread with orange mixture. Roll up like jelly roll. Cut into 1 inch slices and place, cut side down, in buttered muffin tins or in baking pans. Cover and let rise until double in bulk. Bake at 350° for 20 to 25 minutes until tops are golden. Mix frosting and pour over warm rolls.

These rolls sell like hot cakes at bake sales for very good prices. Double the recipe and freeze a few. Try them and you'll love them.

Donald and Betty Whiteman, South Jefferson Lions Club
Adams, NY

DUTCH BABY

4 Tbsp. butter	¼ tsp. salt
3 eggs	⅛ tsp. nutmeg
½ c. milk	Confectioners sugar
½ c. flour	Lemon juice

Heat oven to 425°. In a 10 inch ovenproof frying pan, melt the butter. Meanwhile, combine eggs, milk, flour, salt, and nutmeg until almost smooth, but still slightly lumpy. When butter in the frying pan is hot, pour in batter. Bake until puffed and golden brown, 15 to 20 minutes. Sprinkle with confectioners sugar and drizzle lemon juice over the top. Makes 4 servings.

Per serving: 233 calories, 7 g protein, 16 g fat, 199 mg sodium, 14 g carbohydrate, 195 mg cholesterol.

Joann M. Brownell, Clarence Lions Club
Clarence Center, NY, USA

"On the dance floor, as in life, you're only as good as your partner."
Robin M. Henig

KOLACHES - CESKE KOLACE

½ c. water (lukewarm)
1 tsp. sugar
2 pkg. dry yeast
2½ c. milk (lukewarm)
1 stick oleo, melted

⅓ c. sugar
2 tsp. salt
2 eggs, well beaten
6¼ c. flour
Melted lard

In a large bowl, dissolve water, 1 teaspoon sugar, and yeast and allow to set, covered with cloth, until bubbles, about 10 minutes. Add milk, oleo, sugar, salt, eggs, and flour to the mixture; beat well. Cover with cloth and let rise until double. Turn out on floured board. Cut off pieces to make a bun as large as an egg. Place on a greased cookie sheet about 1 inch apart. Brush with melted lard and allow to rise in warm place until double. Make indentation in center and fill with 1 tablespoon filling. Allow to rise. Bake at 375° for 20 minutes. Remove from oven and brush with melted lard. Cover with cloth and allow to cool.

The Czechoslovakians arrived in Nebraska in the 1860s and brought the Kolache recipes with them. My mother made these once a week for her seven children.

Jean Chestnut, Columbus Noon Lions Club
Columbus, NE, USA

BLUEBERRY KLUCKEN

⅓ c. shortening
½ tsp. salt
2 tsp. baking powder
¾ c. milk
1 can blueberries

¾ c. sugar
2 c. flour
2 eggs
1 tsp. vanilla

Streusel:

1¼ c. flour
½ c. butter
½ c. light brown sugar

Pinch of salt
¾ tsp. cinnamon

Cream shortening, sugar, and salt. Add flour and baking powder alternately with milk and beaten eggs. Add vanilla. Grease cookie sheet. Spread mixture on sheet. Spread fruit on top. Blend streusel ingredients until coarse. Spread streusel on fruit. Bake at 375° for 25 to 30 minutes.

Elizabeth Kowalski, Canaan Northwest Lions Club
Canaan, CT, USA

"The definition of the golden age of anything is when you were there."
Justice Anthony M. Kennedy

THE BEST OF SUMMER FRUIT TART

Pastry:

1¾ c. all-purpose flour
1 tsp. grated lemon peel
¼ tsp. salt
⅓ c. canola oil

1 Tbsp. reduced-fat margarine, chilled
5 to 6 Tbsp. ice water

Filling:

½ (8 oz.) pkg. reduced-fat cream cheese
⅓ c. confectioners sugar

2 Tbsp. nonfat Ricotta cheese
2 tsp. grated lemon peel

Fruit Topping:

2 nectarines or peaches, pitted and sliced
2 plums, pitted and sliced
1 kiwi fruit, peeled and sliced

1 c. blueberries
1 c. raspberries
½ c. strawberries, hulled
¼ c. apricot preserves

For pastry, preheat oven to 425°F. In a small bowl, combine flour, lemon peel, and salt. With pastry blender, cut in oil and margarine until coarse crumbs form. Sprinkle in water, 1 tablespoon at a time, stirring until mixture holds together; knead until smooth. Flatten into a disc; place between two sheets of wax paper. Roll out to an 11 inch circle. Fit into a 9 inch round removable-bottom tart pan; trim. Prick pastry all over with fork. Bake until lightly browned, about 17 minutes. Cool on a wire rack.

For filling: In a small bowl, beat cream cheese and confectioners sugar until smooth. Beat in Ricotta and lemon peel. Spread in cooled crust. Arrange fruit decoratively over filling. In a saucepan, melt preserves over low heat; strain, then brush on fruit. Serve immediately. Makes 10 servings.

Work time: 40 minutes. Total time: 1 hour.

Per serving: 251 calories, 5 g protein, 10 g fat, 140 mg sodium, 37 g carbohydrate, 6 mg cholesterol.

Joanne M. Wetzler, Clarence Lions Club
Clarence Center, NY, USA

"Using your imagination is the one time in life you can really go anywhere."
Ann Patchett

SOUR CREAM TWISTS

3 c. flour
1 pkg. (2½ tsp.) dry yeast
1 c. butter
2 tsp. cinnamon
1 tsp. salt

2 beaten eggs
1 c. sour cream
1 c. sugar
1 tsp. nutmeg (optional)

Sift flour and add yeast. Rub in butter and add salt, eggs, and sour cream. Work until dough leaves sides of bowl. Place in a bowl and cover. Store in refrigerator for at least 3 hours or overnight. Mix in a small bowl sugar, cinnamon, and nutmeg. Spread on breadboard and roll one half of dough into sugar and spice mixture to ¼ inch thickness, coating both sides of dough with mixture. Cut into strips, one inch wide by 3 inches long, and twist with strips rolled plain and cut same widths. Place on greased baking pan and bake at 350° for 15 minutes.

Micheal and Ruth Bartolf, Oxbow and District Lions Club
Oxbow, Saskatchewan, Canada

PEAR AND BRIE PUFF ROLL

Pastry:

½ pkg. frozen puff pastry, thawed

Filling:

1 (4 oz.) round Brie cheese
2 Tbsp. raisins
1 Tbsp. chopped walnuts
  (optional)
1 tsp. grated lemon rind

1 tsp. lemon juice
1 unpeeled pear, cored and thinly
  sliced

Cut off top rind of Brie and allow cheese to soften. Combine raisins, walnuts, lemon rind, and juice in a small bowl; set aside. On a lightly floured board, roll puff pastry into a 9x12 inch rectangle. Spread the softened cheese over the rectangle, leaving a 1 inch strip of pastry along all sides. Arrange the pear slices in rows over the cheese. Sprinkle the raisin and walnut mixture over the pears. Fold over the pastry strip on the short edges. Starting with one long edge, roll up jelly roll fashion, pinching the edge and ends to seal. Make 7 slits in the top with a sharp knife. Bake in preheated 400°F. oven for 20 to 25 minutes until pastry is cooked and golden. Allow the pastry to cool for 5 minutes before cutting. Serve as a dessert and cut into smaller portions and serve as an appetizer. Makes 8 dessert or 16 appetizer servings.

Micheal and Ruth Bartolf, Oxbow and District Lions Club
Oxbow, Saskatchewan, Canada

CREAM CHEESE DANISH PASTRY

2 pkg. crescent rolls (refrigerated
   kind)
2 (8 oz.) pkg. cream cheese

1 egg yolk
1 c. regular sugar
1 tsp. vanilla

Mix 2 packages cream cheese, egg yolk, sugar, and vanilla until well blended. Place 1 package crescent rolls in oblong dish - do not grease dish. Layer bottom with this package. Spread cream cheese mixture over rolls. Place the second package of crescent rolls on top. Brush with some of egg white. Bake at 325° for 25 to 30 minutes.

Mix glaze of confectioners sugar and milk. Pour glaze over. Serve warm.
Gloria E. Thompson, Bellville Lions Club
Bellville, GA, USA

OATMEAL AND CURRANT SCONES

1¼ c. flour
½ c. quick-cooking oats
2 Tbsp. sugar
2 tsp. baking powder
½ tsp. salt

4 Tbsp. unsalted butter, cut in
   pieces
¼ c. dried currants
½ c. heavy cream

Heat the oven to 425°. Butter a baking sheet. Combine the flour, oats, sugar, baking powder, and salt. Cut the butter into the flour mixture until it resembles coarse meal. Stir in the currants, Stir in the heavy cream until the mixture forms large crumbs. Gather into a ball and knead on a floured sugar until just combined, about 30 seconds. Pat dough into an 8 inch round and cut in 8 triangles. Transfer the triangles to the prepared baking sheet and bake until the bottoms are golden, about 10 minutes. Transfer to rack and cool. Serve with orange marmalade. Makes 8 scones.

Per scone: 219 calories, 3 g protein, 12 g fat, 213 mg sodium, 25 g carbohydrate, 36 mg cholesterol.
Lion John J. Hess, Clarence Lions Club
Clarence Center, NY, USA

"What the wise do in the beginning fools do in the end."
Warren Buffet

"The great advantage to telling the truth
is that one's so much more likely to sound convincing."
Susan Howatch

LEMON HONEY SCONES

3¼ c. flour
1 Tbsp. baking powder
1 tsp. salt
6 Tbsp. unsalted butter, chilled

1 c. milk
1 egg
¼ c. honey
1¼ tsp. grated lemon zest

Heat oven to 400°. In a large bowl, combine 3 cups of the flour, the baking powder, and salt. Cut in the butter until mixture resembles coarse meal. Combine the milk, egg, honey, and zest and beat until the honey dissolves. Make a well in the center of the flour mixture and pour in milk mixture. Stir until ingredients are just moistened. Dough will be soft. Sprinkle a work surface with the remaining ¼ cup flour and gently knead the dough on the floured surface until smooth. Divide into two round pieces, about 1 inch thick and 5 inches in diameter. With a lightly floured knife, cut each piece into 6 wedges. Bake on ungreased baking sheets until golden brown, 10 to 12 minutes. Cool on wire racks. Makes 12 scones.

Per scone: 215 calories, 5 g protein, 7 g fat, 322 mg sodium, 33 g carbohydrate, 36 mg cholesterol.

Joanne M. Wetzler, Clarence Lions Club
Clarence Center, NY, USA

CINNAMON WALNUT SCONES

1¾ c. all-purpose flour
¼ c. finely chopped walnuts
4½ tsp. sugar
2¼ tsp. baking powder
½ tsp. salt

½ tsp. ground cinnamon
¼ c. cold butter or margarine
2 eggs
⅓ c. whipping cream
¼ c. buttermilk

In a bowl, combine the first six ingredients; cut in butter until the mixture resembles coarse crumbs. Combine eggs and cream; stir into dry ingredients just until moistened. Turn onto a floured surface; gently pat into a 7 inch circle, ¾ inch thick. Cut into eight wedges. Separate wedges; place on a lightly greased baking sheet. Brush tops with buttermilk. Let rest 15 minutes. Bake at 450° for 14 to 16 minutes or until golden brown. Yield: 8 servings.

"People who believe a problem can be solved tend to get busy solving it."
William Raspberry

"Eccentricity is like having an accent. It's what other people have."
Oliver Sacks

PAM'S HOT YEAST ROLLS

2 c. warm water
1 pkg. dry yeast
½ c. sugar

6 c. flour
6 Tbsp. oil
1½ tsp. salt

Put dry yeast in warm water; add sugar and salt. Add 3 cups of flour; beat with hand mixer until smooth. Add 6 tablespoons oil; heat with hand mixer. Add 3 more cups of flour. (Do not use mixer.) Work with hands. Form into ball. Let rise for 45 minutes to 1 hour. Punch down. Pinch off to make rolls. Let rise. Bake for 25 minutes or until golden brown.

It took me 15 years to learn how to make homemade rolls. They are wonderful. Thanks to my friend, Phyllis Silver.

Pam Caldwell, Mexico Sunrise Lions Club
Mexico, MO

"Heroes and winners aren't the same thing."
Michael Kevin Farrell

"Misers are no fun to live with, but they make great ancestors."
Tom Snyder

"Society works by putting opportunity and responsibility together."
Tony Blair

"Manners are just a formal expression of how you treat people."
Molly Ivins

Pies,
Pastries

CRUSTS FOR ICE CREAM PIES

No rolling, no shaping. No patching, no baking. The secrets to carefree ice cream pies — a favorite summer dessert. Combining coolness and crunch, these make-ahead creations stimulate all sorts of imaginative combinations. Mix and match complementary crusts and ice cream flavors all summer long. Fun family fare, yet perfect for dinner parties.

The simple preparation steps begin with combining your choice of crumbs with sugar, the optional additions suggested, and the melted margarine in a small bowl. Press the mixture in the bottom and up the side of an 8 or 9-inch pie pan or in the bottom of a 9-inch springform pan. Refrigerate for 10 to 15 minutes before filling with ice cream, then freeze until solid. Wrap carefully and store in the freezer. When ready to serve, remove the pie from the freezer 5 to 10 minutes before serving for easier cutting. Dip the knife into warm water to facilitate serving.

Kind	Amount of Crumbs	Sugar	Optional Additions	Margarine or Butter, Melted
Graham Cracker	1½ cups (21 squares)	¼ cup	½ tsp. cinnamon	⅓ cup
Graham Cracker-Walnut	1 cup (14 squares)	2 Tbsp.	½ cup finely chopped walnuts	¼ cup
Vanilla Wafer	1½ cups (30 wafers)	—	—	¼ cup
Chocolate Wafer	1¼ cups (20 wafers)	¼ cup	—	¼ cup
Creme-filled Choc./Vanilla Cookie	1½ cups (15 cookies)	—	—	¼ cup
Crisp Macaroon Cookie	1½ cups	—	—	¼ cup
Gingersnap Cookie	1½ cups	—	—	¼ cup
Shortbread Cookie	1¼ cups	¼ cup	¼ cup sliced almonds (chopped)	¼ cup
Pretzel *	1¼ cups	¼ cup	—	½ cup
Granola	1½ cups (coarsely crushed)	—	—	¼ cup
Coconut	2 cups	—	—	2 Tbsp.
Popcorn *	7 cups popcorn = 3½ cups coarsely ground popcorn	¼ cup (brown sugar)	⅛ tsp. cinnamon	½ cup
TIP: *For ease in serving, butter pan before preparing crust.				

PIES, PASTRIES

VELVETY CUSTARD PIE

4 eggs, slightly beaten
½ c. sugar
¼ tsp. salt
1 tsp. vanilla

2½ c. scalded milk
1 (9 inch) pie shell
Nutmeg

Mix eggs, sugar, salt, and vanilla. Add to hot milk. Pour into unbaked pie shell. Sprinkle with nutmeg. Bake at 475° for 5 minutes. Reduce heat to 375°. Bake for 25 minutes.

Teresa White, Graysville-Proctor Lions Club
Proctor, WV, USA

CUSTARD PIE

4 eggs, slightly beaten
¼ tsp. salt
½ c. sugar

3 c. milk, scalded
½ tsp. vanilla
Nutmeg

Combine eggs, salt, and sugar. Scald milk and add to egg mixture. Add vanilla. Pour into an unbaked pie shell. Sprinkle nutmeg over the top. Bake in a very hot (450°) oven for 10 minutes. Reduce heat to 350° for 30 to 40 minutes or until knife inserted comes out clean.

I like this recipe because the custard doesn't get watery as it stands.

Jennie Ludwick, Lyons-Muir Lions Club
Muir, MI, USA

COCONUT CUSTARD PIE

1 c. coconut
3 eggs
1 can Eagle Brand
1 tsp. vanilla

1¼ c. water
¼ tsp. salt
⅛ tsp. nutmeg

Preheat oven to 425°. Reserve ½ cup of the coconut. Toast the remainder. It toasts quickly so watch and stir. Bake pastry for 8 minutes. Cool slightly. Beat eggs. Add Eagle Brand, water, vanilla, salt, and nutmeg. Stir in reserved ½ cup of coconut. Pour into the pie shell. Sprinkle with toasted coconut. Bake for 10 minutes. Reduce heat to 350°. Bake 25 to 30 minutes longer or until knife comes out clean. Refrigerate.

Janie Fox, Saginaw Lions Club
Saginaw, TX

FRENCH CHOCOLATE CREAM PIE

1 pkg. Dream Whip, prepared
  according to instructions
4 oz. unsweetened chocolate
½ lb. butter
1½ c. sugar

1 tsp. vanilla
4 eggs
2 (8 inch) graham cracker crumb
  crusts

Melt unsweetened chocolate and butter in a bowl. Beat in sugar and vanilla until well mixed. Add eggs, one at a time, and beat until well blended. Blend in whipped cream. Will fill two 8 inch graham cracker crumb pies. Keep in refrigerator.

Vic Dreyer, Sr., Keiser Lions Club
Salem, OR

CHOCOLATE PIE

1 c. sugar
3 Tbsp. cornstarch
3 egg yolks
2 c. milk (2%)

2 Tbsp. Hershey's cocoa
Pinch of salt
1 tsp. vanilla extract
1 tsp. butter or oleo

Meringue:

3 egg whites
⅓ tsp. cream of tartar

6 Tbsp. sugar

In medium saucepan, beat egg yolks; add sugar, cornstarch, cocoa, and salt and mix well. Add milk; mix well and cook over medium heat until thick. Remove from heat and add vanilla and butter. Pour into baked 8 inch pie shell.

Beat egg whites and cream of tartar until soft peaks form. Add sugar gradually and continue beating until stiff peaks form. Cover pie with meringue and bake at 350° for 15 minutes or until golden brown.

Mildred Court, Stafford-Missouri City Lions Club
Stafford, TX, USA

FUDGE PIE

8 oz. butter
6 oz. unsweetened baking
  chocolate
2 c. sugar
4 eggs

1 c. flour
Pinch of salt
2 tsp. vanilla
Whipped cream

Preheat the oven to 300°. Melt the butter and chocolate in a pan over low heat. Cool. Add the sugar, eggs, flour, salt, and vanilla. Pour into a greased pie plate. Bake for 20 minutes. Refrigerate until firm. Serve topped with whipped cream and/or chocolate shavings.

Joan Katz, Stafford-Missouri City Lions Club
Stafford, TX, USA

CHOCOLATE CHIP PECAN PIE

¾ c. butter, melted and cooled
6 eggs
1½ c. sugar

1½ c. light corn syrup
2 c. pecan pieces
1 c. semi-sweet chocolate chips

Divide nuts and chips between two pastry lined 9 inch pie plates. Combine rest of ingredients and blend thoroughly. Pour into crust and bake at 350° for 35 to 40 minutes.

Variation: Stir 2 tablespoons of your favorite bourbon into the batter.

Frances T. Langley, Shelbyville Lions Club
Shelbyville, TN, USA

BUTTERMILK PIE

1 c. margarine
½ c. flour
6 eggs, slightly beaten
1 tsp. vanilla

3¾ c. sugar
¼ tsp. salt
1 c. buttermilk

Lightly cream margarine and sugar. Add salt, eggs, and buttermilk. Add flour and vanilla. Pour into uncooked pastry shells. (It is good to brown crusts a few minutes first.) Cook 8 minutes at 400°, then 30 to 40 minutes at 300° or until knife inserted in center comes out clean. This recipe makes 3 small pies or 2 large ones. Don't need a thick filling (it is very rich).

Esther Akiyoshi, Bothell Lions Club
Bothell, WA, USA

BUTTERMILK PIE

1 unbaked pie shell
1½ c. sugar
2 Tbsp. flour
2 eggs

1 stick melted margarine
¾ c. buttermilk
2 tsp. vanilla

Add the flour to sugar. Add eggs, one at a time, and mix. Add melted margarine. Stir. Add buttermilk and vanilla. Mix well. Pour into pie shell and bake at 400° until brown on top (about 25 minutes). Reduce heat to 200° and bake until pie will barely shake (about 20 minutes).

Deryl Fox, Saginaw Lions Club

"Your children make it impossible to regret your past. They're its finest fruits."

Anna Quindlen

OLD-FASHIONED CREAM PIE

1½ c. sugar
2 heaping Tbsp. flour
Pinch of salt
1 c. cream

½ c. milk
Pie shell
Butter
Nutmeg

Combine sugar, flour, and salt in bowl. Add cream and milk. Blend well. Pour into unbaked 9 inch pie shell. Dot with butter and sprinkle lightly with nutmeg. Bake 10 to 15 minutes in preheated 425° oven; reduce heat to 350° and bake 35 to 40 minutes longer.

Lion Wilma Ell, Southport Lions Club
Indianapolis, IN, USA

SUGAR-FREE CHIFFON PIE

1 pkg. jello sugar-free (any flavor)
1 c. boiling water

1 container Cool Whip
1 (9 inch) pie shell, baked

Dissolve jello in boiling water. Set aside to thicken just slightly. Beat with mixer until light and foamy. Mix in the Cool Whip, reserving enough for topping. Pour into baked pie shell. Top with reserved topping; chill and enjoy.

This can also be done with pudding mix using 1½ cups milk. Hope you enjoy these - my husband does. You may come up with some of your own ideas. If you do, you too can put them in the next cookbook.

Lion Janice Elliott, Meredith Lions Club
Meredith, NH, USA

EASY PEANUT BUTTER PIE

1 (8 oz.) pkg. cream cheese,
  softened
1 c. powdered sugar

1 c. crunchy peanut butter
1 (8 oz.) ctn. Cool Whip
1 graham cracker crust

Cream the cream cheese. Add sugar and peanut butter. Beat till smooth. Fold in Cool Whip. Place in graham cracker crust. Refrigerate or freeze. This is very good!

Mrs. Duane (Pam) Bennett, Mad River Lions Club
Riverside, OH, USA

Save the whales. Collect the whole set.

MOCHA PIE

1 prepared chocolate graham
   cracker pie crust
2 env. Dream Whip
1 c. skim milk

1 Tbsp. instant coffee
1 Tbsp. hot water
1 (8 oz.) pkg. nonfat vanilla
   yogurt
⅓ c. reduced-fat chocolate syrup

Prepare Dream Whip using milk and vanilla according to package directions. In small bowl, dissolve coffee in water. Stir in yogurt and chocolate syrup. Fold yogurt mixture into Dream Whip. Pour mixture into pie crust. Cover and freeze overnight. Transfer to refrigerator 15 minutes before serving. Garnish with drizzled chocolate syrup if desired. Serves 8.

Contains 186 calories, 8 g fat (5 g saturated), 4 g protein, 24 g carbohydrate, 0 g fiber, 150 mg sodium, 9 mg cholesterol.

Supporter of Lions, Princeton Lions Club
Princeton, IL, USA

BRICKLE DELIGHT PIE

1 (3 oz.) pkg. cream cheese,
   softened
2 Tbsp. sugar
½ c. milk

1 (6 oz.) pkg. Bits 'O Brickle
   (Heath Bits), divided
1 (8 oz.) container Cool Whip
1 (9 inch) graham cracker pie
   crust

Combine cream cheese, sugar, and milk. Add ¾ cup Bits 'O Brickle; fold in whipped topping. Spoon into pie crust. Sprinkle remaining bits over filling. Freeze about 4 hours before serving.

Frances Tays, New Braunfels Lioness Club
New Braunfels, TX, USA

IMPOSSIBLE PIE

1 c. sugar
4 eggs
½ stick butter, melted

½ c. Bisquick
1 tsp. vanilla
1 c. coconut

Put all ingredients, except coconut, in blender. Blend one minute. Add coconut (1 cup) and stir. Pour in a greased and floured pie plate (9 inches). Bake at 350° for 45 minutes or until set.

I would like to dedicate this recipe to my mother, Grace Myers.

Doris Brewer, Silver Run Union Mills Lions Club
Silver Run, MD, USA

CHOCOLATE NUT PIE

1 stick butter
¾ c. white sugar
¼ c. light brown sugar
1 tsp. vanilla
1 c. white Karo syrup

1 Tbsp. flour
1 (6 oz.) pkg. chocolate chips
1 c. pecans or walnuts
2 unbaked pie shells (9 inches)

Divide chocolate chips and pecans between pie shells. Melt butter. Stir eggs. Mix everything together. Pour into pie shells over chips and nuts. Bake at 350° for 40 to 45 minutes.

Dorothy Freeman, Travelers Rest Lions Club, District 32-A
Greenville, SC, USA

MONTGOMERY PIE

1 unbaked pie shell

Top:

⅔ c. sugar
⅓ c. buttermilk
3 Tbsp. butter

1 egg
⅓ tsp. baking soda
⅔ c. plus 3 Tbsp. flour

Bottom:

⅓ c. molasses
⅓ c. sugar
⅔ c. cold water

1 egg white
2 tsp. lemon juice
2 tsp. flour

Mix top and pour into unbaked pie shell first. Mix bottom and pour over mixture already in pan. Bake at 350° for 45 to 60 minutes. Makes one 9 inch pie.

Lion Sandy Clever, East Prospect Lions Club
East Prospect, PA, USA

RITZ CRACKER PIE

Beat stiff 3 egg whites with beater. Gradually add 1 cup sugar and 1 teaspoon vanilla. Fold in 20 Ritz crackers, crumbled, and ½ cup pecans. Pour into ungreased pie plate. Bake *exactly* 30 minutes (no longer, no less) at 325°. Cool and frost with whipped cream. Refrigerate.

Barbara Vaughn, Conroe Lioness Club
Conroe, TX, Montgomery County

Ambition without knowledge is like a boat on dry land.
Mark Lee

CREAM FILLING FOR PIES

⅔ c. sugar
⅛ tsp. salt
3 c. milk
1 tsp. vanilla (after filling is
  cooked)

3 Tbsp. cornstarch
3 egg yolks
2 Tbsp. butter

Stir ingredients together in saucepan. Cook in microwave for 3 minutes. Remove and stir. Return to microwave and cook for another 3 minutes. Remove and stir. If more cooking needed, return to microwave and repeat procedure.

Peanut Butter Pie: Use above cream filling for pies and add the following. Cream ¾ cup powdered sugar and ½ cup crunchy peanut butter together until crumbly. Sprinkle ⅔ of the peanut butter mixture in bottom of baked pie shell. Add 1 tablespoon peanut butter to the pudding and pour filling over the mixture. Use remainder of peanut butter mixture on top of filling. Cover with meringue. Brown meringue.

Banana Meringue Pie: Use above cream filling for pies and add the following. Stir in ¼ teaspoon banana flavoring. Slice two medium size bananas and arrange in a layer in the bottom of a baked pie shell. Cover with filling and meringue. Brown meringue.

Coconut Meringue Pie: Use above filling for pies and add the following. Stir in ½ teaspoon coconut flavoring and ⅔ cup shredded coconut. Pour filling into the baked pie shell and top with meringue. Brown meringue.

Carl D. Hoyt, Hutchinson Breakfast Lions Club
Hutchinson, KS, USA

FLAKY PIE CRUST

1½ c. shortening (except butter,
  margarine or salad oil)
½ c. boiling water

2 Tbsp. milk
4 c. sifted all-purpose flour
2 tsp. salt

Add boiling water and milk to shortening. With fork, break up shortening, then beat until mixture is smooth and thick. Add flour and salt into shortening. Stir quickly, forming dough that clings together. Makes enough for two 8 or 9 inch pies.

This dough is very easy to work with because it is warm. Rolls out great between two sheets of wax paper. Just pull the top sheet off and flip into your pie plate.

2075-99

TOMATO PIE

2 c. biscuit mix
⅔ c. milk
Tomatoes, peeled and sliced
Salt and pepper to taste

Crushed basil leaves
Chopped chives
1 c. grated sharp cheese
1 c. mayonnaise

Combine biscuit mix and milk; mix like pie crust. Put into 13x9 inch baking pan. Fill with tomatoes. Sprinkle with salt, pepper, and spices. Mix cheese and mayonnaise; spread over tomatoes. Bake at 400°F. for 35 minutes. Let set 10 minutes before cutting.

Elizabeth Maddock, Canaan Northwest Lions Club
Canaan, CT, USA

GREEN TOMATO PIE

2 (9 inch) unbaked pie crusts
2½ c. green tomatoes, cut up fine
1 c. (scant) dark raisins
½ c. brown sugar
½ c. white sugar
1 tsp. cinnamon

¼ tsp. nutmeg
¼ tsp. cloves
Pinch of salt
1 Tbsp. cornstarch
1 Tbsp. butter or margarine

Combine all ingredients, except pie crust, cornstarch, and butter, in a saucepan. Cook on top of stove about 8 to 10 minutes, stirring and watching so it won't scorch. Cool mixture. Add 1 tablespoon cornstarch and 1 tablespoon butter. Pour into bottom crust and cover with top crust. Bake at 350° until crust is brown, about 30 to 35 minutes.

This is my husband's favorite pie. I have won several blue ribbons and awards at the County Fair and area Festivals. We have it often late summer and fall before frost. I also chop and freeze the tomatoes in 2½ cup packages to have on hand year 'round. Much like a mince pie.

Janet Johnson, Treasurer, Princeton Lions Club
Princeton, IL, USA

August is nature's nap.

Bern Williams

The best things in life are postage paid, batteries included,
guaranteed forever, and tax-free.

Jacqueline Schiff

GREEN TOMATO PIE
(Two crust pie)

Filling:

½ c. sugar
1 Tbsp. vinegar
2 Tbsp. water
1 Tbsp. flour
⅛ tsp. salt
A dusting of allspice, cloves,
  nutmeg, and cinnamon to
  taste

1 Tbsp. butter (dot over top of
  filling)
Half grown green tomatoes (with
  tinge of color), peeled and
  cut very thin

Make pie crust for 2 crust pie and make it on the rich side. Slice tomatoes and place in pie shell, then sprinkle other ingredients over top of tomatoes. Place top crust on pie and bake at 375°F. for about 50 to 60 minutes.

Norma Sands, Rootstown Township, 13-D
Rootstown, OH, USA

CARROT PIE

1 lb. carrots, peeled and sliced
1½ c. water
1 tsp. salt
4 eggs
6 oz. evaporated milk
1 c. sugar

1 Tbsp. flour
1 tsp. ginger, ground
1 tsp. cinnamon, ground
½ tsp. nutmeg, ground
⅛ tsp. cloves, ground
Unbaked 9 inch pastry shell

Place carrots, water, and ½ teaspoon salt in saucepan and bring to boil; cook until tender. Drain. Place carrots, eggs, milk, and all dry ingredients in blender and blend until smooth. Pour into pastry shell. Bake in preheated 400° oven for 45 to 50 minutes. Serve warm or cold topped with whipped cream. When pie is done, insert a knife in center and it will come out clean. Yield: 1 pie.

Author of "The Best of Mayberry" cookbook, honored in "America's Best" recipes by Oxmoor House, Inc.

Betty Conley Lyerly, Mount Airy Foothill Lions Club
Mount Airy, NC, USA

I do not believe things happen accidentally. I believe you earn them.
Madeleine Albright

PRALINE PUMPKIN PIE

2 c. plus 1 c. brown sugar, firmly packed
2/3 c. finely chopped pecans
4 Tbsp. plus 1 Tbsp. unsalted butter (at room temperature)
2 large eggs, slightly beaten
1 (16 oz.) can solid pack pumpkin
1/2 tsp. salt
2 tsp. ground cinnamon
1/2 tsp. ground nutmeg
1/2 tsp. ground ginger
1/4 tsp. ground cloves
1 Tbsp. all-purpose flour
1 (12 oz.) can evaporated milk
2 unbaked 9 inch pie crusts

Preheat oven to 425°. Combine 2 cups brown sugar, pecans, and 4 tablespoons butter. Sprinkle evenly over pie crusts. Bake 10 minutes. Remove from oven and reduce to 350°. Combine remaining ingredients in a large bowl and mix well. Divide evenly between 2 pie crusts. Bake 30 minutes or until tester inserted into center comes out clean.

Nettie Favara, Greenwood Lions Club
Greenwood, MS, USA

TRADITIONAL PUMPKIN PIE

1 pkg. refrigerated pie crusts

Filling:

3/4 c. sugar
1 1/2 tsp. pumpkin pie spice
1/2 tsp. salt
1 (16 oz.) can pumpkin
1 1/2 c. evaporated milk
2 eggs, beaten

Topping:

Reddi-Whip whipped topping

Heat oven to 425°. In large bowl, combine all filling ingredients; blend well. Pour into pie crust-lined pan. Carefully transfer to oven rack. Bake at 425°F. for 15 minutes. Reduce oven temperature to 350°F.; continue baking 40 to 50 minutes or until knife inserted near center comes out clean. Cool; refrigerate until serving time. Top with Reddi-Whip whipped topping. Store in refrigerator. Serves 8.

Lion Robert Dobson, Mount Airy Foothills Lions Club
Mount Airy, NC, USA

CREAMY PECAN PIE

3/4 c. sugar
3 Tbsp. flour
1 c. dark corn syrup
3/4 c. evaporated milk
1 tsp. vanilla
2 eggs, beaten
1 c. pecan pieces
1 deep dish pie crust

Mix ingredients as listed. Mix well and pour in unbaked pie crust. Bake at 350° for about 45 minutes or until pie is set and golden brown.

Janie Phillips, Iron City Lions Club
Iron City, TN

PECAN PIE

3 eggs
½ c. brown sugar
½ c. white sugar
¼ tsp. salt
1 rounded Tbsp. flour

2 or 3 Tbsp. melted butter
2 to 3 Tbsp. evaporated milk
1 c. white Karo
1 tsp. vanilla
1 c. chopped pecans

Beat eggs slightly. Add all ingredients, except pecans, and mix well. Add pecans and mix. Pour into 9 inch unbaked pie crust. Bake 15 minutes at 425°, then 30 to 35 minutes at 350°. Wonderful.

Mildred Court, Stafford-Missouri City Lions Club
Stafford, TX, USA

MAMA'S PECAN PIE

1 c. sugar
1 c. Karo syrup
¾ stick butter, melted
2 eggs

1 tsp. vanilla
1 c. pecans
1 unbaked pie crust or 1 pkg.
   mini-tart pie crusts

Preheat oven to 350°. Lightly toast pecans while mixing first 5 ingredients. Add pecans to syrup mixture. Pour into pie crust. Bake 30 to 35 minutes.

Lion Connie Hughes, Foley Lions Club
Foley, AL, USA

PECAN PIE

1⅓ c. pecans, chopped fine
1⅓ c. white sugar
1⅓ c. white Karo syrup

4 eggs
1⅓ sticks margarine, melted
2 Pet-Ritz pie crusts (not deep
   dish)

Beat eggs until lemon colored. Add sugar; stir well. Add syrup; stir well. Add pecans; stir. Add margarine and stir well. Pour into 2 crusts. Bake at 300° for 1 hour or longer until the pies are golden to dark brown. Can be frozen.

Ardis Rittenberry, Shelbyville Lions Club
Shelbyville, TN, USA

JELL-O PUDDING PECAN PIE

Preheat oven to 375°.

1 (3¼ oz.) pkg. regular vanilla
   pudding and pie filling
1 c. white Karo syrup
¾ c. evaporated milk

1 egg, slightly beaten
1 c. chopped pecans
1 unbaked 8 or 9 inch pie shell

Blend pudding mix with Karo syrup. Gradually add milk and egg, then add pecans. Pour into pie shell. Bake until top is firm, about 40 minutes. Cool 3 hours.

Joyce Werkmeister, Elberfeld Lions Club
Elberfeld, IN

WALNUT PIE

3 eggs, well beaten
1 c. sugar
1¼ c. graham cracker crusts

¾ c. walnuts, chopped
Pinch of salt
½ tsp. vanilla

Beat the eggs and add your sugar. Keep beating. Add vanilla and pinch of salt. Fold in graham cracker crumbs, then the walnuts. Bake in 9 inch pie plate for 25 minutes at 325°. Do not overbake. Serve with whip topping or vanilla ice cream.

This is so easy and needs no crust.

Lion Ann K. Brumback, Silver Run Union Mills Lions Club
Westminster, MD, USA

RHUBARB PIE

2 eggs, beaten
2 Tbsp. lemon juice
1½ c. sugar
Pinch of salt

3 slices bread
3 c. rhubarb, cut into ½ inch
  pieces
Pastry for 2 crust pie

Remove crust from bread. Soak bread under faucet and squeeze out the water. Add bread to beaten eggs, lemon juice, sugar, and salt. Mix and then add rhubarb. Line pan (9 inch) with pastry; add filling and top with pastry. Brush with milk and sprinkle with sugar. Bake at 350° for 1 hour or until rhubarb is soft.

Janet Johnson, Treasurer, Princeton Lions Club
Princeton, IL, USA

An enjoyable job is like the fountain of youth.
Mike Thomas

Success has always been easy to measure.
It is the distance between one's origins and one's final achievement.
Michael Korda

Change is not merely necessary to life. It is life.
Alvin Toffler

Most people don't mind criticism as long as it's about someone else.
Suzan L. Wiener

FRENCH RHUBARB CUSTARD PIE

Pastry:

⅓ c. Crisco
1 c. flour
¼ tsp. salt

1 Tbsp. sugar
Ice water

Filling:

2 egg whites
2 whole eggs
3 Tbsp. milk
1½ c. sugar

¼ c. flour
¾ tsp. nutmeg
4 to 6 c. cut-up rhubarb

Topping:

⅓ c. butter or oleo
½ c. brown sugar, packed

1 c. flour

Pastry: Blend Crisco, flour, salt, and sugar till crumbly. Add ice water until pastry holds together and forms ball. Roll out dough to fit 9 inch deep-dish pie pan. Fit into pan and flute edges above rim of pie pan.

Filling: Beat together all ingredients, except rhubarb, till very well blended. Add rhubarb. Pour filling into pie crust.

Topping: Blend all ingredients until crumbly. Sprinkle, then pat, over filling. Bake at 425° for 10 minutes, then 350° for 30 to 40 minutes until nicely browned.

Martin Findling, Princeton Lions Club
Princeton, IL, USA

RHUBARB BANANA PIE

Pastry for 2 crust pie
2 c. diced rhubarb
½ tsp. cinnamon
1 egg + 1 egg yolk

1 c. sugar
1 Tbsp. flour
1 banana

Slice banana into bottom of pie crust. Combine remaining ingredients and pour over banana. Cover with top crust and seal edges. Bake at 400° for 15 minutes, then at 350° for 45 minutes more.

This is a new recipe to me, but we have enjoyed it this spring. Always looking for new and different rhubarb recipes; seems we love rhubarb any way we have tried it!

Janet Johnson, Treasurer, Princeton Lion Club
Princeton, IL, USA

2075-99

MY RHUBARB PIE

1 recipe 2 crust pie pastry
1 c. sugar
4 Tbsp. cornstarch

1 beaten egg
⅛ tsp. salt
4 c. rhubarb, cut ½ inch pieces

Combine in mixing bowl sugar, cornstarch, and salt. Blend thoroughly. Add beaten egg and blend well. Stir in the rhubarb. Make sure each piece is coated. Pour into your pastry lined pie dish. Dot with butter. Cover with vented pastry. Flute edge. Bake at 425°F. for 15 minutes. Reduce temperature to 375°F. and bake for 40 minutes longer and crust is golden brown.

Mildred Weir, Bentleyville Lioness Club
Bentleyville, PA

RHUBARB CREAM PIE

Pastry for 2 pie crusts
1½ c. white sugar
3 Tbsp. flour
½ tsp. nutmeg

3 c. fresh rhubarb, cut in 1 inch
    pieces
2 eggs

Prepare your favourite pie crust. In a bowl, blend together the sugar, flour, nutmeg, and rhubarb; spread into pie crust. In a separate bowl, beat eggs until foamy and pour over rhubarb mixture; dot with 1 tablespoon of butter. Cover with top crust. Bake for 10 minutes at 450°F. Reduce to 350°F. and bake another 30 minutes. Delicious.

Lion Violet Labelle, Lake of the Woods Lions Club
Kenora, Ontario, Canada

RHUBARB PIE

4 c. rhubarb, cut in pieces
1¼ c. sugar
⅓ c. flour

1 Tbsp. tapioca
Pastry for 9 inch double crust pie

Mix rhubarb, sugar, flour, and tapioca together. Put mixture in unbaked pie crust. Cover with slashed top crust. Brush milk over top. Bake at 400° about one hour or until done.

Double recipe to make cobbler.

Teresa Jett, West Milford Lions Club
West Milford, WV, USA

We all live every day in virtual environments, defined by our ideas.
Michael Crichton

CHERRY ALMOND-CRUMB PIE

9 inch unbaked pie shell
¾ c. flour
¼ c. sugar
¼ tsp. salt
¼ tsp. nutmeg

6 Tbsp. unsalted butter
⅓ c. sliced almonds
⅛ tsp. cinnamon
21 oz. can cherry pie filling

Heat the oven to 425°. Line the pie shell with a double thickness of foil and bake 10 minutes. Remove from the oven, take off the foil, and let cool. Combine the flour, sugar, salt, and nutmeg. Cut the butter into small pieces and rub it into the flour mixture with your fingers until crumbly. Add the almonds. Add the cinnamon to the pie filling. Pour the pie filling into the pie shell. Sprinkle with the crumb mixture. Bake 10 minutes. Reduce heat to 350° and continue baking until brown, about 35 minutes. Makes 6 servings.

Work time: 20 minutes. Total time: 1 hour.

Per serving, 515 calories, 5 g protein, 27 g fat, 276 mg sodium, 66 g carbohydrate, 31 mg cholesterol.

Barbara Joy Hess, Clarence Lions Club
Clarence Center, NY, USA

PERFECT APPLE PIE

1 pkg. refrigerated pie crusts

Filling:

6 c. thinly sliced, peeled apples
¾ c. sugar
2 Tbsp. flour
¾ tsp. cinnamon

¼ tsp. salt
⅛ tsp. nutmeg
1 Tbsp. lemon juice

Heat oven to 425°F. Prepare pie crust according to package directions for two crust pie, using 9 inch pie pan.

In large bowl, combine remaining ingredients; mix lightly. Spoon into crust lined pan. Top with second crust and flute. Cut slits in several places. Bake at 425°F. for 40 to 45 minutes or until apples are tender and crust is golden brown. Serves 8.

Suggested apple varieties: Golden Delicious or Granny Smith.
Lion Louise Hines, Mount Airy Foothills Lions Club
Mount Airy, NC, USA

A window of opportunity won't open itself.
Dave Weinbaum

STRAWBERRY PIE

2 pie crusts
2 pt. fresh strawberries
1 c. water
3 Tbsp. red jello

½ c. sugar
3 Tbsp. cornstarch
Whipped topping

Put strawberries in baked pie shell. Cook jello, water, sugar, and cornstarch until thick. Stir constantly. Pour over strawberries. Top with whipped topping.

Pam Caldwell, Mexico Sunrise Lions Club
Mexico, MO

MAPLE APPLE PIE WITH MAPLE GLAZE

4 c. apples, peeled, cored, and
    sliced thin
1 c. maple syrup
¼ tsp. salt
¼ tsp. cinnamon

3 Tbsp. flour
1 Tbsp. cornstarch
2 Tbsp. butter
Pastry for a two crust pie

Glaze:

½ c. powdered sugar

3 Tbsp. maple syrup

Preheat oven to 450°. Line 9 inch pie plate with pastry crust. In a bowl, combine the sliced apples, maple syrup, salt, cinnamon, flour, and cornstarch. Pour this into pastry crust. Dot with butter. Cover with top crust and cut air vents. Bake in a 450° oven for 10 minutes, then reduce heat to 350° and bake 40 minutes or until done.

Glaze: In a small bowl, combine ingredients and drizzle over pie after it has cooled a little but is still warm.

Elaine (Pepin) Howes, Northfield Lions Club
Northfield, MA

APPLE PIE MIX

Apples to fill 7 qt. canning jars
4½ c. sugar
1 c. cornstarch
1 tsp. cinnamon
¼ tsp. nutmeg

1 tsp. salt
10 c. water
3 Tbsp. lemon juice
3 drops of yellow food coloring

Combine sugar, cornstarch, salt, cinnamon, nutmeg, and water. Cook and stir until thick. Add lemon juice and food coloring. Peel and slice apples. Pack in widemouthed quart jars. Fill with syrup. Process 20 minutes. Makes 7 quarts.

Use one and a half quarts per pie.

Liz Birchen, O'Fallon Lions Club
O'Fallon, MO, USA

SUGAR FREE APPLE PIE

12 oz. can frozen apple juice
(concentrate)
3 Tbsp. cornstarch

1 tsp. cinnamon
4 to 5 apples, pared and sliced
Crust for double crust pie

Peel apples and slice into bottom crust. Cook apple juice, cornstarch, and cinnamon until thickened. Pour over apples. Add top crust and bake at 325° for 40 minutes. This is delicious.

Leola C. Jurrens, Downtown-Bartlesville Lions Club
Bartlesville, OK, USA

MOM'S APPLE PIE

Crust:

2½ c. flour
2 tsp. baking powder
2 Tbsp. sugar

1 c. butter or margarine
1 egg white
1 tsp. vanilla

Additional ingredients:

3 lb. apples (or 18 to 20)
1½ c. sugar

2½ Tbsp. flour

Peel and core apples into ½ pieces. Press dough into baking dish, 9x12 inches. Place apples in dish and sprinkle sugar mixture over the apples. Sprinkle cinnamon and pats of butter over apples. Bake at 350° for 1 hour.

Antoinette Merlo, Plainfield Township Lions Club
Easton, PA

RITZ APPLE PIE
(2 crust pie)

Filling:

2 c. water
1½ c. sugar

2 tsp. cream of tartar

Boil 2 minutes. Add 20 whole Ritz crackers. Boil 2 minutes. Add 1 teaspoon butter and cinnamon or nutmeg to taste. Make pie crust for 2 crust pie. Place filling inside and bake at 350°F. for 30 to 35 minutes.

Norma Sands, Rootstown Township, 13-D Lions Club
Rootstown, OH

People used to live lives of quiet desperation - now they go on talk shows.
Bob Thaves

BANANA PIE

2 c. softened vanilla ice cream
1 c. milk
1 pkg. instant banana or vanilla
    pudding

1 pie shell, baked

Beat all ingredients for 1 minute. Pour into baked pie shell lined with bananas. Top with whipped topping if desired.

Norma Murray, Bryan Lioness Club
Bryan, OH, USA

FROSTY ORANGE PIE

1 (8 oz.) pkg. cream cheese,
    softened
1 (6 oz.) can frozen orange juice
    concentrate, thawed
1 (8 oz.) ctn. whipped topping,
    thawed

1 (9 inch) graham cracker crust
1 (14 oz.) can sweetened
    condensed milk

In mixing bowl, beat cream cheese and condensed milk till smooth. Beat in orange juice concentrate. Fold in whipped topping. Spoon into crust. Cover and freeze for up to 3 months. Serves 6 to 8.

"Some minds are like concrete - all mixed up and permanently set."

Doris (Cricket) Kimbrell, Iron City Lions Club
Iron City, TN, USA

Modesty is the proof that morality is sexy.
Wendy Shalit

❦ ❦ ❦

The ego is the ugly little troll that lives
underneath the bridge between your mind and your heart.
Dennis Miller

❦ ❦ ❦

Love is how we feel toward those who show us
that which is lovable about ourselves.
Gerry Spence

❦ ❦ ❦

Doing the best at this moment puts you in the best place for the next moment.
Oprah Winfrey

FROSTED ORANGE PIE

¾ c. sugar
½ c. all-purpose flour
¼ tsp. salt
1¼ c. water
2 egg yolks, lightly beaten

2 to 3 Tbsp. grated orange peel
½ tsp. grated lemon peel
½ c. orange juice
2 Tbsp. lemon juice
1 pastry shell (9 inches), baked

Frosting:

½ c. sugar
2 egg whites
2 Tbsp. water
⅛ tsp. cream of tartar

⅛ tsp. salt
½ c. flaked coconut, toasted
    (optional)

In a saucepan, combine sugar, flour, and salt; gradually add water. Cook and stir over medium-high heat for 2 to 3 minutes or until thickened and bubbly. Remove from heat. Gradually stir ½ cup into egg yolks; return all to pan. Bring to a gentle boil; cook and stir for 2 minutes. Remove from the heat; stir in orange and lemon peels. Gently stir in juices. Pour into pastry shell. Cool on a wire rack for 1 hour. Chill at least 3 hours.

In a heavy saucepan or double boiler, combine sugar, egg whites, water, cream of tartar, and salt. With a portable mixer, beat on low speed for 1 minute. Continue beating on low over low heat until frosting reaches 160°, about 8 to 10 minutes. With a stand mixer, beat on high until frosting forms stiff peaks, about 7 minutes. Spread over chilled pie. Just before serving, sprinkle with coconut. Store in the refrigerator. Yield: 6 to 8 servings.

TRIPLE FRUIT PIE

1¼ c. fresh blueberries*
1¼ c. fresh raspberries*
1¼ c. chopped rhubarb*
½ tsp. almond extract
1¼ c. sugar
¼ c. quick-cooking tapioca

¼ tsp. ground nutmeg
¼ tsp. salt
1 Tbsp. lemon juice
Pastry for double-crust pie (9
    inches)

In a large bowl, combine fruits and extract; toss to coat. In another bowl, combine sugar, tapioca, nutmeg, and salt. Add to fruit; stir gently. Let stand for 15 minutes. Line a 9 inch pie plate with bottom crust; trim pastry even with edge. Stir lemon juice into fruit mixture; spoon into the crust. Roll out remaining pastry; make a lattice crust. Seal and flute edges. Bake at 400° for 20 minutes. Reduce heat to 350°; bake 30 minutes longer or until the crust is golden brown and the filling is bubbly. Yield: 6 to 8 servings.

* Note: Frozen berries and rhubarb may be substituted for fresh; thaw and drain before using.

LEMON CHIFFON PIE

1 env. unflavored gelatin,
    dissolved in ¼ c. water
4 egg yolks
1½ c. sugar
⅓ c. lemon juice
½ tsp. salt

1½ tsp. grated lemon rind
4 egg whites
Whipped cream or Cool Whip for
    top
1 (9 inch) pastry shell

Soften gelatin in water. Beat egg yolks; add ¾ cup sugar, lemon juice, and salt. Cook over hot water, stirring constantly, until thickened. Add dissolved gelatin and lemon juice. Stir until gelatin is dissolved. Cool.

Beat *egg whites* stiff. Gradually add remaining sugar, beating constantly. Continue beating until egg whites are very stiff. Fold into cooled egg yolk mixture. *Do not beat.* Fold until thoroughly mixed. Pour into pie shell. Chill until firm.

This pie can be frozen. Add whipped cream or Cool Whip before serving.

Goldie Fultz, Bullhead City Lions Club
Bullhead City, AZ, USA

BEST-EVER LEMON PIE

1 baked 9 inch pie shell
6 Tbsp. cornstarch
⅓ c. lemon juice (fresh squeezed)
1½ tsp. lemon extract
3 Tbsp. butter

1¼ c. sugar
2 c. water
3 egg yolks
2 tsp. vinegar

Mix sugar and cornstarch together in top of a double boiler. Add the 2 cups of water. Combine egg yolks with lemon juice and beat until well mixed. Add to the rest of the sugar mixture. Cook over boiling water until thick, about 25 minutes. This does away with the starchy taste. Now, add the lemon extract, butter, and vinegar and stir thoroughly. Pour mixture into deep 9 inch shell and let cool. Cover with meringue and brown in oven at 350° for 10 minutes or until lightly browned.

Shirley J. Hoyt, Hutchinson Breakfast Lions Club
Hutchinson, KS, USA

Fear can keep us up all night long, but faith makes one fine pillow.
Philip Gulley

If you don't risk anything, you risk even more.
Erica Jong

LEMON SUPREME PIE

1 unbaked deep-dish pastry shell
  (9 inches)

Lemon Filling:

1¼ c. sugar, divided
6 Tbsp. cornstarch
½ tsp. salt
1¼ c. water
2 Tbsp. butter

2 tsp. grated lemon peel
4 to 5 drops of yellow food
  coloring (optional)
½ c. fresh lemon juice

Cream Cheese Filling:

2 pkg. (one 8 oz., one 3 oz.)
  cream cheese, softened
¾ c. confectioners sugar

1½ c. whipped topping
1 Tbsp. fresh lemon juice

Line unpricked pastry shell with a double thickness of heavy-duty foil. Bake at 450° for 8 minutes. Remove foil; bake 5 minutes longer. Cool on a wire rack.

In a saucepan, combine ¾ cup sugar, cornstarch, and salt. Stir in water; bring to a boil over medium-high heat. Reduce heat; add remaining sugar. Cook and stir for 2 minutes or until thickened and bubbly. Remove from the heat; stir in butter, lemon peel, and food coloring if desired. Gently stir in lemon juice (do not overmix). Cool to room temperature, about 1 hour. Do not stir.

In a mixing bowl, beat cream cheese and sugar until smooth. Fold in whipped topping and lemon juice. Refrigerate ½ cup for garnish. Spread remaining cream cheese mixture into shell; top with lemon filling. Chill overnight. Place reserved cream cheese mixture in a pastry bag with a No. 21 star tip; pipe stars onto pie. Store in the refrigerator. Yield: 6 to 8 servings.

PEACH PARFAIT PIE

1 small lemon jello
1½ c. juice from peaches and
  water
1 pt. ice cream (vanilla)

1 can sliced peaches
⅛ tsp. almond extract
1 baked pie shell

Boil juice and add jello. Add ice cream. Chill until thickened, about 35 minutes. Add drained peaches and almond extract. Put into pie shell and refrigerate until set. Ice with whipped cream. Keep in refrigerator.

Olive Higinbotham, Bentleyville Lioness Club
Bentleyville, PA, USA

PEACH PIE

2¼ c. hot water
1 c. sugar
½ c. cornstarch

1 (3 oz.) pkg. peach jello
Yellow food coloring (as desired)

Cook above items until thick, then cool.

8 or 9 peaches, sliced

Place sliced peaches in cooked pie shell and top with cooled jello mixture. Top with whipped cream.

I like to mix my peaches and jello mixture together before placing in the pie crust.

Shirley J. Hoyt, Hutchinson Breakfast Lions Club
Hutchinson, KS, USA

FRESH PEACH PIE

1 c. water
⅔ c. sugar
2 Tbsp. corn starch
1 (3 oz.) box peach jello

1 Tbsp. lemon juice
3 large peaches
1 baked pie crust
Cool Whip

Boil water, sugar, and corn starch until thick and clear. Add jello and lemon juice. Cool a little. Peel peaches and slice. Put peaches in baked pie shell. Pour glaze over peaches. Refrigerate. When set, add Cool Whip.

Mary Sekse, Dixon Sunrise Lions Club
Dixon, IL, USA

PEACH CARAMEL PIE

¾ c. brown sugar, packed
¼ c. white syrup
¼ c. butter

3 Tbsp. flour
2 Tbsp. water
Pinch of salt

Combine these ingredients in a saucepan and cook over low or medium heat until completely dissolved. Put 5 cups of sliced fresh peaches into an unbaked 9 inch pie shell. Pour caramel mixture over peaches and put on a lattice crust. Bake at 400° about 10 to 15 minutes and then at 350° for 35 minutes.

Canned peaches that are drained well may be substituted. (Fresh peaches are better.)

Learn to laugh at yourself; you'll be a lifelong source of amusement.

Lion Dorothy Moras, Westbrook Lions Club
Westbrook, MN

PEACH PLUM PIE

2 c. sliced, peeled fresh or frozen peaches, thawed and drained
2 c. sliced, peeled fresh purple plums
1 Tbsp. lemon juice
¼ tsp. almond extract
1½ c. sugar
¼ c. quick-cooking tapioca
½ to 1 tsp. grated lemon peel
¼ tsp. salt
Pastry for double-crust pie (9 inches)
2 Tbsp. butter or margarine

In a large bowl, combine the peaches, plums, lemon juice, and extract. In another bowl, combine sugar, tapioca, lemon peel, and salt. Add to fruit mixture and stir gently; let stand for 15 minutes.

Line a 9 inch pie plate with bottom crust; add the filling. Dot with butter. Roll out remaining pastry to fit top of pie; cut slits in pastry. Place over filling. Trim, seal, and flute edges. Cover the edges loosely with foil. Bake at 450° for 10 minutes. Reduce heat to 350°. Remove foil; bake 35 minutes longer or until crust is golden brown and filling is bubbly. Yield: 6 to 8 servings.

HOLLY'S STRAWBERRY PIE

1 graham cracker pie crust
1 qt. strawberries
1 large sugar-free jello (strawberry or raspberry)
2 c. diet Seven-Up
⅛ tsp. lemon juice
4 Tbsp. cornstarch
1 pkg. Equal or Sweet 'N Low (or whatever)

Cut berries and stir into pie shell. Heat Seven-Up with cornstarch until thick. Add jello, Equal, and lemon juice. Spoon over berries. Refrigerate. Serve with Cool Whip.

Plan to make another one real soon!!!
Holly Schoff Tobin, Porter Schoff, PID, Portsmouth Lions Club
Portsmouth, NH, USA

STRAWBERRY PIE

1 qt. strawberries
1 c. sugar
1 c. water
3 Tbsp. cornstarch

Wash and hull berries. Measure 1 cup of small ones and mash them. Add sugar, water, and cornstarch. Cook until clear and slightly thickened. Put remaining berries in 8 or 9 inch baked pie shell. Pour cooked mixture over them, chill, and serve with whipped cream.
Pauline and PGD Gerald Nuffer, South Jefferson Lions Club
Adams, NY

2075-99

STRAWBERRY PARFAIT PIE

1 small strawberry jello
1½ c. juice from frozen
   strawberries and water

1 pt. ice cream (vanilla)
1 pkg. strawberries (frozen)
Baked pie shell

Boil juice and add jello. Add ice cream and stir until dissolved. Chill until set, approximately 30 minutes. Add strawberries. Put in pie shell. Place in refrigerator until firm. Ice with whipped cream. Keep in refrigerator.

Olive Higinbotham, Bentleyville Lioness Club
Bentleyville, PA, USA

GOOSEBERRY PIE

⅔ c. water
2 c. sugar
6 c. fresh stemmed and cleaned
   gooseberries

¼ c. cornstarch
Pastry for 2 crust (9 inch) pie

Cook ⅓ cup water and sugar in saucepan over low heat 2 to 3 minutes. Add berries. Simmer gently until cooked and opaque looking. Use small strainer and remove berries from syrup. Reserve in large bowl.

Dissolve cornstarch in remaining ⅓ cup water. Stir into syrup. Cook over moderate heat until thick and clear, stirring constantly. (May need to add a little more cornstarch if it doesn't thicken.) Cool to lukewarm. Add to berries. Stir gently and pour into prepared pie crust. Top with second crust. Bake at 425° for 20 minutes. Turn down to 350° and bake 30 minutes more or until done.

Lion Cheryl Kastle, Berthoud Lions Club
Berthoud, CO, USA

RAISIN AND PECAN PIE

4 egg yolks
2 Tbsp. butter or margarine
2 c. sugar
1 c. raisins

1 c. pecans
3 tsp. vinegar
1 tsp. vanilla
4 egg whites

Beat egg whites. Cream together butter, sugar, and egg yolks. Add raisins, pecans, vinegar, and vanilla, mixing well. Pour into a 9 inch unbaked pie shell and bake at 325°F. for about 50 minutes. Remove from oven, put meringue on top, and return to oven until brown. Cool before cutting.

This pie has been in family for 4 generations.

Barbara Kelly, Iron City Lions Club
Iron City, TN, USA

RAISIN CREAM PIE

1 baked pie shell
1 c. sugar
2/3 c. raisins
1/2 c. water
Dash of salt

3 Tbsp. cornstarch
1/2 c. milk
1/2 c. water
2 egg yolks

Combine sugar, raisins, 1/2 cup water, and salt and simmer. Prepare cornstarch, milk, water, and egg yolks and cook until thick. Add raisin mixture and pour into pie shell. Make meringue using egg whites and 2 tablespoons sugar. Bake at 325° for 10 minutes.

Pauline and PDG Gerald Nuffer, South Jefferson Lions Club
Adams, NY

RAISIN PIE

2 eggs, beaten separately
1 c. sugar
1/2 c. raisins
1/2 c. pecans

1/2 c. cocoanut
1 tsp. vanilla
1/2 to 3/4 stick oleo, melted

Separate eggs and beat; mix all together. Fold in egg whites and pour in unbaked pie shell. Bake at 325° until semi-firm in middle.

Lion Jane McCune, Huffman Lions Club
Huffman, TX

SOUR CREAM RAISIN PIE

Boil together for 5 minutes:

1 c. raisins
3/4 c. sugar

3/4 c. water

Mix:

1 c. sour cream
1/2 tsp. cinnamon
3 beaten egg yolks

3 Tbsp. flour
1 tsp. vanilla

Add to raisin mixture and cook until thick. Pour into baked pie crust.

Beat until stiff:

3 egg whites
5 to 6 Tbsp. sugar

Little vanilla

Put on pie and bake at 350° for 12 minutes or until brown.

Carol Waller, Stewart Lions Club
Stewart, MN, USA

2075-99

PINEAPPLE CHEESE PIE

2 (8¼ oz.) cans crushed
   pineapple (undrained)
¼ c. sugar
2 Tbsp. cornstarch
2 Tbsp. water
¼ c. sifted flour

1 c. cottage cheese
1 tsp. vanilla
½ tsp. salt
2 eggs, slightly beaten
1¼ c. milk

    Custard layer:

⅔ c. sugar

1 Tbsp. butter

    Crust:

1 unbaked 9 or 10 inch pie shell

    Combine pineapple, sugar, cornstarch, and water in small saucepan; bring to a boil. Cook for 1 minute, stirring constantly. Let cool; set aside.

    Custard layer: Blend sugar and butter; add flour, cottage cheese, vanilla, and salt. Beat until smooth. Add the eggs, then the milk, beating constantly. Spread the pineapple mixture over the crust. Gently pour the custard mixture over the pineapple, being careful not to disturb the pineapple layer. Bake at 400° for 10 minutes, then reduce heat to 325° and bake for about 40 more minutes.

    An unusual pie that's loaded with flavor. It forms a custardlike base as it bakes.

Lion Micheal and Ruth (Sauskojus) Bartolf, Oxbow and District Lions
Club
Oxbow, Saskatchewan, Canada

COCONUT-PINEAPPLE PIE

4 eggs
1 can coconut
1½ c. sugar

1 stick margarine, melted
1 small can crushed pineapple

    Melt the margarine; add sugar and beat well. Add the eggs and beat. Works better if you drain part of the pineapple. Add the pineapple and can of coconut. Pour into a deep dish pie shell. Bake 45 minutes at 350°.

Linda Fox, Saginaw Lions Club
Saginaw, TX

It takes considerable knowledge just to realize
the extent of your own ignorance.
Thomas Sowell

Desserts

Common Baking Dishes and Pans

Spring Form Pan

Layer Cake or Pie Pan

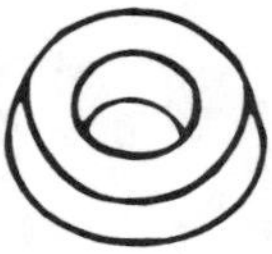

Ring Mold

Baking or Square Pan

Loaf Pan

Brioche Pan

Angel Cake Pan

Bundt Tube

Equivalent Dishes

4-CUP BAKING DISH
= 9″ pie plate
= 8″ x 1¼″ layer cake pan
= 7⅜″ x 3⅝″ x 2¼″ loaf pan

6-CUP BAKING DISH
= 8″ or 9″ x 1½″ layer cake pan
= 10″ pie pan
= 8½″ x 3⅝″ x 2⅝″ loaf pan

8-CUP BAKING DISH
= 8″ x 8″ x 2″ square pan
= 11″ x 7″ x 1½″ baking pan
= 9″ x 5″ x 3″ loaf pan

10-CUP BAKING DISH
= 9″ x 9″ x 2″ square pan
= 11¾″ x 7½″ x 1¾″ baking pan
= 15″ x 10″ x 1″ flat jelly roll pan

12-CUP BAKING DISH OR MORE
= 13½″ x 8½″ x 2″ glass baking dish
= 13″ x 9″ x 2″ metal baking pan
= 14″ x 10½″ x 2½″ roasting pan

Total Volume of Pans

TUBE PANS

7½″ x 3″ Bundt tube	6 cups
9″ x 3½″ fancy or Bundt tube	9 cups
9″ x 3½″ angel cake pan	12 cups
10″ x 3¾″ Bundt tube	12 cups
9″ x 3½″ fancy tube mold	12 cups
10″ x 4″ fancy tube mold	16 cups
10″ x 4″ angel cake pan	18 cups

SPRING FORM PANS

8″ x 3″ pan	12 cups
9″ x 3″ pan	16 cups

RING MOLDS

8½″ x 2¼″ mold	4½ cups
9¼″ x 2¾″ mold	8 cups

BRIOCHE PAN

9½″ x 3¼″ pan	8 cups

DESSERTS

FRUIT SQUARES

1 c. butter or margarine (I use
   one stick of each)
⅔ c. confectioners sugar
1¾ c. (rounded) flour

1 can apple/cherry/peach pie
   filling
¾ c. coconut (optional)*
½ c. nuts (optional)*

Combine first three ingredients till well blended. Press ⅔ of this mixture in a well-greased 10x7 or 9 inch square pan. Spread pie filling over top and then cover with remaining crumbs (patting down lightly). Bake for 45 minutes to 1 hour until golden brown. Cool completely before cutting.

* Options: Add coconut to first 3 ingredients. Add nuts to pie filling.

This is so easy and quick to make for the "Help! What am I going to serve" committee meetings at your house.

Lion Gloria Sikorski, East Haddam Community Lions Club
East Haddam, CT, USA

PEACH AND PLUM CROUSTADE

2 peaches
2 plums
¼ c. sugar
2 Tbsp. cornstarch

2 tsp. grated fresh ginger
1 refrigerated pie crust (½ of a
   15 oz. pkg.)
1 egg

Heat oven to 375°. Slice the peaches and plums and put in a mixing bowl. Sprinkle fruit with the sugar, cornstarch, and ginger and toss gently to coat. Unfold dough and put in the middle of a baking sheet. Mound fruit mixture in the center of the crust and fold the edges of the crust over the fruit to form a triangle. Moisten overlapping edges with a bit of water and pinch together to seal. Beat egg with 1 tablespoon water and brush pie crust lightly with some of the egg mixture. Bake until fruit is tender and the crust is golden brown 40 to 45 minutes. Makes 4 servings.

Work time: 20 minutes. Total time: 1 hour and 5 minutes.

Per serving: 347 calories, 3 g protein, 15 g fat, 267 mg sodium, 51 g carbohydrate, 14 mg cholesterol.

Lion John J. Hess, Clarence Lions Club
Clarence Center, NY, USA

Before you can win, you have to believe you are worthy.
Mike Ditka

APPLE-BUTTERSCOTCH-WALNUT PUDDING

3 c. peeled, cored cooking
  apples, sliced
1 pkg. instant butterscotch
  pudding
1½ c. milk

Cinnamon
⅓ c. finely chopped walnuts
Whipped cream or lite Cool Whip

In a little water, simmer apples until tender crisp. Drain. Cool. Make up pudding using 1½ cups milk. Spice with cinnamon. Fold in apples and walnuts. Pour into dessert dishes and chill. To serve, top with cream and sprinkle with more chopped walnuts.

PDG Doris J. Myers, Mexico Noon Lions Club
Mexico, MO

CRACKER COCOANUT PUDDING

24 crushed saltine crackers
1 c. cocoanut
1 c. sugar

4 to 6 eggs, separated
1 qt. milk
1 tsp. vanilla

Cream egg yolks and sugar together. Add crackers and cocoanut. Slowly add milk and vanilla. Cook at 350° about 1 hour or until it thickens. As the top tans, stir under to prevent burning on top. When pudding is thickened to liking, top with whipped egg white icing and brown.

Agnes Williams, Alpha Lions Club
Brookhaven, MS, USA

EASY BAKED CHERRY PUDDING - GRANDMA KEISER'S

2 eggs
2 tsp. sugar
2 tsp. butter
2 c. flour

1 tsp. salt
2 tsp. baking powder
1 c. milk
2 c. pitted semi-sweet cherries

Cream eggs, sugar, and butter until fluffy. Sift flour, salt, and baking powder together. Alternately add milk and flour to creamed mixture, beating smooth after each addition. Fold in 1 cup cherries. Put in 9x13 inch greased pan; top with remaining cherries. Bake at 350° approximately 50 minutes. Serve warm with Cool Whip or ice cream.

Note: When using presifted flour, just combine with baking powder and salt.

This brings back childhood memories in Pennsylvania.

Lion Louise K. Berdick, Western Branch Lions Club
Chesapeake, VA

452

BANANA PUDDING

1 large box vanilla instant
   pudding
3 c. milk
1 can Eagle Brand milk

1 (8 oz.) Cool Whip
4 or 5 bananas

In a 9x13 inch cake pan, place a layer of vanilla wafers, then a layer of sliced bananas, then the pudding mixture. Refrigerate and top with Cool Whip.

It is much wiser to take advice than to give it.

Lion Jane McCune, Huffman Lions Club
Huffman, TX, USA

BANANA PUDDING

3 lb. bananas
1 small box banana instant
   pudding
1 large box vanilla instant
   pudding

1 (8 oz.) sour cream
1 (8 oz.) Cool Whip
1 box vanilla wafers

Mix banana and vanilla pudding with 3½ cups milk. Mix well. Add sour cream and Cool Whip. Mix well. You may layer pudding, bananas, and wafers or just stir into pudding. Works great both ways.

I use fat free sour cream and puddings, reduced fat wafers, lite Cool Whip, and skim milk. You may use just vanilla pudding.

Lion Wanda Ramos, Foley Lions Club
Foley, AL

BANANA PUDDING

2 c. milk
¾ c. sugar
¼ tsp. salt
⅓ c. flour

2 eggs, separated
1½ tsp. vanilla
2 to 3 bananas
1 box vanilla wafers

Scald milk in double boiler. Thoroughly blend sugar, salt, and flour. Add gradually to milk, stirring until thoroughly blended. Add beaten egg yolks, stirring rapidly. Stir slowly and cook until it begins to thicken. Remove from heat; add flavoring and let stand while fixing wafers and bananas in bowl.

Line bottom and sides of a 7 inch casserole or pudding dish with vanilla wafers. Add a layer of bananas, sliced in ¼ inch or less. Repeat until about ½ inch from top of dish. Pour in custard. Fix meringue and spread on top. Place in a hot 350°F. oven until lightly browned. Remove and let cool.

Barbara Kelly, Iron City Lions Club
Iron City, TN, USA

2075-99

WASHINGTON PUDDING

Sauce:

1 c. sugar
2 c. water

Pinch of salt

Cake:

½ c. sugar
1 Tbsp. shortening
1 Tbsp. cocoa
½ c. nuts
½ c. milk
1 c. flour

½ c. raisins
1 tsp. vanilla
½ tsp. nutmeg
½ tsp. cinnamon
2 tsp. baking powder

Bring sauce mixture to boil in small roaster. Combine cake ingredients and mix well, then add to sauce mixture. Boil up, then bake slowly at 325° for 1 hour until cake is done.

This is a very old recipe and does not have a baking temperature. We baked this in a coal cookstove.

Bert Morgan, Broken Bow Lions Club
Broken Bow, NE

SUET PUDDING

1½ c. chopped suet
1 c. raisins
1 c. currants
1 c. sour milk
2 eggs
½ c. brown sugar
3½ c. flour

1 tsp. cinnamon
1 tsp. soda
1 tsp. cloves
1 tsp. nutmeg
1 c. molasses
½ c. granulated sugar

Combine all ingredients and mix well. Steam 3 hours in 325° oven or 8 hours in crock pot on LOW.

This is a very old recipe.

Bert Morgan, Broken Bow Lions Club
Broken Bow, Custer County, NE

Integrity is telling myself the truth.
And honesty is telling the truth to other people.
Spencer Johnson

❦ ❦ ❦

Politeness is the art of choosing among your thoughts.
Madame De Stael

GAJAR HALWA - CARROT PUDDING

4 medium carrots (little more
    than ½ lb.)
1 c. sugar
1½ c. full cream milk
½ c. pure ghee or melted butter

¼ c. sultanas
4 cardamom pods, bruised
1 tsp. sliced almonds
1 tsp. coarsely ground pistachios
A pinch of ground nutmeg

    Peel and grate the carrots. In a medium saucepan, add ghee or melted butter and grated carrots. Saute on reduced heat for two minutes. Add milk and simmer until the liquid is evaporated. Stir in sugar, sultanas, nutmeg, cardamoms, and pistachios. Remove from the heat. When warm, serve with vanilla ice cream or put in the fridge and serve cold by itself.

    It's the India sweet dish served with meal but loved by everyone when served with ice cream as a dessert.

Lion Mrudulla Amalean, Wellawatte Lions Club
Colombo, Sri Lanka

HOLLY'S DIRT CAKE

1 (8 oz.) cream cheese, softened
4 Tbsp. butter/margarine (½
    stick)
1 c. powdered sugar
12 oz. Cool Whip (1½ c.)
3½ c. milk

2 small pkg. vanilla instant
    pudding
2 (1 lb.) pkg. Oreo cookies
1 new 8 inch flower pot
1 new trowel

    Cream together cream cheese, butter, and sugar. Prepare pudding with the milk (3½ cups). Blend Cool Whip into pudding when it begins to thicken. Gradually add this mixture to cream cheese mixture. Combine well. Grind Oreo cookies (a food processor works good).

    Line the bottom of the pot with foil if it has holes. Beginning with the ground cookies, alternate one-inch layers with the mixture, ending with a layer of cookies on top. Chill. Decorate with gummy worms, flowers, or whatever!!! Serve with the trowel. Serves 8 to 10. Delicious and fun.

Holly Schoff Tobin, Porter Schoff, PID, Portsmouth Lions Club
Portsmouth, NH, USA

Peace has no borders.

Yitzhak Rabin

Life is like a ten-speed bicycle. Most of us have gears we never use.
Charles M. Schultz

2075-99

DIRT DESSERT

1¼ or 1½ lb. bag Oreo cookies
1 (8 oz.) pkg. cream cheese, softened
1 c. 10X sugar

3 c. milk
2 small boxes vanilla instant pudding
1 (16 oz.) container Cool Whip

Crumble cookies in blender. Spread ⅓ of the crumbs on the bottom of 13x9 or 14x11 inch pan. Mix pudding and milk in a small bowl and set aside.

Cream cream cheese and 10X sugar. Mix pudding with cream cheese mixture. Fold in Cool Whip. Spread ½ of the filling on cookie crumbs. Sprinkle ½ of the remaining crumbs on top of filling. Spread remaining filling on crumbs. Top with remaining crumbs. Refrigerate.

Sue Bubb, Burnham Lions Club
McClure, PA

BREAD PUDDING

1½ c. dry stale bread, broken up
3 c. milk
2 Tbsp. melted butter
⅓ c. sugar
½ tsp. salt

½ tsp. cinnamon
½ tsp. nutmeg
2 eggs
½ c. raisins (if desired)

Mix together and pour into buttered baking dish. Bake at 350° for 1 hour.

Eric and Karen Dutton, South Jefferson Lions Club
Adams, NY

BREAD PUDDING

1 (12 inch) loaf French bread
4 c. milk
½ c. (1 stick) butter, melted
½ c. sugar
1 tsp. ground cinnamon

6 eggs
2 tsp. vanilla
⅓ c. dark raisins
⅓ c. golden raisins

Slice bread into 1 inch thick slices. Cut slices into quarters. Whisk together milk, melted butter, sugar, cinnamon, eggs, and vanilla in large bowl. Pour into 2½ quart casserole. Add bread and raisins. Push down bread to cover with liquid. Refrigerate 1 hour or until bread absorbs liquid.

Heat oven to 350°. Bake one hour or until skewer inserted in center comes out somewhat clean. If pudding begins to brown too quickly, cover loosely with aluminum foil. Let stand 30 minutes. Serve warm, at room temperature or cold, with vanilla ice cream.

Lion Mary Clark, Foley Lions Club
Foley, AL, USA

BREAD PUDDING

4 eggs
2 c. milk
⅓ c. sugar
½ tsp. cinnamon

½ tsp. vanilla
¼ tsp. salt
2½ c. dry bread cubes
⅓ c. raisins

Beat together eggs, milk, sugar, cinnamon, vanilla, and salt. Place dry bread cubes in an 8 x 1½ inch round baking dish. Sprinkle raisins over bread. Pour egg mixture over all. Bake in a 325°F. oven for 40 to 45 minutes or till a knife inserted near center comes out clean.

Elizabeth Maddock, Canaan Northwest Lions Club
Canaan, CT, USA

BREAD PUDDING

4 c. bread cubes
1 qt. hot milk
3 Tbsp. butter
4 eggs, separated

Dash of salt
1 c. sugar
½ tsp. vanilla

After milk has been boiled, combine it with bread cubes and butter. Allow to stand for 10 minutes. Beat egg yolks and salt until light. Add sugar and vanilla; beat until lemon colored. Add bread mixture. Pour into greased 2 quart baking dish. Bake at 350° for 50 minutes.

Norma Murray, Bryan Lioness Club
Bryan, OH, USA

The greatest thing you can do is surprise yourself.
Steve Martin

Status symbols are poor excuses for values.
Merry Browne

Searching is half the fun: Life is much more manageable when thought of as a scavenger hunt as opposed to a surprise party.
Jimmy Buffet

A leader's role is to raise people's aspirations for what they can become and to release their energies so they will try to get there.
David Gergen

2075-99

BARBARA'S PUMPKIN PIE SQUARES

Crust:

1 c. flour
½ c. quick cooking oats

½ c. margarine, cut in pieces
½ c. packed brown sugar

Filling:

1 large can pumpkin
2 Tbsp. flour
2 tsp. ginger
1 tsp. cinnamon
1 tsp. nutmeg
1 tsp. salt

5 to 6 eggs
1 large can evaporated milk
1 c. orange juice
1 tsp. grated orange rind
2 c. packed brown sugar

Topping:

½ c. chopped walnuts
½ c. brown sugar

2 Tbsp. margarine
Whip cream

Crust: Combine flour, oatmeal, brown sugar, and margarine. Mix till crumbly. Press into greased 9x13 inch pan. Bake at 350° for 15 minutes. Remove from oven.

Filling: Mix all filling ingredients and pour into hot crust. Return to oven. Bake at 350° until knife inserted in center comes out clean. Remove from oven.

Topping: Combine walnuts, brown sugar, and margarine. Sprinkle over filling and bake 15 to 20 minutes longer. Cool. Top with whip cream.

Barbara Rozelle, West Lind Riverview Lions Club
Portland, OR, USA

PUMPKIN CRUNCH

1⅛ c. milk
3 eggs
3 Tbsp. sugar
3 Tbsp. brown sugar
½ tsp. salt

6 Tbsp. flour
¾ tsp. ground cinnamon
½ tsp. ground nutmeg
¼ tsp. ground allspice
3 c. pumpkin or squash

Topping:

6 Tbsp. butter
½ c. flour

1 c. oats
¼ to ½ c. brown sugar

Mix all the filling ingredients together and pour into ungreased 8x8 inch pan. Mix topping ingredients separately until crumbly, then sprinkle on top of pumpkin filling. Bake at 350° for 20 to 25 minutes.

Our family likes this instead of pumpkin pie.

James R. Schiebel, Hilton Lions Club
Hilton, NY, USA

FROZEN PUMPKIN DESSERT

1 qt. vanilla ice cream, softened
   in refrigerator
1 c. pumpkin
⅓ c. sugar
1⅔ c. crumbs (vanilla wafers or
   graham crackers or half and
   half)

½ tsp. salt
½ tsp. ginger
½ tsp. cloves
1 tsp. cinnamon
¼ c. chopped nuts
½ c. sugar
½ c. melted butter or margarine

Mix crumbs, ½ cup sugar, and melted margarine. Press into pan, reserving some of mixture to mix with nuts, and sprinkle on top. Bake crust about 7 minutes at 350°. Mix pumpkin, sugar, and spices. Beat in ice cream and quickly turn into cooled crust. Sprinkle with reserved crust mixture and nuts. Freeze. Makes a 9x13 inch pan or 1 pie pan.

Mary L. Coon, Hutchinson Breakfast Lions Club
Hutchinson, KS, USA

RHUBARB TORTE

Bottom layer:

½ c. butter
2 c. flour

2 Tbsp. sugar

Filling:

5 c. rhubarb, cut fine
½ tsp. salt
4 to 6 egg yolks, beaten

1 c. whipping cram
2 c. sugar
1 heaping Tbsp. flour

Topping:

4 to 6 egg whites
12 Tbsp. sugar

1 tsp. vanilla
½ tsp. salt

Mix first three ingredients together like pie crust and pat in bottom of 9x13 inch pan. Bake 7 minutes at 350°.

For filling, beat egg yolks well. Add sugar, salt, flour, and whipping cream together. Beat well. Add rhubarb. Pour over baked crust and bake 45 minutes or until done at 375°.

Topping: Beat 4 to 6 egg whites with salt until frothy. Add sugar, 2 tablespoons at a time. Continue beating until egg whites hold peaks. Add vanilla. Spread over custard and bake until meringue is golden brown in 375° oven.

Delicious with fresh or frozen rhubarb. Can also use 2 deep pie shells for rhubarb pie.

Myra Franke, Plato Lions Club
Plato, MN, USA

RHUBARB DUMPLINGS

Sauce:

1½ c. sugar
1 Tbsp. flour
½ tsp. cinnamon
¼ tsp. salt

1½ c. water
⅓ c. butter or margarine
1 tsp. vanilla
Red food coloring (optional)

Dough:

2 c. flour
2 Tbsp. sugar
2 tsp. baking powder

¼ tsp. salt
2½ Tbsp. butter or margarine
¾ c. milk

Filling:

2 Tbsp. butter or margarine,
    softened
2 c. finely chopped rhubarb

½ c. sugar
½ tsp. cinnamon

In saucepan, combine sugar, flour, cinnamon, and salt. Stir in water; add butter. Bring to a boil; cook and stir 1 minute. Remove from heat. Add vanilla and, if desired, enough food coloring to tint a deep pink; set aside.

For dough, in a medium bowl, combine flour, sugar, baking powder, and salt. Cut in butter until mixture resembles coarse crumbs. Add milk and mix quickly. Do not overmix. Form dough into ball and roll out on floured surface to a 9x12 inch rectangle. Spread with softened butter; arrange rhubarb evenly on top. Combine sugar and cinnamon; sprinkle over rhubarb. Roll up from long side and cut into 12 equal slices; arrange in greased 9x13 inch pan. Pour sauce over all and bake at 350° for 35 to 40 minutes or until golden brown.

We love it with milk or cream poured over when serving or with ice cream. Best when served warm, but also good cold.

Janet Johnson, Treasurer, Princeton Lions Club
Princeton, IL, USA

Everybody thinks of changing humanity and
nobody thinks of changing himself.

Leo Tolstoy

After climbing a great hill, one only finds
that there are many more hills to climb.

Nelson Mandela

RHUBARB TORTE

Crust:

½ lb. butter
2 c. flour

2 Tbsp. sugar

Filling:

5 c. rhubarb, cut fine
6 egg yolks, beaten with 1 c.
    cream
½ tsp. salt

2 c. sugar
4 Tbsp. flour

Topping:

6 egg whites, beaten
1 tsp. vanilla

2 Tbsp. sugar
½ tsp. salt

Crust: Mix like pie crust. Pat in bottom of 9x13 inch pan and bake 15 minutes at 350°.

Filling: Mix all together. Pour over baked crust and bake for 45 minutes at 375°.

Topping: Beat 6 egg whites. Add 1 teaspoon vanilla. Add 2 tablespoons sugar. Spread over custard; bake until golden brown in a 350° to 375° oven.

Wilma Arens, Plato Lions Club
Plato, MN, USA

RHUBARB-BERRY DESSERT

5 c. rhubarb (fresh or frozen), cut
    in pieces
1 c. sugar
1 (3 oz.) pkg. jello (strawberry or
    raspberry)

2 c. miniature marshmallows
1 pkg. white cake mix

Place cut-up rhubarb in a 9x13 inch pan. Sprinkle sugar over rhubarb, then sprinkle jello. Add the marshmallows, then cover with white cake mix that has been mixed as directed on the package. Pour over fruit and bake in 350° oven until cake is done. Serve with whipped cream or ice cream.

Lion Amy L. Kastle, Kirwin Lions Club
Kirwin, KS, USA

There is the risk you cannot afford to take,
and there is the risk you cannot afford not to take.
Peter F. Drucker

2075-99

APPLE RHUBARB STRITZEL

Filling:

½ c. sugar
4 tsp. flour
½ tsp. salt
1 tsp. nutmeg

1½ tsp. cinnamon
1 c. sliced apple
1 c. rhubarb, chopped fine

Topping:

⅔ c. oatmeal
⅓ c. chopped walnuts
¾ c. brown sugar
¾ c. flour

¼ tsp. baking soda
½ tsp. baking powder
⅔ c. butter

Mix sugar, flour, salt, nutmeg, and cinnamon. Add apple and rhubarb. Mix, then set aside. Combine topping mixture in order given and mix well with hands (mixture should look like crumbs). Put one third of mixture in 10 inch square cake pan and pat down firmly. Add filling; pat down. Last, add remaining topping and pat down. Bake at 350°F. for 60 minutes or until top is golden brown.

Micheal and Ruth Bartolf, Oxbow and District Lions Club
Oxbow, Saskatchewan, Canada

BUTTERFINGER TORTE

4 egg yolks, beaten
1 c. soft margarine
1 tsp. vanilla
2 c. powdered sugar

2 c. whipping cream
1 angel food cake
6 large Butterfingers, crushed in
    food processor or plastic bag

Beat together first 4 ingredients. Whip cream and fold into mixture. Tear cake into 1 inch pieces and place half in 9x13 inch pan. Pour half of cream mixture over cake. Sprinkle with half the crushed candy. Repeat cake, cream, candy layers with remaining ingredients. Refrigerate overnight.

Mrs. Tim (Linda) Lyons, Elburn Lions Club
Batavia, IL, USA

Maintaining a complicated life is a great way to avoid changing it.
Elaine St. James

❧ ❧ ❧

It is almost impossible to watch a sunset and not dream.
Bern Williams

BUTTERFINGER DELIGHT

2 c. powdered sugar
1 stick butter
4 egg yolks
1 large angel food cake, cut in
   half and torn into chunks

16 oz. Cool Whip
6 regular Butterfingers, crumbled
   into chunks

Cream powdered sugar, butter, and egg yolks together until smooth; add Cool Whip. Layer half of angel food cake in bottom of bowl; layer half of cream mixture and layer half of Butterfingers. Repeat.

Be sure to use very large bowl.

Nancy Pence, Elizabethtown Lions Club
Elizabethtown, KY, USA

TOFFEE BAR CRUNCH SLICE

1 tin butterscotch sauce
1 graham wafer crust
1½ c. milk or cream
1 large Cool Whip

1 (4 serving) pkg. Jell-O vanilla
   instant pudding powder
1 c. chopped chocolate bar (Skor)

Make crust according to directions. Spread into 9x11 inch baking pan. Pour half can butterscotch sauce over crust. Prepare pudding with milk or cream and fold in Cool Whip and chocolate bar (keep 2 tablespoons for garnish). Spread over crust and top with remaining sauce and chocolate garnish. *Freeze* for several hours.

This dessert is very good and easy to make.

Lion Jean Ukrainec, Lake of the Woods Lions Club
Kenora, Ontario, Canada

TOFFEE MOCHA DESSERT

1 angel food cake (8 inches), cut
   into 1 inch cubes
¾ c. strong brewed coffee, cooled
1 (8 oz.) pkg. cream cheese,
   softened

½ c. chocolate syrup
2 to 4 Tbsp. sugar
2 c. whipped topping
2 (1.4 oz.) Heath bars, crushed
Additional Heath bars (optional)

Place cake cubes in an ungreased 13x9x2 inch dish. Add coffee and toss lightly. In a mixing bowl, combine cream cheese, chocolate syrup, and sugar until blended. Fold in whipped topping. Spread over cake. Sprinkle with crushed Heath bars. Cover and refrigerate for at least 1 hour. Garnish with additional Heath bars if desired. Yield: 16 to 20 servings.

CRUNCHY BROWNIE SUNDAES

Brownie:

12 Tbsp. unsalted butter
4 oz. unsweetened chocolate,
   chopped
2 c. sugar
1¾ c. flour
¼ c. unsweetened cocoa powder

½ tsp. baking powder
½ tsp. salt
3 eggs
2 tsp. vanilla extract
½ c. milk

Heat oven to 350°. Butter a 13x9 inch baking pan. In a medium-size saucepan, melt the butter and chocolate together. Remove from heat and stir in the sugar. Set aside to cool. Combine flour, cocoa, baking powder, and salt. Stir the eggs into butter mixture, one at a time, until well-blended. Add the vanilla. Stir in the flour mixture, alternating with the milk, until the batter is smooth. Spread batter in the prepared pan and bake until edges pull away from sides of the pan, about 30 minutes. Cool completely in the pan before cutting.

Work time: 20 minutes. Total time: 50 minutes.

Per brownie: 282 calories, 4 g protein, 14 g fat, 94 mg sodium, 38 g carbohydrate, 64 mg cholesterol.

Caramel Sauce:

1 lb. dark brown sugar
½ c. maple syrup
8 oz. unsalted butter
½ tsp. salt

1 tsp. vanilla extract
½ tsp. almond extract
2 c. heavy cream

In a medium saucepan, combine the brown sugar, maple syrup, and the butter. Bring the mixture to a boil and boil 10 minutes, stirring constantly with a whisk. Remove from the heat and cool slightly, about 5 minutes. Stir in the salt, vanilla and almond extracts, and heavy cream. Chill Caramel Sauce for at least 4 hours (or overnight). Any remaining sauce can be refrigerated for up to 4 weeks, stored in a tightly covered container.

Work time: 30 minutes. Total time: 4 hours and 30 minutes.

Per ¼ cup serving: 285 calories, 1 g protein, 17 g fat, 140 mg sodium, 35 g carbohydrate, 56 mg cholesterol.

For sundae:

½ gal. vanilla ice cream

6 (1.4 oz.) chocolate coated
   toffee bars (2½ c. coarsely
   chopped)

Place a brownie square on an individual plate. Top with a scoop of vanilla ice cream, ¼ cup Caramel Sauce, and 1½ tablespoons chopped chocolate-coated toffee. Makes 16 sundaes.

Per sundae: 804 calories, 8 g protein, 47 g fat, 334 mg sodium, 292 g carbohydrate, 150 mg cholesterol.

Lion John J. Hess, Clarence Lions Club
Clarence Center, NY, USA

CHOCOLATE ECLAIR CAKE

1 box graham crackers
2 boxes vanilla instant pudding

1 (12 oz.) container Cool Whip
3 c. milk

Line the bottom of a 9x13 inch pan with graham crackers. Mix together the pudding and milk, then add the Cool Whip, mixing well. Spread half of the pudding on top of the layer of graham crackers. Put a layer of graham crackers on top of the pudding, then spread the rest of the pudding on that layer of crackers. Put a layer of crackers on the pudding. Make a chocolate frosting that is runny and spread on the top layer of crackers.

Best when made the night before - graham crackers will soften.

CHOCOLATE COCONUT NESTS

2 (14 oz.) pkg. flaked coconut
1⅓ c. semi-sweet chocolate
  chips, melted

3 qt. mint chocolate chip ice
  cream

In a bowl, toss coconut and chocolate until well blended. On baking sheets covered with waxed paper, shape about ⅓ cupfuls into 2½ inch nests. Chill until firm. Just before serving, top each nest with ½ cup of ice cream. Yield: 24 servings.

STRAWBERRY DESSERT

2½ c. vanilla wafers
1 stick butter
1 small box instant vanilla
  pudding

1 env. Dream Whip or 1 small
  Cool Whip
1 qt. strawberries

Mix crushed vanilla wafers and melted butter. Reserve ⅓ cup crumbs for topping. Press vanilla wafer mixture into 9x13 inch pan. Mix small box instant pudding as directed. Spread over crushed wafer mixture. Spread sliced strawberries over pudding mixture. Mix envelope Dream Whip as directed or use 1 small Cool Whip. Spread over mixture. Sprinkle remaining crumbs on top. Refrigerate several hours or overnight.

Lion Ronald Wilson, Graysville-Proctor Lions Club
Proctor, WV, USA

If you are lucky enough to find a way of life you love,
you have to find the courage to live it.
John Irving

Autumn is that season when nature seems to stop growing and start glowing.
William Arthur Ward

VANILLA WAFER SALAD

1 lb. vanilla wafers
¾ c. soft margarine
1 c. powdered sugar
½ tsp. vanilla
3 small eggs

2 (12 oz.) pkg. strawberries,
  drained and chilled
½ c. chopped nuts
1½ c. cream, whipped (can use
  Cool Whip)

Make this salad 2 days ahead: Crush wafers and put ½ on bottom of 12x8x2 inch pan. Mix butter, sugar, and vanilla until fluffy. Add egg yolks, 1 at a time. Beat egg whites till stiff, then fold in with butter mixture. Spread over crumbs. Spoon strawberries on mixture. Sprinkle nuts on top. Spread whipped cream or Cool Whip. Add nuts on top and sprinkle with rest of crumbs.

Ila Harrington, Bryan Lioness Club
Bryan, OH, USA

STRAWBERRY RHUBARB SHORTCAKE

1½ lb. rhubarb
2 c. dark brown sugar
Grated zest of 1 lemon
⅛ tsp. ground nutmeg
2 Tbsp. cornstarch
1 pt. strawberries
2 c. flour
4 Tbsp. granulated sugar

3¼ tsp. baking powder
½ tsp. salt
5 Tbsp. chilled vegetable
  shortening
¾ c. buttermilk
1 c. heavy cream
½ tsp. vanilla extract
Softened butter

Cut rhubarb into approximately ½ inch pieces. In a medium saucepan, combine the rhubarb, brown sugar, lemon zest, nutmeg, and cornstarch. Bring to a simmer over medium heat and cook until the rhubarb is tender and the mixture is slightly thickened, about 10 minutes. Remove from heat.

Meanwhile, cut the strawberries in halves and stir them into the warm rhubarb mixture. Heat the oven to 450°. Combine the flour, 2 tablespoons sugar, the baking powder, and salt. Cut in the shortening until the mixture resembles coarse meal with a few pea-sized pieces remaining. With a fork, stir in the buttermilk until the mixture comes together in a ball. Dough will be moist. On a lightly floured work surface, knead the dough gently two or three times. Pat or roll out dough to about ½ inch thick. With a 3 inch cutter, stamp out 8 biscuits. Cook on ungreased baking sheet until golden, 8 to 12 minutes. Let cool. Beat the cream with the remaining 2 tablespoons sugar and the vanilla until the cream holds stiff peaks. Split the biscuits and spread with butter. Spoon some of the warm fruit and sauce over the biscuit bottoms. Top them with whipped cream, the biscuit tops, and the rest of the fruit and whipped cream. Makes 8 servings.

Work time: 40 minutes. Total time: 1 hour.

Per serving: 560 calories, 6 g protein, 24 g fat, 367 mg sodium, 94 g carbohydrate, 52 mg cholesterol.

Joann M. Brownell, Clarence Lions Club
Clarence Center, NY, USA

QUICK STRAWBERRY SHORTCAKE

1 c. miniature marshmallows
2 c. fresh or 2 (10 oz.) pkg.
    frozen strawberries in syrup,
    completely thawed
3 oz. pkg. strawberry Jell-O
2¼ c. all-purpose flour
1½ c. sugar

½ c. butter
3 tsp. baking powder
1 c. milk
3 eggs
1 tsp. vanilla
½ tsp. salt

Generously grease bottom only of 13x9 inch pan. Sprinkle marshmallows over bottom of pan. Thoroughly combine Jell-O and strawberries. Set aside. Combine rest of ingredients and blend at low speed until moistened. Pour batter evenly over marshmallows. Spoon strawberry mix over all. Bake at 350°F. for 45 to 50 minutes. Delicious with whipped cream.

Micheal and Ruth Bartolf, Oxbow and District Lions Club
Oxbow, Saskatchewan, Canada

PLUM CORNMEAL SHORTCAKES

1 lb. plums, cut into 1 inch
    chunks
¾ c. + 2 Tbsp. sugar
1 c. flour
⅓ c. cornmeal
1½ tsp. baking powder

¼ tsp. salt
5 Tbsp. unsalted butter
About ½ c. milk
1 c. heavy cream
¼ tsp. vanilla extract

In a saucepan, combine plums, ½ cup sugar, and ⅓ cup water over medium-high heat. Cover and simmer about 15 minutes. Let cool. Heat oven to 400°. Combine flour, cornmeal, 1 tablespoon sugar, baking powder, and salt. Cut in butter until mixture resembles coarse meal. Stir in just enough of the milk to form a dough. On a floured work surface, pat into a disk about ½ inch thick. Cut out 6 biscuits. Brush with milk. Sprinkle with 1 tablespoon sugar. Bake on an ungreased baking sheet about 15 minutes. Whip cream, ¼ cup sugar, and vanilla. Split biscuits. Sandwich with plum sauce and whipped cream. Top with more fruit and cream. Makes 6 servings.

Barbara Joy Hess, Clarence Lions Club
Clarence Center, NY, USA

Anyone who takes himself too seriously always runs the risk of looking ridiculous; anyone who can consistently laugh at himself does not.
Vaclav Havel

People are pretty much alike. It's only that our differences are more susceptible to definition than our similarities.
Linda Ellerbee

STRAWBERRY DELIGHT

Crust:

½ c. melted butter or margarine
¼ c. brown sugar

1 c. flour
1 c. chopped nuts

Press into a 13x9 inch dish. Bake at 350° for 20 minutes. Cool.

2 egg whites
¾ c. sugar
1 tsp. vanilla

2 (10 oz.) pkg. frozen
   strawberries
8 oz. Cool Whip
Pecans

Beat 2 egg whites until stiff. Add ¾ cup sugar and 1 teaspoon vanilla. Fold in 2 (10 ounce) packages frozen strawberries, partially thawed, then fold in 8 ounce carton Cool Whip. Pour over crust and sprinkle with pecans. Freeze.

Leola C. Jurrens, Downtown Bartlesville Lions Club
Bartlesville, OK, USA

DELIGHTFUL STRAWBERRY DESSERT

3 egg whites
1½ c. sugar, *divided*
¾ tsp. cream of tartar
½ c. crushed saltines (about 15
   crackers)

½ c. flaked coconut
½ c. chopped pecans
2 c. whipping cream
½ tsp. unflavored gelatin
1 qt. fresh strawberries, sliced

In a mixing bowl, beat egg whites until soft peaks form. Gradually add 1 cup sugar and cream of tartar, beating until stiff peaks form. Gently fold in crumbs, coconut, and pecans. Spread onto the bottom and up the sides of a 9 inch pie plate. Bake at 375° for 20 to 22 minutes or until lightly browned. Cool completely.

In a mixing bowl, beat cream, gelatin, and remaining sugar until stiff peaks form. Fold in strawberries; pour into shell. Refrigerate for 2 hours. Yield: 10 to 12 servings.

Talent is the gift plus the passion - a desire to succeed
so intense that no force on earth can stop it.
Neil Simon

In the New Year, may your right hand always be stretched
out in friendship, but never in want.
Irish toast

STRAWBERRY PIZZA

Crust:

1½ c. all-purpose flour
1½ sticks oleo, melted

1 c. chopped pecans

Mix ingredients until well mixed and spread in a 12 or 13 inch pizza pan. Bake at 350° for 15 minutes or until lightly browned. Cool.

Filling:

1 (8 oz.) pkg. softened cream cheese
1 c. powdered sugar

1 (4 oz.) container whipped topping
1 qt. fresh strawberries

Combine cream cheese and powdered sugar and mix well. Beat in whipped topping until mixture is smooth. Spread over crust, leaving ¼ to ½ inch of crust exposed. Pile slightly higher at edges than in the center. Arrange strawberries attractively over filling. Spoon cooled glaze over strawberries (recipe follows).

Glaze:

1 c. sugar
2 Tbsp. cornstarch
4 to 5 drops of red food coloring

1 c. Sprite or 7-Up
1 Tbsp. strawberry gelatin

Combine all ingredients in medium-sized saucepan and cook over medium heat until thick and sauce is a clear red color. Refrigerate until ready to serve (2 to 3 hours). To serve, cut in wedges as you would pizza.

Nettie Favara, Greenwood Lions Club
Greenwood, MS, USA

HEAVENLY STRAWBERRY TRIFLE

1 pkg. white angel food cake mix (optional - ladyfingers)
½ pkg. (28 oz.) whipped topping mix (1 env.)
2 ctn. (6 oz.) non-fat strawberry yogurt

1 pt. strawberries, sliced
3 kiwi, sliced
¼ c. slivered almonds, toasted*

Bake and cool cake as directed on package. Cut cake vertically into halves. Freeze one half for future use. Layer half each of the cake pieces, yogurt, whipped topping, strawberries, and kiwi fruit in a 2 quart serving bowl; repeat. Sprinkle with almonds on top. Garnish with whole strawberries if desired. Refrigerate until firm, at least 2 hours. Makes 12 servings.

* To toast almonds, heat oven to 350°. Bake in ungreased pan 10 minutes. Stir occasionally.

Lion Mickey McConnell, Foley Lions Club
Foley, AL, USA

2075-99

STRAWBERRY MANGO TART

When shopping for mangoes and strawberries, be sure to smell the fruit before you buy. Those with a particularly sweet scent will have the best flavor.

1 refrigerated pie crust (½ of a
    15 oz. pkg.)
1 egg
2 c. strawberries
1 mango

½ c. heavy cream
2 tsp. sugar
¼ tsp. vanilla
2 Tbsp. apricot preserves

Heat oven to 425°. Unfold dough and put on a baking sheet. Fold edge of the dough over about ½ inch and crimp to make a decorative border. Prick surface of dough with a fork. Beat egg with 1 tablespoon water. Brush crust with the egg mixture. Bake until golden brown. Cool. Slice strawberries. Peel mango and cut it into thin slices.

In a small bowl, combine cream, sugar, and vanilla and beat until stiff. Spread whipped cream over cooled crust. Arrange mango slices around the edge of the cream to form a border. Arrange strawberry slices in overlapping rings over cream, covering it completely.

In a small saucepan, melt the preserves with 2 tablespoons water over medium-low heat, stirring until the preserves are smooth. Brush the melted preserves over the strawberries and refrigerate tart until ready to serve. Makes 6 servings.

Work time: 25 minutes. Total time: 40 minutes.

Per serving: 282 calories, 3 g protein, 18 g fat, 197 mg sodium, 27 g carbohydrate, 72 mg cholesterol.

Mrs. Lucy Aiken, Clarence Lions Club
Clarence Center, NY, USA

We never really grow up, we only learn how to act in public.
Bryan White

The most important lesson you can learn from winning is that you can.
Dave Weinbaum

Money is a singular thing. It ranks with love as man's great source of joy ...
and with death as his greatest source of anxiety.
John Kenneth Galbraith

STRAWBERRY BANANA SPLIT CAKE

2 c. graham cracker crumbs
(about 32 sq.)

½ c. butter or margarine, melted
¼ c. sugar

Filling:

½ c. butter or margarine,
softened
2 c. confectioners sugar
1 Tbsp. milk
1 tsp. vanilla extract
3 large firm bananas, cut into ¼
inch slices

2 (8 oz.) cans crushed pineapple,
drained
2 qt. fresh strawberries, sliced

Topping:

2 c. whipping cream
¼ c. confectioners sugar

1½ c. chopped walnuts

Combine the crumbs, butter, and sugar; press into an ungreased 13x9x2 inch dish. Chill for 1 hour. In a mixing bowl, cream butter, confectioners sugar, milk, and vanilla. Spread over crust; chill for 30 minutes. Layer with bananas, pineapple, and strawberries.

In a small mixing bowl, beat cream until soft peaks form. Add confectioners sugar; beat until stiff peaks form. Spread over fruit. Sprinkle with nuts. Chill until serving. Yield: 12 to 15 servings.

Unsolicited advice is the junk mail of life.
Bern Williams

❧ ❧ ❧

If you smile when no one else is around, you really mean it.
Andy Rooney

❧ ❧ ❧

Government is like junior high. Your status depends upon whom you're able to persecute.
Jonathan Kellerman

❧ ❧ ❧

You can't be brave if you've only had wonderful things happen to you.
Mary Tyler Moore

2075-99

BANANA SPLIT CAKE

First layer:

2 c. crushed graham crackers   **⅔ c. butter, melted**

Mix and press in bottom of pan.

Second layer:

2 sticks softened butter   **2 c. powdered sugar**
2 eggs   **1 tsp. vanilla**

Beat until thick. Spread over crackers.

Third layer:

**3 large sliced bananas, dipped in
    pineapple juice**

Fourth layer:

**1 (16 oz. or larger) can well
    drained crushed pineapple**

Fifth layer:

1 large container Cool Whip

Sixth layer: Sprinkle with chopped nuts and cherries.

Use 9x13 inch pan. Chill 8 hours before serving.
Donna Silbaugh, Bullskin Township Lioness Club
Mt. Pleasant, PA

A common enemy does not a true friendship make.
Richard Stengel

❧ ❧ ❧

We're all only fragile threads, but what a tapestry we make.
Jerry Ellis

❧ ❧ ❧

*No one can pick a peck of pickled peppers,
they have to be picked before they can be pickled.*

❧ ❧ ❧

The person who knows everything has a lot to learn.

472

BANANA SPLIT DESSERT

1 box powdered sugar
2 sticks oleo
2 eggs

1 large can crushed pineapple
12 oz. ctn. Cool Whip
6 bananas

Crust:

1⅓ pkg. graham crackers,
crushed

1 stick oleo

Mix first 3 ingredients together and beat 15 minutes. Prepare cooking pan with crust flattened out. Use 9x13 inch pan.

First layer - Crust.

Second layer - Sugar, oleo, and egg mixture.

Third layer: Cut bananas and spread over above mixture. Spread crushed pineapple.

Fourth and fifth layers: Spread Cool Whip over above. You can add chopped pecans and cherries on top if desired.

Put in refrigerator until ready to use.

Unexpected company? This is a good, quick dessert to make for your club or bake sale - goes a long way. No cooking involved.

Doris L. Mahalak, Biloxi Lions Club

PINEAPPLE REFRIGERATOR DESSERT

1 pkg. Jiffy yellow cake mix
1 large vanilla instant pudding
mix
2 c. milk
1 (8 oz.) cream cheese, softened

1 large (20 oz.) can crushed
pineapple
1 (18 oz.) Cool Whip

Make Jiffy cake according to directions, using a 9x13 inch pan. Cool. Beat together pudding, milk, and cram cheese. Spread on cooled cake. Drain pineapple and spread on top of pudding layer. Top with Cool Whip. Refrigerate overnight.

We all smile in the same language.

**Lioness Joni Arvidson, South-West Lioness Club
South St. Paul, MN, USA**

If your view of life is cloudy, maybe your windows need washing.

PINEAPPLE TORTE

Crust:

2¼ c. Oreo cookies (I prefer double stuffed)

½ c. butter/margarine

Crush the cookies in a blender to make fine crumbs. Spread on the bottom of a spring-form pan. Melt the butter/margarine and mix with crumbs so they become moist. This will form a crust. If you use double stuffed Oreos, you may not need as much margarine.

Filling:

1 (8 oz.) pkg. cream cheese
1⅓ c. sugar
½ tsp. lemon peel
1 (15¼ oz.) can Del Monte crushed pineapple in juice

1 (8 oz.) can pineapple "tidbits" (chunks will do in a pinch)
2 env. Knox gelatine
2¼ c. whipping cream, whipped

Blend cheese, sugar, and lemon peel. For best results, soften the cheese and blend long enough so sugar dissolves as much as possible. Drain crushed and tidbit pineapple, retaining the juice. Put juice in a saucepan and sprinkle the gelatine over it. Heat until dissolved. Add juice/gelatine to cheese mixture. Add *crushed* pineapple and mix all together well. Fold in whipped cream and pour into spring pan over the cookie crust. Chill for 5 hours or overnight. Garnish with pineapple *tidbits* and shaved milk chocolate. (I just use an oversized Hershey's bar and shave it with a vegetable peeler.)

Note: If the crushed pineapple can't be found in a 15¼ ounce can, you can use a larger can without much worry.

Lion Wanda Ramor, Foley Lions Club
Foley, AL

PINEAPPLE CREAM SLICE

Crust:

2½ c. graham wafer crumbs

½ c. melted butter

Additional ingredients:

½ c. butter
1½ c. icing sugar
1 egg, lightly beaten

1 can crushed pineapple
Whipping cream

Preheat oven to 325°F. Combine ingredients for crust and spread into 8x11 inch cake pan. Bake for 15 minutes. Cool. Cream together butter, icing sugar, and egg and spread evenly over crust. Drain pineapple and spread over cream mixture. Chill for several hours. Before serving, whip cream until stiff and spread over entire top.

Easy to prepare, delicious to eat.

Lion Marie Allanson, Lake of the Woods Lions Club
Kenora, Ontario, Canada

PINEAPPLE CUSTARD BRULEE

1 Tbsp. cornstarch
1 Tbsp. sugar
1 large egg yolk
1 c. low-fat milk
½ tsp. vanilla

½ c. plain low-fat yogurt
1 (8 oz.) can pineapple chunks (in natural juice), well drained
¼ c. packed light brown sugar

In small saucepan, stir cornstarch and sugar. In cup, whisk egg yolk into milk, then whisk into saucepan. Cook, stirring, over medium heat until mixture thickens, about 4 minutes. Remove from heat; stir in vanilla. Cool slightly, then stir in yogurt. Chill until cold.

Preheat oven to broil. Divide pineapple chunks among four 6 ounce custard cups. Pour cooled custard evenly over each. Sieve brown sugar evenly over each. Broil 3 inches from heat source until sugar melts and is bubbly, about 5 minutes. Serve at once or chill. Makes 4 servings.

Per serving: 171 calories, 4 g protein, 3 g fat, 58 mg sodium, 32 g carbohydrate, 60 mg cholesterol.

Barbara Joy Hess, Clarence Lions Club
Clarence Center, NY, USA

PINEAPPLE DESSERT

1 can crushed pineapple
½ c. sugar
Regular size lemon jello

3 oz. cream cheese
½ pt. whipping cream

Boil pineapple and sugar. Add lemon jello and mix well. Cool. Add cream cheese. Refrigerate until mixture starts to set. Whip whipping cream until soft peaks form. Add to partially set mixture.

Lion Dan Clever, East Prospect Lions Club
East Prospect, PA, USA

Man's ears aren't made to shut, but his mouth is.

❧ ❧ ❧

When all think alike, no one thinks very much.

❧ ❧ ❧

Believe in yourself and what others think won't matter.

HAWAIIAN DREAMS

Crust:

3 egg whites
½ tsp. baking powder
1 c. sugar

28 Ritz crackers, crushed*
½ c. chopped nuts

Whip egg whites till peaks form. Add baking powder and sugar. Beat till stiff on medium speed. Fold in crackers and nuts. Grease 13x9 inch pan. Spread evenly; press into pan. Bake 15 to 20 minutes at 325°.

Filling:

1 (8 oz.) cream cheese (room
temperature), cut into pieces

1 pkg. Dream Whip

Make Dream Whip according to directions, then beat in softened cream cheese, then fold in 1 can crushed pineapple (no juice). Spread on top of cooled crust. Top with toasted coconut. Cut into squares. Enjoy.

* Use rolling pin and wax paper to crush crackers.

Whenever I bring this dessert, I'm always asked for the recipe.
Dot WOCL, President, East Haddam Community Lions Club
East Haddam, CT

QUICK DESSERT

1 box Betty Crocker cake mix
(use 1 step)
1 (20 oz.) can crushed Dole
pineapple

Real whipping cream

Mix cake mix and pineapple together in bowl until combined. Pour into 13x9 inch pan. Bake in 325° oven for 25 to 35 minutes until golden brown on top. Serve with real whip cream.
LaVerne Childers, Kal-Haven Trail Lions Club
Gobles, MI, USA

PRETTY CHERRY PARFAITS

1 (21 oz.) can cherry pie filling
¼ tsp. almond extract
1 c. (8 oz.) sour cream
1 c. cold milk
1 (3.4 oz.) pkg. instant vanilla
pudding mix

Whipped topping, chopped
almonds, and fresh mint
(optional)

Combine pie filling and extract; set aside. In a mixing bowl, combine sour cream and milk. Stir in pineapple mix; beat on low speed for 2 minutes. Spoon half into parfait glasses; top with half of the pie filling. Repeat layers. Garnish with whipped topping, almonds, and mint if desired. Refrigerate until serving. Yield: 4 to 6 servings.

LEMON-RASPBERRY PARFAIT

¼ c. cornstarch
⅔ c. sugar
⅛ tsp. salt
2½ c. milk
2 egg yolks

1 tsp. vanilla
1 lemon
10 oz. pkg. whole raspberries
(packed in lite syrup)
½ c. heavy cream

In a saucepan, combine cornstarch, sugar, and salt. Mix together milk and yolks and slowly stir into cornstarch mixture. Cook over medium-low heat, stirring constantly, until mixture thickens and comes to a boil. Boil, stirring, 1 to 2 minutes. Remove from heat and pour through a sieve. Stir in vanilla and lemon zest and refrigerate. Drain raspberries, puree them, and pour through a sieve. Whip cream until it holds soft peaks. Fold whipped cream into cooled pudding. Halve pudding and fold raspberry puree into one half. Spoon alternating layers of puddings into parfait glasses. Refrigerate until ready to serve. Makes 4 servings.

Per serving: 468 calories, 8 g protein, 19 g fat, 161 mg sodium, 71 g carbohydrate, 168 mg cholesterol.

Lion John J. Hess, Clarence Lions Club
Clarence Center, NY, USA

CREAMY LIME SHERBET

1 (3 oz.) pkg. lime gelatin
1 c. boiling water
1¼ c. sugar
1 (6 oz.) can frozen limeade
concentrate, thawed

Dash of salt
1 qt. milk
1 pt. half & half cream
8 drops of green food coloring
(optional)

In a large bowl, dissolve gelatin in water. Add sugar, limeade, and salt; mix until sugar is dissolved. Add remaining ingredients; blend well. Freeze in an ice cream freezer according to manufacturer's directions. Yield: About 2 quarts.

CRANBERRY-PEAR SORBET

⅔ c. sugar
⅔ c. water
3 c. fresh or frozen whole
cranberries
2 ripe pears, peeled, cored, and
pureed

2 tsp. cinnamon
Zest of 2 oranges, minced
1 egg white

Combine sugar and water in a small pan on medium heat. Stir until sugar dissolves. Bring almost to a boil. Remove from heat and let cool. Cover and chill.

Combine syrup, cranberries, pears, and cinnamon and blend. Place in a metal ice cube maker and freeze. Remove from freezer; partially thaw. Spoon into blender and beat until fluffy. Add egg white and beat again. Refreeze; serve when frozen.

Lion Albert A. Ramsay, East Anne Arundel Lions Club, District 22A
Pasadena, MD, USA

SUGAR-FREE FROZEN DESSERT

1 pkg. sugar-free pudding mix
  (any flavor)
1½ c. cold milk

1 large container frozen dessert
  topping (Cool Whip)

Mix milk and pudding mix with wire whisk; set aside to thicken. Fruit may be added at this time, if you wish. Mix into dessert topping until evenly mixed. Cover and freeze until firm.

This can also be done with fruit flavored jello, with 1 cup of boiling water. Thicken slightly. With wire whisk, beat into Cool Whip and freeze.

This makes great fruit flavored ice cream for people who can't have dairy products. Leave some out to soften slightly and then spoon into an ice-cream cone for the little ones, if you wish.

Lion Janice Elliott, Meredith Lions Club
Meredith, NH, USA

NECTARINE ICE CREAM WITH HONEYED KIWI

1 lemon
1 c. heavy cream
1 c. milk
⅛ tsp. ground nutmeg

½ c. plus 2 tsp. honey
3 nectarines (about 1 lb.)
2 kiwi

Squeeze 2 tablespoons plus 2 teaspoons juice from lemon. In a stainless steel or glass bowl, combine heavy cream, milk, nutmeg, 2 tablespoons of the lemon juice, and 6 tablespoons of the honey. Stir until the honey dissolves. Put in freezer. When the mixture starts to set around the edges, stir and return to freezer. Stir once an hour for next two hours.

Meanwhile, peel and chop 2 of the nectarines. Toss with 2 tablespoons of the honey and 2 teaspoons of the lemon juice. When the ice cream has thickened slightly, fold in the nectarine mixture. Return to freezer to set, 1 to 2 hours. Peel kiwi and slice. Slice remaining nectarine. Toss the fruit with the remaining 2 teaspoons honey. Serve with the ice cream. Makes 4 servings.

Per serving: 460 calories, 5 g protein, 25 g fat, 57 mg sodium, 61 g carbohydrate, 90 mg cholesterol.

Joann M. Brownell, Clarence Lions Club
Clarence Center, NY, USA

Man's ears aren't made to shut, but his mouth is.

❧ ❧ ❧

Believe in yourself and what others think won't matter.

HOMEMADE ICE CREAM

4 c. milk
4 large eggs
2¼ c. sugar
Dash of salt
Large mixing spoon vanilla

1 qt. half & half
½ pt. heavy cream
Approx. 10 lb. ice
Freezer salt
1 gal. freezer

Scald milk. Beat eggs in large bowl until thick and lemon colored. Continuing to beat, add sugar and salt gradually. Pour scalded milk into beaten egg mixture while continuing to beat. Chill mixture thoroughly. When ready to freeze, add vanilla and cream.

Carol Chrisp, Sargent Lions Club
Sargent, NE, USA

ICE-CREAM ILLUSION

1 pt. heavy cream
6 slices firm white bread

¾ c. firmly packed light brown
sugar

In large bowl, with electric mixer at medium, beat heavy cream until soft peaks form. Pour into 13x9 inch cake pan; smooth surface. Cover with foil and freeze. Once mixture begins to solidify at edges (about 20 to 30 minutes), stir mixture from edges to center, smooth surface, and return to freezer for 30 minutes.

Meanwhile, preheat broiler. In food processor, process bread just until crumbs form, 5 to 10 seconds. Evenly spread crumbs on baking sheet; sprinkle with brown sugar. Broil until sugar melts and crumbs are lightly browned, stirring occasionally, 2 to 6 minutes. Watch carefully to prevent burning. Cool, then break any large chunks into small crumbs. Stir into semi-frozen cream. Return to freezer to harden, about 2 hours or overnight. Before starting to pack for the picnic, thaw in refrigerator 30 minutes. Makes 8 servings.

Work time: 20 minutes. Total time: 2 hours and 40 minutes.

Per serving: 348 calories, 3 g protein, 34 g carbohydrate, 23 g fat, 82 mg cholesterol, 159 mg sodium.

Mrs. Lucy Aiken, Clarence Lions Club
Clarence Center, NY, USA

Live so you're neither afraid of tomorrow nor ashamed of yesterday.

Be like a postage stamp - stick to it until you get there.

2075-99

STRAWBERRY TOFU ICE CREAM

2 lb. soft tofu
1 c. soy milk
2 c. sugar
1⅓ c. oil
¼ c. fresh lemon juice

2 (20 oz.) frozen unsweetened
   strawberries
2 Tbsp. vanilla
¼ tsp. salt

Blend in a blender in four equal parts until smooth and creamy. Freeze in a home hand operated or electric ice cream maker and serve. Makes 12½ cups.

Per ½ cup serving: 204 calories, 3 g protein, 14 g fat, 20 g carbohydrate.
Evelyn Thompson, Mount Airy Foothills Lions Club
Mt. Airy, NC, USA

CHOCOLATE FUDGE ICE CREAM

2 (14 oz.) cans sweetened
   condensed milk
2 (4 oz.) pkg. chocolate instant
   pudding mix

2 qt. milk

Combine all ingredients in large bowl. Pour mixture in freezer can of a 5 quart hand turned or electric freezer. Freeze according to instructions with freezer. Serve at once. Makes 1 gallon.

When life gets hectic and it's hard to cope, repeat these words: "Love and hope."

Doris (Cricket) Kimbrell, Iron City Lions Club
Iron City, TN, USA

CHOCOLATE ICE CREAM

12 Milky Way candy bars, diced
   and melted thoroughly
1 (5 oz.) can Hershey's chocolate
   syrup

1 can Eagle Brand sweetened
   condensed milk

Mix together. Put into ice cream freezer can. Fill can with milk to fill line. Freeze in electric or hand turned ice cream freezer. Freeze as directed by freezer instructions. Serve at once. Yummy.

Amy Bromley, Iron City Lions Club
Iron City, TN, USA

If you don't grow vegetables, it pays to praise your neighbor's garden.

ALZETTE FRUIT CRUMBLE

1 medium sized can apple, peach, cherry, or blueberry pie filling
1 small spice cake mix or 2 c. full-size spice cake mix
½ c. chopped pecans
¾ stick melted butter or margarine
2 Tbsp. hot water

Spread pie filling in 7x11 inch pan. Sprinkle cake mix over filling. Sprinkle nuts over mix. Mix melted butter and hot water; pour over mixture. Bake in preheated oven at 350°F. for 45 minutes. Serve with whipped cream or vanilla ice cream.

This makes an easy last-minute dessert.

Carol Speicher, Columbus Lions Club
Columbus, NE, USA

FRUIT PIZZA

1 (20 oz.) pkg. cookie dough
1 (8 oz.) pkg. cream cheese
⅓ c. sugar
½ tsp. vanilla
Any fresh fruit
1 c. orange marmalade
2 Tbsp. water

Crust: Press cookie dough into a pizza pan, distributing evenly. Bake at 325° for 15 minutes. Let cool.

Pizza filling: Blend cream cheese, sugar, and vanilla and spread on the crust.

Topping: Use any fruit, such as kiwi, peaches, pineapple, cherries, and strawberries. Cut the fruit into shapes and place on the filling.

Glaze: Mix marmalade and water and drizzle over the pizza. Chill and serve.

Lion Kendrick Sisk, Mount Airy Foothills Lions Club
Mount Airy, NC, USA

Two of the most beautiful words in
the English language are "check enclosed."

❧ ❧ ❧

Learn to laugh at yourself; you'll have a lifelong source of amusement.

❧ ❧ ❧

Win without boasting; lose without excuse.

FRUIT COCKTAIL CAKE

Cake:

1½ c. sugar
2 c. self-rising flour

2 eggs
2 c. fruit cocktail

Topping:

1 c. chopped pecans
½ c. dark brown sugar
1½ c. sugar

1 c. Pet milk
¾ c. margarine
1 tsp. vanilla flavoring

Mix all cake ingredients and pour into sheet cake pan. Sprinkle over cake in pan, 1 cup chopped nuts and ½ cup dark brown sugar. Bake at 350° for 40 minutes or until done.

In saucepan, combine 1½ cups sugar, Pet milk, and margarine. Boil for 2 minutes, then pour over cake in pan. Sprinkle vanilla over top of cake. Let cake cool. Delicious.

This is absolutely delicious.

Janet Brown, Covington Lions Club
Covington, GA, USA

FRUIT SALAD PIE

1 can water packed cherries
1 can crushed pineapple
1 c. sugar
¼ c. flour
1 small box cherry gelatin

1 c. chopped pecans
4 to 6 bananas
Graham cracker crumbs for 2 pie
   crusts

Prepare 2 graham cracker crusts. Cook cherries, pineapple, sugar, and flour in pan on medium heat till thick. Remove from heat; add gelatin, pecans, and bananas. Pour into crusts; cool and put in refrigerator.

Excellent if topped with whipped topping.

Lion Nelson Bonager, East Prospect Lions Club
East Prospect, PA, USA

Tact is making a point without making an enemy.

❧ ❧ ❧

Today should always be our most wonderful day.

❧ ❧ ❧

A word to the wise is often enough to start an argument.

WHITE CHOCOLATE FRUIT TART

¾ c. butter, softened
½ c. confectioners sugar

1½ c. all-purpose flour

Filling:

1 (10 oz.) pkg. vanilla baking
   chips, melted
¼ c. whipping cream
1 (8 oz.) pkg. cream cheese,
   softened
1 (20 oz.) can pineapple chunks
   (undrained)

1 pt. fresh strawberries, sliced
1 (11 oz.) can mandarin oranges,
   drained
2 kiwi fruit, peeled and sliced

Glaze:

3 Tbsp. sugar
2 tsp. cornstarch

½ tsp. lemon juice

In a mixing bowl, cream butter and sugar. Gradually add flour; mix well. Press into an ungreased 11 inch tart pan or 12 inch pizza pan with sides. Bake at 300° for 25 to 30 minutes or until lightly browned. Cool.

In a mixing bowl, beat chips and cream. Add cream cheese and beat until smooth. Spread over crust. Chill for 30 minutes. Drain pineapple, reserving ½ cup juice; set juice aside. Arrange strawberries, pineapple, oranges, and kiwi over filling.

In a saucepan, combine sugar, cornstarch, lemon juice, and reserved pineapple juice; bring to a boil over medium heat. Boil for 2 minutes or until thickened, stirring constantly. Cool; brush over fruit. Chill 1 hour before serving. Store in the refrigerator. Yield: 12 to 16 servings.

CREAMY FROZEN FRUIT CUPS

1 (8 oz.) pkg. cream cheese,
   softened
½ c. sugar
1 (10 oz.) jar maraschino
   cherries, drained
1 (11 oz.) can mandarin oranges,
   drained

1 (8 oz.) can crushed pineapple,
   drained
½ c. chopped pecans
1 (8 oz.) ctn. frozen whipped
   topping, thawed
Fresh mint (optional)

In a mixing bowl, beat the cream cheese and sugar until fluffy. Halve 9 cherries; chop the remaining cherries. Set aside halved cherries and 18 oranges for garnish. Add the pineapple, pecans, and chopped cherries to cream cheese mixture. Fold in whipped topping and remaining oranges. Line muffin cups with paper or foil liners. Spoon fruit mixture into cups; garnish with reserved cherries and oranges. Freeze until firm. Remove from the freezer 10 minutes before serving. Top with mint if desired. Yield: 1½ dozen.

2075-99

APPLE DUMPLINGS

1 can Hungry Jack biscuits

Syrup:

1 (12 oz.) can 7-Up
1 tsp. cinnamon

6 apples, peeled and diced

1 c. sugar
1 stick margarine, melted

Put syrup ingredients into a saucepan and bring to a boil. Let boil for 2 minutes.

Roll biscuits thin. Fill with diced apples. Pinch edges together after folding over in half. Place dumplings in a baking dish. Pour syrup over dumplings and bake at 350° for 30 minutes.

Lion Shirley Jones, Mount Airy Foothills Lions Club
Mount Airy, NC, USA

APPLE CRISP

12 apples
½ c. brown sugar
2 c. flour
1½ c. white sugar

1 tsp. baking powder
¼ tsp. salt
2 eggs
⅔ c. margarine

Peel and slice apples. Combine with brown sugar. Place in 9x13 inch pan. Mix flour, sugar, baking powder, salt, and eggs. Place on top of apples. Melt margarine and pour over topping. Sprinkle with cinnamon. Bake in preheated oven at 350° for 1 hour.

Ardist Ferris, Lyons-Muir Lions Club
Lyons, MI, USA

If you can't be a lifter, don't be a leaner.

After you've heard two eyewitness accounts of an auto accident,
it makes you wonder about history.

Bits & Pieces

The highest reward for a person's toil is not
what they get for it, but what they become by it.

John Ruskin

You can live to be a hundred if you give up
all the things that make you want to live to be a hundred.

Woody Allen

APPLE CRISP

Time: 45 minutes.

6 to 8 cooking apples
1 c. sweet cider or apple juice
¼ tsp. cinnamon
1 c. unbleached white flour
1 c. whole wheat pastry flour
1 c. rolled oats

Pinch of sea salt
½ to 1 c. chopped walnuts
½ c. corn oil
⅓ c. pure maple syrup
¼ tsp. vanilla (optional)

Peel, core, and slice apples into a 9x12 inch baking dish. Mix the cinnamon with the sweet cider or apple juice and pour over the apples. Set aside while you prepare the topping.

Combine the flours, oats, sea salt, and nuts in a large mixing bowl. Add the oil, maple syrup, and vanilla if using. Mix all together until crumbly. Sprinkle the topping over the apples and press lightly with hands to firm. Bake at 350°F. for about 40 minutes or until the top begins to brown and the apples are tender. Serves 6 to 8.

Comments: For special occasion, serve with tofu whipped cream.

PDG Jim Schiebel, Hilton Lions Club
Hilton, NY, USA

LEMON CHEESE TORTE

1 large Cool Whip
1 (8 oz.) cream cheese
3 c. milk
1 c. 10X sugar
1 c. finely chopped nuts

2 small boxes instant lemon
    pudding
2 c. flour
2 sticks margarine

Crust: Melt 2 sticks of margarine. Mix with 2 cups flour and spread in bottom of 9x13 inch pan. Sprinkle half of the nuts on top. Bake at 350° for 20 minutes. Cool completely!

First layer: Mix ½ container of Cool Whip, 1 cup 10X sugar, and 8 ounces cream cheese (softened).

Second layer: Mix all the lemon pudding with 3 cups milk. Spread.

Third layer: Spread the rest of the Cool Whip and sprinkle on rest of the nuts.

Gail Kemmerer, Green Lane-Marlboro Lioness Club
Sumneytown, PA, USA

4-LAYER LEMON DESSERT

1 c. margarine
2 c. flour
1 c. chopped pecans
8 oz. pkg. cream cheese
1 c. powdered sugar

4 c. Cool Whip
2 boxes lemon instant pudding
3 c. milk
1 tsp. lemon flavoring

Melt margarine and mix with flour and pecans. Put in bottom of 9x13 inch pan for a crust. Bake at 350° for 15 minutes. Let cool.

Soften cream cheese and mix with powdered sugar. Add 1 cup of Cool Whip and mix. Spread this layer on cooled crust. Mix pudding, milk, and lemon flavoring. Spread over second layer. Spread remaining Cool Whip on top. Refrigerate.

Can be made the day before serving.

Lynne Swanson, Princeton Lions Club
Princeton, IL

LEMON-RASPBERRY TART

1½ lemon zest*
8 to 9 Tbsp. sugar (7 Tbsp. for a
  tart flavor)

2 eggs
1 yolk
¾ c. cream

Place all ingredients into blender and mix. Add zest. Continue beating for a couple of seconds and pour through strainer. Add raspberries and cook for ½ hour or until firm.

Crust for Lemon-Raspberry Tart:

1½ c. confectioners sugar
9 Tbsp. butter
Pinch of salt

1¾ c. flour, sifted
1 egg

Place all the ingredients into a mixing bowl and combine well. Divide in half and chill. Roll out and place in tart pan (one with a removable bottom). Place beans, for weight, in pan and bake for 15 minutes at 350°.

* Cut skin off of lemons, remove seeds, put into blender, and blend.

Martha Stewart, October, 1998.

Marilyn Redifer, Whitehall Area Lions Club
Columbus, OH

The best preparation for tomorrow is to do today's work superbly well.
Sir William Osler

LEMON TRIFLE

1 (14 oz.) can sweetened
   condensed milk
1 (8 oz.) ctn. lemon yogurt
⅓ c. lemon juice
2 tsp. grated lemon peel
2 c. whipped topping

1 angel food cake (10 inches), cut
   into 1 inch cubes
2 c. fresh raspberries
½ c. flaked coconut, toasted
Fresh mint (optional)

In a bowl, combine the first four ingredients. Fold in whipped topping. Place half of the cake cubes in a trifle bowl or 2 quart serving bowl. Top with half of the lemon mixture. Repeat layers. Top with raspberries. Garnish with coconut and mint if desired. Yield: 14 servings.

LEMONADE ANGEL FLUFF

1 c. evaporated milk
2 env. unflavored gelatin
1 c. cold water
½ c. sugar

¾ c. pink lemonade concentrate
Red food coloring (optional)
4 c. angel food cake cubes

Pour milk into a small metal mixing bowl; place mixer beaters in the bowl. Cover and chill for at least 2 hours.

In a saucepan, sprinkle gelatin over cold water; let stand for 2 minutes. Stir in sugar; heat until sugar and gelatin are dissolved. Remove from the heat; stir in lemonade concentrate and food coloring if desired. Cover and chill until slightly thickened. Gradually add to chilled milk; beat until light and fluffy. Fold in cake.

Pour into an 8x4x2 inch loaf pan coated with nonstick cooking spray. Cover and chill for at least 2 hours. Remove from pan; cut into eight slices. Yield: 8 servings.

BLUEBERRY DESSERT

2 c. graham cracker crumbs
⅔ c. butter
2 (3 oz.) pkg. cream cheese

1 c. powdered sugar
1 (12 oz.) Cool Whip
1 can blueberry pie filling

Melt butter. Mix with graham cracker crumbs. Press into a 12x8 inch pan. Bake 8 minutes at 350°. Cool.

Beat cream cheese and add powdered sugar; beat till smooth. Fold in Cool Whip. Spread ½ mixture over crust. Add can of blueberry pie filling over cream cheese. Spread remaining cream cheese mixture over blueberry pie filling. Refrigerate overnight. Cut into serving squares.

Mrs. Gordon (Linn) Dierschow, Elburn Lions Club
Elburn, IL

BLUEBERRY CRUMBLE

3 c. blueberries
6 Tbsp. sugar
Juice of 1 lemon
¼ tsp. cinnamon

¾ c. flour
⅓ c. butter
6 Tbsp. sugar
½ tsp. salt

Wash berries and put in a buttered square baking dish. Add sugar, lemon juice, and cinnamon and stir to coat the berries. Combine flour, butter, sugar, and salt and mix with fork or fingers till mix is crumbly. Sprinkle mix over berries and bake at 350° for 30 to 40 minutes. Makes 4 to 6 servings.

You can top this with ice cream.

This has been a family favorite for many years.
Mrs. Duane (Pam) Bennett, Mad River Lions Club
Riverside, OH, USA

BLUEBERRY KUCHEN

Batter:

½ c. butter
1 c. sugar
1 tsp. vanilla
3 eggs
2 c. sifted flour

½ tsp. salt
1 tsp. baking powder
1¼ c. sour cream
2 c. blueberries

Topping:

½ c. chopped pecans
⅔ c. packed brown sugar

½ tsp. cinnamon
2 Tbsp. melted butter

Preheat oven to 350°F. Batter: Cream together butter, sugar, and vanilla and beat until light and fluffy. Add eggs, one at a time, beating well after each. Sift flour, salt, baking powder, and baking soda. Add by thirds into butter mixture. Alternate with ½ sour cream, mixing well after each addition. Spread half of the mixture into a 10 inch spring form pan. Spread layer of blueberries and remainder of batter mixture. In a separate bowl, mix together topping and spread over batter. Bake for 55 to 60 minutes.
Lion Carol Anderson, Lake of the Woods Lions Club
Kenora, Ontario, Canada

Success is more attitude than aptitude.

A small town is a place where there's no place to go where you shouldn't.
Burt Bacharach

BLUEBERRY STRIP

1 refrigerated pie crust (½ of a
  15 oz. pkg.)
1 egg
1 lemon

8 oz. cream cheese, softened
¾ c. sugar
1 pt. blueberries
Confectioners sugar (optional)

Heat the oven to 425°. On a lightly floured work surface, roll out pie dough to an oval, about 16 inches wide. Trim a strip about 1½ inches wide off each long side and discard. Fold over a 1 inch border along each long side. Put dough on a baking sheet and prick surface with a fork. Beat egg with 1 tablespoon water and brush the dough lightly with some of this egg mixture. Bake until golden brown, about 10 minutes. Cool.

Grate 1 tablespoon of the yellow zest from the lemon and squeeze 2 tablespoons juice.

In a bowl, combine cream cheese, sugar, lemon zest, and juice and beat until smooth. Chill. Spread cream cheese mixture over the bottom of the baked crust and arrange blueberries on top. Refrigerate until ready to serve. Just before serving, sprinkle tart with confectioners sugar, if you like. Makes 6 servings.

Work time: 30 minutes. Total time: 40 minutes.

Per serving: 427 calories, 5 g protein, 24 g fat, 303 mg sodium, 49 g carbohydrate, 86 mg cholesterol.

Mrs. Lucy Aiken, Clarence Lions Club
Clarence Center, NY, USA

BLUEBERRY BUCKLE

Base:

¼ c. butter
½ c. sugar
2 eggs
1½ c. flour
½ c. milk

2 tsp. baking powder
½ tsp. salt
½ tsp. nutmeg
¼ tsp. ground cloves

Blend butter, sugar, eggs, and milk. Stir in flour, baking powder, salt, nutmeg, and cloves. Spread in a 9x9 inch pan.

Filling: Spread base with 1 pint fresh blueberries or 10 ounce frozen (dry pack) blueberries.

Topping:

⅓ c. sugar
⅓ c. flour

½ tsp. cinnamon
¼ c. butter

Combine ingredients; mix until crumbly. Sprinkle over top. Bake at 350°F. for 45 minutes. Serve with whipped cream.

Micheal and Ruth Bartolf, Oxbow and District Lions Club
Oxbow, Saskatchewan, Canada

PEACH CRUNCH

1 qt. fresh peaches (can use
    blueberries, apples or
    strawberries)
2 Tbsp. cornstarch
1 c. sugar

1 c. water
1 c. flour
1 stick margarine
½ c. sugar

Bring water, sugar, and cornstarch to a boil and stir until mixture is clear. Add 1 quart fresh peaches. Place fruit mixture in baking dish.

Topping: Cut flour, margarine, and sugar with a pastry blender until mixture resembles coarse crumbs. Spread on top of fruit and bake 30 minutes at 450°.

May use Cool Whip or ice cream as topping.

Lion Irene Shuff, Mount Airy Foothills Lions Club
Mount Airy, NC, USA

PEACH DESSERT

Bottom crust - Mix:

¾ c. butter
1½ c. flour

½ c. chopped pecans

Press into 9x12 inch pan. Bake for 10 minutes in a 350° oven.

Middle layer: Beat ⅞ cup powdered sugar with 8 ounces cream cheese. Fold in 1 cup Cool Whip. Put on the cooled crust.

Top layer: Lay sliced peaches over the middle layer. (Fresh peaches are best.)

Mix:

1 c. sugar
3 tsp. corn starch

2 Tbsp. white syrup
1 c. water

Cook until thick, then add 3 tablespoons peach dry gelatin. Cool and pour over the peaches. Refrigerate until serving time.

If your view of life is cloudy, maybe your windows need washing.

Robert Maras, Windom Lions Club
Windom, MN, USA

The older you get, the more you like to tell it like it used to be.

Consumers are statistics. Customers are people.
Stanley Marcus

NO SUGAR PEACH COBBLER

1 (12 oz.) frozen apple juice
  concentrate, thawed
3 Tbsp. cornstarch
4 c. sliced peaches (or use frozen
  natural peaches)
1 c. flour

1½ tsp. baking powder
3 Tbsp. melted butter
¼ tsp. almond extract
2 Tbsp. chopped almonds
  (optional)

Mix cornstarch with 1 cup apple juice and almond extract in saucepan. Heat, stirring often, until thickens to a glaze. Takes about 5 minutes. Add peaches and stir until peaches are well coated. Pour into 8 inch square glass pan or 2 quart casserole.

In small bowl, mix flour and baking powder. Add butter and remaining ½ cup apple juice. Spread in almonds. Drop batter on top of fruit and spread. Bake at 400°F. for 25 to 30 minutes. Serve warm.

Marty Clark, Hutchinson Breakfast Lions Club
Hutchinson, KS, USA

PEACH COBBLER FOR A CROWD

2 large cans peaches, sliced
1 c. brown sugar
1 stick butter or margarine,
  melted
2 c. biscuit mix

1 egg
Cinnamon
½ c. milk

In a 9x13 inch pan (deep), place peaches and juice. Sprinkle cinnamon over all. Mix biscuit mix and egg with milk. Drop 12 spoonfuls evenly. (I use an ice cream scoop.) Place a spoonful of brown sugar on each spoonful of batter. Pour butter over everything. Bake at 350° for 20 minutes or till biscuits are done and light brown. Makes 12 servings.

Serve with a scoop of vanilla ice cream.

Lions serve this at the Portage County-Randolph Fair. It's a favorite of the senior citizens and sold out every year!

King Shirley Riemenschneider, Rootstown Township, 13-D Lions Club
Rootstown, OH

PEACH COBBLER

1 c. sugar
1 c. Bisquick
½ stick butter

1 c. milk
1 large can peaches
Cinnamon-sugar

Melt butter in 9x13 inch cake pan. Mix sugar and Bisquick together. Pour on top melted butter, then pour peaches on top. Sprinkle with cinnamon sugar. Bake at 350° for 45 minutes.

Mrs. Bill (Candy) McCartney, Elburn Lions Club
Elburn, IL, Kane County

PEACH COBBLER

¼ c. butter
1 c. flour
1 c. sugar
1 Tbsp. baking powder

⅔ c. milk
3 c. fresh peaches (slices)
¼ tsp. nutmeg
¼ tsp. cinnamon

Melt butter in a 7x11 inch baking dish. Sift dry ingredients; add milk and stir well. Pour this mixture into baking dish. Do not stir. Top with peaches. Sprinkle nutmeg and cinnamon over peaches. Do not stir. Bake in 350°F. oven for 40 minutes or until golden brown. Serve warm. Serves 6 to 8.

Doris Brewer, wife of Lion Guy Brewer,
Silver Run Union Mills Lions Club
Silver Run, MD, USA

CHERRY CRUMB DESSERT

½ butter or margarine, chilled
1 (18½ oz.) pkg. yellow cake mix
1 (21 oz.) can cherry or blueberry
   pie filling

½ c. chopped walnuts
Whipped cream or ice cream

In a mixing bowl, cut butter into cake mix as for pastry dough. Set aside one cup. Pat remaining crumbs onto the bottom and ½ inch up the sides of a greased 13x9 inch baking pan. Spread pie filling over crust. Combine the walnuts with reserved crumbs and sprinkle over top. Bake at 350° for 30 to 35 minutes. Serve warm with whipped cream or ice cream if desired. Yield: 12 to 16 servings.

Bernice Kniceley, Rivesville Lions Club
Rivesville, WV, USA

CHERRY ANGEL FOOD DESSERT

1 pt. whipping cream
1 pkg. Philadelphia cream cheese
1 can cherry pie filling

1 small bar angel food or about
   ½ regular angel food cake
1 or 2 Tbsp. sugar

Place ½ inch slices of angel food cake or cover bottom of 9x13 inch cake dish with angel food cake, broken in small pieces, then whip the whipping cream and combine softened Philadelphia cream cheese. Spread this mixture over angel food cake. Top with cherry pie filling and sprinkle sugar on top. Refrigerate until serving.

Can be made a day or two before using.

Nancy Lansky, Tuscola Lions Club
Tuscola, IL, USA

Everything that is done in the world is done by hope.
Martin Luther

CHERRY CRUNCH

1 stick butter
1 yellow cake mix

1 can cherry pie filling
½ c. chopped nuts

Mix butter with cake mix. Keep out 1 cup of mixture. Place rest of mixture into a 13x9 inch oblong pan. Spread cherries over mixture. Mix chopped walnuts with remainder of dry cake mix and sprinkle over top. Bake 45 to 50 minutes at 350°.

Debra James, Beekmantown Lions Club
West Chazy, NY

CHERRY DESSERT

1 (8 oz.) pkg. cream cheese
¼ c. lemon juice

1 can sweetened condensed milk
½ tsp. vanilla

Crust:

1 packet graham crackers,
    crushed
⅓ c. butter, melted

½ c. sugar

Additional ingredient:

1 can cherry pie filling

Beat cheese; add milk gradually. Mix together with rest of filling ingredients. Pour into prepared graham cracker crust. Chill 2 to 3 hours. Pour a can of cherry pie mix over the cheese mixture.

For crust: Mix all ingredients together; press into a 9x11 inch pan.

Any kind of pie filling works well.

P. Diane Baldwin, Broken Bow Lions Club
Broken Bow, NE, USA

CHERRY COBBLER

1 (16 oz.) can unsweetened
    cherries
1 c. sugar
1 c. sugar

1 c. flour
2 Tbsp. butter
1 tsp. baking powder
½ c. milk

Combine 1 cup sugar and cherries and let stand. Sift into a mixing bowl the other cup of sugar, flour, and baking powder. Add milk. Melt butter and add to the batter. Grease baking dish. Pour in the batter; add cherries on top of the batter. Bake about 45 minutes at 375°.

Bert Morgan, Broken Bow Lions Club
Broken Bow, NE, Custer County

QUICK CHERRY DESSERT

1½ c. flour
1 tsp. salt
½ tsp. soda
1 c. brown sugar

¾ c. oatmeal
½ c. shortening
2 (No. 2) cans Thank You Brand
  cherry pie filling

I add a drop or two of lemon juice and a little sugar to the pie filling.

Mix together first 6 ingredients. Place ½ of the mixture in bottom of 9x13 inch Pyrex baking dish. Add pie filling. Top with remainder of crumb mixture. Bake at 325° for about 45 minutes.

Alyce Reinking, Princeton Lions Club
Princeton, IL (Bureau County), USA

MINI CHERRY POCKETS

1 (15 oz.) pkg. Pillsbury
  refrigerated pie crusts

Filling:

1 (21 oz.) can Comstock cherry
  pie filling

Heat oven to 450°F. Place pie crust on cutting board and remove plastic sheets. Cut each crust into quarters, making 8 wedges. Top one half of each triangle with 2 tablespoons pie filling. Fold remaining pie crust half over filling. Press edges with fork to seal. Place on cookie sheet. Bake at 450°F. for 11 to 15 minutes or until light golden brown. Makes 8 pockets.

Lion Clinton Brim, Mount Airy Foothills Lions Club
Mount Airy, NC, USA

CHERRY CRANBERRY CUPS

1 pkg. refrigerated pie crusts

Filling:

1 (21 oz.) Comstock cherry pie
  filling

½ c. Ocean Spray craisins
  (sweetened dried cranberries)

Heat oven to 425°F. With 3½ inch round cookie cutter, cut 12 rounds from pie crusts; reserve remaining crust pieces. Fit rounds into ungreased muffin pan cups, pressing in gently.

Combine pie filling and craisins. Spoon 2 tablespoons filling into each cup. Bake at 425°F. for 14 to 18 minutes or until edges are golden brown and filling is bubbly.

Cut small shapes from remaining crust pieces with 1 inch cookie cutters. Place on ungreased cookie sheet. Bake at 425°F. for 4 to 6 minutes or until golden brown. Place shapes on baked pie cups. Makes 12 pie cups.

Lion Marie Hatcher, Mount Airy Foothills Lions Club
Mount Airy, NC, USA

CHERRY-PINEAPPLE DESSERT

1 (21 oz.) can cherry pie filling
  (Thank You)
1 can crushed pineapple, drained

1 can sweetened condensed milk
  (Eagle Brand)
1 (8 oz.) dish Dairy Whip

Put all ingredients into dish at once and mix together. Put in the refrigerator to cool. Put into a nice glass dish to serve. Decorate. Top with maraschino cherries and walnut or pecan half nutmeats.

Makes a beautiful dessert or can be used as a salad.

I use this a lot of times for a potluck. I never have to worry about taking any home. You will get a lot of comments on it.

Jennie Ludwick, Lyons-Muir Lions Club
Muir, MI, USA

RED RASPBERRY FREEZER DESSERT

1 stick oleo
1 c. flour
¼ c. brown sugar
1 c. chopped nuts

2 egg whites
1 c. sugar
1 pkg. red raspberries
2 c. Cool Whip

Combine the oleo, flour, brown sugar, and nuts and spread on cookie sheet. Flatten out with your hands. Bake 10 minutes at 350° or until light brown only. Crush it by running spoon back and forth through it, making crumbs. Put it in 9x13 inch pan. (Reserve a few crumbs for top.) Pat down good.

Blend egg whites, sugar, and red raspberries (thawed, without the juice). Add 2 cups Cool Whip and beat at high speed. Spread over crumbs and freeze overnight.

Lion Ida Rohrer, Moundbuilders Lions Club
Newark, OH, USA

Common sense is genius dressed in its working clothes.
Ralph Waldo Emerson

❦ ❦ ❦

Comedy is simply a funny way of being serious.
Peter Ustinov

❦ ❦ ❦

Few things are more satisfying than seeing
your children have teenagers of their own.
Doug Larson

RASPBERRY CRUNCH

¼ c. brown sugar
½ c. butter or margarine
½ c. chopped pecans
1 c. flour

1 (15 oz.) pkg. raspberries,
    thawed
2 large or 3 small egg whites
¾ c. white sugar
1 pkg. Dream Whip

Preheat oven to 325°F. In a bowl, mix together melted butter, brown sugar, pecans, and flour to make crumbs. Spread on cookie sheet and bake for 15 minutes, stirring once. Remove and crumble fine while still warm; set aside to cool. Using a large bowl, beat egg whites, thawed raspberries, and sugar until stiff and you will get stiff peaks. (Wrap a tea towel around bowl to prevent splashing.) Whip Dream Whip until stiff peaks form and fold into raspberry mix. Spread crumbs into 9x13 inch baking pan and spread whipped mixture over crumbs. *Freeze* for several hours.

When ready to serve, remove from freezer and let sit on counter for a few minutes. Cut into squares. M-M-M-good.

Lion Jean Ukrainec, Lake of the Woods Lions Club
Kenora, Ontario, Canada

FROZEN ORANGE DESSERT

60 round buttery crackers,
    crushed (about 3 c.)
½ c. butter or margarine, melted
¼ c. sugar
1 (14 oz.) can sweetened
    condensed milk

1 (6 oz.) can frozen orange juice
    concentrate, thawed
    (undiluted)
1 (8 oz.) container frozen
    whipped topping, thawed
2 (11 oz.) cans mandarin
    oranges, drained

Combine first 3 ingredients; reserve ¾ cup crumb mixture. Press remaining crumb mixture into 2 ungreased 8 inch square disposable baking pans or baking dishes; set aside.

Combine sweetened condensed milk and orange juice concentrate; fold in whipped topping and oranges. Spoon evenly into prepared pans and sprinkle with reserved crumb mixture. Cover and freeze up to 1 month. Makes 6 servings per pan.

I have brought this dessert to our annual picnic and everyone enjoyed it.

Mary Ruff, Springfield Lioness Club
Springfield, PA, Delaware County

Drive-in banks were established so most of the cars today
could see their real owners.

E. Joseph Cossman

PUNCH BOWL CAKE

1 box yellow (or lemon) cake mix
2 (4 oz.) boxes instant vanilla
    pudding
3 bananas, sliced
2 cans cherry pie filling
2 cans fruit cocktail, drained

2 cans pineapple tidbits, drained
1 c. chopped nuts
2 (6 oz.) containers shredded
    coconut
2 (8 oz.) containers frozen
    whipped topping

Mix and bake cake mix as directed on box, making two layers, and let cool. Prepare instant pudding as directed; refrigerate. Using a 6 quart punch bowl or large glass bowl, place 1 cake layer (intact or broken in pieces) in punch bowl. Add half of each of the following ingredients in this order: Pudding, bananas, cherry pie filling, fruit cocktail, pineapple, nuts, coconut, and whipped topping. Place second cake layer (whole or broken) on top and repeat layering of remaining ingredients; refrigerate.

This makes a big dessert. It can sit for quite a long time - the "soak" improves the quality.

Lion Wilma Ell, Southport Lions Club
Indianapolis, IN, USA

DAD'S WHOOPIE PIES

Mix together the following five *dry* ingredients:

2 c. flour
1 tsp. soda
¼ tsp. salt

⅓ c. cocoa
1 c. sugar

Add the following four *wet* ingredients and beat all together:

1 egg
⅓ c. salad oil

1 tsp. vanilla
¾ c. milk

When thoroughly mixed, drop by tablespoon onto *greased* cookie sheet. Bake in 350° oven for about *12 minutes*. Allow to cool. (These will be the "tops" and "bottoms.") Make as many as the batter will allow (probably 16 to 20).

Beat together the following *four* ingredients for filling:

1 stick margarine
1 c. *confectioners* sugar

3 heaping Tbsp. marshmallow
    fluff
1 tsp. vanilla

Spread the filling between the *cooled* chocolate cookies and enjoy!!!

The secret of this recipe is in the filling. It's great!!!

One "batch" makes 8 to 10 Whoopie Pies. Three "batches" will fit in a standard Kitchen Aid mixer.

Porter Schoff, PID, Portsmouth Lions Club
Portsmouth, NH, USA

QUICK AND EASY DESSERT

2 pkg. chocolate chip cookies
  (about 100 cookies)
3 env. Dream Whip

2 to 3 c. liqueur (Tia Maria,
  Kahlua, or Amaretto)
2 to 3 c. milk

Mix Dream Whip according to directions until stiff peaks form. Set aside. In a 9x13 inch glass dish (at least 2 inches deep), spread bottom with thin layer of Dream Whip. Take cookies and alternately dip each one in milk, then in liqueur. Layer over topping - cookies can overlap. Spread a layer of whipped topping. Continue dipping each cookie and layering between whipped topping until pan is full, ending with whipped topping. If you have cookies left over, crumble and sprinkle over top. Cover with plastic wrap, using toothpicks if necessary, to keep away from topping. Refrigerate for several hours, preferably overnight. Cut in squares and serve.

An alternate topping is roasted slivered almonds. The liqueur is not over-whelming and you can drink any leftover liquids. This is a nice light dessert following any main course. Your adult guests will love it.

Lion Lillian Marchant, Lake of the Woods Lions Club
Kenora, Ontario, Canada

*Too bad that all the people who know how to
run the country are busy driving taxicabs and cutting hair.*
George Burns

*I was thrown out of college for cheating on the metaphysics exam;
I looked into the soul of the boy next to me.*
Woody Allen

When we ask for advice, we are usually looking for an accomplice.
Marquis De La Grange

Respect cannot be learned, purchased, or acquired - it can only be earned.
Bits & Pieces

DESSERT CREPES WITH APRICOT SAUCE

1 c. all-purpose flour
1½ c. milk
2 eggs
½ gal. vanilla ice cream

2 Tbsp. sugar
1 Tbsp. cooking oil
⅛ tsp. salt
Apricot Sauce (see following recipe)

Combine flour, milk, eggs, sugar, oil, and salt in a bowl; beat with a rotary beater until blended. Heat a lightly greased 6 inch skillet. Use a 1 inch wide spatula. Set out a small dish of oil and a basting brush. Spread three feet of wax paper on your counter as a cooling surface.

Heat the pan and oil it with a brush. Remove the pan from the heat and pour in about ¼ cup of batter. Swirl the pan to coat the bottom with batter. Swirl the pan over the heat until the bottom surface of the crepe is brown. Remove the crepe from the pan when the top is dry and place it on the wax paper while it cools. Re-oil the pan and heat the pan to the proper temperature. Test several degrees of heat to find the temperature that makes a crepe that is golden brown on one side. Continue making crepes, one at a time. After they are cool, fill each crepe with vanilla ice cream (3 or 4 tablespoons), then roll the crepe around the ice cream. Place them in a freezer until about 10 minutes before serving. Serve two crepes to a plate and cover with Apricot Sauce. Makes 12 crepes.

A man can do this.

Apricot Sauce for Dessert Crepes:

8 oz. apricots
Corn starch
½ tsp. almond flavoring
3 oz. slivered toasted almonds

¼ c. apricot brandy
12 dessert crepes (see preceding recipe)

Mix a little corn starch (scant tablespoon) in 3 tablespoons water. Add to sauce made by chopping apricots in their liquid. Heat until thick. Add only enough corn starch to make sauce the consistency of maple syrup. Add nuts and flavoring. Pour over crepes. Flambe with ¼ cup apricot brandy. To flambe, heat the brandy slightly and pour over the crepe and sauce immediately before serving. Ignite the brandy with a match and serve after the flames go out. Makes 1½ cups of sauce.

Keep a fire extinguisher handy.

Larry L. Mengel, Elizabethtown Lions Club
Elizabethtown, KY, USA

The way I see it, if you want the rainbow, you gotta put up with the rain.
Dolly Parton

COOKIE SALAD

1 c. buttermilk
1 (5 oz.) pkg. instant vanilla
   pudding
1 (12 oz.) Cool Whip

1 (8 oz.) can crushed pineapple
1 (8 oz.) can mandarin oranges
1 pkg. fudge stripe cookies

Mix buttermilk and pudding together; add Cool Whip and mix well. Drain pineapple and oranges, then add by folding in. If not eating at once, should be refrigerated.

Crush cookies and fold into mixture *just before eating* so they will be crisp.

This has been a favorite no matter where I've taken it.

Lee Kerley

INGERSOLL BLACK TOP COBBLER

2 bananas
6 Oreo cookies, filling removed
1 can fruit (with juice)
1 can fruit pie filling

1 oz. crushed nuts
7 oz. shredded coconut
¼ stick margarine
1 yellow cake mix

To be cooked in a Dutch oven, over a campfire. Pour fruit and pie filling into Dutch oven. Mix. Spread ½ of coconut and all the nuts over the fruit. Cover with dry cake mix. Level, but do not compress. Slice margarine over top in thin slices. Do the same with the banana. Crumble cookies over banana and sprinkle remaining coconut on top. Bake 45 minutes or until done. Bake with 8 briquettes on bottom of oven and 20 or so on top.

The appearance of this cobbler is revolting but taste is excellent. Go by taste, not by looks. Try it, you'll like it! (Scoutmaster with 17 years experience.)
Larry Johnson, Secretary, Princeton Lions Club
Princeton, IL, USA

We experience moments absolutely free from worry.
These brief respites are called panic.
Cullen Hightower

Nothing in fine print is ever good news.
Andy Rooney

The point of living, and of being an optimist,
is to be foolish enough to believe the best is yet to come.
Peter Ustinov

500

WHISKEY CAKE

1 box yellow cake mix (without pudding)
1 box instant vanilla pudding
4 eggs
½ c. oil
1 c. milk
1 shot whiskey (1½ oz.)
1 c. walnuts, chopped

Combine all ingredients. Mix 3 minutes. Pour into a well-greased tube pan. Bake at 350° for 50 to 60 minutes.

Topping:

1 stick butter
1 c. sugar
½ c. whiskey

Melt butter. Add sugar and whisky. Cook until sugar is dissolved and of syrup texture. After removing cake from oven, poke holes (with fork) in the top. (Leave cake in pan while doing this.) Pour some of the syrup mixture over cake. Let cake sit in pan 15 to 20 minutes. Remove cake from pan and brush remaining syrup on sides and top of cake.

This is one of my favorite cakes to take to a potluck or buffet dinner, because it makes so many servings - the cake is so rich, you only need a small slice! Enjoy!

Lioness Cheryl Edelen, Erlanger Lioness Club
Erlanger, KY, USA

DREAM WHIP TORTE

½ c. flour
1 c. chopped nuts
1½ c. graham cracker crumbs
1 stick butter or margarine

Mix and bake 15 minutes in 9x13 inch pan at 350°.

Filling:

1 (8 oz.) pkg. cream cheese
1 c. confectioners sugar

Add sugar slowly to cream cheese. Make 2 packages of Dream Whip (directions on box). Fold this into cream cheese mixture. Pour into cooled shell. Spoon 2 cans of cherry pie filling on top and refrigerate until ready to use (at least two hours before serving).

Elizabeth Kowalski, Canaan Northwest Lions Club
Canaan, CT, USA

Obstacles are things a person sees when he takes his eyes off his goal.
E. Joseph Cossman

GRAHAM CRACKER DESSERT

½ c. milk
2 packets graham crackers
1 pt. whip cream or Cool Whip
1 small can crushed pineapple

Green food coloring
⅔ c. butter, melted
1 c. sugar
1 (16 oz.) pkg. marshmallows

Heat milk; add marshmallows. Melt and let cool. Whip cream. Add coloring and pineapple. Use graham cracker crust for top and bottom. Refrigerate.

For crust, mix 2 packets graham crackers (crushed), ⅔ cup melted butter, and 1 cup sugar.

This is an old-fashioned recipe, from my grandmother 70 years old and is easy (given to me as a new bride) and very good to this day.

P. Diane Baldwin, Broken Bow Lions Club
Broken Bow, NE, USA

COBBLER

1 c. sugar
1 c. flour
1 c. milk
1 tsp. baking powder

1 pt. blueberries or raspberry or
    blackberries
1 stick margarine or butter

Mix sugar, flour, baking powder, and milk in bowl. Set aside. Melt butter in 9x9 inch pan in oven. When butter is melted, pour batter evenly in melted butter, then sprinkle 1 pint berries over top. Bake 25 to 30 minutes in 400° oven.

Best when served warm with ice cream.

Lion Amy Von Scyoc, Graysville-Proctor Lions Club
Glen Easton, WV, USA

CARAMEL DUMPLINGS

Syrup:

2 c. brown sugar
2 c. boiling water

Pinch of salt

Dumplings:

1¼ c. flour
1½ tsp. baking powder
⅓ c. sugar

2 Tbsp. shortening
⅔ c. milk

Combine sauce ingredients in heavy saucepan. Have boiling.

Combine dumpling ingredients. Mix and drop by spoonfuls into boiling syrup; cover and boil slowly 20 minutes, *without removing lid*.

If you're a peeker, use glass lid of Pyrex pie plate.

Bert Morgan, Broken Bow Lions Club
Broken Bow, NE, Custer County

502

COCONUT DESSERT BREAD

12 c. flour
4 c. sugar
4 Tbsp. baking powder
1½ tsp. salt
5 c. coconut

2 c. semi-sweet chocolate morsels
2 c. chopped nuts
4 c. milk
4 eggs, beaten
3 tsp. vanilla extract

Preheat oven to 350°F. In large bowl, combine flour, sugar, baking powder, and salt. Mix thoroughly. Stir in coconut, chocolate morsels, and nuts. Combine milk, eggs, and vanilla. Add to dry ingredients and stir until well blended. Let stand 20 minutes. Spread into 4 well greased loaf pans. Bake at 350° for 1 hour and 5 minutes. Cool. Remove from pans.

Recipe may be halved for smaller amount.

Lydia Lamy, Plymouth Lions Club
Terryville, CT, USA

Nothing lasts forever - not even your troubles.
Arnold H. Glasow

The trouble with jogging is that, by the time you realize
you're not in shape for it, it's too far to walk back.
Franklin P. Jones

Instead of giving a politician the keys to the city,
it might be better to change the locks.
Doug Larson

Before I got married I had six theories about bringing up children;
now I have six children and no theories.
John Wilmot

CHEESECAKE

Crust:

1 c. graham cracker crumbs
2 Tbsp. sugar

2 Tbsp. butter or margarine, melted

Filling:

5 (8 oz.) pkg. cream cheese
1⅓ c. sugar
3 Tbsp. flour
3 large eggs

½ c. sour cream
Juice from 1 lemon
1 tsp. vanilla

Topping:

Fresh fruit or pie filling of your choice

Preheat oven to 325°F. Combine graham cracker crumbs, sugar, and butter. Mix well and press onto the bottom of a 10 inch springform pan.

Beat cream cheese for 2 minutes with an electric mixer on medium speed. Add sugar and mix together. Slowly add flour and mix until combined. On low speed, beat eggs in, one at a time, until just blended. Add sour cream, lemon juice, and vanilla; beat until just blended. Pour into springform pan and bake for 1 hour and 15 minutes. Turn off oven and let it sit with the door closed for 30 minutes.

Take cake out of the oven and run a thin-bladed knife between the cake and the pan. Return to oven and let it sit with the door open slightly for 30 more minutes.

Take cheesecake out of the oven and let it cool on a wire rack, away from drafts, for 2 to 3 hours or until completely cool. Refrigerate at least 6 hours before serving. To serve, cut into wedge-shaped slices and top with fruit or pie filling.

Tips:

Make sure all ingredients are at room temperature.

Scrape sides of bowl and beaters to prevent lumps.

Use a flat paddle attachment on the electric mixer. You will get a creamier texture as it incorporates less air.

Do not overmix; it should be a smooth, creamy batter, not a whipped batter with lots of air.

Center of cake will be softer than the edges, but will firm up as it cools.

For a marble cheesecake: Add 6 ounces semi-sweet chocolate, melted and cooled, to 2½ cups of cheesecake batter. Drop spoonfuls of chocolate batter randomly over white batter (do several layers) and pull a table knife through cake to marble. Do not touch sides or bottom of pan with knife. Bake as above.

Judy Rannow, Arlington (SEA) Lions Club
Arlington, MN, USA

CHEESECAKE

2 (8 oz.) pkg. cream cheese, softened
1 lb. creamed cottage cheese
4 eggs, slightly beaten
3 Tbsp. cornstarch
3 Tbsp. flour
1 Tbsp. lemon juice
2 tsp. vanilla extract
½ c. butter, melted
1 pt. dairy sour cream
Fresh strawberries, blueberries, or pineapple

Preheat oven to 325°. Grease spring form pan. In large bowl, beat at high speed cream cheese with cottage cheese until creamy and well blended. Gradually beat in sugar, then beat in eggs until well blended. At low speed, beat in cornstarch, flour, lemon juice, and vanilla. Add melted butter and sour cream. Beat just until smooth.

Pour into prepared pan. Bake 1 hour and 10 minutes (or until firm around edges). Turn off oven and let cake stay in oven for 2 hours. Remove from oven and let cool completely. Refrigerate until well chilled.

To serve, run spatula around side of cheesecake to loosen. Remove side of spring form pan. Leave bottom of pan in place. Serves 12 to 20.

Janet Colbert, Bullskin Township Lioness Club
Mt. Pleasant, PA

DREAM CHEESE CAKE

¼ c. butter or margarine, melted
1 c. fine graham cracker crumbs (about 16 large crackers)
1 tsp. cream of tartar
6 eggs, separated
Sugar
19 oz. cream cheese
½ tsp. salt
1 pt. dairy sour cream
1 tsp. vanilla extract
3 Tbsp. flour

Have all ingredients at room temperature. Butter generously a 9 inch spring form pan. Mix butter and crumbs well. Reserve ¼ cup of graham crackers. Press the rest of the crumbs to the sides and the bottom. Add cream of tartar to the egg whites and beat until foamy. Gradually add 3 tablespoons of sugar until stiff; set aside.

Beat cheese until soft. Mix 1½ cups of sugar. Add the flour and salt. Gradually beat into the cheese. Add egg yolks, one at a time; beat thoroughly after each. Add sour cream and vanilla; mix well. Fold in egg whites thoroughly and pour mixture into prepared pan. Sprinkle with reserved ¼ cup crumbs. Bake in preheated slow oven (325°F.) for 1¼ hours or until firm. Turn off heat, open door, and leave cake in oven for 10 minutes. Remove from oven and let stand on cake rack away from drafts until cool.

MOM'S CHEESE CAKE

1¼ c. graham cracker crumbs
¼ c. granulated sugar
¼ c. melted butter or margarine
1 lb. cream cheese (2½ - 8 oz. pkg.)
½ c. granulated sugar

3 medium or 2 very large eggs (½ c.)
¾ tsp. vanilla
2 pt. sour cream (16 oz.)
¼ c. granulated sugar
1 tsp. vanilla

Combine cracker crumbs, ¼ cup sugar, and melted margarine and mix vigorously with fork. Grease a spring form pan with shortening, covering bottom and up sides of pan one inch from top. Keep in refrigerator until filling made.

Combine cream cheese, ½ cup sugar, eggs, and ¾ teaspoon vanilla with mixer. Pour into prepared pan of cracker crust. Bake in preheated oven (375°) for 20 minutes. Remove from oven and put on cake rack for about 15 minutes. Raise oven temperature to 475°.

Prepare topping - sour cream, ¼ cup sugar, and 1 teaspoon vanilla. Mix these ingredients until well blended. Working from sides of pan, spoon the topping, spreading gently and evenly. Bake at 475° for 10 minutes. Remove from oven and cool on rack. When completely cool, keeping in pan, store in refrigerator for 6 hours till cold. Using knife or metal spatula, loosen sides. Release clamp and remove cake carefully.

Dottie Sabo, Bellville Lions Club
Bellville, GA, USA

EMIL'S CHEESECAKE

2½ c. firmly packed graham cracker crumbs
¼ c. sugar
½ c. butter or margarine, softened
5 pkg. cream cheese (8 oz.), softened
1¾ c. sugar

3 Tbsp. flour
1 Tbsp. grated lemon peel
¼ tsp. vanilla
5 eggs
2 egg yolks
¼ c. heavy cream
½ c. sour cream

Mix graham cracker crumbs, ¼ cup of sugar, and the butter. Press into bottom and up the sides of a 9 inch springform pan.

Preheat oven to 500°. Using electric mixer, combine cream cheese, 1¾ cups of sugar, the flour, lemon peel, and vanilla. Beat at high speed to blend. Beat in eggs and yolks, 1 at a time. Add heavy cream, beating just until well-combined.

Pour into crust-lined pan. Bake 10 minutes, reduce temperature to 250°, and bake for 1 hour longer. Spread top of hot cake with sour cream. Let cool in pan on wire rack. Refrigerate at least 3 hours or overnight. Serve, removing the side of pan loosening with spatula. Decorate with fresh fruit.

Marilyn Redifer, Whitehall Area Lions Club
Columbus, OH

MARBLED PUMPKIN CHEESECAKE

12 cinnamon graham crackers
(each 5 x 2½ inches)
3 Tbsp. butter or margarine,
softened
1 (16 oz.) can solid pack pumpkin
(not pumpkin pie mix)
1 tsp. ginger (ground)
½ tsp. salt
4 large eggs

1 c. walnuts, chopped
4 (8 oz.) pkg. cream cheese,
softened
1¼ c. sugar
1½ tsp. cinnamon (ground)
1 tsp. nutmeg (ground)
1 tsp. vanilla extract
⅓ tsp. cloves (ground)
1 oz. semi-sweet chocolate,
melted

Early in day or day ahead: In food processor with knife blade attached or in blender at medium speed, blend graham crackers until fine crumbs form. In a 9 x 2½ inch springform pan, with hand, mix graham crackers, walnuts, and margarine or butter. Press mixture onto bottom and up side of pan to within 1 inch from top of pan.

Preheat oven to 350°. In a large bowl, with mixer at medium speed, beat cream cheese until smooth; slowly beat in sugar. With mixer at low speed, beat in pumpkin, cinnamon, nutmeg, ginger, vanilla, salt, cloves, and eggs; beat 3 minutes, occasionally scraping bowl with a rubber spatula. Remove ½ cup pumpkin batter to a small bowl. Stir in melted chocolate until blended. Pour remaining pumpkin batter into pan. Spoon dollops of chocolate mixture onto batter. With knife, cut and twist through mixtures to obtain marbled effect. Bake 1 hour. Turn off oven; let cheesecake remain in oven 1 hour longer. Remove cheesecake from oven; cool in pan on wire rack. Cover and refrigerate cheesecake at least 6 hours or until well chilled. Makes 16 servings.

Mike Hazzard
Littleton, CO

LEMON CHEESECAKE

Chill 1 tin evaporated milk very well. May be put in freezer while following rest recipe.

2½ c. graham wafer crumbs   ¾ c. melted butter

Mix together and press into 9x13 inch pan, then prepare 1 package lemon jello in 1 cup boiling water and 3 tablespoons lemon juice. Stir till dissolved and allow to cool, but not set. Beat together 1 (8 ounce) package cream cheese and 1 cup sugar with electric mixer, then add to cooled jello. Now, whip the chilled evaporated milk till it forms peaks. Stir in the cream cheese and jello mixture and pour over the crumbs in pan. Garnish the top with a few graham crumbs. Refrigerate at least 24 hours before using.

Micheal and Ruth Bartolf, Oxbow and District Lions Club
Oxbow, Saskatchewan, Canada

STRAWBERRY GLAZE CHEESE CAKE

1¼ c. graham wafers, rolled fine
⅓ c. butter, melted
½ c. white sugar
1 lb. pkg. Philadelphia cream
  cheese
¾ c. white sugar
1 tsp. vanilla
3 eggs
1 pkg. frozen strawberries
2 Tbsp. corn starch

Prepare oven to 350°F. Mix together first three ingredients and press into 9x13 inch pan. Soften cream cheese and add sugar, vanilla, and eggs. Beat until smooth. Spread over graham crumb crust and bake for 30 to 35 minutes. Cool.

Heat frozen strawberries and thicken with corn starch (shiny appearance). Cool and spread over cheese cake.

Lion Irene Johnson, Lake of the Woods Lions Club
Kenora, Ontario, Canada

STRAWBERRY CHEESECAKE TRIFLE

2 pt. fresh strawberries, sliced
1 c. sugar, *divided*
2 (8 oz.) pkg. cream cheese,
  softened
3 Tbsp. orange juice
3 c. whipping cream, whipped
1 (10¾ oz.) loaf frozen pound
  cake, thawed and cut into ½
  inch cubes
3 (1 oz.) sq. semi-sweet
  chocolate, grated
Chocolate curls and additional
  strawberries (optional)

In a bowl, toss strawberries with ½ cup sugar; set aside. In a mixing bowl, beat cream cheese, orange juice, and remaining sugar until smooth. Fold in the whipped cream; set aside.

Drain strawberries, reserving juice; set the berries aside. Gently toss cake cubes with reserved juice. Place half of the cake in a 4 quart trifle dish or serving bowl. Top with a third of the cream cheese mixture, half of the strawberries, and half of the grated chocolate. Repeat layers. Top with remaining cream cheese mixture. Garnish with chocolate curls and strawberries if desired. Cover and refrigerate for at least 4 hours. Yield: 14 to 16 servings.

Everyone is in awe of the lion tamer in a cage with half a dozen lions -
everyone but a school bus driver.

CHOCOLATE ALMOND CHEESECAKE

1¼ c. graham cracker crumbs
(18 crackers)
¾ c. very finely chopped
unblanched almonds (3½ oz.)
½ c. melted butter or margarine
2 Tbsp. sugar
4 eggs

1 c. sugar
3 (8 oz.) pkg. cream cheese
2 sq. unsweetened chocolate
2 tsp. vanilla
1 c. dairy sour cream
Glace fruit mix
Toasted slivered almonds

Combine crumbs, chopped almonds, butter, and 2 tablespoons sugar; mix well. Line sides and bottom of 9 inch springform pan with mixture, pressing firmly against pan with back of spoon. Beat eggs well; gradually add 1 cup sugar, beating until mixture is lemon-colored. Add cheese in small amounts, beating until smooth after each addition. Melt chocolate over hot water; blend into beaten mixture along with vanilla.

Pour into crumb-lined pan. Bake in moderate oven (350°) for 35 to 40 minutes or until cake is set in center. Remove from oven and cool thoroughly. Loosen up ring and remove side of pan.

Blend sour cream with 1 tablespoon sugar. Spread over torte, making wreath around the edge and a medallion in the center. Garnish with glace fruit and slivered almonds. Makes 16 servings.

Roxie Bradney, Berthoud Lions Club
Berthoud, CO, USA

ALMOND CHEESECAKE WITH RASPBERRIES

1¼ c. graham cracker crumbs
⅓ c. margarine, melted
¼ c. sugar
1 (16 oz.) can vanilla cake
frosting
1 Tbsp. lemon juice

1 Tbsp. grated lemon peel
3 c. Cool Whip, thawed
Raspberries
Sliced almonds

Stir together crumbs, margarine, and sugar in small bowl; press onto bottom and ½ inch up sides of 9 inch springform pan or pie plate. Chill.

Beat cream cheese, frosting, juice, and peel in large mixing bowl at medium speed with electric mixer until well blended. Fold in whipped topping; pour over crust. Chill until firm. Arrange raspberries and almonds on top of cheesecake.

Lion Ida Rohrer, Moundbuilders Lions Club
Newark, OH, USA

Human beings are the only creatures on earth that
allow their children to come back home.

Bill Cosby

BANANA SPLIT CHEESECAKE

Crust:

2 c. graham cracker crumbs
1/3 c. butter or margarine, melted

1/4 c. sugar

Filling:

3 (8 oz.) pkg. Philadelphia cream
  cheese, softened
3/4 c. sugar

1 tsp. vanilla
3 eggs
1/2 c. mashed bananas

Topping:

1 c. halved strawberries
1 banana, sliced and tossed with
  1 tsp. lemon juice

1 (8 oz.) can pineapple chunks,
  drained

Crust: Mix crumbs, butter, and sugar. Press onto bottom of 13x9 inch baking pan.

Filling: Mix cream cheese, sugar, and vanilla with electric mixer on medium speed until well blended. Add eggs; mix until well blended. Stir in mashed bananas. Pour into crust. Bake at 350°F. for 30 minutes or until center is almost set. Cool. Refrigerate 3 hours or overnight.

Topping: Top with strawberries, sliced banana, and pineapple. Drizzle with melted Baker's semi-sweet baking chocolate and sprinkle with nuts if desired. Cut into squares. Serves 18.

Regina Gish, Mexico Sunrise Lions Club
Mexico, MO

A committee is a group that keeps minutes and loses hours.
Milton Berle

Autumn is a season followed immediately by looking forward to spring.
Doug Larson

The best way to remember your wife's birthday is to forget it once.
E. Joseph Cossman

If you watch a game, it's fun. If you play it, it's recreation.
If you work at it, it's golf.
Bob Hope

PINA COLADA CHEESE CAKE

4 (8 oz.) cream cheese
¾ c. sugar
4 large eggs
1 pt. sour cream
1 (16 oz.) cream of coconut
1 (15 oz.) crushed pineapple,
    drained

2 Tbsp. corn starch
1 tsp. vanilla, 1 tsp. rum extract,
    and 1 tsp. lemon juice (or 2
    oz. rum)

Topping:

¼ c. melted butter
1½ c. flaked coconut

½ c. chopped nuts

Crust:

2 c. graham cracker crumbs

¾ stick melted butter

Use a graham cracker crust in a spring bottom pan. Crust: Press in bottom of pan and 1 inch up side of pan. Chill.

Combine cream cheese. Add sugar. Stir in one egg at a time. Stir in sour cream and the rest of the ingredients. Bake at 350° for 1 hour and 20 minutes. Turn oven off. Sprinkle on the topping mixture. Return cake to oven and leave cake in oven with door closed and heat off for ½ hour. Chill in pan overnight before removing from pan.

Sue Hopkins (Mrs. John), Silver Run-Union Mills Lions Club
Westminster, MD, USA

RICE PUDDING

⅓ c. uncooked rice
¼ tsp. salt
2 Tbsp. butter

4 c. scalded milk
¼ c. sugar

Put all together in a baking dish. Bake at 300° for 1½ hours or until thick, stirring about every 20 minutes. When done, sprinkle with cinnamon.

Make a lot and often - the children and grandchildren love it!
Genny Leiser, Plainfield Lions Club
Nazareth, PA, USA

If at first you succeed, don't take any more stupid chances.

Comedy is tragedy - plus time.

Carol Burnett

Notes

Never let the seeds keep you from enjoying the watermelon.

Cakes, Bars,
Cookies,
Candies

TEMPERATURE TESTS
FOR CANDY MAKING

There are two different methods of determining when candy has been cooked to the proper consistency. One is by using a candy thermometer in order to record degrees, the other is by using the cold water test. The chart below will prove useful in helping to follow candy recipes:

TYPE OF CANDY	DEGREES	COLD WATER
Fondant, Fudge	234 - 238°	Soft Ball
Divinity, Caramels	245 - 248°	Firm Ball
Taffy	265 - 270°	Hard Ball
Butterscotch	275 - 280°	Light Crack
Peanut Brittle	285 - 290°	Hard Crack
Caramelized Sugar	310 - 321°	Caramelized

In using the cold water test, use a fresh cupful of cold water for each test. When testing, remove the candy from the fire and pour about ½ teaspoon of candy into the cold water. Pick the candy up in the fingers and roll into a ball if possible.

In the SOFT BALL TEST the candy will roll into a soft ball which quickly loses its shape when removed from the water.

In the FIRM BALL TEST the candy will roll into a firm, but not hard ball. It will flatten out a few minutes after being removed from the water.

In the HARD BALL TEST the candy will roll into a hard ball which has lost almost all plasticity and will roll around on a plate on removal from the water.

In the LIGHT CRACK TEST the candy will form brittle threads which will soften on removal from the water.

In the HARD CRACK TEST the candy will form brittle threads in the water which will remain brittle after being removed from the water.

In CARAMELIZING the sugar first melts then becomes a golden brown. It will form a hard brittle ball in cold water.

CAKES, BARS, COOKIES, CANDIES
CAKES

SIMPLICITY CAKE

2 c. all-purpose flour
¾ c. Hershey's cocoa
2 eggs
½ tsp. baking powder
½ c. milk

2 c. sugar
½ tsp. salt
2 tsp. baking soda
½ c. salad or vegetable oil
1½ c. brewed black coffee

Mix all together in large mixing bowl. Beat with electric mixer for 5 minutes. Batter will be thin. Bake in tube pan at 350° for 1 hour or when depressed cake springs back up. Enjoy.

Lion Cheryl Gifford, East Anne Arundel Lions Club
Pasadena, MD, USA

MILK CHOCOLATE BUNDT CAKE

1 (7 oz.) milk chocolate candy bar
½ c. chocolate syrup
1 c. butter or margarine, softened
1½ c. sugar
4 eggs
1 tsp. vanilla extract

2¾ c. all-purpose flour
½ tsp. salt
½ tsp. baking soda
1 c. buttermilk
Confectioners sugar (optional)

In a saucepan, heat the candy bar and chocolate syrup over low heat until melted; set aside to cool. In a mixing bowl, cream butter and sugar. Add eggs, one at a time, beating well after each addition. Stir in chocolate mixture and vanilla. Combine flour, salt, and baking soda; add to creamed mixture alternately with buttermilk.

Pour into a greased and floured 10 inch fluted tube pan. Bake at 350° for 65 to 70 minutes or until a toothpick inserted near the center comes out clean. Cool in pan on a wire rack for 15 minutes. Remove from pan and cool completely. Dust with confectioners sugar if desired. Yield: 12 to 14 servings.

Irony is when you buy a suit with two pairs of pants,
and then burn a hole in the coat.

HOT FUDGE CAKE

1 c. all-purpose flour
¾ c. sugar
6 Tbsp. baking cocoa, *divided*
2 tsp. baking powder
¼ tsp. salt
½ c. milk

2 Tbsp. vegetable oil
1 tsp. vanilla extract
1 c. packed brown sugar
1¾ c. hot water
Whipped cream or ice cream
(optional)

In a medium bowl, combine flour, sugar, 2 tablespoons cocoa, baking powder, and salt. Stir in the milk, oil, and vanilla until smooth. Spread in an ungreased 9 inch square baking pan. Combine brown sugar and remaining cocoa; sprinkle over batter. Pour hot water over all; do not stir. Bake at 350° for 35 to 40 minutes. Serve warm. Top with whipped cream or ice cream if desired. Yield: 9 servings.

CHOCOLATE SHEET CAKE

2 c. sugar
2 c. flour
2 sticks oleo
4 Tbsp. cocoa
1 c. water

2 eggs
1 tsp. vanilla
Pinch of salt
½ c. sour milk with 1 tsp. baking soda added

Frosting:

⅓ c. milk
3 Tbsp. cocoa
3½ c. powdered sugar

Pinch of salt
Chopped nuts (optional)

Boil oleo, cocoa, and water (just bring to a good boil). Add flour and sugar. Mix, then add rest of ingredients. Mix and pour into greased sheet cake pan. Bake for 20 to 25 minutes in 350° oven. Note: Cake mixture will be thin.

Frosting: Boil milk and oleo; add cocoa. Bring to a boil to dissolve cocoa. Remove from heat. Stir in powdered sugar and nuts. Spread on warm cake.

Note: Frosting may run off a bit; simply spread back on cake gently. It will cool and stay in place.

A family favorite. Very easy. Freezes well. Travels well.
P. Diane Baldwin, Broken Bow Lions Club
Broken Bow, NE, USA

What I admire in Columbus is not his having discovered a world but his having gone to search for it on the faith of an opinion.
A. Robert Turgot

COOKIE SHEET CAKE

4 Tbsp. cocoa　　　　　　　　1 c. butter
1 c. water

    Bring just to boil.

    Add:

2 c. flour　　　　　　　　　　1 tsp. soda
2 c. sugar

    Mix.

    Add:

½ c. buttermilk　　　　　　　2 eggs
1 tsp. vanilla

    Spread in greased cookie sheet. Bake in 350° oven for about 15 to 20 minutes.

    Frosting:

¾ c. sugar　　　　　　　　　¼ c. butter
¼ c. milk

    Boil for 1 minute, then take off heat.

    Add:

1 c. chocolate chips　　　　　1 c. mini marshmallows

    Stir and spread on cake.

    This goes a long way. It's great for potluck dinners.

Lion Micheal and Ruth (Sauskojus) Bartolf, Oxbow and District Lions Club
Oxbow, Saskatchewan, Canada

TRIPLE FUDGE CAKE

1 pkg. chocolate pudding (not　　½ c. semi-sweet chocolate chips
   instant)　　　　　　　　　　½ c. walnuts, chopped
1 devils food cake mix

    Cook chocolate pudding as directed on package. Blend in dry cake mix. Pour into prepared oblong pan, 15x9x2 inches. Sprinkle with chocolate chips and walnuts. Bake at 350° for 30 to 35 minutes.

    May also be baked in a 9x13 inch pan. I leave walnuts whole so people not eating nuts may pick them off.

Lion Nelson Bonager, East Prospect Lions Club
East Prospect, PA, USA

DEEP CHOCOLATE CAKE

1¾ c. all-purpose flour
½ c. unsweetened cocoa
1½ tsp. baking powder
½ tsp. salt
½ lb. unsalted butter (room
    temperature)

1½ c. sugar
4 eggs
2 tsp. vanilla
½ c. sour cream
1 tsp. confectioners sugar

Heat oven to 350°. Butter a 12 cup Bundt pan. In a medium bowl, combine flour, cocoa, baking powder, and salt. In another bowl, using an electric mixer at medium speed, beat butter and sugar until light and fluffy. Add eggs, one at a time, beating well after each addition. Beat in vanilla. Beat in flour mixture in three parts, alternating with sour cream.

Spoon batter into prepared pan. Bake until a toothpick stuck in the center comes out almost clean and cake springs back when pressed lightly, about 45 minutes. Cool in pan 10 minutes. Unmold and cool completely on wire rack. Sift confectioners sugar over the cake and, if desired, serve with whipped cream. Makes 12 servings.

Per serving: 356 calories, 5 g protein, 20 g fat, 154 mg sodium, 42 g carbohydrate, 117 mg cholesterol.

Lion John J. Hess, Clarence Lions Club
Clarence Center, NY, USA

If you wish to forget anything on the spot,
make a note that this thing is to be remembered.
Edgar Allan Poe

Happiness is having a large, loving, caring, close-knit family in another city.
George Burns

Middle age is when your broad mind and narrow waist begin to change places.
E. Joseph Cossman

Be thankful for problems. If they were less difficult,
someone with less ability might have your job.
Bits & Pieces

RED VELVET CAKE

2 c. shortening
1½ c. sugar
2 eggs
2 oz. red food coloring
2 Tbsp. cocoa
1 tsp. salt

1 c. buttermilk
2½ c. *sifted cake flour*
1 tsp. vanilla
1 Tbsp. cider vinegar
1 tsp. soda

Cream shortening and sugar; add eggs and beat well. Add food coloring and cocoa; mix and add salt and vanilla. Mix well. Add sifted cake flour alternately with buttermilk, mixing well after each addition. Fold in vinegar and baking soda, either by hand or at slowest speed with mixer.

Pour into two 9 inch round layer cake pans which have been greased and floured. Bake at 350° for 30 to 35 minutes. Place pans on rack to cool completely.

While cake is cooling, prepare the following icing: Cook 3 tablespoons flour and 1 cup milk until thick, stirring constantly. Cool *well*. (This mixture must be *completely cool* before adding to the following creamed mixture.)

Cream 1 cup *butter* (must be butter, *not* margarine) and 1 cup sugar. Add above milk and flour mixture (which is completely cool) and 1 teaspoon vanilla. Mix well.

When cake is cool, split each layer (as for a torte) and ice the tops only of each layer (4).

I use powdered buttermilk (follow instructions on can) and sift it in with the cake flour. If you do this, add flour and buttermilk alternately with 1 cup water. Otherwise, follow instructions as given above.

This makes a very pretty red and white cake for Valentine's Day or Christmas (or anytime). I have been making this cake since 1959 when my college roommate made one for my birthday and shared the recipe with me. It is my husband's favorite cake and he gets at least two a year - Valentine's Day and birthday! Enjoy!!

Janet Johnson, Princeton Lions Club
Princeton, IL, USA

"What do you mean we don't communicate? Just yesterday I faxed you a reply to the recorded message you left on my answering machine."
The Wall Street Journal

Motivation is what gets you started. Habit is what keeps you going.
Jim Ryun

CHOCOLATE SHEATH CAKE

Mix in large bowl:

2 c. flour
2 c. sugar

1 tsp. soda

Additional ingredients:

⅓ c. buttermilk
3 eggs

1 tsp. vanilla

Mix together in saucepan:

1 stick oleo
4 Tbsp. cocoa or 3½ Tbsp.
   chocolate syrup

1 c. water
½ c. Crisco

Bring chocolate mixture to boil. Add to dry ingredients, then add buttermilk. In small bowl, mix eggs and vanilla well together. Add to other ingredients and beat well. Pour into long pan, 11x17 inches. Bake at 350° for 25 minutes.

Frosting: Bring to boil 1 stick oleo, ½ cup milk, 3½ tablespoons chocolate syrup or 3 tablespoons dry cocoa, and 1 teaspoon vanilla. Pour over 1 box sifted powdered sugar. Add ½ cup chopped pecans. Beat well. Pour over cake while both cake and frosting are hot.

Frances Blount, Saginaw Lions Club
Saginaw, TX, USA

CHOCOLATE CAKE

Cake:

2 c. all-purpose flour
1 tsp. salt
1 tsp. baking powder
2 tsp. baking soda
¾ c. unsweetened cocoa
2 c. sugar

1 c. vegetable oil
1 c. hot coffee
1 c. milk
2 eggs
1 tsp. vanilla

Frosting:

1 c. milk
5 Tbsp. flour
½ c. softened butter

½ c. shortening
1 c. sugar
1 tsp. vanilla

Sift dry ingredients in a mixing bowl. Add oil, coffee, and milk; mix at medium speed for 2 minutes. Add eggs and vanilla; beat 2 minutes. (Batter will be thin.) Pour in 2 greased and floured 9 x 1½ inch pans. Bake at 325° for 25 to 30 minutes. Cool cake and set aside.

Frosting: Combine milk and flour in saucepan. Cook until thick. Cover and refrigerate. In a mixing bowl, beat butter, shortening, sugar, and vanilla until creamy. Add chilled milk/flour mixture and beat 10 minutes. Frost cooled cake.

Diana Risha, Diana McHugh, Conroe Noon Lions Club
Conroe, TX

CHOCOLATE SOUR CREAM CAKE

1¾ c. unsifted flour
1¾ c. sugar
¾ c. unsweetened cocoa
1½ tsp. baking soda
1 tsp. salt

⅔ c. butter, softened
2 c. sour cream
2 eggs
1 tsp. vanilla

Combine dry ingredients in large bowl of electric mixer. On low speed, blend in remainder of ingredients. Beat 3 minutes on medium speed. Pour batter into greased and floured 9x13 inch pan or 2 (9 inch) round pans. Bake at 350°F. for 40 to 45 minutes. Cool completely. Frost.

Joan Katz, Stafford-Missouri City Lions Club
Stafford, TX, USA

CHOCOLATE MAYONNAISE CAKE

3 c. unsifted all-purpose flour
1½ c. sugar
⅔ c. unsweetened cocoa
2¼ tsp. baking powder

1½ tsp. baking soda
1½ c. Hellmann's real
   mayonnaise
1½ c. water
1½ tsp. vanilla

Grease 2 (9 x 1½ inch) layer pans; line bottoms with waxed paper. Sift together dry ingredients into large bowl. Stir in real mayonnaise. Gradually stir in water and vanilla until smooth and blended. Pour into prepared pans. Bake in 350°F. (moderate) oven about 30 minutes or until cake tests done. Cool completely. Remove from pans. Makes 2 layers.

Elizabeth Maddock, Canaan Northwest Lions Club
Canaan, CT, USA

CHOCOLATE MAYONNAISE CAKE

2 c. flour
1 c. sugar
2 tsp. soda
½ tsp. salt

4 Tbsp. cocoa
1 c. mayonnaise
1 c. cold water
1 tsp. vanilla

Combine in order given. Pour into 9x13 inch pan and bake 30 to 35 minutes at 375°.

Wonderful for someone who is allergic to eggs or milk.

Bert Morgan, Broken Bow Lions Club
Broken Bow, NE, Custer County

Creativity is allowing yourself to make mistakes.
Art is knowing which ones to keep.

Scott Adams

CHOCOLATE MAYONNAISE CAKE

2 c. flour
⅔ c. cocoa
1¼ tsp. baking soda
¼ tsp. baking powder
1⅔ c. sugar

4 eggs
1 tsp. vanilla
1 c. mayonnaise
1⅓ c. water (or coffee - I use coffee)

Mix first four ingredients. Set aside. In large bowl, mix next three ingredients at high speed three minutes or until light and fluffy. At low speed, beat in mayonnaise. Add flour mix, beginning with flour and adding water or coffee, ending with flour mix. Grease and flour two 9 inch cake pans or three 8 inch cake pans. Bake at 350° for 30 to 35 minutes.

I use coffee instead of water for a darker richer cake!

Margaret Kiefer, Plainfield Township Lions Club
Nazareth, PA, USA

CHOCOLATE PEANUT CAKE

1⅔ c. cake flour
1¾ tsp. baking powder
¼ tsp. salt
⅔ c. smooth peanut butter
3 Tbsp. butter (at room temperature)
1¼ c. sugar

½ tsp. vanilla extract
3 eggs
¾ c. milk
½ c. roasted peanuts, chopped
7 oz. milk-chocolate candy bar, chopped

Heat oven to 350°. Butter and flour a 13x9 inch baking pan. Combine flour, baking powder, and salt. With an electric mixer set at low speed, beat peanut butter and butter until smooth. Beat in sugar and vanilla. Beat in eggs, one at a time. Beat in flour mixture, alternating with milk, until just smooth. Stir in half the peanuts. Pour into pan. Bake until a toothpick stuck in the center comes out clean, 25 to 30 minutes. Immediately sprinkle candy bar on the hot cake. Let stand 1 minute. Spread over cake. Sprinkle with remaining peanuts. Cool before cutting. Makes 8 servings.

Per serving: 593 calories, 15 g protein, 31 g fat, 401 mg sodium, 70 g carbohydrate, 99 mg cholesterol.

Mrs. Lucy Aiken, Clarence Lions Club
Clarence Center, NY, USA

Good manners will open doors that the best education cannot.
Clarence Thomas

CHOCOLATE-CHIP CUPCAKES

1 c. flour
½ c. sugar
1¼ tsp. baking powder
¼ tsp. salt
4 Tbsp. unsalted butter (at room temperature)

⅓ c. milk
1 egg
½ tsp. vanilla extract
½ c. + 3 Tbsp. miniature chocolate chips

Heat oven to 350°. Line a 9 inch muffin pan with paper baking cups. In a mixing bowl, combine flour, sugar, baking powder, and salt. Cut the butter into pieces and add to flour mixture. Gradually pour milk into flour mixture and, with an electric mixer set at low speed, beat until ingredients are just moistened. Combine egg and vanilla and gradually beat into batter. Stir in ½ cup chocolate chips. Spoon batter into prepared pan. Sprinkle remaining chips on top of cupcakes. Bake until a toothpick inserted into a cupcake comes out clean, about 25 minutes. Makes 9 cupcakes.

Mrs. Lucy Aiken, Clarence Lions Club
Clarence Center, NY, USA

MARBLE CHIFFON CAKE

⅓ c. baking cocoa
¼ c. boiling water
1½ c. plus 3 Tbsp. sugar, *divided*
½ c. plus 2 Tbsp. vegetable oil, *divided*
2¼ c. all-purpose flour

1 Tbsp. baking powder
1 tsp. salt
7 eggs, *separated*
¾ c. water
½ tsp. cream of tartar
2 tsp. grated orange peel

Orange Glaze:

2 c. confectioners sugar
⅓ c. butter, melted

3 to 4 Tbsp. orange juice
½ tsp. grated orange peel

In a bowl, combine cocoa, boiling water, 3 tablespoons sugar, and 2 tablespoons oil; whisk until smooth. Cool. In a mixing bowl, combine flour, baking powder, salt, and remaining sugar. Whisk egg yolks, water, and remaining oil; add to dry ingredients. Beat until well blended. Beat egg whites and cream of tartar until soft peaks form; fold into batter. Remove 2 cups of batter; stir into cocoa mixture.

To the remaining batter, add orange peel. Alternately spoon the batters into an ungreased 10 inch tube pan. Swirl with a knife. Bake at 325° for 70 to 75 minutes or until top springs back when lightly touched. Invert cake pan on a wire rack; cool.

For the glaze, combine sugar, butter, and enough orange juice to reach desired consistency. Add orange peel; spoon over cake. Yield: 12 to 14 servings.

2075-99

CHOCOLATE ORANGE CAKE

1½ c. flour
½ c. cocoa powder
1 tsp. baking soda
¾ tsp. baking powder
½ tsp. salt
8 Tbsp. unsalted butter (at room temperature)

1 c. granulated sugar
1 Tbsp. grated orange zest
2 eggs
1 tsp. vanilla extract
¾ c. sour cream
1 c. semi-sweet chocolate chips
Confectioners sugar for sprinkling

Heat oven to 350°. Butter and flour a 9 inch square baking pan. Combine flour, cocoa, soda, baking powder, and salt. Beat butter, sugar, and zest until fluffy. Beat in eggs and vanilla. Stir in half the flour mixture, then sour cream, then remaining flour. Stir in chocolate chips. Spread batter in pan. Bake until a toothpick stuck in center comes out clean, 60 to 70 minutes. Cool in pan 10 minutes, remove to rack, and cool completely. Sprinkle with confectioners sugar. Makes 9 slices.

Per slice: 388 calories, 6 g protein, 19 g fat, 55 mg sodium, 55 g carbohydrate, 78 mg cholesterol.

Mrs. Mike Nowicki, Clarence Lions Club
Clarence Center, NY

COFFEE-ORANGE FUDGE CAKE

1 (2 layer size) pkg. devils food or German chocolate cake mix
1 (8 oz.) ctn. dairy sour cream
½ c. cooking oil
½ c. water
4 eggs
1 (4 serving size) pkg. instant chocolate fudge pudding mix

¼ c. coffee liqueur
2 Tbsp. finely shredded orange peel
1 tsp. ground cinnamon
1 (12 oz.) pkg. semi-sweet chocolate pieces
Powdered sugar

Grease and flour a 10 inch fluted tube pan. In large mixer bowl, combine pudding mix, cake mix, sour cream, oil, water, eggs, liqueur, orange peel, and cinnamon. Beat with an electric mixer on low speed until blended, scraping sides of bowl constantly. Beat on medium speed for 4 minutes. Stir in chocolate pieces. Pour into prepared pan. Bake in a 350°F. oven for 50 to 60 minutes or until toothpick inserted near the center comes out clean. Cool on wire rack for 10 minutes.

Although I am unable to eat chocolate, I made this cake with a group of senior citizens. They enjoyed it very much.

Lion Ann K. Brumback, Silver Run Union Mills Lions Club
Westminster, MD, USA

AMARETTO FUDGE BUNDT CAKE

4 eggs
½ c. oil
1¼ c. cold water
18 oz. devils food cake mix

2 tsp. almond extract
2 tsp. vanilla
1 small box instant chocolate
   pudding mix

Beat eggs, oil, water, and flavorings at high speed until blended. Add cake mix and pudding mix; beat 4 minutes at medium speed. Grease Bundt cake pan with shortening. Spread batter and bake at 350° for one hour or until done. Cool in pan 15 minutes. Sprinkle powdered sugar on cake platter. Turn out cake.

Mix and then drizzle over warm cake:

½ c. 80 proof vodka
1 Tbsp. almond extract

½ tsp. vanilla
1 c. powdered sugar

Today should always be our most wonderful day.
Lion Dorothy Maras, Westbrook Lions Club
Windom, MN, USA

HO HO CAKE

Prepare chocolate mix as directed.

First topping:

5 Tbsp. flour

1¼ c. milk

Cook and stir constantly until thick. Let cool.

Cream:

1 c. sugar
1 stick oleo

½ c. Crisco

Mix with cooled mixture. Beat well for 8 minutes. Spread on cake. Refrigerate till set.

Second topping: Melt 1 stick oleo. Let cool.

Beat:

1 egg
1 tsp. vanilla

3 pkg. premelted cocoa
3 Tbsp. oil

Mix with cooled oleo. Mix 2 teaspoons hot water and 1½ cups powdered sugar. Mix with chocolate mixture over cream topping. Keep refrigerated.

For premelted cocoa, substitute 9 tablespoons of cocoa or 3 (1 inch) unsweetened chocolate.
Edith VanHorn, Fairmont East Grafton Road Lions Club
Fairmont, WV

EASY GOURMET ICE CREAM CAKE

Cake:

1 pkg. chocolate fudge cake mix
(or any flavor)
½ gal. dark chocolate or vanilla
ice cream (top quality brand)

10 oz. seedless red raspberry
preserves

Ganache Frosting:

18 oz. semi-sweet chocolate chips
or bittersweet chocolate,
chopped

1½ c. heavy cream
2 Tbsp. butter, cut up
1 tsp. almond or vanilla extract

Prepare cake mix as directed on package. Prepare and fill only one 8 inch round cake pan. Bake as directed. Cool completely. (Use remaining cake batter for cupcakes, etc.)

Line another 8 inch round cake pan with a long sheet of plastic wrap and other sheet crossing over the first. Make certain enough plastic wrap hangs off in all four directions. Fill this pan with softened ice cream, leveling at top. Fold over plastic wrap to cover top of ice cream. Place in freezer to reharden.

Next, make Chocolate Ganache: In a large glass bowl, combine chocolate chips and heavy cream. Heat in microwave oven on HIGH for 2 to 3 minutes, until melted and smooth when stirred. (Be careful not to overheat chocolate. When chips are glossy, stir to test for melted smoothness.) Add butter and almond extract. Cover and refrigerate 1 hour, stirring occasionally, until Ganache holds its shape and can be spread or poured on cake.

Assemble cake: Place completely cooled cake layer on a large plate or platter. Place foil or wax paper strips under edge of cake to catch Ganache excess. Unwrap plastic wrap from ice cream and pull ice cream quickly out of pan, maintaining its shape, and place on top of cake layer.

In a small bowl, stir raspberry preserves to slightly thin; spread over top of ice cream. (This step can also be done in between cake and ice cream layers.) Finally, pour or spread Ganache completely over cake, covering sides. Return to freezer until ready to serve.

To many, chocolate is essential to self-indulgence. This is a great cake for a special birthday or even a sophisticated dinner!

Lion Christina Sikorski, IPP, East Haddam Community Lions Club
East Haddam, CT, USA

Men are like steel. When they lose their temper, they lose their worth.
Chuck Norris

COAL MINERS CAKE

Cake:

1 box devils food cake mix
1 can cherry pie filling (Thank
   You Brand is best for me)

2 eggs
1 tsp. vanilla flavor
¼ c. water

Preheat oven to 350°. Mix all ingredients in a 9x13 inch bake pan and bake for 30 to 35 minutes.

Topping:

1 c. white sugar
¼ c. evaporated milk
1 stick margarine

1 (6 oz.) pkg. chocolate chips
1 c. pecans

Use a saucepan to warm mixture of sugar, margarine, and milk over a low heat, bring it to a boil for 1 minute. Add chips and pecans and pour over cake. While cake is still warm, punch holes into cake. Let cool and serve.

Cornelius A. and Estelle Wahl, Elizabethtown, District 43N Lions Club
Elizabethtown KY, USA

TURTLE CAKE

1 German chocolate cake mix
⅔ c. evaporated milk
¼ c. margarine

1 (14 oz.) pkg. caramels
6 oz. chocolate chips
1 c. nuts

Mix cake according to directions, but add ⅓ cup evaporated milk and ¼ cup margarine in addition to the oil and water the mix calls for. Put half of batter in a 9x13 inch pan and bake 15 minutes at 350°. Melt caramels and ⅓ cup evaporated milk. Pour over warm cake. Sprinkle chocolate chips and nuts over this. Pour remainder of batter over this and bake 15 to 20 minutes or until done.

Cindy Bamburg, Biloxi Lions Club
Biloxi, MS, USA

Dreams that do come true can be as unsettling as those that don't.
Brett Butler

Friendship is certainly the finest balm for the pangs of disappointed love.
Jane Austen

EARTHQUAKE CAKE
(Wonderful! Easy!)

1 small bag or can coconut
1 stick oleo
8 oz. cream cheese (soft)

1 c. chopped pecans
1 box powdered sugar
1 box German chocolate cake
   mix

Spray 9x13 inch pan with Pam. Layer coconut and nuts on bottom. Mix cake according to box instructions; pour over coconut and nuts. Combine in another bowl the cream cheese, sugar, and oleo and drop by spoonfuls into the cake batter. Bake at 350° for 40 minutes.

Looks just like an earthquake - but oh, so good. Can serve ice cream with this.

Barbara Vaughn, Conroe Lioness Club
Montgomery County, Conroe, TX

EARTHQUAKE CAKE

1 c. nuts
1 c. coconut
1 c. chocolate chips
1 pkg. chocolate cake mix

1 pkg. cream cheese
¼ lb. butter
2 c. confectioners sugar

Note: Do not use a glass dish for this recipe. Use an aluminum pan (13x9 inches). Glass will burn cake.

Mix nuts, coconut, and chocolate chips together and place in bottom of greased or sprayed pan. Mix together 1 package chocolate cake mix according to instructions. Pour this over the above mixture.

Blend together until creamy, 1 package cream cheese, ¼ pound butter, and 2 cups confectioners sugar and glob anywhere onto top of cake. Bake at 350° for 50 minutes or until cake is done.

Cynthia Robinson is the daughter of Eleanor Reuter, Landisville Lions Club, Landisville, PA, USA.

Cynthia Robinson
Harrisburg, PA, USA

Some are born great, some achieve greatness,
and some hire public-relations writers.
Daniel J. Boorstin

There is nothing like returning to a place that remains unchanged
to find the ways in which you yourself have altered.
Nelson Mandela

EARTHQUAKE CAKE
(Upside-down German chocolate)

1 small can coconut
1 c. pecans
1 German chocolate cake mix

1 stick oleo
1 box powdered sugar
1 (8 oz.) cream cheese

Spray 9x13 inch pan with Pam. Sprinkle coconut and pecans on bottom of pan. Mix cake mix according to directions. Pour over pecans. Beat oleo, powdered sugar, and cream cheese together. Pour over cake batter. Bake for 45 minutes at 375°. Yum!!

Shirley Ward, Levelland Evening Lions Club
Levelland, TX

YELLOW CAKE

2½ c. cake flour
1⅔ c. sugar
⅔ c. shortening

½ tsp. salt
¾ c. milk

Blend with mixer for 2 minutes. Stir in 3½ teaspoons baking powder.

Add:

½ c. milk
3 eggs

Orange extract
Yellow cake coloring

Blend for 2 minutes. Pour into 2 (9 inch) pans. Bake at 375°.

I like to put a whipped icing on this cake and coconut. Delicious.

Olive Higinbotham, Bentleyville Lioness Club
Bentleyville, PA, USA

WHITE CAKE

½ c. butter
1½ c. sugar
2½ c. sifted cake flour
2½ tsp. baking powder

1 c. milk
1 tsp. vanilla
⅛ tsp. salt
4 egg whites

Cream butter and sugar. Sift flour with baking powder. Add to butter mixture in about 3 parts alternately with milk to which vanilla has been added. Beat batter after each addition until blended. Add salt to egg whites. Whip until stiff, but not dry. Fold lightly into batter. Bake cake in a greased 7 inch tube pan in moderate oven for about 20 to 40 minutes or two 9 inch layer cake pans for about 12 to 25 minutes.

My grandmother also baked this cake for my grandfather on his birthday and their wedding anniversary.

Lion Carol Van Scyoc, Graysville-Proctor Lions Club
Glen Easton, WV, USA

2075-99

POPPY SEED CAKE

1½ c. sugar
½ c. butter
4 egg whites, beaten till stiff
1 tsp. baking powder
2 c. white flour

¼ tsp. salt
1 Tbsp. vanilla
½ c. poppy seeds, soaked in ¾ c.
    milk for at least 2 hours

Sift dry ingredients together and set aside. Cream sugar and butter together. Add dry ingredients alternately with the milk and poppy seeds. Last, fold in stiffly beaten egg whites. Pour into greased tube pan. Bake at 350° for 35 minutes when golden brown. Cool on wire rack.

Serve plain or make a lemon butter drizzle icing using 2 tablespoons butter, 10X sugar, and lemon juice. Melt butter; add powdered sugar and lemon juice to taste. Mix until smooth.

I never had a measurement for the 10X sugar so start with 1 cup.

In honor of Hubert K. Brumback who has had this as his February birthday cake for many years - through college and military service.

Lion Ann K. Brumback, Silver Run Union Mills Lions Club
Westminster, MD

LOWFAT POPPY SEED CAKE

1 pkg. yellow cake mix
1 small pkg. instant lemon
    pudding
3 eggs or equivalent Egg Beaters
¼ c. oil

¼ c. applesauce
1 c. fat free lemon yogurt
½ c. water
⅓ c. poppy seeds

Combine all ingredients. Pour in greased and floured Bundt or tube pan. Bake at 350° for 45 to 50 minutes. Dust with powdered sugar before serving.

Incredible Lions International women don't get hot flashes, we get power surges!

Mrs. Tim (Linda) Lyons, Elburn Lions Club
Batavia, IL, USA

It is better to ask some of the questions than to know all the answers.
James Thurber

POPPY SEED CAKE

Mix:

2/3 c. milk
2 tsp. vinegar

1/4 c. poppy seeds

Let stand 20 minutes.

Mix:

1¾ c. flour
¼ tsp. salt

½ tsp. baking soda
1½ tsp. baking powder

Cream together:

3 eggs (room temperature)
¾ c. white sugar

2/3 c. butter
½ tsp. vanilla

Add poppy seed mixture. Blend, then add flour mixture and mix well.

Mix:

1/3 c. white sugar

1 tsp. cinnamon

Spread ½ batter in Bundt or 9 inch square pan, buttered. Sprinkle with sugar and cinnamon mixture, then spread on rest of batter. Bake at 350°F. for 40 minutes.

Micheal and Ruth Bartolf, Oxbow and District Lions Club
Oxbow, Saskatchewan, Canada

EDNA'S POUND CAKE

3 c. sugar
1½ c. Crisco
6 eggs
1 can evaporated milk

¾ c. self-rising flour
1 Tbsp. vanilla
1 tsp. lemon

Frosting:

1 box (2 c.) confectioners sugar
1 stick margarine

3 oz. cream cheese
Milk

Cream Crisco and sugar. Add eggs, 1 at a time, beating well after each addition. Sift flour and add alternately with milk, beginning and ending with flour. Add extracts and blend well. Pour into a greased and floured tube pan at 275° for one hour. Cool on rack.

Combine all ingredients for frosting. Add only enough milk to make frosting spread easily. Spread over cooled cake.

This is a family recipe and makes a large delicious pound cake. It is a favorite at family dinners.

Martha C. Cox, Travelers Rest Lions Club
Travelers Rest, SC

2075-99

POUND CAKE

3 sticks margarine or butter
1 box confectioners sugar
1 confectioners sugar box cake
    flour (scant full)

6 eggs (add one at a time)
1 tsp. vanilla flavoring
1 tsp. almond flavoring

Margarine needs to be room temperature. Blend until smooth with electric mixer. Add remaining ingredients in order as given. Bake in greased and floured Bundt pan for 1½ hours at 300°.

Margaret Hicks, Shelbyville Lions Club
Shelbyville, TN, USA

BROWN SUGAR POUND CAKE

½ c. shortening
1½ sticks margarine
1 lb. light brown sugar
1 c. white sugar
5 eggs

1 c. milk
3 c. plain flour
1 tsp. baking powder
Pinch of salt
2 tsp. vanilla extract

Cream shortening and margarine. Add the sugars and cream well. Beat in the eggs, one at a time. Mix well, then add sifted dry ingredients alternately with the milk. Stir in the vanilla. Pour into a greased and floured tube pan. Bake at 325° for 1½ hours. Cool on rack 15 minutes.

Martha C. Cox, Travelers Rest Lions Club
Travelers Rest, SC

SOUR CREAM WALNUT POUND CAKE

3 c. flour
½ tsp. soda
2 sticks butter
3 c. sugar

6 eggs, separated
1 c. sour cream
1 tsp. vanilla
1 c. ground walnuts

Sift flour with soda. Cream butter and sugar, then beat in egg yolks. Add flour mixture alternately with sour cream. Add vanilla and ground walnuts. Fold in stiffly beaten egg whites. Bake at 300° for 1 hour and 30 minutes. Remove from pan and cool with top side up.

If you can wait, this cake is best if you wait a day to eat. It gets more moist each day.

Mrs. Donna Hayes, Dover Lions Club
Dover, PA, USA

Values are not trendy items that are casually traded in.
Ellen Goodman

CREAM CHEESE BUTTERSCOTCH PECAN POUND CAKE

1 (8 oz.) cream cheese
1 c. margarine
2½ c. sugar
6 eggs

3 c. flour
1 Tbsp. vanilla
1 (6 oz.) pkg. butterscotch
   morsels
1 c. chopped pecans

Cream the cream cheese, margarine, and sugar. Add eggs, one at a time, and mix well. Add flour slowly and beat. Add vanilla. Fold in butterscotch morsels and pecans. Place in greased tube pan. Bake at 325° for 1½ hours. Do not overbake.

Deryl Fox, Saginaw Lions Club

APPLE CAKE

3 c. flour
3 tsp. baking powder
1 c. Crisco oil
3 tsp. vanilla flavoring
2½ c. sugar
½ tsp. salt
7 Tbsp. orange juice
4 eggs

3 to 4 Granny Smith apples,
   peeled, cored, and sliced thin
   (mix with ¼ cup sugar, pinch
   of ground cloves, 2 tsp.
   cinnamon and sprinkle of
   nutmeg)
2 oz. pkg. pecan pieces

Mix first 8 ingredients in order by hand (no mixer needed). Grease and flour pan well. Pour layer of batter, place layer of apples on that, and sprinkle with layer of pecan pieces. Repeat until pan is full. Bake approximately 1 hour and check. Let bake 10 to 15 minutes longer if needed. Sprinkle with cinnamon sugar while cake is still warm. Cool and serve.

Lion Cheryl Gifford, East Anne Arundel Lions Club
Pasadena, MD, USA

Hard work spotlights the character of people: Some turn up their sleeves, some turn up their noses, and some don't turn up at all.
Sam Ewing

❦ ❦ ❦

When you can't have what you want, it's time to start wanting what you have.
Kathleen A. Sutton

❦ ❦ ❦

Ultimately, the only power to which man should aspire is that which he exercises over himself.
Elie Wiesel

2075-99

APPLE WALNUT CAKE

Medium bowl:

4 c. coarsely chopped apples | 1½ c. sugar

Small bowl:

2 c. flour | 2 tsp. cinnamon
1 tsp. baking powder | 1 tsp. baking soda
½ tsp. salt | ½ c. chopped walnuts (optional)

Largest bowl - wet ingredients:

2 eggs | 1 tsp. vanilla
½ c. oil

Beat wet ingredients with mixer until well blended. Add dry ingredients and apple mixture alternately with mixer. (Chop apples even finer.) Bake 40 to 50 minutes in a Bundt or angel food pan in 350° oven.

Elizabeth Kowalski, Canaan Northwest Lions Club
Canaan, CT, USA

FRESH APPLE WALNUT CAKE

1 c. butter | 1 tsp. cinnamon
2 c. sugar | ¼ tsp. mace
3 eggs | 3 c. chopped apples
3 c. sifted all-purpose flour | 2 c. chopped nuts
1½ tsp. baking soda | 1 tsp. vanilla
½ tsp. salt

Cream butter and sugar until fluffy. Add eggs, one at a time, beating well after each addition. Sift together flour, baking soda, salt, cinnamon, and mace; add gradually. Stir in vanilla, apples, and walnuts. Batter will be stiff. Spoon into a greased and floured 10 inch tube pan. Bake in a 325° oven for 1½ hours. Let cool in pan for 10 minutes. Remove from pan and cool on a wire rack.

Note: During baking, a macaroon type crust forms on the top so it needs no icing.

Dorothy Coon, Hutchinson Breakfast Lions Club
Hutchinson, KS, USA

The pleasure you get from life is equal to the attitude you put into it.

❦ ❦ ❦

Always give people more than they expect to get.

CINNAMON APPLE CAKE

1 pkg. spice or yellow cake mix
1 (21 oz.) can apple or peach pie
   filling

3 Tbsp. sugar
3 eggs
1 tsp. cinnamon

Heat oven to 350°. Blend together cake mix, pie filling, and eggs in large mixing bowl. Beat at medium speed for 2 minutes. Combine sugar and cinnamon. Spread half the batter in greased 13x9 inch pan. Sprinkle with half the sugar-cinnamon. Repeat with remaining batter and cinnamon-sugar. Bake 30 to 35 minutes until wooden pick inserted in center of cake comes out clean.

Luetta Smitley, Bullskin Township Lioness Club
Mt. Pleasant, PA

APPLE CAKE

2 eggs

1 c. oil

Beat until stiff.

Add:

2 c. white sugar
2 c. flour
1 tsp. soda
1 tsp. vanilla
2 tsp. cinnamon
1 tsp. salt

4 c. thinly sliced apples (I soak
   mine in the oil before adding
   others)
1 c. chopped walnuts
1 Tbsp. butter

Mix well. Bake at 350° for 45 to 60 minutes. Ice when cold.

Icing:

8 oz. cream cheese
1 tsp. vanilla

3 Tbsp. butter
1½ c. powdered sugar

Mix well together.

Thelma Richter, Bullskin Township Lioness Club
Mt. Pleasant, PA

Happiness often sneaks in through an open door
you didn't know you left open.

❦ ❦ ❦

Persistence prevails when all else fails.

2075-99

ONE BOWL APPLE CAKE

4 c. diced apples

2 c. sugar

Let stand for 2 hours.

Add the following:

¾ c. oil
¼ c. melted butter
2 whole eggs
½ tsp. vanilla or almond extract

2¼ c. flour
1 tsp. baking soda
½ tsp. salt
1 c. chopped walnuts

Mix well together and pour into an ungreased pan. Bake for one hour at 350°.

Comments: All the ingredients are easy to find at home and if you like apples and the fact you only need one large bowl, it should be a welcome recipe.

Lion Evelyn M. Mongesku, Western Branch Lions Club
Chesapeake, VA, USA

FRESH APPLE CAKE

4 c. chopped apples
1 c. nuts
2 c. flour
2 tsp. baking soda
1½ tsp. cinnamon

1 tsp. salt
1½ c. vegetable shortening
2 c. sugar
2 eggs

Chop apples and nuts; set aside. Sift together flour, soda, cinnamon, and salt. Cream together shortening, sugar, and eggs. Stir in dry ingredients until blended. Stir in apples and nuts until well blended. Bake at 350° for about 40 minutes.

Lion Paul Murphy, Tuscola Lions Club
Tuscola, IL, USA

Secrets are things we give to others to keep for us.

❧ ❧ ❧

No matter what you undertake, you will never do it until you think you can.

❧ ❧ ❧

Confidence comes from experience ... experience comes from know-how.

FRESH APPLE CAKE

2 eggs
2 c. sugar
½ c. Wesson oil
1 tsp. vanilla
2 c. flour

2 tsp. baking soda
2 tsp. cinnamon
¼ tsp. salt
4 c. finely chopped apples
1 c. chopped nuts

Icing:

1½ c. 10X sugar
1 (8 oz.) pkg. cream cheese

3 Tbsp. butter
½ tsp. vanilla

Beat eggs. Continue beating and add sugar, oil, and vanilla. Sift together flour, soda, cinnamon, and salt. Stir in apples and nuts. Bake in greased 13x9x2 inch pan at 350° for 45 minutes. Cool.

Icing: Beat together until smooth.

Betty Swope, Elizabethtown Lions Club
Elizabethtown, KY, USA

FRESH APPLE CAKE

1¼ c. Wesson oil
2 c. sugar
1 tsp. salt
1 tsp. soda
3 c. flour

3 eggs
2 tsp. vanilla
1 c. chopped nuts
3 c. chopped fresh apples
½ can flaked coconut

Mix oil and sugar together. Combine dry ingredients and add to sugar mixture. Add eggs, beating after each addition. Add vanilla, nuts, apples, and coconut. Batter is thick. Pour in greased tube pan. Bake at 350° for 1 hour and 15 minutes.

Top with:

½ c. white sugar
½ c. brown sugar

¼ c. milk
1 stick margarine

Cook 2½ minutes. Pour while hot over cake in pan and let set until cool.

Mrs. John Fairey, Elizabethtown Lions Club
Elizabethtown, KY, USA

Live life with intensity.

❧ ❧ ❧

The greatest power that a person possesses is the power to choose.

APPLE CAKE SQUARES

2½ c. flour
2 tsp. baking powder
2 tsp. cinnamon
3 c. peeled and chopped apples
2 c. sugar

1 c. margarine (soft)
2 eggs
Pinch of salt
1 tsp. baking soda

Beat eggs, sugar, and margarine together. Add flour, baking powder, baking soda, and salt at a low speed of mixer. Fold in apples. Place in greased 9x12 inch pan. Bake at 350° for 1 hour or until toothpick comes out clean. Serve with Cool Whip or ice cream.

Mrs. Don (Marge) Zahn, Elburn Lions Club
Elburn, IL, USA

APPLESAUCE CAKE

½ c. shortening
1 c. sugar
1 egg
2 c. flour
2 tsp. baking soda
¼ tsp. salt

½ tsp. ground cloves
½ tsp. allspice
½ tsp. cinnamon
1½ c. applesauce
1 c. raisins
1 c. chopped nuts

Topping:

¼ tsp. cinnamon
¼ tsp. sugar

¼ c. chopped nuts

Cream shortening and sugar; add egg and beat well. Sift together dry ingredients. Add alternately with applesauce. Stir in raisins and nuts. Spread in greased 9x13 inch pan. Sprinkle on topping. Bake for 35 to 40 minutes at 350°.

APPLESAUCE CAKE

½ c. butter
1 c. sugar
1¾ c. flour
1 c. nuts, chopped
1 c. raisins
2 eggs
¼ tsp. salt

1 tsp. soda
1 tsp. cinnamon
½ tsp. cloves
2 Tbsp. cocoa
1 c. hot applesauce, sweetened
1 c. crushed pineapple

Add soda to hot applesauce and add last to cake batter. Bake for 1 hour at 325°.

I like to make this in an angel food pan and top with candied cherries and pecans.

Lion Ida Rohrer, Moundbuilders Lions Club
Newark, OH, USA

536

GRANDMOTHER BYWATERS' APPLESAUCE CAKE

½ c. margarine or butter
1 c. sugar
1 egg
¼ tsp. salt
1 c. applesauce
1 c. raisins

1¾ c. sifted flour
1 tsp. soda
1 tsp. cinnamon
½ tsp. cloves
1 c. chopped nutmeats

Sift a couple tablespoons flour over nuts and raisins; set aside. Sift dry ingredients together and set aside. Cream butter and sugar together; add egg and blend well. Add applesauce. Spoon in dry sifted ingredients. Mix floured raisins and nuts into mixture; blend well. Pour into large loaf pan or small tube. Be sure to grease pan. Bake 1¼ hours at 325°.

Double recipe if you need a larger cake. Use large tube pan if you double the ingredients.

This is in memory of Isabell Bywaters and in honor of Pastor H. Lee Brumback, II, Pastor of St. Mary's Lutheran Church.

Lion Ann K. Brumback, Silver Run Union Mills Lions Club
Westminster, MD

APPLE BUTTER CUPCAKES

1¾ c. all-purpose flour
1½ tsp. baking powder
1 tsp. baking soda
¼ tsp. salt
1 stick margarine
1 c. sugar

1 egg
1 c. apple butter
1 tsp. vanilla
2 Tbsp. lemon juice
1 (5 oz.) can evaporated milk

Stir dry ingredients. Set aside. Cream margarine and sugar until fluffy. Add egg and beat well. Beat in apple butter and vanilla. Stir lemon juice into milk, then add flour and milk mixtures alternately to apple butter mixture until just combined. Fill greased muffin cups ⅔ full. Bake at 350° for 20 to 25 minutes.

Hazel Bailey, Iron City Lions Club
Iron City, TN, USA

All dreams come true - if we have the courage to pursue them.

❦ ❦ ❦

A mind once stretched by a new idea never regains its original dimensions.

❦ ❦ ❦

Have faith in what you believe and don't give up on the future.

BANANA SHEET CAKE

2 c. sugar
1 c. Crisco
4 eggs
4 ripe bananas

2 c. flour
1 tsp. baking soda
1 tsp. vanilla

Icing:

1 (8 oz.) pkg. cream cheese,
  softened

¼ c. margarine, softened
1 (1 lb.) box powdered sugar

Cream sugar and Crisco. Add remaining ingredients. Pour batter into a greased 11x16 inch jellyroll pan. Bake at 350° for 30 minutes.

To prepare frosting, mix all ingredients together and spread on cooled cake. This will freeze either before or after frosting. This keeps real well and will even be better after freezing.

Can be baked in a larger cake pan.

Leola C. Jurrens, Downtown Bartlesville Lions Club
Bartlesville, OK, USA

BANANA NUT CAKE

2¼ c. cake flour
1⅔ c. sugar
1¼ tsp. baking powder
1¼ tsp. baking soda
1 tsp. salt
⅔ c. shortening

⅔ c. buttermilk
3 eggs
1¼ c. mashed bananas (about 3
  medium)
⅔ c. chopped nuts (optional)

Heat oven to 350°. Grease and flour oblong pan, 13x9 inches or 2 (9 inch) layer pans. Measure all ingredients into large mixing bowl. Blend ½ minute on low speed, scraping sides of bowl constantly. Turn on high speed for 3 minutes. Bake oblong 45 to 50 minutes and layers 35 to 40 minutes. Add nuts before putting in baking pans.

Olive Higinbotham, Bentleyville Lioness Club
Bentleyville, PA, USA

GRANDMA'S BANANA CAKE

1½ c. white sugar
¼ c. shortening
3 eggs
4 Tbsp. sour cream
1 tsp. soda

3 mashed bananas
2 c. flour
1 tsp. vanilla
1 c. chopped nuts
Pinch of salt

In a bowl, put sour cream and soda together and set aside. Mix other ingredients together and then put sour cream in. Pour into a Bundt pan or 2 greased loaf pans. Bake at 350° for 45 to 50 minutes or until done.

Mary Ann Corbett, South-West Lioness Club
So. St. Paul, MN

BANANA NUT CUPCAKES

2¼ c. flour
1½ c. sugar
1 tsp. soda
1 tsp. salt
1 tsp. vanilla

½ c. shortening
2 eggs
⅔ c. buttermilk or sour milk
2 bananas (very ripe), sliced
½ c. nuts, chopped

Combine all the above ingredients in a mixing bowl and beat at medium speed for 2 minutes. Fill paper-lined cupcake pans ⅔ full. Bake at 375° for 20 to 25 minutes or until cake springs back when touched lightly in center. Cool and frost. Makes 24.

Banana Frosting: Combine 3 tablespoons butter, ½ small ripe banana, 1 teaspoon lemon juice, and ½ teaspoon vanilla. Blend in 2 cups powdered sugar. Add milk, if necessary, until of spreading consistency.

Note: To sour milk, combine 1 tablespoon vinegar with ⅔ cup milk.

Can be made either as a cake in 9x13 inch pan or cupcakes. Quick and easy.

Myra Franke, Plato Lions Club
Plato, MN, USA

BANANA CAKE

1 box yellow cake mix
½ c. self-rising flour
1 Tbsp. apple pie spice
½ c. buttermilk
1¾ c. banana, blended

1 box instant vanilla pudding mix
⅔ c. sugar
½ tsp. soda
4 eggs

Sift cake mix, pudding mix, flour, sugar, and spices together. Put soda into buttermilk and add mixture, then add eggs and bananas and mix. Pour into a greased and floured tube pan. Bake until toothpick comes out clean.

Melba Johnson, Brookhaven Alpha Lions Club
Brookhaven, MS

Today's dream is the threshold of tomorrow's discovery.

Most problems don't exist until a government agency is created to solve them.

Kirk Kirkpatrick

DUTCH BANANA CAKE

1½ c. flour
½ c. sugar
2 tsp. baking powder
⅓ tsp. salt

About ½ c. milk
1 egg
4 or 5 bananas
3 Tbsp. butter

Sift the dry ingredients twice and soften the butter. Beat egg light and add part of milk to it, then stir this into prepared flour, adding also the butter. The dough should be too stiff to pour so the milk is added by degrees; with a soft batter, the fruit sinks into it instead of remaining on top. As flour varies somewhat, the amount of milk cannot be exact. After the dough is spread on the greased pan or glass bake dish, the halved bananas are pressed uniformly over the top, then the whole is sprinkled with sugar and baked in a quick oven (about 400° oven) for 15 to 20 minutes or until brown. Serve hot with butter as a tea cake or as a pudding with either hard or liquid sauce or with sugar and cream.

Micheal and Ruth Bartolf, Oxbow and District Lions Club
Oxbow, Saskatchewan, Canada

BANANA SPLIT CAKE

2 c. graham wafer crumbs
½ c. butter, melted
1 c. soft butter
2 c. icing sugar

2 eggs
2 cans crushed pineapple
3 bananas
1 pt. whipping cream

Preheat oven to 375°. Combine the first two ingredients and press into baking pan. Bake for about 8 minutes. Let cool. Combine next three ingredients and whip together for 15 minutes; do not skimp on time. Spread on cooled crust. Drain pineapple and slice bananas and layer on top of butter mixture. Whip cream and spread over entire cake. Decorate top with fresh fruit and nuts. Refrigerate until ready to serve.

Lion Irene Johnson, Lake of the Woods Club
Kenora, Ontario, Canada

LEMON JELLO CAKE

1 pkg. yellow cake mix
1 (3 oz.) pkg. lemon Jell-O
½ c. Wesson oil

3 tsp. lemon extract
¾ c. apricot nectar (can)

Add 4 eggs, 1 at a time. Beat after each.

Glaze:

1 c. powdered sugar

¼ c. lemon juice

Mix together. Pour into greased and floured Bundt pan. I have also baked it in a 9x13 inch pan and does well. Bake at 350° for 50 minutes.

This is my husband's favorite cake.

Shirley Ward, Levelland Evening Lions Club
Levelland, TX, USA

LEMON BUNDT CAKE

3 c. sugar
1 c. oil
5 eggs
3 c. flour

1 c. milk
½ tsp. salt
1 tsp. baking powder
1 tsp. lemon extract

Cream sugar, oil, and eggs. Mix flour, 1 cup at a time. Add milk, salt, baking powder, and lemon extract. Bake in a greased and floured Bundt pan in a 350° oven for 55 to 60 minutes.

GRANDMA'S LEMON CAKE

1 yellow cake mix
4 eggs

1 can lemon pie mix

Beat eggs. Add cake mix and pie filling and mix. Put in 9x13 inch pan. Bake according to directions on package. Glaze with powdered sugar frosting.

Karen Prescher, Avenue of Pines Lions Club
Deer River, MN, USA

BLUEBERRY CAKE

2 eggs, separated
½ c. shortening
1½ c. flour
1 tsp. baking powder
1½ c. blueberries

⅓ c. milk
1 c. sugar
¼ tsp. salt
1 tsp. vanilla

Beat 2 egg whites until stiff. Add about ¼ of the sugar to keep them stiff. Cream shortening. Add salt and vanilla. Add remaining sugar gradually. Add 2 egg yolks and beat until creamy. Sift flour. Measure and mix with baking powder. Add alternately to creamed mixture with ⅓ cup milk. Fold in beaten egg whites mixture. Add an extra 1 tablespoon flour to berries to coat them. Fold in berries. Turn into a well-greased 8x8 inch pan. Sprinkle top of batter with granulated sugar. Bake at 350° for 50 minutes.

Carolyn Hale, Eliot Lions Club
Eliot, ME, USA

BLUEBERRY CAKE

4 eggs
¾ c. cooking oil
2 c. fresh or frozen blueberries

2 c. granulated sugar
3 c. self-rising flour
1 tsp. vanilla

Beat eggs. Slowly add sugar and beat well. Gradually add cooking oil. Add flour, reserving ⅓ cup for berries. Roll berries in ⅓ cup flour and add to mixture. Bake for 1 hour at 300° in a large baking dish.

Delicious with good fresh milk.

Gloria E. Thompson, Bellville Lions Club
Bellville, GA, USA

BLUEBERRY RIPPLE CAKE

1 c. light brown sugar
1 c. flour
1 Tbsp. cinnamon
½ c. butter or margarine

½ c. pecans
1 box white cake mix
1 (12 oz.) pkg. fresh or frozen
   blueberries, thawed

Mix sugar, flour, cinnamon, salt, and butter well with pastry blender. Add pecans and blend thoroughly. Prepare cake mix according to directions. Sprinkle ½ of the sugar mixture over bottom of greased 9x13 inch baking pan. Spread cake batter evenly over sugar mixture. Sprinkle blueberries and remaining sugar mixture over cake batter. Run knife through to swirl for ripple effect. Bake at 350° for 40 minutes.

BEST BLUEBERRY COFFEE CAKE

Cake:

2 c. flour
¾ c. sugar
2 tsp. baking powder
¼ tsp. salt
1 egg, beaten
½ c. milk

½ c. butter, softened (no
   margarine)
1 c. fresh or thawed, drained
   blueberries
1 c. chopped pecans (optional)

Streusel Topping:

½ c. sugar
⅓ c. flour

¼ c. cold butter

Cake: In mixing bowl, mix flour, sugar, baking powder, and salt. Add and beat on low speed the egg, milk, and butter. When smooth, fold in berries and nuts. Spread in greased 9x9 inch pan.

Streusel Topping: In small bowl, mix flour and sugar. Cut in cold butter until crumbly. Sprinkle over cake batter. Bake at 375° for 35 to 40 minutes or until toothpick tests clean.

I didn't like blueberries until I tried this recipe.
Lioness Denice Riley, South-West Lioness Club
So. St. Paul, MN, USA

You know you are middle-aged when your children tell you that you're driving too slowly and your parents tell you that you're driving too fast.
Caren Wlodarski

ORANGE CAKE

1 c. sugar
½ c. butter
2 eggs

1 tsp. soda
1 c. sour cream
2 c. flour

Mix all of the ingredients well. Pour into a well greased tube pan. Bake in 325° oven for 1 hour and 15 minutes. Check with toothpick. While still warm, leave in pan. Pour ½ cup sugar and add orange juice to make 1 cup. Mix sugar and juice well.

This has been my favorite birthday cake.

Mrs. Arnie (Lou Ann) Anderson, Elburn Lions Club
Elburn, IL

ORANGE CAKE

1 box yellow cake mix
1 (3 oz.) box orange gelatin
⅔ c. water
⅔ c. vegetable oil

4 eggs
1½ c. sugar
1 c. orange juice

Mix cake mix and orange gelatin together. Add water and oil. Stir until well mixed. Add one egg at a time; stir after each addition. Pour mixture into greased square pan. Bake for 1 hour at 300°. While cake bakes, dissolve sugar in orange juice. When done, while cake is still hot, punch holes in it with a fork. Dribble orange juice mixture over hot cake.

Cynthia Hall, Huffman Lions Club
Huffman, TX, USA

SUNSHINE CAKE

1 box Duncan Hines orange
    supreme cake mix
½ c. cooking oil

1 can mandarin oranges
4 eggs

Frosting:

1 (8 oz.) ctn. Cool Whip
1 small pkg. instant vanilla
    pudding

1 large can crushed pineapple in
    heavy syrup

Combine cake mix, oil, oranges, and eggs. Beat 2 minutes. Bake in 3 (9 inch) pans at 325° for 20 to 25 minutes. Cool. Mix Cool Whip, pudding, and pineapple well. Spread on cake layers and sides. Keep in refrigerator.

Edra Smith Riggs, Bellville Lions Club
Bellville, GA, USA

2075-99

APRICOT UPSIDE-DOWN CAKE

1 (14 oz.) can apricots
¼ c. butter

½ c. lightly packed brown sugar
8 to 10 walnut halves

Place baking pan on low heat to melt butter. Sprinkle sugar on top of melted butter. Drain apricots, reserving syrup. Arrange fruit in design in pan with skin-side down. Place walnuts between fruit.

Batter:

½ c. flour
½ tsp. baking powder
2 large eggs, separated

2 Tbsp. apricot juice
½ c. sugar

Sift flour and baking powder. In separate bowl, beat yolks with apricot juice until thick. Beat egg whites stiff, but not dry. Sprinkle in sugar, then fold in yolk mixture alternately with dry ingredients. Cover fruit with batter. Bake at 350°F. for 35 to 40 minutes. Cool for 5 minutes, then turn upside down on plate. Serve with whipped cream.

Micheal and Ruth Bartolf, Oxbow and District Lions Club
Oxbow, Saskatchewan, Canada

BLACKBERRIES CAKE

2 eggs
½ c. shortening
1 c. sugar
¾ c. berries
½ c. milk
2 c. flour

1 tsp. soda
1 tsp. baking powder
½ tsp. salt
1 tsp. cinnamon
1 tsp. allspice

Beat eggs and set aside. Cream shortening and sugar together; add eggs and cream again. Sift flour, soda, baking powder, salt, cinnamon, and allspice together. Alternately add milk and flour mixture, then mix in blackberries till blended. Add mixture in tube pan or 2 (9 inch) cake pans and bake for 30 to 35 minutes in 375° preheated oven.

Lion Anna Van Scyoc, Graysville-Proctor Lions Club
Glen Easton, WV, USA

Tennis scores go from 1 to 15 to 30 to 40. Sometimes aging seems the same.

❧ ❧ ❧

We grow neither better nor worse as we get older, but more like ourselves.

PFLAUMENPLATTENKUCHEN - PLUM CAKE

½ c. sugar
¼ lb. butter
2 eggs
1 Tbsp. vanilla
4 to 5 c. flour

1 Tbsp. baking powder
Milk
Fresh plums (small blue ones)
Cinnamon and sugar

Preheat oven to 375°F. In a bowl, cream together the butter and sugar; beat in the eggs and add vanilla. Sift together the flour and baking powder; add slowly to creamed mixture, alternating with milk. Add only enough milk to ensure flour is well mixed in. Should be of similar consistency as well blended muffin batter.

Pour mixture onto a greased cookie sheet with at least one inch sides. Wash and dry plums; cut in halves and place on cake layer, cut side up. Plums should cover entire surface of cake. Bake for 40 minutes. Sprinkle with a mixture of cinnamon and sugar. (Combine about ½ the cinnamon to ¼ sugar. It is easiest to put into a shaker bottle and sprinkle all over fruit.) Yummy! Yummy!

Before moving to Canada and Kenora, I lived in Hamburg, Germany with my family. This recipe has been in my family for at least four generations that I know of. My children now enjoy making it and no generation seemed to worry about accurate measurements - you just know when the cake is right for the oven.

Lion Heide Riemann, Lake of the Woods Lions Club
Kenora, Ontario, Canada

Judge your success by the degree that you're enjoying peace, health, and love.

Be bold and courageous. When you look back on your life, you'll regret the things you didn't do more than the ones you did.

Laugh a lot. A good sense of humor cures almost all of life's ills.

PRUNE CAKE

3 eggs
1 c. Wesson oil
1½ c. sugar
2 c. flour
1 c. buttermilk
1 c. cooked prunes

1 c. chopped nuts
1 tsp. baking soda
1 tsp. cinnamon
1 tsp. nutmeg
1 tsp. allspice

Topping (to pour over hot cake):

½ c. buttermilk
1 c. sugar
½ tsp. baking soda

½ stick margarine
1 tsp. vanilla

Blend sugar and oil. Add eggs and beat. Add milk and dry ingredients alternately. Add nuts and prunes. Bake in greased 9x13 inch pan in oven for approximately 1 hour. If glass pan is used, less cooking time will be required. Test cake at 50 minutes.

Topping: Place in medium saucepan the milk, sugar, soda, and margarine. Stir. Let come to a boil on medium heat; boil 1 to 2 minutes. Remove from heat. Stir in vanilla. Pour over warm cake while icing is hot. Icing will absorb more quickly if toothpick holes are punched in cake.

A nice moist cake. Will keep several days in refrigerator.

Leola C. Jurrens, Downtown Bartlesville Lions Club
Bartlesville, OK, USA

EASY CHERRY CAKE

1 box white cake mix
1 pkg. Dream Whip
1 (8 oz.) pkg. Philadelphia cream
   cheese

½ c. powdered sugar
1 can cherry pie filling

Bake cake as directed on package in 9x13 inch pan. Prepare Dream Whip as directed. (I use Cool Whip.) Cream softened cream cheese and powdered sugar until fluffy; fold in Dream Whip. Spread over cooled cake and top with pie filling.

Helen Leggett, Sherrodsville Lions Club
Sherrodsville, OH, USA

Become the most positive and enthusiastic person you know.

PEACH UPSIDE-DOWN CAKE

¼ c. butter or margarine
¼ c. packed brown sugar
4 peaches, peeled and sliced
2 Tbsp. sliced almonds, toasted
1½ c. baking mix
1 egg

½ c. packed brown sugar
½ c. half & half or milk
2 Tbsp. vegetable oil
1 tsp. almond extract
½ tsp. vanilla extract
½ tsp. cinnamon

Heat oven to 350°F. Melt butter or margarine in 9 x 1½ inch round pan or an 8 x 8 x 2 inch square pan in oven. Sprinkle ¼ cup brown sugar evenly over melted butter. Arrange peach slices in single layer on sugar mixture; sprinkle with almonds. Beat remaining ingredients in medium bowl with electric mixer on low speed 30 seconds, scraping bowl constantly. Beat on medium speed 4 minutes, scraping bowl occasionally. Pour batter over peach slices. Bake 35 to 40 minutes or until toothpick inserted in center comes out clean. Immediately invert pan onto heatproof serving plate; leave pan over cake a few minutes. Remove pan. Let cake stand at least 10 minutes before serving with ice cream or whipped cream.

Lion Joan Shores, St. Charles Lions Club
St. Charles, MO, USA

ORANGE PINEAPPLE CAKE

20 oz. can crushed pineapple,
   drained (save juice)
¾ c. pineapple juice
4 eggs

1 (3 oz.) pkg. orange Jell-O
1 yellow cake mix
¾ c. salad oil

Mix all ingredients, except crushed pineapple, about 2 minutes with mixer. Add ¾ cup salad oil. Beat at medium speed about 2 minutes. Fold in crushed pineapple. Bake at 350° for 50 minutes in greased 9x13 inch pan.

Combine 2 cups confectioners sugar and ¼ cup orange juice for glaze. After removing cake from oven, pierce cake all over with fork. Pour on glaze. Holes will allow glaze to seep through cake.

Lion Nelson Bonager, East Prospect Lions Club
East Prospect, PA, USA

Without the human community, one single human being cannot survive.

❧ ❧ ❧

Whatever we do for someone else we do because it fulfills a need we have.

EASY PINEAPPLE CAKE

1 box Duncan Hines yellow cake
   mix
1 (20 oz.) can crushed pineapple

1 can Eagle Brand milk
1 ctn. Cool Whip or other
   whipped topping

Mix cake and bake according to directions on package. After cake is finished baking and while hot, poke holes over top of cake and pour Eagle Brand milk on top, then spoon crushed pineapple on top of cake (not to use a lot of the juice). Before serving, spread on whipped topping. Cake will need to be refrigerated because of whipped topping.

This cake is so easy to make and my family and friends love it.

Linda Cantrell, Conroe Lioness Club
Conroe, TX, USA

MOIST PINEAPPLE CAKE

Cake:

2 c. flour
2 tsp. soda
½ tsp. salt
1½ c. sugar

2 eggs
1 tsp. vanilla
1 (No. 2) can crushed pineapple

Icing:

1 c. sugar
1 stick margarine
1 small can evaporated milk

1 c. coconut
1 c. chopped pecans

Sift together flour, soda, and salt. Add all other ingredients and mix well. Bake in greased and floured 9x13 inch pan for 30 minutes at 350°.

For icing: In small pan, mix sugar, margarine, and milk. Cook until margarine melts, then cook 2 minutes longer. Remove from fire and add coconut and pecans. Pour over cake while icing and cake are hot.

Very simple to make and delicious.

Mildred Court, Stafford-Missouri City Lions Club
Stafford, TX, USA

Be the change you want to see in the world.

Ghandi

Don't allow self-pity. The moment this emotion strikes,
do something nice for someone else less fortunate.

CAKE THAT WON'T LAST

3 c. all-purpose flour
2 c. sugar
1⅓ c. vegetable oil
1 tsp. baking soda
1½ tsp. vanilla extract
½ c. nuts (I use chopped toasted pecans)

1 tsp. ground cinnamon
1 tsp. salt
1 (8 oz.) can crushed pineapple (don't drain)
3 eggs
2 c. diced bananas

Preheat oven to 350°. Mix. Add all ingredients together and pour into a greased and floured Bundt pan. Bake for 1 hour and 20 minutes or until cake tester comes out clean.

Tester Reilly says "the cake was a nice texture and lovely flavors. I'd make it again. I used chopped toasted pecans as my nuts and vegetable oil for the unspecified oil and they worked beautifully together. I cooked it exactly 70 minutes before the tester came out clean, so I think 80 minutes might be a bit long. Don't overmix - the batter or the cake will be tough."

Lioness Diane DeVincent, East Anne Arundel Lioness Club
Pasadena, MD, USA

RITZ CRACKER CAKE

60 Ritz crackers, crushed fine
6 egg whites
2 c. sugar
1 c. chopped pecans

2 pkg. Dream Whip
8 oz. cream cheese
1 can crushed pineapple, drained
1 can fruit cocktail, drained

Beat the egg whites. Slowly add the sugar while beating. Fold in the crackers with the egg whites. Add the pecans. Pour into a greased 9x13 inch pan. Bake at 350° for 20 minutes. Beat the packages of Dream Whip according to the directions. Add the cream cheese. Beat again. Combine the drained fruit with the whipped topping and cream cheese. Spread this over cooled cake. Keep cold.

Lion June Taylor, Foley Lions Club
Foley, AL, USA

Don't expect life's very best if you're not giving it your very best.

The older the violin the sweeter the tune.

SNOWBALL CAKE

2 env. plain no-Nox gelatine
1 Tbsp. lemon juice
1 c. sugar
1 large (No. 2) can crushed
    pineapple, drained

1 small Cool Whip
1 large angel food cake
1 bag flake coconut

Dissolve gelatine in 1 cup boiling water; stir well. Add lemon juice, sugar, and pineapple. Mix well. Chill in refrigerator for 1 hour or until partly set. Stir in ½ Cool Whip. Break angel food cake up in little pieces in a 9x13 inch pan. Pour mixture over. Stir till well mixed. Top with remaining Cool Whip. Sprinkle on coconut.

You can use this with low fat Cool Whip.

Lion Connie Cunningham, Graysville-Proctor Lions Club
Glen Gaston, WV, USA

HUMMINGBIRD CAKE

¾ c. flour
¾ c. sugar
1 tsp. baking powder
1 tsp. cinnamon
1 tsp. vanilla
½ tsp. soda

2 eggs
½ c. cooking oil
1 banana, chopped
½ c. pecans, chopped
½ c. crushed canned pineapple
    with juice

Place all ingredients in mixing bowl. Blend at low speed, then at medium speed 2 minutes. Spread batter in a 9 inch round dish. Microwave on 50% power for 6 minutes and HIGH 2 to 6 minutes until done. Cover with wax paper and let stand directly on countertop 5 to 10 minutes. Cool and frost with cream cheese frosting. Makes one 9 inch cake.

Hummingbird Bundt Cake: Double recipe and bake in a prepared 12 cup ring cake dish (greased and dusted with graham cracker crumbs) 12 minutes on 50% power and 1 to 8 minutes on HIGH. Frost with cream cheese frosting.

Clear glass baking dish enables you to check the bottom for uncooked batter.

Agnes Williams, Alpha Lions Club
Brookhaven, MS, USA

Learn to listen. Opportunity sometimes knocks very softly.

HAWAIIAN CAKE

1 box yellow cake mix
1 (8 oz.) cream cheese (room
   temperature)
1 (8 oz.) pkg. Cool Whip
1 can crushed pineapple

½ c. chopped maraschino
   cherries
½ c. chopped nuts
½ c. coconut
1 pkg. instant vanilla pudding

Prepare cake mix according to package directions. Put in a greased cookie sheet that has edges or 9x13 inch cake pan. Bake 15 minutes or until done. Mix pudding with 1 cup cold milk. Beat cream cheese into pudding mix, then fold in Cool Whip. Spread this pudding onto cooled cake. Drain pineapple. Spread on top of pudding mix. Sprinkle with chopped cherries, nuts, and coconut. Keep in the refrigerator until time to serve.

Peg Cser, Canaan Northwest Lions Club
Canaan, CT

HAWAIIAN ALOHA CAKE

1 pkg. yellow cake mix
1 (8 oz.) pkg. cream cheese
1 c. milk
1 pkg. instant vanilla pudding

1 (14 or 16 oz.) crushed
   pineapple
1 large Cool Whip
Chopped nuts
Coconut and cherry halves

Preheat oven to 350°F. Prepare cake mix according to package directions. Bake on large cookie sheet. Cream the cheese, milk, and instant pudding powder and beat well. Spread over baked cake. Drain pineapple very well. Add to Cool Whip and spread over cream cheese mixture. Garnish with finely chopped nuts, coconut, and cherry halves. Refrigerate until ready to serve.

Lion Helen Oneschuk, Lake of the Woods Lions Club
Kenora, Ontario, Canada

Evaluate yourself by your own standards, not someone elses.

❧ ❧ ❧

I've learned that an insatiable curiosity is important to never feeling old.

❧ ❧ ❧

It's not how old we are, but how we are old.

EASY PINA COLADA CAKE

1 (18½ oz.) pkg. white cake mix
3¾ oz. pkg. *instant* vanilla
   pudding and pie filling mix
1 (15 oz.) can Coco Lopez cream
   of cocoanut, divided
½ c. rum, divided
⅓ c. vegetable oil

4 large eggs
1 (8 oz.) can crushed pineapple,
   well drained
Whipped cream, pineapple
   chunks, and toasted cocoanut
   for garnish

If pudding is in your white cake mix, omit the separate package.

Preheat oven to 350°. In large mixing bowl, combine the cake mix, pudding mix, ½ cup Coco Lopez, ¼ cup rum, oil, and eggs. Using the electric mixer, beat on medium speed for 2 minutes. Stir in drained pineapple. Pour into a well greased and floured 10 inch tube pan. Bake 45 to 50 minutes. Remove from oven and cool slightly, about 20 to 25 minutes. Remove from pan; with a steak knife or skewer, poke holes in the cake about 1 inch apart almost to bottom. Combine remaining Coco Lopez and the balance of ¼ cup rum and pour into holes.

To make your icing, beat up 2 packages of whipping cream with sugar. Completely cover cake and garnish with pineapple chunks or cocoanut.

For you cocoanut lovers, you'll think you've died and gone to heaven!
JoAnn Jones, Mathews Lions Club
North, VA

DUMP CAKE

1 lb. can crushed pineapple
1 lb. can cherry pie filling (or any
   flavor)
1 box yellow or white cake mix
   (dry)

½ to 1 c. chopped nuts
1½ sticks butter, cut in squares

Grease 13x9x2 inch pan. Put pineapple in bottom of pan; add pie filling. Sprinkle cake mix over this and top with nuts and butter squares. Bake at 350° for 35 to 40 minutes. Let cool and serve out of pan.

A dollop of whipped cream may be added if desired.
Lioness Jo Millner, East Anne Arundel Lioness Club
Pasadena, MD, USA

As soon as you feel too old to do something, do it.

WATERGATE CAKE

2 pkg. pistachio pudding mix
1 box white cake mix
1 c. vegetable oil
1 (8 oz.) container frozen
    whipped topping

1 c. ginger ale
3 eggs
1 c. chopped walnuts
1¼ c. milk

Preheat oven to 350°. Mix together 1 package pistachio pudding mix, white cake mix, vegetable oil, ½ cup walnuts, ginger ale, and eggs. Pour into greased 13x9x2 inch rectangular pan. Bake 30 to 40 minutes. Cool before frosting.

Frosting: Mix together whipped topping, 1 package pistachio pudding mix, and milk. Sprinkle rest of walnuts on top of cake. (Use either ½ cup chopped nuts or walnut halves to put on top of cake.)

Lioness Catherine Violette, East Anne Arundel Lioness Club
Annapolis, MD, USA

RHUBARB CAKE

2 c. flour
1½ c. sugar
½ c. shortening
1 c. buttermilk or sour milk
1 tsp. baking soda

1 tsp. vanilla
1 egg
2 c. rhubarb (fold into batter after
    ingredients are mixed)

Cover top with ½ cup sugar with 1 teaspoon cinnamon, mixed. Bake in 10x13 inch pan at 350° for 35 minutes.

This was my grandmother's and my mother's recipe. It is very good. I enjoy baking and cooking, trying new recipes.

Betty J. Kaniper, Plainfield Township Lions Club
Stockertown, PA, USA

RHUBARB CAKE

½ c. butter
1½ c. brown sugar
1 egg
1 c. buttermilk or sour milk

2 c. flour
1¼ tsp. baking soda
2 c. raw rhubarb
1 tsp. vanilla

Topping:

2 Tbsp. flour
2 Tbsp. butter

½ c. brown sugar

Cream together butter and brown sugar. Add egg. Mix remaining ingredients and put in a well greased 9x13 inch pan. Pour topping over batter. Bake in 350° oven for 35 minutes. Serve with real whipped cream.

Lion Micheal and Ruth (Sauskojus) Bartolf,
Oxbow and District Lions Club
Oxbow, Saskatchewan, Canada

RHUBARB CAKE

1 tsp. baking soda
1 c. milk
½ c. margarine
1½ c. sugar
½ tsp. salt

1 egg
1 tsp. vanilla
2 c. flour
3 c. rhubarb

Topping:

½ c. sugar

1 tsp. cinnamon

Put soda in milk. Mix shortening, sugar, salt, egg, and vanilla. Add flour. Add soda and milk mixture. Stir well. Slowly add rhubarb. Pour into 9x12 inch pan.

Mix topping and sprinkle on cake evenly. Bake at 350° for 45 minutes.

RHUBARB MERINGUE CAKE

Crust:

1¾ c. flour
3 Tbsp. sugar
1 tsp. baking powder
½ c. + 2 Tbsp. margarine

2 egg yolks, beaten
2 Tbsp. milk
½ c. chopped nuts

Filling:

8 c. sliced rhubarb
3 egg yolks

1⅔ c. sugar
4 Tbsp. flour

Meringue:

5 egg whites
¼ tsp. cream of tartar

10 Tbsp. sugar

Crust: Mix the first 6 ingredients well. Add the chopped nuts. Press onto the sides and bottom of a well greased 9x13 inch pan.

Filling: Mix all filling ingredients well and pour into the crust lined pan. Bake at 350° for 45 minutes.

Meringue: Combine egg whites and cream of tartar. Beat until peaks are formed when beater is lifted. Add sugar and continue beating until stiff peaks are formed. Put meringue on baked cake, then bake again for about 18 minutes or until light brown.

"Older" is when you feel your oats less, and your corns more.

ZUCCHINI CAKE

2½ c. all-purpose flour
2 c. sugar
1½ tsp. ground cinnamon
1 tsp. salt
½ tsp. baking powder

½ tsp. baking soda
1 c. vegetable oil
4 eggs
2 c. shredded zucchini
½ c. chopped walnuts (optional)

Frosting:

1 (3 oz.) pkg. cream cheese,
  softened
¼ c. butter or margarine,
  softened
1 Tbsp. milk

1 tsp. vanilla extract
2 c. confectioners sugar
Additional chopped walnuts
  (optional)

In a mixing bowl, combine flour, sugar, cinnamon, salt, baking powder, and baking soda. Combine oil and eggs; add to dry ingredients and mix well. Add zucchini; stir until thoroughly combined. Fold in walnuts if desired.

Pour into a greased 13x9x2 inch baking pan. Bake at 350° for 35 to 40 minutes or until a toothpick inserted near the center comes out clean. Cool.

For frosting, in a small mixing bowl, beat cream cheese, butter, milk, and vanilla until smooth. Add confectioners sugar and mix well. Frost cake. Sprinkle with nuts if desired. Store in the refrigerator. Yield: 20 to 24 servings.

DARK FRUIT CAKE

1½ c. dark molasses
1½ c. dark sugar
½ lb. lard*
1 pkg. dark raisins
1 pkg. currants
1 pkg. orange peel, ground
1 pkg. lemon peel, ground
1 pkg. citron, ground
1 lb. English walnuts, ground

1 lb. pecans, ground
4 eggs
1 c. buttermilk
1 tsp. baking soda
2 tsp. cloves, cinnamon, and
  allspice
½ c. currant jelly
Sufficient flour to hold together

Grind nuts and peels while warming molasses and mix all ingredients. Add soda to buttermilk before adding. Stir well and add flour to make stiff dough. Place in greased pans and cook at 275° for 3 or 4 hours. Test with a toothpick. Good luck.

* This is for savory. You can use any type of solid fat.

This is a French recipe from my great-uncle, Harry Thevenot.

**Vic Dreyer, Sr., Keiser Lions Club
Salem, OR**

EASY FRUITCAKE

2½ c. flour
1 tsp. baking soda
2 eggs
28 oz. jar mincemeat

15 oz. can condensed milk
1 lb. mixed candied fruit
1 c. coarsely chopped walnuts
½ lb. candied cherries

Mix eggs, mincemeat, condensed milk, fruit, and nuts together. Fold in the sifted dry ingredients. Makes 2 small loaf pans and 2 dozen mini muffins, which baked at 300° for 1 hour. Or, it can be baked in 2 large loaf pans at 300° for 1½ hours or until done.

A member of my ceramic class gave us this recipe after she had brought in a cake for us as a snack. We all loved it. It's different than the average fruitcake.

Lion Virginia Bayer, Franklin Park Lions Club
Park Ridge, IL

FRUIT CAKE BONBONS

1 c. flour
1 tsp. baking powder
½ tsp. salt
½ tsp. allspice
1 tsp. cinnamon
3 c. chopped pecans
3 c. chopped walnuts
1 c. candied pineapple

1 c. chopped citron
1 c. golden raisins
¾ c. margarine
¼ c. packed light brown sugar
⅓ c. light corn syrup
4 large eggs
⅓ c. brandy or apple juice

In a small bowl, stir together flour, baking powder, salt, allspice, and cinnamon. In large bowl, stir together pecans, walnuts, pineapple, citron, and raisins, all chopped the size of peas. In mixer bowl, cream sugar, corn syrup, and margarine until smooth. Beat eggs in one at a time, blending after each. Stir in flour mixture alternately with brandy or apple juice in 3 additions. Pour batter over fruit mixture until coated. Spoon 1 tablespoon mix into 1¾ x 1 inch paper cups. Bake in oven at 300° for 30 minutes. Cool completely.

May be frozen in one layer shallow dish in freezer. Thaw at room temperature.

Lydia Lamy, Plymouth Lions Club
Terryville, CT, USA

If you do not climb the mountain, you will not see the plain.
Chinese Proverb

❧ ❧ ❧

Life is like a scooter car; not much happens unless you do some peddling.

PUMPKIN PIE CAKE

¾ c. granulated sugar
½ tsp. salt
1 tsp. cinnamon
½ tsp. ground ginger
¼ tsp. ground cloves
2 eggs
1¾ c. (15 oz. can) solid packed
   pumpkin

1½ c. evaporated milk
1 box yellow cake mix
1 c. coconut
1 c. chopped nuts
1 c. butter or margarine, melted

Preheat oven to 350°F. Combine sugar, salt, cinnamon, ginger, and cloves in small bowl. Beat eggs lightly in large bowl. Stir in pumpkin and sugar-spice mixture. Gradually stir in evaporated milk. Pour in a 9x13 inch greased baking dish. Take one box yellow cake mix and sprinkle over pie filling, then sprinkle with coconut and chopped nuts. Pour melted butter or margarine over cake. Bake for 55 to 60 minutes.

Lion Joan Shores, St. Charles Lions Club
St. Charles, MO, USA

PUMPKIN ROLL

1 c. white flour
1 c. granulated sugar
1 tsp. baking soda
1 tsp. ground cinnamon

1 tsp. vanilla
3 eggs
⅔ c. canned pumpkin
Sprinkle of nutmeg

Filling:

1 (8 oz.) cream cheese
4 Tbsp. melted butter

1 tsp. vanilla
1 c. confectioners (10X) sugar

Mix above ingredients in medium bowl. Pour mixture onto greased cookie sheet with sides. Bake in preheated oven at 350° for 15 to 20 minutes (until sides of cake pull away from pan). Cool cake in cookie sheet 5 minutes. Sprinkle 1½ tablespoons 10X sugar on one side. Flip cake onto waxed paper and sprinkle other side with 1½ tablespoons 10X sugar. Roll cake with wax paper into jellyroll form. Cool cake completely while preparing filling.

Blend filling ingredients until very smooth. Unroll cake with waxed paper on bottom. Spread filling onto cake and reroll without waxed paper. Cover with plastic wrap. Refrigerate until ready to use. Cut and serve.

This is the best dessert I ever had.

Enza Spence, Plainfield Township Lions Club
Nazareth, PA, USA

Every great achievement was once considered impossible.

2075-99

SPICY PUMPKIN SHEET CAKE

4 eggs
1¾ c. Libby's pumpkin (16 oz.)
1 c. sugar
¾ c. brown sugar
1 c. oil
2 c. flour

2 tsp. baking powder
1 tsp. baking soda
1 tsp. cinnamon
½ tsp. ginger
½ tsp. nutmeg
½ tsp. salt

Beat eggs in large mixing bowl. Add pumpkin, sugars, and oil. Beat well. Add remaining above ingredients and beat until well blended. Spread onto greased 15x10x1 inch jellyroll pan. Bake at 350° for 25 minutes or until toothpick inserted into center comes out clean. Cool. Frost with the following frosting.

Combine 3 ounces cream cheese, ¼ cup butter, 1 teaspoon vanilla, and 2 cups powdered sugar in small mixing bowl. Beat until light and fluffy.

Betty Rutledge, Bryan Lioness Club
Bryan, OH

SUPER SPICE CUPCAKES

1 c. raisins
1 c. chopped nuts
1 c. boiling water
1 tsp. soda
1 c. sugar
1½ c. flour

1 Tbsp. cocoa
½ tsp. cinnamon
½ tsp. cloves
½ tsp. nutmeg
½ c. salad oil
1 egg

Pour water over nuts and raisins. Add soda and let stand until cold. Sift dry ingredients and add to above. Beat salad oil and egg together and add last. Bake in paper cups at 350° for 15 to 20 minutes.

This has always been a favorite at potlucks and picnics.

Barbara J. Pedersen, Othello Lions Club
Othello, WA, USA

SPICE MAYONNAISE CAKE

2 c. flour
1 c. sugar
2 tsp. soda
½ tsp. salt
1 tsp. cocoa

4 tsp. cinnamon
1 tsp. cloves
1 c. mayonnaise
1 c. cold water
1 tsp. vanilla

Combine in order given. Pour into 9x13 inch bake pan and bake 30 to 35 minutes at 375°.

Wonderful for someone who is allergic to eggs or milk.

Bert Morgan, Broken Bow Lions Club
Broken Bow, NE, Custer County

ANGEL FOOD PINEAPPLE CAKE

1 box angel food cake mix
1 (20 oz.) can crushed pineapple
　　with its own juices

Mix or beat together. Put in tube pan. Do not grease pan. Bake at 350° for 40 to 45 minutes (no less).

Doris G. Brey, Upper Perkiomen Lioness Club
Harleysville, PA, USA

HOMEMADE ANGEL FOOD CAKE

1 c. cake flour
1 c. confectioners sugar
1½ c. egg whites (about 12)
1 tsp. cream of tartar

Pinch of salt
1 tsp. vanilla extract
1¼ c. sugar

Frosting:

1 (7 oz.) plain milk chocolate
　　candy bar
2 c. whipping cream

3 Tbsp. confectioners sugar
1 tsp. vanilla extract
Chocolate shavings (optional)

Sift flour and confectioners sugar together twice; set aside. In a mixing bowl, beat egg whites, cream of tartar, and salt on medium speed until soft peaks form. Add vanilla. Gradually beat in sugar, about 2 tablespoons at a time, until stiff peaks form, scraping bowl occasionally. Gradually fold in flour mixture, about ½ cup at a time. Pour into an ungreased 10 inch tube pan. Bake at 325° for 50 to 60 minutes or until lightly browned.

PUNCH BOWL CAKE

1 pineapple cake, baked as
　　directed from a mix
2 (5½ oz.) boxes vanilla instant
　　pudding
5 c. milk

2 (21 oz.) cans cherry pie filling
2 (8 oz.) cans crushed pineapple
1 (12 oz.) container whipped
　　topping
1 c. pecans

Bake cake as directed. Cool and crumble half of cake in bottom of bowl. Mix pudding, using five cups of milk. Pour half of pudding over cake. Spoon one can pie filling over pudding, then add one can pineapple and half the container of whipped topping. Repeat with the rest of the ingredients; chill well before serving.

Note - Substitute: Good with yellow cake mix and strawberry pie filling.

Lion Lucille Caruso, wife of PDG James "Jim" Caruso,
Delta Lions Club, District 8-S
Metairie, LA, USA

2075-99

PUNCH BOWL CAKE
(Good at Christmas)

1 box angel food cake (cook)
2 cans cherry pie filling
2 (16 oz.) cans crushed pineapple
2 bananas, sliced
1 medium size Cool Whip

2 small boxes instant vanilla
   pudding
Chopped pecans, coconut,
   maraschino cherries (for top
   garnish)

Layer all ingredients (twice) in punch bowl. Leave overnight.

Barbara Vaughn, Conroe Lioness Club
Conroe, TX, Montgomery County

SOUR CREAM COFFEE CAKE

1 c. sugar
½ c. butter
2 eggs
½ tsp. salt
1 tsp. vanilla

1 tsp. baking soda
1 tsp. baking powder
2 c. flour
1 c. sour cream

Mix all the above by hand.

Put ½ of the following in center and on top:

⅓ c. brown sugar
¼ c. white sugar

1 tsp. cinnamon
1 c. nuts, chopped

Put in 8x8 or 9x9 inch pan. Bake 40 minutes at 350°.

Karen Cornell, Elburn Lions Club
Elburn, IL, USA

Getting fired can be the best thing that can happen to you.

❦ ❦ ❦

It's hard to argue with someone when they're right.

❦ ❦ ❦

Marrying for money is the hardest way of getting it.

❦ ❦ ❦

Even the simplest task can be meaningful if you do it in the right spirit.

OATMEAL CAKE

Cake:

1½ c. boiling water
1 c. quick oats
1 c. brown sugar
1 c. white sugar
½ c. butter
2 eggs

1½ c. flour
1 tsp. cinnamon
1 tsp. baking soda
1 tsp. salt
1 c. nuts (if desired)

Frosting:

1 stick butter
1 c. brown sugar
½ c. canned milk (evaporated)

1 c. cocoanut
1 tsp. vanilla

Cook oats and let cool. Cream butter, sugars, and eggs. Add flour, cinnamon, baking soda, and salt. Mix well, then add oats. Mix well. Pour into greased and floured pan. Bake at 350° for 35 minutes. Pour hot frosting over cake. Enjoy!!

Frosting: Cook, stirring constantly, until thick. Remove from heat. Add cocoanut and vanilla. Pour over cake.

In loving memory of my grandma, Mary Hamilton.

Lion Linda Hamilton, Graysville-Proctor Lions Club
Proctor, WV, USA

CHEESE MERINGUE

½ c. flour
¼ c. sugar
¼ c. butter

1 c. ground walnuts (fine)
¼ tsp. almond extract

Mix together well, then spread in an 8x8 inch pan.

2 c. dry cottage cheese
4 eggs, separated
½ c. sugar
1 tsp. vanilla

1 tsp. flour
Pinch of salt
Juice and rind from orange

Sieve cheese. Mix yolks, sugar, and the rest of the ingredients. Put on top of the first mixture. Bake at 325°F. to 350°F. for 40 to 45 minutes.

Meringue: Beat egg whites until frothy. Add 6 tablespoons sugar and beat until stiff. Spread on baked cake and return to 400°F. oven for about 10 to 15 minutes.

Micheal and Ruth Bartolf, Oxbow and District Lions Club
Oxbow, Saskatchewan, Canada

2075-99

PATTY'S CRUMB CAKE

2½ c. flour
1¾ c. sugar
1 tsp. baking soda
1 tsp. cream of tartar
½ tsp. salt

Dash of nutmeg
¾ c. shortening
2 eggs
1 c. milk

Sift all dry ingredients together and add shortening. Mix to crumb consistency. Reserve 2 tablespoons of this mixture for top of cakes. Beat eggs well and add milk. Add to crumb mixture and mix well. Put in two 9 inch pans and top with crumbs. Bake 25 minutes in 350° oven. My family's favorite!

Pat Wheeler, Green Lane-Marlboro Lioness Club
Green Lane, PA, USA

FOURTH OF JULY CAKE

2 c. + 1 Tbsp. cake flour
2 tsp. baking powder
Salt
½ c. fresh raspberries
½ c. fresh blueberries
14 Tbsp. unsalted butter (at room temperature)

1⅓ c. granulated sugar
1¼ tsp. vanilla extract
1 c. + 2 Tbsp. milk
4 egg whites (at room temperature)
4 oz. cream cheese
2½ c. confectioners sugar, sifted

Heat oven to 350°. Butter a 13x9 inch pan. Combine 2 cups flour, the baking powder, and ½ teaspoon salt. Toss berries with 1 tablespoon flour. Beat 10 tablespoons butter, the granulated sugar, and 1 teaspoon vanilla about 5 minutes. Beat in flour in thirds, alternating with milk using 1 cup. Beat whites until stiff and fold into batter. Fold in berries. Pour into pan. Bake until done, about 30 minutes. Beat 4 tablespoons butter, the cream cheese, and a pinch of salt. Beat in confectioners sugar, ¼ teaspoon vanilla, and 2 tablespoons milk. Frost the cake. Makes 12 servings.

Per serving: 434 calories, 4 g protein, 18 g fat, 244 mg sodium, 65 g carbohydrate, 52 mg cholesterol.

Lion John J. Hess, Clarence Lions Club
Clarence Center, NY, USA

After age 50 you get "furniture disease."
That's when your chest falls into your drawers.

Anticipation is often better than the real thing.

CREAM PUFF CAKE

1 c. water
1 c. flour

1 stick oleo
4 eggs

Filling:

3 c. milk
2 small boxes vanilla instant
    pudding

8 oz. cream cheese, softened
1 large Cool Whip
Chocolate syrup (to drizzle on
    top)

Boil water and oleo. Remove from heat and add flour. Mix well. Let cool, then beat in one egg at a time. Spread on 11x15 inch pan. Bake at 400° for ½ hour. Let cool.

Prepare vanilla pudding using 3 cups milk. Add the softened cream cheese and spread on cooled crust. Top with the Cool Whip. Drizzle chocolate syrup all over the Cool Whip. Keep refrigerated.

Carol Bilek, Bullskin Township Lioness Club
Mt. Pleasant, PA

BAKE AND TAKE CAKE

1¼ c. warm water
1 c. rolled oats
1 c. white sugar
1 c. brown sugar
½ c. shortening

2 eggs
1½ c. flour
½ to 1 tsp. salt
1 tsp. baking soda
1 tsp. vanilla

Pour warm water over rolled oats and set aside. Mix shortening and both sugars together well, then add eggs and mix. Next, add the rolled oats that was set aside. Add flour that was mixed with salt and baking soda. Last, add vanilla and mix well. Pour into a 9x13 inch well greased pan. Bake at 350° till done, about 20 to 25 minutes. After cake is baked, make topping.

Topping:

1 c. cocoanut
½ c. butter
2 egg yolks

½ tsp. vanilla
1 c. brown sugar

Mix all together and spread on cake, then bake for 10 more minutes.

Lion Micheal and Ruth (Sauskojus) Bartolf,
Oxbow and District Lions Club
Oxbow, Saskatchewan, Canada

Enthusiasm is caught, not taught.

HEATH CAKE

2 c. brown sugar
2 c. flour
½ c. margarine
1 egg, beaten
1 tsp. soda

1 tsp. vanilla
Pinch of salt
6 Heath candy bars, broken into
    small pieces
½ c. nuts, chopped

Mix brown sugar, flour, and margarine like a crust. Take out 1 cup of crumbs for topping. To the rest of the mixture, add the egg, soda, vanilla, and salt. Mix and pour into a 13x9x2 inch pan.

Mix reserved cup of crumbs with Heath bars and nuts. Pour on top of batter. Bake at 350° for 30 minutes.

My son got this recipe from a friend when he was in 4-H.

Nancy Poole, Bend Lions Club
Bend, OR

HAPPINESS CAKE

1 c. good thoughts
1 c. nice deeds
1 c. thoughtful intentions

2 c. understanding and patience
3 c. forgiveness
2 c. well-beaten faults

Mix well. Add tears of joy, sorrow, and sympathy. Flavor with love and kindly service. Fold in 4 cups prayers and faith. After pouring all this into daily life, bake well with the heat of human kindness. Serve with a smile anytime and it will satisfy the hearts of starving souls.

East Haddam Community Lions Club
East Haddam, CT

PEANUT BUTTER "TANDY" CAKE

1 c. milk
2 Tbsp. butter
4 eggs
2 c. flour
2 tsp. baking powder

2 c. sugar
Pinch of salt
1 large (7 oz.) Hershey's bar
Peanut butter (approx. 1 c.)

Scald the milk and add the butter; set aside to cool. Mix the dry ingredients and add the slightly beaten eggs and milk/butter mixture. Beat until just smooth. Pour into a greased and floured 10½ x 15 inch jellyroll pan. Bake 15 to 18 minutes in a 350° oven. Immediately spread the peanut butter over the top of the cake. (Hint: Drop the peanut butter by spoonfuls over the top.) Refrigerate the cake until the peanut butter is "set." Melt the Hershey's bar in the top of a double boiler and spread over the peanut butter. Re-refrigerate for approximately ½ hour. *Do not store* permanently in refrigerator since this will make chocolate too hard.

Richard Koskey, Plainfield Township Lions Club
Easton, PA, USA

LAZY GOB CAKE

1 box yellow cake mix	4 eggs
1 (3¾ oz.) box instant pudding*	1½ c. milk
¼ c. oil	

Filling:

1 (3¾ oz.) box instant pudding	1 c. Crisco shortening
(same as in cake)	1 c. milk
1 c. sugar	

Mix cake mix, instant pudding, oil, eggs, and milk together. Pour batter into 2 jellyroll pans (11x17 inches), dividing batter equally. Bake one pan at a time at 350° for 15 minutes.

Filling: Mix pudding, sugar, Crisco, and milk, beating at high speed until all sugar is dissolved. Spread filling over cooled first layer of cake; top with second layer. Cut into squares.

   * Use flavor of your choice - lemon, chocolate, pistachio, coconut, banana, etc.

Donna King, York Springs Lions Club
York Springs, PA

JELL-O NO BAKE PUDDING CAKE

2 cans cherry pie filling	1 (8 oz.) thawed Cool Whip
1 box graham crackers	
4 c. cold milk	
2 (6 oz.) pkg. Jell-O *instant*	
pudding and pie filling	
(vanilla and chocolate flavor)	

Get 2 bowls. Pour 2 cups of cold milk in one bowl. Add vanilla pudding mix. Use electric mixer on low speed until well blended, 1 to 2 minutes, then let stand for 5 minutes and fold in ½ container of Cool Whip. Set aside.

Pour 2 cups of cold milk in other bowl. Add chocolate pudding mix. Use electric mixer on low speed until well blended, 1 to 2 minutes, then let stand for 5 minutes and fold in ½ container of Cool Whip. Set aside.

Line 13x9 inch throw away aluminum deep dish lasagna pan with graham crackers. Spread one mixture of pudding over crackers evenly and add another layer of crackers. Spread the other mixture of pudding evenly over and then add another layer of graham crackers. Spread 2 cans of cherry pie filling on top. Chill overnight.

Enza Spence, Plainfield Township Lions Club
Nazareth, PA, USA

LINDY'S CAKE

Mix 1 yellow cake mix according to the directions on the box. Place in 2 (9 inch) cake pans.

3 to 4 egg whites (depending on size of eggs)

1 tsp. vanilla
½ c. sugar

Beat egg whites till stiff. Add vanilla and sugar. Spread egg white mixture over the cake batter and top with 1 cup chopped pecans. Bake at 350° for 35 to 40 minutes or until toothpick comes clean. Cool in pan for 10 minutes. Remove from pan and place on a wire rack with meringue right side up and finish cooling.

Filling:

1 (8 oz.) container Cool Whip
1 (15 oz.) can crushed pineapple, drained completely

Mix the ingredients and spread on top of first layer with meringue side up. Top with remaining layer, meringue side up, and serve.

Marilyn Redifer, Whitehall Area Lions Club
Columbus, OH

SOC-IT-TO-ME CAKE

1 box yellow butter cake mix
4 eggs
¾ c. Wesson oil

1 tsp. vanilla
½ c. sugar
1 c. sour cream

Put all ingredients in large bowl and mix until fluffy, then in tube pan, put layer of cake mix, then sprinkle nuts, then brown sugar, then cinnamon and then repeat with another layer of cake mix, nuts, brown sugar, and cinnamon. Bake at 350° for 1 hour.

Diana Risha, Conroe Noon Lions Club
Conroe, TX

ECLAIR CAKE

1 c. water
4 eggs
2⅔ c. milk
1 c. flour

1 stick butter
1 large pkg. vanilla instant pudding
8 oz. cream cheese
8 oz. Cool Whip

Boil water and butter together. Remove from heat and add flour. Stir until it forms a ball. Add eggs, one at a time. Spread in greased 9x13 inch pan. Bake at 400° for 35 minutes. Cool. Mix milk and cream cheese. Add pudding and mix well. Spread on cooled pastry. Spread Cool Whip on pudding mixture. Drizzle chocolate syrup on top.

Judy Brasgalla, VDG, Cass Lake Lions and Lioness Club
Cass Lake, MN, USA

HAZEL'S CANADIAN WAR CAKE

Cake:

2 c. brown sugar
2 c. hot water
4 tsp. margarine
1 tsp. allspice
1 tsp. cinnamon
1 tsp. nutmeg

1 box raisins
1 lb. chopped nuts
1 tsp. baking soda
4 Tbsp. cold water
2 c. self-rising flour

Frosting:

1 box brown sugar
1 c. margarine

¾ c. sweet milk
1 Tbsp. vanilla

Put first 8 ingredients in saucepan and boil for 5 minutes. Cool and add baking soda and water. Stir in self-rising flour. Mix well and pour into greased and floured tube pan. Bake at 325° for 1½ hours. Cool and frost with topping.

Frosting: Cook all ingredients till mixture forms a soft ball when dropped in cold water. Cool. Whip until thick. Spread over cake.

Martha C. Cox, Travelers Rest Lions Club
Greenville, SC

SNOWBALL CAKE

2 env. plain gelatin
4 Tbsp. cold water
1 c. boiling water
1 small pkg. strawberry gelatin
1 c. or a little less sugar
Juice of 1 large lemon
1 (1 lb.) box frozen strawberries,
    partially thawed

1 large container Cool Whip
1 large angel food cake, torn into
    bite-size pieces
Grated coconut
Whole fresh strawberries
    (optional)

Dissolve plain gelatin in cold water. Add boiling water, strawberry gelatin, and sugar. Stir until dissolved. Add lemon juice and frozen strawberries. When mixture begins to jell, add half of Cool Whip. In a large round mixing bowl lined with plastic wrap, put a layer of angel food cake bits in bowl. Add a layer of strawberry gelatin mixture. Continue to layer until bowl is full. Cover and chill overnight. Turn out on cake plate. Remove plastic wrap. Cover with remaining Cool Whip and sprinkle with coconut. Garnish with whole fresh strawberries if desired.

For a different experience, you may layer ingredients in large baking dish. Cut and serve in squares with fresh strawberry on top. If done in dish, call it Strawberry Surprise.

This is in honor of Dollie S. Cartwright of Bristol, Tennessee, who was my first landlady in 1967.

Lion Ann K. Brumback, Silver Run-Union Mills Lions Club
Westminster, MD, USA

2075-99

PRALINE TOPPED CAKE

Base:

1 pkg. Duncan Hines butter
   recipe golden cake mix

Topping:

⅔ c. firmly packed brown sugar
¼ c. butter or margarine,
   softened

2 Tbsp. milk
1 c. finely chopped pecans

Preheat oven to 375°F. Grease and flour 9x13x2 inch pan. Prepare and bake cake following package directions.

For topping: Combine brown sugar, butter or margarine, and milk in small bowl. Mix thoroughly. Stir in finely chopped pecans. Spread mixture over warm cake. Broil 2 or 3 minutes or until topping bubbles.

Helen Leggett, Sherrodsville Lions Club
Sherrodsville, OH, USA

FROSTED BANANA BARS

½ c. butter or margarine,
   softened
2 c. sugar
3 eggs
1½ c. mashed ripe bananas (3)

1 tsp. vanilla extract
2 c. all-purpose flour
Pinch of salt

Frosting:

½ c. butter or margarine,
   softened
1 (8 oz.) pkg. cream cheese,
   softened

4 c. confectioners sugar
2 tsp. vanilla extract

In a mixing bowl, cream butter and sugar. Beat in eggs, bananas, and vanilla. Combine the flour, baking soda, and salt; add to creamed mixture and mix well. Pour into a greased 15x10x1 inch baking pan. Bake at 350° for 25 minutes or until bars test done. Cool. Gradually add confectioners sugar and vanilla; beat well. Spread over bars.

I call this cake or banana stuff, not bars. You can call it what you want.
Pam Caldwell, Mexico Sunrise Lions Club
Mexico, MO

Untold treasures are found in the imagination of a child.

COCONUT CAKE

1 box white cake mix
1 can coconut

1 can cream of coconut
8 oz. Cool Whip

Mix cake mix according to directions, but add ½ can of coconut. After it has cooled, punch full of holes. Pour 1 can of cream of coconut over cake. Frost with 8 ounce tub of Cool Whip, mixed with ½ can of coconut. Keep refrigerated.

Nancy Pence, Elizabethtown Lions Club
Elizabethtown, KY, USA

KID PLEASIN' CUPCAKES FOR ST. PATRICK'S DAY

1¾ c. flour
1 (4 oz.) pkg. instant pistachio
    pudding mix
¾ c. mini chocolate pieces
⅔ c. sugar
2½ tsp. baking powder

½ tsp. salt
2 beaten eggs
1¼ c. milk
½ c. oil (cooking)
1 tsp. vanilla

In large mixing bowl, stir together flour, pudding mix, chocolate pieces, sugar, baking powder, and salt. In small mixing bowl, combine beaten eggs, milk, oil, and vanilla. Stir into flour mixture just till combined. Fill muffin tins ⅔ full. Bake at 375° for 18 to 20 minutes. Cool. Frost with Cream Cheese Frosting. Sprinkle with green sugar and colored chocolate pieces. Makes 18 cupcakes.

Cream Cheese Frosting:

1 (3 oz.) pkg. cream cheese
2 Tbsp. butter

1½ c. powdered sugar
1 tsp. vanilla

Mix until creamy. Add color if desired.

Doris Faulds, Plainfield Township Lions Club
Pen Argyl, PA, USA

SHORTCAKE

2 c. sugar
4 eggs
¾ c. butter, softened
1 c. milk

2 c. flour
¼ tsp. salt
2 tsp. baking powder
2 tsp. vanilla

Beat sugar and butter together. Add eggs and beat well. Mix in milk and vanilla. Mix dry ingredients together; beat into butter mixture for about 2 minutes. Pour into greased and floured 13x9 inch pan or two loaf pans. Bake at 350° for 55 minutes for 13x9 inch pan or 45 minutes to an hour for loaf pans or until toothpick comes out clean.

Lion Melba Johnson, Brookhaven Alpha Lions Club
Brookhaven, MS

2075-99

A. BRUMBACK'S RUM CAKE

1 butter/moist cake mix
4 eggs
½ c. oil
¼ c. water
¾ c. rum

1 pkg. white chocolate fat free
   instant Jell-O pudding mix or
   French vanilla instant
   pudding mix
¼ to ½ c. chopped pecans

Boiled Syrup:

1 stick butter
1 c. sugar

½ c. rum
1 tsp. water

Heat oven to 350°. Grease Bundt pan with butter flavor Crisco or cooking spray. Sprinkle pan with chopped pecans. Beat 4 eggs with electric mixer. Add oil, a little at a time, then add water and rum. Add your cake mix and instant pudding mix. Bake cake at 350° until done (about an hour).

While cake is baking, make your Boiled Rum Syrup (stir constantly). Boil syrup about three minutes. When cake is done and still hot, pour syrup over cake until it is all absorbed. Use all the syrup.

This is in honor of Lion Doug Timmons, our 1998 to 1999 Past President of Silver Run-Union Mills, Westminster, Maryland.

Lion Ann K. Brumback of Littlestown, PA,
Silver Run-Union Mills Lions Club
Westminster, MD, USA

RUM CAKE

Cake:

½ c. chopped pecans
1 (18½ oz.) pkg. yellow cake mix
½ c. cooking oil
1 (3¾ oz.) pkg. vanilla pudding
   (instant or noninstant)

½ c. rum
½ c. water
4 eggs

Grease and flour tube or Bundt cake pan. Sprinkle nuts into bottom of pan. Mix other ingredients with electric mixer for 2 to 3 minutes. Bake at 325° for 40 to 60 minutes. Pour hot rum glaze over cake while hot. Cool glazed cake in pan 30 minutes and turn out. May be frozen.

Glaze:

1 c. sugar
½ c. butter

¼ c. rum
¼ c. water

Place ingredients in small saucepan and boil 2 to 3 minutes.

Variation - Rum Pound Cake: Omit water in both cake and glaze. Use ½ cup rum in glaze.

Cindy Bamburg, Biloxi Lions Club
Biloxi, MS, USA

BLACK WALNUT CAKE

2 sticks margarine
3 c. sugar
3 c. flour
1 c. milk
1 c. black walnuts, chopped

½ c. Crisco
5 eggs
1 tsp. baking powder
2 tsp. walnut extract

Cream together margarine, Crisco, and sugar; add eggs one at a time, beating after each egg is added. Sift together flour and baking powder; add alternately with milk. Stir in walnuts. Grease and flour pans. Bake at 325° for 1 hour and 45 minutes.

Use either Bundt pan or 3 small loaf pans.

Lion Jerrie Jefferson, East Anne Arundel Lions Club
Pasadena, MD, USA

ITALIAN CREAM CAKE

1 stick margarine
2 c. sugar
5 egg whites, stiffly beaten
1 c. buttermilk
1 tsp. soda
1 c. sliced pecans

½ c. Crisco
5 egg yolks, beaten
2 tsp. vanilla
2 c. flour
1 small can Angel Flake coconut

Cream margarine, Crisco, and sugar well. Add egg yolks and vanilla. Combine flour and soda. Add to creamed mixture alternately with buttermilk. Add coconut and pecans. Fold in beaten egg whites. Pour into 2 (9 inch) pans, greased and floured. Bake at 325° until done 25 to 30 minutes.

Cream Cheese Icing: Cream 1 (8 ounce) package of cream cheese and ½ stick margarine. Add ½ teaspoon vanilla and 1 pound box powdered sugar. Beat well. Freezes well.

The above cake was our daughter's wedding cake and it was a big hit with all ages.

Barbara J. Pedersen, Othello Lions Club
Othello, WA, USA

CARAMEL FROSTING

1 c. brown sugar
½ c. granulated sugar

1 c. whipping cream
Dash of salt

Combine all above ingredients and cook in a saucepan or iron skillet. Cook until soft ball forms when dropped in cup of cold water. Remove from heat and beat until the frosting loses its glossy appearance and reaches a consistency to spread.

Marie Alicie, North Tazewell Lions Club
North Tazewell, VA

2075-99

FLUFFY WHITE FROSTING

6 Tbsp. all-purpose flour
½ c. shortening
½ c. butter or margarine

1 c. sugar
1 Tbsp. vanilla
½ c. warm milk

Mix all ingredients with electric mixer at high speed for at least 10 minutes. Beat longer for fluffier texture. Makes enough for 1 (9 inch) cake.

Food coloring can be used for color.

Joyce A. Relihan, Plymouth Lions Club
Terryville, CT

Generous people seldom have emotional and mental problems.

❦ ❦ ❦

In every face-to-face encounter, regardless of how brief,
we leave something behind.

❦ ❦ ❦

The ache of unfulfilled dreams is the worst pain of all.

❦ ❦ ❦

Why is it that even when you schedule a doctor's appointment at 8:00 a.m.,
you still have to wait an hour?

BARS

"BEST-EVER" BROWNIES

½ c. butter (or oleo)
2 sq. chocolate (or 2½ Tbsp. cocoa)
1 c. sugar
2 eggs, well-beaten

1 tsp. vanilla
½ c. flour
¼ tsp. salt
1 c. nuts (walnuts or pecans)
1 c. chopped dates

Melt butter and chocolate together in saucepan. Remove from heat and add other ingredients in order given. Spread in buttered pan, 8x8 inches, for 20 to 25 minutes in 325° oven. (Brownies should be soft when taken from oven.) Mark into 1½ inch squares while hot, but cool before removing from pan. Dust with powdered sugar. Keep in airtight container. Makes 3 dozen squares.

These brownies stay moist and chewy because of the dates. Best ever!!!

Edith C. Rich (Dee), Bullhead City Lions Club
Bullhead City, AZ, USA

FROSTED FUDGE BROWNIES

1 stick oleo
2 sq. bitter chocolate
¾ c. flour
1 c. sugar

1 tsp. baking powder
1 tsp. vanilla
2 eggs, beaten
1 c. chopped nuts

Frosting:

¼ c. oleo
2 c. powdered sugar
2 Tbsp. milk or cream
⅛ tsp. salt

1 tsp. vanilla
1½ sq. unsweetened chocolate, melted

Preheat oven to 350°. Melt oleo and chocolate. Remove and add sifted dry ingredients. Stir in eggs, vanilla, and nuts. Pour in greased and floured pan (8x8 inches) and bake 25 to 30 minutes until batter leaves sides of pan. Cool.

Frosting: Beat on low all ingredients except chocolate. Add chocolate. Beat on high until blended well.

Mrs. Gordon (Linn) Dierschow, Elburn Lions Club
Elburn, IL

Even when you have pains, you don't have to be a pain.

2075-99

BEST BROWNIES

¾ c. butter
1½ c. sugar
2 eggs
½ tsp. vanilla
¾ c. flour

½ c. cocoa
¼ tsp. salt
½ c. chocolate chips
½ c. walnuts or pecans, chopped

Cream together butter and sugar. Add eggs and vanilla. Mix well. Add salt, flour, and cocoa. Mix thoroughly. Add chocolate chips and nuts. Pour into 9x9 inch greased pan. Bake at 350° for 30 to 40 minutes.

Great size for bake sales or small families.

Lioness Denice Riley, South-West Lioness Club
So. St. Paul, MN, USA

BROWNIES

4 eggs
2 c. white sugar
1 c. melted butter
¼ c. milk
2 c. scant flour

½ tsp. salt (optional)
1 tsp. vanilla
½ c. cocoa
1 c. walnuts

Beat 4 eggs and the 2 cups sugar well, then add the melted butter and ¼ cup of milk. Add flour, cocoa, and vanilla. Stir in walnuts. Put in well greased 9x13 inch pan. Bake in 350° oven for 35 minutes.

May frost or just sprinkle with powdered sugar. Very good and easy.

Lion Micheal and Ruth (Sauskojus) Bartolf,
Oxbow and District Lions Club
Oxbow, Saskatchewan, Canada

No matter how thin you slice it, there are always two sides.

People allow themselves to be only as successful
as they think they deserve to be.

Never praise your mother's cooking when
you're eating something fixed by your wife.

BUTTERMILK BROWNIES

2 c. sugar
2 c. flour
4 Tbsp. cocoa
1 c. cold water
½ c. (1 stick) margarine

½ c. oil
½ c. buttermilk
1 tsp. baking soda
2 eggs

Frosting:

½ c. margarine
¼ c. cocoa
⅓ c. buttermilk

1 box powdered sugar
½ tsp. vanilla

Sift sugar, flour, and cocoa together. In saucepan, bring water, oleo, and oil to a boil. Pour over dry ingredients and beat until creamy. Add buttermilk, soda, and eggs. Beat thoroughly. Bake in a greased jellyroll pan for 18 minutes at 400°F.

For frosting, bring margarine, cocoa, and buttermilk to a boil. Add powdered sugar and vanilla. Mix until smooth. Frost warm brownies. Top with nuts if desired.

Delicious home-from-school treat for the youngsters.

Janice Robison, Mexico Sunrise Lions Club
Benton City, MO, Audrain County

DOUBLE CHOCOLATE MARSHMALLOW BROWNIES

2 eggs
1 c. sugar
8 Tbsp. cocoa
5 Tbsp. oleo
1 tsp. vanilla

⅔ c. flour
½ tsp. baking powder
¼ tsp. salt
½ c. chocolate chips
¾ c. mini marshmallows

Beat eggs. Add sugar. Stir in cocoa, oleo, and vanilla, then add flour, baking powder, and salt. Stir in chips and marshmallows. Spread in 11x7 inch pan. Bake at 350° for 25 minutes.

My revelation: Nothing really bad happens when you tear those little "do not remove" tags from pillows.

Eating chocolate won't solve your problems.
But it doesn't hurt anything either.

2075-99

CANDY BAR BROWNIES

¾ c. butter or margarine, melted
2 c. sugar
4 eggs
2 tsp. vanilla extract
1½ c. all-purpose flour
⅓ c. baking cocoa

½ tsp. baking powder
¼ tsp. salt
4 (2.07 oz.) Snickers bars, cut
   into ¼ inch pieces
3 (1.55 oz.) plain milk chocolate
   candy bars, coarsely chopped

In a bowl, combine butter, sugar, eggs, and vanilla. Combine flour, cocoa, baking powder, and salt; set aside ¼ cup. Add remaining dry ingredients to the egg mixture; mix well. Toss Snickers pieces with reserved flour mixture; stir into batter.

Transfer to a greased 13x9x2 inch baking pan. Sprinkle with milk chocolate candy bar pieces. Bake at 350° for 30 to 35 minutes or until a toothpick inserted near the center comes out clean (do not overbake). Cool on a wire rack. Chill before cutting. Yield: 3 dozen.

BLONDE BROWNIES

2 c. all-purpose flour
1 tsp. baking powder
¼ tsp. salt
1¼ sticks unsalted butter,
   softened
2 c. brown sugar
2 eggs

1 Tbsp. vanilla
1 c. semi-sweet chocolate chips
1 c. peanut butter chips
½ c. pecans, chopped
½ c. walnuts, chopped

Preheat oven to 350°F. In a bowl, sift together flour, baking powder, and salt. In another bowl, cream butter and brown sugar together until light and creamy. Mix in eggs, one at a time, then vanilla. Add flour mixture and blend well. Stir in chips and nuts. Pour into a 13x9x2 inch buttered and floured baking pan. Bake for 30 minutes until golden. Let cool before cutting into squares and serving. Makes 2 dozen 2 inch square "blondies."

Elizabeth Maddock, Canaan Northwest Lions Club
Canaan, CT, USA

Kindness is more important than perfection.

Education, experience, and memories are
three things no one can take away from you.

MARBLED BROWNIES

2 oz. unsweetened chocolate
2¼ c. flour
2 tsp. baking powder
¾ tsp. salt
12 Tbsp. unsalted butter

1 c. granulated sugar
1 c. light brown sugar
1 tsp. vanilla extract
3 eggs

Heat oven to 325°. Butter a 9 inch baking pan. Chop and melt chocolate. Cool. Combine flour, baking powder, and salt. In a large saucepan, melt butter over low heat. Add both sugars and stir until smooth. Remove from heat and cool. Stir in vanilla. Stir in eggs, one at a time. Add flour mixture gradually, stirring all the while.

Divide batter in half and stir melted chocolate into one half. Drop batters by large tablespoonfuls alternately over bottom of pan. With the tip of a knife, swirl the batters to marbleize. Bake until edges start to pull away from sides of pan, about 55 minutes. Cool before cutting. Makes 16 brownies.

Per brownie: 181 calories, 2 g protein, 8 g fat, 116 mg sodium, 27 g carbohydrate, 42 mg cholesterol.

Barbara Joy Hess, Clarence Lions Club
Clarence Center, NY, USA

ZUCCHINI BROWNIES

2 c. shredded zucchini
¾ c. nuts
½ c. milk
2 c. sugar
2 c. flour
2 eggs

1 tsp. baking soda
1 tsp. salt
1 tsp. cinnamon
1 Tbsp. vanilla
4 Tbsp. heaping cocoa
1 c. margarine

Mix margarine, cocoa, and milk in pot. Stir over heat until margarine melts; cool. Add sugar, flour, etc., except zucchini. Mix. Add zucchini mix. Batter will be thin. Pour into 9x13 inch greased pan. Bake at 350° for 35 to 40 minutes.

If you like chocolate cake, you will like these brownies.

Maria Gaso, Bentleyville Lioness Club
Bentleyville, PA, USA

The best way to lose a friend is to lend him money.

❦ ❦ ❦

More comfort doesn't necessarily mean more happiness.

MAPLE BUTTERSCOTCH BROWNIES

1½ c. packed brown sugar
½ c. butter or margarine
1½ tsp. maple flavoring
2 eggs

1½ c. all-purpose flour
1 tsp. baking powder
1¼ c. chopped walnuts
Confectioners sugar (optional)

In a bowl, combine brown sugar, butter, and maple flavoring. Beat in eggs, one at a time. Combine flour and baking powder and add to mixture. Stir in chopped walnuts. Pour into a greased 9 inch square baking pan or dish. Bake in 350° oven for 30 minutes or until brownies test done. Cool. Dust with confectioners sugar. Cut into squares.

Ann K. Brumback, Silver Run Union Mills Lions Club
Westminster, MD, USA

HEAVENLY HASH

4 eggs, slightly beaten
2 c. sugar
2½ sticks margarine, melted
3 Tbsp. cocoa

1½ c. self-rising flour
2 c. pecans
2 tsp. vanilla
Marshmallows to cover

Icing:

3 Tbsp. cocoa
1 box confectioners sugar

½ c. can milk
4 Tbsp. melted margarine

Mix by hand (spoon) eggs, sugar, and margarine. Mix and add to above cocoa, flour, pecans, and vanilla. Bake in 13x9x2 inch pan at 350° for 50 to 60 minutes. Remove from oven. Cover with marshmallows and return to oven until partly melted.

Mix cocoa, confectioners sugar, milk, and melted margarine. Pour over marshmallows.

Lion June Taylor, Foley Lions Club
Foley, AL, USA

Anger manages everything poorly.

*The secret to growing old gracefully is never to lose
your enthusiasm for meeting new people and seeing new places.*

PECAN PIE SURPRISE BARS

1 pkg. yellow cake mix
1 egg

Filling:

⅔ c. reserved cake mix
1½ c. dark corn syrup
3 eggs

½ c. butter, melted
1 c. chopped pecans

½ c. firmly packed brown sugar
1 tsp. vanilla

Grease bottom and sides of 13x9 inch baking pan. Reserve ⅔ cup dry cake mix for filling. In large mixing bowl, combine remaining dry cake mix, butter, and 1 egg; mix until crumbly. Press into prepared pan. Bake at 350° for 15 to 20 minutes until light golden brown.

Meanwhile, prepare filling by mixing ingredients together. Pour filling over baked crust; sprinkle with pecans. Return to oven and bake for 30 to 35 minutes until filling is set.

P. Diane Baldwin, Broken Bow Lions Club
Broken Bow, NE, USA

SCOTCH-A-ROOS

1 c. sugar
1 c. light corn syrup

Topping:

1 (6 oz.) pkg. chocolate chips

1 c. peanut butter
6 c. Rice Krispies

1 (6 oz.) pkg. butterscotch chips

Cook sugar and corn syrup until it bubbles. Remove from heat and stir in peanut butter. Mix well, then add Rice Krispies. Mix thoroughly and press into buttered 9x13 inch pan. Melt chocolate and butterscotch chips together and spread on top. Chill and cut into small squares.

Carol Hag, Bryan Lioness Club
Bryan, OH, USA

Some money costs too much.

It's easier to stay out of trouble than to get out of trouble.

If you allow someone to make you angry, you have let him conquer you.

2075-99

LIME CHEESECAKE BARS

4 Tbsp. unsalted butter
2 large limes
1 c. graham cracker crumbs
1 Tbsp. plus ⅔ c. sugar
1 lb. cream cheese (at room
    temperature)

2 eggs
1 Tbsp. cornstarch
¼ c. sour cream
Pinch of salt

Heat the oven to 325°. Line a 9 inch baking pan with a sheet of foil extending 2 inches beyond 2 sides of the pan. Melt the butter. Grate 1 tablespoon zest from the limes and squeeze 2 tablespoons juice. Combine the melted butter, graham cracker crumbs, and 1 tablespoon sugar. Press evenly into the bottom of the prepared pan. With an electric mixer set at medium-low speed, beat the cream cheese and the remaining ⅔ cup sugar until smooth. Beat in the lime zest and juice, eggs, cornstarch, sour cream, and salt. Pour into the pan. Bake until firm, 45 to 50 minutes. Cool completely before cutting. Makes 18 bars.

Per serving: 186 calories, 3 g protein, 13 g fat, 131 mg sodium, 14 g carbohydrate, 60 mg cholesterol.

Barbara Joy Hess, Clarence Lions Club
Clarence Center, NY, USA

CHEESECAKE BARS

1¼ c. flour
1 c. graham cracker crumbs
    (about 16 sq.)
½ c. plus ⅔ c. sugar
¼ tsp. baking soda
⅛ tsp. salt
¼ lb. unsalted butter (at room
    temperature)

2 (8 oz.) pkg. cream cheese (at
    room temperature)
¼ tsp. grated lemon zest and 2
    Tbsp. lemon juice
¼ tsp. vanilla extract
2 eggs
⅓ c. semi-sweet chocolate chips
¼ c. golden raisins

Heat oven to 350°. Line bottom and two sides of a 9 inch square pan with foil. Butter remaining two sides. Combine flour, crumbs, ½ cup sugar, the soda, and salt. Cut in butter until crumbly. Reserve 1 cup of this mixture and press the remaining crumbs in the bottom of the pan. Beat cream cheese and ⅔ cup sugar. Beat in the lemon zest and juice, the vanilla, and eggs until just combined. Stir in the chocolate chips and raisins. Pour into pan. Crumble the reserved crumbs on top. Bake until golden brown, about 40 minutes. Cool and chill before cutting. Makes 24 bars.

Per bar: 203 calories, 3 g protein, 12 g fat, 117 mg sodium, 22 g carbohydrate, 49 mg cholesterol.

Joanne M. Wetzler, Clarence Lions Club
Clarence Center, NY, USA

APPLE SQUARES

4 c. diced apples (or slice thin) 1 c. salad oil
2 c. sugar

Put together and let soak ½ hour.

3 c. flour   1 tsp. baking soda
1 tsp. cinnamon   2 slightly beaten eggs

Combine the two mixtures and bake at 350° for 40 minutes. Add nuts if you wish. Glaze top. (Grease pan size 15½ x 10½ x 1 inch.)

Clarissa Fry, Bullskin Township Lioness Club
Mt. Pleasant, PA

APPLE SQUARES

6 Tbsp. butter   1 c. all-purpose flour
2 eggs   2 c. tart apples, peeled and
1 c. white sugar   chopped
1 tsp. baking soda   ½ c. chopped walnuts
1 tsp. vanilla   Icing sugar
¼ tsp. cinnamon

Combine butter, eggs, sugar, baking soda, vanilla, cinnamon, and flour in large bowl. Beat until well mixed. Add apple and nuts. Stir to mix. Scrape into greased 9x9 inch pan. Bake in 350° oven for 40 to 45 minutes. Cool for 15 minutes. Sift icing sugar over top. Cut into 36 squares.

Lion Micheal and Ruth (Sauskojus) Bartolf,
Oxbow and District Lions Club
Oxbow, Saskatchewan, Canada

APPLE BARS

1 c. flour   ½ c. shortening
½ tsp. salt   2½ c. sliced apples
½ tsp. soda   ½ c. sugar
½ c. brown sugar   ½ tsp. cinnamon
1¾ c. rolled oats   2 tsp. butter

Mix flour with salt and sugar. Add brown sugar and rolled oats and mix. Cut in shortening until mixture is crumbly. Spread half mixture in greased 7x11 inch baking dish. Add apples. Sprinkle with sugar and cinnamon that has been blended. Dot with butter. Cover with remaining crumb mixture. Bake at 350° for 40 to 45 minutes. Cut into bars. Serve cold or hot with lemon sauce.

This is my family's favorite. Use a good cooking apple, such as Winesap or McIntosh.

Teresa Jett, West Milford Lions Club
West Milford, WV, USA

2075-99

MOIST APPLE BARS

2 c. flour
1 tsp. soda
1½ c. brown sugar
½ c. shortening
½ tsp. salt
1 tsp. cinnamon

1 egg
½ c. milk
1½ c. chopped apples
1 c. raisins
½ c. nuts

Cream shortening, salt, brown sugar, and cinnamon. Add ½ of the flour, soda, apples, raisins, nuts, and milk. Stir well. Add last portion of flour. Grease 13x9 inch pan or small jellyroll pan. Bake in 350° oven for 25 to 30 minutes or 15 to 20 minutes according to the size pan used.

Frost while hot with:

1½ c. powdered sugar
2 tsp. cream

1 tsp. vanilla

Veleta Young, Bellingham Harborview Lions Club
Bellingham, WA, USA

FIG BARS

3 c. figs (sprinkle with ½ lemon
  juice)
2 c. sugar
1½ c. butter
4 eggs

2 tsp. vanilla
2¾ c. bread flour
3 tsp. baking powder
1½ tsp. salt

Beat butter and sugar together till creamy. Add eggs, 2 at a time. Add vanilla. Add flour, baking powder, and salt that have been mixed. When mixed well, add 2 cups broken nutmeats. Butter an 8x12 inch pan. Bake at 325° for 40 minutes. Cool and cut into bars.

Betty A. Birch, Bullhead City Lions Club
Bullhead, AZ

There are no unimportant acts of kindness.

❧ ❧ ❧

If you wait until retirement to really start living, you've waited too long.

❧ ❧ ❧

You can't change the past, but you can let it go.

DATE BARS

Pour 1 cup boiling water over 2 cups of pitted dates, cut fine.

1 tsp. baking soda	**2 c. flour**
1 c. sugar	**1 Tbsp. baking powder**
2 eggs	**½ tsp. salt**
2 Tbsp. butter	**1 c. nutmeats**

Cream together sugar and butter. Add eggs. Beat until light and fluffy, then add date mixture. Add 2 cups flour, 1 tablespoon baking powder, salt, and 1 cup nutmeats. Spread on cookie sheet. Bake at 350° for about 25 minutes. When you get ready to serve them, put some powdered sugar in a small plastic bag and put some of the bars in and shake to coat the bars.

Best to coat the bars as used.

I use these bars for the holidays. They go real good as a special treat.
Jennie Ludwick, Lyons-Muir Lions Club
Muir, MI, USA

DATE-CHIP BAR

1 c. chopped dates	**1¼ c. boiling water**
1 tsp. soda	

Put in a bowl; mix and set aside.

½ c. shortening	**2 c. flour**
1 c. white sugar	**½ tsp. soda**
2 eggs	**½ tsp. salt**

Mix shortening, sugar, and eggs together. Sift together flour, soda, and salt. Put flour and date mixture in with other mixture and mix well. Pour into a greased large cake pan or jellyroll pan. Sprinkle on top with a chip mixture.

Mix together:

½ c. brown sugar	**1 (8 oz.) pkg. chocolate chips**
½ c. chopped nuts	

Bake at 300° for 30 to 40 minutes.
Mary Ann Corbett, South-West Lioness Club
So. St. Paul, MN

If you keep doing what you've always done, you'll keep getting what you've always gotten.

OATMEAL DATE NUT BARS

1 c. pitted dates
⅔ c. flour
¼ tsp. baking powder
¼ tsp. ground nutmeg
¼ tsp. salt
8 Tbsp. unsalted butter (at room
    temperature)

½ c. dark brown sugar
1 egg
½ tsp. vanilla extract
¾ c. quick-cooking oats
1 c. chopped walnuts

Heat oven to 325°. Line the bottom and two sides of a 9 inch square pan with foil and butter the unlined sides. Chop the dates. Combine the flour, baking powder, nutmeg, and salt. Beat the butter and sugar until creamy. Beat in egg and vanilla. Stir in flour mixture until smooth. Stir in oats, dates, and walnuts. Press the mixture into the prepared pan. Bake until edges are golden brown, 25 to 30 minutes. Cool completely before cutting. Makes 24 bars.

Per bar: 130 calories, 2 g protein, 7 g fat, 33 mg sodium, 15 g carbohydrate, 19 mg cholesterol.

Lion John J. Hess, Clarence Lions Club
Clarence Center, NY, USA

RAISIN BARS

1 c. raisins
½ c. water
¼ c. margarine
1 c. sugar (brown or white)
1 egg

1 tsp. vanilla
1½ c. flour
½ tsp. cinnamon
1 tsp. soda
¼ tsp. salt

Boil raisins in ½ cup water 5 to 10 minutes or until nearly dry. Cream margarine, sugar, egg, and vanilla. Add flour, cinnamon, soda, and salt. Add raisins and water.

Bert Morgan, Broken Bow Lions Club
Broken Bow, NE, Custer County

If you keep doing what you've always done,
you'll keep getting what you've always gotten.

If you want to cheer yourself up, try cheering up someone else.

RAISIN ALMOND BARS

½ c. whole unblanched almonds
1¼ c. flour
¼ tsp. baking soda
¼ tsp. salt
10 Tbsp. unsalted butter (at room temperature)

½ c. light brown sugar
½ tsp. grated lemon zest
¼ tsp. vanilla extract
¼ tsp. almond extract
1 egg
½ c. raisins

Heat oven to 375°. Line the bottom and two long sides of a 13x9 inch pan with foil. Butter the foil and exposed sides of the pan. Chop almonds. Combine flour, soda, and salt. With an electric mixer set at medium speed, beat butter, sugar, and lemon zest until creamy. Beat in vanilla, almond extract, and egg. Gradually beat in flour mixture. Stir in raisins. Spread dough in the prepared pan. Sprinkle with almonds and lightly press them into the dough. Bake until golden brown, about 5 minutes. Cool on a rack. Use the foil to lift cookies from pan and cut into bars. Makes 32 bars.

Per bar: 86 calories, 1 g protein, 5 g fat, 31 mg sodium, 10 g carbohydrate, 17 mg cholesterol.

Joanne M. Wetzler, Clarence Lions Club
Clarence Center, NY, USA

SOUR CREAM RAISIN BARS

1¾ c. oatmeal
1 c. margarine
1 tsp. soda
4 egg yolks
3 heaping Tbsp. cornstarch

2½ c. raisins
1 c. brown sugar
1¾ c. flour
2 c. sour cream
1½ c. sugar

Mix first five ingredients like a pie crust. Save 1½ cups of this mixture for the top. Spread the rest in a jellyroll pan. Bake at 350° for 10 minutes.

Beat egg yolks well and mix with remaining ingredients. Place in saucepan and boil. Keep stirring about 5 to 10 minutes or until thick. Pour over baked crust. Top with remaining crumbs. Bake another 20 minutes.

Lion Theresa Hill, Hector Lions Club
Hector, MN

If you stay focused on yourself, you are guaranteed to be miserable.

SOUR CREAM RAISIN BARS

1¾ c. oatmeal
1¾ c. flour
1 tsp. soda
1 c. brown sugar
1 c. margarine, melted
4 egg yolks, beaten slightly

1 c. sugar
3 Tbsp. cornstarch
2 c. sour cream
2 c. raisins
1 tsp. vanilla

Mix the first 5 ingredients as for pie crust. Save 1½ cups for topping. Press remaining mixture in 9x13 inch pan. Bake 10 to 15 minutes at 350°.

Make filling; put egg yolks, sugar, cornstarch, and sour cream in saucepan. Bring to boil and stir constantly. Cook 5 minutes or until thick. Add raisins. Pour over crust. Put remaining crumbs on top. Bake another 20 minutes at 350°.

Wilma Arens, Plato Lions Club
Plato, MN, USA

PUMPKIN BARS

Crumb Crust:

1½ c. rolled oats
1¼ c. all-purpose flour
¾ c. brown sugar

½ tsp. salt
½ tsp. baking soda
¾ c. margarine, melted

Filling:

2 c. pumpkin
⅔ c. milk
⅓ c. brown sugar

1 egg
1 Tbsp. pumpkin pie spice

Preheat oven to 375°F. Lightly grease a 9x13 inch baking pan. In a large mixing bowl, stir together rolled oats, all-purpose flour, ¾ cup brown sugar, salt, baking soda, and melted margarine until mixture is crumbly. Pat ½ of the mixture into prepared pan and bake for 8 to 10 minutes.

Stir together pumpkin, milk, ⅓ cup brown sugar, egg, and pumpkin pie spice. Spread filling over partially baked crust. Dot remaining crumb mixture over top. Bake for 25 minutes.

Lion Susan E. Shaffer, Connumach Lions Club
Davidsville, PA, USA

If you want to go to parties, you have to give some parties.

PEANUT BUTTER SWIRL BARS

½ c. crunch style peanut butter
⅓ c. margarine, softened
¾ c. brown sugar
¾ c. granulated sugar
2 eggs

2 tsp. vanilla
1 c. flour
1 tsp. baking powder
¼ tsp. salt
1½ c. chocolate chips

Preheat oven to 350°. In large bowl, combine peanut butter, softened margarine, brown sugar, and granulated sugar. Beat until creamy. Gradually beat in eggs and vanilla. Add flour, baking powder, and salt and mix well. Spread into greased 13x9x2 inch baking pan. Sprinkle with chocolate chips. Place in oven for 5 minutes. Remove from oven and run knife through to marbleize. Return to oven and bake 25 minutes. Cool. Cut into 2x1 inch bars. Makes 4 dozen.

Lynne Swanson, Princeton Lions Club
Princeton, IL

PEANUT BUTTER OATMEAL TREATS

Mix together:

1 c. butter
¾ c. sugar
¾ c. brown sugar

2 eggs
1 tsp. vanilla
1 (16 oz.) jar smooth peanut
  butter

Add and mix well:

1¼ c. flour
½ tsp. salt

1 tsp. baking soda

Add 2 cups oats and mix well. Add 1 cup mini chocolate chips. Using ungreased 15½ x 10½ x 1 inch baking pan, press mixture into pan. Bake at 350° for 15 to 17 minutes. Cool, then cut into bars.

Lion Sandy Clever, East Prospect Lions Club
East Prospect, PA, USA

PEANUT BUTTER CUPS OR SQUARES

2 sticks melted margarine
1½ c. crushed graham crackers
1 c. peanut butter (creamy or
  crunchy)

2½ c. sifted confectioners sugar
1 (12 oz.) pkg. chocolate chips

Mix crumbs and margarine; add peanut butter and sugar. Mix well. Pat evenly into 9x13 inch pan. Melt chocolate chips and spread evenly. Refrigerate. Take out ½ hour before serving. Cut into squares.

For less sweetness, melt 1 square bitter sweet chocolate with chocolate chips.

Elizabeth Maddock, Canaan Northwest Lions Club
Canaan, CT, USA

HONEY PEANUT SQUARES

1 c. honey or light corn syrup
(honey preferred)
½ c. sugar

1 c. peanuts (optional)
1 c. creamy peanut butter
8 c. corn flakes

Spray or butter a 10x15 inch bar pan. Spray a large pot with pan spray. Mix honey, sugar, and peanuts in pan. Heat just to boiling over medium heat, stirring constantly. Remove from heat. Stir in peanut butter until smooth. Fold in cereal until well coated. Press mixture firmly in pan with a spoon or your hands. (Press or pound as firmly as possible.) Let stand 1 hour. Cut into squares.

Lion Diane Pfotenhauer, DePere Lions Club
DePere, WI, USA

CHOCOLATE-CHIP WHEAT-GERM BARS

1⅔ c. flour
⅓ c. wheat germ
¾ tsp. baking soda
¾ tsp. salt
10 Tbsp. unsalted butter (at room
temperature)

½ c. brown sugar
⅓ c. granulated sugar
¾ tsp. vanilla extract
1 egg
1¾ c. semi-sweet chocolate chips

Heat oven to 325°. Butter a 15x10 inch jellyroll pan or cookie pan with sides. Combine flour, wheat germ, soda, and salt. With an electric mixer set at medium-low speed, beat butter, brown and granulated sugars, and the vanilla until fluffy. Beat in egg. Reduce speed and gradually add flour mixture. Beat until just combined. Stir in chocolate chips. Dough will be stiff. With lightly moistened fingers, press dough into pan. Bake until lightly browned, 20 to 25 minutes. Let cool slightly before cutting into bars. Makes about 25 bars.

Per bar: 155 calories, 2 g protein, 8 g fat, 96 mg sodium, 21 g carbohydrate, 21 mg cholesterol.

Joann M. Brownell, Clarence Lions Club
Clarence Center, NY, USA

The wealthy person is the one who is content with what he has.

❧ ❧ ❧

If you can't forgive and forget, you can at least forgive and move on.

MARBLE SQUARES

1 c. flour
½ tsp. baking soda
½ tsp. salt
½ c. soft butter (or shortening)
6 Tbsp. granulated sugar
6 Tbsp. brown sugar

½ tsp. vanilla
1 egg
1 tsp. water
1 c. chocolate bits
½ c. chopped nuts (optional)

Mix together flour, baking soda, and salt; set aside. Mix well shortening, sugar(s), vanilla, water, and egg. Add dry ingredients, blending well. Spread in greased (not floured) 13x9x2 inch pan. Sprinkle chocolates over top of batter. Place in oven for 2 to 3 minutes. Remove from oven and run knife through batter to marbleize. Return to oven and continue to bake 12 to 14 minutes at 375°. Cool and cut into 2 inch squares.

Quick and easy recipe to slip into oven just before the kids get home from school. Also, good for "treats" your kids may have to supply.

Margaret Wooden, Princeton Lions Club
Princeton, IL, USA

CHOCOLATE CARAMEL BARS

2¼ c. flour, divided
2 c. quick cooking oats
1½ c. brown sugar
1 tsp. baking soda
1½ c. cold butter or oleo

2 c. semi-sweet chips
1 c. chopped pecans
1 (12 oz.) jar caramel ice cream
   topping

In bowl, combine 2 cups of flour, oats, brown sugar, baking soda, and salt. Cut in butter until crumbly. Set half aside for topping. Press the remaining crumb mixture into a 9x13 inch greased pan. Bake at 350° for 15 minutes. Sprinkle with chocolate chips and nuts. Whisk caramel topping and ¼ cup flour until smooth. Drizzle over top of chips and nuts. Sprinkle with remaining crumb mixture. Bake 18 to 20 minutes or until golden brown. Cool on wire rack 2 hours before cutting.

Karen Cornell, Elburn Lions Club
Elburn, IL, USA

Ultimately, takers lose and givers win.

CHOCOLATE COCONUT BARS

2 c. graham cracker crumbs
½ c. butter or margarine, melted
¼ c. sugar
2 c. flake coconut

1 c. sweetened condensed milk
½ c. chopped pecans
1 (7 oz.) plain chocolate candy
   bar
1 Tbsp. peanut butter

Combine crumbs, butter, and sugar. Press in 9x13 inch pan. Bake at 350° for 10 minutes. Combine coconut, milk, and pecans. Spread over crust. Bake at 350° for 15 minutes. Cool.

In a small saucepan, melt candy and peanut butter. Spread over bars. Cool. Makes 3 dozen.

This was served at one of my clubs. There were so many requests for the recipe it was put into the monthly newsletter.

Lion Virginia Bayer, Franklin Park Lions Club
Park Ridge, IL, USA

CARAMEL CHOCOLATE SQUARES

1 (14 oz.) pkg. Kraft caramels
⅓ c. evaporated milk
1 pkg. German chocolate cake
   mix
¾ c. melted oleo

⅓ c. evaporated milk
1 c. chopped nuts
1 (6 oz.) pkg. chocolate chips

Grease and flour 9x13 inch pan. Heat the caramels in ⅓ cup evaporated milk. Stir until melted; remove from heat and let cool. Mix cake mix, oleo, ⅓ cup evaporated milk, and nuts until dough holds together. Press half into pan. Bake at 350° for 6 minutes. Remove from the oven. Sprinkle chocolate chips over baked crust, then spread melted caramel over chips. Crumble remaining dough over top. Return to the oven for 15 to 18 minutes (longer if necessary, depending on your oven, even 20 minutes). Cool and put in refrigerator until set.

Mary Mitchell, Bullskin Township Lioness Club
Mt. Pleasant, PA

CINDY'S CHOCOLATE ALMOND BARS

1 c. butter
2 c. flour
1 tsp. vanilla

¾ c. brown sugar
¾ c. finely chopped almonds
6 oz. semi-sweet chocolate chips

Put butter, sugar, flour, and vanilla in a large mixing bowl; mix until crumbly. Pat into ungreased 10x15 inch pan. Bake at 350° for 15 to 20 minutes. Remove and sprinkle with chocolate chips. Let stand until beginning to melt; spread evenly. Sprinkle with chopped nuts. Let cool. Cut into bars.

Note: I've used other nuts.

Lioness Marie C. Beatty, East Anne Arundel Lioness Club
Pasadena, MD, USA

TWINKIE BARS

Bake 1 yellow cake mix as directed.

Filling:

1 c. milk
½ c. shortening
5 Tbsp. flour

½ c. margarine or butter
1 c. sugar
1 tsp. vanilla

Gradually mix cold milk with flour; cook over medium heat until very thick. Cover and cool. Cream together sugar, shortening, butter, and vanilla. Add cooled flour mix and beat at high speed for 5 minutes. Spread between layers. Cut into bars.

To cut cake: When cake is cool, place a string around center of cake horizontally, then pull through, cutting cake into layers.

P. Diane Baldwin, Broken Bow Lions Club
Broken Bow, NE, USA

PAYDAY BARS

1 yellow cake mix
5⅓ Tbsp. oleo
1 egg
3 c. mini marshmallows
⅔ c. corn syrup

1 bag peanut butter chips
¼ c. oleo
1 tsp. vanilla
2 c. peanuts
2 c. Rice Krispies

In bowl, mix on low speed cake mix, oleo, and egg. Bake at 350° on ungreased cookie sheet for 10 to 12 minutes. Take out of oven, put marshmallows on top, and bake in oven 1 to 2 minutes or until puffy.

In saucepan, melt corn syrup, oleo (¼ cup), and peanut butter chips. Cool and cut.

Mary Alice Millward, Bullskin Township Lioness Club
Mt. Pleasant, PA

Insatiable curiosity is important to never feeling old.

*You can't expect your children to listen
to your advice and ignore your example.*

2075-99

KIT KAT BARS

These bars are similar to the Kit Kat candy bar.

Butter crackers (e.g. Waverly crackers)
1½ c. graham crackers, crushed
¾ c. brown sugar
1 c. white sugar
¾ c. butter or margarine
⅓ c. milk
1 c. butterscotch chips
1 c. semi-sweet chocolate chips
¾ c. peanut butter

Put graham crackers, brown sugar, white sugar, butter, and milk into a saucepan and bring to a boil. Boil for 5 minutes. Put a layer of Waverly crackers in a 9x13 inch pan and pour ½ of the mixture over it. Put another layer of crackers and pour the remaining mixture. Add last row of crackers.

To make topping: Melt over low heat the butterscotch chips, chocolate chips, and peanut butter. Melt at low heat and spread over the top. Makes 2 dozen.

Barbara K. Hugus, West Milford Lions Club
West Milford, WV, USA

O'HENRY BARS

4 c. oatmeal
1 c. brown sugar
1 c. sugar
1 c. butter
1½ c. chocolate chips
1 heaping c. peanut butter

Mix oatmeal, sugar, and butter together. Spread in a jellyroll pan. Bake 12 minutes at 350°. Cool. Melt chips and peanut butter. Spread over top. (Don't overbake.)

DREAM BARS

¾ stick margarine
1 c. sifted flour
½ c. brown sugar

Mix together and press into 9x9 inch pan. Bake 8 to 10 minutes at 350° (be careful not to burn).

Beat 2 eggs and mix in:

1 c. brown sugar
1 tsp. vanilla
2 tsp. flour
½ tsp. baking powder
½ c. coconut
½ c. chopped nuts

Pour second mixture onto first. Bake 15 to 20 minutes at 350°. When cool, cut in squares.

Bobbie Seiter, Lubbock South Plains Lions Club
Lubbock, TX, USA

JO'S YUMMY BARS

1 box whole graham crackers
8 oz. peanuts
1 c. brown sugar

1 (12 oz.) chocolate chips
1 c. butter
2 Tbsp. Karo syrup

Place whole graham crackers on bottom of 9x13 inch pan. Sprinkle chocolate chips on graham crackers. Add peanuts. Melt together butter, brown sugar, and Karo syrup; boil for 3 minutes. Pour over peanuts; refrigerate.

Jo Klawitter, Caterer, Hector Lions Club
Hector, MN

CARAMEL APPLE OAT BARS

1¾ c. unsifted flour
1 c. quick cooking oats
½ c. firmly packed brown sugar
½ tsp. baking soda
½ tsp. salt
1 c. cold margarine or butter

20 caramels (unwrapped)
1 (14 oz.) can sweetened
  condensed milk
1 (21 oz.) can apple pie filling
1 c. chopped walnuts

Preheat oven to 375°. In a large bowl, combine flour, oats, sugar, baking soda, and salt; cut in margarine until crumbly. Reserving 1½ cups crumb mixture, press remainder on bottom of 13x9 inch baking pan. Bake 15 minutes. Add nuts to reserved crumb mixture.

In heavy saucepan over low heat, melt caramels with condensed milk, stirring until smooth. Spoon apple filling over prepared crust; top with caramel mixture, then reserve crumb mixture. Bake 20 minutes or until set. Cool. Serve warm with ice cream if desired.

Denise Cain, Alpha Lions Club
Brookhaven, MS

COCONUT CREAM BARS

1 stick oleo
1 box yellow cake mix
3 eggs
8 oz. cream cheese

1 tsp. vanilla
1 box confectioners sugar
1 c. coconut
1 c. chopped pecans

Heat oven to 325°. Lightly spray a cookie sheet with Pam. Melt 1 stick oleo. Mix in 1 box yellow cake mix and 1 egg. Pat mixture in the bottom of the cookie sheet. Mix cream cheese, 2 eggs, confectioners sugar, and vanilla. Add coconut and pecans. Pour over cake crust and bake 30 to 40 minutes at 325°.

Jeanette Simpson, Stafford-Missouri City Lions Club
Stafford-Missouri City, TX, USA

PUFF WHEAT BARS

1 c. Karo syrup

1 c. white or brown sugar

Heat to start to boil. Add 1 cup peanut butter. Stir well. Pour over 6 cups of Puff Wheat cereal. Put in buttered 9x13 inch pan. Cool and serve.

Our family enjoyed these on camping trips. They are very healthy.

Elvera Trettin, Stewart Lions Club
Stewart, MN, USA

BREAKFAST JAM BARS

3 c. plain flour
2 tsp. baking powder
½ tsp. salt
3 c. quick oatmeal

2 c. packed brown sugar
1½ c. butter or shortening
2 c. any flavor jam or jelly

Preheat oven to 375°. Mix first five ingredients. Cut in butter or shortening. Pat ⅔ of this mixture in a 9x13 inch pan. Beat jam or jelly with a fork and spread on top of crust. Sprinkle with remaining crumb mixture. Bake 30 to 35 minutes until lightly browned. Cut while still warm and cool completely. Makes 36 bars.

Lion Connie Hughes, Foley Lions Club
Foley, AL, USA

GAIL'S BUTTER BARS

1 Duncan Hines yellow cake mix
¼ lb. butter, melted

1 egg
¾ c. chopped walnuts

Filling:

1 (8 oz.) cream cheese
1 lb. confectioners sugar

2 eggs

Mix together yellow cake mix with melted butter. Press into bottom of jellyroll pan or cookie sheet with sides. Sprinkle chopped walnuts over the pressed mixture.

Filling: Beat cream cheese, eggs, and sugar well. Pour over top of walnuts. Spread out to edges.

Bake at 350° for 35 minutes. When cool, sprinkle with confectioners sugar and cut into squares.

This recipe came from my friend, Gail Buss, who is Maryland's Field Editor for "Taste of Home" magazine.

Nicki Florentine, Silver Run-Union Mills Lions Club
Westminster, MD, USA

FRUIT PIZZA

1 roll Pillsbury sugar cookie mix
1 (8 oz.) Philadelphia cream
   cheese
½ c. sugar
2 tsp. vanilla
⅛ c. lemon juice
½ c. orange juice

½ c. water
2 Tbsp. corn starch
Sliced fresh fruit - grapes,
   bananas, kiwi, strawberries,
   pineapple, etc.

Press cookie mix onto pizza pan. Bake at 350° for 15 minutes. Mix cream cheese, sugar, and vanilla. Spread over cooled cookie pizza. Cover cookie pizza with sliced fruit. Boil lemon and orange juices, water, and corn starch for 1 minute. Cool and pour over whole pizza. Makes 2 (14 inch) pizzas or 1 (16 to 18 inch) pizza.

So easy to make - beautiful on your table. So delicious to eat!

Lion Judy Hoffman, Southport Lions Club
Indianapolis, IN, USA

PIZZA BARS

Cream:

1 c. brown sugar

1 c. oleo

Add:

1½ c. flour
½ tsp. soda

2 c. oatmeal

Pat in jellyroll pan. Bake at 350° for 13 minutes. Spread ½ to ¾ jar Mrs. Richardson butterscotch caramel/fudge sauce on hot crust.

Sprinkle with:

1 c. mini M&M's

1 c. mini chocolate chips

Drizzle with 3 squares melted white almond bark. Chill.

Carol Waller, Stewart Lions Club
Stewart, MN, USA

Honesty in little things is not a little thing.

MUD HENS

1 c. butter or margarine
1 c. granulated sugar
2 eggs (save one white for last)
1½ c. plain flour, sifted
1 tsp. baking powder

½ tsp. salt
½ tsp. vanilla
1 c. chopped nuts (walnuts or
    pecans)
1 c. dark brown sugar

Sift together flour, baking powder, and salt. Mix all together, then spread mix on cookie sheet (greased lightly). Beat one egg white with one cup dark brown sugar and spread on top. Bake in 300° oven about 25 minutes until light brown. Cool completely before cutting in squares.

Dottie Sabo, Bellville Lions Club
Bellville, GA, USA

KUCHEN BARS

Crust:

1 c. butter, melted
1 c. sugar
2 eggs

1 tsp. vanilla
2 c. flour

Mix all together and spread crust into a greased jellyroll pan.

Fruit:

2 large cans peaches, sliced and
    drained or 2½ c. fresh
    peaches or 3 to 4 c. chopped
    rhubarb

Arrange evenly on crust.

Filling:

4 eggs
1½ c. sugar

2 Tbsp. flour

Mix ingredients and pour over fruit on crust. Sprinkle with cinnamon and bake in 350° oven for 30 minutes or longer until filling is set.

Lion Micheal and Ruth (Sauskojus) Bartolf,
Oxbow and District Lions Club
Oxbow, Saskatchewan, Canada

Being a grandparent is God's compensation for growing older.

LEMON CUSTARD SQUARES

Bottom:

1 c. flour
1 c. graham wafer crumbs
1 c. coconut
1 c. brown sugar

½ tsp. baking soda
½ tsp. salt
½ c. butter

Rub together and press half of mixture into 8x8 inch pan.

Filling:

1 tin condensed milk
2 egg yolks

½ c. lemon juice

Beat milk. Add egg yolks and lemon juice. Beat 1 minute. Put on bottom mixture.

Topping:

2 egg whites

2 Tbsp. sugar

Beat egg whites and sugar. Spread on top of filling. Sprinkle with remaining crumbs. Bake in 350° oven until brown, about 20 minutes.

Lion Micheal and Ruth (Sauskojus) Bartolf,
Oxbow and District Lions Club
Oxbow, Saskatchewan, Canada

CALIFORNIA APRICOT POWER BARS

2 c. California dried apricots,
  coarsely chopped (12 oz.)
2½ c. pecans, coarsely chopped
  (10 oz.)
1¼ c. pitted dates, coarsely
  chopped (8 oz.)

1¼ c. whole wheat flour
1 tsp. baking powder
1 c. firmly packed brown sugar
3 large eggs
¼ c. apple juice or water
1½ tsp. vanilla

Preheat oven to 350°F. Line a 15½ x 10½ x 1 inch jellyroll pan with foil. In a large bowl, stir together apricots, pecans, and dates; divide in half. In a small bowl, combine flour and baking powder; add to half of the fruit and nut mixture. Toss to coat.

In a medium bowl, combine brown sugar, eggs, apple juice, and vanilla; stir into flour mixture until thoroughly moistened. Spread batter evenly into prepared pan. Lightly press remaining fruit and nut mixture on top. Bake 20 minutes or until bars are golden and spring back when pressed lightly. Cool in pan 5 minutes. Turn out onto wire rack; cool 45 minutes. Peel off foil and cut into bars. Store in an airtight container. Bars freeze well.

Lion Ruth McGregor, Lake of the Woods Lions Club
Kenora, Ontario, Canada

PINEAPPLE SQUARES

2 eggs
1½ c. sugar
1 (16 or 20 oz.) can crushed
　pineapple
2¼ c. flour

1½ tsp. soda
½ tsp. salt
1 tsp. vanilla
1½ c. coconut
½ c. nuts (optional)

Beat eggs and sugar together. Add pineapple (do not drain). Add flour, soda, salt, vanilla, and nuts. Spread coconut over top of cookies, after pouring on baking sheet (greased and floured). Bake at 350° for 20 to 25 minutes.

Glaze:

¾ c. sugar
½ c. oleo

¼ c. canned milk
½ tsp. vanilla

Boil all ingredients for 2 minutes. Do not cool. Pour over bars approximately 5 minutes after they come from oven. Delicious!!

Olive Higinbotham, Bentleyville Lioness Club
Bentleyville, PA, USA

There is no elevator to success. You have to take the stairs.

The only thing you owe life is to become the best you can be.

It's easier to keep up than to catch up.

Going the extra mile puts you miles ahead of your competition.

COOKIES

CHIP AHOY CHOCOLATE CHIP COOKIES

⅔ c. shortening
⅔ c. butter or margarine,
   softened
1 c. sugar
1 c. brown sugar, packed
2 eggs, slightly beaten
2 tsp. vanilla

3½ c. all-purpose flour
1 tsp. baking soda
1 tsp. salt
1 c. pecans, chopped
2 (6 oz.) pkg. chocolate chips

Cream in a large mixing bowl shortening, butter or margarine, sugar, and brown sugar until fluffy. Add slightly beaten eggs and vanilla. Stir in flour, soda, and salt. Mix well, then stir in pecans and chocolate chips and stir until mixed well. Drop by rounded teaspoonfuls 2 inches apart onto an ungreased baking sheet. Bake in a preheated 375° oven until light brown, 8 to 10 minutes. Cool slightly before removing from baking sheet. Yield: About 4 dozen cookies.

Dorothy Coon, Hutchinson Breakfast Lions Club
Hutchinson, KS, USA

CHOCOLATE CHIP NEW MOON COOKIES

2 sticks margarine
10 Tbsp. powdered sugar
6 oz. chocolate chips
2 c. chopped pecans

2½ c. sifted flour
3 tsp. vanilla
Extra powdered sugar

Mix the margarine and sugar together. Add rest of the ingredients except for the extra powdered sugar. Make cookies, shaping each one like a "moon." Place the cookies on an ungreased baking sheet. Bake at 350° for 15 to 20 minutes or until brown. Cool and roll in the extra powdered sugar.

Joan Katz, Stafford-Missouri City Lions Club
Stafford, TX, USA

Choices made in adolescence have long-term consequences.

It is impossible to teach without learning something yourself.

CHOCOLATE CHIP COOKIES PLUS

4 sticks oleo or butter, softened
1½ c. granulated sugar
1½ c. firmly packed brown sugar
4 eggs
2 tsp. vanilla
4½ c. presifted flour
2 tsp. baking soda
2 tsp. salt (less if desired)
1 (24 oz.) pkg. chocolate chips
1 c. chopped nuts (cashews, pecans, almonds, or mixed)
1 c. oatmeal
½ c. shredded coconut
¼ c. water

Preheat oven to 375°. Beat oleo or butter, sugars, eggs, and vanilla in large bowl until light and fluffy. Mix in flour, baking soda, and salt, then rest of the ingredients. Drop dough with scoops (mounded) from ice cream scoop on ungreased cookie sheets, at least 2 inches apart. Bake 10 minutes or until golden brown.

This makes man-sized cookies, not like the dainty ones my wife makes. I put in anything I can find in the kitchen, but draw the line at raisins!

Jim Ball, Columbus Noon Lions
Columbus, NE

NEIMAN-MARCUS COOKIES
(Recipe may be halved)

2 c. butter
4 c. flour
2 tsp. soda
2 c. sugar
5 c. blended oatmeal (measure oatmeal and blend in a blender to a fine powder)
24 oz. chocolate chips
2 c. brown sugar
1 tsp. salt
1 (8 oz.) Hershey's bar, grated
4 eggs
2 tsp. baking powder
2 tsp. vanilla
2 c. chopped nuts (your choice)

Cream the butter and both sugars. Add eggs and vanilla; mix together with flour, oatmeal, salt, baking powder, and soda. Add chocolate chips, Hershey's bar, and nuts. Roll into balls and place two inches apart on a cookie sheet. Bake for 10 minutes at 375°. Makes 112 cookies.

Have fun!!! This is not a joke - this is a true story. Ride free citizens!

Carol Waller, Stewart Lions Club
Stewart, MN, USA

If you depend on others to make you happy, you'll be endlessly disappointed.

CHOCOLATE-CHIP FRUIT DROPS

2⅓ c. flour
1 tsp. baking soda
¾ tsp. salt
¾ tsp. ground nutmeg
¼ tsp. ground cinnamon
1 c. whole candied cherries
½ lb. unsalted butter (at room temperature)

⅔ c. granulated sugar
⅓ c. light brown sugar
½ tsp. vanilla extract
2 tsp. rum or brandy extract
2 eggs
1 c. chocolate chips
1½ c. pecan pieces
1 c. diced candied orange peel

Heat oven to 325°. Combine flour, soda, salt, and spices. Cut cherries in halves. Beat butter and sugars until fluffy. Beat in extracts and the eggs. Beat in flour mixture. Stir in cherries, chocolate chips, pecans, and orange peel. Drop dough by rounded teaspoonfuls on ungreased baking sheets, about 2 inches apart. Bake until edges just start to brown, about 12 minutes. Let stand on baking sheets 1 minute. Remove and cool on wire racks. Makes about 84 cookies.

Per cookie: 78 calories, 1 g protein, 4 g fat, 32 mg sodium, 10 g carbohydrate, 11 mg cholesterol.

Barbara Joy Hess, Clarence Lions Club
Clarence Center, NY, USA

ORANGE CHOCOLATE-CHIP COOKIES

1 orange
1¾ c. flour
¾ tsp. baking soda
½ tsp. salt
6 oz. unsalted butter (at room temperature)
½ c. granulated sugar

¼ c. brown sugar
1 egg
1 egg yolk
½ tsp. vanilla extract
12 oz. semi-sweet chocolate chips (2 c.)

Heat oven to 325°. Grate 1½ teaspoons of the colored zest from the orange and squeeze 2 tablespoons juice. Combine the flour, soda, and salt. Beat butter, sugars, and orange zest until fluffy. Beat in egg, yolk, vanilla, and orange juice. Beat in flour mixture. Stir in chocolate chips with a spoon. Drop by teaspoonfuls, about 2 inches apart, onto ungreased baking sheets. Bake until edges start to brown, about 15 minutes. Let stand on baking sheets 1 minute and remove to wire racks. Makes about 3 dozen.

Per cookie: 115 calories, 1 g protein, 6 g fat, 48 mg sodium, 14 g carbohydrate, 21 mg cholesterol.

Barbara Joy Hess, Clarence Lions Club
Clarence Center, NY, USA

You shouldn't fight a battle if there's nothing to win.

CHOCOLATE M&M'S COOKIES

1¾ c. flour
½ c. unsweetened cocoa powder
¾ tsp. baking soda
½ tsp. salt
6 oz. unsalted butter (at room temperature)

1 c. sugar
2 eggs
1 tsp. vanilla extract
1 c. miniature semi-sweet M&M's
+ more for decorating

Heat the oven to 325°. Combine the flour, cocoa, soda, and salt. With an electric mixer set at medium speed, beat butter and sugar until creamy. Beat in the eggs and vanilla. Reduce speed and beat in flour mixture. Stir in 1 cup M&M's. Drop the dough by rounded teaspoonfuls onto ungreased baking sheets, about 2 inches apart. Press a few extra M&M's onto the top of each cookie. Bake until edges are firm, but centers are still slightly soft, 12 to 15 minutes. Makes 3 dozen cookies.

Per cookie: 120 calories, 1 g protein, 6 g fat, 52 mg sodium, 15 g carbohydrate, 22 mg cholesterol.

Mrs. Mike Nowicki, Clarence Lions Club
Clarence Center, NY, USA

COOKIE JUMBLES

1 c. sugar
1 c. brown sugar
1 c. peanut butter
2 sticks butter

2 eggs
2 c. flour
1 tsp. baking soda
1½ c. M&M's

Cream first 4 ingredients until fluffy. Mix in remaining ingredients. Drop by spoonful on greased cookie sheet. Bake at 350° for 12 minutes.

M&M'S COOKIES

1 c. shortening
1 c. brown sugar
½ c. granulated sugar
2 tsp. vanilla
2 eggs

2¼ c. sifted all-purpose flour
1 tsp. soda
1 tsp. salt
1½ c. M&M's plain chocolate pieces

Blend shortening and sugars. Beat in vanilla and eggs. Sift dry ingredients; add to the sugar and egg mixture. Mix well. Stir in ½ cup M&M's. Reserve remaining candies for decorations. Drop from teaspoon onto ungreased cookie sheet. Decorate tops of cookies with remaining candies. Bake at 375° for 10 to 12 minutes or until golden brown. Makes about 6 dozen.

I have been making these since my son was small. As an adult, he still says, make M&M's.

Lion Gloria Bonager, East Prospect Lions Club
East Prospect, PA, USA

GRAN'S MOLASSES SUGAR COOKIES

¾ c. butter
1 c. sugar
¼ c. molasses
1 egg
2 tsp. baking soda

2 c. flour
½ tsp. cloves
½ tsp. ginger
½ tsp. salt
1 tsp. cinnamon

Melt butter; add sugar, molasses, and egg. Beat well. Fold in flour and spices. *Chill thoroughly.* Roll on floured pastry sheet and cut into shapes. Bake at 375° for 8 to 10 minutes. Yield: 4 dozen.

Wonderful old-time cookies. Happy baking!

Lion Carol Kellner, Annapolis Lions Club
Annapolis, MD, USA

MELTING MOMENTS

2 sticks butter, softened
⅓ c. powdered sugar

2 c. sifted all-purpose flour

Cream butter and sugar until fluffy. Gradually blend in flour. Beat at low speed until smooth. Roll ½ teaspoon of dough into marble sized balls. Place on ungreased cookie sheet or baking stone and flatten with a fork. Bake at 350° for 10 to 15 minutes. Put 2 cookies together with frosting when they are cool.

Frosting:

1½ c. powdered sugar
3 Tbsp. butter

¼ tsp. almond extract
2 Tbsp. cream

Blend all ingredients until creamy. For variation, divide frosting and use other flavors. Lemon or coconut is good.

Nettie Favara, Greenwood Lions Club
Greenwood, MS, USA

If you want to do something positive for your children,
try to improve your marriage.

❧ ❧ ❧

Everyone has something to teach.

BASIC ICEBOX SUGAR COOKIES

These are recipes I have found in the "Cooking Light Magazine" and have added my own touches.

1 c. all-purpose flour
¼ tsp. baking soda
⅛ tsp. salt
¼ c. stick margarine, softened

⅔ c. sugar
1 tsp. vanilla extract
1 large egg white (I use 1 whole egg)

Combine first 3 ingredients in a bowl and set aside. Beat margarine and sugar; add vanilla and egg until light and fluffy. Add flour mixture and stir until well blended. Turn dough out onto wax paper; shape into a 6 inch log. Wrap log in wax paper and freeze 3 hours or until very firm.

Preheat oven to 350°. Cut log into 24 (¼ inch) slices and place slices 1 inch apart on baking sheet coated with cooking spray or very lightly greased. Bake at 350° for 8 to 10 minutes (I bake for 9 minutes). Remove from baking sheets and cool on wire racks. Store in your favorite cookie jar.

You can add ¼ cup peanut butter and just a little more flour so the dough will be stiff enough to make into a log. You can roll the logs into brown sugar or finely chopped nuts before slicing. Just a slight variation.

My grandchildren love them. I hope yours will too.

Lion Janice Elliott, Meredith Lions Club
Meredith, NH, USA

SUGAR COOKIES

4 c. flour
1 tsp. cream of tartar
½ tsp. salt
1 c. shortening
1 tsp. soda

1 c. milk
2 eggs
1 c. sugar
1 tsp. vanilla
½ tsp. nutmeg

Mix together flour, cream of tartar, and salt. Cut in 1 cup shortening. Dissolve soda in milk and add. Mix 2 eggs with sugar, vanilla, and nutmeg and stir all together. Chill. Roll out and cut as desired. Bake at 350° for 8 to 9 minutes.

Pauline and PDG Gerald Nuffer, South Jefferson Lions Club
Adams, NY

How people treat you is more a reflection of
how they see themselves than how they see you.

SUGAR COOKIES

1 c. sugar
1 c. shortening
1 c. sour milk
1 tsp. baking soda

1 egg
1 tsp. nutmeg
1 tsp. vanilla
Approx. 3½ c. flour

Put baking soda in the sour milk and let sit while doing the following. Cream together shortening, sugar, nutmeg, and vanilla. Add egg and mix well, then add milk and stir together. Add flour slowly until you have a soft mix. Place dough in refrigerator overnight. Roll out and cut. Bake at 375° in oven approximately 15 minutes.

Karen is a quilter and made a beautiful Lions quilt using her own created pattern to celebrate South Jefferson Lions Club 50th anniversary!

Eric and Karen Dutton, South Jefferson Lions Club
Adams, NY

SUGAR COOKIES

1 c. powdered sugar
1 c. white sugar
1 c. butter
1 c. oil
2 eggs

1 tsp. vanilla
4 c. flour plus 4 heaping Tbsp.
1 tsp. salt
1 tsp. soda
1 tsp. cream of tartar

Mix all ingredients. Roll dough into small balls. Place on ungreased cookie sheet. Press down with glass dipped in sugar. Bake at 350° for 10 to 15 minutes until golden brown. Makes about 4 dozen.

Lion Bev Wilkes, Plato Lions Club
Young America, MN, USA

THE BEST SUGAR COOKIES

1½ c. butter flavor Crisco
2 c. sugar
4 c. flour
3 tsp. baking powder

1 tsp. baking soda
1½ c. sour milk or buttermilk
4 eggs
1¼ tsp. vanilla

Color sprinkles can be used at holiday times (optional). If used, sprinkle on cookies before they go into oven.

Cream shortening and sugar. Add eggs and vanilla. Alternate 1 cup sour milk and dry ingredients. Put soda in ½ cup sour milk and add last. Drop by tablespoonfuls onto greased cookie sheet. Bake at 375° until lightly browned.

In honor of Guy, Doris, and Doug Brewer, who have given jobs to countless individuals at Brewer's Market in Silver Run, Maryland.

Lion Ann K. Brumback, Silver Run Union Mills Lions Club
Westminster, MD, USA

SUGAR AND SPICE GIFT COOKIES

2 c. flour
¾ tsp. salt
½ tsp. baking powder
1 tsp. ground ginger
¾ tsp. ground cinnamon
½ tsp. ground allspice
¼ tsp. ground nutmeg

5 oz. unsalted butter (at room temperature)
⅔ c. light brown sugar
½ tsp. vanilla extract
1 egg
3 c. confectioners sugar
Green and red food coloring

Combine flour, salt, baking powder, and spices. Beat butter and sugar until fluffy. Beat in vanilla and egg and then flour mixture. Divide in thirds and chill 1 hour. Heat oven to 350°. Roll dough, a piece at a time, between sheets of floured waxed paper to ⅛ inch thick. With knife or pastry cutter, cut into 1½ x 2½ inch rectangles. Bake on ungreased baking sheets until edges brown, 8 to 12 minutes. Cool. Stir ¼ cup water into confectioners sugar. Divide in three and tint ⅓ red and ⅓ green. Frost and decorate as desired. Makes about 48 cookies.

Per cookie: 83 calories, 1 g protein, 3 g fat, 41 mg sodium, 14 g carbohydrate, 11 mg cholesterol.

Joann M. Brownell, Clarence Lions Club
Clarence Center, NY, USA

CHRISTMAS CUT-OUTS

2 c. sugar
4 c. oleo or butter (preferred)
¼ tsp. salt

5 tsp. baking powder
2 c. milk
9 c. flour (about)

Cream sugar and butter thoroughly. Add baking powder and salt. Add milk and flour alternately, adding only enough flour to handle. Roll on well-floured cloth, ⅛ to ¼ inch thick. Cut into desired shapes. Bake on ungreased cookie sheet at 350° for 10 to 12 minutes or until edges are light brown. When cool, frost and decorate. Yield: Approximately 18 dozen.

Note: Dough does not toughen if rerolled. Recipe can be divided successfully for smaller batches.

Thousands were made by a Wausau, Wisconsin, doctor and his wife to share with children hospitalized over Christmas. This is a 1930's recipe.

Martin Findling, Princeton Lions Club
Princeton, IL, USA

Envy is the enemy of happiness.

SOUTHERN PRALINES

2 c. white sugar
5 Tbsp. light brown sugar
Dash of salt (about ⅛ tsp.)
⅔ c. pure whipping cream

⅓ c. white Karo syrup
1 tsp. vanilla
¼ tsp. soda
2 or 3 c. chopped pecans

Cook first five ingredients till soft ball forms in cold water. Remove from heat; add soda, vanilla, and pecans. Beat until gloss is gone. Dip by tablespoon onto wax paper.

Not once has this recipe failed with me.

Katie Nell Smith, Brookhaven Alpha Lions Club
Brookhaven, MS, USA

MAPLE BUTTERNUT CHEWIES

½ c. melted butter flavor Crisco
2 eggs
2 c. firmly packed light brown
  sugar
1½ tsp. maple flavoring

1½ c. unsifted flour (all-purpose)
2 tsp. baking powder
½ tsp. salt
1 c. finely chopped nuts
White chocolate bits (optional)

Preheat oven to 350°F. Grease 13x9x2 inch pan with butter flavor Crisco. Beat eggs until light and foamy in large bowl of electric mixer with baking powder and salt. Beat in sugar, maple flavor, and butter flavor Crisco until creamy. Combine flour, baking powder, and salt. Add to egg mixture. Mix at low speed until blended. Mixture will be stiff. Use wooden spoon to stir in nuts. Spread evenly in prepared pan. Bake at 350° for 25 to 30 minutes. Do not overbake. Cool 10 to 15 minutes. Cut into bars. Makes two dozen.

This is for all of us who cannot eat chocolate. You may add a cup of white chocolate or vanilla bits to this recipe if you wish.

Lion Ann K. Brumback, Silver Run Union Mills Lions Club
Westminster, MD

Love is a great investment. No matter whom
you give it to, it returns great dividends.

❦ ❦ ❦

The two happiest days of my life were the day I bought my boat,
and the day I sold my boat.

2075-99

CAROL'S SOFT COOKIES

2 c. sugar
1 c. margarine
3 eggs
1 c. sour cream
2 tsp. vanilla

4 c. flour
1 tsp. baking powder
1 tsp. baking soda
Dash of salt (optional)

Preheat oven to 350°. Cream sugar and margarine. Add eggs, sour cream, and vanilla, then add dry ingredients. Use electric mixer and mix thoroughly. Drop by tablespoon on greased sheets. Bake 8 minutes. Watch closely. Cookies should be light in color. Do not brown. Remove from oven and cool.

Frost with a thin icing made from confectioners sugar and a little milk. Decorate with colored sprinkles or color as desired.

These are very versatile for any holiday or special function.

Carol Ludwick, Lyons-Muir Lions Club
Muir, MI, USA

FORGOTTEN COOKIES

2 egg whites
⅔ c. white sugar
Dash of salt

1 c. chocolate chips
1 c. nuts (coarse)

Preheat oven to 350°. Beat whites until stiff. Add salt. Add sugar, small amount at a time, and continue beating until like meringue. Blend in nuts and chocolate chips. Drop by spoonfuls on foil. Place in heated oven. Turn oven off. Cookies are done when oven is cool, preferably overnight. Makes 24 medium size.

Nancy Pence, Elizabethtown Lions Club
Elizabethtown, KY, USA

MOLASSES COOKIES

1 c. shortening
1½ c. sugar
½ c. molasses (light)
2 eggs

4 tsp. soda
1 tsp. cinnamon
4½ c. flour
1 tsp. salt

Cream shortening and sugar. Add molasses and eggs. Sift flour, salt, soda, and cinnamon together and add to above mixture. Shape into small balls. Roll in sugar and place on cookie sheet. Bake in preheated oven at 375° for 10 to 12 minutes.

Mrs. Max (Minna) Kennedy, Princeton Lions Club
Princeton, IL, USA

ZUCCHINI COOKIES

Beat ¾ cup sugar and ¾ cup melted butter.

Blend in:

1 egg	1 tsp. baking soda
2 c. flour	1 c. zucchini
2 tsp. vanilla	¼ c. walnuts
1 tsp. cinnamon	¼ c. raisins

Bake in 350° oven for 10 to 15 minutes.

Debra James, Beekmantown Lions Club
West Chazy, NY

SAND TARTS

2 c. margarine, softened	1½ tsp. clear vanilla
2½ c. sugar	4 c. flour
2 eggs	

Use a pastry blender to mix the margarine and sugar together. Beat eggs in a separate bowl. Add to margarine and sugar mixture with the clear vanilla.

Mix in the sifted flour until it forms like dough. Chill for 3 hours or overnight in the refrigerator. Roll out dough on floured surface, making a thin layer. Form the Sand Tart with any cookie cutter. Place on cookie sheet. Sprinkle with decorator colored sugars. Bake at 350° for 10 minutes. Keep checking to make sure the cookies don't get dark brown around edges.

This recipe brings a family together. Everybody wants a part in making these. In memory of my mom and many happy times in the kitchen.

Nicki Florentine, Silver Run-Union Mills Lions Club
Westminster, MD, USA

MARIAN'S CREAM DELIGHTS

2 c. granulated sugar	1 tsp. vanilla
2 c. butter or margarine	½ tsp. baking soda
2 eggs	6 Tbsp. cream (or milk)
4½ c. plain flour	

Cream sugar and butter until light and fluffy. Add eggs. Mix until well blended. Sift flour and baking soda; add to mixture. Add vanilla and cream. Mix until blended. Drop by teaspoon onto ungreased cookie sheet. Bake in 350° oven about 12 minutes, or until lightly browned around edges.

You may decorate with chopped nuts, sprinkles, or chocolate chips, then bake.

Dottie Sabo, Bellville Lions Club
Bellville, GA, USA

NUTTY CLUB CRACKER COOKIES

42 club crackers (2½ x 1 inch)
½ c. butter or oleo
½ c. sugar

1 tsp. vanilla
1 c. slivered almonds

Place crackers on a greased (oleo) 15x10 inch pan in a single layer. In a saucepan over medium heat, melt butter. Add sugar. Bring to a boil, stirring constantly. Boil slowly for 2 minutes. Remove from heat. Add vanilla. Pour evenly over crackers; sprinkle with nuts. Bake at 350° for 10 minutes or until lightly browned. Immediately remove from the pan. Cool on wire racks. Store in an airtight container. Makes 3½ dozen.

Katheryn Thompson, Ave. of Pines Lions Club
Deer River, MN

ANISE CHRISTMAS MERINGUES

4 egg whites
½ tsp. cream of tartar
Pinch of salt

1 c. sugar
¼ tsp. anise seeds
Red and green colored sugars

Heat the oven to 250°. Line baking sheets with foil. With an electric mixer set at medium speed, beat the egg whites with the cream of tartar and salt until they hold soft peaks. Increase speed to high and beat in the sugar gradually. Continue beating until the whites hold stiff peaks. Beat in the anise seeds. Drop by heaping teaspoonfuls, about 2 inches apart, onto the baking sheets. Sprinkle with colored sugar. Bake until firm to the touch, 40 to 45 minutes. Centers will still be soft. Let stand about 30 seconds on baking sheets before removing. Makes 40 meringues.

Per meringue: 21 calories, 0 g protein, 0 g fat, 9 mg sodium, 5 g carbohydrate, 0 mg cholesterol.

Barbara Joy Hess, Clarence Lions Club
Clarence Center, NY, USA

ANISE CHRISTMAS COOKIES

3 eggs
1 c. sugar

1 Tbsp. anise seed
1½ to 2 c. flour

Beat eggs very light. Add sugar. Continue beating for about 10 minutes. Best using an electric mixer. Add flour, 1 teaspoon baking powder and anise seed, rolled fine. Beat again. Drop by ½ teaspoon in well greased and floured pans, 1 inch apart. Let stand overnight or about ten hours at room temperature to dry. Bake in a 350°F. oven till light brown.

Micheal and Ruth Bartolf, Oxbow and District Lions Club
Oxbow, Saskatchewan, Canada

SUNFLOWER SEED COOKIES

1 c. butter
1 c. firmly packed brown sugar
1 c. sugar
2 eggs
1 tsp. vanilla

1½ c. unsifted flour
½ tsp. soda
3 c. quick-cooking rolled oats
1 c. shelled sunflower seeds

Thoroughly cream together butter and sugar; add eggs and vanilla. Blend well. Add flour, salt, soda, and oatmeal. Mix thoroughly. Gently blend in sunflower seeds. Form in long rolls, about 1½ inches in diameter; wrap in plastic wrap. Chill thoroughly. Slice ¼ inch thick. Bake on ungreased sheet for 10 minutes at 350°. Store airtight. Yields 9 dozen.

Sarah Wehling, Bothell Lions Club
Bothell, WA, USA

STARS AND STRIPES COOKIES

1 c. butter (at room temperature)
¾ c. sugar
1 egg
2 tsp. vanilla
3 c. all-purpose flour, divided
2 tsp. baking powder
¼ c. peanut butter

4 (1 oz.) sq. semi-sweet
   chocolate, melted
¾ c. confectioners sugar
1 Tbsp. milk
1 Tbsp. blue colored sugar
1 Tbsp. red colored sugar

Preheat oven to 350°F. In medium bowl, with electric mixer at high, beat butter and sugar until fluffy. Reduce speed to low; add egg and vanilla. Stir in 2¾ cups flour and baking powder until just blended. Divide dough into 2 equal halves. Remove one half of dough to medium bowl; stir in peanut butter and 2 tablespoons flour just until blended.

To remaining dough, stir in chocolate and remaining 2 tablespoons flour just until blended. On lightly floured sheet of waxed paper, roll out each ball of dough ¼ inch thick. Chill 10 minutes to firm dough. Using a 2 inch and a 3 inch star cookie cutter, cut out 16 shapes of each size from each dough. If necessary, roll up scraps and chill again to get the required number of cutouts. Place larger stars onto greased cookie sheets. Place smaller stars on top of opposite-colored larger ones. Bake 12 to 14 minutes or until lightly browned. Remove to wire racks to cool.

In small bowl, stir together confectioners sugar and milk until smooth. If needed, add more drops of milk in order to achieve a ribbon-shaped drizzle. To insure easy cleanup, place a piece of wax paper beneath wire rack before glazing. Dip tines of fork into glaze and drizzle over cookies. Lightly sprinkle with colored sugars. Let stand until glaze is firm and set. Makes 32 cookies.

Work time: 45 minutes. Total time: 1 hour and 15 minutes.

Per cookie: 154 calories, 2 g protein, 19 g carbohydrate, 8 g fat, 22 mg cholesterol, 79 mg sodium.

Mrs. Lucy Aiken, Clarence Lions Club
Clarence Center, NY, USA

2075-99

BROWN SUGAR BUTTER COOKIES

¾ c. butter or margarine,
   softened
½ c. brown sugar
½ c. white sugar
1 egg

1½ tsp. vanilla extract
2¼ c. flour
½ tsp. baking soda
½ tsp. cream of tartar

Heat oven to 350°. Cream together butter and sugars. Add egg and vanilla; beat until smooth. Sift in dry ingredients and mix until a soft dough forms. Wrap dough in plastic wrap and chill for 2 hours. On a floured surface, roll out ½ of the dough to ¼ inch thickness. Cut out cookies with cutters and place on a lightly greased cookie sheet. Bake 7 to 9 minutes or until bottoms are lightly browned.

I roll the dough into balls (without chilling), place onto a cookie sheet, and stamp with a cookie press. Bake 10 to 12 minutes or until lightly browned.

Judy Rannow, Arlington (SEA) Lions Club
Arlington, MN, USA

GRANDMA'S ICEBOX COOKIES

1 c. butter
1 c. sugar
1 c. brown sugar
3 eggs
3½ c. flour

1 tsp. baking soda
2 tsp. cinnamon
½ tsp. salt
1 c. finely chopped pecans

Cream butter and sugars. Add eggs, beating well. Sift flour with baking soda, cinnamon, and salt. Add to sugar mixture along with chopped pecans, kneading into a stiff dough. Divide dough into portions on wax paper and roll into 1½ inch diameter. Chill thoroughly and cut into ¼ inch slices. Place on lightly greased cookie sheet and bake in 400° oven until lightly browned. Remove from pan while still warm. Makes approximately 6 dozen cookies.

Dough may be frozen and baked as needed.

Rose Scanlin, Stafford-Missouri City Lions Club
Missouri City, TX, USA

ICEBOX COOKIES

2 c. brown sugar
1 c. butter or oleo
2 beaten eggs
3½ c. flour

1 tsp. salt
1 tsp. soda
½ c. nuts, chopped
1 tsp. vanilla

Mix above. Make 3 rolls. Refrigerate overnight. Slice and bake at 350°. Freeze well to bake later. Garnish, if desired, with nuts or cherries.

Bliss Hammaker, Bullskin Township Lioness Club
Mt. Pleasant, PA

ICEBOX COOKIES

1 c. margarine
2 c. packed brown sugar
3½ c. all-purpose flour
1 tsp. soda

1 tsp. cinnamon
1 tsp. vanilla extract
2 eggs
1 c. chopped pecans

Cream margarine and sugar. Add flour with soda in last cup. Add cinnamon, nuts, eggs, and vanilla. Mix well with hands. Make into rolls, about 1 to 1½ inches round and 8 to 10 inches long. Wrap in wax paper and refrigerate overnight. Cut in thin slices and bake on ungreased cookie sheet at 375° for 10 to 12 minutes.

Rolls may frozen and baked as needed.

Mildred Court, Stafford-Missouri City Lions Club
Stafford, TX, USA

VANILLA GOBS AND ICING

2 c. sugar
1 c. milk
½ tsp. salt
4½ c. flour
1 tsp. vanilla

½ c. Crisco
2 tsp. baking powder
2 eggs
1 tsp. soda

Mix all together. Roll in small balls in powdered sugar. Bake 10 minutes at 375°. When cool, cut in half and ice. (Dough will be sticky.)

Icing:

½ c. oleo
1 c. sugar
1 c. milk

½ c. Crisco
1 large instant pudding
1 tsp. vanilla

Beat at high speed until thick and fluffy.

Bullskin Township Lioness Club
Mt. Pleasant, PA

COWBOY COOKIES

2 c. flour
1 tsp. baking soda
1 c. margarine, softened
2 eggs
2 c. quick oats

1 tsp. vanilla
2 c. raisins
½ tsp. baking powder
1 c. sugar
1 c. packed brown sugar

Blend margarine and sugars. Add eggs and vanilla and beat until fluffy. Add flour mixture and mix well. Add oatmeal and fold in raisins carefully. Drop by teaspoon onto a greased cookie sheet. Bake at 350° for 12 minutes.

One-half cup nutmeats may be added.

Leola C. Jurrens, Downtown Bartlesville Lions Club
Bartlesville, OK, USA

2075-99

AMARETTO BISCOTTI (TWICE BAKED COOKIE)

1 c. sugar
½ c. butter or margarine, melted
3 Tbsp. Amaretto liqueur
¾ tsp. almond extract
¾ tsp. vanilla extract

3 eggs
3 c. all-purpose flour
1½ tsp. baking powder
¾ c. sliced almonds, toasted
¾ c. maraschino cherries

Note: For a more flavorful cookie, marinate the maraschino cherries, quartered, in the Amaretto liqueur overnight. Before starting to make batter, drain cherries and reserve the Amaretto.

In a large bowl, stir together sugar, butter, Amaretto, almond extract, and vanilla extract. Beat in eggs. In another bowl, stir together flour and baking powder; gradually add to sugar mixture, blending thoroughly. Mix in almonds and cherries. Cover tightly with plastic wrap and refrigerate for 2 to 3 hours. Directly on greased baking sheet, shape dough with your hands to form two loaves about 2 inches wide the length of the baking sheet. Place loaves about 4 inches apart. Bake in a preheated 375°F. oven for 20 minutes, or until lightly browned. Remove from oven and let cool on baking sheet about 15 minutes. Cut diagonally into ½ inch thick slices. Place slices close together, cut sides down, on baking sheet; bake for 10 minutes. Turn slices over and bake for another 10 minutes. Cool on a rack. Store in an airtight container.

Lion Joan Shores, St. Charles Lions Club
St. Charles, MO, USA

CUTE KITTY COOKIES

½ c. butter or margarine,
    softened
¼ c. shortening
1 c. sugar
2 eggs
1 tsp. vanilla extract
2¼ c. all-purpose flour
¾ tsp. baking powder
½ tsp. salt

1 c. quick-cooking oats
2 (1 oz.) sq. unsweetened
    chocolate, melted and cooled
Semi-sweet chocolate chips
Red-hot candies
Black shoestring licorice, cut into
    1½ inch pieces

In a mixing bowl, cream butter, shortening, and sugar. Add eggs, one at a time, beating well after each addition. Beat in vanilla. Combine flour, baking powder, and salt; gradually add to the creamed mixture. Stir in oats. Divide dough in half. Add melted chocolate to one portion. Roll plain dough into an 8 inch log. Roll chocolate dough between waxed paper into an 8 inch square. Place log at one end of square; roll up. Wrap in plastic wrap; refrigerate for at least 3 hours. Cut into ¼ inch slices. Place on ungreased baking sheets. To form ears, pinch two triangles on the top of each cookie. Bake at 350° for 8 to 10 minutes or until lightly browned. Immediately place two chocolate chips for eyes, a red-hot for the nose, and six pieces of licorice on each for whiskers. Cool on wire racks. Yield: 3 dozen.

VANILLA WAFER COOKIES

½ c. butter (no substitutes),
   softened
1 c. sugar
1 egg

1 Tbsp. vanilla extract
1⅓ c. all-purpose flour
¾ tsp. baking powder
¼ tsp. salt

In a mixing bowl, cream butter and sugar. Beat in egg and vanilla. Combine dry ingredients; add to creamed mixture and mix well. Drop by teaspoonfuls 2 inches apart onto ungreased baking sheets. Bake at 350° for 12 to 15 minutes or until edges are golden brown. Remove to a wire rack to cool. Yield: About 3½ dozen.

DELICIOUS COOKIES

1 c. brown sugar
1 c. white sugar
1 c. shortening
1 c. oil
1 egg
1 tsp. soda
1 tsp. cream of tartar

1 c. coconut
2 tsp. vanilla
1 tsp. coconut flavoring
4 c. flour
1 tsp. salt
1 c. Rice Krispies

Drop by teaspoon on cookie sheet. Press down with fork. Bake at 350° for 12 to 15 minutes.

They are so good that they melt in your mouth.

Lion Bev Wilkens, Plato Lions Club
Young America, MN, USA

RICE KRISPIES COOKIES

1 c. brown sugar
½ c. white sugar
1 c. shortening (or use ½
   margarine)
2 eggs
1 tsp. vanilla
1 c. oatmeal

2 c. Rice Krispies
1 c. coconut
1 c. flour
1 tsp. baking powder
1 tsp. baking soda
½ tsp. salt

Preheat oven to 350°F. In a large bowl, beat together the sugars, shortening, eggs, and vanilla until well blended. Add the remaining ingredients and mix well. Drop by spoonfuls onto greased cookie sheet. Bake for 15 minutes.

Kids love these cookies ... grown up kids too.

Lion Gwen Holmstrom, Lake of the Woods Lions Club
Kenora, Ontario, Canada

2075-99

FARM MOUSE COOKIES

1 c. creamy peanut butter
½ c. butter or margarine,
   softened
½ c. sugar
½ c. packed brown sugar
1 egg
1 tsp. vanilla extract

1½ c. all-purpose flour
½ tsp. baking soda
Peanut halves
Black shoestring licorice, cut into
   2½ inch pieces

    In a mixing bowl, cream peanut butter, butter, and sugars. Beat in egg and vanilla. Combine flour and baking soda; gradually add to creamed mixture. Cover and chill dough for 1 hour or overnight. Roll into 1 inch balls. Pinch one end, forming a teardrop shape. Place 2 inches apart on ungreased baking sheets; press to flatten. For ears, press two peanuts into each cookie near the pointed end. Using a toothpick, make a ½ inch deep hole for the tail in the end opposite the ears. Bake at 350° for 8 to 10 minutes or until golden. While cookies are warm, insert licorice for tails. Cool on wire racks. Yield: 4 dozen.

BUTTERFINGER COOKIES

½ c. butter, softened
¾ c. sugar
⅔ c. packed brown sugar
2 egg whites
1¼ c. chunky peanut butter
1½ tsp. vanilla extract

1 c. all-purpose flour
½ tsp. baking soda
¼ tsp. salt
5 (2.1 oz.) Butterfinger candy
   bars, chopped

    In a mixing bowl, cream butter and sugars. Add egg whites; beat well. Blend in peanut butter and vanilla. Combine flour, baking soda, and salt; add to creamed mixture and mix well. Stir in candy bars. Shape into 1½ inch balls and place on greased baking sheets. Bake at 350° for 10 to 12 minutes or until golden brown. Cool on wire racks. Yield: 4 dozen.

If you wait until all conditions are perfect before you act, you'll never act.

❦ ❦ ❦

Either you control your attitude or it controls you.

DOUBLE TREAT COOKIES

2 c. sifted flour
2 tsp. baking soda
½ tsp. salt
1 c. shortening (butter flavored Crisco)
1 c. white sugar

1 c. brown sugar, packed
2 eggs
1 tsp. vanilla
1 c. peanut butter
1 (6 oz.) pkg. chocolate chips

Sift together flour, baking soda, and salt. Beat together shortening, white and brown sugars, eggs, and vanilla until fluffy. Blend in peanut butter. Add dry sifted ingredients. Stir in chocolate chips. Shape batter into balls and place about 2 inches apart on ungreased baking sheet. Flatten with a drinking glass dipped in sugar. Bake at 350° for 8 minutes or until brown. Makes 7 dozen.

These taste like a combination of peanut butter, chocolate chip, and sugar cookies - all in one!

Kathy Simmons, Princeton Lions Club
Princeton, IL, USA

ONE CUP COOKIES

1 c. butter
1 c. sugar
1 c. brown sugar
3 eggs
1 c. peanut butter
1 c. flour

1 Tbsp. soda
1 c. oatmeal
1 c. coconut
1 c. chopped walnuts
1 c. raisins
1 c. chocolate chips

Cream together sugars and butter. Add eggs and peanut butter and mix well. Add flour, soda, oatmeal, coconut, chopped nuts, raisins, and chocolate chips and mix again. Drop by teaspoon on cookie sheets and bake at 350° for 10 minutes. Yield: 60 cookies.

Pat Worden, South Jefferson Lions Club
Adams, NY

Success is more often the result of hard work than of talent.

Nothing is more precious than a baby's laugh.

2075-99

YUMMY OATMEAL SCOTCHIES
(Cookie)

1 c. margarine (2 sticks)
¼ c. sugar
¾ c. brown sugar
1 (4 serving size) vanilla instant
    pudding (dry)

2 eggs
1¼ c. flour
1 tsp. baking soda
3½ c. quick oatmeal
1 c. butterscotch chips

Mix flour with baking soda. Combine margarine, sugars, and dry pudding mix in a large mixer bowl. Beat in eggs. Gradually add flour mixture, then stir in oatmeal and chips. Batter will be stiff. Drop by teaspoons on ungreased cookie sheet. Bake at 375° for 10 to 12 minutes. Makes 5 dozen.

Chocolate chips, peanut butter chips, or raisins may be substituted. Very good cookies.

Shirley Petersen, Dix Lions Club
Dix, NE

GRANDMA HOOVER'S OATMEAL COOKIES

2 c. quick oatmeal
2 c. flour
1⅓ c. brown sugar
1 c. shortening
½ tsp. baking powder
½ tsp. soda, dissolved in 1 c. hot
    water

½ tsp. salt
2 eggs
1 tsp. vanilla
1 c. nuts, chopped
1 c. raisins

Cream shortening, brown sugar, and eggs. Add rest of ingredients and mix well. Drop by spoons on cookie sheet and bake at 375°. Ice with powdered sugar icing while still hot.

Mrs. Max (Minna) Kennedy, Princeton Lions Club
Princeton, IL, USA

Whenever you need to borrow money, it's best to look prosperous.

❦ ❦ ❦

You always find time to do the things you really want to do.

FANCY OATMEAL COOKIES

1 c. butter
1 c. brown sugar, packed
1 c. granulated sugar
2 eggs
2½ c. flour
1 tsp. baking soda
1 tsp. cinnamon

1 tsp. salt
2 c. quick cooking oats or old-
  fashioned oats
1 c. raisins
¾ c. chopped pecans
½ c. mini-chocolate chips

In large mixing bowl, cream butter and sugars until fluffy. Beat in eggs. Add flour, soda, cinnamon, and salt; mix well. Stir in oats, raisins, pecans, and chocolate chips. Refrigerate dough, covered, until thoroughly chilled.

Preheat oven to 350°. Shape rounded teaspoonfuls of dough into flat patties, about 2 inches wide. Place on lightly buttered baking sheet, about 1 inch apart. Bake 10 minutes or until lightly browned. Remove from oven. Let cookies cool on sheets for 2 minutes, then transfer to wire racks to cool completely. Serves 3 dozen.

Elaine (Pepin) Howes, Northfield Lions Club
Northfield, MA

OATMEAL MACAROONS

1 c. Crisco
1 c. brown sugar
1 c. granulated sugar
2 eggs (unbeaten)
½ tsp. vanilla
1¼ c. flour

1 tsp. baking soda
½ tsp. salt
½ tsp. cinnamon
3 c. quick oatmeal
½ c. nuts (optional)

Place Crisco, sugar, vanilla, and eggs in large bowl. Beat thoroughly. Mix flour, baking soda, salt, and cinnamon. Add to creamed mixture. Fold in oatmeal and nuts. Make into balls the size of walnuts. Roll in granulated sugar. Bake on ungreased cookie sheet at 350° for 10 to 12 minutes. Makes about 8 dozen.

I flatten cookie balls slightly (before baking). They crackle on top.

Gloria Hansen, Princeton Lions Club
Princeton, IL, USA

I've learned that the time I really need a vacation
is when I'm just back from one.

❦ ❦ ❦

The greatest risk is in thinking too small.

2075-99

ALL SAINTS DAY MACARONI
(November 2)

1 c. unblanched almonds
1⅓ c. sugar
1 tsp. ground cinnamon
1 c. flour

2 Tbsp. butter
Grated rind of 2 lemons
2 eggs, beaten

Grind almonds very fine in a nut grinder or electric blender. Combine almonds, sugar, and cinnamon. Sift together through a strainer in a deep bowl. Add flour, butter, lemon rind, and eggs. Mix with a spoon until mixture clings together. With hands, knead into a smooth paste or until mixture no longer clings to hands. Grease and flour 2 cookie sheets. Bake at 350° for 15 to 20 minutes. Cook until edges are golden brown. Makes 70 cookies.

Sarah Wehling, Bothell Lions Club
Bothell, WA, USA

DATE ICEBOX COOKIES

Cookie Batter:

2 c. flour
½ c. Crisco
½ c. sugar
½ c. brown sugar

½ tsp. soda
½ tsp. baking powder
2 eggs
1 tsp. vanilla

Filling:

¼ c. lemon juice
1 lb. dates, chopped
½ c. water

½ c. sugar
2 Tbsp. flour

Cook filling until thick and cool in refrigerator. Mix cookie batter; set in refrigerator and let cool. Take out and roll out thin. Spread on date filling and roll up like a jelly roll. Set in refrigerator overnight. Slice thin and bake at 375° for 8 to 10 minutes.

Lion Ida Rohrer, Moundbuilders Lions Club
Newark, OH, USA

DATE-OATMEAL COOKIES

1 c. butter or oleo (I use real
    butter)
1 c. white sugar
1 c. brown sugar
2 eggs
1 tsp. vanilla

2 tsp. soda
2 c. flour
2 c. oatmeal
1 c. chopped dates
¾ c. chopped nuts (I use pecans)

Cream butter, white sugar, and brown sugar. Add eggs and vanilla; beat well. Add flour and soda; mix well. Fold in dates, oatmeal, and nuts. Drop by teaspoonfuls on cookie sheet. Bake at 350° for 10 to 12 minutes..

Carrie Tyler, President, Montezuma Lions Club
Copeland, KS

DATE FILLED COOKIES

½ c. shortening
1 c. sugar

2 eggs

    Beat together.

    Add:

2 c. flour
1 Tbsp. milk
1 tsp. vanilla

2 tsp. baking powder
½ tsp. salt

    Dough will be soft. If refrigerated, it will be easier to work with. Roll ½ dough on floured board and cut into rounds. Put rounds on greased cookie sheet. Fill with 1 teaspoon filling and top with another round. Bake at 375° until light brown. Makes about 4 dozen.

    Filling:

½ pkg. pitted dates, chopped
1 c. sugar

1 c. water

    Cook until thick.

    Any fruit can be used, such as raisins, apples, or apricots.

Thelma Cranfill, Marion, IN, submitted by J.V. Vandergrift,
Fairmont East Grafton Road Lions Club
Fairmont, WV

PECAN BUTTER COOKIES

½ lb. real butter, slightly softened
    (no substitution)
1 c. sugar
1½ c. flour (heaping)

1 tsp. baking powder
1 tsp. baking soda
1 tsp. vanilla
½ c. chopped pecans

    Cream butter and sugar. Add vanilla and nuts. Add dry ingredients, which have been sifted together. Drop by small teaspoonfuls on baking sheet. Bake at 325° for about 10 minutes or until brown at edges. Makes approximately 3 dozen cookies.

Deb Fergeson, Kal-Haven Trail Lions Club
Gobles, MI, USA

EASY COCONUT PECAN COOKIES

1 box yellow cake mix
1 box coconut pecan frosting mix

2 eggs
½ c. butter, softened

    In a large mixing bowl, combine all ingredients and mix well. Drop by spoonful onto lightly greased cookie sheet and bake at 350°F. for 10 minutes. Makes 3 to 4 dozen.

Micheal and Ruth Bartolf, Oxbow and District Lions Club
Oxbow, Saskatchewan, Canada

CRUNCHY PECAN CRESCENTS

Cookie:

1 c. margarine
⅓ c. sugar
2 tsp. vanilla
2 c. flour

1 tsp. cinnamon
1 c. crushed corn flakes
1 c. finely chopped pecans

Frosting:

2 Tbsp. margarine
1½ c. powdered sugar
1 Tbsp. hot water

Milk
½ c. chopped pecans

Cookies: Cream margarine, sugar, and vanilla together. Blend in the remaining ingredients. Mix well. Shape level teaspoonfuls of dough into crescents. Place on cookie sheets. Bake at 350° for about 15 minutes. When cool, frost.

Frosting: Brown margarine in saucepan. Remove from heat. Stir in sugar and water. Add enough milk to make frosting of spreading consistency. Frost cookies. Sprinkle with chopped pecans.

SWEDISH COCONUT COOKIES

1 c. butter or margarine
1 c. shortening

2⅓ c. sugar

Add:

1½ tsp. vanilla
3⅔ c. flour
1 tsp. baking powder

1 tsp. soda
Scant tsp. salt
2 c. coconut

Form into 1 inch balls. Press with cookie press. Bake at 350° for 15 minutes.

Barb Tornes, Ave. of Pines Lions Club
Deer River, MN

You should fill your life with experiences, not excuses.

❧ ❧ ❧

Joy is often the ability to be happy in small ways.

❧ ❧ ❧

A good feeling gets even better when it's shared.

WHITE-CHOCOLATE ALMOND BALLS

½ c. blanched silver almonds
12 Tbsp. unsalted butter (at room temperature)
½ c. confectioners sugar
½ tsp. salt
¼ tsp. almond extract
2 c. flour
10 oz. white chocolate
2⅓ c. flaked coconut

Heat oven to 325°. Spread nuts on a baking sheet and toast in the oven until golden brown, 8 to 10 minutes. Cool and chop. With an electric mixer set at medium-low speed, beat butter, sugar, salt, and almond extract until creamy. On low speed, beat in flour until mixture just comes together. Stir in nuts. Chill until firm. Roll into approximately 1 inch balls. Put on ungreased baking sheets. Bake until golden brown on bottom, 15 to 18 minutes. Cool completely on wire racks.

Chop chocolate, put in a small bowl, and melt in a 250° oven. Put coconut in a bowl. Drop cookies, one at a time, into the chocolate. Coat and remove with a fork, letting excess drip off. Drop the cookies into coconut. Lightly press coconut onto the cookies. Set on a rack to dry. Makes about 40 cookies.

Per cookie: 128 calories, 2 g protein, 8 g fat, 45 mg sodium, 13 g carbohydrate, 11 mg cholesterol.

Barbara Joy Hess, Clarence Lions Club
Clarence Center, NY, USA

ALMOND BISCOTTI (TWICE BAKED COOKIES)

½ c. butter or margarine, softened
1¼ c. sugar, divided
3 eggs
1 tsp. anise flavoring
2 c. all-purpose flour
2 tsp. baking powder
Dash of salt
½ c. sliced almonds, toasted
2 tsp. milk

Preheat oven to 375°F. In a mixing bowl, cream butter and 1 cup sugar. Add eggs, one at a time, beating well after each addition. Stir in anise flavoring. (If anise is not available, vanilla extract can be substituted.) Combine dry ingredients added to creamed mixture and stir in almonds. Line a baking sheet with foil and grease foil. Divide dough in half; spread into two 12x2 inch rectangles, four inches apart, on foil. Brush with milk and sprinkle with remaining sugar. Bake for 15 to 20 minutes or until golden brown and firm to the touch. Remove from oven and reduce heat to 300°F. Lift rectangles with foil onto wire rack; cool for 15 minutes. Place on a cutting board; slice diagonally into ½ inch thick slices. Place slices with cut side down on ungreased baking sheet. Bake for 10 minutes. Turn cookies over; bake 10 minutes more. Turn oven off, leaving cookies in oven with door ajar to cool. Store in airtight container.

Lion Joan Shores, St. Charles Lions Club
St. Charles, MO, USA

ALMOND CRESCENTS

1 c. slivered almonds, chopped
7 oz. pkg. almond paste
½ c. confectioners sugar

1 egg
¼ tsp. vanilla
½ c. flour

Heat oven to 300°. Scatter the almonds over a baking sheet and toast them in the oven until golden, about 8 minutes, stirring them up occasionally so they don't burn. Set aside to cool. In a small bowl, beat the almond paste and confectioners sugar until smooth. Add egg and vanilla and beat again until smooth. Beat in flour. Chill dough until firm, about 30 minutes.

Heat the oven to 325°. Lightly butter a baking sheet. Roll a heaping ½ tablespoon of dough into a log, about 4 inches long. Roll the log in almonds, shape into a crescent, and place on prepared baking sheet. Repeat with remaining dough. Bake crescents until golden brown, 15 to 20 minutes. Makes 24 cookies.

Per cookie: 91 calories, 3 g protein, 5 g fat, 4 mg sodium, 9 g carbohydrate, 9 mg cholesterol.

Lion John J. Hess, Clarence Lions Club
Clarence Center, NY, USA

BUTTERSCOTCH CHIP PUDDING COOKIES

2¼ c. flour
1 tsp. baking soda
1 c. butter or margarine
¼ c. sugar
¾ c. light brown sugar
½ c. Bits 'O Brickle

1 small pkg. instant pudding
   (vanilla or chocolate)
1 tsp. vanilla
2 eggs
1 small pkg. butterscotch chips
1 c. chopped nuts

Mix flour with baking soda. Combine butter with sugars, pudding mix, and vanilla in large mixing bowl. Beat until smooth and creamy. Beat in eggs and gradually add flour mix. Stir in chips and nuts. Drop by teaspoonfuls onto greased cookie sheet. Bake at 375° for 8 to 10 minutes.

Norma Murray, Bryan Lioness Club
Bryan, OH, USA

It is impossible to accomplish anything worthwhile
without the help of other people.

If you like yourself and who you are, then you'll probably
like almost everyone you meet regardless of who they are.

LEMON POPPY-SEED PRETZELS

2¾ c. flour
1 Tbsp. poppy seeds plus more
   for sprinkling
¾ tsp. salt
6 oz. unsalted butter (at room
   temperature)

2½ c. confectioners sugar
1¼ tsp. grated lemon zest
¼ tsp. almond extract
1 egg
3 Tbsp. milk
Yellow food coloring

Combine flour, 1 tablespoon poppy seeds, and the salt. Beat butter, 1 cup of the confectioners sugar, and 1 teaspoon of the lemon zest until creamy. Beat in almond extract and the egg. Beat in flour mixture. Chill dough.

Heat oven to 325°. Divide dough into 25 pieces and roll each into a 10 inch length. Shape into pretzels and put on ungreased baking sheets. Bake until edges start to brown, 15 to 20 minutes. Cool on wire racks.

Combine remaining 1½ cups confectioners sugar, ¼ teaspoon lemon zest, and milk. Add food coloring to tint the icing pale yellow. Spoon icing over cookies. Let excess drip back into the bowl. Put cookies on wire racks and sprinkle with poppy seeds. Let dry. Makes 25 cookies.

Per cookie: 151 calories, 2 g protein, 6 g fat, 70 mg sodium, 23 g carbohydrate, 24 mg cholesterol.

Barbara Joy Hess, Clarence Lions Club
Clarence Center, NY, USA

LEMON CRISP COOKIES

1 (18¼ oz.) pkg. lemon cake mix
1 c. crisp rice cereal
½ c. butter or margarine, melted

1 egg, beaten
1 tsp. grated lemon peel

In a large bowl, combine all ingredients until well mixed (dough will be crumbly). Shape into 1 inch balls. Place 2 inches apart on ungreased baking sheet. Bake at 350° for 10 to 12 minutes or until set. Cool for 1 minute; remove from pan to a wire rack to cool completely. Yield: About 4 dozen.

Lion Sue Leidel, De Pere Lions Club
De Pere, WI

You should make money before you spend it.

❦ ❦ ❦

Heroes are the people who do what has to be done
when it needs to be done, regardless of the consequences.

AMMONIA COOKIES (LEMON CRACKERS)

2 eggs, beaten
1 c. lard (or shortening)
1 pt. milk
2½ c. sugar
½ tsp. salt

2 Tbsp. baker's ammonia (not
   household ammonia)
1 Tbsp. oil of lemon
Flour

Cream shortening and sugar. Add beaten eggs and salt. Mix the baker's ammonia (found in drugstores) in warm milk; add oil of lemon. Add the milk mixture and flour alternately until you have a stiff dough. Roll out the dough until it is half as thick as you want the cookies to be. Cut into squares with a pizza cutter and place on ungreased cookie sheet. Prick each cookie with fork tines. Bake at 375° for 10 minutes. The cookies should be fairly thick and slightly browned when done.

This recipe was a favorite years ago.
Lion Barbara Hugus, West Milford Lions Club
West Milford, WV, USA

LEMON DROP COOKIES

2 Tbsp. butter
¼ c. sour cream
½ c. sugar
Grated rind of 1 lemon
3 Tbsp. lemon juice

1 egg
1½ c. flour
1½ tsp. baking powder
½ tsp. baking soda
Pinch of salt

Melt butter. Add cream (sour), sugar, lemon juice, rind, and egg. Beat well and add dry ingredients, which have been sifted together. Drop by teaspoon on greased baking sheet and bake in moderately hot oven till delicately browned.

This recipe should be welcome by all ages.
Lion Evelyn M. Mongesku, Western Branch Lions Club
Chesapeake, VA, USA

It's better to be decisive, even if it means you'll sometimes be wrong.

It's better not to wait for a crisis to discover what's important in your life.

GLAZED APPLE COOKIES

½ c. shortening
2 c. flour
¼ c. apple juice or milk
½ tsp. cloves
½ tsp. salt
1 c. finely cut apples

1 tsp. cinnamon
1⅓ c. brown sugar
1 c. nuts, chopped
1 c. raisins
1 egg
1 tsp. soda

Blend together and drop onto cookie sheet. Bake for 15 minutes at 400°. Glaze while hot.

Glaze:

1½ c. powdered sugar
2½ Tbsp. apple juice or cream
⅛ tsp. salt

½ tsp. butter
½ tsp. vanilla

Blend well and ice cookies.

Evelyn Hershgerger, Bullskin Township Lioness Club
Mt. Pleasant, PA

ORANGE COOKIES

1 c. Crisco shortening
2 c. granulated sugar
1 whole orange, seeds removed
    and ground
2 eggs

1 c. sour milk
4½ c. Gold Medal flour
2 tsp. baking powder
1 tsp. baking soda

Icing:

1 whole orange, ground

1 lb. box 10X sugar

Mix ingredients in order given. Drop by spoonful onto greased cookie sheet. Bake in a 375° oven for 10 to 12 minutes. Makes about 5 dozen cookies.

Icing: Mix icing ingredients together and put on cooled cookies.

To grind up the orange a food processor can also be used and don't forget to use the rind of the orange; it gives it color and flavor.

Store in airtight container. They disappear fast.

Donna King, York Springs Lions Club
York Springs, PA

Failures always blame someone else.

ORANGE PISTACHIO BELLS

¾ c. pistachios
1¾ c. flour
½ tsp. salt
¼ tsp. baking soda
8 Tbsp. unsalted butter (at room temperature)
½ c. sugar

1 tsp. orange zest
1 egg yolk
1 Tbsp. orange juice
¼ tsp. vanilla extract
1 c. apricot preserves, melted and strained

Shell pistachios. Put in a bowl and cover with water to remove salt. Combine flour, salt, and soda. Beat butter, sugar, and orange zest until light and fluffy. Beat in yolk, orange juice, and vanilla. Gradually beat in flour mixture. Divide in half, wrap, and chill until firm, about 1 hour.

Meanwhile, drain pistachios. Rub dry between paper towels. Heat oven to 350°. Roll each piece of dough between sheets of lightly floured waxed paper to about ³⁄₁₆ inch thick. With a 2 inch cookie cutter, stamp out cookies. Put on ungreased baking sheets. Bake until edges are golden brown, 10 to 12 minutes. Remove from pans and cool on wire racks. Brush some of the melted jam on the bottom edge of each cookie and sprinkle with pistachios. Makes about 54 cookies.

Per cookie: 65 calories, 1 g protein, 3 g fat, 25 mg sodium, 10 g carbohydrate, 9 mg cholesterol.

Barbara Joy Hess, Clarence Lions Club
Clarence Center, NY, USA

BANANA PEANUT COOKIES

½ c. peanuts
2 c. flour
½ tsp. baking soda
½ tsp. salt
¼ tsp. nutmeg
1 large banana (about ½ c. pureed)

6 oz. unsalted butter (at room temperature)
⅔ c. brown sugar
1 egg
½ tsp. vanilla extract

Heat oven to 350°. Chop peanuts. Combine flour, soda, salt, and nutmeg. Puree banana in a food processor or mash until smooth. With an electric mixer set at medium speed, beat butter and sugar until fluffy. Add egg and vanilla and beat until well combined. Beat in pureed banana. Reduce speed and beat in flour mixture until just combined. Drop dough by heaping teaspoonfuls about 2 inches apart onto ungreased baking sheets. Press chopped nuts onto the tops of the cookies. Bake until bottoms are browned, 8 to 10 minutes. Remove and cool on racks. Makes about 42 cookies.

Per cookie: 79 calories, 1 g protein, 4 g fat, 39 mg sodium, 9 g carbohydrate, 14 mg cholesterol.

Mrs. Mike Nowicki, Clarence Lions Club
Clarence Center, NY, USA

PUMPKIN-CRANBERRY COOKIES

2 c. flour
1 tsp. baking soda
½ tsp. salt
1 tsp. ground cinnamon
½ tsp. ground nutmeg
½ tsp. ground allspice
¼ tsp. ground cloves
1½ c. cranberries, chopped

3 Tbsp. sugar
¾ c. unsalted butter (at room
    temperature)
1 c. brown sugar
1 egg
¾ tsp. vanilla extract
1 c. canned pumpkin puree
1 c. coarsely chopped walnuts

Heat oven to 375°. Combine flour, soda, salt, and spices. Combine cranberries and sugar. Beat butter with brown sugar until creamy. Beat in egg, vanilla, and pumpkin. Beat in flour mixture. Stir in cranberries and walnuts. Drop dough by teaspoonfuls onto greased baking sheets. Bake until just beginning to brown, about 20 minutes. Makes about 45 cookies.

Per cookie: 93 calories, 1 g protein, 5 g fat, 57 mg sodium, 11 g carbohydrate, 13 mg cholesterol.

Lion John J. Hess, Clarence Lions Club
Clarence Center, NY, USA

CHERRY DREAMS

2 c. sugar
1⅓ c. butter
4 eggs
4 tsp. vanilla
10 Tbsp. juice from maraschino
    cherries
4 c. flour

1 tsp. salt
1 tsp. baking soda
2 tsp. baking powder
2 c. chopped nuts
4 c. corn flake crumbs
Maraschino cherries, halved

In large mixing bowl, cream butter and sugar. Add eggs, vanilla, and juice from cherries and mix well. In a separate bowl, combine flour, salt, baking soda, and baking powder and stir into egg mixture. Add nuts and mix well. Drop by spoonful into crushed corn flakes and coat well. Place cookie on lightly greased cookie sheet and flatten slightly. Press a cherry half into each cookie. Bake at 350°F. for 10 minutes or until lightly browned. Makes 6 dozen.

Micheal and Ruth Bartolf, Oxbow and District Lions Club
Oxbow, Saskatchewan, Canada

ALMOND BARK COOKIES

1 lb. white almond bark
1 c. crunchy peanut butter
2 c. Rice Krispies

2 c. miniature marshmallows
1 c. salted peanuts (with skins)

Preheat oven to 200° to melt almond bark or use microwave. When melted, mix all above remaining ingredients. Drop by spoonful on wax paper, cool, and store or eat.

Zona Roberts, Bullhead City Lions Club
Bullhead City, AZ, USA

CHRISTMAS SPICE COOKIES

¾ c. butter, softened
1 c. light brown sugar
1 egg, well beaten
¼ c. molasses
2¼ c. all-purpose flour
2 tsp. baking soda

2 tsp. cinnamon
2 tsp. ginger
¾ tsp. cloves
¼ tsp. salt
2 Tbsp. sugar (for rolling dough in)

Cream together butter and brown sugar. Add egg and molasses. Stir dry ingredients and stir into batter. Wrap in wax paper and chill thoroughly. Shape into balls the size of walnuts (or smaller). Dip balls in sugar and place 3 inches apart on buttered cookie sheets. Bake in oven at 350°F. about 10 minutes or until firm. Cool on racks.

Lydia Lamy, Plymouth Lions Club
Terryville, CT, USA

SOFT GINGER COOKIES

Mix in order:

1 c. baking molasses
1 c. sugar

1 c. sour milk or buttermilk
2 eggs

Sift together and mix in:

5 c. flour
2 tsp. soda
1 tsp. cinnamon

1 tsp. cloves
1 tsp. ginger
½ tsp. salt

Add last:

1 c. melted butter flavor
   shortening

Mix thoroughly, then let stand 10 minutes. Drop by teaspoon (or half tablespoons for larger cookies) onto greased and lightly floured cookie sheet. Brush with beaten egg, if desired, before baking. Bake at 375° until done, 6 to 10 minutes, depending on your oven.

In honor of all my senior friends.
Lion Ann K. Brumback, Silver Run-Union Mills Lions Club
Westminster, MD, USA

If you want the circumstances of your life to change for the better,
you must change for the better.

GINGERSNAPS

1½ c. shortening
2 c. sugar
2 eggs
¼ c. light molasses
4 c. flour

1 tsp. salt
2 tsp. baking soda
2 tsp. ground ginger
2 tsp. ground cinnamon
2 tsp. ground cloves

Preheat oven to 350°F. Beat shortening and sugar until light and fluffy. Beat in eggs and molasses until blended. Beat in one cup flour, salt, baking soda, and spices until well mixed. Stir in enough of remaining flour to make a stiff dough. Shape into 1½ inch balls and place 3 inches apart on greased cookie sheet.

Lightly grease bottom of 3 inch glass, dip in sugar, and flatten cookie balls. Bake 15 minutes or until firm and lightly browned.

Elizabeth Maddock, Canaan Northwest Lions Club
Canaan, CT, USA

SO GOOD SNICKERDOODLES

1 c. low-fat margarine
2½ c. powdered sugar
1 Tbsp. vanilla extract

2 tsp. almond extract
2 Egg Beaters (½ c.)
2½ to 3 c. self-rising flour

For rolling dough:

3 Tbsp. sugar

1 Tbsp. cinnamon

Cream together margarine, powdered sugar, vanilla, almond, and Egg Beaters until smooth. Add flour and stir thoroughly. Chill dough 30 to 40 minutes. On a small plate, mix together sugar and cinnamon with fork. Dip by teaspoonfuls into the cinnamon-sugar mixture. (The dough will be sticky.) Sprinkle mixture over dough until coated enough to roll. Next, place coated balls on cookie sheet sprayed with Pam. Bake at 375° for 8 to 10 minutes.

Hazel Bailey, Iron City Lions Club
Iron City, TN, USA

SNICKERDOODLES

1 c. shortening
1½ c. sugar
2 eggs
2¾ c. flour

2 tsp. cream of tartar
1 tsp. baking soda
¼ tsp. salt
Cinnamon-sugar

Mix shortening, sugar, and eggs together. Sift together flour, cream of tartar, soda, and salt. Mix with shortening mixture. Roll dough into ball-shaped cookies, then roll in cinnamon-sugar. Bake in a 375° oven 8 to 10 minutes until lightly browned. Cool. Freezes well.

P. Diane Baldwin, Broken Bow Lions Club
Broken Bow, NE, USA

BASIC CHOCOLATE ICEBOX COOKIES

¾ c. all-purpose flour
¼ c. unsweetened cocoa
¼ tsp. baking soda
⅛ tsp. salt
¼ c. stick margarine, softened

⅔ c. sugar
1 tsp. vanilla extract
1 large egg white (I use 1 whole egg)
2 Tbsp. turbinado sugar

Combine first 4 ingredients in a bowl and set aside. Beat margarine, sugar, vanilla, and egg until fluffy. Add flour mixture and mix until well blended. Turn dough out onto wax paper. Shape into a 6 inch log. Wrap in the wax paper and freeze for 3 hours or until very firm.

Preheat oven to 350°. Roll log in turbinado sugar. Cut into 24 (¼ inch) slices; place on cookie sheet, 1 inch apart, sprayed with cooking spray or very lightly greased. Bake at 350° for 8 to 10 minutes (I bake for 9 minutes). Remove from sheets and cool on wire racks. Store in your favorite cookie jar.

You can add ¼ cup peanut butter and just a little more flour so the dough will be stiff enough to make into logs. You can roll the logs into brown sugar or finely chopped nuts before slicing.

Lion Janice Elliott, Meredith Lions Club
Meredith, NH, USA

CHOCOLATE PEANUT BUTTER COOKIES

1 can chocolate fudge frosting
1 c. chunky peanut butter
1 egg

1½ c. flour
Sugar

Heat oven to 375°. Lightly grease cookie sheets. Reserve ⅓ cup frosting. In large bowl, combine remaining frosting, peanut butter, and egg; blend well. Lightly spoon flour into measuring cup; level off. By hand, stir in flour. Shape dough into 1 inch balls. Place 2 inches apart on greased cookie sheets. Flatten each to 2 inch diameter with bottom of glass dipped in sugar. Bake at 375° for 4 to 7 minutes or until set. *Do not overbake.* Cool 1 minute. Remove from cookie sheets. Cool completely. Lightly frost with reserved frosting. Makes 4 dozen.

Eleanor McFadden, West Milford Lions Club
West Milford, WV, USA

The purpose of criticism is to help, not to humiliate.

Nothing very bad or very good ever lasts very long.

CHOCOLATE BISCOTTI (TWICE BAKED COOKIE)

4 (1 oz.) sq. unsweetened
   chocolate
½ c. butter or margarine
½ tsp. vanilla extract
3 large eggs
1¼ c. sugar

3 c. all-purpose flour
½ tsp. baking powder
1 c. chopped walnuts, toasted
1 egg white, lightly beaten

Preheat oven to 350°F. Melt chocolate and butter in a heavy saucepan over low heat; remove from heat. Stir in vanilla and cool. Beat eggs at medium speed with an electric mixer until frothy; gradually add sugar, beating until thick and pale (about 5 minutes). Add chocolate mixture, stirring until blended. Combine flour and baking powder; stir into chocolate mixture. Stir in nuts. Flour hands and form dough into a 13 inch log. Place on a lightly greased baking sheet. Brush with egg white. Bake for about 45 minutes; cool on a wire rack. Cut log with a serrated knife crosswise into 24 (½ inch) slices and place on an ungreased cookie sheet. Bake at 350°F. for 10 minutes on each side. Remove to wire rack to cool. Store in an airtight container.

Lion Joan Shores, St. Charles Lions Club
St. Charles, MO, USA

DOUBLE-CHOCOLATE ALMOND BISCOTTI

2 c. flour
⅓ c. unsweetened cocoa powder
1½ tsp. baking powder
½ tsp. salt
¼ lb. unsalted butter (at room
   temperature)
1¼ c. sugar

2 eggs
1 tsp. vanilla extract
½ tsp. almond extract
1 c. blanched almonds, coarsely
   chopped
⅔ c. semi-sweet chocolate chips

Heat oven to 325°. Combine flour, cocoa, baking powder, and salt. Beat butter and sugar until light and fluffy. Beat in eggs and the vanilla and almond extracts. Gradually beat in flour mixture. Stir in almonds and chocolate chips. Shape dough into two logs, about 1½ inches wide by 15 inches long. Put logs about 3 inches apart on a baking sheet. Bake until edges start to brown and top becomes firm, 50 to 55 minutes. Cool. Cut into ½ inch diagonal slices. Return to baking sheet, cut-side down, and bake until dried, 30 to 40 minutes. Makes 3 dozen.

Per cookie: 125 calories, 2 g protein, 6 g fat, 55 mg sodium, 17 g carbohydrate, 19 mg cholesterol.

Mrs. Mike Nowicki, Clarence Lions Club
Clarence Center, NY, USA

CHOCOLATE SPICE CRINKLES

¼ lb. butter
1½ c. sugar
2 tsp. baking powder
1½ tsp. cinnamon
¼ tsp. salt
3 eggs

1 tsp. vanilla
4 oz. unsweetened baking
chocolate
2 c. flour
½ c. confectioners sugar

Beat butter, sugar, baking powder, cinnamon, and salt until creamy. Add eggs, vanilla, and melted chocolate; mix thoroughly. Add flour and beat at low speed until well blended. Cover and refrigerate for 2 hours (a must). Roll into balls and roll in confectioners sugar. Place on lightly greased cookie sheet. Bake 12 minutes or until tops are puffed and cracked. Remove to wire rack and cool.

Carol Hug, Bryan Lioness Club
Bryan, OH, USA

AUNT HILDA'S CHOCOLATE COOKIES

Cookie mix:

1 c. light brown sugar
½ c. butter
½ c. sour (or butter) milk
1½ c. flour (plain)

¾ c. walnut meats, cut fine
1 egg
½ tsp. soda
1½ sq. melted chocolate

Frosting mix:

1½ c. powdered sugar
1 small egg
2 Tbsp. cream

1½ sq. melted chocolate
½ Tbsp. vanilla

Mix ingredients, 1 item at a time, until all are well mixed; drop by teaspoon onto greased cookie sheet. Bake at 350° until done; brown. Ice them while hot - icing will run. Beat thoroughly and spread on hot cookies. Sprinkle a few nuts on icing.

To make them last, hide them!!!!!

My Aunt Hilda made these every time I took my family home to visit. They would be gone in an instant. I also made these for P.T.A. meetings.

Delores Wilkerson, Bellville Lions Club
Bellville, GA, USA

You should treasure your children for what they are,
not for what you want them to be.

VELMA'S CORN FLAKES COOKIES

1 c. sugar
1 c. white syrup

1 c. peanut butter
8 c. corn flakes

Bring to boil sugar and white syrup. Add peanut butter and let melt. Add 8 cups corn flakes. Spoon out the size wanted on wax paper. Let set.

These are fast and easy. Grandma Velma Caldwell made these when my kids were growing up.

Pam Caldwell, Mexico Sunrise Lions Club
Mexico, MO

The important thing is not what others think of me, but what I think of me.

❦ ❦ ❦

The worst decisions made in your life are the ones ·
you make when you are angry.

❦ ❦ ❦

Bigger is not always better, and going faster is not necessarily progress.

❦ ❦ ❦

You can always get more money, but you can never get more time.

CANDIES

BEST PEANUT BUTTER FUDGE

½ c. margarine (1 stick)
1 (12 oz.) can evaporated milk
2 (1 lb.) boxes confectioners
    sugar (or a 2 lb. bag)
1 tsp. vanilla

1 (1 lb.) jar peanut butter
1 (7 oz.) jar marshmallow creme
1 c. chopped nuts (or use crunchy
    peanut butter - optional)

In a large heavy saucepan, melt the margarine, then add the evaporated milk, then gradually stir in the confectioners sugar. Cook the mixture, while stirring, to the soft ball stage (candy thermometer at 235°). Remove from heat, then add the remaining ingredients. Stir until well blended. Pour into a buttered 9x13 inch pan. Cool. Cut into squares.

Don't try to understand me - just love me.

Lion Ellen Thornton, Butler Lions Club
Butler, OH, USA

PEANUT BUTTER FUDGE

4½ c. sugar
1 stick butter or oleo
1 can evaporated milk

1 pt. marshmallow creme
1 jar peanut butter

Combine sugar, butter, and milk. Boil 9 minutes (soft ball stage). Remove from heat and add marshmallow creme and peanut butter. Beat until it loses its glossy look. Pour into buttered pan. Delicious and easy.

Olive Higinbotham, Bentleyville Lioness Club
Bentleyville, PA, USA

PEANUT BUTTER FUDGE

4 c. white sugar
1⅓ c. evaporated milk
2 c. peanut butter

1 (7½ oz.) jar marshmallow fluff
2 tsp. vanilla
Nuts (add if desired)

Boil sugar and milk to soft ball stage (238°). Add remaining ingredients. Pour into buttered 9x13 inch pan and cool. Can be put in freezer. Makes a lot!

It's delicious! Have had many requests for copies of the recipe. "Try it, you'll like it." It's great!

Faith Murdock, Scio Lions Club
Scio, NY, USA

A new baby changes all your priorities.

PEANUT BUTTER FUDGE

½ c. milk
2 Tbsp. butter or oleo
1 Tbsp. white corn syrup

2 c. white sugar
1 c. peanut butter
1 tsp. vanilla

Mix milk, butter, and syrup in a heavy saucepan. Boil to soft ball stage (235°F.). Remove from heat. Add peanut butter and vanilla. Stir thoroughly. Pour into buttered 9x9 inch pan. Cut into pieces.

Be careful - if you are like me, you can eat this all yourself!
King Lion Shirley, Rootstown Township, 13-D Lions Club
Rootstown, OH

PEANUT BUTTER BALLS

1⅓ sticks oleo
1 c. peanut butter
1 box powdered sugar

6 to 7 Hershey's bars (chocolate)
3 tsp. paraffin

Mix oleo and peanut butter together. Add powdered sugar; mix well. (I knead a little to make creamier.) Form into small balls. Insert toothpick into ball to dip in milk chocolate mixture. Melt chocolate and paraffin in double boiler. Cool on waxed paper. Yield: 75 balls approximately.
Olive Higinbotham, Bentleyville Lioness Club
Bentleyville, PA, USA

TOFU FUDGE CHEWS

Blend in a blender until smooth:

½ lb. tofu   ½ c. oil

Pour into a medium mixing bowl.

Add:

1½ c. sugar   ½ c. cocoa powder

Stir well.

Mix separately:

3 c. unbleached white flour   1 tsp. salt
1 tsp. baking soda

Add to wet ingredients. Mix well. The dough should be fairly stiff. Roll into 1½ inch balls. In a saucer, put ½ cup sugar. Roll the formed balls in the sugar until they are coated. Place on a lightly oiled cookie sheet, 1 inch apart. Bake for 12 to 15 minutes at 350°F. Cool on a wire rack. Makes 48 cookies.

Per cookie: 92 calories, 1 g protein, 3 g fat, 15 g carbohydrates.
Evelyn S. Thompson, Mount Airy Foothills Lions Club
Mt. Airy, NC, USA

2075-99

ONE BOWL FUDGE
("Easy")

2 pkg. Baker's semi-sweet
   chocolate
1 (14 oz.) can sweetened
   condensed milk

2 tsp. vanilla
1½ c. chopped nuts

Microwave chocolate in large bowl 2 to 3 minutes until almost melted, stirring halfway through time. Keep on stirring until melted. Stir in vanilla and nuts. Refrigerate 2 hours or until firm. Makes 4 dozen pieces.

Carolyn Phillips, Elberfeld Lions Club
Elberfeld, IN

FAILPROOF FUDGE

1 (18 oz.) pkg. chocolate chips
1 (14 oz.) Eagle Brand sweetened
   condensed milk

Dash of salt
1½ tsp. vanilla
½ c. walnuts or pecans

Combine chips and milk together in double boiler and melt. Remove from heat, then add salt, vanilla, and nuts. Pour into buttered pan and cool for 2 hours before cutting into squares.

Lion Micheal and Ruth (Sauskojus) Bartolf,
Oxbow and District Lions Club
Oxbow, Saskatchewan, Canada

MARTHA WASHINGTON FUDGE

Candy:

2 boxes powdered sugar
1 can condensed milk
¼ c. soft butter

2 tsp. vanilla
3 c. chopped nuts

Mix powdered sugar, condensed milk, butter, vanilla, and nuts together. Chill. Roll into balls.

Dipping Chocolate:

1½ to 2 pkg. semi-sweet brick
   chocolate

¾ block paraffin wax

Melt chocolate and paraffin in top of double boiler. Drop one ball at a time into chocolate mixture. Retrieve with a fork and shake off excess chocolate. Dry on waxed paper. Yield: 5 pounds.

Cindy Bamburg, Biloxi Lions Club
Biloxi, MS, USA

JOE'S PEANUT BRITTLE

1 c. sugar
½ c. white corn syrup
¼ c. water

2 c. Spanish peanuts
1 tsp. salt
1 tsp. baking soda

Add salt to peanuts. Measure soda and set aside. Mix sugar, syrup, and water in a skillet. Cook until it forms a thread. Add nuts and cook till it turns a lemon color and smells scorched. Add soda and stir until foamy. Put on a buttered cookie sheet to cool. Break apart.

Martha C. Cox, Travelers Rest Lions Club
Travelers Rest, SC

CHOCOLATE BRITTLE

2 c. butter (I use margarine)
2 c. sugar
¼ c. + 2 Tbsp. water

12 oz. pkg. chocolate morsels
3 c. chopped nuts (pecans)

Combine butter, sugar, and water in an agate pan (or skillet). Cook over low heat until candy reaches hard crack stage (300°F.). Remove from heat; immediately spread thin on greased cookie sheets (the thinner the better). Melt chocolate in top of double boiler (I melt in microwave). Spread chocolate over brittle; sprinkle pecans evenly on top. Press pecans into chocolate. Let stand until firm. Break candy into pieces. It's good!

Barbara Vaughn, Conroe Lioness Club
Conroe, TX, Montgomery County

No one is ever so powerful or successful that they
don't appreciate a sincere compliment.

❧ ❧ ❧

More people are influenced by how much you care
than by how much you know.

❧ ❧ ❧

Plotting revenge only allows the people who hurt you to hurt you longer.

CHOCOLATE CARAMEL CANDY

Bottom layer and top layer:

1 c. milk chocolate chips
¼ c. butterscotch chips

¼ c. creamy peanut butter

Filling:

¼ c. butter
1 c. sugar
¼ c. evaporated milk
1½ c. marshmallow creme

¼ c. creamy peanut butter
1 tsp. vanilla
1½ c. chopped salted peanuts

Caramel layer:

1 (14 oz.) pkg. caramels

¼ c. whipping cream

Combine first 3 ingredients in small saucepan; stir over low heat until melted and smooth. Spread onto the bottom of lightly greased 13x9 inch pan; cool until set.

Filling: Melt butter in saucepan over medium-high heat. Add sugar and milk. Bring to a boil and stir 5 minutes. Remove from heat. Stir in marshmallow creme, peanut butter, and vanilla. Add peanuts. Spread over first layer. Cool till set.

Combine caramels and cream in saucepan; stir over low heat until melted and smooth. Spread over filling; cool till set.

Combine first 3 ingredients again in small saucepan. Melt. Pour over caramel layer. Refrigerate at least 1 hour. Cut in 1 inch squares.

Mrs. Ron (Pat) Henne, Elburn Lions Club
Elburn, IL (Kane)

SOUR CREAM PRALINES

1½ c. sugar
1½ c. packed brown sugar
¼ tsp. salt
¼ tsp. baking soda
1 c. sour cream

1 Tbsp. light corn syrup
2 Tbsp. butter
1 tsp. vanilla
2 c. pecans

Combine sugars, baking soda, salt, sour cream, and corn syrup in a heavy saucepan. Cook over moderate heat to 230° on candy thermometer, stirring constantly. Remove from heat and beat in butter, vanilla, and pecans. Cool to warm, then beat until mixture begins to lose its sheen. Working rapidly, drop by spoonfuls onto wax paper. When candy is set, wrap in plastic wrap. Store in an airtight container.

Dorothy Coon, Hutchinson Breakfast Lions Club
Hutchinson, KS, USA

NUT SURPRISES

3 c. broken nuts
2 c. pitted dates

2 c. seedless raisins
4 Tbsp. honey

Put 1 cup of the nuts through food chopper and set aside. Now put the rest of the nuts, raisins, and dates through the chopper. Add honey and mix well. Butter your hands and roll the mixture into little balls, then roll balls in the 1 cup of ground nuts and your nut surprises are ready to serve.

Mary L. Cool, Hutchinson Breakfast Lions Club
Hutchinson, KS, USA

LEMON-NUT BALLS

1 (16 oz.) pkg. powdered sugar
1 (12 oz.) pkg. vanilla wafers,
  finely crushed
1 (6 oz.) can frozen lemonade
  concentrate, thawed

1 c. chopped nuts, toasted and
  finely ground
½ c. butter or margarine, melted
Powdered sugar and flaked
  coconut

In a large bowl, combine powdered sugar (16 ounces), vanilla wafers, and nuts. Stir in melted butter and lemonade concentrate; mix until well combined. Shape mixture into 1 inch balls. Roll half of balls in powdered sugar and remaining balls in coconut. Store in an airtight container in refrigerator. Yield: About 7 dozen balls.

Mary L. Coon, Hutchinson Breakfast Lions Club
Hutchinson, KS, USA

ANGEL FOOD CANDY

1 c. white sugar
1 c. dark Karo syrup

1 Tbsp. vinegar
1 Tbsp. baking soda

Combine sugar, syrup, and vinegar. Cook over medium heat until candy thermometer reaches 300° (be sure to stir). Remove from heat and quickly add soda, while stirring. Pour into ungreased 9x13 inch pan. When cool, break into pieces and dip in chocolate.

IRISH POTATOES CANDY

1 small to medium potato with
  peeling

Peanut butter
Confectioners sugar

Boil potato in peel. When tender, peel skin off and mash. Add confectioners sugar to potato and stir until mixture is thick enough to roll out with rolling pin. Use sugar to coat to prevent sticking. Roll thinly. Spread the top with peanut butter. Roll up as a jelly roll. Cut into slices and allow to harden. You must work fast in all phases of making this so it will not harden until after you cut it into slices.

Lion Melba Johnson, Brookhaven Alpha Lions Club
Brookhaven, MS

MILLIONAIRE CANDY

1 lb. bag yellow Kraft caramels
3 Tbsp. Carnation evaporated
  milk

3 c. pecans, cut lengthwise

Chocolate coating:

12 oz. Hershey's kisses

½ box paraffin wax

Melt caramels with milk in top of double boiler, then stir in pecans. Coat well and drop by spoonfuls on greased wax paper. Cool and dip in chocolate coating.

Chocolate coating: Melt kisses and wax in double boiler. Dip above candy in it. Cool on wax paper.

Tammy Rawls, Alfa Lions Club
Bogue Chitto, MS

ALMOND BARK TREAT

5 almond bark squares
1 c. Rice Krispies
1 c. M&M's or chocolate chips

2 c. pretzels, broken
1 c. peanuts (optional)

Mix pretzels, Rice Krispies, and peanuts together. Melt almond bark. Pour over pretzel mixture and mix well. Add candies. Pour onto wax paper to cool. Break apart after cooled.

Can melt bark in microwave container and add ingredients.

Nancy Pence, Elizabethtown Lions Club
Elizabethtown, KY, USA

BUTTER BALLS

1 c. butter, softened
½ c. confectioners sugar
1 tsp. vanilla

2¼ c. flour
¼ tsp. salt
¾ c. finely chopped nuts

Heat oven to 400°F. Work all ingredients thoroughly until dough holds together. Shape into 1 inch balls. Place on ungreased cookie sheet. Bake 10 to 12 minutes until set.

Elizabeth Maddock, Canaan Northwest Lions Club
Canaan, CT, USA

Even the most mundane job holds the potential for great achievement.

BUCK EYES

2 sticks margarine
4½ c. confectioners sugar
1½ c. peanut butter

1 tsp. vanilla
1 inch slab wax
12 oz. chocolate chips

Mix and roll up into small balls the first 4 ingredients. Melt the wax and chocolate chips in double boiler and leave on low heat while you dip the balls. Put on wax paper to set. (I use a toothpick in the balls.) If the chocolate does not want to stay on the balls, you can add more wax (a little at a time). This should make 7 dozen buckeyes.

I also dipped the balls into butterscotch chips instead of chocolate chips and they are delicious.

Lion Ida Rohrer, Moundbuilders Lions Club
Newark, OH, USA

BUCKEYES

1½ c. confectioners sugar
1¼ c. chunky peanut butter
4 Tbsp. butter, softened

1 c. semi-sweet chocolate pieces
1 tsp. shortening

Mix sugar, peanut butter, and butter until well blended. Knead with hands if necessary. Shape into 1 inch balls; place in a jellyroll pan, cover, and refrigerate until firm, about 2 hours.

Heat chocolate pieces and shortening in a heavy 1 quart pan over low heat and cool slightly. Remove half of the peanut butter balls from refrigerator. Using a toothpick, carefully dip, one at a time, into chocolate mixture, making sure to leave a small amount of the peanut butter mixture showing on top to resemble an eye. Place chocolate covered ball on waxed paper lined cookie sheet. Remove the toothpick and gently smooth over the hole. Refrigerate balls until coating is firm (about 1 hour). Repeat with remaining balls. Store in covered container in refrigerator. Yield: Approximately 3½ dozen.

Dorothy Coon, Hutchinson Breakfast Lions Club
Hutchinson, KS, USA

MARZIPAN POTATOES
(A German Christmas goodie)

⅔ lb. almond paste or marzipan, diced

⅔ c. (approx.) icing sugar
½ c. unsweetened cocoa powder

On work surface, sprinkle almond paste with sugar. Gently work with hands until smooth; do not overwork. Taste and add additional sugar if desired. Divide mixture into thirds and shape each into long roll. Divide each roll in 10 equal pieces. Roll each piece into ¾ inch diameter ball. Roll balls in cocoa, coating thoroughly and tapping off excess. Place in tiny paper cup. Makes 30.

Micheal and Ruth Bartolf, Oxbow and District Lions Club
Oxbow, Saskatchewan, Canada

2075-99

TUMBLEWEEDS

1 (12 oz.) can salted peanuts   3 c. butterscotch chips
1 (7 oz.) can potato sticks   3 Tbsp. peanut butter

Combine peanuts and potato sticks in a bowl; set aside. In a microwave, heat butterscotch chips and peanut butter at 70% power for 1 to 2 minutes or until melted, stirring every 30 seconds. Add to peanut mixture; stir to coat evenly. Drop by rounded tablespoonfuls onto waxed paper-lined baking sheets. Refrigerate until set, about 5 minutes. Store in an airtight container. Yield: About 4½ dozen.

*It's easy to go from the simple life to the fast track,
but almost impossible to go back the other way.*

❦ ❦ ❦

*Why it is that most people resist change,
and yet it's the only thing that brings progress.*

❦ ❦ ❦

*Meeting interesting people depends less on
where you go than on who you are.*

❦ ❦ ❦

*Regrets over yesterday and the fear of tomorrow are
twin thieves that rob us of the moment.*

Low-Fat,
Healthy

HEART HEALTHY TIPS
Substitutions, Modifications and Equivalents

Instead of	Use	Instead of	Use
1 c. butter 498 mg cholesterol	⅞ c. polyunsaturated oil-0 mg cholesterol 1 c. tub margarine- 0 mg cholesterol 2 stks margarine- 0 mg cholesterol	1 c. whole milk yogurt, plain- 250 calories	1 c. part skim milk yogurt, plain- 125-145 calories
		1 c. sour cream- 416 calories	1 c. blended low-fat cottage cheese- 208 calories
1 c. heavy cream- 832 calories, 296 mg cholesterol	1 c. evap. skim milk- 176 calories 8 mg cholesterol	1 oz. baking chocolate 8.4 gm sat. fat	3 Tbsp. cocoa powder- 1.7 gm sat. fat PLUS
1 md whole egg- 274 mg cholesterol	¼ c. egg sub- 0 mg cholesterol*		1 Tbsp. polyunsaturated oil - 1.1 gm sat. fat TOTAL: 2.8 gm sat. fat

*Some egg substitutes do contain cholesterol. Check label to be sure.

To Reduce Cholesterol or Saturated Fats:

1. Select lean cuts of meat.
2. Serve moderate portions.
3. Replace animal fats with appropriate substitutes.

Examples

Instead of	Use
Butter, lard, bacon or bacon fat, and chicken fat	Polyunsaturated margarine or oil
Sour cream	Low-fat yogurt
Whole milk	Skim milk
Whole milk cheeses	Low-fat cheeses
Whole eggs	Egg whites or egg substitutes

To Reduce Calories or Fats:

1. Brown meat by broiling or cooking in non-stick pans with little or no oil.
2. Chill soups, stews, sauces, and broths. Lift off congealed fat (saves 100 calories per Tbsp. of fat removed).
3. Trim fat from meat. Also remove skin from poultry.
4. Use water-packed canned products (canned fish, canned fruits).
5. In recipes for baked products, the sugar can often be reduced ¼ to ⅓ without harming the final product. Cinnamon and vanilla also give the impression of sweetness.
6. Use fresh fruit whenever possible. If canned fruit must be used, select water-packed varieties, fruit in own juice, or drain heavy syrup from canned fruit.
7. For sauces and dressings, use low-calorie bases (vinegar, mustard, tomato juice, fat-free bouillon) instead of high calorie ones (creams, fats, oils, mayonnaise).

Equivalents for Sugar Substitutes

Brand Name	Amount	Substitution for Sugar
Adolph's Powder	1 tsp. 4 tsp.	= ¼ c. = 1 c.
Equal Powder	1 pkt.	= 2 tsp.
Sweet 'N Low Powder	1 pkt. 1 tsp. 4 tsp.	= 2 tsp. = ¼ c. = 1 c.
Sweet 'N Low Brown	4 tsp.	= 1 c. brown sugar
Sugar Twin Powder	1 tsp.	= 1 tsp.
Sugar Twin Brown Powder	1 tsp.	= 1 tsp. brown sugar
Sweet-10 Liquid	10 drops 2 Tbsp.	= 1 tsp. = 1 c.

LOW-FAT, HEALTHY

POTLUCK PAN ROLLS

1 (¼ oz.) pkg. active dry yeast
⅓ c. plus 1 tsp. sugar, *divided*
1½ c. warm water (110° to
   115°), *divided*
½ c. butter or margarine, melted

2 eggs
¼ c. instant nonfat dry milk
   powder
1¼ tsp. salt
5½ to 6 c. all-purpose flour

In a mixing bowl, dissolve yeast and 1 teaspoon sugar in ½ cup water. Add butter, eggs, milk powder, salt, 3 cups flour, and remaining sugar and water. Beat on medium speed for 3 minutes or until smooth. Stir in enough remaining flour to form a soft dough. Turn onto a floured surface; knead until smooth and elastic, about 6 to 8 minutes. Place in a greased bowl, turning once to grease top. Cover and let rise in a warm place until doubled, about 1½ hours. Punch dough down. Divide into 27 pieces; shape into balls. Place 18 balls in a greased 13x9x2 inch baking pan and remaining balls in a greased 9 inch square baking pan. Cover and let rise until doubled, about 45 minutes. Bake at 375° for 17 to 20 minutes or until golden brown. Cool on wire racks. Yield: 27 rolls.

Nutritional analysis: One roll (prepared with margarine) equals 142 calories, 156 mg sodium, 16 mg cholesterol, 23 g carbohydrate, 4 g protein, 4 g fat. Diabetic exchanges: 1½ starch, 1 fat.

TURKEY CUTLETS WITH APPLE CHUTNEY

1¼ c. chopped Granny Smith
   apples
1 c. diced tomato
¾ c. thinly sliced onion
3 Tbsp. brown sugar
2 Tbsp. cider vinegar
⅛ tsp. ground cloves

½ tsp. ground ginger
4 (2 oz.) turkey cutlets
⅛ tsp. salt
Dash of white pepper
1 tsp. oil
Cooking spray

Combine first 7 ingredients in small saucepan and bring to boil. Cover, reduce heat, and simmer for 45 minutes, stirring occasionally. Remove and let stand 10 minutes. Cover and chill. Sprinkle turkey with salt and pepper. Heat oil in nonstick pan coated with spray. Saute 2 minutes on each side or until done. Serve with apple chutney. Makes 2 servings.

Chutney will keep in airtight container 2 weeks.

Contains 203 calories, 4.6 g fat, 1.7 g fiber.

Joanne Shelley, Windsor Lions Club
Windsor, PA, USA

TURKEY BAYOU BURGERS

1 lb. ground turkey
2 scallions with 3 inches of green
    included, thinly sliced
1 red bell pepper, finely chopped
1 tsp. fresh minced garlic
2 Tbsp. chopped cilantro
¾ tsp. dried thyme

½ tsp. ground cumin
½ tsp. paprika
Red pepper flakes to taste
Salt and pepper to taste
4 hamburger buns
Mayonnaise, lettuce, tomatoes,
    avocado slices (optional)

Prepare BBQ for grilling. Place ground turkey in a bowl and mix well with the scallions, bell pepper, garlic, cilantro, and spices. Season to taste with salt and pepper. Gently form 4 patties. Grill for about 5 to 6 minutes per side, 3 inches from the heat. Serve on buns with mayonnaise, lettuce, tomato (and avocado slice if desired).

Spices turn the blander turkey patty into delicious burger.

Candace Wellman, Bellingham Harborview Lions Club
Bellingham, WA, USA

TENDER TURKEY BURGERS

⅔ c. soft whole wheat bread
    crumbs
½ c. finely chopped celery
¼ c. finely chopped onion
Egg substitute equivalent to 1 egg
1 Tbsp. minced fresh parsley
1 tsp. Worcestershire sauce

1 tsp. dried oregano
½ tsp. salt
¼ tsp. pepper
1¼ lb. ground turkey breast
6 whole wheat hamburger buns,
    split

In a bowl, combine the first nine ingredients. Add turkey and mix well. Shape into six patties. Pan-fry, grill or broil until no longer pink. Serve on buns. Yield: 6 servings.

Nutritional analysis: One burger (calculated without bun) equals 163 calories, 398 mg sodium, 47 mg cholesterol, 10 g carbohydrate, 26 g protein, 2 g fat. Diabetic exchanges: 3 very lean meat, ½ starch, ½ vegetable.

Enthusiasm and success just seem to go together.

You never get rewarded for the things you intended to do.

VENISON TENDERLOIN SANDWICHES

2 large onions, sliced
2 (4 oz.) cans sliced mushrooms,
    drained
1/4 c. butter or margarine
1/4 c. Worcestershire sauce
8 venison tenderloin steaks (12
    oz. - about 3/4 inch thick)

1/2 tsp. garlic powder
1/4 tsp. pepper
1/2 tsp. salt (optional)
4 hard rolls, split

In a skillet, saute the onions and mushrooms in butter and Worcestershire sauce until onions are tender. Flatten steaks to 1/2 inch thick; add to the skillet. Cook over medium heat until meat is done as desired, about 3 minutes on each side. Sprinkle with garlic powder, pepper, and salt if desired. Place two steaks on each roll; top with onions and mushrooms. Yield: 4 servings.

Nutritional analysis: One serving (prepared with margarine and without salt) equals 423 calories, 819 mg sodium, 85 mg cholesterol, 39 g carbohydrate, 30 g protein, 16 g fat. Diabetic exchanges: 3 lean meat, 2 starch, 1 1/2 fat, 1 vegetable.

HAM-BROCCOLI CASSEROLE

2 cans Healthy Request cream of
    mushroom soup
8 oz. jar Cheez Whiz
1/2 c. milk
1/2 c. chopped onions

2 (10 oz.) pkg. frozen broccoli,
    chopped
4 c. cooked ham, diced (1 1/2 lb.)
2 c. Minute rice

In a large bowl, blend soup, Cheez Whiz, and milk. Cook onion in butter until tender. Cook broccoli until almost tender, then drain. Add onion, broccoli, ham, and uncooked rice to soup mixture. This makes 2 1/2 quart casseroles. Bake covered at 350° for 35 to 40 minutes.

Exchanges for 1 cup: 1/2 vegetable, 1 1/4 breads, 1 fat, 1 1/3 meat.

Betty M. Kessler, North Lebanon Lioness Club
Lebanon, PA

CHICKEN POT PIE

1 (10 3/4 oz.) can Campbell's
    condensed 98% fat free
    cream of chicken soup
1 (9 oz.) pkg. frozen mixed
    vegetables, thawed

1 c. cubed cooked chicken
1/2 c. milk
1 egg
1 c. Bisquick reduced fat baking
    mix

Preheat oven to 400°. In a 9 inch pie pan, mix chicken soup, vegetables, and chicken. Mix milk, egg, and Bisquick in a separate container. Pour over top of vegetable, chicken, and soup mix. Bake for 30 minutes at 400° (or until brown).

Regina Gish, Mexico Sunrise Lions Club
Mexico, MO

VEGGIE CALZONES

Crust:

2¼ c. bread flour
⅔ c. oat bran
1½ tsp. RapidRise yeast

1 tsp. sugar
¼ tsp. salt
1 c. water

Filling:

1¼ c. fresh spinach
¼ c. onions, chopped
1¼ c. non/lowfat Ricotta cheese
¾ c. non/lowfat grated
　　Mozzarella cheese

3 Tbsp. non/lowfat grated
　　Parmesan cheese
¾ tsp. dried Italian seasoning

Sauce:

2 c. lowfat tomato sauce

In a large bowl, combine 1¼ cups of the flour with the oat bran, yeast, sugar, and salt and stir well. Place the water in a saucepan and heat on medium heat. Add the water to the flour mixture and stir for 1 to 2 minutes. Stir in enough of the remaining flour, 1 tablespoon at a time, to form a stiff dough. Sprinkle 2 tablespoons of the remaining flour over a flat surface and place the dough onto the surface. Knead the dough for 5 minutes, gradually adding enough of the remaining flour to form a smooth ball. Coat a large bowl with nonstick cooking spray (nonfat) and place the dough in the bowl. Cover the bowl with a towel and let rise for about 30 to 40 minutes.

When the dough has risen, divide it into 6 portions and shape each portion into a ball. Using a rolling pin, roll each ball into a circle.

Combine all of the filling ingredients in a medium-sized bowl and stir well. Spread the filling on the top half of each circle of dough. Brush a little water around the outer edges of each circle. Fold the bottom half over the top half and firmly press the edges together to seal. Place the calzones on the baking sheet. Bake at 450°F. for 15 to 18 minutes. Serve the calzones hot with warm sauce spread over top. Makes 6 servings.

Serving size: 1 calzone. Nutritional information: 290 calories, 1 g fat, 17 g protein, 3.5 g fiber, 35 g carbohydrate, 340 mg sodium.

Francis Sedlacek, Creston Lions Club
Creston, NE

*You shouldn't expect life's very best
if you're not giving it your very best.*

VEGGIE PIZZA

1 (8 oz.) pkg. refrigerated
    crescent rolls
1 (8 oz.) pkg. cream cheese,
    softened
1½ tsp. mayonnaise
1 crushed garlic clove

1 tsp. dried dill weed
Salt and pepper
2 c. assorted veggies - zucchini,
    carrots, green and red
    peppers, broccoli,
    mushrooms, celery, onion,
    etc.

Unroll rolls and divide into triangles. Arrange in circle on pizza pan and smooth edges. Bake at 350° for 12 to 15 minutes till light golden brown.

In 1 quart bowl, mix cream cheese, mayonnaise, garlic, and dill weed. Spread on baked crust. Chop all vegetables together and mix, then spread evenly over the top. Enjoy.

This is a healthy snack and young people like it.

Anne Tibbetts, South Jefferson Lions Club
Adams, NY

CINDI AND JOHN ZANKI'S HEALTHY
PASTA WITH VEGETABLES

2 medium yellow squash
1 medium stalk celery
10 to 14 fresh mushrooms
1 small onion
1 carrot

2 cloves garlic (optional)
1 red pepper
Salt and pepper
Linguini pasta (spinach pasta is
    the best)

Medium dice all vegetables except carrots and mushrooms. Slice carrots and mushrooms. Add 2 tablespoons olive oil to large skillet. Heat. Add carrots, celery, and onion. Saute approximately 10 minutes. Add all other vegetables. Saute until soft. Add salt and pepper. Cook pasta and put in dish. Pour vegetables on top. Serve.

You can add grated cheese or hot sauce. It's a very filling lowfat meal. If you add garlic, it helps colds.

Cindi Zanki, Jackson Lions Club
Jackson, NJ

You can tell how good a parent you were
by observing your children with their children.

2075-99

DOUBLE COATED CRISPY CHICKEN

6 skinless, boneless chicken
    breasts
¼ c. milk
¼ c. flour

1 tsp. salt
¼ tsp. pepper
1 c. crushed corn flakes

Wash chicken. In a bowl, mix milk, flour, salt, and pepper. Dip chicken breasts in the mixture and roll in corn flake crumbs. Place chicken on a greased pan or greased Reynolds Wrap to keep from sticking. Bake about 35 to 40 minutes at 375°.

Can cut chicken with fork and very healthy.

Edwin Young, Elizabethtown Lions Club
Elizabethtown, KY, USA

CHICKEN AND PORK ADOBO

3 chicken breasts, skinned and
    cut into 4 inch cubes
6 pork chops (no fat, use lean),
    cut into 4 inch cubes
3 cloves garlic, minced
1 medium onion, cut into 4
    lengthwise

1 bay leaf
½ tsp. pepper
Salt to taste
½ c. light soy sauce
½ c. water
½ c. vinegar

In a large pan, arrange pork chops, then chicken, onion, 1 bay leaf, pepper, and the mixture of soy sauce, vinegar, and water; pour on top and let it cook for 10 minutes, then let it simmer for another 20 minutes. To taste, add salt as needed or omit salt. Serve hot or cold over rice.

Ruby Thomas, Clairton Lions Club
Clairton, PA

Kids need hugs more than they need things.

The trip is often more fun than the destination.

Position can be bought, but respect must be earned.

OVEN FISH 'N' CHIPS

2 Tbsp. olive or vegetable oil
¼ tsp. pepper

4 medium baking potatoes (1 lb.), peeled

Fish:

⅓ c. all-purpose flour
¼ tsp. pepper
Egg substitute equivalent to 1 egg
2 Tbsp. water
⅔ c. crushed corn flakes

1 Tbsp. grated Parmesan cheese
⅛ tsp. cayenne pepper
1 lb. frozen haddock fillets, thawed
Tartar sauce (optional)

In a medium bowl, combine oil and pepper. Cut potatoes lengthwise into ½ inch strips. Add to oil mixture; toss to coat. Place on a 15x10x1 inch baking pan that has been coated with nonstick cooking spray. Bake, uncovered, at 425° for 25 to 30 minutes or until golden brown and crisp.

Meanwhile, combine flour and pepper in a shallow dish. In a second dish, beat egg substitute and water. In a third dish, combine corn flakes, cheese, and cayenne. Dredge fish in flour, then dip in egg mixture and coat with crumb mixture. Place on a baking sheet that has been coated with nonstick cooking spray. Bake at 425° for 10 to 15 minutes or until fish flakes easily with a fork. Serve with chips and tartar sauce if desired. Yield: 4 servings.

Nutritional analysis for fish: One 4 ounce serving (calculated without tartar sauce) equals 243 calories, 328 mg sodium, 67 mg cholesterol, 28 g carbohydrate, 27 g protein, 2 g fat. Diabetic exchanges: 3 very lean meat, 2 starch. Nutritional analysis for chips: One 4 ounce serving equals 137 calories, 4 mg sodium, 0 cholesterol, 18 g carbohydrate, 2 g protein, 7 g fat. Diabetic exchanges: 1½ fat, 1 starch.

It's never too late to improve yourself.

❧ ❧ ❧

A good deal is a good deal only when it's a good deal for both parties.

❧ ❧ ❧

Fame is written in ice - and eventually the sun comes out.

TURKEY STIR-FRY SUPPER

2¼ lb. boneless, skinless turkey
  breast
2 Tbsp. vegetable oil
¾ c. uncooked long grain rice
2 (14½ oz.) cans chicken broth,
  divided
5 Tbsp. soy sauce
2 garlic cloves, minced
½ tsp. ground ginger

¼ tsp. pepper
1 (10 oz.) pkg. frozen broccoli
  spears, thawed
1 lb. carrots, thinly sliced
3 bunches green onions, sliced
3 Tbsp. cornstarch
1 (14 oz.) can bean sprouts,
  drained

Cut turkey into 2 inch strips. In a Dutch oven or wok, stir-fry turkey in batches in oil for 5 to 7 minutes or until juices run clear. Set turkey aside. Add rice, 3½ cups broth, soy sauce, garlic, ginger, and pepper to pan; bring to a boil. Reduce heat; cover and simmer for 15 minutes or until rice is tender. Cut broccoli into 3 inch pieces. Add broccoli, carrots, and onions to rice mixture; simmer for 3 to 5 minutes. Combine cornstarch and remaining broth; add to pan. Bring to a boil; cook and stir for 2 minutes. Stir in turkey and beans sprouts; heat through. Yield: 14 servings.

Nutritional analysis: One 1 cup serving (prepared with low-sodium broth and light soy sauce) equals 233 calories, 345 mg sodium, 46 mg cholesterol, 19 g carbohydrate, 22 g protein, 8 g fat. Diabetic exchanges: 2 meat, 1 starch, 1 vegetable.

LOW FAT LASAGNA

1 lb. ground turkey
1 large onion
2 (1 lb.) cans stewed tomatoes
1 (6 oz.) can tomato paste
2 Tbsp. parsley flakes
1 tsp. oregano

1 tsp. basil
3 oz. Parmesan cheese
8 oz. dry lasagna noodles (10
  noodles - do not cook)
3 c. low fat cottage cheese
8 oz. low fat Mozzarella cheese

Brown meat and onion. Add all ingredients through Parmesan cheese. In sprayed 9x13 inch pan, layer as follows: ½ of sauce mixture, 5 noodles, cottage cheese, 5 noodles, remaining sauce, and Mozzarella cheese. Bake at 350° for 1 hour covered and 15 minutes uncovered. Let set 15 minutes before cutting. Leftovers can be frozen.

PARTY WALNUT BROCCOLI
(Very heart healthy)

1 (10 oz.) pkg. frozen chopped
   broccoli
3 Tbsp. margarine
2 Tbsp. flour
2 chicken bouillon cubes,
   dissolved in 1 c. hot water

1 c. skim milk
1/3 c. water
1 c. herbed poultry stuffing
   (crumbly type)
1/2 c. chopped walnuts

Preheat oven to 400°. Cook broccoli according to package directions until just barely tender. Drain well and place in an oiled 2 quart casserole dish.

Melt 1 tablespoon margarine in a saucepan. Stir in the flour; cook briefly and add the milk. Add the bouillon and cook, stirring constantly, until thickened. Set aside.

Melt the remaining margarine in the 1/3 cup of water; mix with the herb dressing and walnuts. Pour the bouillon sauce over the broccoli. Sprinkle evenly with the walnut mixture and bake 20 minutes. Serves 4.

CHINESE-STYLE SUMMER VEGETABLES
(Low in fat)

3 Tbsp. soy sauce
1 Tbsp. rice-wine vinegar
1 Tbsp. vegetable oil
2 large scallions, sliced (about 1/4
   c.)
1 clove garlic, minced
2 tsp. minced fresh ginger

1/2 lb. green beans, trimmed and
   cut in halves crosswise (about
   2 c.)
1 medium carrot, cut into thin
   sticks (about 1 c.)
1 medium yellow squash, cut in
   half lengthwise, then
   crosswise into 1/4 inch slices
   (about 1 c.)

In a small bowl, combine soy sauce and rice vinegar. Set aside. In a medium frying pan, heat oil over high heat. Add scallions, garlic, and ginger and cook 1 minute. Add green beans and 1/4 cup water and cook 4 minutes. Add carrot, yellow squash, and half the soy mixture and cook until vegetables are tender-crisp, about 4 minutes. Stir in remaining soy mixture and heat through an additional 2 to 3 minutes. Makes 6 servings.

Per serving: 48 calories, 2 g protein, 2 g fat, 522 mg sodium, 6 g carbohydrate, 0 mg cholesterol.

Lion John J. Hess, Clarence Lions Club
Clarence Center, NY, USA

2075-99

BAKED ONION RINGS

1½ c. crushed corn flakes
2 tsp. sugar
1 tsp. paprika
¼ tsp. seasoned salt

¼ tsp. garlic salt
2 large sweet onions
Egg substitute equivalent to 2
   eggs

In a large bowl, combine the first five ingredients; set aside. Cut onions into ½ inch thick slices. Separate into rings, reserving the small rings for another use. In a small mixing bowl, beat egg substitute until frothy. Dip onion rings into egg, then into crumb mixture, coating well. Place in a single layer on baking sheets that have been coated with nonstick cooking spray. Bake at 375° for 15 to 20 minutes or until onions are tender and coating is crispy. Yield: About 6 servings.

Nutritional analysis: One serving (four onion rings) equals 143 calories, 442 mg sodium, trace cholesterol, 30 g carbohydrate, 5 g protein, 1 g fat. Diabetic exchanges: 2 starch.

SESAME ASPARAGUS

6 fresh asparagus spears,
   trimmed
¼ tsp. salt (optional)
1 tsp. butter or margarine

1 tsp. lemon juice
¾ tsp. sesame seeds, toasted

Place asparagus in a skillet; sprinkle with salt if desired. Add ½ inch of water; bring to a boil. Reduce heat; cover and simmer until crisp-tender, about 4 minutes. Meanwhile, melt butter; add lemon juice and sesame seeds. Drain asparagus; drizzle with the butter mixture. Yield: 1 serving.

Nutritional analysis: One serving (prepared with margarine and without salt) equals 71 calories, 47 mg sodium, 0 cholesterol, 5 g carbohydrate, 3 g protein, 5 g fat. Diabetic exchanges: 1 vegetable, 1 fat.

FAT FREE MASHED POTATOES

6 medium potatoes (2 lb.)
½ c. fat free evaporated skimmed
   milk

3 Tbsp. + 1 tsp. Molly McButter
   natural butter flavor sprinkles
Dash of salt and pepper to taste

Scrub potatoes. Cut potatoes into quarters. Boil until tender (20 to 25 minutes). Drain. Add remaining ingredients and mash to desired consistency.

Tip: Add 2½ teaspoons Dijon mustard to the recipe for added flavor.
Lion Ethel Harbaugh, Tuscola Lions Club
Tuscola, IL, USA

LOADED POTATO

½ c. small-curd cottage cheese
2 Tbsp. shredded Cheddar cheese
2 Tbsp. chopped tomato

1 Tbsp. chopped green pepper
1 Tbsp. chopped green onion
1 hot baked potato

Combine the first five ingredients. With a sharp knife, cut an X in the top of the potato; fluff pulp with a fork. Top with cottage cheese mixture. Serve immediately. Yield: 1 serving.

Nutritional analysis: One serving (prepared with fat-free cottage cheese and fat-free Cheddar cheese) equals 245 calories, 563 mg sodium, 11 mg cholesterol, 38 g carbohydrate, 22 g protein, trace fat. Diabetic exchanges: 3 very lean meat, 2 starch, 1 vegetable.

NANCY WANZEL'S ESCAROLE SOUP

2 big heads escarole
2 large cans chicken broth
5 large kernels garlic

1 can Progresso lentils
Olive oil
Orzo or small pasta

Cut escarole into approximately 1 inch pieces. Put in strainer and wash 3 times to get out sand. Put in large pot with chicken broth. Slice or mince garlic and add to mixture. Add olive oil (approximately 2 to 4 tablespoons). Cook on medium to low heat about ½ hour until escarole cooks down. Add can of lentils and cook another 15 minutes or so. Serve over small macaroni or orzo. Add grated cheese if you wish.

Very healthy for you. Low fat. Great to help stop colds and flu.
Cindi Zanki, Jackson Lions Club
Jackson, NJ, Ocean

To get the right answer, you have to ask the right question.

❦ ❦ ❦

The best way to appreciate something is to be without it for awhile.

❦ ❦ ❦

It takes as much time and energy to wish as it does to plan.

VEGETABLE SOUP
("Think thin")

Carrots
Cabbage
Cauliflower
Onion
Clove of garlic
Peas
Lentils (clean and soak at least 3
   hours in water before starting
   soup)

Celery
Potatoes
Broccoli
Zucchini
Brussels sprouts
Green pepper
Beets
Water

Make your own soup using any combination of the above vegetables in a large cooking pot. Chop vegetables into bite-size pieces. Put 8 cups mixed vegetables into large pot. Add ½ gallon water. Bring to boil. Reduce heat to low, then simmer until vegetables are soft. Add another ½ gallon water. Simmer. Season with herbs or dry vegetable seasoning to taste. Check for doneness. If you wish, you may add a can of stewed tomatoes. The amount depends on your choice. Serving size: 2 cups per meal. Eat only 4 low salt no fat crackers with your meal.

Check with your doctor before going on any diet.

Ann K. Brumback of Littlestown, PA,
Silver Run Union Mills Lions Club
Westminster, MD

EASY - BUT GOOD - VEGETABLE SOUP

½ lb. ground beef
¼ c. dry onion soup mix
1 tsp. sugar
10 oz. pkg. frozen mixed
   vegetables

16 oz. can stewed tomatoes
8 oz. can tomato sauce
1 to 2 tsp. green chillies
2 c. water

In large saucepan, brown meat. Drain off fat. Stir in 2 cups water and remaining ingredients. Bring to boiling. Reduce heat; cover and simmer for 20 minutes.

For fat free soup, I use 2 teaspoons bouillon granules instead of ground beef.

Lion Ethel Harbaugh, Tuscola Lions Club
Tuscola, IL, USA

We grow only when we push ourselves beyond what we already know.

DIET HAMBURG SOUP

1½ lb. hamburg
5¾ c. tomato juice (46 oz. can)
1 c. stewed tomatoes
1 bay leaf, broken up
1 Tbsp. garlic powder
1 c. chopped carrots
2 tsp. basil

2 c. chopped celery
2 tsp. oregano
2 tsp. onion, chopped
1 Tbsp. Worcestershire sauce
2 c. string beans
2 c. shredded cabbage
3 beef bouillon cubes

Brown and drain hamburg. Add all other ingredients and simmer well.

Carrots, celery, and green beans can be fresh or frozen.

Lion Gloria Bonager, East Prospect Lions Club
East Prospect, PA, USA

"FORGOTTEN" MINESTRONE

1 lb. lean beef stew meat
6 c. water
1 (28 oz.) can tomatoes with
    liquid, cut up
1 beef bouillon cube
1 medium onion, chopped
2 Tbsp. minced dried parsley
2½ tsp. salt (optional)
1½ tsp. ground thyme

½ tsp. pepper
1 medium zucchini, thinly sliced
2 c. finely chopped cabbage
1 (16 oz.) can garbanzo beans,
    drained
1 c. uncooked small elbow or
    shell macaroni
¼ c. grated Parmesan cheese
    (optional)

In a slow cooker, combine the first nine ingredients. Cover and cook on LOW for 7 to 9 hours or until meat is tender. Add zucchini, cabbage, beans, and macaroni; cook on HIGH 30 to 45 minutes more or until the vegetables are tender. Sprinkle individual servings with Parmesan cheese if desired. Yield: 8 servings.

Nutritional analysis: One serving (prepared without salt and Parmesan cheese) equals 246 calories, 453 mg sodium, 33 mg cholesterol, 30 g carbohydrate, 19 g protein, 6 g fat. Diabetic Exchanges: 2 vegetable, 1½ starch, 1 meat.

If you don't feel like being pleasant, courteous, and kind,
act that way and the feelings will come.

When things get easy, it's easy to stop growing.

2075-99

SPEEDY VEGETABLE SOUP

2 cans (one 49 oz., one 14½ oz.)
    low-sodium chicken broth
2 celery ribs, thinly sliced
1 medium green pepper, chopped
1 medium onion, chopped
2 medium carrots, chopped

1 env. onion soup mix
1 bay leaf
¼ tsp. garlic powder
¼ tsp. pepper
1 (14½ oz.) can diced tomatoes
    (undrained)

In a saucepan, combine the first nine ingredients; bring to a boil over medium heat. Reduce heat; cover and simmer for 15 to 20 minutes or until vegetables are tender. Add tomatoes; heat through. Remove bay leaf. Yield: 11 servings (about 3 quarts).

Nutritional analysis: One 1 cup serving equals 38 calories, 195 mg sodium, 3 mg cholesterol, 5 g carbohydrate, 3 g protein, 1 g fat. Diabetic exchanges: 1 vegetable.

ALASKAN SALMON CHOWDER

½ c. chopped onion
½ c. chopped celery
¼ c. chopped green pepper
1 garlic clove, minced
1 (14½ oz.) can chicken broth,
    divided
2 c. diced, peeled potatoes
1 c. sliced carrots

1 tsp. seasoned salt (optional)
½ tsp. dill weed
1 small zucchini, thinly sliced
1 (14¾ oz.) can cream style corn
1 (12 oz.) can evaporated milk
2 c. cooked salmon chunks or 2
    (7½ oz.) cans salmon,
    drained and bones removed

In a saucepan, cook onion, celery, green pepper, and garlic in ¼ cup broth until tender. Add potatoes, carrots, seasoned salt (if desired), dill, and remaining broth. Cover and simmer for 20 minutes or until vegetables are tender. Add zucchini; simmer for 5 minutes. Add corn, milk, and salmon; heat through. Yield: 7 servings.

Nutritional analysis: One 1 cup serving (prepared with low-sodium broth, no-salt-added corn and evaporated skim milk and without seasoned salt) equals 225 calories, 147 mg sodium, 27 mg cholesterol, 29 g carbohydrate, 20 g protein, 4 g fat. Diabetic exchanges: 2 lean meat, 1½ starch, 1 vegetable.

*People are in such a hurry to get to the "good life"
that they often rush right past it.*

QUICK JELLO LUNCH

24 oz. cottage cheese
20 oz. can crushed pineapple,
   drained (save juice)

1 (4 serving) box Jell-O (any
   flavor)

Mix Jell-O with ¾ cup hot water. Add pineapple juice (need 1 cup - add water if not enough). In 4 containers put ⅔ cup cottage cheese, ½ cup crushed pineapple, and ½ cup Jell-O liquid.

Each serving: 1 fruit, 2 proteins, 8 optional calories.

Strawberry Jell-O is very good and colorful.

Audrey Leisgang, Ashwaubenon Lioness Club
Green Bay, WI, USA

INDONESIAN-STYLE SALAD

1 c. cantaloupe chunks
1 c. pineapple chunks
1½ c. broccoli florets
1 c. chopped red pepper (sweet)

2 stalks celery, cut up
15 oz. can black beans, drained
   and rinsed
½ c. whole peanuts

Dressing:

2 Tbsp. light molasses
2 Tbsp. lemon juice
1 Tbsp. water

1½ Tbsp. lite soy sauce
1 clove crushed garlic
⅛ tsp. crushed red pepper (hot)

Combine fruit and vegetables and mix. Combine dressing and pour over salad just before serving. This makes 4 servings with 310 calories each.

Don't be afraid to try this - it is very good.

Pat Worden, South Jefferson Lions Club
Adams, NY

STRAWBERRY SPINACH SALAD

2 c. fresh strawberries or
   raspberries
Fresh spinach leaves, washed and
   patted dry

1 Bermuda onion (red), sliced
Lite raspberry vinaigrette dressing

Slice strawberries in halves. Toss with dry, clean, and broken spinach leaves. Add onion slices. Just before serving, toss with small amount of the raspberry vinaigrette, only enough to dampen slightly.

Best served in a glass bowl. All ingredients can be prepared ahead and combined at the last minute.

This odd combination of foods is so intriguing. There will never be any leftovers. It's delicious!

Candace Wellman, Bellingham Harborview Lions Club
Bellingham, WA, USA

2075-99

HEALTH SALAD

5 Tbsp. white wine vinegar
2 Tbsp. olive oil
1 Tbsp. sugar
¾ tsp. salt
⅛ tsp. pepper
2 c. broccoli florets
2 c. cauliflower florets

3 c. cabbage, cut into ½ inch
  pieces
3 scallions, chopped
2 carrots, diagonally sliced
1 large red pepper, cut into 1
  inch pieces

In large bowl, whisk together vinegar, olive oil, sugar, salt, and pepper. In large saucepan, bring 1 inch of water to a boil over high heat. Add broccoli and cauliflower florets; cook 2 minutes or until tender. Drain and rinse with cold water. This method of blanching (rapid boiling followed by quick cooling) helps to set color and preserve crispness. Add broccoli and cauliflower to dressing. Add cabbage, scallions, carrots, and red pepper; toss to combine. Cover and refrigerate 1 hour or overnight. Makes 8 servings.

Work time: 30 minutes. Total time: 1 hour and 35 minutes.

Per serving: 67 calories, 2 g protein, 9 g carbohydrate, 4 g fat, 0 mg cholesterol, 221 mg sodium.

Mrs. Lucy Aiken, Clarence Lions Club
Clarence Center, NY, USA

WINTER-FRUIT COMPOTE
(Low in fat)

4 firm pears (about 2 lb.), peeled,
  cored, and cut into eighths
½ c. dried apricots
½ c. pitted prunes
4 strips lemon zest (about 2
  inches each)

3 whole cloves
1 cinnamon stick
3 c. apple juice

Put pears, apricots, prunes, lemon zest, cloves, and cinnamon stick in medium saucepan. Add the apple juice; bring to a boil, then reduce heat to low. Cover and cook until pears are very tender when pierced with the tip of a knife, about 30 minutes. Drain the fruit, reserving the poaching liquid. Return liquid to saucepan and boil until reduced by about one-third, 15 to 20 minutes. It should become a smooth, thick syrup. Pour this syrup over the fruit and chill before serving. Makes 6 servings.

Per serving: 183 calories, 1 g protein, 1 g fat, 6 mg sodium, 47 g carbohydrate, 0 mg cholesterol.

Joanne M. Wetzler, Clarence Lions Club
Clarence Center, NY, USA

CUCUMBER WITH YOGURT AND MINT
(Low in fat)

2 medium cucumbers, peeled
2 Tbsp. chopped fresh mint
1 clove garlic, minced
¾ tsp. ground cumin

⅛ tsp. cayenne pepper
½ tsp. salt
⅔ c. plain yogurt

Cut the cucumbers in halves lengthwise. Using a spoon, scoop out the seeds from each half. Cut the cucumbers crosswise into thick slices. In a medium bowl, combine the cucumbers with the mint, garlic, cumin, cayenne, and salt. Stir in the yogurt and chill thoroughly. Stir up salad again before serving. Makes 6 servings.

Per serving: 32 calories, 2 g protein, 1 g fat, 193 mg sodium, 5 g carbohydrate, 4 mg cholesterol.

Joanne M. Wetzler, Clarence Lions Club
Clarence Center, NY, USA

BROCCOLI TOMATO SALAD

1 large bunch broccoli, separated
    into florets
2 large tomatoes, cut into wedges

¾ c. sliced fresh mushrooms
2 green onions, sliced

Dressing:

¾ c. olive or vegetable oil
⅓ c. tarragon or cider vinegar
2 Tbsp. water
1 tsp. lemon juice
1 tsp. sugar
1 tsp. salt (optional)
¾ tsp. dried thyme

1 garlic clove, minced
½ tsp. celery seed
¼ tsp. Italian seasoning
¼ tsp. lemon-pepper seasoning
¼ tsp. paprika
¼ tsp. ground mustard

Cook broccoli in a small amount of water for 5 minutes or until crisp-tender. Rinse with cold water and drain. Place in a large bowl; add tomatoes, mushrooms, and onions. Combine dressing ingredients in a jar with a tight-fitting lid; shake well. Pour over salad; toss gently. Cover and chill for 1 hour. Serve with a slotted spoon. Yield: 6 to 8 servings.

Nutritional analysis: One 1 cup serving (prepared without salt) equals 130 calories, 32 mg sodium, 0 cholesterol, 8 g carbohydrate, 3 g protein, 11 g fat. Diabetic exchanges: 2 fat, 1½ vegetable.

You shouldn't speak unless you can improve on the silence.

SALAD WITH OIL-FREE DRESSING

1 Tbsp. powdered fruit pectin
¼ tsp. dried herb (oregano, basil,
    thyme, tarragon, savory or
    dill weed)
Artificial sweetener equivalent to
    2 tsp. sugar
⅛ tsp. ground mustard
⅛ tsp. salt
⅛ tsp. pepper
¼ c. water
2 tsp. vinegar
1 garlic clove, minced
Salad greens, tomatoes,
    cucumbers, and carrots or
    vegetables of your choice

In a small bowl, combine pectin, herb of choice, sweetener, mustard, salt, and pepper. Stir in water, vinegar, and garlic. Chill. serve over greens and vegetables of your choice. Refrigerate leftovers. Yield: ⅓ cup.

Nutritional analysis: 1 tablespoon of dressing equals 13 calories, 60 mg sodium, 0 cholesterol, 3 g carbohydrate, trace protein, trace fat. Diabetic exchange: Free.

BARLEY NUT SALAD

1 c. uncooked barley
3 c. water
3 Tbsp. olive oil
¼ c. lemon juice (fresh is best)
½ tsp. sea salt
2 stalks celery, chopped
1 carrot, finely chopped
1 medium onion, finely chopped
½ c. minced fresh parsley
½ c. roasted nuts (walnuts or
    hazelnuts)

Wash barley and cook in 3 cups water in a 1½ to 2 quart saucepan 50 to 60 minutes. Allow to cool. Wash and chop celery, onion, and carrot; mince parsley and chop nuts. Combine lemon juice, oil, and salt. Combine all ingredients and mix thoroughly. Refrigerate for several hours before serving to blend flavors.

I sometimes add chopped broccoli and/or radishes. It carries well to picnics. Can substitute flax oil for olive oil.

James R. Schiebel, Hilton Lions Club
Hilton, NY, USA

Money is a lousy means of keeping score.

If you wish to do business with honest people, you must be an honest person.

DIET FRUIT BARS
(No sugar)

1 c. flour
1 tsp. baking soda
1 tsp. cinnamon
½ c. raisins
½ c. prunes, cut up

1 c. water
½ c. oleo
2 eggs, beaten well
1 tsp. vanilla
½ c. nuts (optional)

Mix together flour, soda, and cinnamon. Set aside. Combine raisins, prunes, and dates in saucepan with 1 cup water. Bring to boil. Simmer 4 minutes. Add oleo and let cool. Stir in eggs and vanilla. Add dry ingredients and nuts. Spread in 9x9 inch pan. Bake in 350° oven about 30 minutes or until it tests done to your liking.

This recipe has only natural sugars, so may appear ''done'' sooner to one person than to another.

Margaret Wooden, Princeton Lions Club
Princeton, IL, USA

DOUBLE RASPBERRY FRUIT DRIP

½ c. Seven Seas free raspberry
   vinaigrette free dressing
½ c. Breyers lowfat raspberry
   yogurt

1 c. thawed Cool Whip Free
   whipped topping
Cut up fresh fruit

Mix dressing, yogurt, and whipped topping until smooth. Refrigerate. Serve with fruit. Makes 2 cups.

Regina Gish, Mexico Sunrise Lions Club
Mexico, MO

You can inherit wealth but never wisdom.

It's never too late to heal an injured relationship.

I've learned that the little sayings you learn as a child,
such as the Golden Rule, are actually important.

ALMOND BISCOTTI

½ c. butter or margarine (I use
   margarine)
1 c. white sugar
3 eggs
1 tsp. almond flavoring
2 c. flour

2 tsp. baking powder
Dash of salt
½ c. chopped almonds (I use
   chopped pecans)
2 tsp. milk

In mixing bowl, cream butter and 1 cup sugar. Add eggs 1 at a time, beating well after each addition. Stir in almond flavoring. Combine dry ingredients. Add to creamed mixture. Stir in chopped nuts of your choice. Line a baking sheet with foil and spray with Pam.

Divide dough in half. Spread into 12x3 inch rectangles on foil. Brush with milk and sprinkle with sugar. Bake at 375° for 17 minutes or until golden brown. Remove from oven and reduce heat to 300°. Lift rectangles with foil onto wire rack. Cool for 15 minutes. Place on a cutting board. Slice diagonally ½ inch thick. Place slices with cut side down on ungreased baking sheet. Bake for 10 minutes. Turn slices over and bake 10 minutes more. Turn oven off, leaving oven door ajar to cool. Store in airtight container. Yield: 3½ dozen.

Carol Waller, Stewart Lions Club
Stewart, MN, USA

ANGEL MACAROONS

1 (16 oz.) pkg. one-step angel
   food cake mix
½ c. water

1½ tsp. almond extract
2 c. flaked coconut

In a mixing bowl, beat cake mix, water, and extract on low speed for 30 seconds. Scrape bowl; beat on medium for 1 minute. Fold in the coconut. Drop by rounded teaspoonfuls onto a parchment paper-lined baking sheet. Bake at 350° for 10 to 12 minutes or until set. Remove paper with cookies to a wire rack to cool. Yield: 2½ dozen.

Nutritional analysis: One cookie equals 89 calories, 164 mg sodium, 0 cholesterol, 16 g carbohydrate, 2 g protein, 2 g fat. Diabetic exchange: 1 starch.

You are grown up not when you can take care of yourself,
but when you can take care of others.

❧ ❧ ❧

Don't be afraid to take a big step if one is indicated.
You can't cross a chasm in two small jumps.
David Lloyd George

PINEAPPLE COCONUT PIE

1 c. skim milk
1 pkg. instant sugar free vanilla
   pudding mix
½ c. flaked coconut

1 (8 oz.) can crushed
   unsweetened pineapple,
   drained
Whipped topping (optional)
1 pastry shell (9 inches), baked

In mixing bowl, beat milk and instant pudding mix until thickened. Stir in the coconut and drained pineapple. Pour into baked/cooled pie shell. Chill for at least 2 hours. Garnish with whipped topping if desired. Makes 8 servings.

Equals 198 calories, 647 mg sodium, 1 mg cholesterol, 26 g carbohydrate, 3 g protein, 9 g fat. Diabetic exchanges: 2 fat, 1 starch, ½ fruit.

For all our diabetic members.
Lion Ann Brumback, Silver Run Union Mills Lions Club
Westminster, MD, USA

LITE 'N EASY STRAWBERRY TRIFLE

1 angel food cake
1 (4 serving) pkg. strawberry
   sugar-free Jell-O
1 pt. strawberries (fresh or frozen
   unsweetened)

1 qt. cold skim milk (fat free)
2 (4 serving) pkg. vanilla fat-free
   sugar-free instant Jell-O
   pudding
8 oz. lite Cool Whip

Line bottom of a 4 quart shallow baking dish with angel food cake pieces. Prepare Jell-O per package instructions. Pour over cake pieces. Top with halved strawberries, reserving several for garnish. Prepare pudding per package. Spread over strawberry layers. Let stand 5 minutes. Spread Cool Whip over pudding layer. Refrigerate 4 hours. Garnish with Cool Whip and strawberries. Cut into 16 squares.

This is truly lite and refreshing.
Emily Groover, Bellville Lions Club
Bellville, GA, USA

ANGEL CAKE

1 pkg. dry angel food cake mix   1 (20 oz.) crushed pineapple

Mix by hand the dry cake mix by hand with the crushed pineapple juice and all. Mix slowly until all is mixed together. Bake in ungreased 9x13 inch pan for 30 minutes at 350° or until done. Serve with light Cool Whip.

This is a cake diabetics can eat.
Leola C. Jurrens, Downtown Bartlesville Lions Club
Bartlesville, OK, USA

SUGAR-FREE APPLE PIE

⅓ c. frozen apple juice
    concentrate
4 packets artificial sweetener
    (equal to 8 tsp. sugar)
2 tsp. cornstarch
1 tsp. ground cinnamon

Pastry for double-crust pie (9
    inches)
8 c. thinly sliced, peeled baking
    apples
1 Tbsp. margarine

Combine the first four ingredients. Line pie plate with bottom crust; add apples. Pour juice mixture over apples; dot with margarine. Roll out remaining pastry to fit top of pie; cut slits in top. Place over filling; seal and flute edges. Bake at 375° for 35 minutes. Increase oven to 400°; bake for 15 to 20 minutes or until apples are tender. Sweet 'N Low is recommended for baking.

My husband is diabetic so I enjoy fixing this pie. He can enjoy dessert, too.

Georgia Kleeb, Sargent Lions Club
Sargent, NE

"SUGAR FREE" CAKE

2 c. raisins
2 c. water
1 c. plum or prune baby food or
    1 c. unsweetened applesauce
    or unsweetened fruit (plums
    are best)
2 eggs
2 Tbsp. liquid sweetener

¾ c. cooking oil
2 c. self-rising flour (do not sift)
½ tsp. cinnamon
½ tsp. nutmeg or cloves
½ tsp. vanilla
½ tsp. soda
½ c. chopped nuts (optional)

Cook raisins in water until dry. Mix all ingredients well and bake in a Bundt pan (or a greased and floured 9x13 inch pan) for 55 to 60 minutes or until cake pulls away from sides of pan.

Good warm served with cream cheese.

This is very good to take to project suppers and to give as Christmas gifts to diabetic friends.

Lion Gloria Bonager, East Prospect Lions Club
East Prospect, PA, USA

All things are difficult before they are easy.
John Norley and Thomas Fuller

ORANGE PINEAPPLE TORTE

1 (18¼ oz.) pkg. yellow light
    cake mix
2 (1 oz.) pkg. instant sugar-free
    vanilla pudding mix, *divided*
4 egg whites
1 c. water
¼ c. vegetable oil
¼ tsp. baking soda

1 c. cold skim milk
1 (8 oz.) ctn. frozen light whipped
    topping, thawed
1 (20 oz.) can unsweetened
    crushed pineapple, well
    drained
1 (11 oz.) can mandarin oranges,
    drained and *divided*
Fresh mint (optional)

In a mixing bowl, combine cake mix, one package of pudding mix, egg whites, water, oil, and baking soda. Beat on low speed for 1 minute; beat on medium for 4 minutes. Pour into two greased an floured 9 inch round cake pans. Bake at 350° for 25 to 30 minutes or until a toothpick inserted near the center comes out clean. Cool for 10 minutes; remove from pans to a wire rack to cool completely.

For filling, combine milk and remaining pudding mix. Whisk to 2 minutes; let stand for 2 minutes. Fold in whipped topping.

In a medium bowl, combine 1½ cups pudding mixture with pineapple and half of the oranges. Slice each cake layer in half horizontally. Spread pineapple mixture between the layers. Frost top and sides of cake with remaining pudding mixture. Garnish with remaining oranges and mint if desired. Yield: 12 servings.

Nutritional analysis: One serving equals 335 calories, 516 mg sodium, trace cholesterol, 58 g carbohydrate, 4 g protein, 9 g fat. Diabetic exchanges: 2 starch, 2 fruit, 2 fat.

FRUITY DESSERT

1 (0.3 oz.) pkg. sugar-free cherry
    gelatin
1 c. boiling water
1 (20 oz.) can unsweetened
    crushed pineapple

1½ c. hot cooked rice
1 c. light whipped topping

In a bowl, dissolve gelatin in boiling water. Drain pineapple, reserving juice; set pineapple aside. Add juice to gelatin; stir in rice. Chill until mixture begins to thicken. Fold in whipped topping and pineapple. Chill for 1 hour. Yield: 10 servings.

Nutritional analysis: One ½ cup serving equals 79 calories, 19 mg sodium, 0 cholesterol, 16 g carbohydrate, 1 g protein, 1 g fat. Diabetic exchanges: ½ starch, ½ fruit.

2075-99

DIABETIC PINEAPPLE PIE

4 pkg. sugar substitute
3 Tbsp. corn starch

¼ tsp. salt
2½ c. crushed pineapple and
   juice

    Make 2 pie crusts. Line pie pan with one (1) crust. Set aside. Cook all above ingredients over medium heat, stirring constantly, until mixture thickens and boils for one (1) minute. Pour into pie pan. Quickly cover with other crust. Make slits in top crust with knife. Bake at 425° (hot oven) for 25 to 30 minutes.

Carol S. Dowers, Elberfeld Lions Club
Haubstadt, IN, Gibson County

Sometimes you have to sprout your wings after you jump off the cliff.

Even if you're on the right track, you'll get run over if you just sit there.
James Allen

We will not know unless we begin.
Howard Zinn

Once you're moving you can keep moving.
Ronald Alan Weiss

Miscellaneous

FIRST AID IN HOUSEHOLD EMERGENCIES

POISONING: When a poison has been taken internally, start first aid at once. Call doctor immediately.
- Dilute poison with large amounts of liquid — milk or water.
- Wash out by inducing vomiting, when not a strong acid, strong alkali, or petroleum.
- For acid poisons do not induce vomiting, but neutralize with milk of magnesia. Then give milk, olive oil, or egg white. Keep victim warm and lying down.
- For alkali poisons such as lye or ammonia, do not induce vomiting.
- Give lemon juice or vinegar. Then give milk and keep victim warm and lying down.
- If poison is a sleeping drug, induce vomiting and then give strong black coffee frequently. Victim must be kept awake.
- If breathing stops, give artificial respiration.

SHOCK: Shock is brought on by a sudden or severe physical injury or emotional disturbance. In shock, the balance between the nervous system and the blood vessels is upset. The result is faintness, nausea, and a pale and clammy skin. Call ambulance immediately. If not treated the victim may become unconscious and eventually lapse into a coma.
- Keep victim lying down, preferably with head lower than body.
- Don't give fluids unless delayed in getting to doctor, then give only water. (Hot tea, coffee, milk, or broth may be tried if water is not tolerated.)
- Never give liquid to an unconscious person. Patient must be alert.
- Cover victim both under and around his body.
- Do not permit victim to become abnormally hot.
- Reassure victim and avoid letting him see other victims or his own injury.
- Fainting is most common and last form of shock. Patient will respond in 30-60 seconds by merely allowing patient to lie head down, if possible, on floor.

FRACTURES: Pain, deformity, or swelling of injured part usually means a fracture. If fracture is suspected, don't move person unless absolutely necessary, and then only if the suspected area is splinted. Give small amounts of lukewarm fluids and treat for shock.

BURNS: Apply or submerge the burned area in cold water. Apply a protective dry sterile cloth or gauze dry dressing if necessary. Do not apply grease or an antiseptic ointment or spray. Call doctor and keep patient warm (not hot) with severe burns.
- If burn case must be transported any distance, cover burns with clean cloth.
- Don't dress extensive facial burns. (It may hinder early plastic surgery.)

WOUNDS: Minor cuts — Apply pressure with sterile gauze until bleeding stops. Use antiseptic recommended by your doctor. Bandage with sterile gauze. See your doctor. **Puncture Wounds** — Cover with sterile gauze and consult a doctor immediately. Serious infection can arise unless properly treated.

ANIMAL BITES: Wash wounds freely with soap and water. Hold under running tap for several minutes if possible. Apply an antiseptic approved by your doctor and cover with sterile gauze compress. Always see your doctor immediately. So that animal may be held in quarantine, obtain name and address of owner.

HEAT EXHAUSTION: Caused by exposure to heat or sun. Symptoms: Pale face, moist and clammy skin, weak pulse, subnormal temperature, victim usually conscious.
Treatment: Keep victim lying down, legs elevated, victim wrapped in blanket. Give salt water to drink (1 tsp. salt to 1 glass water), ½ glass every 15 minutes. Call doctor.

GENERAL DIRECTIONS FOR FIRST AID

1. Effect a prompt rescue.
2. Maintain an open airway.
3. Control severe bleeding by direct pressure over bleeding site. No tourniquet.
4. Give First Aid for poisoning.
5. Do not move victim unless it is necessary for safety reasons.
6. Protect the victim from unnecessary manipulation.
7. Avoid or overcome chilling by using blankets or covers, if available.
8. Determine the injuries or cause for sudden illness.
9. Examine the victim methodically but be guided by the kind of accident or sudden illness and the need of the situation.
10. Carry out the indicated First Aid.

MISCELLANEOUS

ELDERBERRY JELLY

3¾ c. elderberry juice
¼ c. lemon juice

1 box powdered pectin
5 c. sugar

Wash elderberries and cook with water covering elderberries in pan. Put in jelly bag and drain. Measure elderberry juice into a large enameled or stainless steel pan. Add lemon juice and pectin. Bring to a boil, stirring over high heat. Add sugar, all at once, stirring constantly. Bring to a full rolling boil for 2 minutes. Set off heat and skim off foam. Pour into sterile jars and seal. Turn upside down for 5 minutes. Turn right side up.

Liz Birchen, O'Fallon Lions Club
O'Fallon, MO, USA

QUEEN ANNE'S LACE JELLY

17 large flower heads

3¾ c. boiling water

Place flower heads in boiling water. Remove from heat and allow to steep 15 minutes. This yields about 3 cups of infusion.

3 c. infusion
3¾ c. sugar

1 box powdered pectin
1 Tbsp. lemon juice

Add pectin to infusion and bring to a boil over high heat, stirring constantly. Add sugar, all at once, and lemon juice, stirring over high heat. Bring to a full boil for 2 minutes, stirring constantly. Remove from heat. Skim off foam and pour jelly into sterile jars. Seal and invert for 5 minutes. Turn right side up.

Liz Birchen, O'Fallon Lions Club
O'Fallon, MO, USA

HOT PEPPER JELLY

10 jalapeno chiles, stemmed and
    seeded
2 medium bell peppers
1½ c. vinegar
6 c. sugar

⅓ c. lemon juice
4 oz. liquid pectin
10 drops of red or green food
    coloring (optional)

Puree peppers until finely chopped. Combine peppers and vinegar. Bring to a boil over high heat and boil rapidly for 10 minutes, stirring occasionally. Remove pan from heat and stir in lemon juice and sugar. Return to heat and bring to boil again. Stir in pectin and food coloring and boil again, stirring constantly, for a minute. Remove from heat. Skim off foam and pour into sterile jars.

Extra jalapeno chiles may be used instead of the sweet bell peppers if preferred. To adjust the "hotness" of the jelly, remember that the pith of the jalapeno is where the hot is - more pith, more heat.

2075-99

GOOSEBERRY JAM

2 qt. washed gooseberries
4½ c. brown sugar
1 c. vinegar
1 cinnamon stick

8 cloves
¼ tsp. nutmeg
2 whole allspice
½ c. water

In a pot, combine sugar, vinegar, spices, and water. Boil 5 minutes. Add gooseberries; reduce heat and cook for 30 to 40 minutes until gooseberries are tender and syrup is thick. Seal into hot sterile jars. Makes 3 pints.

Lion Micheal and Ruth (Sauskojus) Bartolf,
Oxbow and District Lions Club
Oxbow, Saskatchewan, Canada

TRIPLE BERRY JAM

14 oz. frozen raspberries
14 oz. frozen blackberries
14 oz. frozen blueberries
4¼ c. sugar

1 box Sure-Jell fruit pectin for
   lower sugar recipes
½ tsp. butter or margarine

Thaw and crush berries with a potato masher. (For less seeds, strain raspberries and blackberries.) Combine ¼ cup sugar with Sure-Jell. In a large kettle, combine fruit with sugar/pectin mixture. Add the butter or margarine. Bring mixture to a full rolling boil; stir constantly. Quickly stir in the remaining 4 cups sugar and return to a full rolling boil. Boil exactly 1 minute, stirring constantly. Remove from heat. Pour into sterilized jars and seal.

You can use fresh berries: Crush berries and measure 2 cups raspberries, 2 cups blackberries, and 1½ cups blueberries.

Judy Rannow, Arlington (SEA) Lions Club
Arlington, MN, USA

STRAWBERRY MARMALADE

2 small or 1½ medium oranges
5 c. quartered strawberries

5½ c. extra fine white sugar
1 (6 oz.) bottle liquid fruit pectin

Cut unpeeled oranges into quarters and remove seeds. Grind or finely chop peel and pulp, reserving the juice. Combine orange, orange juice, strawberries, and sugar in a large saucepan. Place over high heat and bring to a full rolling boil; continue to rapidly boil for 1 minute, stirring constantly. Remove from heat and immediately add the pectin, stirring to mix. Skim off foam with a metal spoon. Continue to stir and skim for 5 minutes. Fill hot, sterilized jars, and adjust caps. Makes about 6½ pints.

Lion Micheal and Ruth (Sauskojus) Bartolf,
Oxbow and District Lions Club
Oxbow, Saskatchewan, Canada

CARROT MARMALADE

3 oranges
3 lemons

4 c. carrots
8 c. water

Grind oranges, lemons, and carrots; add water and let set overnight. Cook till soft, then measure pulp. Add 2 cups more of sugar, then pulp. Let set overnight, then next day, cook till clear and thick. Pour in sterilized jars and seal while hot with sterilized 2 piece lids with new centers.

Micheal and Ruth Bartolf, Oxbow and District Lions Club
Oxbow, Saskatchewan, Canada

TROPICAL-FRUIT SAUTE

1 papaya
1 mango
1 pt. strawberries
1 lime

4 Tbsp. butter
½ c. sugar
1 tsp. coriander

Peel the papaya and cut into slices. Cut the mango into chunks. Cut the strawberries in halves. Grate the green zest from the lime and squeeze 2 tablespoons juice. In a frying pan, melt the butter over medium-high heat. Add the papaya, mango, lime juice, sugar, and coriander. Reduce the heat to low and continue to cook the mixture, stirring occasionally, until the sugar has dissolved and the fruit has softened slightly, about three minutes. Stir in the strawberries and the lime zest. Makes 3½ cups.

Mrs. Lucy Aiken, Clarence Lions Club
Clarence Center, NY, USA

MICROWAVE CARAMEL CORN

1 c. brown sugar
1 stick butter or margarine
¼ c. white corn syrup

½ tsp. salt
½ tsp. baking soda
3 to 4 qt. popped corn

Combine all ingredients, except soda and popcorn, in 1½ to 2 quart dish. Bring to boil, then cook on FULL power for 2 minutes. Remove from microwave and stir in soda. Put popped corn in grocery bag. Pour syrup over corn. Close bag and shake. Cook in bag on HIGH in microwave for 1½ minutes. Shake and cook another 1½ minutes. (May need another 1½ minutes.) Pour into pan and allow to cool.

Pam Caldwell, Mexico Sunrise Lions Club
Mexico, MO

I'm a slow walker, but I never walk back.
Abraham Lincoln

BASIC SEASONED FLOUR

4 c. all-purpose flour
¼ c. salt
2 Tbsp. pepper
2 Tbsp. dry English mustard
1 Tbsp. paprika

1 tsp. basil
1 tsp. chervil
1 tsp. thyme
1 tsp. parsley flakes

Sift flour, salt, pepper, mustard, and paprika together. Stir in the herbs and store in an airtight container for use as needed. Makes about 4½ cups seasoned flour.

Long term shelf life. Good on oven baked chicken. Great gift idea.

Sarah Wehling, Bothell Lions Club
Bothell, WA, USA

SESAME SALT - GOMASHIO

Time: 15 minutes.

1 c. unhulled sesame seeds   ½ Tbsp. sea salt

Wash seeds. Drain well. Dry roast salt in a heated skillet over medium heat. Remove to suribachi or a dish. Do the same procedure for the washed seeds, stirring constantly until they give off a nutty aroma and start to turn a golden brown color and begin to pop. Remove from skillet immediately so they do not burn.

Grind with a suribachi (mortar) and pestle or in a blender at low speed until each seed is half-crushed. Store in a glass jar with tight cover. Use in place of salt for flavor. Sprinkle on grains and cereals. Good source of calcium, iron, and vitamins A and B. Serves 16.

Comments: Aids digestion; adds minerals and vitamins to a meal.

PDG Jim Schiebel, Hilton Lions Club
Hilton, NY, USA

CRANBERRY HONEY

2 c. cranberry cocktail
3 c. sugar
1 tsp. grated orange rind

1 c. honey
½ bottle pectin

Bring first 3 ingredients to a boil. Simmer 10 minutes, then add honey. Bring to a rapid boil and boil 1 minute. Remove from heat. Add pectin and skim. Pour in sterilized jars and seal.

Micheal and Ruth Bartolf, Oxbow and District Lions Club
Oxbow, Saskatchewan, Canada

HOW TO PRESERVE A HUSBAND

Be careful in your selection. Do not choose too young. When once selected, give your entire thought to preparation for domestic use. Some insist on keeping them in a pickle, others are constantly getting them in hot water. This makes them sour, hard, and sometimes bitter. Even poor varieties may be made sweet, tender, and good by garnishing them with patience, well sweetened with love, and seasoned with kisses. Wrap them in a mantle of charity. Keep warm with a steady fire of domestic devotion and serve with peaches and cream. Thus prepared, they will keep for years.

East Haddam Community Lions Club
East Haddam, CT

APPLE PECTIN

7 large apples
4 c. water

2 Tbsp. lemon juice

Wash tart apples. Cut in pieces, but do not peel. Add water and lemon juice. Boil for 40 minutes. Press through jelly bag, then strain juice through another bag without pressure. Boil juice rapidly 15 minutes. Pour boiling juice into sterilized jars and seal. Process 5 minutes in boiling water bath. Use for jelly, making from such fruits as peaches, strawberries, cherries, and so forth or any fruits that are lacking in pectin. Add 1 cup apple pectin for each cup of fruit juice used. Usually ¾ cup sugar to 1 cup of the combined juices is correct. Yield: 4 half pint jars.

Micheal and Ruth Bartolf, Oxbow and District Lions Club
Oxbow, Saskatchewan, Canada

PICKLED PIGS FEET

Pigs feet
Vinegar

Sugar
Water

Cook pigs feet until done. Remove some of the rind and fat from cooked feet. Cut and break apart. Put in stone jar or crock. Make sweetened vinegar. Boil to dissolve sugar. Pour over feet and cover with cloth (piece of sheet or pillowcase works great). Put some place cool. Let stand about 2 weeks. Keep an eye on them - they might run away.

Happy eating from many moons ago.

In loving memory of my mom, Olive Hibbs.

Lion Rae Hamilton, Graysville-Proctor Lions Club
Proctor, WV, USA

The difference between ordinary and extraordinary is that little extra.

PICKLED CRAB APPLES

4 lb. crab apples
2 c. white vinegar
1 c. water or beet juice

4 c. sugar (white)
20 cinnamon heart candies
1 tsp. ground mace

Use only varieties of crab apples that remain firm when cooked. Select unblemished crab apples with stems. Wash and remove blossom end. Make syrup of vinegar, water, candies, and sugar. Add apples; simmer until apples are heated through, but not soft. Pack apples carefully in hot, sterilized jars. Cover with boiling syrup. Seal. If crab apples do not remain firm, they may have been overcooked or may be of a variety unsuitable for pickling. If the crab apples become wrinkled during storage, it is probably due to the syrup having become too concentrated for the type of apples used. This may occur in a dry year with apples that otherwise would pickle satisfactorily. Skins may be pricked before boiling to avoid bursting.

Micheal and Ruth Bartolf, Oxbow and District Lions Club
Oxbow, Saskatchewan, Canada

CINNAMON PICKLE RINGS

1 gal. cucumber slices
1 c. lime
4½ qt. water or enough to cover
   pickles

½ c. vinegar
½ large bottle red food coloring
½ tsp. alum

Peel and slice cucumbers into ¼ inch rings. To 1 gallon rings, mix: 1 cup lime and 4½ quarts water or enough to cover pickles. Let stand 24 hours. Drain. Wash in clear water and soak in cold water 3 hours. Drain. Combine ½ cup vinegar, ½ large bottle red food coloring, ½ teaspoon alum, and enough water to cover. Simmer 2 hours with rings. Drain.

Bring to a boil:

2 c. vinegar
10 c. sugar
2 c. water

1 c. red hot candies
8 cinnamon sticks

Add pickles and let set overnight. Heat the juice, then add pickles and heat 30 minutes. Pack and seal in hot jars.

You will think these are apple rings.

Bert Morgan, Broken Bow Lions Club
Broken Bow, NE, Custer County

The speed of the leader determines the rate of the pack.
Ralph Waldo Emerson

RAISIN JACK

4 lb. raisins
10 lb. white sugar
1 pt. grape juice

1 pkg. dry yeast
4 gal. water

Mix all together and let ferment until quits working. Keep in warm place.

Do not give the raisins to animals - *believe me they will see 3 of everything.*
Lion Jack Hamilton, Graysville-Proctor Lions Club
Proctor, WV, USA

MAITRE D'HOTEL BUTTER

½ c. softened butter
Juice of ½ lemon

Salt and pepper to taste
1 heaping Tbsp. dry parsley

Blend all ingredients. Shape into a ball or square and chill firmly.

When steaks come off the barbecue, put one pat on each steak just at serving.

Sarah Wehling, Bothell Lions Club
Bothell, WA, USA

HOT PEPPER BUTTER

Hot peppers (enough to make 4
   qt. after they are cleaned and
   ground)
6 c. sugar
1 qt. regular mustard

1 qt. vinegar
1 tsp. salt
1½ c. flour and enough water to
   make a paste for thickening

Mix first 5 ingredients together and bring to a rolling boil. Slowly add the flour and water paste until it thickens. Fill sterilized jars while still hot and seal.

You can use red, yellow, and green peppers to make a pretty combination.
Teresa Jett, West Milford Lions Club
West Milford, WV, USA

MAPLE DRESSING

1 c. maple syrup
2 Tbsp. vegetable oil
1 Tbsp. lemon juice
½ tsp. paprika

¼ tsp. celery seed
¼ tsp. salt
¼ tsp. onion powder
¼ tsp. ground mustard

Combine all ingredients in a jar with tight-fitting lid; shake well. Serve over salad greens.

Elaine D. Howes, Northfield Lions Club
Northfield, MA, USA

2075-99

APPLE BUTTER
(Crock pot)

3 c. white sugar
½ tsp. cloves

Apples
2 tsp. cinnamon

Fill crock pot with quartered and cored (but not peeled) apples. Cook 3 hours on HIGH. Add other ingredients and cook 9 more hours on LOW. Do not remove lid. Put 3 cups in blender for 5 seconds. Makes 4½ pints.

I make this overnight - it makes the house smell wonderful.

President Shirley, Rootstown Township, 13-D Lions Club
Rootstown, OH

BEST PICKLES IN THE WORLD

3 slices onion per jar
1 qt. pure vinegar
1 c. sugar

½ c. water
⅓ c. salt (pickling)

Use small and medium size cucumbers. Cut in 4 strips. Pack cucumbers very closely in quart jars with 3 slices of onion. Heat vinegar, sugar, water, and salt together; bring to a boil. Pour over cucumbers, sealing at once. This makes 3 or 4 quarts. Let stand 4 weeks before opening.

Sometimes a hot water bath may help to seal jars quicker - just a few minutes.

Linda Fox, Saginaw Lions Club
Saginaw, TX

ICEBOX PICKLES

Soak large pickles in very cold water (ice cubes) for five or more hours. Cut lengthwise without paring into about five pieces. Pack very close in jars with 3 slices of onions on the top of each jar, also 3 stalks of celery or one teaspoon of celery seed may be added if desired. Drain off any juice after packing. Heat 1 quart of vinegar, 1 cup sugar, ½ cup of water, and ⅓ cup of salt. Boil mixture well. Pour over cucumbers while hot until jar is full. Seal at once. They are ready to use in about six weeks.

Micheal and Ruth Bartolf, Oxbow and District Lions Club
Oxbow, Saskatchewan, Canada

Please make me the kind of person my dog thinks I am.
Warren J. Keating

AUNT VIOLET'S BREAD AND BUTTER PICKLES

4 qt. sliced medium unpeeled
    cucumbers
8 small white onions, sliced thinly
2 green peppers (one may be
    red), cut in strips

1 to 3 cloves garlic, sliced very
    thin
½ c. salt

Syrup:

5 c. white sugar
3 c. vinegar (add another c. if
    needed)
1½ tsp. turmeric

½ tsp. ground cloves
2 tsp. celery seed
2 Tbsp. mustard seed

Mix salt with vegetables and bury ice in them. Let stand for 3 hours. Drain. Add the hot syrup; bring slowly to a boil, but do not boil. Can in sterilized jars.

This recipe is in memory of my Aunt Violet B. Keister, who gave it to me July 1977.

Lion Ann K. Brumback, Silver Run-Union Mills Lions Club
Westminster, MD, USA

BREAD AND BUTTER PICKLES

2 c. sugar
2 c. cider vinegar
3 Tbsp. coarse salt (kosher)
2 Tbsp. mustard seed
1 tsp. dry mustard
1 tsp. turmeric

1 tsp. hot red pepper flakes or
    less
½ tsp. celery seeds
12 small pickling cucumbers (2½
    lb.), cut into ¼ inch slices
1 medium onion, sliced

In large pot, bring all ingredients, except cucumbers and onions, until sugar is dissolved. Add cucumbers and onions. Cook over high heat, stirring for 1 minute. Remove from heat. With slotted spoon, transfer cucumber and onions to 4 clean pint jars. Pour hot pickling juice over pickles to cover. Loosely cover with lids. Let cool. Tighten bands or lids. Refrigerate and use within 2 weeks.

Doris G. Brey, Upper Perkion Lioness Club
Harleysville, PA, USA

Some people can dish it out, but they can't cook it.

❧ ❧ ❧

Where there's smoke there's toast.

2075-99

BREAD AND BUTTER PICKLES

6 qt. cucumbers (medium sized), thinly sliced
6 medium white onions, sliced
2 c. water
4 c. sugar

2 Tbsp. mustard seed
¾ c. sugar
1 qt. cider vinegar
2 Tbsp. celery seed

Wash cucumbers thoroughly before slicing. Arrange cucumbers and onions in layers in an earthenware crock or bowl. Sprinkle each layer with salt. Cover and let stand 3 hours. Drain off accumulated juice. Combine water, vinegar, sugar, celery seed, and mustard seed. Bring to a boil, stirring until sugar is dissolved; boil 3 minutes. Add cucumber mixture and bring once more to the boiling point, but do not boil. Pack immediately into hot sterilized jars. Seal at once. Makes about 8 pints.

Mike Hazzard
Littleton, CO

REFRIGERATOR PICKLES

8 c. sliced cucumbers
2 sliced green peppers
1 c. sliced onions
1 tsp. mustard seed

2 c. sugar
1 tsp. celery seed
4 tsp. pickling salt
1 c. vinegar

In a large bowl, place all ingredients in order given. Mix together well and pour into an ice cream pail or glass jar. Store in refrigerator.

If you like stronger flavour, add garlic and dill.

Lion Carol Anderson, Lake of the Woods Lions Club
Kenora, Ontario, Canada

SWEET SOUR PICKLES

1 gal. pickles
2 Tbsp. alum
2 Tbsp. pickling salt

¼ to ½ c. pickling spices
4 c. white vinegar
4 c. white sugar

Step 1: Fill clean glass gallon jar with any size pickles. Add alum, pickling salt, and pickling spices. Pour white vinegar into jar over pickles. Fill remaining space in jar with water. Place on lid and tilt jar to mix vinegar and water. Put in dark cool place one month (in basement).

Step 2: After one month, remove pickles. Rinse out jar. Cut pickles crosswise. Return to jar. Add sugar. Return to cool place. Let stand two weeks. Ready to eat. Will keep one year.

Everyone will say "don't you add liquid?" No, they make their own after you add sugar. Do not refrigerate. Real good.

Margie E. Conley, Boaz Lions Club
Blue River, WI

DOCTORED DILL PICKLES

½ gal. dill pickles

Drain off liquid and quarter the pickles.

In a saucepan:

1 c. vinegar
1½ c. water

4 c. sugar
1 pinch of alum

Bring to boil 15 minutes. Pour over pickles. Hold and refrigerate three days.

Kenneth C. Bloss, Hilton Lions Club
Hilton, NY

BEET PICKLES

2 gal. small beets
10 c. sugar
10 c. vinegar

2 c. water
½ c. pickling spice

Boil beets; peel and cut into small pieces if beets are large. Add to the mixture of sugar, vinegar, water, and pickling spice. Boil 10 minutes. Pack into hot jars and add juice. Seal.

Bert Morgan, Broken Bow Lions Club
Broken Bow, NE, Custer County

GOLDEN PUMPKIN PICKLES

2 Tbsp. stick cinnamon, broken
    up
2 Tbsp. whole cloves
4 lb. sugar

1 qt. cider vinegar
5 lb. pumpkin, pared and cut in 1
    inch cubes

Tie cinnamon and cloves in a double thickness of cheesecloth. Combine sugar and vinegar in a large saucepan; add spice bag and bring to a boil. Add pumpkin. Cook until pumpkin is tender. Remove spice bag and spoon pumpkin into hot, sterilized jars. Cover with syrup and seal. This pickle should come out clear and golden in color. Overcooking darkens the color, but does not spoil the flavor or texture.

Micheal and Ruth Bartolf, Oxbow and District Lions Club
Oxbow, Saskatchewan, Canada

Why is it those who can wait 3 hours for a fish to bite
can't wait 5 minutes for dinner?

BUDGET DIAPER WIPES

1 roll Bounty towels, cut in half
1 (10 c.) Rubbermaid container
   and lid
1 squirt of baby shampoo or baby
   bath soap

1 squirt of baby oil
2 c. warm water

Put water in container. Slowly add oil and shampoo or soap. Stir gently. Soak ½ roll of paper towels in upright position. Use anytime after 1 hour. Keep lid on when not in use.

We have 15 grandchildren and I've used these for them all. They cost pennies.

King Shirley, Rootstown Township, 13-D Lions Club
Rootstown, Portage County, OH

CANDY CLAY

⅓ c. vegetable shortening
⅓ c. light corn syrup
1 (1 lb.) box powdered sugar
½ tsp. salt

2 tsp. extract (your choice for
   flavoring)
Food coloring (paste preferred)

Beat the vegetable shortening with the corn syrup, salt, and flavoring until creamy and well blended. Gradually add the powdered sugar, beating constantly. Mixture will be crumbly. Squeeze mixture together with your hands until it forms a large ball. Knead until smooth and pliable. Divide and tint as desired, kneading in the color. Package tightly in plastic bags and store in sealed container until ready to use. Makes 1 pound.

Note: Paste food coloring - available where cake decorating supplies are sold - produces a richer color, but liquid food coloring will work also.

Mary L. Coon, Hutchinson Breakfast Lions Club
Hutchinson, KS, USA

CHANNEL CAT DOUGH BAIT

10 slices wheat bread
½ c. sugar

1 small ripe banana
Crushed wheat flour (as needed)

Knead ingredients together. Add enough wheat flour to make a good dough. Place in a bread wrapper and keep in refrigerator until ready to use.

Peanut butter and strawberry pop may be substituted for the banana.

Marty Clark, Hutchinson Breakfast Lions Club
Hutchinson, KS, USA

NATURAL EGG DYES

Green: Blueberry juice and turmeric, mixed with water.

Purple: Beet juice and blueberry juice.

Yellow to orange to brown: Onion skin, cooked in water.

Pink: Beets (fresh), cooked in water.

Light blue: Red cabbage, cooked in water.

Blue: Blueberry juice.

Yellow: Turmeric, cooked in water.

Liz Birchen, O'Fallon Lions Club
O'Fallon, MO, USA

RECIPE FOR A HAPPY HOME

4 c. love
2 c. loyalty
3 c. forgiveness
1 c. friendship

5 heaping Tbsp. hope
3 spoonfuls tenderness
4 qt. faith
1 barrel laughter

Take love and loyalty; mix it thoroughly with tenderness, kindness, and forgiving. Add friendship and hope. Sprinkle abundantly with laughter. Bake it with sunshine in 350° heat. Serve daily with generous helpings.

East Haddam Community Lions Club
East Haddam, CT

*Some people are so argumentative they won't even
eat food that agrees with them.*

❧ ❧ ❧

*The things we sweep under the rug have a disconcerting habit
of creeping out on the other side.*

❧ ❧ ❧

Influence is something you think you have until you try to use it.

❧ ❧ ❧

A Bible in the hand is worth two in the bookcase.

2075-99

Notes

Our five senses are incomplete without the sixth - humor.

INDEX OF RECIPES

SNACKS, APPETIZERS, BEVERAGES

684

SOUPS, SANDWICHES, SAUCES

SOUPS

SANDWICHES

VEGETABLES

MEAT, SEAFOOD, POULTRY

MEAT

SEAFOOD

CASSEROLES, MAIN DISHES, BREAKFASTS

CASSEROLES

BREADS, ROLLS

DESSERTS

CAKES, BARS, COOKIES, CANDIES

CAKES

694

You may order as many single copies of The Lions Clubs Cookbooks (Volumes 1, 2, & 3) as you wish. Simply contact your local Lions Club at the address or phone below:

If you are unable to obtain a book from the local Lions Club above, you may contact us at the address below for information on how to receive your new cookbooks:

Cookbooks Unlimited
P.O. Box 1865
Loveland, CO 80539

Phone: (970) 663-6767
Fax: (970) 663-6760

Cook Up a Fundraising Success!

Lions Clubs are entitled to purchase these books at considerably reduced prices with easy payment terms to enable you to use them as a great fundraising project for your local club. Using this cookbook to earn thousands of dollars is a great way to accomplish your club's goals quickly and easily with very little work on anyone's part. Just send a copy of this form to the address above or call to request further information.

☐ Please send more information on using this cookbook as a fundraiser for my club.

Name _____

Address _____

City, State, Zip _____